SCOTTISH ROCK CLIMBS

SCOTTISH ROCK CLIMBS

Andy Nisbet

With contributions from
Rab Anderson, Joanna George,
Dave MacLeod, Colin Moody, Stephen Reid
and Simon Richardson

Series Editor: Brian Davison

SCOTTISH MOUNTAINEERING CLUB
CLIMBERS' GUIDE

Published in Great Britain by The Scottish Mountaineering Trust,
2005

ISBN 0-907521-86-X

Front Cover: Crocodile, E3 5c, Lower North-East Nose of Aonach Dubh, Glen Coe

Frontispiece: Punster's Crack, Severe 4a, The Cobbler (photos Cubby Images)

A catalogue record for this book is available from the British Library

This guidebook is compiled from the most recent information and
experience provided by members of the Scottish Mountaineering
Club and other contributors. The book is published by the Scottish
Mountaineering Trust, which is a charitable trust.
Revenue from the sale of books published by the Trust is used for the
continuation of its publishing programme and for charitable
purposes associated with Scottish mountains and mountaineering.

Production: Scottish Mountaineering Trust (Publications) Ltd
Typesetting: Ken Crocket, Tom Prentice
Diagram & map graphics: Tom Prentice
Colour separations: Core Image, East Kilbride
Printed & bound in Spain by Elkar, Bilbao

Distributed by Cordee, 3a DeMonfort Street, Leicester. LE1 7HD
(t) 0116 254 3579, (f) 0116 247 1176, (e) sales@cordee.co.uk

For details of other SMC guidebooks see inside rear endpaper

6 CONTENTS

8 CONTENTS

Introduction & Acknowledgements

The aim of this guidebook is to provide a selection of the best rock climbs through-out Scotland for those more likely to visit the area infrequently. To that end the crags and climbs selected for inclusion are biased towards the middle grades on the established crags. Though a selection of higher grade routes have been included, not all the E5 or E6s which get most of the stars in the comprehensive guides have been transferred into this guide.

Scotland has some wonderful climbing in beautiful places. Beautiful places are perhaps the attraction because with worldwide transport now available, you can always find somewhere bigger and steeper but not as beautiful as the Highlands on a sunny day. But some work is needed to find this wonderful climbing, mostly due to a reputation for changeable weather and slow drying mountain cliffs. But reputations are usually exaggerated so with flexible planning and the acceptance of the odd wet day, very few trips will be wasted. On every cliff there are quick drying routes, perhaps not the three star route that first attracted you, but every route in this book is good, and you will always have a good day. Unless it is actually raining of course, but it will probably be dry if you head to the opposite side of the country. As this usually means away from the spectacular but wetter west coast several dry eastern crags have been included.

While May is drier on average than other months from April to August, there has been little difference in recent years, possibly due to climate change. Also in May, the hills may still be wet from the winter and many of Scotland's best climbs are in the hills. But every year is different and our winters are shortening. Remaining as flexible as possible and picking a good week at short notice is much more success-ful. As for tactics once you're there, just go for a good day out; it doesn't have to be perfect sunshine and the glamour presented in the magazines (people and rock) for you to enjoy yourself.

Midges can also be troublesome, but rarely during the day and even more rarely in the mountains. The same may not apply evening and overnight, but avoid camp-ing in July and August, and take midge repellent.

And finally, don't let the pace of modern life dominate; make time for your climbing.

Andy Nisbet
Summer 2005

For their invaluable contribution and helpful comments, thanks to Rab Anderson, Roger Everett, Allen Fyffe, Cynthia Grindley, Mark Hudson, Ross Jones, Julian Lines, Graham Little, John Lyall, Dave MacLeod, Wilson Moir, Colin Moody, Neil Morrison, Grahame Nicoll, Tom Prentice, Jonathan Preston, Mike Reed, Simon Richardson, Ian Taylor and Noel Williams.

As a selected guide, this book is based on the work of authors of previous and cur-rent guides. Particular thanks go to the following authors of current guides, listed in the order of the chapters to which they contributed.

Mark Robson (Lowland Outcrops); Graham Little (Arran); Tom Prentice (The Cobbler, Ullapool to Reiff); Ben Ankers, George Ridge (Highland Outcrops South); Rab Anderson, Ken Crocket, Dave Cuthbertson (Glen Coe & Glen Etive, Ardgour & Ardnamurchan, Lewis); Allen Fyffe (Cairngorms North, Ullapool to Reiff); Alastair Ross, Neil Morrison (Cairngorms South); Grant Farquhar, Kevin Howett, Gary Latter (Highland Outcrops Central); John Mackenzie, Noel Williams (Skye); Geoff Cohen (Applecross & Torridon); Dougie Dinwoodie (North-West Gneiss); Andy Cunningham (Ullapool to Reiff, Far North), Dave Turnbull (Orkney sea-stacks), Bob Christie (Caithness sea-cliffs and stacks).

Production of the first SMC colour guide with photodiagrams has been a huge task, meticulously undertaken by Tom Prentice. This stage has been underpinned by Brain Davison's painstaking editing and the amassing of almost 1000 photos by Grahame Nicoll, for the selection of action shots.

General

Maps

The relevant maps are given under the chapter introduction, with L or E and the sheet number. L stands for Ordnance Survey (OS) 1:50000 scale Landranger series, and E for (OS) 1:25000 scale, Explorer series. Maps produced by Harvey are also listed where relevant, the Superwalker series being at 1:25000 scale. Symbols are used on chapter maps to indicate different categories of summit. Munro – black triangle; Corbett – black circle; Graham – black diamond; Other – crossed circle.

Books

The SMC produces a comprehensive series of climbing guidebooks and the relevant book is listed in each chapter. The following SMC and SMT publications, *The Munros, The Corbetts, North-West Highlands, Cairngorms, Islands of Scotland Including Skye, Central Highlands, Southern Highlands, Southern Uplands, Scottish Hill and Mountain Names* and *Scottish Hill Tracks* may also proove useful. For more information and to order SMC and SMT publications, visit the SMC website <www.smc.org.uk>. See also the publications list at the end of this guide.

Sun, Rain and Forecasts

Ben Nevis has the highest annual rainfall, followed by Glen Coe, The Cobbler and the Cuillins of Skye (in no order). Of middle rainfall are Arran, Torridon and the North-West (but sunshine amounts decrease further north) and central venues like Binnein Shuas. The Cairngorms are the driest mountains.

Valley crags follow a similar pattern, but are always drier. Sea-cliffs are drier again, but with the pattern of the nearest mountains. So Glen Nevis is wettest, then Skye sea-cliffs, the North-West (the further north, the drier), with the driest being the Highland Outcrops, particularly the Moray Firth coast.

Such wide geographical coverage and varied weather patterns makes weather forecasting important. The problem is finding a sufficiently accurate local forecast. The following may help, but there is something to be said for "go anyway".

Radio Scotland: In summer 2005 the Outdoor Activities forecast was at 6.58pm, and 7.58pm on Sunday, with an additional one at 6.58am on Saturday.

TV: Reporting Scotland forecast at 6.50 to 6.55pm is the only good daily one.

Internet: <www.onlineweather.co.uk>, <www.bbc.co.uk/weather> Good mountain forecasts can be found at <www.mwis.org.uk> and <www.metcheck.com>.

Telephone: These forecasts are expensive but handy: **Climbline** (0900 654 669): +601 West Highlands, +602 East Highlands; **Weather Check** (0900 654 660): +101 West Highlands, +102 East Highlands; **The Weather Centre** (09063 666 070): West/North-West Highlands, East Highlands.

Public Transport

Details of public transport have been given where possible. Firstscotrail train tickets can be booked on (0845 601 5929). <www.firstscotrail.com> has links to all Scottish and British transport websites from taxis to ferries and buses and tourist boards. It also links to Traveline (0870 608 2608), <www.traveline.org.uk> a very useful organisation for information about UK wide public transport.

Accommodation

Tourist Offices are the best source of general information. VisitScotland handles accommodation bookings (0845 225 5121) or <www.visitscotland.com>. The website details accommodation and lists phone numbers for direct bookings.

Camping: The best known campsites are listed. Camping is possible in the hills or out of sight of civilisation, away from the road and farmland.

Mountaineering Huts: These are usually only available to members of clubs affiliated to the MCofS or BMC. Addresses and phone numbers of current hut custodians can be obtained through clubs or from the McofS (see below).

SYHA Youth Hostels: Centralised booking (0870 1553 255), <www.syha.org.uk>.

Independent Hostels: The Blue Hostel Guide lists independent hostels (01479 831331), <www.hostel-scotland.co.uk> Booking is with the individual hostel.

Climbing Walls

There are around 25 climbing walls of variable quality in Scotland, but only the ones near the climbing areas are mentioned in the chapter introductions. There are walls in all the cities; <www.thebmc.co.uk/ indoor/walls> has information and links. Also worth checking out in the main cities are: Glasgow – Glasgow Climbing Centre (0141 427 9550, <www.glasgowclimbingcentre.co.uk>, Edinburgh – Alien Rock (0131 552 7211), for leading and top-roping and Alien Rock 2 (0131 555 3650), for bouldering <www.alienrock.co.uk> and Edinburgh – Ratho, Ratho Quarry (0131 333 6333), <www.adventure scotland.com>. The latter is a multi-faceted 30m leading and top-roping wall with extensive bouldering. The quarry outside has numerous traditional routes.

Technical

Summer Grades

The grading system ranges from Easy, Moderate, Difficult, Very Difficult, Severe, Hard Severe, Very Severe (VS), Hard Very Severe (HVS) to Extremely Severe. The Extremely Severe grade has been subdivided into E1, E2, E3, E4, E5, E6 and E7 and so on. Technical grades are given for routes of VS and above where known, also sometimes for Severe and Hard Severe. The normal range for technical grades expected on routes of the given overall grade are as follows; Severe – 4a, 4b; Hard Severe – 4a, 4b, 4c; VS – 4b, 4c, 5a; HVS – 4c, 5a, 5b; E1 – 5a, 5b, 5c; E2 – 5b, 5c, 6a; E3 – 5c, 6a; E4 – 5c, 6a, 6b; E5 – 6a, 6b. Routes with a technical grade at the lower end of the range will be sustained or poorly protected, while those with grades at the upper end, are likely to have a shorter and generally well protected crux. French grades have been given for bolted climbs.

Equipment and Style

Scotland has a tradition of climbs with leader placed protection. Pegs are nowadays considered unacceptable in summer rock first ascents due to improved equipment and the option of move rehearsal as an alternative to hammered protection. Some established climbs depend on peg runners to keep their grade; these are acceptable. Bolts are also considered unacceptable on mountain cliffs. However, bolt protected sport climbs are accepted on low lying cliffs which are not adventurous in nature, do not have a history of established traditional routes and have been agreed to be better suited to sport climbing by the local climbing community. Retrobolting of traditional routes is considered unacceptable without agreement from the first ascentionist and the local climbing community.

Left and Right

The terms generally refer to a climber facing the cliff. This always applies for route descriptions and usually for descents, which are often planned before the downhill movement starts. But for a few complex descents from mountain cliffs, the direction is facing downhill (but then the direction is specified by the name of features or by the compass point). Routes are generally described from left to right, and this should be assumed, unless indicated otherwise in the text.

Pitch Lengths

Pitch lengths are often rounded to the nearest 5m, although pitches below 20m are sometimes rounded to the nearest 2m. The descriptions assume the use of 50m ropes.

Diagrams

If a route has been numbered, this indicates that there is a diagram depicting the cliff, which will be found close to the relevant text. The numbers of the climbs in the text correspond to the numbers on the diagrams.

Recommended Routes

A star quality system has been used, from one to four stars indicating the best climbs of their class in Scotland. All the routes in this guide are good and many would get three stars in a comprehensive guide, so the star assessment has been stricter. But since this guide covers everything from mountain cliffs to sport climbing crags, from friction slabs to overhanging walls, and on many different rock types, the star rating is more subjective than ever.

First Ascensionists

If climbed originally using aid, then the first free ascent (FFA) is also given. PA is a point of aid, usually a peg because NA is nut for aid if originally specified. Where an artificial grade is given (e.g. A2), then long sections of aid climbing were used. The first ascensionists of variations are given if the variation is considered important.

Environment
Access

Part 1 of the Land Reform (Scotland) Act 2004 gives everyone statutory access rights to most land and inland water including mountains, moorland, woods and forests, grassland, paths and tracks, and rivers and lochs.

People only have these rights if they exercise them responsibly by respecting people's privacy, safety and livelihoods, and Scotland's environment. The Scottish Outdoor Access Code provides detailed guidance on the responsibilities of those exercising access rights and of those managing land and water.

• Take personal responsibility for your own actions and act safely.
• Respect people's privacy and peace of mind.
• Help land managers and others to work safely and effectively.
• Care for the environment and take your litter home.
• Keep your dog under proper control.
• Take extra care if you're organising an event or running a business.

Stalking, Shooting & Lambing

The stag stalking season is from 1st July to 20th October, although few estates start at the beginning of the season. Hinds continue to be culled until 15th February. There is no stalking anywhere on the hills on Sundays, although requests to avoid disturbing deer on the hills may still be made, and there is no stalking on land owned by the National Trust for Scotland.

Most of the areas in this guide are not affected by stalking. At the few where restrictions may be encountered, this is been noted in the introduction to the cliff. North Glen Sannox, North Arran, (01770 302363) and Beinn a' Bhuird, Invercauld, (01339 741911) are covered by the Hillphones scheme <www.hillphones.info>, run by Scotland's Natural Heritage (SNH) and the Mountaineering Council for Scotland (MCofS, see below), which provides daily stalking information.

The grouse shooting season is from 12th August until 10th December, although the end of the season is less used. It is also important to avoid disturbance to sheep, especially from dogs and particularly during the lambing season between March and May.

Bird Life

When climbing, don't cause direct disturbance to nesting birds, particularly the rarer species, which are often found on crags (eg. Golden Eagle, White Tailed (Sea) Eagle, Peregrine Falcon, Razorbill, Guillemot, Puffin, Fulmar, Kittiwake, Cormorant, Shag, Buzzard, Kestrel, Raven). Often this is between 1st February and the end of July. Intentional disturbance of nesting birds is a criminal offence and if convicted, you face a fine of up to £5000 and confiscation of climbing equipment.

It is the individual's responsibility to find out from the MCofS (see below) about voluntary restrictions at any particular location and to obtain advice as to whether their presence might disturb any nesting birds.

Mountaineering Council of Scotland

The MCofS is the representative body for climbers and walkers in Scotland. One of its primary concerns is the continued free access to the hills and crags. Information about bird restrictions, stalking and general access issues can be obtained from the MCofS. Should you encounter problems regarding access you should contact the MCofS, whose current address is: The Old Granary, West Mill Street, Perth PH1 5QP, tel (01738 638 227), fax (01738 442 095), email <info@mountaineering-scotland.org.uk>, website <www.mountaineering-scotland.org.uk>.

Footpath Erosion & Bicycles

Part of the revenue from the sale of this and other Scottish Mountaineering Club books is granted by the Scottish Mountaineering Trust as financial assistance towards the repair and maintenance of hill paths in Scotland. However, it is our responsibility to minimise our erosive effect, for the enjoyment of future climbers. Bicycles can cause severe erosion when used 'off road' on footpaths and open hillsides and should only be used on vehicular or forest tracks.

Safety

Participation

"Climbing and mountaineering are activities with a danger of personal injury or death. Participants in these activities should be aware of and accept these risks and be responsible for their own actions and involvement."
UIAA participation statement.

Liabilities

You are responsible for your own actions and should not hold landowners liable for an accident (even if a 'no win, no fee' solicitor tempts you), even if it happens while climbing over a fence or dyke. The same is true of bolted sport climbs, or routes with any protection in place. It is up to you to assess the reliability of bolts, pegs, slings or old nuts on the understanding that they may, over time, become eroded and therefore fail.

Mountain Rescue

Contact the police, either by phone (999) or in person. Give concise information about the location and injuries of the victim and any assistance available at the accident site. It is often better to stay with the victim, but in a party of two, one may have to leave to summon help. Leave the casualty warm and comfortable in a sheltered, well marked place.

Equipment and Planning

Good navigation skills, equipment, clothing and planning can all reduce the risk of accident. Mobile phones and GPS can help in communications and locating your position, but mobiles do not work in many places in the North of Scotland and both rely on batteries and electronics which can fail or be damaged. Consequently, they can never be a substitute for good navigation, first aid or general mountain skills.

LOWLAND OUTCROPS

This chapter covers the climbing away from the Highlands: both the Central Lowlands (Edinburgh and Glasgow) and South-West Scotland (Dumfries and Galloway). In the Central Lowlands where many of the crags are small, only two of the best have been included, Dumbarton Rock near Glasgow and Cambusbarron Quarries near Stirling. Dumfries and Galloway is represented by one mountain crag, Dungeon of Buchan and one roadside crag, Clifton.

Dumfries & Galloway

The hills and crags of Dumfriesshire and Galloway are known to relatively few climbers compared with far more popular Highland destinations, and they are generally bypassed by Scottish and English alike in their headlong rush northwards to Fort William or Aviemore. There are however some excellent crags hereabouts – and the area is noted for enjoying a milder climate than much of the rest of Scotland.

Maps: OS L77, L84, E313, E318, Harvey Superwalker Galloway

SMC Climbers' Guide: *Lowland Outcrops* (2004)

Access: The normal route by car is via Dumfries which is easily reached from the M6/A74. For Clifton take the A710 Solway Coast road, whilst those intent on the Galloway Hills should follow the A75 Stranraer road to Newton Stewart.

Public Transport: Dumfries & Galloway Council <www.dumgal.gov.uk> travel information helpline (0870 608 2608). Train from Glasgow and Carlisle to Dumfries and Glasgow to Stranraer. Clifton is accessible by the Dalbeattie bus from Dumfries – ask to get off at the Clifton Road end south of the crag. For the Galloway Hills, there are regular buses to Newton Stewart, though this is still distant from The Dungeon of Buchan.

Amenities: Information Office at Dumfries, (01387 245 550). <www.dumfries andgalloway.co.uk>, Castle Douglas and Newton Stewart.

Camping: Sandyhills Bay Leisure Park (01387 780 257) is just south of Clifton. Creebridge Caravan Park, Newton Stewart (01671 402 324).

SYHA Youth Hostels: Minnigaff (NX 411 663), (0870 004 1142), April to September, is just a short walk from Newton Stewart.

Independent Hostels: Stranraer Hostel (01776 703 395), Galloway Sailing Centre Castle Douglas, (01644 420 626), Marthrown of Mabie, nr. Dumfries, (01387 247 900).

Hotels and Cafes: Creebridge House Hotel, Newton Stewart or the Ken Bridge Hotel, New Galloway are worth visiting. Near Clifton, The Anchor at Kippford can be recommended as is the Garden Room, on the left as you enter Rockcliffe.

Shops and Petrol: A limited range of climbing gear is available at Patties of Dumfries (01387 252 891). Petrol can be found in most towns but Dumfries is probably the only place where some are open 24hrs.

DUNGEON OF BUCHAN

(NX 462 848)   Alt 450m   South-East facing

This superb crag of sound clean granite lying in splendid isolation on Dungeon Hill in the heart of the Galloway Hills offers some wonderful climbing, particularly to lovers of remote solitude. The arduousness of the approach is somewhat mitigated by the quality of the climbing and the rugged beauty of the surroundings, and though there can be some seepage early in the season, by mid-summer the crags take only a day or two to dry after rain. The many jamming cracks warrant doubling, (or even trebling) up on Friends, not to mention taping up for the squeamish. Midges can be a problem in summer – repellent and a stiff breeze are useful.

DUNGEON BUTTRESS

1. Carrick Corner	VS 4c *
2. Scots Wha' Hae	HVS 5b **
3. Incy Wincy Spider	E2 5b ***
4. Parcel of Rogues	E3 6a, 5b ***
5. Bannockburn	E1 5b **

Approach: The easiest access is from the A712 New Galloway to Newton Stewart road. Immediately west of the Clatteringshaws Loch dam is a single-track road, signed Craignell and Loch Dee (NX 545 749). Follow the road north-westwards to where it ends under the crag of Craigencallie at a car park next to the forestry gates (NX 503 781). Continue on foot or bike up the forest track, taking a right turn over the River Dee after 1.5km, followed by a left turn immediately thereafter and bearing left at the next major junction, to the Backhill of Bush Bothy, a good base for this crag.

Opposite the bothy, take either of the firebreaks in the forest to the edge of the marsh known as the Silver Flowe. This is a Site of Special Scientific Interest and it is requested that climbers skirt the boggy central area slightly to the north; 10.5 km, 2hrs 30mins from Craigencallie (1hr 30mins using a mountain bike). Walking from Glen Trool takes 3hrs.

DUNGEON BUTTRESS

This is the small but steep rectangular buttress on the very far left-hand side of the hill. Belays are well back, but an intermediate belay can be taken on a terrace which splits the crag near the top.

Descent: To the left of the buttress.

1 Carrick Corner   35m   VS 4c *
S.Reid, J.Grinbergs   24 Apr 1991
The obvious corner on the left side of the crag leads to an awkward exit and a detached block. The slab slightly left is climbed to an overhung niche and a skin rasping finish.

2 Scots Wha' Hae   35m   HVS 5b **
S.Reid, J.Grinbergs   24 Apr 1991
Excellent climbing. Just right of the right arete of Carrick Corner is a steep crack with several large half jammed flakes. Climb the crack to a tiny ledge and make a hard move up and right to a shallow niche. Pull left over the roof to regain the arete, which is followed to slabs. Trend right then left to finish.

3 Incy Wincy Spider   35m   E2 5b ***
S.Reid, J.Grinbergs   20 Aug 1991
A superb route, strenuous and intimidating. Climb the steep jamming crack 2m right of Scots Wha' Hae to a niche. Reach over the roof and hand-traverse right to grasp a reverberating pinnacle. Pull over the roof leftwards using the pinnacle (!) and step left. Go up the unlikely wall to a thread and continue to the terrace, finishing up the corner right of the cracked arete.

4 Parcel of Rogues   35m   E3 ***
D.Wilson, W.O'Connor, S.Reid   3 Sep 1991
Technical, strenuous and sustained climbing with good protection. Start below a crack leading to a huge overhung niche 10m right of Incy Wincy Spider.
1. 30m 6a Climb up to the crack and follow it to a small ledge. Make a difficult jamming traverse left and climb the clean undercut groove, exiting right at the top. A bold move leads to the terrace.
2. 5m 5b Climb the prominent impending right-slanting crack in the narrow arete. The obvious *Direct Finish* to Pitch 1 up the hanging niche is E3 6a.

5 Bannockburn   35m   E1 5b **
J.Grinbergs, S.Reid   20 Aug 1991
A sound test of jamming technique – or lack of it. Climb the triple crack system in the centre of the wall to a ledge on the left. Force yourself back into the cracks and make hard but well protected moves to gain the large heather ledge. The final impending off-width is a piece of cake (by comparison).

COORAN BUTTRESS

The major central buttress that runs the full length of the hillside to the right of Dungeon Buttress has numerous good routes, though all are split by heather ledges. The obvious huge corner on the right side of the buttress is The Colonel's Corner.

Descent: By an easy grass ramp on the left that finishes at Dungeon Buttress (this ramp passes under Silver Slab which contains a number of good single pitch climbs of VS and below).

The first route tackles the broken ridge of clean rock that bounds the far left-hand side of the buttress.

6 Traitor's Gait   115m   VS **
A.Fraser   10 Jun 1984
Fine pleasant climbing and very quick to dry. Low in the grade. Start at a crack splitting the slab at the toe of the ridge.
1. 25m 4b Climb the crack to a ledge on the left at 8m, then continue up leftwards to the left edge and either finish up this, or toe traverse right and move up. Belay on a large ledge.
2. 30m 4a Cross the slab on the right for 5m to a vague ridge and follow it to a

COORAN BUTTRESS

Silver Slab   descent

A

10

8

6   7   9

6. Traitor's Gait	VS **	9. The Colonel's Corner	HVS ***
7. The Highway Man	HVS *	10. Cyclopath	E1 **
8. Heir Apparent	HVS **	A. Leaning Block	

terrace and thread belay on a leaning block. A lovely pitch.

3. 20m 4b A few metres left of the leaning block are two short steep cracks. Climb the left-hand one directly (or move onto the left arete at 5m) to a terrace below the headwall.

4. 40m 4b Follow the cracks directly above which lead up to parallel cracks just to the right of the left arete of the final wall (and a few metres to the left of the long overhang). Move left to the arete and climb it to easy ground. Alternatively finish up the cracks direct at 4c.

To the right are two grassy fault-lines separated by a broken buttress. Right again is the most continuous area of rock with the obvious line of The Colonel's Corner on its right.

The Highway Man   130m   HVS *

G.Little, J.Dykes   12 Apr 1968

The original hard route of the crag is actually quite easy for the grade. Start below cracks at the lowest point of the buttress, mid-way between the right-hand grassy fault-line and The Colonel's Corner.

1. 45m 5a Climb a shallow groove to the central crack which is followed to slabs. After about 2m, traverse 3m right under a bulge, then climb a groove to a large spike. Move left onto an upper slab and climb a crack just left of the rib, then go left and over a bulge to a heather terrace (or climb the arete direct). Belay at the right-hand end below a tiny roof.

2. 25m 4c Climb directly up a crack just left of the roof to a narrow terrace and belay at the obvious short crack in the centre of the wall.

3. 30m 4a Climb the crack and scramble up heather to just below the final wall.

4. 30m 4a Climb the broken crack-groove line a few metres up and left of the impressive central crack of Cyclopath.

8 Heir Apparent   130m   HVS **

S.Reid, J.Grinbergs   17 Jul 1991

A fine sustained way up the crag and at the top end of the grade. Start at the foot of The Colonel's Corner.

1. 45m 5a Climb steeply up the left wall to a good flake, then swing up left and make an awkward pull on to a small ledge. The groove above leads to an easier groove in the left arete of the corner; follow this and then go up and left to a large spike. Stand on this and swing back right into a corner which is followed to a belay under a tiny roof at the right-hand end of the terrace.

2. 25m 5a Pass the roof on the right and continue, moving slightly right to a very awkward move on to a sloping ledge. Easier climbing via a niche leads to a heather ledge.

3. 30m 4c Climb the wall above, via a crack in the rib 2m right of the short central crack taken by The Highway Man (and just down and left of the wide crack taken by The Colonel's Corner and Cyclopath), and scramble to a belay under a blunt nose at the right-hand end of the final headwall, 5m right of the impressive crack of Cyclopath.

4. 30m 5b Just up and left on the smooth wall is a long thin flake. Gain it directly with difficulty, then follow it past a small ledge until just below its top, where a step right onto a sloping foothold can be made. Swing right into the groove of the Colonel's Corner and climb the overhanging jamming crack direct.

Variation: **Direct Finish   30m   E3 5b ** **

S.Reid, J.Grinbergs   17 Jul 1991

"Excellent climbing but leave your brain at home". Follow the long thin flake to its top (last runners), swing up left to holds, stand on them, and then go straight up the slight flake above to good handholds. Hand-traverse left into a scoop and finish more easily. Add a technical grade if you are short, maybe even two if you are very short.

9 The Colonel's Corner   130m   HVS ***

S.Reid, J.Grinbergs   5 May 1991

A popular classic – at the top end of the grade, particularly if you find jamming a challenge. Take lots of Friends and start up the huge corner on the right of the crag.

1. 45m 5b Climb the corner to a steep finish and exit left by a poised flake. Cracks above lead to a finish up the left-hand of two short V-grooves and a good stance (as for Cyclopath).

2. 25m 4a Follow the right-slanting groove above to a narrow ledge which is traversed rightwards to its end. Move up left to a square grass ledge, then go up a short crack to a higher ledge and belay under the obvious wide crack at the far right end of the wall.

3. 30m 4c Follow the crack for a short distance before quitting it for the arete on its right. Climb this rightwards in an unlikely and sensational position before moving up to a spike. Scramble up to a belay under a blunt nose at the right-hand end of the final headwall, 5m right of the impressive crack of Cyclopath.

4. 30m 5a On the right is an overhung groove with two large poised blocks. Climb the groove with trepidation to the top of the second block. Either climb the

jamming crack of Heir Apparent above (5b) or avoid it by stepping right into either of twin grooves and an awkward finish.

0 Cyclopath   130m   E1 **
J.Fotheringham, P.Whillance   Jul 1982
Bold slab climbing (and/or desperate jamming) on the first pitch just pushes this fine route into the Extreme grade. Start at the foot of the slabby right wall of The Colonel's Corner.
1. 45m 5b Climb a groove in the slab, move left onto the wall and go up flakes to the start of a crack. Follow this widening crack to the right-hand of twin V-chimneys, which is followed to a belay on the right. An excellent pitch.
2. 25m 4c Climb the wall behind the stance to a blunt spike in the right-slanting groove of The Colonel's Corner. Follow a thin crack through the bulge above and move up to a belay as for The Colonel's Corner under a wide crack at the far right end of the terrace.
3. 30m 4c Climb the wide crack direct, then scramble up to the obvious central crack in the final wall.
4. 30m 5a The fine crack, which will be found to have a sting in its tail.

CLIFTON

(NX 909 571)   Alt 150m   South facing

Clifton is one of Southern Scotland's best kept secrets. South facing, quick drying, close to the road, and in a beautiful location: its only weak point is the diminutive stature of the climbs. However, these pack such a punch into their short length that they are guaranteed to leave you just as drained as a 50m pitch would on most other crags.

Approach: Usually via the A710 south from Dumfries. South of Criffel, 1.5km after the junction with the B793 at Caulkerbush (and 2.5km north of Sandyhills Beach) there is a narrow lane on the right (west) signed variously to Southwick Cemetery, Nether Clifton and Clifton Farm. Some outcrops can be seen on the hillside to the north of this lane. Follow the lane for about 2km to Upper Clifton Farm: there is room for a few thoughtfully parked cars hereabouts. Just past the farm there is a small passing place on the left and opposite this a granite stile leads into a paddock.

Squelch straight across this (wellies advised), to the left of the farm buildings, to an angle in the far wall. A second stile is hidden some 15m to the right, just before a fence. Cross the next field, keeping an eye out for bulls, to a gate in the far corner, under Hollowstones Wall. Please keep dogs on a lead when in the fields. There is a possibility of restrictions due to nesting birds on part or all of Clifton in the spring (February 15 to June 30) and climbers are advised to check with the MCofS (see Environment notes) prior to visiting.

HOLLOWSTONES WALL

At the far left-hand end of the crag, not far above the field gate, is a yellow wall, flanked on the left by a hawthorn tree, and with a pleasant gearing up area below.

1 Sidekick   15m   Hard Severe 4b *
Take the groove behind the tree, finishing up the steep crack, or wimp out by moving right and finishing up Jeune Ecole.

2 Jeune Ecole   15m   Severe 4b **
Superb. Start at a shallow, blocky chimney-crack just right of the tree and climb the crack to a platform on the right. Climb the steep crack in the wall to gain a standing position on a ledge on the left. Traverse to the arete and finish up a groove. The crack can also be finished direct **Overground** (Severe 4b).

Dirl Chimney Area

This area is immediately above and 10m right of Hollowstones Wall. A path leads up and rightwards, then back left, to a bay behind an oak tree.

Dirl Chimney   13 m   VS 4c ***

A classic! Dirl means "a tremulous stroke; a sharp blow; a resonating sound; an anxious haste or hurry; a twinge of conscience; an exhilarating pleasure of mind and body". All these, and more, may happen when you undertake this interesting exercise in back and footing up the chimney on the left-hand side of the bay. Start below and left of the chimney, at a crack with a wobbly block in it. Climb the crack without hesitation, repetition, deviation or repetition and move rightwards into the chimney. Follow it over a roof to easier slabs.

Gibbon in Wonderland   13m   VS 5a *

The obvious handjam crack through the roof is made considerably less daunting by modern camming devices. Start opposite the oak tree. Climb a short way up a groove and avoid loose debris above by taking the slab on the right to finish up the blood stained crack. Probably HVS if you don't know how to jam!

Tour de Force   15m   VS 4c *

Well named. Start below a steep cracked arete just right of Gibbon. Traverse rightwards along a large flake for 2m until a series of mantelshelves lead to a bulge. Surmount this and finish up a short corner.

Main Wall

Main Wall lies 40m to the right of the Hollowstones Wall/Dirl Chimney area. A large beaked roof dominates this area which is defined by a steep corner behind a tree on the left **Ratten's Rest** (HVS 5b) and a fine arete on the right. Gain the foot of the wall by scrambling up from the right to a lower ledge known as Coffin Stone Ledge. Another move up and left leads to Main Wall Ledge from which the routes start.

Liplet   10m   Severe 4b **

Short but sweet. Start left of the tree on the left end of Main Wall Ledge, and climb a short groove to a roof, which is overcome with trepidation and technique.

Wall Street   13m   E1 5b ***
C.MacAdam, G.MacAdam   1977

Easy for the grade and possibly only sustained HVS if you've done it before. Nevertheless a truly superb route – strenuous, technical and well protected. Follow the thin crack just left of centre of the wall to a break and then finish up the awkward hanging groove immediately left of the roof, avoiding the temptation to rest on the gear.

The obvious groove leading to the right of the roof is **The Groove** (VS 4c), and the gnarly looking off-width in the corner is **Kenny's Chimney** (ungradeable!). **Novice Crack** (VS 4b) starts as for The Groove and makes a rising traverse right into the top of Kenny's Chimney. The next routes finish on the slanting gangway of **The Esplanade** (Difficult), which makes a good descent route, except for the last 2m.

The Arete   15m   E2 5b ***
C.MacAdam   1978

Exciting climbing up the arete with the prominent knob on it and quite easy for the grade. Start down and right from Coffin Stone Ledge at the foot of Elders Crack.

Jeune Ecole, Severe 4b, Clifton. Climber Jill Reid
(photo Stephen Reid)

Climb up to a roof and traverse left under it. A difficult move leads round the arete and into a groove on the left. (Many parties start from Coffin Stone Ledge and gain this groove easily but thus miss out the first of the climb's two cruxes – deduct one E point for this). Climb the short corner until it is possible to reach right to grasp the knob and swing right. Move up with difficulty and finish by a short crack up on the right. It is also possible, but difficult and serious, to climb the arete direct without moving into the corner (E4 6a).

9 Elders Crack   15m   VS 4b
A great little climb up the crack to the right of The Arete. Start down and right of Coffin Stone Ledge directly under the crack and behind some elders.

THE RED SLAB

To the right of The Esplanade is a complex area of walls and roofs half hidden behind some pinnacles.

10 D.I.Y.   15m   HVS 5a *
Climb the crack flanking the obvious red slab on its right, followed by a hand-traverse right to finish up an awkward break in the roof. Surmount this by use of a dubious block which in retrospect you would probably much rather not have touched.

11 Fingerlust   12m   E4 6a **
C.MacAdam   1979
The thin crack in the leaning tower on the far right gives a tremendous route; short, but very strenuous and technical, with excellent protection (but only if you can hang around and place it).

TWIN CRACKS BUTTRESS

About 100m right of the Red Slab is a buttress marked by an obvious crack on the left and a large detached pinnacle below on the right.

12 Crawl Wall   14m   VS 4c *
Start from a ledge up under the left-hand side of the buttress. Climb the wall just right of the left arete of the buttress until it is possible to move right into a crack which leads to a ledge. Finish up the wide crack on the right. Alternatively, climb strenuously up the crack all the way **The Direct** (HVS 5a).

13 Twin Cracks   15m   VS 4b **
Fine climbing up the twin crack system starting just left of the pinnacle on the right-hand side of the buttress.

JUGULAR VEIN BUTTRESS

A bushwhack 30m down and to the right leads to a steep buttress with a double tier of roofs on the left.

14 The Slash   15m   HVS 5a *
The central crack is a classic of its type, and those who like that sort of thing will find that this is the sort of thing they like.

15 Jugular Vein   15m   E1 5b ***
C.Macadam, G.Macadam   1977
Fine climbing up the wall to the right of The Slash and quite low in the grade. Start up and right of that route. Puzzle your way up the wall leftwards to a resting position on the arete. Take deep breath, step right, and climb the intimidating crack above.

Glasgow Area - Dumbarton

DUMBARTON ROCK

(NS 400 745)   Alt 5m   North-West facing

Sitting by the river Clyde near the town of Dumbarton, this 70m high volcanic plug is one of Scotland's finest low lying outcrops. Combining excellent bouldering on the huge basalt boulders with spectacular sport and traditional climbing on the main face, it offers varied and exhilarating climbing. The crag is often buzzing with climbers on summer evenings, when it is a sun trap, but is also frequented even in the depths of winter due to its quick drying and accessible nature. The boulders dry very quickly after rain, as do most of the routes.

March and April are excellent months for friction, but conditions are frequently good all year and midges are rarely experienced, except during very still summer evenings. 'Dumby' has always retained a reputation for danger and seriousness and almost all the routes feature spectacular exposure disproportionate to their length, with a very pleasant outlook to the Clyde estuary.

Approach: From Glasgow follow the A82 to the Little Chef and turn off for Dumbarton on the A814. Take the second left after Dumbarton East train station. Follow this to a small car park on the right. From here the alleyway leads round the rock to the boulders. There are also frequent trains from Glasgow running via Queen St or Central stations to Balloch and Helensburgh. Get off at Dumbarton East station. There are 4 trains every hour.

Descent: Generally by abseil from the top of nearby sport routes.

The awe inspiring face above the boulders is home to some of Scotland's finest crack climbs as well as numerous other classic traditional and sport routes, which have a reputation for being bold, exposed and intimidating.

Stonefall Crack   20m   HVS 5a *
N.Macniven   1963
The wide crack below the square cut roof and chimney is climbed direct, or with a deviation out left at mid-height to finish up the chimney. Big cams or hexes useful.

The Big Zipper   30m   E3 5c **
B.Shields, A.Baillie   1964 (aid); FFA: M.Hamilton   1983
The smooth corner above the ledge to the right gives an excellent pitch of bridging and finger jamming with good protection. Climb Stonefall Crack until it is possible to traverse right along the ledge to the base of the corner. Continue up the excellent but strenuous corner (bolt belay). The corner can also be gained from the steep finger crack below **Woops** (E4 6a).

Omerta   30m   F7c **
A.Gallagher   1993
The stunning and exposed left arete of the main wall. Climb the direct start to The Big Zipper via a desperate move then continue up the technical arete.

Chemin de Fer   30m   E5 6a ***
N.MacNiven, B.Shields   1964 (aid); FFA: D.Cuthbertson   1980
One of the finest crack-lines in Scotland and a test piece at the grade. The curving crack on the left side of the main face has hard moves in the first half, then eases very slightly towards the top. However, there is excellent protection. Bolt belay at the top. The obvious direct finish on the smooth wall above is taken by **Achemine** (E9 6c), Scotland's hardest route at present.

Requiem   35m   E8 6b ***
B.Shields, M.Connolly   1965 (aid); FFA: D.Cuthbertson   1983
This central crack-line remains one of the very hardest and best routes in Scotland

with F8a+ climbing and few repeats. This may have been the world's hardest route when first done. From a bolt belay on the ledge, climb the sustained crack then follow the line of holds leading right on the headwall (bold). The crux is the last move!

Persistence of Vision   15m   F7a+ ***
A.Gallagher   1997
This recent addition is now the most popular sport route in the area. Follow the line of bolts on the slab directly below Requiem to a lower off. Moving out left then back right at the fourth bolt is the crux. Perma-dry.

Sufferance   18m   F8a *
A.Gallagher   1993
A first class sport route up the very smooth left-facing wall to the right of a grassy ledge and corner. The route is sustained and technical on small edges, with a traverse at half-height being the crux. Start up a corner and follow the right-hand line of bolts to a ledge. The left-hand line is also F8a.

Fever Pitch   25m   E4 5c *
N.Colton   1976
An exciting but serious pitch with some dirty rock and the odd rattling hold, taking the big right arete of the left-facing wall. The crux is much harder than anything else on the route. Start just right of the arete. Climb easily straight up to a resting place at the horizontal break (large Friend). Climb past the thin crack beside the roof (crux) and finish rightwards up the wall above.

Longbow   30m   E1 5b ***
S.Belk   1960s
Exhilarating and well protected climbing up the left-hand of three corner-lines on the wall to the right. Much better than it looks from below. Exit right at the top.

Windjammer Crack   30m   HVS 5a ***
B.Shields   1964
A classic sustained pitch up the soaring right-hand corner. Again the climbing is considerably better than it looks. Well protected (large Friends useful for the lower section).

Unforgiven   18m   F7b **
A.Gallagher   1993
On the compact wall to the right, the right-hand of three bolt routes gives excellent but blind, technical climbing. The other two lines are also F7b.

Natural Born Drillers   8m   F7a
C.Phair   1996
From the edge of the shelf, follow the diagonal line of bolts across the wall to a crack. Climb this and use a finger lock over the bulge to pull over (crux) and reach the lower-off. Regularly failed on. The line to the left is F7c.

Plunge   30m   Difficult **
L.Mitchell   1960s
An excellent climb in a good situation and on good rock. Also a handy access route to the top of the crag. Best done when the tide is in. Start at the large mooring ring round to the right of the main face and follow steepening grooves in the clean rock rib to the castle wall. Avoid this on the right and finish on the balcony. Abseil off or continue up and left and abseil off the main face for extra enjoyment!

Mark Garthwaite steaming up Chemin de Fer, E5 6a, Dumbarton Rock
(photo Cubby Images)

DUMBARTON BOULDERS

Gorilla   6b ***
P.Greenwell   1978
A brilliant classic climbing the wildly overhanging arete to the right of the cave on the first boulder on the approach. From the starting crimps, slap for the large, smooth layaway and make a long reach left to a jug on the lip. Move right and pull over.

The Blue Meanie   5c **
Right of Gorilla is a long overhanging wall. Near the top of the path running underneath this is an attractive bulging wall. Start at a flat jug and some undercuts. Move up to the smooth layaway in the roof and make a technical move to gain a line of good finishing jugs.

Zig Zag   5b *
This varied problem weaves through the stepped roofs at the right end of the wall facing the castle on the first boulder. Start left of a bush and climb steeply on good holds moving left, then back right until a rock over left onto the slab is possible. Finish directly.

Mestizo   6a **
Gary Latter 1985
A brilliant problem climbing the left arete of the graffiti covered wall on the tall boulder underneath Requiem. Climb the arete to a good hold and move left on edges. A thin rock over leads to the easy groove and the top. Good landing. The wall just to the left is **Mugsy** (6c).

Friar's Mantle   5b **
The obvious stepped central line on the short wall directly below the graffiti covered wall has one tricky move on slopers. Brilliant! The crack to the left is 4a and the wall on the right is 5a.

Toto   6a *
G.Latter 1985
Another Dumbarton classic, not to be missed. Follow the through route under Mestizo and as you emerge there is a short thin crack on the left. Climb the left-slanting crack, then use a high pinch to gain the jug on the left. Finish here or climb the right-hand finish at 6b. Every ascent seems to use a different sequence! Traversing in from the right on crimps is Font 7a+.

Pongo   6b ***
The obvious grossly overhanging crack on the right of the next through route gives powerful moves, starting by swinging in from the left. A hard move at mid-height is eased by a foothook on the right arete. Classic! The sitting start is one of the hardest problems in the country at Font 8a.

Consolidated   6b (Font 7b+) **
A.Gallagher 1994
A classic traverse not to be missed by any dedicated boulderer. It is situated on the same boulder as Pongo, facing the river and is recognised by the long series of stepped ramps running along the bottom of the wall. A sustained eliminate problem which is somewhat difficult to describe, but a good rule of thumb is if you think it might be too high, it probably is! Start at the left arete on a sidepull and undercut. Traverse right on small holds on the lip and then drop down to better holds. Follow the line of parallel holds to the blunt arete of Cheddar Direct. Pause here for a moment on an upside down rest on a toe hook, then layback past the niche and continue right past a complex sequence on holds below the lip to reach triangular hold below the right arete. Finish up the arete.

**Cheddar Direct   4b ** **
An excellent varied problem, with a good landing. Start at a blunt arete with a little niche in it, facing the river. Climb past this until standing on the smooth slab above. Move rightwards across the slab to finish on a ledge between the two boulders.

Pendulum   4c * **
Forming the roof of the through route is a high boulder with an high and smooth slab above a roof **B.N.I.** (5c). Just right of the slab facing the main crag is a large flake running up above a ledge. Climb onto the ledge and follow good holds in the flake steepy to the spike on the arete. Move round and make a delicate move to stand on the spike to finish. Bold.

Stirling Area - Cambusbarron Quarries

The two dolerite quarries at Cambusbarron are the best in the central belt.

Access: If approaching from the south, leave the M90 at junction 9 and head towards Bannockburn Heritage Centre. At the next roundabout take the first exit, continuing towards the town centre. Now take the first left and where the road curves back right after a few hundred metres, turn left on to a bridge over the motorway. On the far side, turn right towards Cambusbarron. Follow the main street through the village, and turn left at Quarry Road (about 200m after the centre of the village).

THORNTONS QUARRY

(NS 772 922)   Enclosed, North & West facing

This fine abandoned quarry bowl offers a good selection of high standard single pitch routes, mostly following prominent cracks or grooves. The routes are generally well protected. The quarry is very sheltered, consequently staying dry in poor weather in summer. The main face catches the evening sun in the summer, though the routes are seldom dry in winter.

Approach: The quarry is accessed from Quarry Road (see above). The entrance to the quarry is at the top of the road, with limited parking next to the public information board which has a useful display map showing the various quarry trails. Walk through the overgrown old quarry access track into the main amphitheatre. The routes lie mainly on the back wall of the quarry.

Power of Endurance   25m   E5 6b *
G.Latter   1984
A very powerful route requiring strong shoulders. Near the left end of the wall is a thin crack which leads to an obvious small pod. Follow good but spaced holds to the thin crack. Climb this (small wires for protection) until it is necessary to crank wildly to reach the pod (crux). Slightly easier climbing leads to the final wall, which is best avoided by an awkward exit right.

Quantum Grunt   25m   E3 6a *
G.Pedley   1984
Strenuous and technical climbing. Start below the groove a few metres right of the previous route. Make difficult initial moves to gain the groove proper (large Friend useful). Mantel into the niche using a doubtful looking flake and continue up the groove above. A thin fingery crux leads to good holds and an awkward pull out right to finish.

Big Country Dreams   25m   E4 6a * **
A.Kay, R.Cowels   1984
The classic of the quarry, taking the striking S-shaped crack-line. Start just right of the main crack-line. Climb onto a jutting block and pull up and left to follow a thin

crack which leads to a good rest below the final crack. Climb this with increasing difficulty to a pumpy finish. The obvious direct start gives a bold and reachy **Cumacoma** (E5 6b).

Grace Under Pressure   25m   E1 5b
Just right of Big Country Dreams, gain the shallow flared chimney from the left and follow it past an undercut (crux) to an easier finish. Good protection.

The Purr Blind Doomster   25m   E5 6a **
C.Macadam   1984
About 10m right of Big Country Dreams is a thin crack with a slot near the top, just left of an arete. Climb the thin crack with difficulty to the vertical slot. Move delicately right to the arete (crux) and boldly climb this on sloping holds to reach the 'thank god' spike at its top. Stand on this and move right to an easier finish.

Both Ends Burning   25m   E5 6b **
D.McCallum   1984
Well right of The Purr Blind Doomster is a smooth chimney just left of an obvious smooth black arete. This route climbs the thin crack just right of the arete, giving sustained technical and varied climbing. Climb the crack with increasing difficulty to reach an obvious hold on the left. Stand on this (crux), step blindly back into the crack and continue with more difficult moves to reach an easier finish.

At the back of the quarry is a huge smooth corner. Just right of this is a curious leaning boulder with two excellent boulder problems. The left arete of the rectangular slab is **Spanking the Monkey** (6c, Font 7b), the right arete is **LDV** (5c, Font 4).

Anabolic Steroids   25m   E6 6b *
G.Lennox, C.Adam   1996
Reasonably well protected climbing taking the thin crack in the wall above the boulder problems. Low in the grade. A difficult start leads to a line of edges leading out left from the crack. From the top of these pull back right into the crack and follow it (crux) to the obvious large pod. Move up and follow the right-hand of two cracks on good fingerlocks and wires (strenuous) to easier climbing below the top.

Moving Shadow   25m   E5 6c *
M.Tweedly, L.Byrnes   2001
This route climbs the obvious V-groove in the middle of the back wall of the quarry. Small wires now protect the hard crux, which used to have a peg. Climb the groove to a series of desperate moves to gain a bridging position. Continue up the groove with excellent bridging to a ledge on the right. Lurch leftwards to gain a small crack and headwall.

FOURTH QUARRY

(NS 772 920)   South-West facing
This quarry dries quickly and year round climbing is possible. The face sees the sun in the afternoon and has a pleasant outlook to the Trossachs. Some of the routes still have some loose rock, particularly near the top and care must be taken with both holds and gear. However many of the routes are very popular due to their good protection and accessibility.

Approach: From the car park for the main quarry, walk along the track blocked by the fence and boulders and break left after a minute or two up a gentle incline to reach the open quarry floor.

Descent: By a small path returning to the left end of the wall. It is handy to fix an abseil rope from the fence posts above the face for a quicker descent.

The routes start at the isolated pillar at the extreme left of the face.

Ninety-Five   10m   E1 5b *
G.Szuca   1993
This takes the small isolated pillar, with good Friend protection in horizontal breaks. Start on a small block and foot traverse right along the obvious fault. Move up past horizontals, make an awkward move right to the arete, then finish back left with a long reach to the top.

Scales of Injustice   10m   F7b+ *
M.Somerville   2000
This is the line of bolts behind the trees, about 10m left of Production Line. It gives interesting and unusual technical slab climbing, easing slightly near the top.

Production Line   12m   E6 6b/c *
G.Lennox   1997
This hard but safe route takes the thin crack in the slab a few metres left of the start of the trees. Start by climbing up the wide crack to the right and place a high side runner. Climb back down and left to below the crack. Climb to a break from where a series of difficult moves lead to a triangular hold in the crack. Gain a series of good finger locks in the crack above which lead to a worrying loose finish.

Cross in Oz   14m   E1 5b ***
R. Wallace, A. Wallace   1993
The left-hand crack in the slabby undercut buttress 20m right of Production Line gives an excellent and varied route. Pull over the overhang at the left end of the buttress and climb the fine crack and slab above. The slab looks dirty but isn't.

Cha   10m   Hard Severe
G.Szuca, D.Gregg   1993
Climb the blocks on the small pillar to the right (look for the graffiti) until it is possible to move right on to good holds. Climb to the horizontal break, then finish up the crack. The short rounded arete leading to the finishing section of this route is taken by **Looney Tunes** (E4 6a).

Some 50m right of a tall dubious looking pinnacle is a thin crack in a smooth wall with chipped finger locks at its base – **Chisel** (E4 6a). The cracked buttress to the right provides the best climbing in the quarry, following a series of interconnected cracks. The following route starts just right of Chisel, at a triangular recess.

Gobi Roof   10m   E2 5c *
M.Garthwaite, G.Szuca, G.Campbell   1990
Climb up to a small roof, pull over (crux) and follow the fault to the top. Good protection.

Not Easy Contract   10m   E1 5b **
C.Hewitt, N.Sheperd, K.Clark   1985
This good route follows the wide crack near the left end of the buttress to a small ledge at the base of a short shallow groove. Climb this and the vertical crack above and finish direct.

Malky The Alky   12m   E1 5b *
G.Harrison, P.Laughlan   1980s
A few metres right of Not Easy Contract is a large scrappy corner. Start just right of this and climb up through a bulge to the large ledge, then continue up the corner.

The Doobie Brothers   12m   E1 5b **
M.Garthwaite, G.Szuca   1991
Start 5m right of the central corner, just left of a tottering pillar which marks the right end of the buttress. Climb the obvious crack and avoid the large loose looking block near the top on the left.

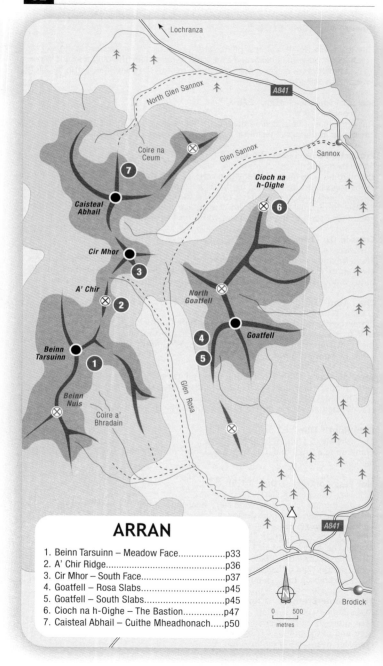

ARRAN

ARRAN

Tucked in between the coast of Ayrshire and the Kintyre peninsula and accessed only by ferry, Arran has more of a highland atmosphere than its position near central Scotland might suggest. The island is quite mountainous with a group of seven granite peaks around 800m in height. The main approach glen (Glen Rosa) cuts northwards into the massif from near the largest town (Brodick) and ferry terminal to provide a cirque of generally south facing cliffs.

Arran granite has obvious similarities to its Cairngorm cousin, although more crystalline and weathered, and away from the better climbs the rock can be vegetated and crumbling. The cliffs display a striking architecture, the great 'Cyclopean' block walls and vast bare boilerplate slabs so characteristic of granite erosion. Many of the climbs are slabby with friction moves, but sometimes with steep jamming or laybacking cracks. The open face routes dry quickly after rain, but the fault and corner-lines require three to four days of dry weather.

Maps: OS L69, E361 Harvey Superwalker Isle of Arran

SMC Climbers' Guide: *Arran, Arrochar and the Southern Highlands* (1997)

Access: Caledonian MacBrayne operate a regular passenger and vehicle ferry service from Ardrossan to Brodick (55mins) (01294 463470), (01770 302166), <www.calmac.co.uk>. During holiday periods, bookings for vehicles should be made well in advance. Another ferry service runs between Claonaig in Kintyre and Lochranza on Arran (April to October, 30mins). A car is not necessary for a short visit, since reasonably priced taxis can be used to access Glen Rosa or Glen Sannox.

Public transport: A bus service synchronised with the ferry timetable, provides a reasonable round island service; Traveline (0870 608 2 608). Ardrossan is easily reached by bus and rail from Glasgow.

Amenities: Brodick is a small holiday town with shops, hotels, post office and B&Bs. For more information on accommodation and tourist activities, see <www.ayrshire -arran.com>. The Sannox Bay Hotel is some 200m south of the start of the path; the food is good but slightly more expensive than usual climbers' fare. A tearoom just to the north has cheaper food.

Camping: Glen Rosa (NS 000 377) lies at the end of the public road up the glen, 3km from Brodick ferry terminal, and has basic facilities. Sannox is very small, with no campsite.

SYHA Youth Hostels: Lochranza and Whiting Bay are less convenient for climbing.

Glen Rosa

A horseshoe of peaks surround Glen Rosa, their cliffs facing into the glen. Moving in a clockwise direction, at the south-west tip (actually in a subsidiary corrie) is Beinn Nuis, then Beinn Tarsuinn with its Meadow Face. Next up the west side is the rocky crest of A' Chir before reaching Cir Mhor at the head. Although slightly lower than the peaks either side, Cir Mhor's dominant position matches the high quality of its climbing. The east side of the horseshoe is the highest but least dramatic peak, Goatfell, but still with some fine sheets of slab facing Glen Rosa.

BEINN TARSUINN - MEADOW FACE

(NR 962 412)   Alt 650m   South facing   Diagram p35

The long ridge of Beinn Tarsuinn (NR 959 412) has two tops. All the climbing is on the east flank of the peak facing Coire a' Bhradhain and Ealta Choire, known as the Meadow Face. Its unfortunate name is after a distinctive patch of turf at its base, not on the face itself. Despite enjoying a sunny aspect it does take a while to dry out after rain. The rock is generally good but can be gritty in the cracks. The climbs on this relatively remote face are long and serious undertakings and although not of the very highest quality, they offer grand mountaineering experiences. The most prominent features of the face are a great edge (dividing the long slabby south-east face from the narrow south face) and two parallel crack-lines to the right, splitting the face from bottom to top. To the right of the parallel cracks, the south-east face comprises a fan of great curving, overlapping slabs, expanding from right to left. Left of the great edge, on the south face, is a big corner-crack (The Blinder) and further left a prominent gully and chimney high on the face.

Approach: Follow the path up Glen Rosa and turn left immediately after a bridge across the Garbh Allt. Follow this new path into a fenced area and after the gate back out, leave the path to go right and follow the Beinn a' Chliabhain path over the first hillock. From the slight col beyond this, contour down into Coire a' Bhradain, then follow the burn into Ealta Choire to the base of the face. 2hrs.

1 The Blinder   140m   E1 *
W.Skidmore, J.Crawford   21 Aug 1971 (2PA); FFA: J.Perrin   Aug 1976.
A superb line up the striking corner-crack immediately left of the great edge gives a good struggle, although somewhat vegetated and friable. Some parties do the first pitch (35m 5b) and abseil off. The continuation is 5a, 5a, 4c, 4c.

2 Brobdingnag   205m   E2 **
I.F.Duckworth, J.Fraser, W.G.Smith   9 Apr 1975 (4PA); FFA: unknown
A spectacular route taking a line just to the right of the great edge and parallel to it. Start at a sloping grass ledge to the right of the corner of Blinder.
1. 30m 4b Traverse right into a small corner, climb it and continue straight up to a large grass ledge.
2. 20m 5b Climb a grassy groove to an overhang (often wet), then turn it on the left to reach a belay below twin cracks.
3. 20m 5a Climb the cracks to an overhang, then step right to a shelf below a shallow chimney. Climb the chimney to a belay below a thin crack in a wall.
4. 45m 5b Climb the crack and swing left to a ramp. Move right then left on good holds, then follow the corner to belay on chockstones below a small cave.
5. 10m Climb easily up left through a remarkable rock arch to belay in a deep hole.
6. 20m 5a Climb a loose slab to a ledge. From the ledge climb directly up a good jamming crack and exit right onto a large stance.
7. 15m 5a Follow the left-hand crack, then transfer to the right-hand crack to pull over a jammed block.
8. 45m 4c Climb the corner and slabs to the top.

3 Blundecral   215m   E2 *
G.E.Little, K.Howet   5 Aug 1995; Finish as described: A.Fraser, R.McAllister   31 Aug 1995
This varied and interesting route climbs a line on the wall between Brobdingnag and Brachistochrone, taking the obvious break through the band of overhangs at the end of the long roof running left from Brachistochrone. Scramble up to below the chimney of Brachistochrone, then traverse left to a vegetated ledge.
1. 25m 4c Climb a flake, then move right to an obvious groove (which runs parallel to the Brachistochrone chimney). Ascend the groove, then move left to a pointed turf ledge.
2. 25m 5c Follow the line of a thin diagonal crack up and left to a left-trending ramp which leads to the base of a right-facing corner. Climb this, then step left to grasp a huge (detached!) block come flake. From its top make a difficult step right to gain a ramp.
3. 15m 5c Climb the diagonal undercling to reach a hidden left-trending groove. Ascend this for 3m, then traverse back right across the wall to gain an obvious thin rock ramp. Move right to a small turf ledge. A spectacular pitch.
4. 25m 5a Climb the fine diagonal rock ramp to step left on to a continuation ramp and follow it for 7m to a spectacularly situated belay.
5. 25m 5a Continue up the ramp for 3m, then move up to a higher ramp. Follow this leftwards until it leads to a wide grassy fault on Brobdingnag. Ascend this for 7m to a cave under a rock arch.
6. 25m 5a Quit Brobdingnag by jumping on to a grass ledge to the right of the belay. Follow this rightwards and down to its end. Above this is a flake-crack leading

35

BEINN TARSUINN
Meadow Face

ARRAN

1. The Blinder	E1 *	
2. Brobdingnag	E2 **	
3. Blundecral	E2 *	
3a. Direct Finish	E5 6a *	
4. Brachistochrone	E1 *	

up to a narrow chimney. Climb these, taking either fork of the chimney to reach a wide ledge.

7. 50m 4c Climb a slab at the extreme left of the upper face to its apex, move right, then continue to and climb left-trending flake-cracks above.

8. 25m Pleasant climbing up walls and cracks leads to the top.

Variation: **Direct Finish   130m   E5 6a** *

R.McAllister, D.McGimpsey   14 Aug 1996 (pitch 4a climbed on original ascent)

A more direct and independent version, bold and poorly protected on the crux traverse.

4a. 25m 5c From the continuation ramp on pitch 4, climb a knobbly vein on the wall above. Pull up on to a shelf and move left up this to gain the obvious flake-crack which leads to a ledge above. Belay on the right.

5a. 30m 6a Move left and ascend a steep slab on tiny holds to a wide horizontal break. Move left along this break until a hard step up on to a narrow sloping ramp can be made. Move left again (rejoining the normal route, pitch 6) to reach and climb the flake-crack and narrow chimney. Finish as for the normal route (75m, 4c).

4 Brachistochrone   230m   E1 *

M.Galbraith, A.McKeith   18 Sep 1966 (aid); FFA: J.Perrin   Aug 1976

A fine line following the left-hand of two long parallel cracks that split the front face of the cliff; the right is **Bogle** (E2 5c). The situations are good particularly in the lower half, although there is a little gritty rock in places. The highlight is unlocking the secret which allows such a large roof to be climbed at 5b. The route needs dry conditions. Scramble up a groove to the foot of a chimney.

1. 45m 4c Climb the chimney, then a flake-overhang to twin cracks leading to a belay on a ledge below a huge roof.

2. 15m 5b Climb the strenuous twin overhanging cracks through the roof to a block in a chimney.

3. 45m 5a Traverse left up a layback shelf, then go back right to a grass ledge and a crack. Follow the crack over a smooth bulge to the next roof. Climb the overhanging crack to a recess in the roof, swing down left onto a steep slab, then go straight up to a grass ledge.

4., 5. and 6. 80m Continue up the same general line by grassy grooves, slabs and flakes to reach the continuation crack in the upper slabs.

7. 45m 4b Climb the crack over three overlaps, turning the middle one on the right.

A' CHIR

(NR 966 421)   Alt745m   Map p32

This peak of lies on the narrow rocky ridge between Beinn Tarsuinn and Cir Mhor. The actual summit of A' Chir is a massive block, climbable in a number of ways (all requiring some ingenuity!).

A' Chir Ridge Traverse   1.5km   Moderate ***

T.F.S.Campbell, W.Douglas, J.H.Gibson, H.Fleming, R.A.Robertson and Dr Leith   30 Jan 1892

This fine ridge, one of the best in Scotland outside Skye, gives a splendid outing. Much variation is possible and the grade given is for the easiest line traversing the crest from south to north. The most problematic section of the traverse is at the Mauvais Pas about 300m to the north of the summit. After a steep step in the ridge, turned on the west flank, a narrow gap is reached which can be stepped across without difficulty. Beyond this lies a short level section terminating in a vertical rock wall dropping to a little col. The correct route is to descend the right (east) side of the ridge, roughly mid-way between the gap and the termination, initially by a steep wall with good holds, then by a grassy ledge, becoming a rock trench, across an exposed wall. At the end of the trench a short chimney gives access to the col (in reverse this short polished chimney becomes the crux of the route – Very Difficult). The section to the north of the col is particularly enjoyable and the ridge continues with decreasing difficulty towards the Cir Mhor col.

CIR MHOR - SOUTH FACE (ROSA PINNACLE)

(NR 972 431)   Alt 540m   South facing   Map p32   Diagram p39

This magnificent peak, the finest on Arran and one of the most striking in Scotland, sits at the top of Glen Rosa. It presents a delightful South Face with impeccable granite slabs which hold a selection of the finest routes on Arran at all grades. The main buttress dropping from the summit of the mountain, also known as the Rosa Pinnacle, dominates the face. Despite the relatively long walk in, it is the most popular climbing venue on the island.

Approach: Access is via the main Glen Rosa path to take the left fork at NR 978 414 which leads up into Fionn Choire. 2.5hrs.

CALIBAN'S BUTTRESS

A separate ridge which lies immediately left of the West Face. It has a slabby west face and a vertical east face (forming the left retaining wall of the gully which bounds the main slabs on the left).

**1 Caliban's Creep   150m   Very Difficult ** **
G.C.Curtis, G.H.Townend   25 Jul 1943
This is an unusual route with some splendid situations. Start on the right of the toe of the buttress which forms a square-cut overhang.
1. 25m Climb slabs diagonally leftwards to belay in a pile of boulders under an overhang and left of a shattered looking wall. This pitch can be avoided by entry from the left.
2. 25m Traverse across the wall on good holds, move down and round the edge and gain an easy chimney which leads to an area of slabs.
3. 15m Cross the slabs to below a vertical wall and belay at its right-hand edge.
4. 20m Crawl through a narrow rock tunnel (the Creep), then cross a narrow exposed ledge on the east face to reach a deep chimney. Climb this into the floor of a great fissure and belay.
5. and 6. 65m Escape from the fissure, then climb slabs near the right edge for two pitches to the top.

WEST FACE

This is the wide area of immaculate slabs on the west flank of the buttress. Most of the routes are quick to dry and the rock is superb.

**2 Arctic Way   65m   VS * **
W.Hood, C.Moody   19 Jun 1982
High on the left, an obvious left-facing corner-crack runs up the slabs, providing a fine and sustained pitch. Start as for Sou'wester Slabs, at the foot of a long slanting groove, level with the foot of the vertical wall on Caliban's Buttress. Follow the groove to reach the foot of the corner (about Difficult).
1. 40m 4c Climb the corner to its top, then follow the continuation crack over a bulge to another bulge which is climbed directly, then ascend the slab above to belay under an overlap.
2. 25m 4c Move left to a crack through the overlap and go left again to a bulge above an old peg. Climb over the bulge, then trend left up the slab for a metre or so. Traverse right to below a thin crack, climb it, then trend left to a block at the top.

3 Sou'wester Slabs   190m   Very Difficult ** **
G.H.Townend, G.C.Curtis, M.J.H.Hawkins, H.Hore   3 Sep 1944
A much celebrated route and the finest of its grade in Scotland. Start at the foot of a long slanting groove, level with the foot of the vertical wall on Caliban's Buttress.
1. and 2. 50m Follow the groove to a point level with the foot of an open chimney/corner on the slabs to the right.

3. 20m Traverse easily right to the foot of the chimney/corner, then climb it to a spike belay below prominent twin parallel cracks.

4. 30m Climb the parallel cracks to the right edge of the slab, drop down onto the lower slab on the right, then climb a right-trending groove to belay under the great overhang.

5. 10m Traverse easily right under the roof to join South Ridge Direct under the Three-Tier Chimney.

6. 30m Above the platform, on the left side of the ridge crest, lies an obvious chimney in three sections, the Three-Tier Chimney. Climb it to gain the ridge crest.

7. and 8. 50m Two easy pitches along the crest lead to The Terrace below the Upper Pinnacle. The Upper Pinnacle can be climbed as for South Ridge Direct (90m, Very Difficult) and leading to the summit of the mountain. Or the Upper Pinnacle can be avoided by walking off the Terrace.

4 Vanishing Point   100m   E4 **

C.MacAdam, S.Steer   9 May 1985

An excellent and very bold route starting up the crack system to the left of the chimney-line of West Flank Route, just left of the bottomless flake-crack in the slab above.

1. 30m 6a Climb the crack system, then traverse right to gain the obvious flake-crack and follow it to belay on the edge above the second chimney of West Flank Route.

2. 45m 4c Step right on to the slab, then follow a direct line to below the layback crack on South Ridge Direct.

3. 25m 5c Climb the layback crack for 3m, then break out left to gain a sandwiched slab and groove. Climb this, then go up the headwall above to finish at the top of Sou'wester Slabs.

5 West Flank Route   155m   E1 ****

W.Skidmore, R.Richardson, J.Crawford, J.Madden   3 Aug 1963

A truly classic route following a natural line of chimneys and cracks running diagonally leftwards across the huge central slab. Although at the lower end of its grade, the initial chimneys will provide even the most stylish performer with moments of doubt and a deeper insight into the joys of Arran climbing!

1. 20m 5a Climb the first chimney to a belay.

2. 15m 5a Climb the second chimney to a ledge below a small overlap in the slab.

3. 25m 4b Follow the long diagonal crack in the slab above to a big overlap. Move right around the corner into a niche.

4. 30m 5b Step up and left from the niche round an edge into a groove and crack. Follow these to reach a small spike and flake by a rounded layback. The crack now branches. Take the right-hand crack for a metre or so until a move can be made across the slab. Climb to a horizontal crack, then traverse left across the slab (crux) and up to gain a thread belay on Sou'wester Slabs (at the top of a groove). The crux traverse can be avoided by descending to the left from the horizontal crack to the base of a groove which leads to the belay.

5. 35m 4c Climb the corner above the belay, then step left onto a small ledge on a slabby rib. Ascend the rib to the great overhang, then traverse left to gain a wall and continue left around a bulge. Climb up to easier ground and belay.

6. 30m Ascend broken slabs above to a short wall and climb through a recess, moving up a crack to finish on The Terrace.

6 Hammer   85m   VS **

R.Sim, D.Cameron   6 Aug 1960

A good route starting at a tapering slab just to the right of West Flank Route.

1. 25m 4b Climb up onto the slab, then go left to a crack. Follow the crack which becomes a small groove to belay above the first chimney of West Flank Route.

2. 20m 4c Descend a short distance until it is possible to traverse right a metre or so into a good crack containing a few tufts of grass. Climb the crack to belay on a large ledge.

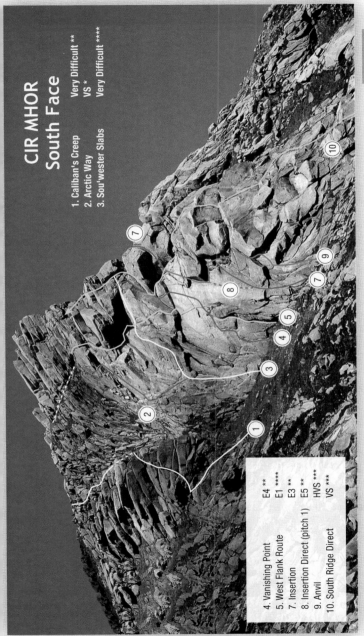

39

ARRAN

CIR MHOR
South Face

1. Caliban's Creep   Very Difficult **
2. Arctic Way   VS *
3. Sou'wester Slabs   Very Difficult ****

4. Vanishing Point   E4 **
5. West Flank Route   E1 ****
7. Insertion   E3 **
8. Insertion Direct (pitch 1)   E5 **
9. Anvil   HVS ***
10. South Ridge Direct   VS ***

3. 40m 4b Climb the crack in the slab above to reach a microgranite vein 5m from its end. Follow the vein rightwards (delicate in places) to a crack, then climb up to belay on South Ridge Direct.

7 Insertion   105m   E3 **

R.Carrington, I.Fulton   15 Jun 1969

A hard slab climb. Start about a metre to the right of a broad crack which is a short distance right of Hammer.

1. 45m 5c Climb straight up a steep slab to an overlap. Surmount this, continue up another steep slab, then trend right to belay a little way below the cave on Anvil.
2. 30m 4c Traverse up and left under the big overhang and climb the bulging rounded groove of Anvil to beneath the overhang. Move out right up a slab, then climb a groove to below a roof. Pull out right onto a slab and move easily left, crossing South Ridge Direct, to belay below a steep slab.
3. 30m 4c Move up left, then traverse horizontally right below an overhanging wall. Continue round an edge to a crack which is climbed to the big platform below the Three-Tier Chimney on South Ridge Direct.

8 Insertion Direct   95m   E5 **

M.Charlton, K.Howett   Jun 1986

A very bold first pitch, requiring continuous motion (upwards!). Start as for Insertion.

1. 50m 5c Climb a steep slab to an overlap. Surmount this, then climb straight up into a scoop in the centre of the slab. Ascend this, then teeter rightwards to take a hanging belay under the big overhang at the base of the bulging rounded groove of Anvil Variation Finish.
2. 25m 4c Gain and climb the groove to below a roof. Move out right up a slab and climb to belay at its top below a bulging wall containing a large round pocket.
3. 20m 5c Pull past the pocket and smaller ones above. Swing round the edge, then climb to reach easier ground on South Ridge Direct.

9 Anvil (Recess Start – Variation Finish)   65m   HVS ***

D.McKelvie, R.Richardson   6 Aug 1964; Recess Start: W.Skidmore, J.Crawford, J.Madden 16 Jul 1964; Variation Finish: R.Richardson, J.Madden   1965

Start at a corner-crack directly below the huge inverted-V recess on the front face of the ridge.

1. 15m 4b Climb the corner-crack to its finish.
2. 25m 5a Pull round left on to the slab and climb up until it is possible to move right to gain a large flake lodged under the right wall of the recess. Climb the flake, then step left to the opposite wall and gain the slab above by a strenuous pull-up out of the recess. Continue more easily by a crack on the right, then move left to reach a cave.
3. 25m 4c From the cave, traverse left under the big overhang and climb a bulging rounded groove to beneath an overhang. Move right up a slab, then climb a groove and more slabs to finish on South Ridge Direct. The original route broke out right from the cave.

10 South Ridge Direct   395m   VS ***

J.F.Hamilton, D.Paterson   Sep 1941

This splendid long and varied climb, one of the most popular on the island, has achieved classic status. The Y-cracks pitch is considerably harder than the rest and quite stiff for VS. From Fionn Choire the ridge rises as a steep nose out of a jumble of vegetated slabs. A very distinctive elongated S-shaped crack splits the face of the nose and this is the first main pitch of the route.

1. to 4. 130m Climb the vegetated slabs, by the line of least resistance (at most Very Difficult), to the base of the S-Crack and a large flake on the left.

Sou'wester Slabs, Very Difficult, South Face of Cir Mhor. Climber Melanie Nicoll (photo Grahame Nicoll)

5. 15m 4c Climb the S-Crack to a wide shelf with a block.

6. 10m 5a The overhanging Y-Cracks. A meaty little pitch! The obvious method is not necessarily the best.

7. 45m Move up to a block strewn terrace, step around a rib on the left, then make an easy ascending diagonal traverse across the top of the great western slabs to take an awkward belay in the far corner below the Layback Crack.

8. 20m 4b Climb the Layback Crack until a vein runs out to the right. Follow it across the slab (good hand holds above) to reach a large platform via a short corner. A very fine pitch.

9. 30m Above the platform, on the left side of the ridge crest, lies an obvious chimney in three sections, the Three-Tier Chimney. Climb it to gain the ridge crest.

10. and 11. 55m Two easy pitches along the crest lead to The Terrace below the Upper Pinnacle. The Upper Pinnacle can be avoided by walking off The Terrace, but it gives good quality climbing at about Very Difficult standard and should not be omitted.

12. 40m Start on the left and climb a short steep wall, via two undercut flakes, to gain a slab. Climb straight up this, near the ridge crest, to gain a fault coming in from the right. Follow this, then climb a chimney to a grass ledge.

13. 35m Move left across the grass ledge to a little chimney. Climb the slab on its right to the ridge crest. Move round right onto the east face, then make an exposed traverse right to a corner. Climb the corner to a crevasse belay.

14. 15m Climb a corner and short slab to the top of the Upper Pinnacle. A short descent leads to a path traversing westward to join the descent path of Cir Mhor's South-West Ridge. If time and energy allow, an ascent of The Rosetta Stone (see below) en route to the summit of Cir Mhor provides a fitting climax.

Variation: **South Ridge Original   60m   VS** *****

J.A.Ramsay and party   1935

Provides a more consistent grade for those who might find the Y-Cracks too hard, or a good alternative for climbers who find themselves queuing below the S-Crack.

1. 30m From the foot of the S-Crack, traverse right below the steep wall, then move up into a turfy recess below a big undercut corner.

2. 30m 4b Climb out of the recess (problematic) into the corner above. Ascend it until cracks running up the steep left wall can be climbed to the block strewn terrace above.

LOWER EAST FACE

The east flank of South Ridge is divided into Lower and Upper Faces by a break **Old East** (Moderate). The base of the East Face is gained via an ascent or descent of the gully on its right, Sub Rosa Gully.

Ariel's Arete   40m   E1 5b *******

M.Reynard, D.Musgrove   6 May 1995

Despite the initial messy scramble this is a really excellent pitch, which gains and follows flakes and cracks up the striking edge (flanked on its right by a massive slab), to the left of a wide vegetated open corner rising out of Sub Rosa Gully. A second 'first ascent' named it Squids and Elephants. Start at a messy bay just right of two parallel cracks in a proud buttress of poor rock beneath a flake-crack, which is **The Crack** (HVS 5a). Scramble up the bay, then move left to a ledge. Ascend a tricky little wall, then pull right into the flake crack system. Climb this, then take a remarkable thin crack seaming the very edge, to chill out on a rock ledge above. Ascend a slab past large pockets to belay at a horizontal fault. A short descent to the left, down a rock ramp, leads to the block strewn terrace on South Ridge Direct.

UPPER EAST FACE

This fine and very steep cracked wall overlooks the upper reaches of Sub Rosa Gully. The Sub Rosa Gully face forms a monolithic wall low down, bounded on its left by an unpleasant curving crack-line and on it right by chimney and crack-lines. Pinnacle Gully lies further right again.

Skydiver 80m E3 ****
G.E.Little, C.Ritchie 1 Aug 1981 (4PA); FFA and as described: C.MacLean, A.Nisbet, 7 May 1984
A brilliant route on excellent rock. Start at the foot of an arete, below a big lug of rock high up, about 15m left of the unpleasant curving crack-line.
1. 30m 5b Climb the left side of the arete via a corner and pull right on to the edge. Enter a superb twin cracked corner and climb it to a sloping stance below a roof. A magnificent pitch.
2. 10m 6a Make a contorted move left below the roof to enter a groove behind the lug. Follow the groove to a small stance beside a detached flake.
3. 40m 5a Stand on the detached flake, then climb a crack to a horizontal break. Move right to reach a flake. Climb this and the twin roofs above to enter a recess. Pull out right and move up slabs to reach a good ledge. Finish up an overhanging corner.

The Sleeping Crack 55m E6 ***
D.MacLeod, D.Honeyman Aug 2001
This stunning line climbs the attractive intermittent crack-line in the monolithic wall right of the curving crack-line. Unrepeated; four stars has been suggested. The second pitch gives bold exposed climbing followed by difficult moves in the crack.
1. 15m 6a Gain the first crack and follow it with increasing difficulty until it is possible to escape left on to a slab. Take a hanging belay on the huge thread.
2. 40m 6b Traverse right from the belay and boldly climb a sloping shelf to regain the crack-line. Follow this with hard moves (crux), but excellent protection to an undercut flake. Follow this leftwards, then up until below the final bulge. Climb rightwards up another flake, then make a difficult move up left on finger pockets to gain the finishing slab. Pad easily up this to a flake belay on the terrace (large Friends useful).

Labyrinth 120m VS 4b *
G.C.Curtis, H.K.Moneypenny 26 Sep 1943; Direct Finish: J.C.MacLaurin, J.S.Orr May 1951
The general line of the central chimney-crack gives a strenuous but fun start (if you like that sort of thing) and a fine finish. Start at a short rock alleyway just below the bottom right-hand corner of the monolithic wall.
1. 20m Enter the alleyway, moving behind an enormous jammed block. Exit left and continue up to a grass platform abutting the monolithic wall.
2. 10m Ascend a right-slanting groove to a sloping grass patch; the crack of **Easter Route** (HVS 5a) lies just to the right.
3. 15m A horizontal ledge runs across the wall on the left. Traverse across to reach a little undercut corner. Belay in the groove above.
4. 30m Climb the chimney-line above, initially grassy, then holding two groups of chockstones above a grass platform (optional belay), to belay in a rocky recess (The Eyrie) below the slightly overhung edge sweeping down from the summit – The Prow.
5. 40m 4b The original route traverses rightwards but this provides a much better finish, although VS instead of Severe. Climb straight up a big corner for about 5m to reach two horizontal faults running out left. Traverse these (crux) moving round a corner to join the final pitch of South Ridge Direct.

The Rosetta Stone 15m 5a **
R.Smith May 1955
This huge block lies on the west side of the Pinnacle summit, near the top of Pinnacle Gully. It is climbable on its west side – an exercise in pure friction! Descend by the same line on all fives.

GOATFELL

The highest mountain on the island lacks the steep walls that flank almost every other peak, but has extensive areas of slab on its western flanks.

ARRAN

ROSA SLABS

(NR 986 415)   Alt 460m   West facing   Map p32

The larger left-hand area, known as the Rosa Slabs, is directly under the summit. Two grass rakes, known as the First and Second Terraces, run up from left to right to form three sections. From the Glen Rosa path and on the approach, the slabs are much foreshortened and the rakes not immediately obvious. Except in dry weather, there can be wet streaks which often dry out during a sunny afternoon.

Approach: The slabs are best reached by toiling up the heather covered hillside from the Glen Rosa path. 2hrs.

Angel's Pavement   80m   Severe **
G.Kilgour, N.MacNiven   27 Jul 1960

An excellent clean route on the bottom right section. The lowest point of this section is a large undercut slab. Start at the highest point of the grassy rake which runs rightwards above this slab.
1. 20m Climb slabs to the right-hand of two cracks splitting the overlap above. Climb the crack to a small stance and spike belay.
2. 25m 4b Follow an obvious line diagonally left, then a prominent chain of pitted holds leading right. The holds give out 3m below a rounded ledge which must be gained. Traverse easily left to a small belay.
3. 35m Climb straight up the slab over two small overlaps to finish on the upper reaches of the First Terrace.
Fool's Causeway (see below) is the traditional continuation.

The Perfect Fool   170m   HVS **
A.Nisbet, A.Robertson   19 Apr 1981

Described as the best non-line on the slabs, it tackles the blankest and steepest section. Start about 10m right of Angel's Pavement. Climb diagonally leftwards across the clean slab, crossing a small overlap, until it is possible to climb straight up to the First Terrace at the foot of Fool's Causeway (4c). Traverse left and up on to the slab. Fool's Causeway now follows a very thin grassy crack slanting rightwards, but instead climb straight up the slab to an overlap. Surmount this and continue straight up, keeping to the rock (4c). Protection is scarce and belays should be taken as available.

Fool's Causeway   90m   HVS *
G.Kilgour, N.MacNiven   27 Jul 1960

This route starts on the First Terrace and finishes on the Second Terrace. Angel's Pavement is the traditional means of access. Start lower down the First Terrace from the top of Angel's Pavement, below a smooth water streaked slab, where two blocks form a thread belay. The climb is slow to dry.
1. 25m 4c Traverse left and up on to the slab. A metre or so higher, follow a very thin grassy crack slanting rightwards. From its finish, move up a short distance to a rock pocket. Poor belay.
2. 35m 4c Pad up right to a line of pockets leading to a tiny groove. This develops into a layback crack curving left to a small overlap. An easier groove and a slab now lead to a ledge.
3. 30m Easier slabs lead to the top of the Second Terrace.

SOUTH SLABS

(NR 986 409)   Alt 440m   West facing   Map p32

This clean and compact triangle of slab lies some 400m before the Rosa Slabs when

Tidemark, Severe 4b, Cioch na h-Oighe. Climber Dave MacLeod
(photo Dave MacLeod collection)

approaching up the Glen Rosa path. The rock is excellent, clean and continuous, and provides some of the best middle grade slab climbing on the island. The shorter access makes it convenient before catching the ferry. The climbing style is similar to the more famous Etive Slabs, but the rock is rougher and with more holds, although similarly few runners. The routes can be climbed with increasing ease as confidence in the excellent friction grows.

Approach: From the main Glen Rosa path cross the burn, then head up the line of a stream which descends from the right side of the slabs. A small path then leads diagonally left to the base and a worn patch on a grass ledge at the foot of the cleanest section of slab. 1hr 45mins.

Descent: Scramble down grass and heather on the right (south) side.

Dogleg   110m   VS *
J.R.Brumfitt, A.McKeith   21 Jun 1964
Start immediately left of the worn patch.
1. 25m 4b Climb a little ramp leftwards, then go up to a break in a thin overlap at 6m. Cross this, then climb a flake edge. Move right, then go up into a flake-groove, climbed to small ledges (the cracks may need some cleaning).
2. 45m 4b Continue up the flake-groove to its top (Blank now joins from the right). Climb up pockets in a slight scoop to reach a flake-corner. Traverse left until a line of pockets leads straight up to a small spike in a corner.
3. 40m 4b Climb the rib on the left of the corner (you should be getting more confident in the friction now!) to reach and climb the easier upper slabs.

Blank   110m   VS ***
B.Kelly, A.McKeith   13 Sep 1963
A fine route, best of the three because it climbs up the centre of the slabs. Start at the worn patch, just right of Dogleg.
1. 30m 4b Climb boldly up the slab to gain a line of scoops and flakes, trending slightly right to a small gravelly ledge in a heather groove off to the right of the main slab.
2. 45m 4b Step left, move up, then follow a wide vein running left across the slab until 5m before a heather groove. Climb up pockets in a slight scoop to reach a flake-corner. At its top, traverse 3m right, surmount an overlap, then follow a line of pockets straight up to a ledge.
3. 35m 4b Climb directly up the centre of a big slab (superb but unprotected).
Direct Variation: Even better, but spoils Dogleg as a second route. Start as normal but climb directly up the slab to join Dogleg at the flake-groove. Follow this to where Blank is joined again.

Blankist   100m   HVS **
G.E.Little, K.Howett   20 Aug 1995
Takes a direct line up the right side of the slab. Start just right of a black streak, 5m right of Blank. Only marginally harder than the other two routes.
1. 30m 4c Climb straight up the holdless slab (crux) to reach flakes. Ascend these to join Blank and belay on the same gravelly ledge on the right.
2. 25m 4c Step left and climb straight up a line of perfect pockets, trending left to gain an obvious long thin downward-facing flake. Thin moves above the flake lead to more flakes.
3. 45m 4b Climb straight up a bare slab to the right end of the ledge on Blank. Continue straight up to follow an obvious rib (overlooking a long corner to the right), then easier-angled slabs to the top. An exhilarating unprotected pitch.

Glen Sannox & North Glen Sannox

The spectacular Cioch na h-Oighe and Cuithe Mheadhonach on Caisteal lie at the northern end of the range, outwith the Glen Rosa horseshoe, and are best approached from Glen Sannox and North Glen Sannox.

CIOCH NA H-OIGHE

(NR 999 439)   Alt 470m   South-East facing   Map p32   Diagram p49

This excellent little mountain presents one of the most spectacular mountain views on Arran. Although all sides of the mountain are rocky, it is Coire na Ciche, also known as The Devil's Punchbowl, that contains its true pride; a long cliff rising over 200m from the corrie floor to the summit ridge, with the very best and the very worst that Arran rock has to offer. The Bastion, the great clean wall in the centre of the face, holds a concentration of high standard climbs, some of the best on the island and comparable with the best in Scotland. All have a serious mountaineering feel about them. Unless otherwise indicated, the routes dry quickly after rain.

Five roughly parallel rakes run diagonally upward across the face from left to right. Numbered 1 to 5 from the right, these infamous ledges consist of crumbly rock and unstable vegetation and are best avoided other than the necessity of Ledge 3 which gives access to the base of The Bastion and the upper part of Ledge 4 which provides access to the summit ridge.

Approach: From the car park at Sannox Bay (NS 016 454) follow the main Glen Sannox track to the ford over the Allt a' Chapuill, the burn draining from Coire na Ciche. A path follows the east (left) side of this burn up into the floor of the corrie. 1hr.

The main features of The Bastion are the great parallel grooves of **Klepht** (E2 5c) and Armadillo on the left and the striking horn like flake of Rhino on the right. A rock shelf cuts across this great wall at two-thirds height (the line of Tidemark). Another enormous flake sits below this shelf on the left, forming the reversed image of the Rhino flake which in combination resemble the pincers of a giant crab's claw.

◀ **Armadillo   100m   E3 *****
W.Skidmore, R.Richardson   14 Jul 1977 (3PA); FFA and Direct Variation: C.Macadam, S.Steer   29 May 1985
A brilliant climb up the prominent roofed groove to the right of Klepht. It is worth its three stars, despite a rather messy top pitch.
1. 25m 6a Climb the groove until hard under the second roof. Desperate but well protected moves lead left around this to a ledge and belay under the third and biggest roof.
2. 35m 5b Re-enter the groove and climb it to near the top where a hard traverse left gains a ledge. Climb an awkward slab wall to reach a grass rake and bolt belay. Alternatively (and more logically), instead of taking the left traverse, continue straight on up into a slabby groove to gain the grass rake. Although it is possible to drop down and traverse off left above Klepht at this point, the character building pleasures of the final pitch should not be missed!
3. 40m 5b Climb a hard scoop, then take the short overhung corner above to gain a grass ledge. Traverse left, move up, then step back right to gain an easy turfy groove leading left to a flake belay on Ledge 4.

2 Abraxas   105m   E4 **
G.E.Little, R.J.Little   26 May 1980 (12PA); FFA: C.Macadam, S.Steer   1 Jun 1985
A fine but originally controversial route due to the aid, taking a sensational line across the bare central section of The Bastion. Pitch 2 is rarely dry. Start directly below the right-hand end of a prominent arched overhang.
1. 30m 6a Traverse leftwards and slightly up to the left end of the arch. Move left around the edge to the base of a yellow roof-capped corner. Climb this, then pull right on to the wall. Move slightly left at a horizontal break, then move up to gain a hidden finger pocket. Climb up from this to gain a hand-traverse line leading right to a belay on a small rock ledge just above.
2. 35m 6a Climb a diagonal finger crack to a narrow sloping shelf. Gain this awkwardly, then undercling left to reach a vertical waterworn groove. At the top of this

groove, step left on to a sloping rock ledge (two bolts in-situ just above, optional belay). Cross the thin ledge (initially rock, then turf) with some difficulty (often wet) to gain a niche and bolt belay.

3. 40m 5b Climb a crack on decomposing rock to an undercut flake. Pull left on good holds to reach a crack which leads to a heather ledge. Follow a narrowing slab ramp leftwards to join the easy turfy groove on the final pitch of Armadillo and climb this to Ledge 4.

3 The Great Escape   100m   E8 ***
J.Dunne, A.Jack   21 Jun 2001
The last guide stated: "A tenuous line running up the blank wall to nearly reach the left-hand pincer presents Arran's 'last great problem' and a major challenge for the 21st century." Six months into the new millennium the 'last great problem' was solved, with the unknowing second ascent following on a week later.

1. 30m 6b Climb the open groove right of the 1st pitch of Abraxas, over a roof to an obvious ledge.

2. 40m 6c The awesome main pitch. From the belay climb directly up the stunning leftward trending groove line to a poor in-situ thread runner. Make difficult moves diagonally leftwards to gain the left-hand pincer. Follow this in a spectacular position to a belay on the Tidemark ramp.

3. 30m 6b Climb the obvious scoop above the belay, with a hard move at roughly 5m, to a spike runner. Ascend the slab above and finish up easier ground and the top of Ledge 4.

4 Rhino   85m   E2 *
G.E.Little   3 Jun 1979 (2PA); FFA: P.Whillance and party   1983
This fine line climbs the crack defining the left side of the great horn like flake on the right side of the wall. Start directly below the flake.

1. 25m 5b Gain and climb a short left-facing flake. Mantelshelf up, go straight up to a bulge, then pull left to reach a small ledge. Climb to a curious hole, then up the left-hand of the twin grooves above (the right-hand one has an old peg and is slightly harder). Traverse right to reach a grass ledge and belay below the horn.

2. 20m 5b Climb straight up on good flakes, then by a crack to enter the widening flake-crack which leads to an exit around a chockstone at the top. Belay on the ledge of Tidemark.

3. 40m 5b Walk right and climb the corner above a big block (often wet). Make a slight detour on the left wall, then continue up the corner to a large grass ledge (optional belay). Climb a short overhanging corner to a ledge and belay. An alternative, harder and better start (5c) to this pitch is to climb the slabby pocketed wall directly above the horn to gain some small flakes and a right-trending ramp which leads back to the original line. Quite bold! Ledge 4 can be reached via a short scramble.

5 Tidemark   75m   Severe **
A.J.Maxfield, J.Peacock   9 Jun 1960
A delightful and exposed girdle provides a great mountaineering expedition with tremendous situations following the striking curving rock shelf that divides the lower two-thirds from the upper third of The Bastion's main wall. The shelf can be clearly seen from the main Corrie to Sannox road. Ascend Ledge 3, passing below The Bastion and scramble across to the start, which is near the upper end of and well above Ledge 3 at a rounded flake close to the obvious start of the line

1. 30m Cross two slabs (often wet) to reach a grassy corner and a split block. Climb over the block, then follow the grass ledge to take an eyehole belay a short distance up the clean rock gangway.

2. 30m Follow the exposed gangway to its end and belay on a small ledge just left of an overhang. A splendid pitch!

3. 15m 4b Climb an awkward flake-crack, then traverse left into a heather groove to finish on Ledge 4.

CIOCH NA H-OIGHE

1. Armadillo	E3 ***
2. Abraxas	E4 **
3. The Great Escape	E8 ***
4. Rhino	E2 *
5. Tidemark	Severe **

A. Klepht corner

Armadillo, E3 6a, Cioch na h-Oighe. Climber Derek Austin
(photo Andrew Fraser)

CAISTEAL ABHAIL - CUITHE MHEADHONACH

(NR 970 451) Alt 500m East facing Map p32

This striking slabby wall lies on the east flank of the north ridge of Caisteal Abhail facing into Coire nan Ceum. Cuithe Mheadhonach means Central Stronghold, a very appropriate name. The following routes, on the pale wall on the left of the crag, are quick drying, although the rest of the crag is not.

Approach: From the A841 in North Glen Sannox a fairly wet path runs from the bridge car park (NR 993 467) along the south side of the burn. The walk is rather uninspiring until the cliff comes into sight before quitting the forestry plantation. The side of a picturesque small gorge then leads to the burn junction. Cross the burn just above this junction, then head straight up to the crag. 1hr 15mins. There may be restrictions during the stalking season (see Environment notes).

Ulysses 50m E2 **
G.E.Little, W.Skidmore 9 May 1982
This route takes a left of centre line up the pale wall. A fine climb despite the presence of some crumbly rock. Start on a vegetated terrace (accessed by scrambling in from the left) 6m right of the obvious vegetated crack.
1. 25m 5c Trend right, bypassing the right end of a thin roof, to gain a slight right-facing scoop. Move up, then take a left-trending line to reach the right end of the long roof. Move left under the roof to a good thread runner. Surmount the roof directly, then climb the short wall above (crux) until a short left traverse can be made to a small ledge and bolt belay.
2. 25m 5c Traverse right to reach crumbling flakes. Climb these and the crack above to reach a small flake. Traverse hard right to shallow corner-cracks which lead to a traverse left for 3m under bulging rock. Strenuous moves over the bulge and short rock steps lead to the top.

Icarus 55m E5 **
K.Howett, G.E.Little 22 Jul 1995
A sustained line starting on the wall between Ulysses and Achilles, then crossing Ulysses to tackle the headwall to its left, giving an amazing pitch. Start, as for Ulysses, 6m right of the vegetated crack.
1. 30m 6b Trend right, bypassing the right end of a thin roof, to gain a slight right-facing scoop and small ledge above (Ulysses goes up and left from here). Traverse hard right to gain big flat holds. From the top of these traverse slightly left, then move up via a finger pocket to reach an undercling. Move left to an incipient flake, climb this, then make precarious moves over a bulge and go up to reach a deep horizontal break. Traverse left strenuously to below twin flakes (Friend 0). Pull up to stand in the break, then teeter left to reach the left traverse leading to the bolt belay of Ulysses. Very sustained climbing.
2. 25m 6b Climb up the flakes and cracks of Ulysses to a jug where that route traverses right. Traverse left to a big flake. Pull up, then ascend a line of small pockets in the wall above with desperation to a horizontal break. Finish straight up.

Achilles 50m E5 **
G.E.Little 29 Apr 1984 (2PA); Free variation: G.E.Little, K.Howett, 6 Aug 1995
A spectacular and excellent climb taking a fairly central line on the pale wall on the left side of the crag. The route can be led as a single pitch, but a double set of small Friends is required to protect it adequately. Start about 10m right of Ulysses at the highest point of the vegetated terrace.
1. 20m 5c Climb the slabby wall to reach an easy left-facing flake system. From the top of this a second and fragile flake is gained by difficult moves on the left. A long stretch allows a step up on to the top of the fragile flake, from where a bombproof Rock 9 belay can be placed in a short deep vertical crack.
2. 30m 6c The belay crack curves left to become a horizontal break. Hand-traverse this break until a step up can be made onto a higher break. Move right, then make desperate moves to gain a fat left-facing flake (crux). Pull over this to reach a horizontal break, then reach left to gain another flake edge. A horizontal crack, becoming a rail, runs out left. Follow it to reach the obvious vertical crack and flake system which leads strenuously but more easily to the top.

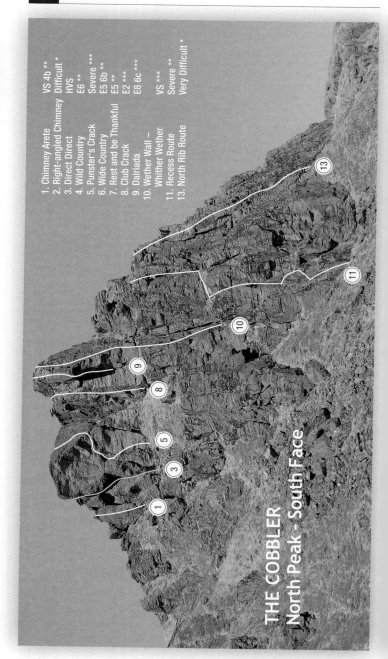

THE COBBLER
North Peak - South Face

1. Chimney Arete — VS 4b **
2. Right-angled Chimney — Difficult *
3. Direct Direct — HVS
4. Wild Country — E6 **
5. Punster's Crack — Severe ***
6. Wide Country — E5 6b **
7. Rest and be Thankful — E5 **
8. Club Crack — E2 ***
9. Dalriada — E8 6c ***
10. Wether Wall – Whither Wether — VS ***
11. Recess Route — Severe **
13. North Rib Route — Very Difficult *

THE COBBLER

This rocky peak rises above Arrochar and Loch Long, to the west of Loch Lomond. Its North and South Peaks are two of the most distinctive mountain silhouettes in the Southern Highlands, and its highest point, the Central Peak, is one of an exclusive club of Scottish summits that can only be ascended by rock climbing. Some of the climbs are quite short for mountain routes but follow well defined features on formations which are unlike anywhere else. The views from the cliffs are excellent.

Maps: OS L56, E364; Harvey Superwalker Arrochar

SMC Climbers' Guide: *Arran, Arrochar and the Southern Highlands* (1997)

Public Transport: Tarbet, approximately 3km from Arrochar, has a station on the Glasgow to Fort William line. Many buses run daily to Arrochar from Glasgow.

Amenities: Arrochar at the foot of the mountain, has shops, cafes, hotels and petrol. Information Centre at Ardgarten (08707 200606).
Camping: Ardgarten (01301 702293).

THE COBBLER

(NN 259 058)   Alt 884m   Map p60

The Cobbler's convenient location and easy road access made it the focus of Glaswegian climbers since the birth of climbing in the 19th Century when transport was more difficult. Starting with The Cobbler Club formed in 1866 by Professor Gordon Ramsay, its history progressed through the early days of the SMC at the end of the century to Jock Nimlin who climbed 11 routes in the 1930s. Soon after, the Creagh Dhu, from the shipyards of the Clyde and including John Cunningham, climbed many of the harder and cleaner features in the late 1940s and '50s. This left the smooth and serious faces to be climbed in more modern times, particularly by Dave Cuthbertson, not forgetting the awesome hooked arete of Dalriada, the Cobbler's defining feature, redpointed by Gary Latter in 1994. The mica schist can be alternatively smooth and slabby, then steep and pocketed, covered in a fine patina of tough, grey lichen and protection ranges from bomb proof through fiddly to non-existent. Accordingly, some routes are quite serious for their grade.

Approach: Park at a large car park beside the A83 at the head of Loch Long (NN 292 050). Follow the new track which zigzags through the felled forest to meet the Allt a' Bhalachain and a dam. Follow the path alongside the burn, past the Narnain Boulders and across the burn. Ascend the corrie below the South Face of North Peak to arrive at the col between the North and Centre Peaks in about 1hr 45mins.

Despite the implication that the North, Centre and South Peaks lie in a straight line, they actually surround the corrie facing Arrochar and Loch Long. The South Face of North Peak faces into the corrie, whereas the South Face of South Peak faces out of the corrie and across Glen Croe.

NORTH PEAK - SOUTH FACE

Alt 800m   South facing

Two impressive and wildly overhanging prows of compact mica schist give this face its distinct profile. They lie on the upper left, above a terrace. The right side of the face is more broken and vegetated and offers routes of a traditional mountaineering nature. The routes are described from left to right, starting from the col.

**Chimney Arete   25m   VS 4b ** ✱✱
J.Cunningham, I.Dingwall   Jun 1947
The arete left of the obvious corner-chimney gives a fine route with minimal protection until mid-height. Previously graded Severe! Climb the arete, with one difficult move on to a flat hold to avoid a bulge at mid-height.

2 Right-Angled Chimney   30m   Difficult *
Climb the obvious big open chimney to pass the roof via sloping polished holds on the slabby left wall.

3 Direct Direct   30m   HVS 5a
J.Cunningham   1948
The overhanging crack above a recess at the lowest point of this buttress leads to a big groove which passes left of the prow and finishes up an off-width crack in a chimney.

4 Wild Country   50m   E6 **
D.Cuthbertson, R.Kerr   4 Jul 1979
The original route on this wildly overhanging wall gives bold and powerful climbing. Despite repeats it still awaits an on sight ascent. Start in the recess of Direct Direct.
1. 20m 5c Climb the strenuous overhanging crack on the right, then go up to the block belay on Punster's Crack.
2. 30m 6b Climb leftwards up the wall, then continue up the quartz blotched wall to a ledge (runners in a thin crack on the right). Ascend overhung ledges rightwards and where they peter out, step up and then right to a good hold at the foot of a thin overhanging crack. Climb the crack (Friend 1.5 at the top) heading for a small but good sidepull on the left, before reaching a recess below the top. Good flake belay well back.
Variation: **Wild at Heart   6b**
From the ledge on pitch 2, this route climbs out left past a number of pegs to good finishing holds near the arete of the prow.

5 Punster's Crack   45m   Severe ***
J.Cunningham, W.Smith   Aug 1949
An excellent route taking the easiest line through some impressive scenery. Start below a slabby wall leading to a short corner which is right of the recess of Direct Direct and just left of a deep chimney to the left of the deep corner-gully between the two buttresses with the prows (Right-Angled Gully).
1. 20m 4a Climb the wall and corner, then continue up and left to a large block belay below the overhanging wall.
2. 15m 4a Traverse up and right, passing below the wide crack taken by Wide Country, to an obvious gap. Bridge the gap and continue more easily to a belay at the right end of the ledge overlooking Right-Angled Gully.
3. 10m 4a Step left and follow cracks up the slabby wall in a fine position. A good flake belay well back.

6 Wide Country   E5 6b **
R.Campbell, P.Thorburn   20 Jul 1994
The striking off-width in the headwall above Punster's Crack gives a memorable experience; tape and large camming devices de rigeur.

Right of the wildly overhanging wall is the open corner of **Right-Angled Gully** (Very Difficult). Right of that is an impressive steep wall with a prominent groove to the left of centre, the line of Rest and Be Thankful. The prominent jagged crack right of the groove is Club Crack, while Dalriada climbs the edge of the prow forming the wall's right arete.

7 Rest and be Thankful   45m   E5 **
D.Cuthbertson, K.Johnstone   25 May 1980
A classic Cobbler wall climb. Start at the foot of the obvious groove, often wet at the top, in the left-hand side of the wall.

Punster's Crack, Severe 4a, The Cobbler. Climber Bitta Dost
(photo Cubby Images)

1. 35m 6a Follow the groove to its top, traverse left then step down and left to good holds. Traverse about 3m left, go up to a good foothold, then move up and right to a horizontal break. Continue up and left to a good ledge. Climb the wall, then move easily right to a thread belay.

2. 10m 4c Climb the wall above at its highest point.

Variation: **E5 6b** ✳✳

P.Laughlan May 1987

Climb diagonally up and left from the top of the initial groove.

8 Club Crack   40m   E2 ✳✳
P.Walsh and party   1957

The steep crack springing from the cave is sustained, strenuous and technical with fiddly protection. Start below and left of the cave. A direct start is also possible through the roof above the cave at 5b.

1. 35m 5c Traverse awkwardly right to gain the crack and climb it past a wilting rusty peg and a good spike runner disturbingly far out right. A difficult move where the crack closes brings better holds, protection and respite. A final steep wall leads to the terrace.

2. 10m 4c Climb the wall behind at its highest point.

The next route starts from a higher grass ledge on the right, gained by squeezing through a fissure in the cave below Club Crack, not as narrow or as awkward as it looks.

9 Dalriada   40m   E6 6b ✳✳✳
G.Latter   20 Sep 1995

An awe inspiring line up the superb jutting prow right of a slabby open corner **Right-Angled Groove** (VS 4c). It is sustained and technical but well protected by nine peg runners, although a small rack is still required. The grade will increase to E7 as the pegs deteriorate. Start up the slabby corner, which rises above the cave exit, for 3m to a ledge, then climb the flake-crack above to two peg runners. Move right round the arete and go up to a superb thread. Climb straight up a thin finger crack and the arete past a poor peg to a hands-off rest under the roof. Steep moves out left and up lead to a prominent diagonal crack and a line of incut jugs which lead past more pegs to the capping wall. Continue with interest past two small fingerpockets to pull out right to a ledge, then move up to a belay.

10 Wether Wall – Whither Wether   85m   VS ✳✳✳
J.Cunningham, H.MacInnes   Sep 1951 (Wether Wall); H.MacInnes, W.Smith   Aug 1952 (Whither Wether)

This combination makes a very fine excursion. Whither Wether is one of the finest VS pitches in Scotland, taking a tremendous exposed line up the right side of the jutting prow, with a minimum of protection. At the base of a lower tier but still directly below the prow, is a wide bay which leads up right into a chimney. Left of the chimney is an arete directly in line with the prow above. Wether Wall climbs its right wall. Scramble up the easy initial section of the gully to where it steepens.

1. 40m 4c Step left on to the wall, move up and continue to an obvious left-pointing flake. Pull over this and climb the groove above to belay just right of the cave exit (and Right-angled Groove).

2. 45m 4b Climb the steep wall up and right, then move round the edge on to the slabby wall. Climb the wall, keeping close to the left edge (crux) to gain the right side of a niche at 25m. Finish by going slightly right and up, or step left and climb the edge to the top.

11 Recess Route   85m   Severe ✳✳
J.B.Nimlin, J.Fox, R.Ewing   May 1935

One of The Cobbler's best known climbs, Recess Route has a distinct mountaineering ambience and is deservedly popular. Some of the holds are very polished, and

care should be taken in damp conditions. Start at the left side of the lowest rocks.
1. 20m Climb a clean crack diagonally left, then go up and right to climb a wide curving crack to below a deep chimney.
2. 25m Climb the chimney passing an overhang and continue by the deep chimney above to a big terrace.
3. 5m Traverse easily right along the terrace to a belay.
4. 10m From the right-hand end of the terrace step into and ascend a steep groove (crux) to a cave.
5. 25m   Climb round the overhang above on either side and finish by a final chimney.

On the right side of the face is the wide Great Gully. The following route climbs the prominent rocky rib flanking it on the right.

Spinal Rib   30m   VS 4b *
P.Walsh   Sep 1952
A steep, sustained and well protected route with amazing exposure. Start 2m right of an obvious V-corner in the right wall of Great Gully, below an undercut rib. Pull up on to the rib and climb it over several bulges to a resting spot under the final overhang. Climb this to the right (strenuous) or the left (technical) to join North Rib Route. Go a short way up to belay below a short wall.

North Rib Route   90m   Very Difficult *
J.B.Nimlin, J.Fox   1935
A traditional mountaineering route with good rock and situations up short steep walls. Start about 5m right of the gully at a steep shallow recess. Gain the rib and cross grass to belay in a corner. Surmount a block, then traverse left for a few metres to the rib which leads to the top.

CENTRE PEAK

This is the highest of The Cobbler's three peaks and since the summit can only be gained by climbing, most will wish to pay it a visit, particularly if heading from the climbing on North Peak to the climbing on South Peak.

Doorway Route   15m   Moderate **
The north face of the summit pinnacle is cut through by a 'doorway' in the rock. Squeeze through this to the south side and follow an exposed ledge from where a high step gains the top. Return by going out through the in door.

The Arete   60m   Difficult **
W.W.Naismith, G.Thomson   Jul 1989
The south ridge of Centre Peak provides a pleasant traverse. Begin at the col between the South and Centre Peaks, climb a 15m crack and follow the arete to the summit with good situations and rapidly polishing holds. Descend by Doorway Route.

SOUTH PEAK - SOUTH FACE

Alt 750m   South-west facing   Diagram p58

This steep slabby wall overlooks Glen Croe and contains some of the best and cleanest rock on The Cobbler. It receives a considerable amount of sunshine and offers tremendous, but often quite serious rock routes.

Approach: The most direct approach is direct from the dam, via a good path up the south-east ridge. From climbs on the North Peak, traverse the corrie bowl and ascend to the col left of the South Peak's North Face, before dropping down to the South Face. However, it is much more fun to follow the well-worn path round the

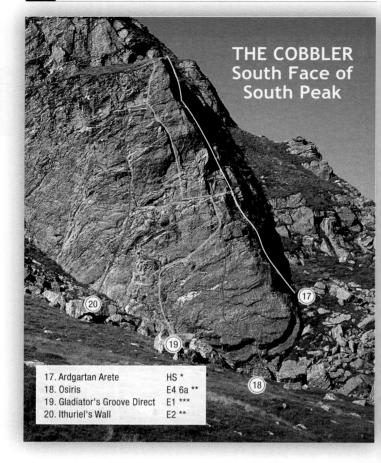

THE COBBLER
South Face of
South Peak

17. Ardgartan Arete	HS *
18. Osiris	E4 6a **
19. Gladiator's Groove Direct	E1 ***
20. Ithuriel's Wall	E2 **

top of the corrie taking in the Centre Peak's summit en route, before dropping down to the South Peak's South Face.

Descent: Traverse terraces right to a vegetated face and descend this. Or scramble over the summit and descend its Original Route, polished but well protected, or abseil from the block near the top of Original Route, overlooking the col between South Peak and Centre Peak (25m).

The first route lies on the lower left-hand section of the North-East, corrie face, of South Peak, which is separated from the main South Face by the south-east crest of the buttress. If approaching up the south-east ridge it is on the right. If traversing the corrie bowl from the North Peak you will pass below it before reaching the col on the south-east ridge.

16 S-Crack   40m   VS 4c **
J.Cunningham, W.Smith   Jun 1948
Left of the lowest rocks and right of a short gully blocked by an overhang is an

COBBLER

obvious clean corner crack. Climb the superb sustained crack over two bulges to finish on a ledge. Walk off left to grassy ledges.

The following routes lie on the steep slabby wall overlooking Glen Croe.

Ardgartan Arete   55m   Hard Severe *
J.Cunningham   Jun 1948
This enjoyable bold route follows the prominent arete forming the right side of the wall. Originally graded Severe and many still think it is. Start about 15m up right from the toe of the buttress where an obvious shallow groove slants up left to join the arete.
1. 30m 4a Follow the groove with little protection over a bulge at 5m, then continue up grooves in the arete to belay at the end of the terrace which slants up below the corners of Gladiator's Groove and Ithuriel's Wall.
2. 10m 4a Climb the wall above, then continue up cracks to belay on the left at a block on the arete.
3. 15m 4a Follow the crack in the wall above to finish on the terrace. This is the descent terrace used by climbs on the South Face. The wall can also be climbed on the left, overlooking the South Face.

Osiris   30m   E4 6a **
D.Griffiths (unseconded)   6 Apr 1988
The original route on the slab gives brilliant climbing with a steep, strenuous and technical crux, followed by a bold and delicate slab of excellent rock. High in the grade. The pegs look rusty, so an abseil down to check is recommended. Start at the lowest point of the slab to the right of a boulder, at an obvious cleaned ledge. Climb to ledges (peg runner), then go out leftwards under the overlap to an inset slab. Pull over the overlap to a peg and climb direct to an in-situ thread runner, then straight up to a small overlap and a runner in a slot. Move left to large pockets, then go straight up to the quartz band and a peg runner. Climb up slightly right until below the prominent block on the arete and finish up its left side.

Gladiator's Groove Direct   65m   E1 ***
W.Smith, H.MacInnes   Aug 1951; Direct start: W.Smith, R.Hope   Jun 1952
A Cobbler classic which takes the left edge of the impressive quartz banded slab which lies at the base of the wall and the right-facing corner above. Much of the route is straightforward for the grade, but the two hard cruxes are characterised by poor protection and a confident approach is essential. Start at steep rock below the left end of the broad quartz band, at a grassy triangular recess.
1. 35m 5a Awkward, strenuous and unprotected moves up the overhanging wall lead to the quartz. Continue up the steep slab to a ledge, then traverse delicately right to the large block. Continue up past a peg and flake to belay on the broad ledge below the corner.
2. 20m 5b The corner gives enjoyable climbing until a step left and an awkward move gain a disturbingly overhanging groove which can only be protected through effort, care and cunning. A difficult and committing udge up and left usually gains the ledge. Belay on wires in the corner on the right.
3. 10m 4c Climb the corner, to finish as for Ithuriel's Wall at the terrace.

Ithuriel's Wall   45m   E2 **
H.MacInnes   Aug 1952 (aid); FFA: J.Hutchison 1976
A prominent left-facing corner about 10m left of the right arete of the face, combining increasingly tenuous climbing with diminishing protection. Start at easy broken grooves below and left of the corner.
1. 10m 4a Climb the grooves to a block belay on the broad ledge below the corner.
2. 25m 5c Follow the fine corner past bulges to the large ledge on Gladiator's Groove. Belay on wires in the corner on the right.
3. 10m 4c Climb the arete on the right of the corner to the top.

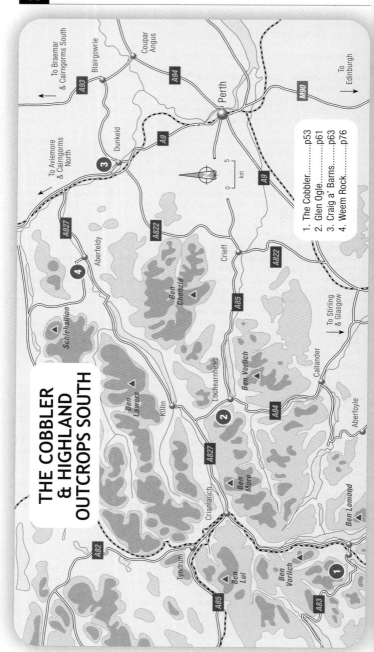

THE COBBLER
& HIGHLAND
OUTCROPS SOUTH

To Braemar & Cairngorms South

Blairgowrie

Coupar Angus

A93

A94

Perth

To Edinburgh

M90

A9

Dunkeld

To Aviemore & Cairngorms North

A827

Aberfeldy

A822

Crieff

A822

N

0 5
km

Schiehallion

Ben Chonzie

Ben Lawers

Killin

Lochearnhead

Ben Vorlich

Callander

To Stirling & Glasgow

Ben More

Crianlarich

Aberfoyle

A827

A84

A85

A82

Tyndrum

Ben Lui

Ben Vorlich

Ben Lomond

A85

A83

HIGHLAND OUTCROPS SOUTH

These three venues lie in the southern part of the Highlands, away from the mountains and with a generally drier and sunnier climate, particularly when the wind is in the northern half of the compass. Craig a' Barns offers mostly traditional routes at all grades; Weem and Glen Ogle sport routes in the middle or hard grades.

Maps: OS L52, L51

SMC Climbers' Guide: *Highland Outcrops* (1998)

Public Transport: Dunkeld is easily reached by train from Glasgow, Edinburgh or Inverness. Many buses per day run from either Edinburgh or Glasgow, via Perth. Aberfeldy (Weem) is also accessible by bus, but Glen Ogle is less convenient.

Amenities: Dunkeld and Weem are near towns and villages, Glen Ogle less so.

Glen Ogle

There are a number of recently developed sport crags on either side of the glen.

DARK SIDE

Approach: Park at a large lay-by near the top of the glen (NN 562 275), just beyond a small bridge (a short way south of the snack van). Drop down through trees to the old railway line and follow this down the glen. For The Diamond, walk along the line until you reach the viaduct and then break rightwards uphill to reach the crag in 20mins (recognised by the steep diamond shaped wall near the left end). To reach Bond Buttress follow sheep paths leftwards from The Diamond to reach open hillside. The tall buttress at the top of the slope can be recognised by the large blunt arete in the centre, 15mins, 35mins total.

BOND BUTTRESS

(NN 568 261) Alt 350m East facing

This wall is more exposed to breezes than the Diamond and gives long airy routes on vertical walls and grooves.

Scaramanga 20m F7a+ **
N.Sheperd 1993
Climb the big flake come groove just right of the blunt arete on good holds to a resting ledge below the roof. A technical section leads leftwards to a difficult swing onto the arete. The arete direct is **Solitaire** (F8b).

Boldfinger 22m F7a ***
D.Redpath 2003
A superb varied route, one of the best in the area. Follow the Scaramanga groove to the ledge. Break out right through roofs on big holds to gain the superb pockety headwall. This leads with sustained interest to the top.

THE DIAMOND

(NN 568 265) Alt 250m North-East facing

Probably the best and most popular crag in the glen, with many routes at a good spread of grades. It seeps after prolonged wet periods, but once dry it can be climbed on during wet weather. The climbing is fairly short, steep and pumpy.

Easy Over 12m F7a *
R.Anderson 1993
Good climbing up a steep pocketed wall to the ledge (there is a small flake just before the ledge). Above this, jugs lead through the roof at the left edge of the diamond shaped wall to an easy finishing slab.

Spiral Tribe 15m F8a ***
D.McCallum 1993
The excellent smooth overhanging wall in the centre of the diamond. Pull over a short bulge to a stopping place, then launch up the steep wall above with great moves and increasing difficulty to a crux last move.

Off the Beaten Track 15m F8a **
P.Thorburn 1993
Difficult fingery climbing up the right side of the diamond wall, pulling through the roof to start. The crux is at mid-height on small pockets.

Chain Lightning 15m F7b+ ***
R.Anderson 1993
The steep hanging right arete of the diamond shaped wall. Superb technical moves through the roof lead to easier climbing.

Old Wives' Tale 15m F6b *
N.Sheperd 1993
The crag warm-up takes the corner and ramp right of the steep arete. Good climbing.

Metal Guru 15m F6c **
R.Anderson 1992
The thin crack on the vertical wall just right of Old Wives' Tale. The climbing gets increasingly difficult towards the top.

SUNNY SIDE

The east side of the Glen has over 80 short sport routes on the many scattered buttresses. Mirror Wall gives the best range of grades on good quick drying rock.

MIRROR WALL

(NN 568 275) Alt 450m South-West facing

This smooth slabby wall is situated up and left of the main group of crags on the sunny (east) side of the glen, near the top of a small valley formed by a burn. It features fingery, off vertical climbing on excellent pocketed rock.

Approach: From the lay-by at the top of the glen (NN 562 275), cross the road and climb over the fence. Follow a rising traverse southwards passing under the electricity lines. Once you reach a burn (forming a shallow valley), the smooth light coloured wall can be seen at the top of the valley. Walk up the burn to reach the wall, 20mins.

Munrobagger 15m F6b+ *
G.Ridge 1998
The wide crack at the left end which shapes the left side of the wall.

Blind Faith 15m F7b+ *
D.Redpath 1997
Make a series of hard moves on two finger pockets to gain the small pod. Continue with less difficulty.

Take a Hike 15m F7a **
J.Horrocks 1998
A line of staple bolts. Pass the shield of rock on its left and follow the blank looking wall with a thin crack in it.

Cony the Calvinist 15m F6c *
D.Redpath 1998

Pass the shield of rock via some cracks in its left side to a standing position. Keep hunting for pockets in the top wall.

**Fat Eagles Fly Low   15m   F6a+ ** **
J.Horrocks   1998
The best of the easier routes on the wall.

Right again are **Retribution** (F6c+) and **Bad Religion** (F6c).

Carry On Up the Corbetts   15m   F6a+
G.Ridge   1998
The rightmost line of bolts finishes at the same lower-off as Fat Eagles Fly Low.

Craig a' Barns (Dunkeld)
Map p60

This is the name given to the craggy wooded hillside that overlooks the village of Dunkeld. Its south side nearest the road presents the most obvious cliff, Polney Crag, named after the small curling pond below it. Polney contains some excellent easy and middle grade climbs as well as a few harder serious ones. Higher up and right on Craig a' Barns are very steep twin crags partially hidden in the trees (on the spur of the hill known locally as Cave Craig), a stark contrast to the slabbier Polney. Together all these crags offer an excellent selection of contrasting climbs, on excellent rock and are easily accessible (and popular) at all times of the year.

POLNEY CRAG

(NO 011 431)   Alt 160m   South-East facing   Diagram p64

Approach: The old A9 passes through Dunkeld and continues north to skirt the base of Polney Crag. The crag lies somewhat diagonally above the road with the left end being much lower. For the central and right section of the crag, park on the east side of the road directly below the centre of the crag, where a small path goes through the trees and up the steep hillside to the base of Hairy Gully which separates the central from the smaller right section of the crag. 5mins. For the left end of the crag (Ivy Buttress, Upper Buttress and Kestrel Crack area), park on the verge 150m north, around a bend, and head direct to Ivy Buttress, which is very close. 1min.

Descent: The walking descent (easy scramble) from all the crag except the right section is to traverse left and follow a small path descending under Upper Buttress, then down a short gully and open ground to arrive under Ivy Buttress. Take care not to go too high and above Upper Buttress; this is much longer. From the right section, go round the right end of the crag. Hairy Gully is also a popular descent (Moderate), often by abseil.

IVY BUTTRESS

A complex little area of projecting walls and deep recessed corners which lost its ivy years ago. On the left is a smooth vertical wall, the right arete of which contains an impressive hanging groove **Hot Tips** (E5 6c). The right side of the arete forms a deep corner (Ivy Crack) and just right again behind a beech tree is the final corner-line of Consolation Corner.

1 Ivy Crack   15m   VS 4c *
P.Brian   1958
The polished corner-line gives a popular climb. After the initial difficulties it is possible to move left on to the rib to finish easily or to continue with difficulty up the corner to a tree belay. Walk off to the left.

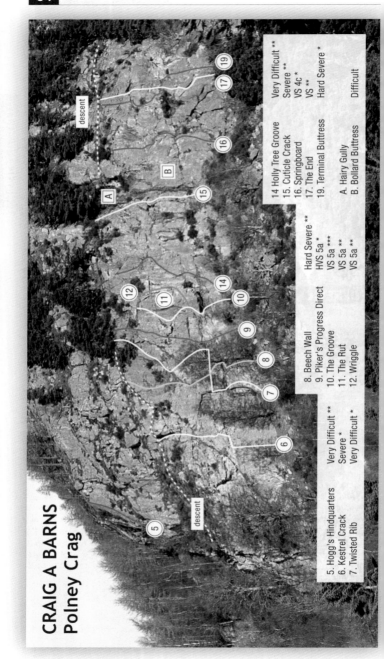

CRAIG A BARNS
Polney Crag

64

5. Hogg's Hindquarters   Very Difficult **
6. Kestrel Crack   Severe *
7. Twisted Rib   Very Difficult *

8. Beech Wall   Hard Severe **
9. Piker's Progress Direct   HVS 5a *
10. The Groove   VS 5a ***
11. The Rut   VS 5a **
12. Wriggle   VS 5a **

14 Holly Tree Groove   Very Difficult **
15. Cuticle Crack   Severe **
16. Springboard   VS 4c *
17. The End   VS **
19. Terminal Buttress   Hard Severe *

A. Hairy Gully
B. Bollard Buttress   Difficult

Poison Ivy   15m   VS 5a *
R.N.Campbell   1961
To the right of Ivy Crack is another large corner that splits at half-height.
Consolation Corner takes the right-hand main corner-line. This route takes the left
exit. Gain a flake leading to the base of the overhanging corner. Layback or jam to
the top.

Consolation Corner   30m   Very Difficult **
P.Brian   1957
A popular route and now quite polished. Climb the easy corner to an impasse, then
move out right and go up to a ledge. The corner above gives interesting climbing
to a ledge and tree (possible belay). Climb the groove and rib above to finish.

UPPER BUTTRESS

This sits above and left of Ivy Buttress and provides good continuation climbs. To
walk to its base, go up a path left from Ivy Buttress, then up a gully (reversing the
descent) to the buttress close on the right. Twin corner-cracks provide an obvious
landmark.
Descent: Abseil, or a tricky scramble right or left.

Left-Hand Crack   10m   E2 5c **
N.MacNiven (aid)   1961; FFA: J.Mackenzie   1974
The superb curving corner-crack gives a sustained, well protected climb (2 pegs). It
is possible to scuttle out right at the top of the corner, but it is arguably purer to
exit directly. Finish up the rib.

The shorter **Right-Hand Crack** (VS 5a) is obvious. Right again, hidden in the trees,
the next route is reached by a scramble up a mass of blocks to the recess of Duncan
Hogg's Hole, one time residence of an old cattle rustler.

Hogg's Hindquarters   30m   Very Difficult **
R.N.Campbell   1959
A fine route with a strenuous start and a delicate finish. Start in the recess of
Duncan Hogg's Hole beneath a steep groove. Step off a large boulder on to the left
wall of the groove, then climb up and exit right, step back left and climb a wrin-
kled slab to the top.

THE MAIN CLIFF - CENTRAL SECTION

About 50m right of the Ivy Buttress area, beyond a huge beech tree and at a higher
level, is the left end of the Central and Main section of cliff. The main feature is a
large slab with a giant arching flake above its right side. Right again is a prominent
rib above which are short corners and ledges. Right of the rib the wall is steeper
and hidden by another big beech tree. Twenty metres right of the beech tree is a
big roof low down with a tree growing below it. Wriggle finds a way past this roof.
The wall continues rightwards as a more slabby affair with the occasional roof to
terminate in the deep-set Hairy Gully.

Kestrel Crack   35m   Severe *
R.N.Campbell   1957
A good climb that ascends first the slab, then the huge flake and corner above.
Start in the centre of the slabs at a crack. Climb the crack-line and move diagonally
right to climb the big flake to a grassy bay and finish up an easy slabby corner above.

Twisted Rib   45m   Very Difficult *
R.N.Campbell   1957
A wandering but interesting route taking the easiest way up this section of crag.

Start at the obvious rib bounding the right side of the slab.

1. 15m Climb the rib to a ledge, poorly protected. Move left into a short easy corner and go up to a tree, then move back right to a second long rock ledge and a huge flake.

2. 30m Make a long rightwards traverse on disjointed ledges until below a slab. Climb this diagonally left to gain a grassy bay. Finish up the grooved slabby rib on the right.

8 Beech Wall   35m   Hard Severe **
R.N.Campbell   1959

An excellent enjoyable route up the steep wall behind the beech tree, right of Twisted Rib.

1. 15m 4c Climb an undercut corner and a further corner on the right to exit left at its top on to a ledge. Move up then gain the long ledge of Twisted Rib. Belay on the huge flake on the left.

2. 20m 4a Climb left and ascend a clean wall direct into the grass bay. Finish up a distinctive left-facing groove in the left-hand side of the headwall. Steep and awkward.

9 Piker's Progress Direct   30m   HVS 5a *
I.G.Rowe   1969

Stretching rightwards from the big beech tree is a line of overhangs about 10m up. This route breaks through these at a little corner near the left end. Climb a slight rib to a ledge, then leftwards up a small ramp and through the overhang to a ledge above and on the right. Continue up the wall above to the top.

The next three routes have a common start at an obvious break in the lower roofs, 20m right of the big beech. Wriggle is painted below a roof at the base. This is arguably the crux for all the routes. Above, they diverge and climb separate grooves or cracks.

10 The Groove   30m   VS 5a ***
R.Smith   1960

One of the best routes on Polney. Gain the break in the lower roof via a traverse in from a tree on the right. Step up, then make hard moves right below a bulge (peg runner) on to a wrinkled slab (there is also a is more elegant high method). Climb up, then go left to gain hanging blocks under more roofs. Climb the fine clean-cut groove slanting up to the right to finish.

11 The Rut   30m   VS 5a **
N.MacNiven   1960

The central line of the wall climbing the short deep groove directly above the start. Follow The Groove through the lower roof. Head up into the deep groove above, which gives further hard moves and a strenuous pull out left into the final section of The Groove.

12 Wriggle   35m   VS 5a **
R.N.Campbell   1959

A popular route which was the first to wriggle through the guarding roof. Start as for The Groove and once established on the lip traverse horizontally right across a wrinkled slab to the exposed right edge. Ascend this and follow the bottomless groove and crack on the right (which emanates from a holly bush under the roof) to the top.

To the right of the roofs where Wriggle and its companions start, the guarding lower roof relents at a groove whose base is infested with a holly bush. A slabby right-slanting ramp starts here and forms a right-bounding edge to a steep concave wall above.

13 Twilight   30m   E1 5b *

D.Cuthbertson, R.Kerr   November 1980

A splendid direct route crossing Wriggle. Start below the holly bush. Climb a steep slim groove just left and under the holly and make a strenuous pull out left through the roof on to the steep slab of Wriggle. Ascend leftwards, then directly up the wall on the line of a slight arete with pushy moves up the bulge near the top.

Holly Tree Groove   30m   Very Difficult ✳✳
R.N.Campbell   1960
Pleasant climbing up the diagonal ramp-line. Start just right of the holly bush and follow the ramp under the concave wall through a short corner come niche to gain a ledge in the left side of a large recess. Finish up the chimney on the left.

Cuticle Crack   25m   Severe ✳✳
P.Brian   1960
A classic struggle up the deep crack immediately left of Hairy Gully (about 50m right of Holly Tree Groove). Cuticle Crack is painted on the rock. Follow the crack, then move right at a protruding jammed block in the sidewall. Continue directly to the top.

MAIN CLIFF - RIGHT-HAND SECTION

This begins immediately right of Hairy Gully, where **Bollard Buttress** (Difficult) and **Bollard Buttress Direct** (Severe) climb slabby ground. At the base of the centre of the wall is a jumble of huge boulders. To their right, the crag is split into two tiers, the lower one being a fine smooth slab and the upper tier being undercut and topped by a roof. The upper tier continues rightwards as a steep wall of roofs to then degenerates into the hillside as a sidewall. Between Bollard Buttress Direct (painted on the rock) and the boulders is a smooth wall above an overlap. At the right end of the overlap, a right-facing brown corner leads up to a further roof.

Springboard   45m   VS 4c ✳
R.N.Campbell   1960
A wandering climb, but full of interest. Start at the lowest point of the wall before the jumble of boulders and climb direct just right of a slight rib to a horizontal break under the overlap. Hand-traverse right and enter the brown corner (it is possible to walk off on to the grass to the right here). Climb the corner (no protection) and exit left on to the springboard. Climb left up an overhung recess to a slab which leads rightwards to the top.

Above the boulders is a huge scoop with a bush high up. To the right of this the cliff forms a double tier. The next three routes ascend both tiers. A central right-facing corner in the lower tier (the start of Terminal Buttress) is the most obvious feature.

The End   45m   VS ✳✳
R.N.Campbell   1961
Start at the base of the clean slab of the lower tier.
1. 20m 4b Climb the left side of the slab to a slanting overlap. Either climb up under this (4c) or up the slab on its left, to step right on to the nose above the overlap. Move up and make a similar move on to another nose. Finish delicately above to the ledge.
2. 30m 5a The wall above is guarded by a steep bulge. Climb through this via a slim right-facing groove with difficulty, then go up the slab to step right to below the break in the largest part of the overlap. Pull through and climb the fine slabs to the top.

Barefoot Beginning   45m   E2 ✳✳
D.Cuthbertson, M.Hamilton   Jun 1976 (The Beginning); D.Cuthbertson, P.Hunter (Barefoot) Aug 1980
A natural combination of pitches on each tier. Both are serious and high in the

HIGHLAND SOUTH

grade on immaculate rock. Derek Jameson soloed Barefoot barefoot hours after its first ascent. Start at the base of the slab as for The End.
1. 15m 5c Climb the slab direct to the overlap. Climb a very thin flake in the smooth rock above to snatch out right for tiny sharp holds leading right to the arete. Stand on a small ledge, then climb the right side of the arete to the ledge.
2. 30m 5b Go up a short right-facing tapering corner slightly down and right. Step up and left over the lip of the steep wall on to the slab. Climb directly to a roof and pull over at a flake right of The End, then finish easily.

Terminal Buttress   40m   Hard Severe *
R.N.Campbell   1959
This route crosses The End on the halfway ledge. Start below a right-facing corner.
1. 15m Climb the corner to the ledge.
2. 25m 4c Climb leftwards through the bulge immediately left of The End (crux) and gain a grass recess above. Step right and climb a crack in the overlap, then follow slabs to the top.

LOWER CAVE CRAG

(NO 018 438)   Alt 190m   South-West facing

The Cave Crags are situated nearer Dunkeld and slightly further from the road. This part of the hill is criss-crossed by paths, installed originally for Victorian tourists; these give easy access direct to the base of the crags. The Victorians were more interested in the scenery and the follies, including Lady Charlotte's Cave. Here, it is rumoured that a past Duke of Atholl hid his lover. Lower Cave Crag is partially obscured by trees that encroach right up to the crag. However, there are some excellent routes in the middle grades on very steep rock with wonderful views as one emerges from the tree canopy.

Approach: After turning on to the A923 Blairgowrie Road just out of Dunkeld take the second track on the left, signposted Cally Car Park 500m (small sign under "The Glack"). Drive to this large car park amongst the trees on the left of the track. Take the path behind the notice board and fork left after 50m. As this begins to descend, branch off on to a small path on the right, now more worn by climbers than the original. Crags start to appear on the right and when a stooped yew tree partially blocking the path is reached, you are directly below Lower Cave Crag. Continue across a small stream before cutting back right across the stream again to reach Lady Charlotte's Cave. Continue along the path to Lower Cave Crag, 10mins.

Descent: It is best to continue up the hillside above to the base of the upper crag and descend its access path.

The first piece of rock encountered forms a steep prow overhanging the path. **The Civer** (E4 6b *) takes the obvious hanging cracked groove. Immediately right is a wet corner and right of it there is a low overhang. The wall then turns an arete (the start of The Hood) beyond which are overhanging corners (Hood Direct and Fuck Face), accessed though trees at the base. The crag becomes scrappy after that.

The Hood   35m   VS **
R.N.Campbell   1959
An excellent route with wild exposure and only adequate protection. Start just to the right of the low overhang just before the arete.
1. 20m 4b Climb to a small roof, then hand-traverse right along a juggy break and turn the arete on to a ramp. This leads back left. From its top, step right to gain ledges and easy ground leading up to a large roof. Traverse right to a sloping ledge below the big hooded roofs.
2. 15m 4c Step up on to the slab and traverse left to the arete (delicate). Climb

Twilight, E1 5b, Polney Crag, Dunkeld. Climbers Bill Wright & Ed Douglas
(photo Grahame Nicoll)

up to the base of an obvious overhanging crack (The Direct Finish) and swing out left to finish up a slabby rib.

The Hood Direct   35m   HVS *
B.Robertson   1963

Start just around the arete to the right from the normal route at a short leaning corner cutting through the overhanging walls at the base.

1. 20m 4c Clamber out of a tree and go up the short corner past the lower roofs to below a bigger roof. Traverse awkwardly left to gain the base of the ramp on the normal route. Follow this to the left, then step right on to easy ground at a large roof. Traverse right to a ledge as per the normal route.

2. 15m 5a Follow The Hood on to the slab and climb leftwards to beneath the overhanging crack. Finish strenuously up this crack on painful jams.

Fuck Face   35m   HVS *
D.Haston   1959

Good climbing up the smooth corner 5m right of the start of The Hood Direct.

1. 15m 5a Clamber over a branch to gain the corner and climb it by thin bridging to pull on to a large slabby area.

2. 20m 4c Pull on to the steep wall on the right (peg runner) and climb through on to the easier wall above. Trend right and go up to finish.

UPPER CAVE CRAG

(NO 018 439)   Alt 240m   South to South-West facing   Diagram p73

Upper Cave Crag gives some of the best hard outcrop climbing in Scotland. A sun trap in the summer, it is steep enough to stay dry in a heavy shower. However, the routes can seep after prolonged wet weather. This crag has been a forcing ground for some of the hardest routes of their time and the traditional routes are generally intricate, bold and technical. The sport routes here are stamina climbs with brilliant moves, and are regarded as some of the finest sport pitches to be found anywhere. Once established on a route, the exposure feels a lot greater than it should. As an added bonus the bouldering at the base of the crag is excellent.

Approach: As for Lower Cave Crag until almost at Lady Charlotte's Cave. But instead of crossing the stream here, go up the left bank and cross higher up before heading diagonally rightwards to the crag, which is directly above the Lower Crag, 15mins.

Descent: From the top of most routes, carefully follow an exposed path leftwards to descend down the open slope on the left side of the crag.

The left end of the main steep wall has the line of The Ramp cutting from right to left. There is a steep bouldering wall below this ramp and the big wall of Lady Charlotte is above. Right of this a larch tree grows close to the wall and immediately to its right is the deep open corner-line of Mousetrap. Beyond this the steep central bolted sports wall (capped by roofs) is bounded on the left by the vertical crack-line of Rat Race and on the right by the triangular niche of Squirm Direct and an arete in the upper half. A more broken but still steep section continues into the obvious Coffin Corner with the steep prow of High Performance on the right edge.

1 The Ramp   40m   Hard Severe *
P.Brian   1957

A pleasant easy start contrasts with a steep and bold top pitch.

1. 20m Romp up the large obvious ramp to a spacious platform.

2. 20m Climb the crack above to the top of a pinnacle. Either step left and climb a sandy groove or continue directly up the steep wall. Both options are hard to exit.

2 Lady Charlotte Direct   35m   E5 6a ***

D.Cuthbertson, M.Duff, K.Johnstone   1980; Direct: D.Cuthbertson   1987
A magnificent wall climb, tackling the big steep face above the ramp. Protection is adequate but difficult to locate. Start 5m up the ramp below a small right-trending groove. Climb the wall right of the groove and move left to a good foot ledge at its top. The pocketed wall above leads slightly left to better holds and protection in a horizontal crack. Gain the hanging flake above and follow it to its top. Make a move up to gain a good pocket which allows a move right to a hidden peg runner in a small groove. Climb to a small ledge and finish up the thin crack above and left.

Rat Catcher   35m   E3 5b **
A.Petit, K.J.Martin   1969 (aid); FFA: D.Cuthbertson, M.Hamilton   1976
This good but serious route takes the shallow fault left of the tree. Start below a small corner. Climb the wall and the corner to a small ledge. Ascend right, then go back left (serious) to welcome peg runners. The groove above becomes less taxing and an exit can be made out right at the very top.

Morbidezza   35m   E5 6b **
D.Cuthbertson   24 Jun 1979
Another bold route in a wild position up the left arete of a huge, often wet, open corner right of the larch tree, **Mousetrap** (E4 6b). The start is a bit contrived and is optional. Hard bouldery moves up the wall 3m right of the big corner lead to a scoop. Move left into the corner and go up this until just below the bulge (peg runner). Traverse left on to the arete, move up the arete (reaching left to clip a peg runner), then move left to finish up the left side of the large cracked block.

Warfarin   50m   E2 ***
D.Jameson, G.Nicoll, M.Duff   5 Sep 1978
A tremendous excursion across the central area, bold and surprisingly delicate. Start beneath the short right-facing corner between the big open corner of Mousetrap and the crack of Rat Race.
1. 25m 5c   A boulder problem start leads into the corner (peg runner at its top). Traverse left into the big corner and follow this for a few moves until it is possible to traverse back right under the roofs to a hanging stance (peg).
2. 25m 5b   Climb the slabby wall to a corner under the capping roofs (peg runner). Continue traversing right under the roofs in a spacewalking position, moving up at the end to finish.

Rat Race   45m   E4 ****
B.Robertson, J.MacLean   1963 (aid); Direct: M.Hamilton   1976 (1PA); FFA: M.Graham   1978
The classic hard route of the crag. Rather strenuous. Start below the obvious overhanging crack in the steep central wall.
1. 20m 6a   Climb the pod (or its left edge) and crack (peg runner) to a niche. Continue up the crack (peg runner) past an overhang to a hanging stance on the left shared with Warfarin.
2. 25m 5b   Climb the slabby wall to a corner under the roof (peg runner). Traverse hard under the roof rightwards for 3m (peg runner) and pull left through the roof on large flat holds. Continue directly to the top.

SPORT WALL

The steep area of rock right of Rat Race was the scene of tentative explorations into sport climbing over a period of several years. The routes evolved almost piecemeal leading to a miss-matched assortment of seven different interconnecting lines based on the original two that were bolted (Marlene and Fall Out) and all starting as for either of these two routes. Over time the best lines have become better understood and some bolts re-positioned. The following descriptions are now recognised as the main routes and are the most chalked up. They are all excellent stamina climbs. Opinions vary as to which is the best route, so the choice has been left to personal preference. The most obvious feature is a left-slanting crack starting halfway up the wall and leading to a lower-off below the roofs. The entirety of this crack is the now superseded Rattle Yer Dags.

7 Marlene 20m F7c ***
D.Cuthbertson (2 bolts and natural gear, now fully bolted)   3 Aug 1986
Named after Suzanne Vega song 'Marlene On The Wall'. Start up the left-hand line of bolts, just right of Rat Race. From the second bolt, go up left to a flange (bolt), then up and traverse right to good holds and a high bolt in the centre of the wall. From the end of the handrail, a hard move up and right gains the foot of the left-slanting crack (bolt) and a shake out for the strong. Hard moves up the crack lead to smaller holds and a final technical section before the lower-off. It is quite common to fail mere centimetres from the chain.

8 Hamish Teddy's Excellent Adventure 25m F7b+ ***
D.MacCallum, J.May, R.Anderson   1992
The extra meat of this route takes the arete above the start of the left-slanting crack. Although this is slightly easier than the finish to Marlene, it is still a real pumper. Climb Marlene to the start of the diagonal crack. Move up right and make a couple of very steep moves to reach a good shake out on the arete. Pull back left and climb a crack on good holds to easier ground and the chain below a roof.

9 The Silk Purse 25m F7c+ ***
G.Livingston   April 1987
The right-hand bolt line and the hardest route on the crag. At the fourth bolt hard moves lead up and left to join Marlene at the base of the diagonal crack. Follow this past another bolt, then step right and climb the shallow scoop above precariously to Hamish Ted's lower-off.

10 Squirm Direct 30m E3 *
D.Bathgate   1960 (5PA); FFA: M.Hamilton, A.Taylor   1976
Technical climbing up the slanting niche which bounds the right side of the Sport Wall. Start below and right of the niche in a groove.
1. 15m 5c Climb the groove and transfer left into the slanting niche. Go up this (poor peg runner) and exit leftwards with difficulty to gain a shallow recess below the prow (peg and thread runners). Continue up and traverse right to a ledge.
2. 15m 5c Squirm up a ribbed slab on the left (peg runner) to reach a small ledge. Move back right and finish up a steep groove with a dead tree.

11 Squirm 30m E1 **
N.MacNiven   1959 (aid); FFA: M.Hamilton, A.Taylor   1976
A worthwhile climb with one short hard section and some remarkable exposure for the grade. Start below the scooped wall, right of Squirm Direct.
1. 15m 4b Climb the brown scoop and short contorted rib to a comfortable ledge.
2. 15m 5c Squirm up a ribbed slab on the left (peg runner, crux) to reach a small ledge. Continue leftwards and up large flakes in a sensational position to the top.

12 Corpse 35m E2 5c **
N.MacNiven   1960 (3PA); FFA: M.Hamilton, A.Taylor   1976
A fine pitch. Start beneath a right-facing corner in the upper wall left of the obvious Coffin Corner. Climb easily up ribs to a ledge at the base of the corner. Follow it with increasing difficulty to a hanging glacis under the steep headwall. Traverse right and climb a perplexing crack to the top.

13 Coffin Corner 30m HVS 5a **
P.Smith   1960
The best line on the crag gives awkward climbing up the polished corner-crack. A choice of lines leads up to the base of the corner. Follow it with good protection, exiting right near the top or finishing directly if so inclined.

CRAIG A' BARNS
Upper Cave Crag

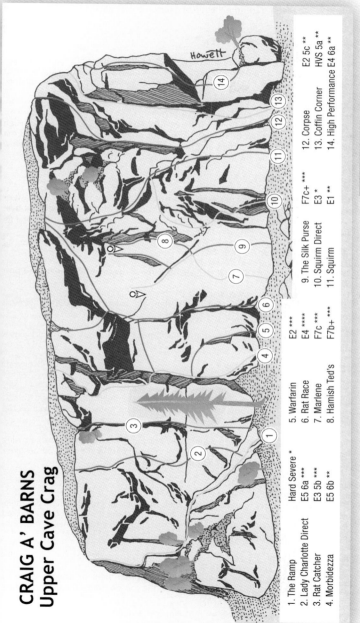

Howett

1. The Ramp   Hard Severe *
2. Lady Charlotte Direct   E5 6a ***
3. Rat Catcher   E3 5b ***
4. Morbidezza   E5 6b **
5. Warfarin   E2 ***
6. Rat Race   E4 ****
7. Marlene   F7c ***
8. Hamish Ted's   F7b+ ***
9. The Silk Purse   F7c+ ***
10. Squirm Direct   E3 *
11. Squirm   E1 **
12. Corpse   E2 5c **
13. Coffin Corner   HVS 5a **
14. High Performance   E4 6a **

The next two routes start from the top of a huge boulder gained from a cave on the right-hand side.

14 High Performance   20m   E4 6a **

D.Cuthbertson 1978

Gymnastic moves over the roof and prow right of Coffin Corner. Start atop the huge boulder. Go easily left up a ramp, arrange protection in the crack above, then leap for the lip of the roof. Pull up, step right and climb an awkward groove to the top.

15 Death's Head   35m   E1 5b *

D.Cuthbertson, A.Taylor, M.Hamilton   Oct 1976

Deceptively steep climbing up the shallow cracked groove right of the prow of High Performance and just left of a sharp arete. Start on top of the boulder. Climb the groove until it bulges, step right on to the arete and go up then back left to below a flying groove. Follow this precariously to finish.

16 Crutch   30m   Severe **

A.Wightman 1959

The best route of its grade at Craig a' Barns. Start 5m right of the cave at a left-slanting ramp. Ascend the ramp to a ledge and climb the short steep corner above. Continue directly up cracked bulges to finish up a prominent crack left of an orange wall.

17 Marjorie Razorblade   30m   E3 *

D.Cuthbertson, M.Hamilton   March 1977

The distinctive crack (straight, then S-shaped) above the ramp of Crutch. Well protected jamming.

1. 15m 5c Ascend the lower wall and the crack.
2. 15m 5a Move left (as for Crutch) and climb the crack right of the orange wall to finish.

The crag now turns to face due south and forms a large mossy slab which has a steep sidewall to the right.

18 Flook   35m   Very Difficult *

R.N.Campbell 1959

A very amenable route up the corner formed by the slab and the steep right-bounding sidewall. Climb the steepening corner to a small rattling block (thread runner) where a left traverse can be made to finish up a steep broken wall on the left side of the capping wall.

Next is the steep side wall with a lone holly bush in the centre of the wall growing from the upper of two diagonal breaks. It is bounded on the right by an overhanging arete, the line of **The Laughing Gnome** (E5 5c).

19 Gnome   25m   E1 5c *

B.Robertson 1960 (aid); FFA: M.Couston 1974

A shallow little corner round the arete from the sidewall provides the main interest of this route. Start at the base of the arete. Climb the lower blunt and cracked arete until it is possible to gain a ledge on the right below the corner. A few technical moves (peg runner) lead to an easy finish.

20 Tombstone   20m   E3 5c **

D.Cuthbertson, M.Duff   10 Oct 1978

Strenuous jamming and bridging up the next corner right of Gnome. Start by scrambling rightwards to a belay ledge below the corner. Follow the diagonal crack

Marlene, F7c, Upper Cave Crag, Dunkeld. Climbers Tracy Harrison & Jo George (photo Cubby Images)

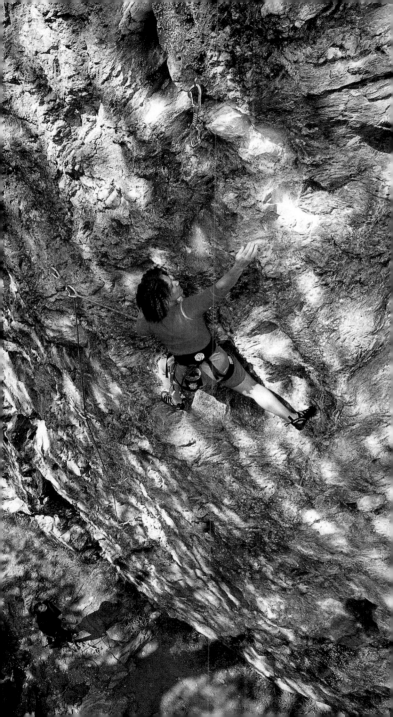

to a triangular overhang, pull over and continue directly up the corner to the top. Deceptively steep but the strong will find it low in the grade.

Weem Crags

Hidden in the beautiful ancient woodlands overlooking the village of Aberfeldy are the Weem Crags, a collection of six quality mica schist crags; Weem Rock is the largest of these.

WEEM ROCK

(NN 845 503)   Alt 200m   South-South-East facing, Side wall West facing   Map p60

Weem Rock holds some 23 sport routes from F5+ to F7b and a handful of traditional lines. The crag comprises of two contrasting facets – a sidewall and a main face. The Sidewall climbs are very overhanging stamina climbs on generally good holds, while the Main Face provides a mixture of long technical walls and shorter lines up a mix of slabby walls, cracks, aretes and small overhangs.

Access: Follow directions to Aberfeldy. Once there, look out for the B846 sign-posted to Weem (the Black Watch Inn is on the corner of the junction). Follow this road over the humpback bridge and into Weem village. Park tight against the stone wall in front of the church (on Sundays please find an alternative parking spot).

Approach: From the church in Weem village, follow the road up hill past the houses (and garages on the right) until you reach a B&B, Tigh na Sgoill. Opposite this house is a wide grassy track; follow this for about 50m, looking out for a small path which breaks up the hillside on the left. Follow this and when it meets the main path, take the right-hand branch. Head uphill, past a left-hand hairpin bend and on for another 100m. Five metres after a rough, sculpted wooden chair on the right side of the path, take a vague path going up the steep hillside (not obvious especially when overgrown in spring/summer). Follow this rocky track over fallen trees and nettles to reach the crag, 15mins.

SIDE WALL

The first line of bolts from the left-hand end is **Every Last Drop** (F7b), the second **One Peg One** (F7b).

High Pitched Scream   15m   F7a **
N.Sheperd   1997
The third line of bolts from the left-hand end – steep and pumpy! Climb the slab then step right on to the main wall. A fingery start leads to crux moves gaining the upper wall, then a jug fest up the top headwall.

The Screaming Weem   18m   F7b ***
G.Ridge   1997
The next line to the right. Superb climbing with a distinct crux sequence between the second and fourth bolts. Gaining the upper headwall can prove tricky so don't relax too much. Power up jugs to finish.

Last Gasp   18m   F7a+ *
G.Latter   1997
Follow The Screaming Weem to the fifth bolt, then traverse hard right and up the arete to the top.

The End of Silence   15m   F7b *
C.Milne   1997
The rightmost line of bolts on The Sidewall. A crimp fest up the bottom wall quickly eases to give easier enjoyable climbing to top.

At the left end is The **Real Mackay** (F6a). A prominent crack and groove line 2m right of the arete is **Back to Basics** (Hard Severe 4b).

The Long Good Friday   20m   F6c+ **
I.Watson   1997
The second line of bolts up the long wall through a series of overlaps. Thin, balancey and interesting climbing.

Confession of Faith   20m   F6c **
J.Horrocks   1997
The third line of bolts. Climb directly up the centre of the wall. A good exercise in footwork with a technical crux – sustained.

Manpower   25m   F6b *
D.Pert   1997
The fourth line of bolts. Climb the tricky slab to the gain the overlap and intermittent crack-line above.

The fifth line of bolts is **Boomhead** (F6a+). The corner right of Boomhead is **Blinded By The Night** (VS). The sixth line of bolts is **Staring at The Sun** (F5+) and the seventh is **Soup Dragon** (F5+).

Scooby Snacks   18m   F6a+ *
G.Ridge, D.Johnson   1997
The eighth line of bolts. After a crimpy start the angle kicks out near the top.

One Step Beyond   18m   F6a *
The next line to the right. Climb the crack and steepening wall above. The crux is saved for last!

Down to the Last Heartbreak   18m   F6a *
G.Ridge   1997
Starts as for One Step Beyond, then step right after the second bolt. A tricky move near the top.

The Trial of Brother Number One   18m   F6a *
C.Miln, I.Watson   1997
The next line of bolts to the right of the previous route – interesting crux move to gain the belay!

The next line is **Lapdancing** (F6b+).

The Llama Parlour   15m   F6c
J.Horrocks, G.Ridge   1997
Climbs the crimpy wall immediately to the left of The Protection Racket to finish on that route.

The Protection Racket   12m   F6a *
D.Johnson, G.Ridge   1997
The steep corner at the right end of the crag. Good bridging up the corner is followed by a tricky move to gain the slab and belay.

Three lines at the right end are **Lighten Up** (F5+), **Crowing at the Enemy** (F6b+) and **Bark Bacherate** (F6b).

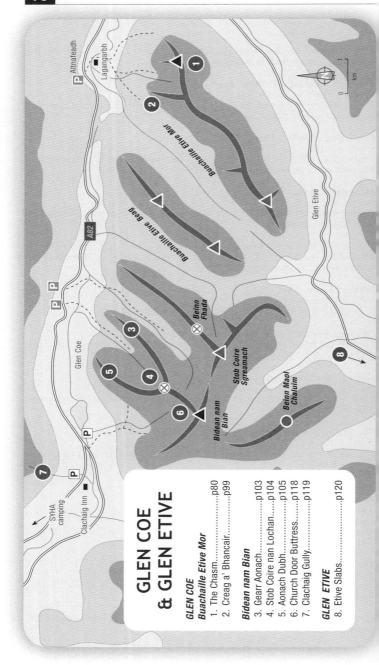

GLEN COE
& GLEN ETIVE

Altnafeadh

Lagangarbh

A82

Glen Coe

Clachaig Inn

SYHA camping

Buachaille Etive Mor

Buachaille Etive Beag

Beinn Fhada

Stob Coire Sgreamach

Bidean nam Bian

Beinn Maol Chaluim

Glen Etive

km

GLEN COE & GLEN ETIVE

Glen Coe has the best selection of mountain rock climbs in Scotland. Whether it has the best climbs is of course debatable, but in the number of good climbs and the range of grades, there can be little argument. Driving up the glen and seeing so much rock almost answers the question. But the Etive Slabs might have to be included to convince those who like slab climbing as against the steep walls of the Coe.

Maps: OS L41, E384; Harvey Superwalker Glen Coe

SMC Climbers' Guide: *Glen Coe* (2001)

Public Transport: Train from Glasgow to Fort William (4 per day, 3 on Sunday), followed by bus to Kinlochleven, which passes through Glen Coe village (10 per day but none on Sunday). Glasgow to Fort William bus (3 per day) passes through Glen Coe.

Amenities: The Glen Coe area is well served for visitor facilities. Fort William is fairly close by car, although a slow and busy road (see Ben Nevis chapter). The nearest Tourist Office is in Ballachulish (01855 811296), where there is also a Ballachulish Visitors Centre (01855 811866).

Camping: There are several campsites at the lower end of Glen Coe, also towards Kinlochleven and Fort William. Wild camping is accepted in Glen Etive (in 2004) but not in Glen Coe, although the Kingshouse Hotel tolerates it just across the bridge from the hotel.

Mountaineering Huts: Blackrock Cottage – Ladies Scottish CC (NN 267 531), Lagangarbh – SMC (NN 222 560) and Kyle MC Memorial Hut (NN 128 567) are in Glen Coe, Inbhirfhaolin – Grampian Club (NN 158 507) and The Smiddy – Forventure (NN 116 457) are in Glen Etive, Alex McIntyre Memorial Hut – BMC and MCofS (NN 046 612) is at North Ballachulish. Manse Barn – Lomond MC (NN 033 613) is at Onich and Waters Cottage – FRCC (NN 183 617) is at Kinlochleven.

SYHA Youth Hostels: Glen Coe (NN 118 577, 0870 004 1122, open all year)

Independent Hostels: Glencoe Bunkhouses (01855 811256), Inchree Hostel (01855 821287). There are others in the area.

Hotels: The two hotels well known by climbers are the Kingshouse Hotel at the top end of the glen (NN 259 543), (01855 851259) and the Clachaig Inn towards the bottom (NN 128 567), (01855 811252).

Shops and Petrol: Several, but nothing down Glen Etive. Climbing equipment is available at Glencoe Guides and Gear (NN 095 586), (01855 811402) as well as at the Kinlochleven climbing wall (see below).

Climbing Wall: The Ice Factor (01855 831100) <www.ice-factor.co.uk> is a new (2003) indoor climbing complex at Kinlochleven with two rock walls, bouldering wall, ice climbing wall, cafe and gym.

Glen Coe

BUACHAILLE ETIVE MOR

(NN 223 543)   Alt 1022m

The famous view of the Buachaille (as it is more popularly known) from the Kingshouse Hotel makes it one of Scotland's best known mountains. It sits at the top of both Glen Coe and Glen Etive and its high quality rock climbing has kept it at the forefront of Scottish climbing history. From the connoisseur of the traditional gully climb to the modern test pieces of Creag a' Bhancair and the daunting Slime Wall. The Buachaille's main climbing is on the great rocky face seen from the A82 and approached from Altnafeadh. The first route (The Chasm), however, has a separate approach.

General Approach: Park on the A82 at Altnafeadh where there is a lay-by on the north side of the road (NN 222 564). Follow the track opposite the lay-by down to the bridge across the river, then approximately 200m beyond the white SMC cottage of Lagangarbh take the left branch of the path. The main branch goes straight on into Coire na Tulaich and is the normal way to the summit. The climbers' path gently rises to cross the outflow of Great Gully (30mins), where the approach to Slime Wall and the Great Gully Buttresses leaves. For the others, continue to the Waterslide slab (another 10mins). Access to the various walls is given from here under the walls themselves; also the descents.

THE CHASM

Map p78

Scotland's best gully climb! Gullies may be out of fashion but this is huge and spectacular, largely on good clean rock and with escapes if needed. It is the deep major gully on the left side of the South-East face, some 400m left of Central Buttress at (NN 228 537). Approach in 20mins from a lay-by (NN 234 532) before a small bridge 2km down the Glen Etive road from its junction with the A82.

The Chasm   450m   VS ***
R.F.Stobart, Mr and Mrs Odell   Apr 1920
The gully can be climbed in the wet, the limiting factor being the volume of water. Difficulty and interest increases with height as does the scenery, culminating in the Devil's Cauldron (Pitch 15). Only this pitch is VS, although more will feel like it in the wet.

The gully starts at an altitude of 360m, with several easy pitches. Pitch 4 is topped by a huge chockstone, best climbed by the groove and crack on its left. Pitch 5, the Red Slab, climbs the left wall (25m). Above, a huge boulder blocks the gully. Climb a crack on the left wall about 6m back from the boulder, then step back right into the gully. The left fork is a short tributary; the true gully is the right fork. Pitch 8 is the Hundred Foot Pitch, where the stream forms a fine waterfall. Pitch 9 is the Piano Pitch. Cross the watercourse to the left wall, and above a small but beckoning pool make a right traverse, ending by a delicate move on to a sloping chockstone. At pitch 10, The Converging Walls, a ramp on the right leads to a 20m cave pitch, with narrowing walls and a waterfall at the back. A few metres out on the left wall is a small ledge. Gain the ledge and then bridge up, facing in, until it is possible to reach good holds on the right wall. This pitch can be avoided by a ridge on the left. Several short pitches then lead to the Devil's Cauldron, a singularly confined and impressive cleft. See below for an exit.

The South Wall   30m   VS 4b
C.M.Allan, J.H.B.Bell, Miss V.Roy   Jun 1934
This is the easiest finish out of the Devil's Cauldron, certainly the chosen route in the wet, when the direct would be an epic. Start up the chimney on the left wall. Climb the chimney for 6m to a runner, then make a very awkward move on to a ledge on the wall on the right. Traverse round the edge on to a broad ledge and take the line of least resistance to the top.

The Direct Route   40m   VS 4c
I.G.Jack, J.G.Robinson   Aug 1931
This would be the normal route but for the ever present stream. Climb straight up the watercourse to a small cave (20m). Now chimney well out from the cave and make for an obvious foothold on the right wall, with a good jug within reach (crux). Beyond are two small chockstones, 3m apart. Back and foot work between them requires care on slabby rock. Above, the climbing gradually eases.

CENTRAL BUTTRESS

Although perhaps central when seen from the Kingshouse Hotel, this is the furthest left of the buttresses described here, left (south) of Curved Ridge.

GLEN COE

South Face

(NN 227 544)   Alt 550m   East facing

This provides excellent climbing which is both secluded and sunny.

Approach: Continue past the waterslide where the path turns uphill. Go up for 50m, from where the most obvious buttress seen in two tiers on the left is Central Buttress. There is a prominent gully right of its top tier. A small path traverses left here, well below any rocks, and in a few minutes a long smooth south face is seen; its far end is where the climbs are found. Go up the hillside diagonally left, initially through heather, taking a direct line for the climbs and passing above a small lower buttress. Bits of path should be found. Near the end, an awkward gully can be climbed, but the face out left is easier although exposed. There is a rocky terrace below the crag.

Descent: By two abseils is easiest, certainly if doing a second route, but the abseil points may not be in place. From the top of Pontoon the first is from a big block and the second from the flake on Pegleg. A scrambling descent is quite complex. First ascend on steep, unpleasant broken ground. Then go left and fairly soon down, contouring back under the foot of the crag. Alternatively, traverse right to join Curved Ridge.

A black watercourse in the centre of the wall is obvious; this flows down into a big gully below. Left of the watercourse is immaculately clean waterwashed rock with the first two routes.

Waterslide Gully   75m   Severe *
D.D.Stewart, C.M.G.Smith   Oct 1951

The scooped shallow gully in the centre of the face. Start from a scree basin directly below the right-facing corners of Waterslide Corner, which are 30m up.
1. 20m Climb a left-hand rake to a grass moustache beneath a shallow groove with a short black groove to the left.
2. 35m Climb the corner for 9m then traverse delicately left to easier ground, follow the line of least resistance to a belay.
3. 20m Continue to the left end of Heather Ledge (the terrace between the two tiers).

Waterslide Corner   70m   E1 **
D.Jenkins, I.Fulton   Aug 1970

This good route continues up the corner where Waterslide Gully goes left.
1. 20m As for Waterslide Gully (it is possible to continue from here in one pitch).
2. 20m 5a Follow the groove with gently increasing difficulty to a peg belay on the left below a steep corner.
3. 10m 5b Climb the smaller corner on the right for 3m, step right on to the wall and climb it delicately to an awkward move on to a sloping ledge and belay or continue.
4. 20m Finish more easily up the groove above.

Pegleg   90m   HVS **
J.R.Marshall, G.J.Ritchie   Sep 1957

A bold and serious climb, the name of which will be apparent at the crux where there may be much standing around on one 'shaky' leg. Start 7m left of Waterslide Gully at a red clean-cut rake.
1. 20m 4a Climb a left-trending weakness to a ledge.
2. 35m 5a Move up and right to another ledge, then climb a jagged right-facing groove of waterworn rock to an awkward move on to a small ledge. Traverse hard left (crux) to a ledge. Climb the groove above then traverse right to a crack. Follow this to the top of a large flake (in-situ slings).
3. 35m 4a Easier rock leads to a steep crack and so to the top.

BUACHAILLE ETIVE MOR

A. Central Buttress
B. Central Buttress, Upper Tier
C. Curved Ridge
D. Rannoch Wall
E. Crowberry Ridge
F. Crowberry Basin
G. North Buttress
H. North Buttress, East Face
I. North Buttress, Upper Tier
J. Raven's Gully
K. Slime Wall
L. Great Gully Upper Buttress
M. Great Gully Buttress, E Face
N. Great Gully
O. Waterslide

Approach from Altnafeadh

Pontoon 75m E1 ***
J.R.Marshall, R.Marshall, J.Moriarty Apr 1959
An excellent climb with two contrasting pitches. In its lower half it follows a thin crack in an otherwise featureless wall, leading to a prominent black crack above. Start 12m up the rake leftwards from the start of Pegleg.
1. 30m 5a Climb the grey wall above (quite bold) to a point 5m to the right of the base of a black crack which splits the upper wall. Traverse into the crack .
2. 45m 5b Climb the steep crack for 25m, then a thin crack running up a smooth slab (crux), until easier ground gains the terrace.

North Face

Approach: Go higher up the path from the waterslide, then head direct for the visible North Face on bits of heathery path to a worn patch below the lower tier and the following route.

North Face Route 220m Severe *
J.H.B.Bell, A.Harrison 1929
This popular climb is often climbed in combination with Agag's Groove or January Jigsaw. The first of many routes by the team of Bell and Harrison in Glen Coe. Scramble up easy slabs to the bottom rocks of the north-east edge of the buttress. Start at a prominent spike just left of a rock niche. Climb a series of corners and walls. The left-hand crack on the last steep wall is exposed but boasts a perfect handhold. Easy scrambling, then an easy slab on the left leads to a ledge below an arete with a crack just left of its edge (Hiccup).

The route goes right round the edge and gains a recess by an obvious and well marked traverse. Now descend rightwards to a ledge and climb an awkward 3m wall to a ledge slanting right. Follow the ledge to a 20m chimney. Climb the chimney, with a long step right at 10m, to a grass ledge. Traverse hard left on sloping holds to a short steep crack near the buttress edge. Follow the edge to the top on splendid rock.

Upper Tier

Approach: Go to the start of North Face Route. Either climb its lower tier or scramble up right of the face on good holds and heather until a few metres below a steep corner, then go out left on to the buttress and finish up the easy top part of North Face Route's lower tier, also the slab on the left to reach the start of the route (Moderate).

Hiccup 75m VS ***
B.W.Robertson, J.Houston Sep 1962
A fine route climbing the steep wall and crack just left of the buttress edge. Recommended as an approach to Rannoch Wall, as it can be climbed with rucksacks. Start below the obvious crack.
1. 25m 4c Climb the crack to a sloping ledge.
2. 45m 4b Climb to a ledge below the right arete of the steep wall. Follow the delicate and exposed arete to the top.

CURVED RIDGE - CROWBERRY RIDGE AREA

The most famous and by far the most popular area on the Buachaille.
Approach: By Curved Ridge (Moderate), described as a route below.
Descent: All the climbs on Crowberry Ridge and Rannoch Wall emerge on to the easy upper section of Crowberry Ridge, a narrow crest leading to the Crowberry. Tower. To avoid the Tower, move left and follow an exposed path (not obvious at first) to the cairn at the top of Curved Ridge. It is easy to go left too soon but

84

BUACHAILLE
ETIVE MOR
Rannoch Wall

1. Grooved Arete   VS **
2. Agag's Groove   Very Difficult ****
3. January Jigsaw   Severe ***
4. Satan's Slit   VS *
7. Engineer's Crack   E1 **
8. Fracture Route   VS **

A. Curved Ridge
B. Easy Gully
C. First Platform

Curved Ridge is visible, so it is easily corrected. Either descend Curved Ridge, or climb with rucksacks and finish over the summit and down the walking route (Coire na Tulaich).

Curved Ridge 240m Moderate ***
G.B.Gibbs Jul 1896

A grand mountain route and a smashing way to the summit. It is remarkable that such a steep line can have so little difficulty, largely due to some unusually good holds. But it does make it rather exposed for a nervous beginner. From just past the Waterslide, continue up the eroded path. The top of Crowberry Ridge and Rannoch Wall can be seen straight ahead but the East Face of North Buttress, in two tiers on the right, is more obvious. When steep rocks are reached, the path becomes less obvious but take a traverse line to the right, then rising with some wet scrambling to reach a basin (Crowberry Basin) from where the view of Crowberry Ridge and the route ahead is much more obvious.

The ridge proper now starts. The climb curves up and under Rannoch Wall (the left face of Crowberry Ridge, with a black corner at mid-height on Agag's Groove particularly obvious), through some impressive rock scenery, and ends at a cairn below the Crowberry Tower. In its middle part and towards the top the ridge is no more than a walk, but in between the rocks steepen to give enjoyable climbing with plenty of scope for variation. The best holds in general are near the crest and keep away from the perhaps tempting but loose gullies on the right. Continue up the crest, with a good snacking platform opposite Rannoch Wall, to the cairn. Go up and slightly left, skirting the lower rocks of the East face of Crowberry Tower, then leading back right to the Crowberry Tower Gap. A short scramble out of the Gap leads to the summit slopes.

Rannoch Wall

(NN 227 545) Alt 700m South-East facing

This face is the most popular on the mountain. The climbs are steep and incredibly exposed and yet it has an open friendly character. Generally speaking, the Rannoch Wall is quick drying and catches the sun until mid afternoon; and the view across Rannoch Moor is a major feature.

The routes are described from the lowest point of the face (not the lowest point of Crowberry Ridge, which carries on below as broken ground) upwards i.e. right to left. Here is a 6m chimney-crack which leads right on to a platform low down on Crowberry Ridge (The First Platform).

Grooved Arete 85m VS **
J.Cuningham, W.Smith Oct 1946

Bold and open climbing on the world's best rock. Start just left of the 6m chimney-crack at a slim left-facing groove 5m down and to the right of the start of Agag's Groove.
1. 20m 4b Climb the groove on small holds and continue to a steep section. Step left to a block belay on Agag's Groove. Avoiding the deviation to belay on Agag's makes the pitch a full 50m, with a top belay slightly lower.
2. 40m 4b Regain the groove in the arete by an awkward traverse. Follow the groove which trends rightwards and becomes less defined as it merges with the crest of the North-East Face. Continue back up and slightly left to the upper of two ledges below a short prominent corner-crack. Crowberry Ridge Direct is 10m to the right. A bold pitch needing some route finding.
3. 25m 4b Above the stance make an awkward move to the foot of a corner. Climb this, then continue up the crest to a ledge.

Agag's Groove 100m Very Difficult ****
J.F.Hamilton, A.Anderson, A.C.D.Small Aug 1936

This is the obvious well defined corner ramp that can be seen rising diagonally across the wall (even from the A82). The route name refers to a biblical character who possessed a decidedly delicate tread. This is a fine climb so expect a lot of traffic on busy weekends. Even the first ascent party only beat the rivals by a few minutes. Look for a large square-cut, detached block come ledge situated at the extreme right edge of the wall, approximately 5m up from the 6m chimney-crack leading to First Platform on Crowberry Ridge.

1. 30m Climb the crack above the block at the right-hand end of the face. The crack develops into a groove and leads to a block at the start of a ramp.
2. 25m Follow the ramp easily up and left to a large block.
3. 25m Up and left a projecting nose of rock will be seen. Continue up the ramp then move left to a hidden crack in the nose (exposed). Climb the crack and narrow groove and go up and left to a block.
4. 20m Move left and continue quite boldly to the top.

Left of Agag's are many small right-facing corners, taken by **Curving Groove** (VS 5a), which starts 8m left at a prominent small flake lying against the wall, and **Juniper Groove** (Hard Severe), a shallow corner 8m left again, but they tend to merge with other routes higher up. January Jigsaw climbs the last set of shallow corners below a huge flake which leans against the wall (Satan's Slit), some 35m up the gully bed from the start of Agag's.

3 January Jigsaw 75m Severe ***
H.I.Ogilvy, Miss E.Speakman Jan 1940
An excellent route, interest increasing with height. The final pitch involves a very exposed right traverse, but fortunately the holds are good. From below the huge flake, go up right for 10m to a flake set away from the wall (22m up and left of the start of Agag's).

1. 20m Climb steep twin right-facing corner cracks for 7m then go up and left by large rock steps until it is possible to move back right to a ledge and square flake situated above the start.
2. 20m Move right and climb by a flake-crack and short steep walls, then go straight up to the block belay below the nose pitch of Agag's.
3. 15m Pull on to the wall above and make an improbable traverse rightwards round the edge of the wall. Climb a hidden groove to re-emerge on the south-east face and continue to the metal spike below the overhanging crack of Satan's Slit.
4. 20m Start a right traverse with a trying move to reach better holds. Swing round an edge to a good stopping place at the foot of a hidden groove. Climb the groove and pull out left on to the wall in a sensational position. Continue on improving holds to the crest of Crowberry Ridge.

4 Satan's Slit 80m VS *
H.I.Ogilvy, Miss E.Speakman Sep 1939
An airy line up the steep wall left of January Jigsaw, also crossing Agag's. Not quite as clean as its illustrious neighbours. Start beneath an obvious chimney forming the left side of the huge detached flake at the base of the wall.

1. 30m 4a Climb the chimney and steep straightforward rock to an obvious flake. Traverse left for 6m, then go up and right to belay above the start.
2. 20m 4b Climb up for 6m on small holds, aiming slightly left, then traverse horizontally right for 12m. This bold and delicate traverse ends in Agag's some 12m below the nose.
3. 10m 4b Follow Agag's for 5m, break out right up a shallow scoop and go up to a small stance with a metal spike below an overhanging crack. Either belay or continue up the strenuous crux.
4. 20m 4c Climb the crack and continue more easily to the ridge.

The next two routes are further up the wall, above the chockstone pitch in the gully. They are easily reached by going further up Curved Ridge and walking in above the pitch. Here is a large red slab, often with wet streaks, at the base of the wall. At the right end of the wall is a prominent small overlap 8m up. A roofed left-facing corner can be seen high up on the wall.

Line Up   75m   HVS ✳✳
C.Higgins, I.Nicolson   1 Jun 1969
A steep and sustained direct line, finishing up the roofed corner. Escapable and a few rattly holds higher up means it 'only' gets two stars. High in the grade. Start towards the right side of the red slab, below the small overlap.
1. 25m 5a Climb to below the overlap, cross the overlap (only 4c at its left end), and continue to a junction with Whortleberry Wall at the left side of a small hanging slab above. Now go right and up (as for Whortleberry) to a ledge.
2. 25m 4c Climb the corner above for 5m, step left and continue to the foot of the roofed corner.
3. 25m 5a Climb the corner above (some vegetation and rattly rock in places) and pull round the roof to easier walls.

Whortleberry Wall   100m   HVS ✳✳
J.Cunningham, W.Smith 16 Sep 1956
A less direct but easier line up the same steep section of face as Line Up. Start to the right of the wet streaks approximately 10m to the left of Line Up. Quite bold.
1. 25m 4c Climb up the slab for 10m, go right 3m and cross a rectangular bulge on small holds. Continue rightwards to the left end of the small overlapping slab and traverse right to a good ledge (as for Line Up).
2. 25m 4c Traverse horizontally left for 5m then gradually upwards to a shallow groove, which is climbed to a small juniper ledge. Directly above are twin cracks; climb the left crack, then transfer to the right one. Easy ground leads to a ledge.
3. 25m 4c Traverse horizontally right for a few metres, go up and right again to a large roofed corner (Line Up). Start up Line Up's corner but 3m below the overhang, step right round an edge and cross the face rightwards to a small ledge.
4. 25m 4b Climb the crack directly above to reach easier ground and large blocks below the Crowberry Tower.

Crowberry Ridge - North-East face

Alt 650m   North-East facing   Diagram p84
This is the narrow face that dominates the head of the Crowberry Basin and overlooks the approach path. The usual approach is via Curved Ridge, moving right to climb the 6m chimney-crack just below the Rannoch Wall. The crack is about Difficult in standard and leads to the First Platform, above which Crowberry Ridge Direct and other climbs on the North-East Face start. Above the Platform is a smooth reddish wall which sports three prominent crack-lines.

Descent: Down the start of Crowberry Ridge (Difficult) back to the Platform, or one abseil from above the main difficulties (sling required). One can of course continue up Crowberry Ridge.

The thin crack-line starting above the left end of First Platform is **Symposium** (E2 5c).

Engineer's Crack   65m   E1 ✳✳
H.MacInnes, C.Vigano, R.Hope   Sep 1951
A fine well protected pitch on excellent rock, taking the next obvious crack starting 3m to the right of Symposium. Low in the grade.
1. 25m 5b Ascend easily to a ledge at 4m. The thin parallel cracks above lead to a good stopping place (this point can be gained more easily from the right). Continue up the crack that bends to the right near the top, to a junction with Fracture Route, at a stance above the second mantelshelf move.
2. 40m Continue up Fracture Route.

Fracture Route   65m   VS ✳✳
K.Copland, W.Smith   Oct 1946
This climb takes the obvious diverging cracks to the right of Engineer's Crack and above a pillar lying against the wall, left of the corner of Dingle. It is possible to

GLEN COE

BUACHAILLE ETIVE MOR
North Buttress
East Face

1. Brevity Crack	VS 5a *		
2. Shackle Route	Severe **		
3. Crow's Nest Crack	VS ***	9. Garrotte	VS 5a **
4. Mainbrace Crack	HVS 5a **	10. Gibbet	HVS 5a *
8. Hangman's Crack	VS 4c **	A. North Buttress	Moderate **

finish up Grooved Arete at 4b.

1. 25m 4c Climb the easy pillar (possible belay) and ascend the left-hand crack above for 5m. Now climb a more difficult and sustained section including two mantelshelf moves which lead to a stance and belay.

2. 40m Either finish direct or better and harder, traverse left around an edge and climb a crack left of the nose. The rock is excellent.

Dingle 35m HVS 5a *
D.Haston, J.Stenhouse Sep 1956
The obvious corner right of Fracture Route. Well protected, providing you can stop to place it.

**Crowberry Ridge Direct Route 225m Severe ** **
G.D.Abraham, A.P.Abraham May 1900
Naismith and Douglas had climbed a less direct version, mostly scrambling, in 1896. But the direct line, very hard for its day, was climbed by the team from the Lake District. There is only one short hard section, the famous left traverse and moves up from Abraham's Ledge. From the right side of the First Platform, turn the corner and take a belay beneath the left-hand side of a pinnacle which lies against the face.

Climb a shallow chimney on the left side of the pinnacle to its top, from which a 5m wall leads to Abraham's Ledge (20m). The crux now looms up on the left and requires a confident approach. Make an exposed left traverse and an upward balance move on sloping footholds to gain a scoop. Go gradually right and climb straight up on large holds to the Upper Ledge (12m). Poorly protected. From the left end of Upper Ledge climb directly up, steeply at first then more easily to easy ground. The steep section of the ridge ends with a long pitch on fine slabby rock. Easy climbing and a narrow ridge lead in a further 75m to the base of Crowberry Tower. This is climbed direct on its north side without difficulty. There is an easy spiral descent from the top by a ledge on the short west flank to reach the Gap.

NORTH BUTTRESS

The broad North Buttress lies between Crowberry Gully and Great Gully.

East Face

(NN 224 546) Alt 700m East facing

The East Face, split into two tiers, is varied and attractive, offering a number of good quality climbs in the VS to HVS grade, several of which can be done in a day. It is very quick drying and catches the morning sun. Although the rock is sound, there are a few hollow blocks.

Approach: Via the Curved Ridge approach until reaching the Crowberry Basin. The corner of Hangman's Crack is well seen in the upper tier. Continue fairly directly to the base. An alternative approach, slightly quicker but the face is not seen until near the end, is, after crossing the outflow from Great Gully, scramble up the well marked path on the east bank of the gully, heading towards split boulders (clearly seen from the approach). North Buttress is the broad buttress straight ahead. Now take a left-trending line following traces of path, to pass just left of the start of the steep section of North Buttress. This is where the face lies. If approaching from the base of Rannoch Wall, Crowberry Gully unexpectedly forces a descent into the Crowberry Basin and back up again.

Descent: To the right by the rocks of North Buttress, which although nowhere particularly difficult, are quite steep and intimidating in parts. There are abseil slings after pitch 1 of Shackle Route. These can be used to descend from all the lower tier routes but are not recommended because the knot tends to jam in the chimney below.

GLEN COE

Lower Tier

The face is well seen from lower Curved Ridge. When close up, a very prominent crack at the right end of red rock is Shackle Route.

1 Brevity Crack   45m   VS 5a *
P.Walsh, C.Vigano   1954
A thin crack 5m left of Shackle Route and starting 5m up. Climb easily to the crack, and a lot less easily up it to attain a standing position on a small ledge (crux). Continue more easily in the same line.

2 Shackle Route   75m   Severe **
S.H.Cross, Miss A.M.Nelson   Jun 1936
The prominent crack, followed by a pitch up the upper tier.
1. 35m 4a   Start on the left wall of the crack, then gain and follow it until it becomes a chimney leading to easier ground.
2. 10m   Continue up easier ground to the terrace between the tiers.
3. 30m   Directly above is a tall pinnacle-flake with a jammed block between it and the left wall. Either climb the black groove right of the pinnacle, or climb over the jammed block, to a left-slanting groove. A steep wall and easier rock lead to the top.

3 Crow's Nest Crack   80m   VS ***
J.Cunningham, J.C.P.McGonigle   Jun 1946
Right of Shackle Route is an arete with a big sharp spike forming its base, then a grassy recess to its right. This route is based on a crack in the groove which springs up from the top of the grassy recess. Fine sustained climbing at 4c after a tricky start (which can be avoided by starting 5m to the left). Start at the sharp spike.
1. 40m 5a   Climb the big sharp spike, pull over the bulge above (crux) and climb a shallow groove to join a line trending slightly right towards the main groove. Traverse right into the main groove and follow it for 6m to a roof. Mainbrace is the wider continuation crack above. Make a long step left below the roof on to a slab. Climb the slab then regain the crack where it is divided by an overhanging nose. Follow the left-hand crack to the terrace between the tiers.
2. 40m 4a   At the lower right end of the terrace is the tall pinnacle-flake of Shackle Route. From a black groove, go right then back left and climb a steep crack left of the arete overlooking Hangman's Crack, taking care of some suspect blocks.

4 Mainbrace Crack   40m   HVS 5a **
P.Walsh, W.Smith   Aug 1955
Another sustained climb with some quite hard sections, especially the start. Start beneath a parallel sided finger crack to the right of the grassy recess, and left of the arete of Bogtrotter. Climb the crack with some moves on the wall to its left to reach a groove that leans to the right. Quit the groove and step left to enter a right-facing corner leading to a bulging wall, which is avoided by going left again to a short wide crack (just above the long step left on Crow's Nest). Climb the crack for a few metres, then traverse right to a foot ledge on the arete. Finish up a groove in the arete in an impressive position.

To the right of Mainbrace Crack, the crag turns a corner forming an obvious prow – the line of **Bogtrotter** (E2 5c).

5 White Wall Crack   45m   E1 5b *
W.Smith, G.MacIntosh   Aug 1955 (2PA); FFA: B.W.Robertson   1963
The green speckled, clean-cut corner behind a large boulder just left of Bottleneck Chimney. Climb the corner-crack (thin) and mantelshelf on to a small ledge. Step

Yamay, E2 5b, Great Gully Upper Buttress. Climber Graeme Robb
(photo Andy Tibbs)

1. 20m Climb to the right of the corner, then easily up and left to below the groove.

2. 20m 5a The next pitch is both steep and sustained. Climb by a detached flake right of the groove, step left into it, then continue on good holds to a good ledge.

3. 15m 5a The link pitch. Move left to the edge, climb up for 2m, traverse left into a vertical crack and follow this to a poor belay on a sloping corner stance (it is perhaps better to continue).

4. 15m 4c Move right round the edge of the wall and gain a broad right-facing ramp of excellent rock. Trend leftwards, then step left again onto a much narrower elevated ramp which leads right to a small stance and block.

5. 35m 5a Swing down and right into the steep groove and follow this for about 6m. Make a difficult right traverse to a flake-crack which is a prominent feature of the climb. Using undercut holds on the flake, swing into the crack (exposed) and climb up to a poor stance below an overhang at 25m. Avoid this on the left and go up 10m to a ledge.

6. 25m 4a Follow the crest of the large flake to the right, and then more easily via a deep corner to finish.

Lecher's Superstition   110m   E2 ***
D.Haston, J.R.Marshall (Lecher's)   Jun 1959; D.Todd, W.Gordon (Superstition)   May 1962; K.Spence, J.Porteous (Lecher's Direct)   Aug 1968
Another combination climb, high in its grade and with two excellent and contrasting pitches. The line of the route follows the parallel corner right of Bludger's Revelation (pitch 2), crosses that route and follows a shallow groove and chocolate coloured wall to the right of Doom Arete.

1. 20m As for Bludger's Revelation.

2. 45m 5c A big pitch, often wet. Climb the detached flake to the foot of the groove. From the top of the flake step left on to a steep wall and pull on to the arete (hard). Regain the groove which is sustained and well protected. Take a semi-hanging belay at the top of the groove, or ropes permitting, cross the slab on the left and go up to the small block belay shared with Doom Arete and Bludger's Revelation, pitch 4.

3. 45m 5c A bold lead. From the Bludger's Revelation stance, climb the dark streak in the wall above and enter a left-facing groove, intricate (not a more prominent groove which is 2 or 3m to the right at this point). Continue up the line of the dark streak to a crack leading to a break with a grass ledge, 2m to the left (possible belay). Continue up the crack to easier ground.

Shibboleth   150m   E2 ****
R.Smith, R.Fraser   June 1958; True Finish (as described): .Smith, J.McLean   Jun 1959
Despite the creation of many harder routes, this great classic maintains its prestige. The route is sustained, serious and intimidating with some complex route finding. Above and right from the parallel grooves of Bludger's and Lecher's, and above the foot of Raven's Gully, is a very prominent hanging corner taken by this route. Start 6m below and left of Raven's Gully.

1. 20m 4a Climb a series of right-trending, slabby grooves to a large flake beneath a black stained crack.

2. 25m 5c Climb the obvious crack for 6m, traverse left for 3m then go up and right with difficulty, poor peg, to enter the corner (often wet). This leads on improving holds to a small ledge.

3. 20m 5a Continue up the corner and its continuation, then make an exposed and poorly protected traverse up and left to belay below the Revelation flake-crack.

4. 25m 5b Follow the groove on the right past protection possibilities, (small wires, thread), until forced onto the wall and follow this to the small overhang. Turn the overhang on its left by means of a hanging groove and crack and continue to a belay.

5. 20m 5a Climb up and left to gain a shallow overhanging corner which is followed to a ledge on the right. The **Original Finish** (4b) climbs the wall and groove above.

6. 20m 5c Traverse right to a good spike. Step up and go right to enter a bottomless

groove that leads to a ledge on the right in a fine position.

7. 20m 5b Traverse right to enter a crack springing up from the Great Cave, the huge recess overhanging Raven's Gully, and climb it to the top.

6 The New Testament   120m   E4 ****
D.Cuthbertson, J.George 6th Aug 1995

A superb route, taking a direct line up the entire cliff. It takes the left-hand of the three prominent grooves in the wall to the right of Shibboleth. Start 6m below and left of Raven's Gully.

1. 20m 4a Climb a series of right-trending slabby grooves to a large flake beneath the black stained crack of Shibboleth. Belay below a prominent dark stained corner on the right.

2. 25m 6a Climb the corner above for 6m, then follow a little stepped overlap going left to enter an obvious groove (the slim hanging groove immediately right of Shibboleth). Negotiate the 'slime factory' to enter the groove. At the top of this groove, move right into another groove (possibly wet). Climb the groove and its right edge (there is another slim groove to the right which is entered towards its top). Climb the mossy thin crack in the short wall above to a small ledge on the left. Although often wet, this pitch has good holds and gear; it is worth persevering (or sending your mate up!).

3. 25m 5c Climb up and left from two fingers of rock (forming a V) and climb a slim groove to a 3m tapering cracked groove. Climb the crack and instead of following the obvious line of stepped holds going up and rightwards, trend left and follow a shallow groove and rib which becomes parallel and close to Shibboleth pitch 4. This leads to the right side of Shibboleth's isolated overhang. From a juggy handrail, climb the tricky wall above and enter a small left-facing corner to reach a narrow ledge and belay on Apparition.

4. 25m 5c Step right and climb two faint, tapering cracks to a ledge. Go up and right to a sloping shelf leading to the right edge of this steep section of cliff, overlooking easier ground on the left wall of Raven's Gully. Climb up and left to a square-cut hold, then continue to a good side pull beneath a bulge. Move left and join Shibboleth at the traverse into the hanging groove. Belay on the ledge above as for Shibboleth.

5. 25m 5c Halfway along the belay ledge, climb a brown streak to gain an obvious stepped, right-trending crack. Climb this in a fine position to easier ground. Pumpy but well protected.

7 Apparition   140m   E2 ***
J.R.Marshall, J.McLean   Sep 1959

Varied climbing with some excellent positions on the slightly less steep section of face above the start of Raven's Gully. Graded HVS in the first Coe guide to use E grades. Start 6m below and left of Raven's Gully.

1. 30m 4a Climb a series of right-trending slabby grooves to a large flake beneath the black stained crack of Shibboleth. Go right towards the foot of a dark stained corner (The New Testament) at the top of a slab corner-crack. Traverse right for 3m round an awkward square-cut edge.

2. 50m 5b Climb the prominent V-groove above the belay. Step left into a parallel groove and continue to an overhang. Climb this and the steep groove above to a stance beneath a right-facing slab corner. Climb the slab and groove on the right to below a thin diagonal crack in the steep wall above, a bold pitch.

3. 30m 5b From the left end of the ledge, climb the diagonal crack in the steep wall above to easier ground leading to a narrow ledge. Move left to gain the ramp on pitch 5 of Shibboleth.

4. 30m 4b Climb the wall above and trend rightwards by grooves to a platform. Finish by an overhanging corner. This is Shibboleth's original finish.

Raven's Gully

Raven's Gully (HVS 5a) is a route for the connoisseur of Scottish gullies, with character and atmosphere and very hard for 1937. Climbed the year before Clachaig Gully, and much harder, although Bill Murray's dramatic writing made Clachaig Gully more famous. A spell of drought is desirable but not essential, although the crux is desperate in the rain. There is an impressive direct finish if there is energy or enthusiasm left.

Raven's Edge   170m   VS **

J.Cunningham, W.Smith, T.Paul   30 May 1948

Climbs a big corner facing Raven's Gully at mid-height. Sensational positions and atmosphere but the climbing is not quite as good as hoped. Start at the foot of Raven's Gully.

1. 60m Climb the left edge of the buttress in one or two rope lengths until about 10m above the crux chockstone of Raven's Gully, at a large block beside a platform on top of the rib, below a vertical wall.
2. 25m 4c Climb the wall above the block and traverse left to a prominent open book corner on the sidewall of Raven's Gully. Climb this to a ledge.
3. 25m 4c Continue up the corner to a platform.
4. 30m Ascend easily to a thread belay below the big roof on the extreme left edge of the buttress.
5. 30m 4c Traverse left under the roof to emerge in a very exposed position on the right wall of Raven's Gully. Climb the deep crack to the top.

Great Gully Buttress - East Face

(NN 224 546)   Alt 600m   South-East facing

This fine cliff lies opposite Slime Wall on the right side of Great Gully and is usually called Great Gully Buttress, although this should strictly refer to the whole right flank of Great Gully. It contains some excellent climbs on rock that is as good as any in the vicinity. The face catches the morning sun.

Approach: Follow the path to Slime Wall. At a point level with the toe of the buttress, Great Gully can be crossed easily.

Descent: A 45m abseil from a flake at the top of July Crack. From June Crack (and the other routes if wished), head left (towards the road) and scramble down until the top of a slab is reached. Cut back right and zigzag rightwards to the base of the cliff.

There are two main cracks seen on the approach; the left-hand crack (June) is fairly central. July and August are further left, thinner and closer together, obvious from the base of Slime Wall but not on the approach.

June Crack   70m   VS ***

W.Smith, J.Cunningham   12 Jun 1948

The most prominent crack. About 15m from the right end of the face there is a rib topped by a grass ledge. Start up the groove to the immediate right of the rib.

1. 20m Climb the groove to the grass ledge.
2. 20m 4b From the left end of the ledge climb up and slightly left for about 5m to reach the crack. Climb the crack with moves on to the left wall at a steepening just below a small rock shelf.
3. 30m 4c Above the crack overhangs. Climb it, using the nose on the right initially, to reach easier ground.

The next two routes are reached by scrambling up a grassy rake going leftwards from the toe of the buttress. Ten metres above a rocky section is a grass ledge on the right.

July Crack   45m   E1 5b ***

R.Smith, A.Fraser   Jun 1958

From the right end of the ledge, go up and right, then back left to a ledge at the base of the crack. The crack gives excellent sustained climbing, low in the grade.

GLEN COE

Fated Path, F7c+, Creag a' Bhancair. Climber Jo George
(photo Cubby Images)

August Crack   50m   HVS *

W.Smith, J.Cunningham 3 Aug 1955

A devious start, but good climbing all the way. There are possible belays if there is rope drag. Start as for July Crack, right and back left to the ledge. Step down and make a descending traverse left for about 5m to a thin ragged crack. Follow this quite steeply at first, then easing but finishing very steeply on huge holds. An independent direct start is possible but harder.

Great Gully Upper Buttress

(NN 223 546)   Alt 800m   South-East facing

This fine little buttress of immaculately clean rock presents a short steep wall some distance above Great Gully Buttress but with the same aspect. The face catches the sun for much of the day, so it is quick drying.

Approach: Up past Slime Wall and the lower buttress (East Face); either side is possible. Climbing June Crack on the way is more fun; carrying boots or trainers is suggested if rucksacks have been left.

Descent: Down the left (Great Gully) side of the buttress, short and straightforward. To return to the base of the lower buttress (and therefore the road), scramble down the crest (not the gully which runs down from the cliff) towards the road until only just above the approach path on the opposite side of Great Gully. Here, the top of a slab is reached. Cut back right and zigzag rightwards to the base of the lower buttress.

Yam   40m   E1 5b *
A.Fulton, J.Cullen   1963
The prominent chimney-crack splitting the centre of the face, with a difficult move over the roof at 15m. Slower to dry.

Yamay   40m   E2 5b ***
I.Nicolson, K.Spence   1 Sep 1968
A steep, well protected and sustained pitch on excellent rock, taking the prominent crack and corner 3m right of Yam. Climb to a small roof, traverse the wall on the right and ascend the corner above. A direct start is a grade harder.

May Crack   35m   VS 5a ***
R.Hope, W.Smith   6 May 1952
Ten metres right of Yamay, and above some scree, pull steeply on to a pointed shelf, gain and climb the fine crack above. Superb.

Facade   40m   VS 4b *
L.S.Lovat   30 Jun 1957
Climbs the mosaic of cracks and blocks at the right end of the wall. Feels bold and exposed, but the holds are excellent, perhaps only Hard Severe. But it was originally graded Very Difficult! To the right of May Crack is an open corner which both leans and faces to the right. Start below the corner and trend right initially, then back left taking the line of least resistance to a short groove at the right end of overhangs. Climb the groove and trend left on the steep wall above to finish.

CREAG A' BHANCAIR

(NN 216 551)   Alt 450m   North-West facing   Map p78   Diagram p100

This superb cliff lies at a relatively low altitude on the west flank of the north spur of Stob Coire na Tuileachan, well to the right (facing) of other described climbs on the Buachaille. Easily distinguished by the prominent reddish wall at its centre (Tunnel Wall), it can be clearly seen when driving south along the straight section of the A82, a couple of kilometres before reaching Altnafeadh. Generally speaking the climbs here are of a high level of difficulty and would rank favourably alongside some of the best and hardest climbs in Scotland. The classic Carnivore was the first line to breach this impressive cliff back in the '60s. Both this and the stunning Whillance '80s test piece, The Risk Business, should not be missed. The Tunnel Wall itself boasts some superb sports climbs – long, intimidating in character and certain to test a climber's reserve of stamina! The cliff is quick drying and enjoys any afternoon or evening sunshine.

Approach: Park as before at the lay-by at Altnafeadh (NN 222 564) on the A82 and follow the path past Lagangarbh, but take the right-hand fork in the path towards Coire na Tulaich. About 15mins after leaving the A82, turn right at a largish boulder that sits on the right side of the path. A few metres beyond this boulder, go past another small boulder and a track (which is vague at first) should be visible. The track leads in a south-westerly direction, crosses a boulder strewn river bed (usually dry) and gently rises under a line of small crags to emerge beneath the foot of the impressive pink coloured Tunnel Wall, 30mins.

BUACHAILLE ETIVE MOR
Creag a' Bhancair

1. Carnivore – Villain's Finish		E2 **
2. The Risk Business		E5 ***
3. Uncertain Emotions *D.Cuthbertson (1986)*	25m	F7b ***
4. The Railway Children *D.Cuthbertson (1987)*	30m	F7c ****
5. Tribeswoman *P.Laughlan (1990)*	30m	F7c+ ***
6. Fated Path *G.Livingston (1986)*	30m	F7c+ ****
7. Fated Mission *D.Birkett (2002)*	30m	F7c+ ***
8. Admission *G.Livingston (1987)*	30m	F7c+ **
9. Axiom *D.MacLeod (2004)*	30m	F8a **
10. The Third Eye *D.MacLeod (2004)*	25m	F7c *

Descent: From the top of the cliff, traverse right on rough rhyolite slabs, then continue leftwards (facing out) and descend a shallow gully watercourse, before traversing back right (facing out) beneath the toe of the buttress.

1 Carnivore – Villain's Finish   160m   E2 **
*J.Cunningham, M.Noon (by original finish – aided)   9 Aug 1958; Villain's Finish:
D.Whillans, D.Walker   1962*
A classic route and the first to breach the central wall. The first pitch is serious and sustained with much traversing. Either a competent second or a very conscientious leader is recommended if the second is to avoid the all too frequent inspection of the grass slope below! Start approximately 10m right of the left end of the crag at a bulge below a right-trending weakness.
1. 45m 5b Pull over the bulge and trend right on good holds to a thread runner (easily missed). Now climb a tricky little wall and continue to a small ledge at the start of the traverse (peg and krab sometimes in-situ for a back-rope – please leave). Follow a descending line of weakness and continue to a point beneath the left end of a long ledge. Climb steeply onto this and walk right to a belay.
2. 20m 4b From the right end of the ledge climb the green, slabby scoop on the right to a ledge and belay.
3. 20m 5a Climb ledges and an obvious line of weakness to a right-slanting crack. Climb the crack to belay on a shelf beneath a black overhung recess.
4. 25m 5c The Villain's Finish. Climb the recess and boldly layback the crack above to the base of a slim groove. Attain a standing position with difficulty and continue more easily to a ledge and belay.
5. 50m Easier climbing leads to ledges and the top

2 The Risk Business   120m   E5 ***
P.Whillance, R.Parker, P.Botterill   28 May and 24 Aug 1980
A modern classic, following the obvious left-rising overlap which issues from a rowan tree on the right side of Tunnel Wall. Friends have made the climb slightly safer, but they involve considerable effort to place.
1. 25m 6a From the rowan tree (now in a poor state), climb up and left on dark slatey rock to a small foot ledge. Traverse left (two peg runners in a poor state) and either step down and re-ascend to a good hold and protection or, go straight left to the same position. Continue more steeply until an exposed left traverse leads to a ledge at the base of a prominent open groove.
2. 15m 5c An easier but unprotected pitch. Climb the groove above, initially by the rib on the left, to a ledge on Carnivore.
3. 30m 6a Move left, then up a short wall to a ledge below a small overhang. Pass this on its left and climb a short groove to another small overhang (protection and poor rest on the right). Move left (strenuous) and pull over the overhang on a thin finger jug in a very airy position. Continue up the groove to a ledge.
4. 50m Continue more easily in the same line to the top.

Tunnel Wall Sport Routes

Topo p100

Eight sport routes are fully bolted with double lower off points, however a stick clip may be advisable to pre clip the first bolt on a few lines. A 60m rope is required for the majority of lines.

Bidean nam Bian Massif

The climbing is centred around three ridges (the Three Sisters) which push into the narrow section of Glen Coe. The highest is Beinn Fhada, the middle is Gearr Aonach and the lowest is Aonach Dubh. The two valleys between them are the Lost Valley (higher) and the Coire nan Lochain valley (lower). The latter, not surprisingly, has the peak and crag of Stob Coire nan Lochain at its top.

The first crag is on the east (Lost Valley) side of Gearr Aonach. Next are the crags up the Coire nan Lochain valley, first the east side of Aonach Dubh, then Stob Coire nan Lochain itself. Then the North Face of Aonach Dubh, facing the main glen, the West Face of Aonach Dubh, clearly seen from lower Glen Coe and finally the high Church Door Buttress, approached up in front of the West Face of Aonach Dubh.

GEARR AONACH

Map p78

This is the middle of the Three Sisters. Where the ridge terminates overlooking the road, it presents a remarkable dome of steep rock as its North Face. Just left of the change of aspect from north to the east facing walls which overlook the Lost Valley is the North-East Face, which shows clean rock overlooking the gorge of the Lost Valley approach. This face is not described although it has some good routes, including **Marshall's Wall** (E2 5b). Further up the Lost Valley is the East Face.

EAST FACE

(NN 162 553)   Alt 650m   South-East facing

The face offers excellent climbing on remarkable holds, despite its slightly vegetated appearance and scrambling approach.

Approach: Park at the westerly of two big car parks (NN 172 568) or slightly nearer but often busy, at a smaller car park 200m east (normally for the Aonach Eagach). Head down to a bridge (NN 173 564) over the River Coe to follow a well made path up the right side of the wooded gorge of the Allt Coire Gabhail. Cross a stile and continue into the gorge, then cross the river and follow the path on the south side of the valley to a high point overlooking the Lost Valley. The crag is the vegetated looking face well ahead on the right side of the valley, above where the path starts to rise after the flat section in the valley. and is flanked by full height shallow gullies on either side; Rev Ted's Gully on the right and Lost Leeper Gully on the left. The climbing is on the upper tier, the lower tier being crossed by many grass ledges.

Descend into the valley and continue until below the crag. From here, the most obvious feature is a long overhang left of centre and high up. The Wabe passes just right of this; Mome Rath Route passes just to the left, while Rainmaker and Snowstormer are well to the left, where the crag turns round into Lost Leeper Gully.

Head upwards by a line near either gully; Rev Ted's is easier but Lost Leeper Gully is more convenient for Rainmaker or Snowstormer. Start on the left of Lost Leeper Gully and zigzag up ledges to a clump of trees at half-height in the gully. If dry, climb the gully bed, which is a remarkable ladder of holds to reach the wall just left of the terrace. Scramble up left for about 30m to the start of Rainmaker and Snowstormer, or up right to the terrace. If wet, a groove leading up right from the trees might be better. For Rev Ted's, find a line through a lower tier to the right of the gully, then go diagonally left to the terrace between the tiers. About 45mins to the Lost Valley and the same again to the terrace.

Descent: It is possible (but not easy) to scramble down the rib beyond Lost Leeper Gully. Abseiling off trees makes it easier but a route here is often done with sacks and walk off via the Zig-Zags. The Zig-Zags is a steep zigzag path with some scrambling on the north (road) side of the North-East Face. From the base of the crag, reversing the gullies is not pleasant. It is easier to make a descending traverse left (facing out) well beyond Rev Ted's Gully and make an abseil down the lower tier (or continue the descending traverse).

**Rainmaker   60m   Hard Severe ** **
R.Marshall, J.Moriarty   13 Sep 1958
This and the next route are well to the left, where the crag turns round into Lost Leeper Gully (see Approach). The deeply recessed corner gives a fine climb.

Snowstormer   85m   HVS 5a *
J.Burns, D.Rubens   May 1974
Climbs quite close to the exposed right arete of Rainmaker corner in three pitches.

Mome Rath Route   135m   Very Difficult *
J.S.Stewart, Mrs M.A.Stewart, Miss C.B.Stewart   16 May 1954
Start up a light grey ramp of rock which slants up and left, some 25m right of the alp's left extremity. Climb the shelf to a flat grassy eyrie at the foot of a steep exposed chimney, on the left of large overhangs three quarters of the way up the face. The chimney leads to the top.

The Wabe   135m   Very Difficult ***
J.M.Brockway, J.S.Orr, D.J.Parlane   15 May 1954
Climbs the right side of steep clean rock above the start of Mome Rath Route's initial ramp. This is right of a very prominent crack **Jabberwock** (VS). Start a few metres right of the ramp. Climb a flake and groove to a stance below a small overhang. Go over this, steep but on good holds, to a slab, then right to a stance in a corner. Traverse left onto the wall and climb up to a large square block under overhangs. Traverse right and up a recessed panel, just right of the overhangs, to a stance on the rib to the right. Cross left to a slab above the overhang and go straight up to the top.

STOB COIRE NAN LOCHAN

(NN 148 551)   Alt 900m   North facing   Map p78

Stob Coire nan Lochan (1115m), the finest attendant peak of Bidean, stands proud 1km north-east of the main summit. The long ridges of Gearr Aonach and Aonach Dubh run north, defining the north-east corrie, before finally plunging down into Glen Coe itself. The andesite is more columnar and cracked than the lower rhyolite. The fine outlook and height make the rock climbing well worth sampling, especially since the snow lasts much of the year, adding an alpine flavour.

Approach: Park opposite where the Coire nan Lochain valley meets the River Coe (NN 168 569). Coming up the valley, this is beyond where the dark slit of Ossian's Cave is seen on the North Face of Aonach Dubh. A bridge can be seen below at NN 167 566. Cross the bridge and continue up the main path. The path runs below some rocky bluffs, crosses the stream below the waterfall issuing from the corrie and climbs up to the right of a small buttress to reach the lip of the corrie. 2hrs to the start of the routes.

Descent: By Broad Gully, the uncomplicated slope left of South and Central Buttresses

The right-hand side of the corrie is dominated by two tall buttresses, South (left) and Central (right). South Buttress is cut by the prominent corner of the following route.

Unicorn   125m   E1 ***
J.R.Marshall, R.N.Campbell   18 Jun 1967
The huge monolithic corner which soars up near the right edge of the buttress provides a classic climb that is low in the grade. Start beneath the corner.
1. 35m 5a Climb the corner for 6m, then move right on to and climb the rib for 5m before re-entering the corner. Continue to a stance.
2. 20m 5a Continue up the corner.
3. 40m 5a Climb the wide crack in the corner to shattered ledges.
4. 30m 5a Carefully climb over loose rock, then climb a chimney for a short way before swinging out right on to the wall where a few steep moves gain the top.

From the top of the third pitch of Unicorn it is possible to abseil down the line (please leave any slings) and climb Scansor, thereby climbing the final chimney common to both routes only once.

Scansor 120m E2 *
P.Braithwaite, G.Cohen 2 Sep 1972

The pillar right of Unicorn gives some fine positions although the climbing is a little disappointing. Start at the foot of Unicorn.

1. 45m 5b Climb the groove right of Unicorn over suspect blocks and flakes to a ledge on the edge. Step up left and steeply climb a crack until level with a small roof on the left. Traverse right, across the wall to the edge and go awkwardly up to a good belay.
2. 25m 5b Awkwardly gain the upper ledge on the left. Move up the wall until it is possible to reach right and climb on to the left end of a ledge. Traverse right to its end (peg runner), then pull up into a groove and go up right to a large stance.
3. 20m 4c Cautiously climb the groove on the right to ledges, then up and left across alarmingly loose ground to belay on Unicorn.
4. 30m 5a Finish up the chimney and wall of Unicorn.

The next route lies on Central Buttress.

Central Grooves 130m VS 4c *
K.Bryan, R.Robb Jul 1960 (1PA); FFA: unknown

The prominent line of corners springing from near the toe of the buttress is a popular winter route and the rock has been well cleaned by axes and crampons. Start just right of the diedre.

1. 30m Climb up and left into the corner and follow it to small ledges.
2. 25m Continue up the corner until it opens out on to mossy ledges.
3. and 4. 50m Follow the grooves above, passing left of a conspicuous overhang, to finish on a broad terrace.
5. 25m Move up right and climb easy ground to the top.

AONACH DUBH

Map p78

The most western (lowest down the Glen) of the Three Sisters offers the best known climbing after the Buachaille.

EAST FACE

Several accessible walls of good clean rock, although the routes are not as long as elsewhere. But the approaches and descents are fairly easy, so several routes can be done in a day.

Approach: Park as for Stob Coire nan Lochan, opposite where the Coire nan Lochain valley meets the River Coe (NN 168 569). Coming up the valley, this is beyond where the dark slit of Ossian's Cave is seen on the North Face of Aonach Dubh. A bridge can be seen below at NN 167 566. From the parking place, the Lower North-East Nose is at the left end of the North Face, although the main climbing wall is only seen in profile. The rest of the East Face crags are also seen in profile but slightly higher up and much closer to the stream. Follow the path across the bridge for about 20min until just past a gully where the path has been washed away. A new pitched section heads steeply uphill. At the first bend beyond this, a small path forks off right contouring towards the Lower Walls and an obvious large boulder beside the burn and just above a waterfall. This is the best crossing point for access to the walls, which are reached in about 1hr, or 45mins if quick.

Lower North-East Nose

(NN 159 562) Alt 490m South-East Facing

Clearly seen from the car park, this steep pale wall, often glinting in the sun, offers some of the finest hard climbing in Glen Coe.

Approach: From the crossing point, head back downstream a little to skirt a line of small crags, then follow grassy terraces up right, then back left to below the crag. A short scramble leads to the base of the wall.

Descent: Down the cliff's left-hand (south) side, or abseil.

Splitting the pale wall is the superb vertical crack of Freak-Out. The wall is bounded on its left side by a big curving corner. This is a bit mossy and often damp, but a stunning line for the grade when dry **Boomerang** (HVS 5a)

Freak-Out   65m   E4 ****
D.Bathgate, A.McKeith   Jul 1967 (aid); FFA: D.Mullin, J.Melrose   1979
One of the Glen Coe Greats, taking the central crack-line up the pale wall, cutting through obvious niche at half-height. Scramble up the lowest rocks to a ledge and tree belay below the crack.
1. 20m 5c Climb the wall to the crack. Follow this to the obvious right traverse to a small ledge and assorted belays.
2. 30m 6a Regain the crack and climb it to a poor rest under the roof. Pull over on good holds then make a few powerful moves to a slightly more relaxed position. Sustained but more reasonable climbing leads to an inverted flake under the final roof. Taking care to absorb the full impact of the situation, climb through the final overhang to a ledge a short distance above.
3. 15m Climb the wall above to the top.

Crocodile   50m   E3 ***
D.Cuthbertson, M.Hamilton   4/5 Jun 1977
A varied climb with a steep and well protected finale up the exposed groove in the right arete of the wall. Low in the grade.
1. 30m 5b Start at a small tree beneath the widest part of the overhang right of Freakout. Climb strenuously up to and round the left side of the overhang to attain a standing position above. Continue up the wall to the girdling ledge common to Freakout and Spacewalk. Either belay here or climb the groove above for 4m (as for Spacewalk), then traverse right round the edge of the face in an exposed position to a ledge beneath the crux groove.
2. 20m 5c Climb the groove with increasing difficulty, culminating in a difficult move (some say 6a) to gain easier ground on the left arete. Belay at a small tree above. Either abseil from the tree or 30m of easy climbing leads to the top.

Spacewalk   50m   E5 **
K.Johnstone, P.Ogden   Apr 1978 (1PA); FFA: D.Cuthbertson, M.Hamilton   6 Jun 1980
A good companion route to Freak-Out, with one very hard move and less than convincing protection. Start down and right of Crocodile, directly below a crack in a steep wall.
1. 25m 5c Climb the crack, then go up and slightly right to roofs. Climb out left then quite boldly across the wall to join and follow Crocodile to the Freak-Out belays. A superb pitch.
2. 25m 6b Climb the groove on the right to a small roof (small wires behind loose flakes). Step left and make a desperate move up a short groove. Continue up then right to the top.

Lower Walls

(NN 159 562)   Alt 450m   South-East facing

These dark water streaked walls are the first rock to be reached after crossing the burn and lie below and left of the North-East Nose. Above and left is Weeping Wall, with a big stepped corner-chimney on its right side. The Lower Walls are

Freak-Out, E4 6a, Aonach Dubh. Climber Emma Williams
(photo Cubby Images)

identified from the burn by a big slimy chimney towards the right end. Descent is easy on the left (south). Their left end is characterised by overhanging corner-grooves flanked by a large wet crack on the right. Right of the crack is the steep wall of Lady Jane, capped by a long horizontal overhang.

Lady Jane   25m   E2 5b ***
D.Cuthbertson, D.Jamieson   Jul 1977

A brilliant pitch with reasonable protection, often possible when adjacent routes are wet. Climb the wall to a right curving crack, follow this then up to the horizontal break at two-thirds height, just left of the wet streak. Step right and up (dryness not essential here) then ascend quite boldly to an easing in angle (crux, although the technical crux is after 8m) leading to a tree on the break. Scramble off left, or abseil from the tree.

Sir Chancealot   45m   E2 *
B.Duff, K.McCluskey   27 May 1978

Good climbing up the centre of the wall about 10m right of Lady Jane, followed by forceful moves over the roof. Start mid-way between the black streak right of Lady Jane and a shallow stepped corner which leads to a tree in the horizontal break (well right of the tree on Lady Jane). Climb the wall more or less directly, taking a small overhang on the right to an awkward thread in a cave, possible belay. Thug over the roof to the right to good holds and easy ground.

Weeping Wall

(NN 157 558)   Alt 530m   South-East facing   Diagram p110

This area lies up and left of the Lower Walls and is defined on its right by an obvious stepped chimney. The routes are described right to left from the lowest point of the crag, which is quite far right and has a flat area below. There is a large block at the crag base about 15m up and left; the biggest wet streak is up and left of this. The wall has few obvious lines but the climbing is better than the appearance might suggest.

Approach: Past the left end of the Lower Walls, 1hr total.

Descent: The routes finish on the Terrace below Terrace Face. Traverse the Terrace right (facing out) and scramble down gravelly ledges with great caution before continuing to traverse to easy ground. An alternative descent, useful if the normal descent is too exposed (say it rains), is to traverse north (towards the valley) for about 200m until the Lower North-East Nose can be seen below. Go down before it and continue diagonally (left) until under its main wall. Now trend right under the Lower Walls to reach the stream at the boulder. Picking the best line is a little tricky; if in doubt follow goat tracks; they usually know the easiest route.

1 Curving Crack   90m   Severe *
L.S.Lovat   Oct 1952

Start at a clean wall some 10m left of the right edge of the face. Climb to a ledge at 10m and continue to another ledge with a tree. Climb the crack above then a steep wall to easier rocks.

2 The Long Crack   90m   Severe **
L.S.Lovat, J.M.Johnstone   Jun 1953

The prominent feature is a long crack which begins in the middle of the wall right of the water streaks (and is therefore not obvious from the very base) and runs diagonally right for 3m, then straight up almost to The Terrace. Start just right of the large block, about 15m left of the right edge, at a fault which goes through a small bulging wall at 10m.

1. 30m Climb to the bulge, then take the fault to a ledge.

2. and 3. 60m Above and right is the crack. Climb it using the wall on the right, crux. Continue more easily to the top.

Weeping Wall Route   105m   Severe **

D.Scott, J.C.Henderson   Aug 1947

Good climbing, but not over endowed with protection, following the cracked fault beginning halfway up the wall and trending slightly left, adjacent to the right edge of the water streaks. Start just left of the detached block.

1. 15m Climb to a recess below the fault.

2. and 3. 90m Climb the steep fault above, trending slightly left, to a bulge with a small block above. Pull over the block and take the line of least resistance on parallel grooves to easier rocks and The Terrace.

Solitude   50m   E3 **

D.Cuthbertson, R.Anderson, W.Todd   3 Jun 1977

Climbs the wall right of the leftmost water streak. It just merits its grade, either for the guile required to protect it, or for the commitment if you can't. Take small wires and cams. Start near the left end of the wall below a depression at the right end of a grass ledge 5m up. Climb the lower wall to the right end of the ledge. Climb a short corner on the right to a higher ledge and a large block. Move boldly up the wall above, slightly right, to the base of short diagonal crack running out left. Follow this then climb with continued interest on superb rock to a large grassy ledge. To descend, walk left past a dilapidated tree and jump to a lower ledge with a good tree. Either abseil (25m) or continue along the ledge and scramble down. The purist will climb an easier second pitch to reach the Terrace Face approach.

Spider Right-Hand   45m   VS 4c ***

The prominent dark brown crack bounding the left side of the leftmost water streak. A superb well protected pitch requiring dry conditions, less so on a sunny day. Climb the lower wall to the ledge at its lowest point (as for Solitude). Climb thin parallel cracks to gain the obvious crack come groove line bounding the left side of the water streak. Climb this with little deviation to the ledge with the dilapidated tree. Descend as for Solitude (or continue).

Spider   45m   HVS **

J.R.Marshall, R.Marshall, A.H.Hendry   Apr 1957

Quite bold. Start just left of Spider Right-Hand/Solitude. Climb the lower wall to the grass ledge. Move up the ramp on the left, then pull on to the wall to gain the base of a small right-facing groove. Climb this to its top, then make a delicate right traverse to a good hold and protection. Either step right into the crack of Spider Right-Hand or, more in keeping, make a tricky move up to gain a fat ledge above. Move left to a hidden crack and follow this to a steepening. Move right and climb steeply to the ledge and dilapidated tree. Descend as for Solitude (or continue).

Terrace Face

(NN 157 558)   Alt 650m   South-East Facing   Diagram p110

This face lies above Weeping Wall and the grassy ledges of The Terrace. Here are some of the best easier routes in Glen Coe. A worn area below the cliff indicates its popularity.

Approach: Either do a route on Weeping Wall, or walk up left from under it. The prominent arete seen above is Archer Ridge. The rocks above become easier angled and a shallow chimney appears, the lower section of **The Bow**. Either climb this, (Difficult for 5m, then Moderate), or miss the first 20m on the left to either join it or continue rightwards beyond it (reversing the descent from Weeping Wall). This reaches The Terrace below the face.

Descent: The safest descent is right (facing out) to descend rocky grassy slopes. To return to The Terrace, walk left (facing out) to the top of a shallow gully formed by an eroded vertical dyke beside a short steep wall. Scramble down the outside of the first section of the gully (a rope may be required), then enter the second section and descend to The Terrace. To descend from The Terrace, see Weeping Wall.

GLEN COE

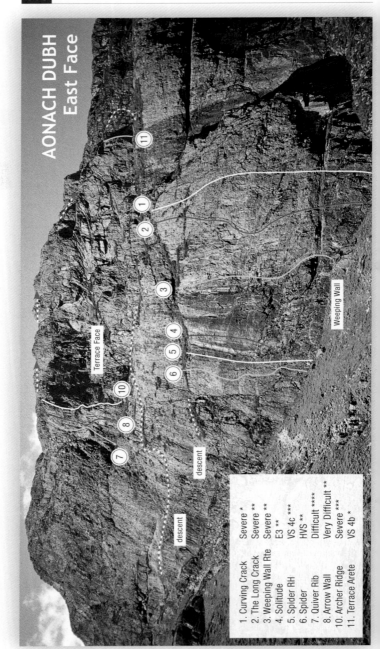

AONACH DUBH
East Face

Terrace Face

Weeping Wall

descent

descent

descent

1. Curving Crack   Severe *
2. The Long Crack   Severe **
3. Weeping Wall Rte   Severe **
4. Solitude   E3 **
5. Spider RH   VS 4c ***
6. Spider   HVS **
7. Quiver Rib   Difficult ****
8. Arrow Wall   Very Difficult **
10. Archer Ridge   Severe ***
11. Terrace Arete   VS 4b *

Quiver Rib   60m   Difficult **

D.B.McIntyre, W.H.Murray   May 1947

At the left end of The Terrace is the dark and damp chimney of The Bow. This fine route, improbable for its grade, climbs the rib and wall immediately right of the chimney.

1. 50m Start up the rib, or climb The Bow for a few metres before stepping on to the rib, then veer rightwards to a small ledge below a black crack on Arrow Wall (possible belay). Continue by some very steep moves to gain a narrow groove trending left up the steep face. Good holds lead to an excellent ledge.

2. 15m Scramble off left, or continue the experience by going back rightwards and up to a block with some slings (abseil descent possible). Easier to the top.

Arrow Wall   70m   Very Difficult **

L.S.Lovat, J.M.Johnstone   Jun 1953

This route, hard for the grade, climbs the steep wall right of Quiver Rib. Start mid-way between Quiver Rib and the arete on the right, below a groove on the wall above.

1. 35m Climb the wall, move slightly right at a bulge at 12m, continue up then left to a ledge. Belay on Quiver Rib.

2. 35m Directly above is a very steep and narrow black groove (left of which the wider groove of Quiver Rib slants up left). Climb the groove on excellent holds to the top.

Wounded Knee   70m   Severe **

K.V.Crocket, B.Dullea   14 Apr 1991

A harder drier alternative to Arrow Wall, this route climbs a shallow groove on the front face parallel to, and left of the arete between Arrow Wall and Archer Ridge, then takes the imposing headwall above. Start mid-way between Arrow Wall and the arete on the right.

1. 30m Climb a steepening groove to a ledge; belay on the left.

2. 40m Step left on to the steep wall. Move up and left a few moves then traverse right across the bulging wall to the edge. Continue on good holds to the top.

Archer Ridge   70m   Severe **

W.H.Murray, D.B.McIntyre   May 1947

This classic climb completes the quartet of good routes on this crag. It takes the blunt arete right of The Bow chimney. Start at the lowest rocks, where the ridge is somewhat rounded.

1. 25m Follow the crest to a good stance just to its right.

2. 20m 4a Directly above on the crest is a steep corner-groove, with a steep rib to its right. Climb up and slightly right under the steep wall for 7m, move up and back left to the crest, then continue to a stance in a corner.

3. 25m 4a Move right a few metres, then up a crack to the final steep wall. Climb this at an obvious breach and continue more easily.

Terrace Arete   45m   VS 4b **

P.Walsh, J.Cullen   May 1954

Bold climbing on excellent rough rock. At the extreme right-hand end of The Terrace, where the descent path turns towards it, a steep arete rises. Start just right of the arete. Climb to a ledge at 5m, then make a delicate step left on to the arete proper. Continue to a recess and finish directly up a groove and a short wall.

NORTH FACE

(NN 152 562)   Alt 600m   North facing

To the north and west, Aonach Dubh presents some of the finest mountain scenery in Glen Coe. Lying above Loch Achtriochtan and the A82 is the massive North Face. The most obvious feature of the face is the great black slot of Ossian's Cave. This has lured unsuspecting climbers into its leafy glade since its first ascent in 1868. Below the cave, a prominent ledge system slopes across the face from middle left to top right marking a geological boundary between vegetated andesite below and the steep and impressive rhyolite above. Particularly distinct in its upper half, where it is known as the Sloping Shelf, this ramp system gives access to some of the finest rock in Glen Coe, only limited by its north facing aspect and consequent slowness to dry.

Approach: Park at NN 148 572, cross the wide but shallow river (often shallow when this crag is in nick) and go up a small path on the left side of a deep gully which leads up the start of the Sloping Shelf (slightly left of Ossian's Cave). Otherwise, cross by the bridge (NN 167 566) and walk slightly downhill to reach the lower continuation of the Sloping Shelf down to the valley bottom. Go up this line to cross one gully and continue to the deep gully. Either approach needs to cross this gully; take the highest traverse line immediately below the cliff. Make an awkward descent, then an awkward climb out (about Difficult, but slippery in its normal wet state) to gain the Sloping Shelf. Go up the Shelf for quite a long way until about 100m in distance short of the big gully at the top. The routes are here, just below a big damp cave on the wall.

Descent: A large ledge runs across the top of the routes towards the big gully at the top of Sloping Shelf. Follow it to its end and descend a chimney. Descend the shallow fault first on its right, then traverse to the left to descend 15m to the Sloping Shelf. The scrambling is exposed and unpleasant.

The obvious feature is a huge left-facing corner, the full height of the cliff (Yo-Yo). In the centre of the wall left of it is a crack-line which starts 10m up (The Clearances). Left again is a more intermittent crack-line which has a definite section low down and another above roofs (Eldorado).

Eldorado   125m   E5 **

K.Johnstone, M.Worsley   22 Jun 1977 (1PA); FFA: M.Hamilton, D.Mullin   17 May 1980
A very strenuous climb, with good protection on pitch 2. An obvious thin crack cuts the wall left of Yo-Yo. About 5m further left is a fainter crack-line, broken by small bulges. Start just right of this crack.
1. 20m 5c Climb up and left into the crack and follow it to a ledge. As this pitch is loose and verdant, it is better to approach from The Clearances by the obvious line.
2. 40m 6b Climb the wall to the overhang, launch into the short corner, then step left above the roof, poor rest. Climb the groove and crack above, passing another small roof by a trying and tiring move, to better holds where the angle eases. Move up slightly left to a crack which is followed to a terrace and awkward belays.
3. 40m 5c Climb the groove just right of the arete (the second most obvious groove left of The Clearances). The groove is barred by a short and difficult bold wall. Once gained, the groove is better protected although mossy, and continues in an impressive position until a right traverse leads to a small ledge and belay on The Clearances.
4. 25m 5a Climb the rib to Pleasant Terrace, as for The Clearances.

Repossessed   125m   E5 6a ***

M.Crocker   30 Jun 1995
The meat of this route is a superb 30m pitch following the obvious crack-line above the roof where Eldorado steps left. Sustained and strenuous, but well protected and not high in the grade.
1. 20m 5c As for Eldorado.
2. 40m 6a Follow the main pitch of Eldorado for 10m to the roof. Step right to an undercut and up a wide crack to better holds. Continue more easily to the overhanging wall above and up this to awkward sloping jugs (crux). A long reach gains better holds and easier ground leading to the terrace.
3 and 4. 40m,25m 5c, 5a As for Eldorado.

The Clearances   105m   E4 ***
E.Grindley, C.Grindley, J.Main   Aug 1976
This fine route climbs the very steep wall left of Yo-Yo. The first pitch is probably the easier, but is not well protected. Some consider the route E3 ****.
1. 40m 6a Climb the slabby breach leading left through the lower bulges, then go left on a slab until it is possible to go right to a thin ledge and poor peg runner. A poor sling is also advisable on an anvil shaped hold. Continue directly up the wall (bold), past a poor peg, then step right into a crack which leads with interest to a ledge.
2. 40m 6a Climb the left wall of the open corner above to an in-situ nut runner. Step right under the roof, pull over and continue to a small ledge and poor belay.
3. 25m Continue more easily to the top.

Yo-Yo   90m   E1 ****
R.Smith, D.Hughes   May 1959
The great corner of the cliff. The first pitch contains some superbly delicate and technical moves. but is a bit scary and slow to dry; the black streaks show up the line well. Once over the initial bulge,however, the protection is excellent. The second pitch is physical and some have fallen off the third through tiredness. Start below the corner at an undercut flake.
1. 40m 5b Step left on to a steep slab and go up and left for 6m then up and right into the corner. Climb this to a shelf and belay on the left.
2. 20m 5a Climb the corner and chimney to a belay above the main overhang.
3. 30m 5a Climb the crack with minor deviations on the left (ignore the left-trending ramp just above mid-way), to Pleasant Terrace.

WEST FACE

This face dominates the lower reaches of the glen, so the cleanest rock can easily be picked out of this complex face. The climbing is at mid-height on the face, a ledge system (Middle Ledge) separating the good rhyolite from vegetated andesite below. The biggest gully on the face is towards its left side (named No.2). The rocks left of it are more broken and soon turn to overlook the road. Just to its left is **Dinner-time Buttress**. To it right, between it and the second biggest gully, are four buttresses forming the main section of the face. B Buttress is the first and clean looking buttress, the next two are less clean, while the steep clean face overlooking the right gully is the famous E Buttress. Right of here the face continues but is more broken.

Approach: Park off the A82, near the entrance to Achnambeithach (NN 139 567). The path begins at a gate 50m away, on the other side of the River Coe. Follow the path under the face towards Coire nam Beith, striking off left below the lowest waterfall and crossing the stream to gain the lower slopes of Dinner-time Buttress. Cross No.2 Gully easily and follow the lower slopes, then scramble up the lower tier of B Buttress to reach Middle Ledge (1hr 15mins). For E Buttress, traverse the ledge right and where it suddenly turns in and down into the gully, the fine walls are seen above (another 10mins).

B Buttress

(NN 145 557)   Alt 520m   West-North-West Facing

The routes are suitable as part of a mountaineering day, heading up to the top after the climbs, when the upper rocks can be climbed by several lines with some good easier pitches. But a scrambling descent is also possible down the gully on the right (looking up).

Direct Route   115m   VS *
A.Parker, H.G.Nicol   Jun 1948
When approaching Middle Ledge, B Buttress is seen to be crested by triple pinnacles,

which cluster on its right-hand section. A long vegetatious groove runs down the buttress to the left of the pinnacles; this route takes the line of the rib to its left. A devious line may be possible at Severe but a more direct line is on cleaner rock, although not well protected. Start at a vertical rib, 10m left of the long groove.

1. 35m 4b Climb the rib (or more easily, the corner on the left of the rib) and continue to slabs below a wall.

2. 35m 4a Move right, climb a steep wall then continue right up another steep wall to the top of a grass rake which plunges down left. Traverse right to the crest.

3. 45m Move straight over a bulge, and continue by clean slabby rock to the top. A nice pitch.

The Pinnacle Face   90m   Very Difficult *
J.H.B.Bell, C.M.Allan   May 1932

Some 20m from the right end of the face the steepest rocks are bounded on the left by a chimney slanting up and left. Climb the chimney to a ledge on the right. Climb trending right to a short chimney. The right-hand pinnacle is now above, with a cracked wall on its right. Climb the wall on good holds to easier ground. Scramble to the top. The starting chimney may be avoided by easier rocks at the right edge of the buttress.

E Buttress

(NN 144 555)   Alt 520m   West to South-West facing

This great buttress has two distinct faces; the west face is above Middle Ledge, and the south-west face soars above the gully. There was much rivalry for the first ascents. The three big routes were shared between the rivals of Robin Smith, Jimmy Marshall and Dougal Haston, with Ian Clough getting the consolation. Just where the path turns the corner and leads into the gully, is a very sharp arete. Right of this is the west face, with an obvious fault-line in its centre and leading to a cave (Consolation). A roof leads right from this to another arete which bounds this face from the gully wall (south-west face). An obvious landmark of the south-west face is the huge corner taken by Trapeze.

Descent: Traverse left (looking down) and descend a sloping shelf into the gully, which gives a scrambling descent, but with no great difficulties.

Consolation   80m   VS *
G.Grandison, I.Clough   23rd Apr 1962

A good warm-up or warm-down. The initial groove is heathery but the climbing is not spoiled. The difficulties are in the first two pitches, from where it is easy to abseil off and save the long descent. Start below the fault at a sharp spike 3m up.

1. 25m 4c Climb the groove to twin cracks. Gain the right-hand crack and follow it to the cave.

2. 20m 4b Move left round a rib to a chimney. Climb this and move left for 5m to a small flake.

3. 35m Pleasant slabs are followed by scrambling.

The Big Top   160m   E1 ***
R.Smith, J.Gardner   Aug 1961

This sustained and exciting route starts up the west face, crosses the exposed edge to the south-west face, then makes a rising traverse across it, in an increasingly spectacular position. Start at a block below the right edge of the west face.

1. 35m 4c Go up and left for 15m, climb a slabby corner and then up and right to a belay on top of a large flake.

2. 35m 5a Climb the bulging arete on the right and continue by a crack on the edge of the arete to an easing of the angle.

Scott Muir on the final pitch of The Big Top, E1 5a, Aonach Dubh
(photo Cubby Images)

3. 45m 5a Move right and climb the obvious diagonal line of slabby grooves and ledges (overlooking the slab of Trapeze) for 40m, then move left to climb the short obvious crack to a large ledge and belay.

4. 45m 5a Climb the large flake on the right to its top. Step left onto the wall then straight up to a peg. Traverse right across a groove (important runner) to a slab. Climb the slab and a wall and finish up a broken groove to the top.

Trapeze 130m E1 **
J.R.Marshall, D.Leaver 1958

The very obvious corner leads to a winding line up the slabs and overhangs above. Start near the left edge of the face.

1. 15m Scramble up grassy rakes to the foot of the corner.

2. 20m 5b Climb the corner, strenuous, to below an overhang.

3. 40m 4c Turn the overhang on the left and follow the easy corner to slabs, continuing to a mossy bay.

4. 5m Traverse right to a well defined platform.

5. 40m 5a Leave the platform on the left and climb a steep wall to a ledge and corner above. The wall is both steep and delicate. **The Direct Finish** (HVS 4c) takes the obvious corner above. Turn the corner on the right and make an ascending traverse right to a groove and crack. Climb these to a slab beneath an overhang and traverse right to a rocky bay.

6. 10m Climb a right-slanting groove and a short crack to the top.

Hee-Haw 135m E1 *
J.Moriarty, D.Haston Jun 1959

This very steep and impressive route climbs the wall up and right of Trapeze. Scramble up the gully for about 50m to a point directly beneath the right-hand of two imposing, hanging cracks on the right-hand section of the buttress. At the foot of the wall projects a small, steep buttress with a groove in it.

1. 25m 5b Climb the groove, or a choice of easier lines to the grass ledge.

2. 25m 5a Climb a crack in a corner for 6m and so up a steep wall to a detached block below a prominent crack.

3. 25m 4c Climb the crack, which overhangs, to a point below a large overhang. Go up right by a steep wall to a ledge.

4. 40m 4c Traverse left to a steep groove, which is followed to its conclusion. Go left to a small stance on a slab.

5. 20m Climb the slab and finish by an overhanging crack near the top of the buttress.

BIDEAN NAM BIAN

CHURCH DOOR BUTTRESS

(NN 143 544)   Alt 950m   North-West to North-East facing   Map p78

The right-hand of the two summit buttresses of Bidean, the left being Diamond Buttress, with Central Gully between them and Collie's Pinnacle at the base of the gully. It was christened by W.Tough from its appearance when seen end on. Immediately right of Collie's Pinnacle a wide spur projects from the buttress, dividing it into two faces; the East Face overlooking Central Gully and, and to its right, the impressive West Face. The rock is andesite; the East Face and the frontal projecting spur are made up of pinnacles, flakes, huge boulders and deep fissures. The West Face, however, is quite different. It is uniformly steep and seamed with grooves and cracks of very rough rock, some of the best in Glen Coe. In addition the elevation and the expansive views over Ben Nevis and the Mamores make this a marvellous place to climb.

Approach: Parking is available off the A82, near the entrance to Achnambeithach (NN 139 567). The path begins at a gate 50m away, on the other side of the River

Coe. Follow the well constructed path which winds up right of the stream. Above the waterfalls the path levels out and soon reaches a fork in the streams. Follow the path up the right fork until the angle eases, then traverse left under Stob Coire nam Beith crag on a path which meets and follows the left fork up into the second of two basins. Church Door Buttress is now on the right up a boulder slope; the less steep Diamond Buttress is to its left and nearer. 2hrs, perhaps a little more.

Descent: Head to the col between Bidean and its west top, then back under the buttress.

East Face

Scramble up the right fork of Central Gully as far as the neck of the pinnacle. Opposite is the obvious chimney of Crypt Route leading to the right end of the Arch, a well named feature formed by two huge jammed boulders and obvious on the approach to the cliff.

Crypt Route   135m   Very Difficult ***
R.Morley, M.Wood, J.Wilding, A.S.Pigott   15 Sep 1920
An atmospheric and unusual route. This is a good option for a wet day, with only the last pitch (Raeburn's Chimney) being much harder, at least Severe, in the wet. Gain the chimney, which starts 10m up, and climb it for 10m until it becomes more difficult. Go inside behind a chockstone and back out above. Continue up until the chimney becomes narrow and smooth, then go in again and return out through a squeeze. Go up to a ledge at the right end of the arch. Go up 10m and walk over the arch to climb a shallow chimney (crux). Grooves and walls on the left of the crest lead to the top. Various subterranean alternatives are either blocked or the pioneers were much thinner!

West Face

Alt 1000m   West-North-West facing   Diagram p118

This steep and impressive face is on the right side of the buttress. There are some fine rock routes but the altitude and aspect ensures slow drying, although the face starts to get the sun at 2pm around mid-summer. The corner system high on the left of the face is **Lost Arrow** (E3 6a). In the middle of the face a long pillar projects slightly. Forming its left side is a groove line, Kingpin, and on its right another groove line, Lost Ark.

1 Kingpin   105m   E3 ****
J.Hardie, W.Thomson   17 Aug 1968 (5-8PA); FFA: D.Cuthbertson, D.Mullin   1978
One of the best high mountain rock routes in Britain, taking a direct line up the left side of the long pillar which projects slightly from the centre of the West Face. High in the grade. Start some 20m right of a chimney-groove which forms the left end of the face, below a short crack and a short hanging chimney.
1. 20m 6a Climb the crack to a slab. Move left and up to a steep groove. Make a few difficult, bold moves, swing right and go up to a poor stance at a groove junction. It is possible to run this and the following pitch together.
2. 20m 5c Climb up right and follow a black groove to a tricky mantelshelf on to a small ledge below the short, hanging chimney. Enter the chimney by an awkward move and at its top step left to a small ledge.
3. 30m 5b Move back right and climb the sloping ramp in a superb position to a small hooded recess. Exit slightly left, then go up to a ledge. Continue to the foot of a prominent corner.
4. 35m 5b Climb the corner to the roof then swing spectacularly right to a ledge. Climb cracks up a groove, then easier ground to the top. Continuing up the corner above the roof is better but more prone to dampness (5c).

118

CHURCH DOOR
BUTTRESS

1. Kingpin   E3 ****
2. The Lost Ark   E4 **
3. Temple of Doom   E3 ***

2 The Lost Ark   85m   E4 **
P.Whillance, R.Parker   27 Jul 1983
The obvious groove and corner system up the right side of the pillar right of
Kingpin. High in the grade. Start at the foot of a white speckled groove.
1. 40m 6a Climb the groove for 20m to a small overlap on its left wall. Move up
and left on to the arete, then climb this for 5m (crux) to pull back right and go up
to ledges. Traverse right a short way and climb to the overhang. Pull right across
the roof to an old peg runner of unknown origin, and climb to a good ledge. Belay
at the foot of a long corner.
2. 45m 5b Step right to climb a crack for 6m, then its right wall for a further 12m.
Move back left and ascend the easy groove to join Kingpin at the top of the pillar.
Climb the groove above to the top.

3 Temple of Doom   75m   E3 ***
M.Hamilton, G.Livingston, R.Anderson   21 Jul 1984
Yet another very fine route, taking the obvious V-groove and hanging, stepped corner system right of Lost Ark. Start at the second groove right of that route: the first
is **The Holy Grail** (E5 6b), a variation start.
1. 30m 6a Climb the groove, then make hard moves up a wall to ledges.
2. 45m 6a Step right to climb a crack for 6m, then step back left and pull over to
the foot of the stepped corner system. Climb this to its top then follow the continuation crack for a short way until it is possible to step into a corner on the right
and make a few moves up this to the top.

CLACHAIG GULLY

Map p78
One of the great Scottish gully climbs; not to be underestimated. The rock is often
compact and does not lend itself to good protection. The grade is for dry conditions but the waterwashed rock is not too slippery in the wet. The climb starts just
above the Clachaig Inn on the south flank of Sgorr nam Fiannaidh. It receives much
sunlight, and is especially pleasant on a warm day in spring, when the gully walls
are covered in wild flowers. Beware of stonefall and avoid large parties. In descent,
follow the steep and eroded path down the west bank with care; there is also a
danger of dislodging stones on to climbers in the gully.

Clachaig Gully   520m   Severe **
W.H.Murray, A.M.MacAlpine, J.K.W.Dunn, W.G.Marskell   May 1938
Several lower pitches, which often have to be climbed on the somewhat vegetated
sidewalls because there is a substantial flow of water, lead up to the Great Cave
Pitch. It is therefore common to start here, at 340m altitude, where there is a short
level section of path and where a side branch of the stream is clearly visible (the
pitches above are therefore drier).
  Descend into the gully on steep vegetation through trees but without difficulty
to finally traverse in to the Great Cave Pitch. This pitch stopped all earlier attempts,
from Collie's in 1894 onwards. Climb the right wall and slab to a small tree. From
the tree traverse down and round a rib, then left to the red wall opposite which
leads to the gully bed. The pitch above is the short but deceptive, crux. Climb the
slabby shelf on the right flank then up a corner. Following a short chockstone pitch,
Jericho Wall is reached. This is on the right of a waterfall, trending up and left to
the top.
  Several good pitches then follow including the Red Chimney, a distinctive 20m
pitch on dark red rock. This pitch may give the biggest soaking in damp conditions.
A shallow cave rises 10m above. From the roof springs a 5m chimney. Climb the
right wall of the cave on the outside to a ledge near the foot of the chimney. Finish
up the chimney and the slab above. A pitch near the top is loose at the start and
some holds have fallen off; it may eventually become the crux.

GLEN COE

Glen Etive

ETIVE SLABS

(NN 097 446)   Alt 300m   East-South-East facing   Map p78, 130
Diagram p122

The Etive Slabs, at the foot of Glen Etive on Beinn Trilleachan, are Britain's most extensive friction slabs. Their granite lies at the crucial angle where one can just climb without holds. Surprisingly, the arrival of sticky rubber doesn't seem to have changed this, so the slabs still provide exhilarating routes. There are two overlap systems across the main slabs so while the slabby pitches are easy to second (with strong calves and a little trust), the overlaps make the routes unsuitable for lower grade climbers to second. The rock is smoother than most of the granite slabs in France or Switzerland, so less steep for the grade, but lack the bolts that pepper those crags. Many of the in-situ pegs have now gone but small wires and cams fit in the same cracks; 0 cams and smaller are particularly useful. The left side of the main face is slightly steeper but has two big corner systems which provide superb routes in a delicate layback style. The slabs catch the sun until mid-afternoon, after which midges can become troublesome. Some routes are prone to wet seeps from under the overlaps, quite serious on friction climbs, so the slabs are not a good choice after a spell of wet weather.

Grading is notoriously difficult and depends on experience of the style of climbing. The technical grades of the friction pitches in the SMC's comprehensive Glen Coe guide have been used for their consistency, whereas some of the overall grades have been reduced to a generally agreed level. The grades of the non-padding pitches are accepted by most.

Approach: Leave the A82 just east of Buachaille Etive Mor and park at the very end of the picturesque Glen Etive road, beside the loch, from where the slabs are easily seen. Leave the more obvious lochside path almost immediately and follow a climbers' path fairly directly to their base. The path arrives at the Coffin Stone, a large flat rock and gearing-up point at the base of the main slab.

Descent: Follow the eroded path that descends the rake running diagonally down right above the steep headwalls. There is some tricky scrambling which is fine for VS leaders, but the nervous might need some assistance. Be very careful not to knock down rocks, since the path runs directly over the routes.

The first two routes start on a smaller right-hand section of slab some 70m right of the Coffin Stone and right of a large heathery slope. They are suitably short for a second route in the day. Descent is best by abseil from trees, but two ropes are required. There are two narrow tongues of clean slab extending from the wall which forms a band across the slab beneath the larger, upper slab. The brownish left-hand tongue is further identified by three short crack-lines on its right side. Above the wall a number of thin crack-lines and seams run up the slab.

1 Vein Rouge   95m   HVS **
R. and C.Anderson   1 Jun 1991
Start left of the three short crack-lines at the base of the brownish left-hand tongue of slab.
1. 35m 5a A few hard moves gain first one pocket, then another. Continue over some small steps, then move up right into an obvious scooped depression in the wall. Climb the depression and continue to a grassy handrail.
2. 30m 4c Climb the crack above and continue to small ledges. A quartz band starts here and runs up the slab above. Move across and up right to a crack.
3. 30m 4c Move back down left to the start of the quartz band and follow this to the top, then scramble to a belay in the corner.

2 Raspberry Ripple   100m   E1 *
R. and C.Anderson   1 Jun 1991

Starts as for Vein Rouge, then goes up just to its left. A very good second pitch.
1. 40m 5a Climb Vein Rouge to where it goes right into the scooped depression. Continue above, passing right of a heather ledge, then go up slightly left and climb to a small ledge at the foot of a crack.
2. 60m 5a The slab above is seamed with ripples. Follow the crack-line which leads to the rightmost ripple, climb this to a small pocket mid-way up it (Friend 1), then continue up the ripple to holds and easier ground leading to a belay in the corner on rope stretch.

The Long Reach   220m   E1 ****
J.McLean, W.Smith   Jun 1963 (1PA); FFA: unknown)
A magnificent sustained route with some quite bold slab sections. It is possible (but normally accidental) to miss the small corner on pitch 4 and climb direct up slabs just to its left; the pitch is then unprotected and will feel like E2. Start directly behind the Coffin Stone at a blank slab.
1. 40m 5b Climb black stained rock to enter a right-facing groove and climb this, then trend up rightwards to cross an overlap. Belay on the ledge above as for Spartan Slab. The blank slab can be climbed by more direct, less protected variants.
2. 40m 5b Climb the twin grooves above on to the slab, step up to a large pocket, then attain a standing position on a quartz band and go horizontally left on this for 5m. Continue up diagonally left to follow a small corner (The Pause) to the main overlap where a left traverse gains the belay of Swastika below the obvious crossing point.
3. 25m 5a Surmount the overlap as for Swastika (Friend 3 protects the second), then go right to small ledges with a thin grassy break above (possible belay). Continue up and right for some 5m to belay in a small left-facing corner on The Pause.
4. 30m 5b Traverse 3m left, then climb the slab past a quartz pocket to a small corner formed by a shallow right-facing groove and its continuation overlap going rightwards. Make a 'Long Reach' out left then go straight up to belay towards the left side of a small overlap.
5. 40m 5b Climb the overlap and a bulge in the slab above then; either climb directly to just below the main terminal overlap (sometimes wet) and traverse right to belay below and right of an overhung groove in the overlap; or climb a black slab going obliquely rightwards to gain a more scooped slab leading to a left trending groove/overlap which is followed to the right end of the main overlap, step right to belay on The Pause. From here many finish up The Pause, because the large overlap that now follows seems out of keeping with the slabs climbed below.
6. 35m 5b Either move up left to below the groove in the large overlap, or make a 4m traverse to it. Using a jug on the left wall gain the groove (bold), then follow it to a ledge and make a traverse left to a sentry box. Thin cracks lead out of this to the tree-lined ledges.
7. 10m 4c The original finish up a small corner in the headwall is dirty and it may be better to climb the vertical corner of The Pause and TheLong Wait.

The Long Wait   255m   E2 **
J.Cunningham, R.Smith   Sep 1959
Start directly behind the Coffin Stone at a blank slab.
1. 40m 5b As for Long Reach. Climb black stained rock to enter a right-facing groove and climb this, then trend up rightwards to cross an overlap. Belay on the ledge above as for Spartan Slab.
2. 40m 5a Climb the twin grooves above to the large pocket on Long Reach. Continue slightly right first up a line of weakness, then a slab to reach the overlap, a traverse up left below which gains the Crevasse.
3. 15m 4c As for The Pause, gain the slab above, move into the groove on the left and climb this over a bulge to The Long Reach ledge.
4. 25m 5b Descend diagonally left until just above the overlap, then go up left to the right end of a grass ledge in a corner.

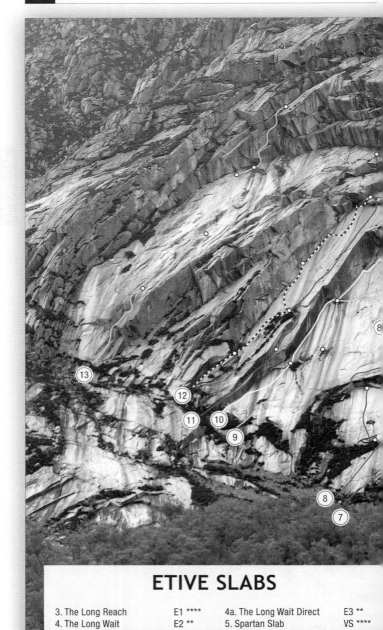

ETIVE SLABS

3. The Long Reach	E1 ****	4a. The Long Wait Direct	E3 **
4. The Long Wait	E2 **	5. Spartan Slab	VS ****

6. The Pause	HVS ****	10. Agony	E2 ****
7. Swastika	E2 **	11. The Pinch Direct	E3 ***
8. The Valkyrie	E2 **	12. Hammer	HVS ***
8a.The Pea Brained Variation	E3 **	13. Jaywalk	E2 ***
9. The Big Ride	E3 *		

5. 25m 5b Climb the corner for 6m to a peg scar, then break out left and move up left to follow the slab on the left of a grass column. Step right to belay.

6. 30m 5a Follow a flange up right and continue to the top of another grass column.

7. 35m 5b Move up left to a diamond shaped break in the overlap, cross this rightwards, then follow a shallow groove and flange left until a traverse left can be made to belay on the right end of grass ledge of Swastika.

8. 35m 5b Ascend the slab to a small niche, move up left and climb to a corner which is followed to the tree-lined ledge. Traverse right to a vertical corner.

9. 15m 5a Climb the vertical corner as for The Pause.

Variation: **The Long Wait Direct** **E3 ****

Climb the normal route to the belay at the start of pitch 5.

5. 25m 5b Climb the corner to the peg scar at 6m, then follow the corner up right and on to a grass ledge. Climb a flange and step left to belay on top of the grass column.

6. 30m 5b Follow the flange up right, then move up left to a corner, step right and climb to the diamond shaped break in the overlap by a ripple and two open quartz seams.

7. 35m 5c Cross the diamond shaped overlap rightwards, then move up and left to runners before heading off up the bold and sometimes wet slab on the right, directly to the sanctuary of the tree-lined ledge.

8. 25m 5b The steep, right-angled corner at the left end of the tree-lined ledge.

5 Spartan Slab   190m   VS ****

E.D.G.Langmuir, M.J.O'Hara, J.A.Mallinson   14 Jun 1954

A classic, offering wonderful and continually interesting climbing. The third pitch is much harder for the short who must layback over the overlap at 5a (but with cunning, can still place the overhead runner). Start 5m left of the Coffin Stone.

1. 40m 4a Climb the groove for 30m, step right on to the lower slab and move up to a ledge.

2. 25m 4a From the right end of the ledge climb the slab and undercut flake to a ledge beneath the overhang.

3. 35m 4c Step left to the overhung recess where an entertaining move enables the overlap to be overcome. There used to be a tree here! Move up a thin crack, then traverse right along a horizontal crack and continue to a belay near the edge.

4. 30m 4c From the right end of the ledge move up a groove containing a thin crack for 5m, step left to a steep slab and follow a thin crack for a short way until a step down right can be made. Climb the overlap and good cracks to a belay.

5. 35m 4b Continue up the right-trending crack to a ledge and tree.

6. 25m 3c Gain the tree-lined ledge via cracked blocks and take the fault on the left to easy ground.

6 The Pause   210m   HVS ****

J.R.Marshall, G.J.Ritchie, G.Tiso, R.Marshall   Jul 1960 (4PA, 1 tension); FFA: unknown

Another superb climb, with no big overlaps but a crux traverse. Pitch 4 is superb and open, the crux when pitch 3 was still tensioned. Start 10m left of the Coffin Stone at a thin peg scarred groove running up the slab.

1. 25m 5a Climb the groove for 18m, move left to climb a bigger groove to reach a spike, then swing out left and belay by a tree.

2. 20m 4c Step right, follow the layback crack on the lip of the groove, then follow easy rock to belay on Swastika.

3. 40m 5b As for Swastika up the small block overlap, then traverse around its right side and up to the main overlap. Go down from the overlap and traverse delicately right into the Crevasse (best to place a high runner in the overlap, but easier to traverse lower down).

Dave Cuthbertson starting off on The Long Reach, E1 5b
(photo Cubby Images)

4. 40m 5a Gain the slab above, move into the groove on the left and climb this over a bulge to a ledge in a short left-facing corner at 15m (Long Reach belay). Traverse 3m right to a faint line of cracks and follow these to a small overlap; move right to a stance.

5. 40m 5a Continue up right to the right end of the higher overlap, then follow a thin crack to an easy groove which leads to a grass ledge beside an overlap.

6. 30m 5a Climb the overlaps on the left to the base of the terminal slab, then traverse left to an undercut edge near the right side of the slab, 5m right of The Long Reach sentry box. Climb the edge to a grass ledge.

7. 15m 5a The vertical corner on the left, common with The Long Wait (or finish more easily out right).

7 Swastika   200m   E2 **

M.Noon, E.Taylor   25 Jun 1957 (aid); FFA: unknown

Excellent climbing with fine situations; pity the last two pitches are much harder than the rest. Often climbed with a point of aid on pitch 8; this reduces the grade to E1. From the Coffin Stone follow the path left for about 40m past a large silver birch tree to the foot of a clean slab. Start below the right-hand of two parallel cracks.

1. 35m 5a Follow the right-slanting crack to a heathery ledge.

2. 25m 4b Move right across the ledge to a slab below a small block overlap.

3. 10m 4c Climb the slab and move directly over a small overlap to beneath the main overlap.

4. 25m 5a Step up right and find a way to attain a standing position on the lip, then traverse left along the Moustache to a grass ledge. It is possible to protect the second by a Friend about 3m along the traverse.

5. 35m 4c Above is the first quartz band. Climb this to a grass ledge, tree belay.

6. 30m 5a Move up right to a ledge, draw breath, and climb the second quartz band.

7. 20m 5c Traverse 2m left beneath the upper overlap to climb a short corner and its ensuing groove, then go up and left to a tree below the final corner.

8. 20m 6a Climb the crack just left of the main crack for 10m, then move up and right to climb the corner to a ledge, finishing by a layback. Or, for a slabbier finish to the route, finish up The Long Wait.

8 The Valkyrie   205m   E2 **

B.W.Robertson, F.Harper   Oct 1965 (1PA); FFA: unknown

A good direct line. Start left of Swastika, at the left-hand of two, long parallel cracks.

1. 25m 4c Climb the crack to a heather ledge and belay.

2. 30m 5a Move up and left to a small ledge, then climb straight up the slab to a cave below the overlap.

3. 15m 5b Traverse 3m left, climb the overlap and follow the lip back right to the Swastika belay at the foot of the quartz band.

4. 30m 5b From the middle of the ledge move up slightly left to a small quartz pocket, then follow a ripple diagonally up right some 5m left of the quartz band to gain a slender corner (long run-out). Climb the corner to the ledge and tree of Swastika.

5. 10m 4b Move up left to a flake belay beneath the overlap.

6. 20m 5b Surmount the overlap and continue up the slab slightly rightwards to a horizontal crack.

7. 30m 5b Continue up the slab and surmount the next overlap, step right, then move up a sloping corner and pull up left to join Agony.

8. and 9. 45m 5a Agony, pitches 4 and 5.

Variation: **The Pea Brained Variation   E3 **

A.Nisbet, A.Clifford   May 1984

Bold and sustained, with some excellent blank padding. Take care with route finding; the consequences are only too obvious below!

4a. 50m 5c From the left end of the Swastika belay ledge go up slightly left, then right, then back left to an obvious red pocket with an ancient chipped spike (poor runner). Climb straight up for 5m to a small ledge (protection on right), then go diagonally up the blank slab to the left end of the overlap. Regain Valkyrie by moving 10m right.

The Big Ride 145m E3 *
D.Haston, R.N.Campbell Aug 1964 (2PA, 2 tension); FFA: R.Carrington, I.Nicolson 1970s
A fine direct line up the steep slab right of the big corner of Agony, a bold second pitch. Scramble to the tree just right of the corner.
1. 30m 5b Climb up right to a peg at 20m, then gain the groove on the right and follow it to ledges.
2. 30m 5c Ascend the obvious thin intermittent flange in the slab above to the haven of a ledge in the corner.
3. 40m 5b Traverse 5m right, then go up to the left end of an overlap, climb a crack and move up left to a ledge, old pegs. Continue above to the overlap and move up into a corner.
4. and 5. 45m 5a and 4c Agony, pitches 4 and 5, also the finish right.

Agony 155m E2 ****
J.Cunningham, M.Noon, W.Smith 6 Apr 1957 (aid); FFA: B.Duff, W.Todd Jun 1978
The great corner bounding the left side of the main slabs gives a magnificent climb, sustained and continually interesting. Unfortunately, it is very slow to dry. Scramble to the base of the corner.
1. 35m 5c Climb the corner for 15m (peg runner), then traverse right on friction to a shallow recess. Now go straight up the slab past a small overlap to a ledge. The corner can be climbed direct but is dirty and often wet.
2. 35m 5c Climb the corner to a ledge.
3. 40m 5c Climb the corner, usually wet, to grass at 25m. Go diagonally right up the slab to a small overlap and continue to a belay.
4. 25m 5a Move up the corner, traverse right, climb a short corner then an overlap and move up to the terminal wall. Traverse left to a tree.
5. 20m 4c Climb the wall behind the belay and continue to easy ground.
Finish diagonally right to gain the path, worth staying roped.

The Pinch Direct 215m E3 ***
J.R.Jackson, R.Carrington 18 Apr 1968; Direct start: M.Hamilton, B.Duff, D.Jamieson Jun 1978
Another magnificent route, taking the corner and slab overlooking the corner of Agony. The original line climbed easier ground to the left to arrive at the current pitch 3, still arguably E3! Start as for Agony.
1. 35m 5c Move up the main corner for 3m, pull into the corner up on the left and follow this to an awkward hanging belay.
2. 25m 5c Continue up the corner then exit left at the top to belay on Hammer below the Scoop. With 60m ropes it possible to climb 1 and 2 as a single stunning pitch.
3. 20m 5b Move up right to a thin crack, then climb up right to the obvious quartz pocket (passing the 'pinch'). Step right almost to the edge and climb a crack to belay a short way below a small overlap.
4. 40m 5b Continue straight up the crack (the original line moved up left to join Hammer) and go over the small overlap to a finger slot 4m below an overlap. Either go up, then left beneath the overlap, or right, then up and left above the overlap; both finish at same belay on Hammer.
5. 40m 5a Move up the slab above to climb corners on to the upper slab and traverse left below the final wall to belay.
6. 25m 5c Climb a steep chimney come crack to a ledge, then walls and across to a recess and a tree.
7. 30m 5a From the top of the recess, climb the crack to the right of twin cracks.

*The crux pitch of The Big Ride, E3 5b. Climbers unknown
(photo Andy Tibbs)*

12 Hammer 150m HVS ✱✱✱

M.Noon, J.Cunningham 7 Apr 1957 (1 tension); FFA: unknown

Justifiably popular, this is a classic which frequently has queues. The route follows the large corner up to the left of the great corner of Agony. Start by following the path from the Coffin Stone and scrambling up to the foot of the corner.

1. 15m 4a Climb the corner to a tree.
2. 35m 4b Follow the cracked slab right of the corner to a stance near the top of a heather cone.
3. 25m 4c Above is the celebrated Scoop, a concave steepening, climbed without protection to gain the safety of the main corner. Continue to a fine belay halfway up the corner.
4. 40m 5b Climb the corner for 20m, tiptoe right for 3m (technical crux), then follow cracks to a large overlap. Move right into a recess and pull over to the base of a corner.
5. 35m 4b Climb the corner, then undercut the overlap and move diagonally up right to gain the descent path.

GLEN ETIVE

3 Jaywalk   210m   E2 ***

J.R.Marshall, J.Moriarty, J.Stenhouse   Sep 1960 (4PA); FFA: unknown

A varied route in a dramatic position with steep but well protected crux sections gaining and leaving the upper slab left of Hammer. This is the slab highest on the left, not seen from the Coffin Stone. Follow the path up past Hammer, up and along a traverse ledge, then up steep grass tufts to start beneath the right edge of the slab, 15m right of a vegetated corner and just left of another.

1. 30m 5b Above is a two tiered groove in the bulging slab. Climb this and its right-trending continuation on to the upper slab, step left at the last peg, then go up to gain a belay.

2. 45m 5a Move right and follow a groove system and its left rib.

3. 45m 5a Follow a groove to a grass patch, move left a metre or so and continue up slabs and a shallow scoop leading left to the main corner.

4. 10m 4b Continue to a grass ledge and prominent small tree. With a longer rope and some courage run the pitches together direct to the ledge and tree.

4. 35m 5c Gain the arete above and climb it using a prominent small spike (hard for the short, but it can be lassoed and aided). Climb a cracked corner and ramp, and move left up a wall. Step right and layback into a grassy corner to a belay.

5. 45m 4c Climb the grassy corner past a short slabby section, then up heather to a right traverse which soon leads to the descent path.

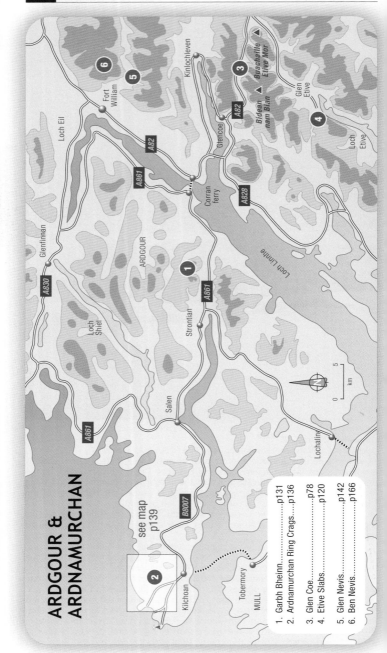

130

ARDGOUR & ARDNAMURCHAN

see map p139

ARDGOUR & ARDNAMURCHAN

The long peninsula north-west of Glen Coe and west of Fort William has Ardgour at its eastern end and Ardnamurchan at its western tip. Access by ferry, or a long drive, means that the area is quiet and the lower mountains attract less rainfall than 'The Coe' or 'The Ben'. There may be restrictions during the stalking season in both areas (see Environment notes).

Maps: OS L40, L47, E390, E391

SMC Climbers' Guide: *Glen Coe* (2001)

Public transport: Possible, but complicated and time consuming.

Ardgour

Garbh Bheinn and the hills of Ardgour are visible across Loch Linnhe from Glen Coe and the A82 from Fort William.

Access: The drive-on Corran Ferry (NN 022 635), just north of Onich on the A82, normally runs from about 7am to 9pm in summer (01855 841243) <www. lochabertransport/corranferry.html>. Ardgour can also be accessed from Fort William by a long drive round Lochs Eil and Linnhe.

ARDGOUR

GARBH BHEINN

(NM 904 623)   Alt 898m

This shapely hill is formed from beautifully striped gneiss which is wonderfully rough even when wet.

Approach: From the ferry, follow the A861 Strontian and Ardnamurchan road to about 3km west of Inversanda and park on the left on a short section of old road just before a cattle grid (NM 897 604). The view from here is deceptive. The summit lies to the right of the obvious central peak, and looks lower and less significant.

On the right is an obvious valley. Follow the rough and steep hillside right of the streams and diverge away from them to arrive at the bealach south of the summit (NM 904 620). Following the more obvious line, a slight ridge with an old fence between two streams leading to a visible col, takes you to the col west of the summit. From the south bealach, continue up the ridge towards the summit but turn down right before the summit to gain the left end of the Upper Tier. Easy slabs continue down, giving access to the Lower Tier, 1.5hrs. A longer but more scenic route up Coire an Iubhair is more suitable for the Great Ridge (see below).

SOUTH WALL

The two tiers of this superb 100m wall are found just under the summit. Some routes climb both tiers and the combinations are endless. Routes on the Upper Tier finish near the summit. The tiers are separated by an easily accessible terrace which cuts across to the final rocks of the Great Ridge.

Lower Tier

(NM 905 622)   Alt 750m   South Facing   Diagram p135

The right side has a flat base. In the centre is a huge boulder leaning against the cliff. Left of here the cliff base rises up left, along the line of the approach ramp.

Gralloch   45m   E2 5b * **
M.Diggins, A.Fyffe   Jun 1981
Start at a shattered ledge about 30m up and left of the huge boulder leaning against the face. After a few moves go up and left via thin cracks and ramps to a big open right-facing corner. Climb this more easily to the terrace.

2 Scimitar 100m VS *
D.D.Stewart, D.N.Mill 13 Apr 1952
This climbs both tiers. Start as for Gralloch, at a shattered ledge about 30m up and left of the huge boulder.
1. 30m 4c Follow the ledge, which curves up and right to where it levels out. From its left end, climb a steep crack to an overhang. Traverse right in a brilliant position to an edge with good holds, move up and left to a ledge and belay at the foot of a corner.
2. 25m 4a Climb easier rocks and an open chimney to the terrace.
3. 45m 4b Continue directly by a well defined vertical groove, which is above a small rock step in the terrace, and move right to a flake. Climb a left-facing corner or the slabs on its left to easier slabs and the ridge crest.

3 Razor Slash 75m Severe *
J.R.Marshall, L.S.Lovat, A.H.Hendry 1 Apr 1956
Start at the huge boulder.
1. 25m Climb the boulder and a corner to a platform beyond the right end of the horizontal section of the shattered ledge.
2. 20m Traverse 10m left along the ledge to a left-sloping, layback slab ledge. Climb this, move delicately over the nose at its top (crux) and go right, then left to a belay.
3. 30m Go up and left by a diagonal fracture, crossing the chimney of Scimitar, to the terrace.

4 The Golden Lance 100m E2 **
R.Anderson, A.Russell 30 Jun 1984
This climbs both tiers, taking the obvious thin crack-line left of Butterknife on the lower tier. Belay on top of the huge boulder at the start of Razor Slash.
1. 20m 5c Climb a thin crack in the steep wall above (crux), pull up left then move up and right to belay on the traverse ledge of Razor Slash.
2. 40m 5c Step right and climb a thin crack-line past an area of loose rock, to pull over a short leaning wall. Continue in the same line to the terrace.
3. 40m 5b Above and just left of Butterknife is a short corner leading to a small roof. Climb this and pull over right to easier ground. Move up and left into the middle of the wall then climb up to a short leaning wall. Pull over this and continue to easier ground.

5 Butterknife 105m VS ***
J.R.Marshall, A.H.Hendry, G.J.Ritchie, I.D.Haig 15 Sep 1956
A classic line up both tiers, starting up the big corner right of centre of the lower tier. Low in the grade. Start at a shallow chimney bounding the right side of a large pillar, immediately right of the huge boulder.
1. 25m 4a Bridge up the chimney and corner (slow to dry), or if wet superb rock on the left. Move left to belay.
2. 25m 4b Gain and climb the prominent and exciting corner-crack to its top. Either belay or continue up the next pitch.
3. 25m 4a Continue to the terrace, reaching a point below an overhang at the far right end of the upper tier.
4. 30m 4a Climb the right end of the overhang and continue to gain the final rocks of the ridge.

6 Bodkin 85m E1 *
K.V.Crocket, S.N.Smith 10 Jun 1979
The wall and steep edge starting immediately right of Butterknife.
1. 25m 5a Climb up rightwards to a steepening at 15m. Step left and continue up left to an edge below bulges.
2. 25m 5a Move right and up to an overhang, then left to and up the edge

overlooking the corner of Butterknife. Bold.
3. 35m Follow Butterknife to the terrace.

7 Mournblade 80m VS *
K.V.Crocket, C.Grant, J.Hutchinson 31 Jun 1976
A corner, some 12m right of and parallel to the corner of Butterknife. Start 6m
right of the initial chimney of Butterknife, at a rough flake.
1. 35m 4b Climb up, then right to the corner. Enter it, step right into a groove and
so to a ledge below a bulge. Climb this using a downward-pointing spike to a ledge
and belay.
2. 45m Climb the wall above on the left. Continue to the terrace.

Upper Tier

(NM 905 623) Alt 800m South facing Diagram p135

8 Sgian Dubh 60m Severe **
J.R.Marshall, L.S.Lovat. 1 Apr 1956
An interesting and varied climb. Near the left end of the upper tier is a chimney
formed by a huge flake.
1. 10m Climb the chimney to a platform.
2. 25m Traverse left and go up cracked ledges to a stance.
3. 25m Move left and over an overhang and follow a groove to the right, then up
a nose and steep rock to finish near the summit.

9 Menghini 30m E1 5a **
A.Taylor, R.Anderson 20 Jun 1982
An obvious crack above the platform gained by the first pitch of Sgian Dubh (or
traverse in from the left).

0 Kelpie 45m E6 ***
M.Hamilton, R.Anderson 21 Jun 1986
Right of Sgain Dubh is a smooth overhanging wall with a central wet seep. Starting
mid-way between the wet seep and a tall thin left-facing corner further right, the
route climbs a prominent left-slanting crack high on the right side of the wall.
1. 25m 6b Gain a groove right of the smooth wall and above an initial overlap
from the left, then move across left to follow a flake-line leading to the halfway
ledge (bold). Struggle up the crack above to a belay perched on the edge of the
leaning wall.
2. 20m 5b Continue up the crack leftwards until a groove can be followed to
easier ground which leads to the top.

1 Tru-Cut 50m E3 5c *
M.Hamilton, R.Anderson 13 Jun 1982
Start as for Kelpie. Gain the groove above the initial overlap from the left, follow
this to pull out left to a junction with the crack of Kelpie at the halfway ledge.
Continue up until a hard move right enables a ramp come groove to be reached.
Follow this over the initial bulge to reach a belay or continue to the top.

2 Chela 45m E4 **
M.Hamilton, A.Murray May 1981
The full height left-facing open corner. The pitch can be split (6a, 5b).

3 The Pincer 50m E2 5c ***
D.Dinwoodie, R.A.Smith Aug 1978
A very fine route up the arete right of Chela, with some excellent positions. Climb
the groove of Chela for a few moves, then move steeply up the sidewall and pull
round rightwards on to the arete. Continue up a groove in the arete to reach a

ARDGOUR

small overhang. Pull round its left side and enter a steep corner. Go up this and the left arete to reach easier ground.

14 The Contender   50m   E3 5c **
R.Anderson, C.Anderson   11 Aug 1994
Excellent climbing up the wall between Pincer and White Hope. Start in the centre of the wall beside White Hope, at an embedded, pointed boulder. Climb 6m to the right end of a short left-slanting crack which is followed to a jug on the left. Move up to a large round pocket, step left to the thin crack-line and continue directly above into a groove, access to which is barred by a bold hard move over a double bulge. At the top of the groove an awkward move over a bulge gains a ramp-line beneath the headwall. Follow the ramp a short way, then swing out right and climb the short crack up the left side of the headwall to reach ledges and a wide groove. Climb the niche on the left, swing out left on to the rib and follow the slab to a thin grassy ledge just below the top.

15 White Hope   55m   E5 **
P.Whillance, R.Anderson, M.Hamilton   5 May 1984
A dazzling and intricate line up the white wall right of The Pincer; barely adequate protection.
1. 45m 6a Start in the centre of the wall below a thin, vertical quartz seam. Climb this to a right-slanting flake at 12m. From its right end hard moves gain jugs below a small, isolated roof. Take the thin crack out left above the roof into the centre of the wall. Continue up and right to blocks below the short, leaning headwall and go up this to a ledge.
2. 10m Continue easily to the top.

16 The Clasp   60m   E1 *
J.R.Marshall   Apr 1960
The white wall has a roof above its right side. This bold route follows a left-trending line below the roof, starting below the right end of the roof.
1. 10m 4b Climb the wall, moving up and left.
2. and 3. 50m 5a Continue up under the roof for 6m, then traverse 10m left to a shallow groove (crux). Climb a chimney above and trend left to the top.

17 Excalibur   55m   HVS ***
K.V.Crocket, C.Stead   10 Jun 1972
Above and right of the roof of The Clasp is a second roof. This route gains then traverses the lip of this upper roof, with some fine (or should that be scary!) situations. Start below the right end of the roof, at a groove with a yellow right wall (the more defined groove on the right is an easier optional first pitch, 4b).
1. 20m 5a Climb the groove, moving right onto the rib. Go up steeply to easier rock and belay at the right end of a large ledge.
2. 15m 4c Traverse hard left above the lip of the roof to a steep corner. Climb this to its top and pull out left on to the flake edge. Step left to a ledge and belay.
2. 20m Go 5m left and climb walls above to the top.

18 Guenevere   40m   HVS 5a **
M.Garthwaite, R.Anderson   3 Sep 2000
A fine direct climb. Climb steeply up the arete immediately to the right of the corner of Excalibur to join it briefly. Move slightly right, then back left to climb a short smooth leaning wall. Bold climbing directly above (passing just to the left of a large detached flake-block) on good holds gains vague crack-lines in the wall of a tower feature above. Climb the cracks moving up left just below the top of the tower.

GARBH BHEINN
South Face
Upper Tier

ARDGOUR

2. Scimitar   VS **
5. Butterknife   VS ***
8. Sgian Dubh   Severe **

9. Menghini   E1 **
10. Kelpie   E6 ***
11. Tru-Cut   E3 *

12. Chela   E4 **
13. The Pincer   E2 ***
14. The Contender E3 **
15. White Hope   E5 **

16. The Clasp   E1 *
17. Excalibur   HVS ***
18. Guenevere   HVS **

GREAT RIDGE

The route is described as a fine mountaineering day, with rucksacks carried. The direct line is described, with the start quite hard for the grade, but there is a vegetated easier option. The highlight is the superb upper ridge, steep and clean on big holds and perhaps only Difficult.

Approach: Park at an old bridge (NM 928 596) and follow the path up Coire an Iubhair to the junction with the Garbh Choire Mor up on the left. The Great Ridge lies ahead, bounded on the right by Great Gully. About 2hrs. The best return is by the long ridge of Sron a' Garbh Choire Bhig, the south ridge of Garbh Bheinn.

The Great Ridge   400m   Very Difficult * * *
J.H.Bell, W.Brown   Apr 1897; D.D.Stewart, D.N.Mill (direct start)   12 Apr 1952
The fine ridge dropping from the summit of Garbh Bheinn into Garbh Choire was first ascended only five years after Tower Ridge. The ridge swells in its lower stretches to form slabby rock, transected by two grassy rakes. Start at the lowest rocks, just right of a twisting crack with a slab on its right. This is well right of a steep wet crack. Climb the slab to gain a prominent, right-running slabby ramp with an overhung left wall; two pitches lead to a broad grass ledge at 65m. Move left round an edge and climb to a second grass ledge, and an obvious flake chimney (12m). Climb the awkward chimney then easy rocks to a grass rake. Move right to follow the lower rake to the beginning of the fine upper ridge, which needs little description. A technically easier but less well protected start is by vegetated slabs near Great Gully.

Ardnamurchan Ring Crags

Map p130, 139
These fine gabbro crags are remote from the usual climbing areas but worth the extra effort to get there. Like nearby Mull, dry rock can often be found when higher hills further east are wet and misty. A day trip is feasible from a base in Glen Coe or Fort William, but spending two days is a more relaxing way to visit. Stalking information can be obtained from Mingary House (01972 510208). R.E.Chapman and G.H.Francis climbed some routes on the gabbro in 1949. Almost 50 years later there was a rush for new routes, with some getting their first and second ascents on consecutive days by rival parties.

Access: From the Corran Ferry (see Garbh Bheinn above) drive west through Strontian to Kilchoan. Turn right just beyond the Kilchoan House Hotel, then right for Sanna about 1km further on. The left branch leads to the lighthouse at the Point of Ardnamurchan. This is 72km (1hr 30mins drive) from the Corran Ferry. There is one bus a day from Fort William to Kilchoan; Sheil Buses, (01967 431 272).

Amenities: There is a shop and filling station at Kilchoan. Open 9am till 5.30pm, closed Sundays, so probably worth stocking up and filling up before Corran. There is no official campsite although the Kilchoan House Hotel and Sonachan Hotel (on the road to the lighthouse) are happy for people to camp nearby, but ask first. There may be a small charge at Kilchoan for a local charity. Both hotels serve bar meals. Wild camping is an alternative. For other accommodation try the Information Office at Kilchoan or <www.ardnamurchan.com>.

MEALL AN FHIR-EOIN BEAG

(NM 482 699)   Alt 110m   South-West facing   Map p139
There are two main masses of rock on the hillside. The lower left-hand mass, Meall an Fhir-eoin Beag, has more exposed rock forming a number of ribs. The higher right-hand hill is Meall an Fhir-eoin.

Approach: Park just beyond the bridge over the Allt Uamha na Muice (NM 473

676), 3km from the Sanna junction. Up the hill over the deer stile and cut through the hillocks on the path to descend on to the landrover track. Slightly longer, but easier route finding, is to park 600m further on (NM 469 677) and follow the landrover track all the way. The track continues to the ruined settlement of Glendrian, with the cliffs beyond, 50mins.

Descent: A convenient way to climb a number of routes is to make a 50m abseil from the right side of the flat ledge at the top of the main section of cliff, or walk off right.

There are some large boulders at the base of the left side of the crag. Just left of the boulders is a slab with a crack on the left side; this is Volcane. The impressive bulging Darth Vadar buttress is just right of the boulders; Star Wars and Return of The Jedi are on this buttress. The rounded rib to the right has a prominent crack, Yir. The slabby rib right again is climbed by Up-Pompeii.

Volcane   50m   E1 **
J.George, D.Cuthbertson   3 Aug 1997
A nice varied route, start just left of the boulders.
1. 25m 4c Climb the thin crack running up the left side of the slab then continue to the shoulder above and to the left.
2. 25m 5b Climb a short steep ramp to a thin break above. Make a delicate step up and go right to a crack leading to a ledge. Continue up the crack and a shallow corner to the flat ledge at the top.

Star Wars   55m   E3 **
R.Anderson, D.Cuthbertson   4 Aug 1997
Climbs the crack up the right side of the Darth Vadar feature (the bulging blank section for those who have not seen the films).
1. 30m 6a Scramble up grass and rock to climb a short crack leading to the leaning cracked wall. Climb through the niche into the diagonal break running up right, then step up left and climb a steep crack to a ledge and a belay just above.
2. 25m 5b Cross the heathery garden above, then climb the centre of the wall to gain and follow a slanting flake-line come crack up right. Finish up a slabby rib.

Return of The Jedi   55m   E2 5c ***
R.Anderson, C.Anderson   3 Aug 1997
From the right side of the buttress scramble up a heathery slab to a steep stepped cracked groove. Climb this up towards the crack of Star Wars, then go up right along a horizontal break to the right edge of the buttress. Step right around the edge and make some bold moves to gain the diagonal break of Star Wars. Climb the crack just right of the edge and continue past a large ledge (possible belay) and up the blunt arete to the top.

Yir   55m   VS 4c ***
C.Prowse, R.Kerr, G.Latter   8 Jul 1997
This prominent line gives fine varied climbing.
1. 40m 4c Follow the crack into the left-slanting groove (the initial section of Minky provides a better and cleaner start) and continue to a ledge at its top. Move right to the crest, and continue up this to a belay.
2. 15m 4b Move left and climb the crack which slants up left then right.

Minky   55m   E2 **
D.Cuthbertson, J.George   3 Aug 1997
A good direct line just right of Yir.
1. 45m 5c Pull over a small overlap and follow a break slanting up to the left to a junction of cracks with Yir (the move into Yir may be avoided at the same grade). Go up a short way, step right and take a direct line up the whaleback by some thin

and poorly protected climbing. Belay where the angle eases.
2. 10m 4b Step left and climb the crack right of Yir.

Up-Pompeii 60m E1 **
R.Anderson, C.Anderson 4 Aug 1997
A good line up the slabby rib to the right.
1. 55m 5a/b Climb a crack up the crest of the initial short buttress, or walk round it. Climb a short crack in the left side of the rib and continue up into the centre. Step up left and climb the left side of the rib to easier ground. Continue to the headwall (possible belay), swing left and climb the short crack to a spacious ledge.
2. 5m Climb the short wall above via the obvious step.

Krakatoa 55m Severe *
The wide crack just right of Up-Pompeii. Move right at the top or finish direct at VS 4c.

An Toiseach 50m Very Difficult *
M.Riley, J.Stevenson 22 Jul 1997
The main crack-line up the next slabby rib, just left of the arete, move leftwards to finish at the top of Krakatoa original finish. The arete is Severe.

MEALL AN FHIR-EOIN

The higher right-hand hill has a number of scattered crags; two are described.
Approach: As for Meall an Fhir-eoin Beag above.

DOME BUTTRESS - CREAG AN FHIR-EOIN

(NM 483 698) Alt 110m South-West facing
This smaller buttress with a slabby right face lies 100m to the right of the crag on Meall an Fhir-eoin Beag.

Claude 25m HVS 5a ***
T.Harper, C.Prowse 17 Jul 1997
The obvious crack on the steeper left-hand portion of the crag gives a great climb. Move up right to gain the crack and go up this to the bulge. Climb the crack out right. The original finish went left below the bulge to finish up a steep groove.

Lava Lout 25m E1 5b *
M.Harris, D.Ballance 29 May 1998
A line close to the left edge of the slabby right-hand side of the buttress. Start at the toe of the slab, climb to the horizontal break, then climb the left-hand groove moving right at the bulge into the other left-facing groove.

Greta Gabbro 25m VS 4b **
J.Stevenson, M.Riley 24 Jul 1997
Pleasant climbing up the right-hand of the left-facing grooves. Start at the toe of the slab and head up right to a detached flake then go up the groove to the top. The difficulties increase with height.

HOODED WALL - LOWER TIER LEFT

(NM 484 697) Alt 140m South-West facing
This slab capped by a huge block is 200m right of Dome Buttress; it has two fine crack-lines and a route of similar grade either side.

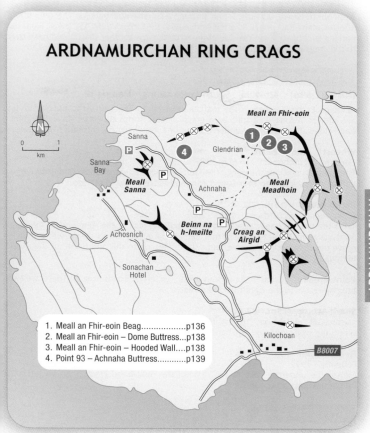

ARDNAMURCHAN RING CRAGS

**Krakatoa 20m HVS 5b ** **
S.Kennedy, C.Grindley   16 May 1998
The left-hand crack. Surmount the overlap and move left to the crack which is climbed to the top.

**Etna 20m E1 5b ** **
S.Kennedy, C.Grindley   16 May 1998
The right-hand crack just left of the crest. Some initial moves up a steep slab lead directly to a steep wall at mid-height (5c for the short), continue above.

POINT 93

Looking north-west from beyond Achnaha, four small hills can be seen stretching back and right. Button Slab is on the left most (nearest) hill. Achnaha Buttress can be seen lower *down* and left.

Approach: Drive towards Sanna through Achnaha and park on the left, 800m after Achnaha and just before the bridge over the stream (NM 457 687). From the parking spot head down the side of the stream, cross another stream and head over to the crags in about 15mins.

ACHNAHA BUTTRESS

(NM 462 696)   Alt 40m   South-West facing   Map p139

Achnaha Buttress is nearer the road than Meall an Fhir-eoin Beag but the routes are shorter. A long wall split by a grassy terrace forms the main face. The right-hand sidewall is steep and undercut. The first route is at the left end of the crag.

Wheest!   20m   E2 5c **
J.George, D.Cuthbertson   16 May 1998
The first thin crack to the right of the left-hand arete is strenuous. Climb the finger and hand-crack to good holds and continue more easily to the top.

Bondi Breach   15m   E2 5b *
C.Cartwright, S.Richardson   10 Oct 1998
Takes the blunt scooped arete left of the bulging rock at the right end of the crag. Start up a small right-facing corner, left of the arete. Climb past a white blotch, move out right and go up to a blunt spike. Step on to this and finish up the excellent wall.

Point Break (E5/6 6a *) is a serious route just left of Bondi Breach. There are two bulging cracks to the right of Bondi Breach.

Shark Attack   15m   E3 6b *
J.George, D.Cuthbertson   16 May 1998
Climb the well-protected left-hand crack by a vicious starting move.

Red Snapper   15m   E3 6a
G.Desroy   1999
Climbs the undercut flake to the right of the right-hand crack, then go left and follow the crack to the top.

BUTTON SLAB

(NM 464 694)   Alt 50m   South facing

A short way east of Achnaha Buttress and seen on the walk in, is a small slab with a pale block (or button) on its face.

Pash   18m   Severe *
M.Riley, J.Stevenson   22 Jul 1997
Start 2m left of a 3m high pinnacle at the base of the slab. Climb up to gain a prominent right-trending crack. Climb straight up to the bulge and go easily through it.

Ludo   18m   Severe *
M.Riley, J.Stevenson   22 Jul 1997
Start just right of the pinnacle, climb boldly straight up to the bulge, step left and pull over the bulge.

Minky, E2 5c, Meall an Fhir-eoin. Climber Dave Cuthbertson
(photo Cubby Images)

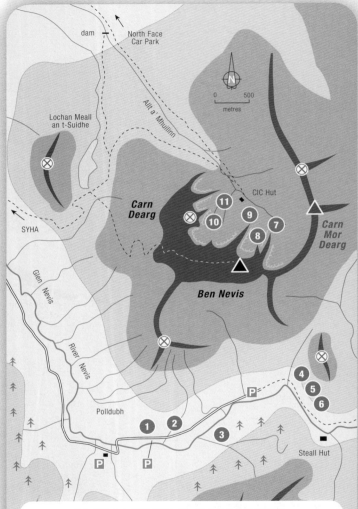

GLEN NEVIS & BEN NEVIS

GLEN NEVIS

This magnificent glen, curving round Ben Nevis from Fort William, offers a multitude of excellent outcrops. The dramatic setting between the glistening screes of Sgurr a' Mhaim and the mighty Ben Nevis mean that it is a tourist magnet in the summer months. The rock is mica schist, scoured by glaciers into wrinkled overhanging walls with slabby front faces. The popular routes are generally very clean, but moss tends to grow on shady or obscure routes. As well as some very hard and serious routes, this is a great place for the lower grades where good footwork and care with protection are important.

Maps: OS L41, E392, Harvey Superwalker Ben Nevis

SMC Climbers' Guide: *Highland Outcrops* (1998)

Access: A small road, signposted to Glen Nevis, leaves the main A82 road from a roundabout at Nevis Bridge, just north of Fort William. The road leads, after 10km, to a dead end at a car park (NN 167 691). Beyond this a path leads up through a gorge to Steall meadow and waterfall

Public Transport: See Ben Nevis. A bus runs up Glen Nevis hourly from Fort William (7 per day on Sunday).

Amenities: See Ben Nevis. Camping is no longer accepted on the river bank below the crags. A bus runs up Glen Nevis hourly (7 per day on Sunday).

GLEN NEVIS

Polldubh Crags

(NN 152 686) Alt 100 to 300m South & West facing Diagram p148

With their ease of access, friendly atmosphere, sunny aspect and wide range of grades, these crags are the most popular in Glen Nevis, perhaps even the most popular in Scotland. This more than compensates for the sometimes unbearable midges and getting lost in the trees looking for your crag. For this reason crags are defined by their approaches, rather than horizontally across the hillside. The name Polldubh, (the black pool) refers to a pool in the River Nevis, just upstream from the lay-by (NN 153 685) below Pinnacle Ridge.

General Approach: Driving up Glen Nevis, the road becomes single track and immediately crosses the river at the lower falls. A further few hundred metres further up the valley brings you to the white speckled wall and big crack of Cavalry Crack Buttress. About 150m further on is Pinnacle Ridge, seen as a smooth slightly rounded top on the lowest buttress.

Cavalry Crack Approach: Cavalry Crack Buttress, Dundee Buttress, Tricouni Buttress, Tricouni Right-Hand Slab, After Crag, Secretaries' Buttress and Nameless Crag are all best approached from the road before Cavalry Crack Buttress (see below).

Pinnacle Ridge Approach: Pinnacle Ridge, Repton Buttress, Pandora's Buttress, Little Buttress, SW Buttress, Pine Wall Crag, Styx Buttress, High Crag and Black's Buttress are all best approached from the road before Pinnacle Ridge (see p150).

CAVALRY CRACK BUTTRESS

Diagrams p144, 148

This is the largest of the lower buttresses. The left-hand face is split by prominent diagonal cracks, easily recognised by a large Scots pine sprouting high up. The lower right end of the wall faces the road and forms a smooth section identified by two big pines. The base of the cliff is overgrown but things improve once on the rock.

Approach: Park just before the crag and approach direct from the road.

Descent: By a steep path beyond Dundee Buttress, the small buttress immediately to the left.

CAVALRY CRACK
BUTTRESS

1. The Long Crack	HVS **	4a. The True Finish	E1 5b
2. The Old Wall	VS 4b ***	5. Heatwave	Severe **
3. Centrefold	HVS *	6. Vampire	Hard Severe *
4. Storm	HVS ****	7. Fang	E2 **

The Long Crack 60m HVS **
D.Nicol and party 29 Oct 1969
This is the left-hand of the two diagonal crack systems splitting the wall.
1. 40m 5a Follow the crack to a point level with the large pine on Storm. Avoid the bulge above on the left, and regain the crack above a tree. Some folk belay on the large pine and climb the route in three pitches.
2. 20m 4b Finish up the easy crack come ramp.

The Old Wall 40m VS 4b ***
I.Jones and party 1963)
Steady open wall climbing on good holds. Protection is noticeably lacking. Start up the left-hand of the two diagonal crack systems (The Long Crack) for 6m to just past a tree. Move right and up before heading across the wall through Storm to finish on the right edge of the wall, level with the pine on Storm.

Centrefold 60m HVS *
E.Grindley, F.Gunn 5 Apr 1982
An eliminate, but on the best wall at Polldubh. This climb takes the wall mid-way between The Long Crack and Storm.
1. 30m 5a From the start of The Long Crack, scramble up steep vegetation right-wards to a ledge. Climb the centre of the narrowing wall between the two diagonal cracks (crossing Old Wall) to the break level with the big pine, then cross the bulge above via a wide crack (crux).
2. 30m 4c Finish up the twin cracks in the rib to the left of the groove of Storm True Finish.

Storm 85m HVS ****
I.Clough, T.Sullivan 3 May 1959 (3PA); FFA: J.A.Austin, J.M.Austin 1962
A classic route with fine situations and generally good protection. One of many fine VS routes climbed by RAF rescue team personnel in the late fifties, the leading light being Ian Clough. Three points of aid were used, soon freed by Allan Austin on honeymoon with his wife Jenny. Start a few metres up left from the very toe of the buttress, at the left-hand and lower of two groove come ramp systems.
1. 30m 4b Climb the groove to belay on a ledge at the foot of a long diagonal crack.
2. 30m 4c Climb the crack to a belay at the large pine.
3. 25m 5a Follow the shallow groove on the right side to cross the bulge (crux), then continue more easily trending slightly right up the wall above.
Variation: **The True Finish E1 5b**
J.Taylor, K.Schwartz 1976
Move out left from above the crux and follow the shallow corner capped by a block overhang.

Heatwave 90m Severe **
I.Clough, J.Pickering, R.Henson, P.Brocklehurst, R.Porteous 22 May 1959
Start just left of the toe of the buttress, at a pair of groove come ramps merging at 5m.
1. 25m Follow either of these ramps to belay below the crack of Storm.
2. 10m Traverse right around the buttress and walk up to a holly beside a large pine.
3. 25m Climb the slabby left wall of the gully to a terrace.
4. 30m Finish up slabs above, trending left to a short groove and continue directly above.

Vampire 80m Hard Severe *
I.Clough, E.Buckley 21 Apr 1959
A varied and enjoyable route. Start 8m right of the buttress edge.
1. 25m 4b Climb a short slab and traverse 3m right to a small tree. Gain and follow a left-trending crack, then traverse left to the pine.

2. 30m 4b Walk 5m left and climb a groove in the edge. Go up the wall veering left to join the buttress edge near the pine break on Storm.

3. 25m Finish up the left edge of the slabs.

Variation: **Alternative Finish   30m   VS 4c** *

E.Grindley and party   Apr 1978

From the pine stance, take the obvious drooping flake to the right, and go up right on to the arete proper. Continue up over the bulge to finish at the second stance, as for Heatwave.

7 Fang   45m   E2 **

W.Skidmore, P.MacKenzie, J.Crawford   Jul 1963 (aid); FFA: E.Grindley, I.Nicolson   19 Apr 1978

Bold open wall climbing. Start beneath an open left-facing groove down and right of the open slab of Vampire.

1. 25m 5b Go up a steep initial groove past an overlap, then move steeply out right on good holds. Move up, then pull leftwards along a diagonal crack to belay on a ledge.

2. 20m 5a Climb the groove above, turning the roof on the right.

DUNDEE BUTTRESS

Diagram p148

This is the small buttress immediately to the left of Cavalry Crack Buttress, about 100m above the road. It is clean and accessible, therefore popular. It is distinguished by a niche in its upper half.

Approach: Park as for Cavalry Crack Buttress and make a slightly rising traverse up and left.

Dundee Weaver   20m   HVS 5b **

R.Gray, G.Low   2 May 1965 (aid); FFA: K.Schwartz, A.Fulton   1967

A popular route with a tricky crux. Climb cracks just right of the left arete to gain a small platform on the left. Hard moves lead up the crack close to the edge to easier ground.

Heading for the Howff   20m   HVS 5b

A.Cameron, J.Stalker   22 Jul 1997

This route takes a line crossing Dundee Weaver. Start as for Dundee Weaver but trend right to a grassy ledge. Pull over the bulge above on good layaways to gain the slab above (crux). Move right to finish up the final niche of Promises.

Promises   20m   Hard Severe 4b *

K.Johnson   1960/61

Climb straight up to the niche near the top. Finish up the crack in its right side.

TRICOUNI BUTTRESS

This is higher than Dundee Buttress and about 150m to the left. The buttress has a big left-facing slabby corner.

Approach: Park as for Cavalry Crack Buttress. It is probably easiest to head direct from the car (apart from the bracken), because the upper right-hand slab is clearly seen from here whereas the main slab is hidden in trees.

Corner   15m   Severe

This route is on a higher left section of crag. Climb a crack formed by a large block leaning against the wall. Step on to the slab and move round the edge on the left to enter a groove between two overhangs.

Tricouni Slab   25m   Very Difficult **

Good climbing up the slab left of the corner. Reach it from the right and climb up almost anywhere on the slab.

Black Slab Edge   25m   VS 4c *
K.Johnson   1960/61
Climb a groove in the right arete of the corner.

TRICOUNI RIGHT-HAND SLAB

About 50m up and right of the main buttress is a prominent clean arete and slab, clearly visible from the road. Unfortunately it's a bit of a fight to get to it.

Fly Direct   25m   HVS 5a **
R.Treadwell, R.Shaw   2 Jun 1983
The arete of the slab, originally gained by traversing across the slab low down, but much better as described. Start at a small rib below the main edge. Move up to a small overlap, turn this on the left, then follow the easier arete. The centre of the slab to the right is **Parisian Walkway** (E2 5b), very serious but fun on a top-rope.

AFTER CRAG

Diagram p148
This crag is situated above and a little left of the top of Dundee Buttress, and to the left of the top of Cavalry Crack Buttress. The features of the crag are those typical of Polldubh – a slabby front face and a steep sidewall to the left.

Approach: Park as for Cavalry Crack Buttress. Make a slightly rising traverse up and left as for Dundee Buttress, pass beneath it and ascend up its left side to its top. Go up and slightly left for about 50m.

Kraut   20m   E1 5b *
K.Schwartz, S.Crymble, D.S.B.Wright   6 Apr 1969 (1PA); FFA: K.Spence   1970
A prominent left-slanting dyke or fault in the left wall, behind a large tree, is strenuous and well protected with good holds.

Rubberface   20m   E1 5b *
K.Schwartz and party   15 Jun 1968; Direct: E.Grindley   2 Mar 1976
Klaus Schwartz's first route in the Glen, first of about 90 in the next decade. Climbed more direct by Ed Grindley, who later moved up to the area. Start on the front wall, 6m right of the lowest rocks and left of a tree. Climb the bulge (crux), step left on to the slab and continue direct. Quite bold.

SECRETARIES' BUTTRESS

Diagram p148
This excellent crag lies directly uphill from Cavalry Crack Buttress and can be seen from the parking place as one of the larger crags in the upper area of Polldubh, with a distinctive slabby right face, a roof on the crest and a steep left wall.

Approach: Park as for Cavalry Crack Buttress. Make a slightly rising traverse up and left as for Dundee Buttress, pass beneath it and ascend up its left side to its top. Either go straight up or head slightly rightwards initially on a well worn path towards the top of Cavalry Crack Buttress, then straight up until the trees begin to thin. Secretaries' can now be seen above.

The crag comprises of slabs on the left of a central gully and a clean buttress with roofs on the right. The routes are described starting from the left-hand end of the steep left-hand face, then working down to the right and on to the slabby front face.

GLEN NEVIS

POLLDUBH CRAGS

Ring of Fire Right-Hand   30m   E3 6a **

M.Hamilton   1984

Fine open wall climbing, with a gymnastic start. Start at the foot of a shallow groove at the far left of the buttress. Swing right to a large flat hold above the lip and go up to a ledge. Break out right and follow an obvious line up the wall leading to a crack (the top crack on Vincent). Follow the crack with interest until a leftward traverse can be made to a ledge. Climb the cracks to the top.

Secretaries' Crack   20m   Moderate *

J.Ness, A.Burgon   11 May 1950

The fault splitting the second and third tiers of the crag gives one of the few deep chimney lines hereabouts. Follow this to a ledge on the front wall. Either walk off rightwards, or continue up the crest of the ridge (the Direct, Severe).

Vincent   60m   E3 ***

D.Cuthbertson, I.Sykes   5 Aug 1981

A diagonal line across the left wall of all three tiers gives fine open climbing. So named, because the rock architecture resembled a Van Gogh painting. Start at the toe of the crag.
1. 20m 5b Climb the wall to join the first diagonal crack and traverse along this to a ledge.
2. 10m 5c Move left round the overhang above and go up the wall (unprotected) to better holds just below the top. Continue up the slab to a ledge.
3. 30m 5c Descend about a metre and pull round onto the wall (hard). Follow the crack with interest until a leftward traverse can be made to a ledge. Climb the cracks to the top.

Secretaries' Super Direct   50m   HVS ***

A.Fulton, K.Schwartz   28 Jul 1969; First pitch: K.Schwartz, J.Mount   19 May 1973

A fine exposed line up the left edge of the slabby face. Another Loch Eil instructor, Alec Fulton, led the thin top pitch (with Klaus Schwartz of course). Start at the left side of the front face, below a shallow left-facing corner.
1. 20m 4c Move left across the steep slab to cross the overlap near the left edge, then go up this to the first ledge system.
2. 30m 5a Follow the thin and exposed left edge of the slab to the second ledge. Cross the gap and finish up easier slabs.

Twitch   15m   E1 5b *

J.Cunningham and party   29 Oct 1969

The thin slab mid-way between the second pitches of the Super Direct and the Direct. Climbed on a visit by John Cunningham; Glenmore Lodge parties instructed here a lot at the time. Gain the start from the right along the first ledge. Although unprotected, the difficulties ease as height is gained.

Secretaries' Direct   80m   Severe ***

I.Clough, E.Buckley   21 Apr 1959

Excellent climbing, giving one of the best lines of its grade in the glen. Start below the shallow left-facing corner.
1. 15m Climb the corner to the first ledge system. Move right to belay below a crack.
2. 20m Follow the central crack on superb quartz holds to the second fault system.
3. 45m Easier climbing up the slab above leads to a horizontal ridge. Continue rightwards over several short steps.

Now above the trees, High Crag with its distinctive skull like feature is clearly seen to the right. The approach to High Crag is described from Pinnacle Ridge approach, but it can also be approached from here. To reach its Lower or Middle Tier, traverse right below a slabby buttress (King Slab, initially hidden). To reach its Upper Tier, make a rising traverse passing under a clearly seen buttress, Nameless Crag.

NAMELESS CRAG

Diagram p148

This is characterised by two steep walls either side of an overhanging nose above a broken rib. The left-hand, west facing wall is composed of slabby grooves, the right-hand side has a smooth wall facing High Crag's 'skull'.

Approach: Park as for Cavalry Crack Buttreess and approach as for Secretaries' Buttress. Nameless Crag lies further up and right.

The first route is situated on the left wall.

Risque Grapefruit   30m   E4 5c **
D.Jamieson, D.Cuthbertson   1981

Thin bold climbing up the slightly slabbier right side of the face, with a run-out crux. Start under a short open groove in the centre of the face. Pull rightwards across the wall and go round the arete on to the slab. Continue direct over a tiny overlap and climb up with some stretchy moves (crux) to reach a shallow scoop. Go up the shallow groove and the left-trending ramp to finish.

Triode   20m   E5 6a ***
D.Cuthbertson, A.de Clerk   19 May 1987

Thin bold climbing up the blankest section of the right-hand face. Start beneath a shallow left-facing groove. Climb this for about 6m, then move right to a crack leading to a horizontal break (protection in a slot above). Move left along the horizontal, then go up to a quartz hold. Continue on small holds to a series of stepped undercuts heading out left to finish.

Diode   20m   E2 5c **
B.Sprunt, C.Hill   29 Jul 1977

A thin crack splits the right end of the face. Climb this direct, passing a narrow roof at mid-height.

PINNACLE RIDGE

Diagram p148

The most popular Polldubh buttress is the closest to the road and the most polished as a consequence. The buttress is composed of a slabby front face and a two tier left wall with a large ledge between. Down its left side flows a small burn, Pinnacle Burn, just a boggy area in dry conditions, with a path to its left.

Approach: Park just before the crag and follow the eroded path beside the Pinnacle Burn.

Pinnacle Ridge   50m   Severe *
J.Ness, D.Duff   1947

This extremely popular route was one of the first routes climbed in the Glen, by local climber Jimmy Ness. Its popularity means it is now somewhat polished, but still a fine route for those who don't realise how rough the rock used to be. Start at the toe of the buttress. Climb near the left edge of the slab to a tree, then go up an easy angled scoop to another tree on the terrace. Move along the top of a large flake and go up rough slabs to the top.

Staircase   15m   Severe *
J.Ness, A.Burgon   28 Sep 1950

An alternative, unpolished and perhaps nicer start to Pinnacle Ridge. Start 6m right of Pinnacle Ridge. Climb staircase like holds to the first tree on that route.

Tip Toe   25m   Hard Severe *
J.Ness, M.Hutchison, R.Corson   23 Sep 1950

Another alternative start to Pinnacle Ridge. Start immediately right of Staircase. Go up the slab to a small foothold, then tip toe left to good hand holds at 10m and traverse left. Climb a niche or the crack to its right to the terrace on Pinnacle Ridge. Poorly protected on the lower slab.

REPTON BUTTRESS

Diagram p148
This crag is on the left of the path, its base level with the top of Pinnacle Ridge, but somewhat hidden by trees. It is distinguished by three big pines growing on a ledge. From the top of the crag Little Buttress is a short traverse right. Continuing the traverse gains the 'Alp' and SW Buttress, Pine Wall Crag and Styx Buttress.

Approach: Park as for Pinnacle Ridge. From Pinnacle Ridge continue up and left.

Descent: On the right, nearer the buttress than the path.

Three Pines 30m Severe 4a *
T.Sullivan, E.Buckley, A.Flegg 27 Mar 1959
A popular route which combines well with Spike Wall on Little Buttress. Climb the rib immediately right of the central gully to the pines. Follow the groove behind the central tree, moving right under the roof to a platform, and continue by a crack.

Right Wall 30m Very Difficult
A pleasant easier route on the higher right-hand side of the crag. Climb up right-wards past big flakes to the right end of a long overhang, step left on to it and go up to a tree. Traverse 3m to another tree and go through yet another tree into a cleft. Finish up behind this.

PANDORA'S BUTTRESS

Diagram p148
This buttress lies immediately up and left of Repton Buttress and 80m right of Cavalry Crack Buttress, their tops being at the same level. A right traverse from the top of Pandora's Buttress passes the base of Little Buttress, then gains the 'Alp' and SW Buttress, Pine Wall Crag and Styx Buttress.

Approach: Park as for Pinnacle Ridge. From Pinnacle Ridge continue up and left, past the base of Repton Buttress.

Descent: Down the left side.

The buttress has a slightly overhanging front face with twin diagonal left-slanting cracks. Two rock tongues extend down on either side of the cracks into the trees. The first two routes start up the left tongue, pass the overhanging wall on the left and climb features on its left side, Phantom Slab a hanging slab and Pandora a big hidden corner. Neither feature is visible from the start.

Phantom Slab 60m VS **
T.Sullivan, I.Clough 3 May 1959
Excellent sustained slab climbing. Start about 20m up left from the left-hand tongue at a groove. If pitch 1 is damp, approach by climbing the first two pitches of Pandora, then descend left to reach the base of the slab.
1. 25m 4b Climb the groove to reach a corner at the bottom right-hand side of the 'Phantom Slab'.
3. 15m 4c Traverse diagonally leftwards and follow a line up the left edge of the slab, and finish by moving slightly rightwards at the top.

Pandora 65m Severe *
I.Clough, E.Buckley 20 Apr 1959
Good varied climbing.

GLEN NEVIS

1. 25m Climb the left-hand of two rock tongues below the diagonal cracks to a large ledge below a corner.
2. 20m Continue up the rib on the left of the corner to a tree on the right wall of a larger corner.
3. 20m Go up the corner to a large ledge, then follow slabs on the left.
Variation: **Pandora Direct   20m   VS 4c**
Climb the corner above the first stance.

Flying Dutchman   60m   Severe **
T.Sullivan, I.Clough   3 May 1959
A deservedly popular route with an exposed and sustained second pitch. Start on the lowest rocks to the right of Pandora (the right tongue).
1. 25m Climb the crest, or heathery grooves just to the right, to a terrace.
2. 25m Go up slabs left of a diedre, then traverse diagonally left on good footholds to a short corner in the left side of an overlap. Pull over, go up the crack and around a rib to a tree on a capacious ledge.
3. 10m Follow the ridge directly, or scramble up easy ledges leading left.
Variation: **Direct Finish   10m   VS 4c**
From the tree belay, follow the thin right-slanting crack.

LITTLE BUTTRESS

Diagram p148

This lies above and slightly right of Pandora's and Repton Buttress. Its base is close to and level with the top of Pandora's Buttress.

Approach: Park as for Pinnacle Ridge. From Pinnacle Ridge follow the path up to the left. Once past the first buttress (Repton Buttress), a boggy section of path and a small tier on the right, go up and left to the crag's base.

Descent: On either side, the right-hand side is slightly easier.

The front of the crag is a slab almost 60m high, divided at half-height by a ledge with a big pine tree above its left end. The sidewall to the left is shorter and divided from the front slab by a rib.

Spike Wall   55m   Severe **
I.Clough, R.Henson, P.Brocklehurst, R.Porteous   28 Jun 1959
A popular and delightful climb which combines well with Three Pines on Repton Buttress below it. Start about 10m right of the rib, near some boulders. The slightly harder Direct starts up a groove immediately right of the rib and climbs direct above the spike.
1. 30m Climb the slab leftwards to reach for a spike at 10m. Go over the spike and traverse left almost to the edge. Climb a recess and the ridge above to the big ledge with the pine.
2. 25m Climb the slab above on small quartz holds to finish on the rounded crest of the ridge.

SW BUTTRESS

Diagram p148
This and the following two crags lie in the 'Alp', a relatively sheltered and partially hidden grassy meadow with an unexpected open aspect. The small but obvious SW Buttress lies at the entrance to the 'Alp' and is characterised by horizontal, vertical and diagonal cracks. It dries very quickly, but is highly polished as a result. The routes were climbed mostly by K.Johnson in 1963 or 1964.

Approach: Park as for Pinnacle Ridge. From Pinnacle Ridge follow the path up the left side of that crag to enter the 'Alp' where the ground flattens out. SW Buttress lies just above the origins of Pinnacle Burn, before reaching the 'Alp' proper.

Three Pines, Severe 4a, Repton Buttress. Climber Ian Dickson
(photo Andrew Fraser)

Tear   12m   Hard Severe *
The vertical crack just left of centre has good holds and protection.

Scratch   12m   VS 4c *
Start immediately right of the crack of Tear. Climb slightly rightwards up thin cracks in the slab.

SW2   15m   HVS 5b *
Climb the tiny corner 3m right of Tear to a diagonal break, step right to a foothold and ascend thin cracks. Thin, poorly protected climbing.

SW Diagonal   18m   HVS 5b *
Climb the diagonal left-slanting crack, with one hard move low down.

Tee   12m   VS 5b
Follow a direct line just right of the diagonal to join a crack above the half-height horizontal fault. There is one hard move.

PINE WALL CRAG

Diagram p148
This crag is situated in the 'Alp' a few hundred metres right of and above Pinnacle Ridge, above the source of the Pinnacle Burn. It is easily identified by a prominent 60m ridge facing the glen, with a large Scots pine at two-thirds height.

Approach: Park as for Pinnacle Ridge. From Pinnacle Ridge follow the path up its left side to enter the 'Alp' where the ground flattens out.

Descent: Via the easy angled left side of the crag, or the steeper gully separating Pine Wall Crag from Styx Buttress.

Eigerwand   45m   Hard Severe **
K.Johnson   1960/61
Start below a large tree right of a tree gully and a quartz wall. Climb up to the tree on the terrace at 8m. Climb a little gully on the left for 3m, then move right and go in a direct line towards the top. Any deviation on the upper part makes the climbing much easier.

Pine Wall   65m   Hard Severe ***
J.Ness, A.Burgon   1 Jun 1950
The ridge gives excellent exposed climbing on superb rock, making it one of the best climbs of its standard at Polldubh. Protection is well spaced on the first pitch. Start at the lowest point of the ridge.
1. 35m 4b Move up to a diedre and climb this to a platform at 12m. Move left and go over a bulge, then climb the immaculate slabs to the immediate right of the rounded ridge to a belay on a platform where the angle eases.
2. 15m Follow the ridge, or grooves left of it, to the prominent pine.
3. 15m Pass an overlap on either side to reach a small recess just left of the crest, and continue more easily up this to finish. Much variation is possible, although the described line gives the best climbing at the grade.

The Gutter   65m   Difficult ***
K.Schwartz   8 Oct 1975
A classic beginner's route, giving pleasant well protected climbing. Follow the twin cracks 4m right of the ridge to a ledge at 12m. Continue in the same line by a deeper crack to a withering sapling at 30m. Either belay just above, or continue up the ridge to the big pine. Move up left to a good flake hold on the wall, then go out right to finish easily up the crest of the ridge.

STYX BUTTRESS

Diagram p148
This lies immediately right of Pine Wall Crag. The crag has a very steep left wall and a slabby front face. A distinctive tapering ramp lies in the arete between the two faces (Resurrection).

Approach: Park as for Pinnacle Ridge. From Pinnacle Ridge follow the path up its left side to enter the 'Alp' where the ground flattens out.

Descent: The steep gully separating Styx from Pine Wall Crag.

Resurrection   35m   VS 4c ***
I.Clough, A.Lakin   5 Apr 1959
A Polldubh classic, sustained and well protected with superb climbing up the tapering ramp in the centre of the crag. Climb the slabby ramp, with the crux (and excellent protection) at the narrow middle section to a slightly easier wide fault-crack
higher up.

Damnation   30m   VS 4c **
I.Clough, J.Alexander   28 Jun 1958
One of the first of many routes climbed at Polldubh by Ian Clough, with rescue
team leader John Alexander. Start on the left side of the wall, 6m right of the left
buttress edge. Climb a ramp until it is possible to traverse right to a vertical rib
which leads to an overhang. Cross this on the left on good holds and continue
straight up the fine slab above to a tree. Improbable looking for the grade.

Iche   30m   HVS 5a *
T.Sullivan, I.Clough   11 Apr 1959
Start just left of a diagonal heather groove. Climb leftwards up a slab and surmount
the overhang 2m from its right end. Traverse left a short way to a thin crack and
go up this to a small tree. Finish up slabs.

Right Wall   50m   Very Difficult *
A good easier route up slabs at the right end of the crag. Start about 10m right of
the central diagonal heathery fault. Climb a slab to a small pine and go along an
edge past another pine. Keep right of a recess to gain the final slab.

HIGH CRAG

Diagram p148, p157
This buttress is composed of three tiers of slabs and is nearly 150m high. The lower
tier is small and scrappy, being split halfway by a ledge with an overlap above and
mostly obscured by trees. The middle tier is about 60m high and more appealing.
Its left side forms a red wall facing west. The upper tier, again 60m, lies above a
large terrace and is undercut along its length. Its left wall forms the crag's distinctive 'skull' shape.

Approach: Park as for Pinnacle Ridge. From Pinnacle Ridge follow the path up its
left side to enter the 'Alp' where the ground flattens out. Gain the top of SW
Buttress, then go diagonally left up a small path, passing the top of Little Buttress
to reach the base of the crag.

Descent: Down open slopes on the left, heading diagonally away from the crag
to pass a slab level with its lower tier (King Slab).

The following route starts from the lower tier.

1 Autobahnausfahrt   170m   VS **
K.Schwartz, B.Chambers   2 Sep 1969
The longest route in the glen is enjoyable and climbs open slabs at the mildest of
VS. Protection is limited but the hard moves are just off the terraces. Start near the
right side of the base of the crag.
1. 35m 4b Climb slabs, crossing a ledge and an overhang with a tiny tree, then
climb steeper slabs to the first terrace.
2. 15m Climb a block and the bulge above to a tree ledge.
3. 45m 4b Surmount the overhang 5m above and head for a small groove. Climb
this to the second terrace.
4. 15m 4b Walk right (not included in the length) to climb the steep slabs at the

right end of the overhanging base, passing a heather groove at 8m on its left.
5. 40m Continue straight up over a bulge to easier slabs, climbed through two sections.

MIDDLE TIER

2 Crag Lough Grooves   135m   HVS **
T.Sullivan, I.Clough   29 Mar 1959 (Combined tactics and 2PA); FFA: J.A.Austin, J.M.Austin   1962
Varied climbing, with a hard crux section through the steeper final tier. Start left of a cave overhang, at the bottom left of the middle tier.
1. 30m 5a Scramble to overhangs at 10m. Traverse 3m right across three small ribs into a red groove, and follow this to a ledge and tree.
2. 40m Climb a groove slightly to the right and continue up slabs to the second terrace. A better alternative is to follow the crack up the edge of the slabs to finish up easier slabs on the right and so reach a thread belay on the top (4c).
3. 15m 5b Walk to the right a few metres to a large diagonal break in the largest part of the overhanging base of the upper tier. Cross the initial bulge and follow a prominent right-trending gangway to a small stance around the rib.
4. 20m 4c Follow a steep groove above to slabs and a ledge.
5. 30m Finish up easy slabs.

3 Kinloss Grooves   65m   VS *
I.Clough, T.Sullivan   11 Apr 1959
Start at a tree below the first break in the overhang right of the start of Crag Lough Grooves, left of a red wall.
1. 35m 4c Climb to a small niche below the overhang at 10m, exit right and go up to another niche. Continue up the slabs to a ledge.
2. 30m 4a The slabs above can be climbed anywhere to the second terrace.

4 Cervix   30m   VS 4c *
K.Schwartz, B.Chambers   11 Oct 1969
Start on the left wall of the second tier, above the gully separating High Crag from King Slab on its left. Climb the initial wall by a left-slanting crack, with a strenuous crux at 10m. Continue along the fine steep slanting chimney above.

UPPER TIER

This tier has an overhanging wall across its grassy base (popular hard bouldering). Crag Lough Grooves climbs the obvious break, Sky Pilot is right of this.

5 Sky Pilot   30m   E5 6b **
D.Cuthbertson   1981
The centre of the overhanging 45 degree wall is breached by a hanging crack, forming a block near the lip. Climb up and out on improving holds (crux at half-height) to the lip, and step left to gain easy slabs.

6 Slatehead Slab   30m   E2 5b **
D.Cuthbertson, G.Latter   27 Oct 1985
High on the left of the front face, right of the rightmost eye of the skull, is a fine slab above a tree with a short wall at its foot. Start below this. Traverse left from the tree, then move up the wall to pull left on to the slab at good sidepulls. Follow an obvious line right across the slab to a good pocket at a break. Continue past another break to the top. The route can also be gained from the right.

BLACK'S BUTTRESS

Diagram p148
This buttress is situated far to the right and on the same level as the Upper Tier of

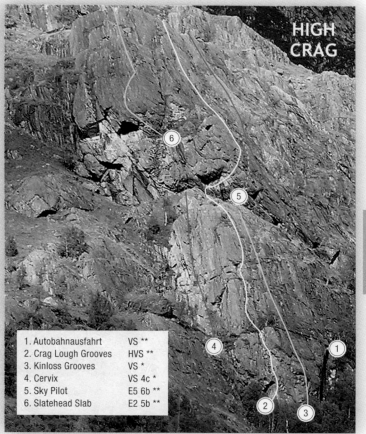

HIGH CRAG

1. Autobahnausfahrt   VS **
2. Crag Lough Grooves   HVS **
3. Kinloss Grooves   VS *
4. Cervix   VS 4c *
5. Sky Pilot   E5 6b **
6. Slatehead Slab   E2 5b **

GLEN NEVIS

High Crag, approximately 60m above Pine Wall Crag. The buttress is composed of a vegetatious lower tier marked by a clean left edge. Immediately above, separated by a flat grassy terrace, is a smooth 30m slab of immaculate white rock.

Approach: Park as for Pinnacle Ridge. From Pinnacle Ridge follow the path up its left side to enter the 'Alp' where the ground flattens out. From the top of Pine Wall Crag go diagonally rightwards to reach a terrace leading back left. Alternatively, follow a small sheep path along the natural terrace from the base of the Upper Tier of High Crag; 'The John Muir Sheep Trail'.

Shergar   30m   HVS 4c **
E.Grindley, C.Grindley, P.Long, G.Higginson   13 Sep 1981
Start to the left of the main crag. Climb thin right-slanting cracks to gain a shallow left-facing corner. A great route, adequately protected, low in the grade.

Land Ahoy   30m   E3 5b ***
E.Grindley, D.Gunn   25 Oct 1981
Start mid-way between Shergar and a thin vertical crack to the right (Kaos), at an

Plague of Blazes, E2 5b, Gorge Crag. Climber Tess Fryer
(photo Ian Taylor)

arrow. Climb the wall direct to a crack in the upper half of the wall, then finish more easily. Brilliant climbing, sustained and unprotected before the crack.

Centrepiece   30m   E6 6b ***
K.Howett, G.Latter, D.Griffiths   11 Oct 1987
Superb fingery climbing directly up the centre of the slab, right of Land Ahoy. Start at some quartz in the centre of the wall. Climb up to a prominent small L shaped hold at 5m (tied down skyhook on this). Hard climbing past this leads to the thin horizontal. Pull direct past this to better holds and a reasonable stopping place. Poor RP placements in the incipient crack system above protect a further tricky move to reach a large flat hold. Easy climbing remains.

Kaos   30m   E2 5c *
K.Schwartz, P.Logan   7 Jul 1968 (aid); FFA: K.Spence   1980
Follow the obvious thin vertical crack, then climb up and left with difficulty to gain a further crack and small ledge at 10m. Continue in the same line to the top. Delicate and fingery, and a bit run-out at the crux.

Crybaby   20m   VS 4c *
K.Schwartz, M.Horsburgh   29 Jun 1970 (1PA); FFA: K.Schwartz and Loch Eil party   1972

Start mid-way between Kaos and the rib on the right side of the crag. Follow the crack rightwards past a small triangular niche to a ledge at 12m, and continue by a crack on the left.

SCIMITAR BUTTRESS

(NN 156 686)   Alt 170m   North-West facing   Map p142

This buttress lies on the left side of a spur about 300m beyond the Polldubh crags and facing them. It is a pleasant venue for a sunny evening.

Approach: There is a parking place for one or two cars before a bridge and a small path heads fairly directly to the crag.

Nutcracker Chimney   25m   Hard Severe 4b **

R.Wilkinson, D.Pipes   8 Apr 1958

Climb the shallow flared chimney at the upper left-hand side of the crag.

Diagonal   20m   VS 4c *

R.Wilkinson, D.Pipes   8 Apr 1958; FFA: A.Fulton, B.Chambers   1968

The left-hand and more obvious of two right-slanting crack-lines towards the right side of the wall is well protected and on good holds.

Razor   20m   VS 4c **

B.Sprunt, A.Slater   1978

From the start of the right crack, climb straight up to join Diagonal. Step left and follow a thin crack to the top.

SCIMITAR UPPER BUTTRESS

This is the steep isolated gritstone like slab 50m further up and close to the top of the 210m knoll. All three routes are unprotected and were done by D.Cuthbertson, June and July 1984.

Sweet Little Mystery   10m   E4 6a *
From the bottom left end of the crag, ascend diagonally rightwards to a steepening. Make an awkward step up to a good break and finish directly.

Jahu   10m   E6 6a **
Climb the right-trending scoop in the centre of the slab in its entirety. Very thin and committing.

Where the Mood Takes Me   10m   E5 6a *
Start at a thin crack on the right side of the crag. Climb up to a flat hold, stand awkwardly on this, then move up and slightly right to finish.

Car Park & Steall Area

Whale Rock lies on the opposite side of the River Nevis from the road, on the northern slopes of Sgurr a' Mhaim and is accessed from the road via a bridge over the river. Gorge Crag (nestling in the trees) and Wave Buttress (on the open hillside directly above, with a prominent quartz patch in the centre) are clearly seen by looking east from the car park at the end of the road (NN 167 691). The Meadow Walls are only visible after passing through the Steall gorge (NN 175 689).

WHALE ROCK

(NN 163 684)   Alt 150m   North-West-facing   Map p142

A few hundred metres beyond Polldubh, Whale Rock comes into view on the opposite side of the river. The frontal wall of this excellent crag is split by the central crack of Earthstrip. Steepening and sweeping round to the right, the crag forms a series of discontinuous scoops, with striking twin ragged cracks up the blunt prow.

Approach: A short wide section of road with good parking is only 30m away from the visible bridge (NN 158 684). Cross the river at the bridge, then cross the stream (Allt an t-Snaig) low down (near where it joins the river) and follow a diagonal line direct to the crag, 10mins.

The Fascination Trap   25m   E1 5c *
D.Armstrong, D.Borthwick   4 Jul 1984
This route follows the right-slanting diagonal line across the wall, with a bouldery start. Just right of the heather gully is a thin crack. Climb this to ledges, then follow the obvious slightly rising traverse line, with a further hard move across the slab to reach good holds leading into the top of Earthstrip. Continue in the same line to the top right of the crag.

Earthstrip   20m   E2 5c ***
D.Armstrong, A.Wright   7 Sep 1983
The central widening crack-line gives excellent sustained climbing, easing towards the top.

There are E5 lines either side of Earthstrip but may need re-cleaning at the start of each season. **Femme Fatale** (E8 6c) provides very serious and technical climbing up the bulging scoops in the steepest section of the crag. The route has repulsed all on sight attempts so far, but is reported to be one of the very best hard routes in Scotland.

Just a Little Tease   25m   E5 6b **
D.Cuthbertson   Jun 1984
Excellent climbing up the scoop and twin ragged cracks at the point where the crag bends around the hillside. Make difficult moves across the scoop (runners used in opposition) to gain good holds and protection. Attain a standing position on a good hold (rest possible) before following the cracks which lead strenuously to the top.

GORGE CRAG

(NN 175 691)   Alt 230m   South-West & North-West facing   Map p142 Diagram p162

This crag lies above a wooden walkway on the path and is the first crag encountered on the path through Steall gorge. A slabby left wall sweeps round into a steep and imposing frontal face, with a couple of corner systems bounding the right side.

Approach: Follow the road to the car park at its end (NN 167 691), then the path towards Steall gorge. The crag squats in the trees about 20m above the path and 15mins from the car park.

Descent: Abseil from trees at the top of Plague of Blazes and Travellin' Man, or contour left from the top of the crag and descend a steep slab just before a stream.

1 Plague of Blazes   30m   E2 5b ***
E.Grindley, F.Gunn, N.Williams, W.Lawrie   27 May 1982
An excellent and popular route with varied, interesting climbing up the slabby sidewall of the crag proper. Start 5m up and left from the toe of the crag, at the left-hand of two thin crack systems running up the slab. Follow the zigzag crack for 12m to a flake. Move left, then go up into a recess. Step right and climb the slab to the final wall. Pull up this on good holds to finish at a Scots pine.

The following two routes climb the grooves in the arete between the two faces.

2 In the Groove   40m   E3 *
D.Cuthbertson, G.Latter   May 1982; First pitch: G.Latter, I.Campbell   24 Jul 1984
Another good route with an awkward finish.
1. 15m 5b Climb the diagonal thin cracks in the right side of the slab. The shorter, right-hand crack in the slab above leads to a ledge.
2. 25m 5c Climb the groove above, then trend right into a subsidiary right-hand groove on the frontal face. Exposed moves past an obvious block lead to a potentially inelegant roll on to the slab above. Easier climbing up the ramp above leads rightwards to the top.

3 Travellin' Man   35m   E2 ***
D.Cuthbertson, G.Latter   22 May 1982
The groove system splitting the rib between the left-hand and front faces provides an outstanding climb which challenges both technique and the ability to place protection.
1. 10m 5b Climb the strenuous cracked groove just right of the toe of the buttress to a ledge.
2. 25m 5c Follow the right-slanting groove above until it is possible to step left (crux) to reach a crack in the slab. Climb this and finish up the easy ramp above.

4 Cosmopolitan   30m   E5 ***
D.Cuthbertson, G.Latter   21 May 1982
The original and best line on the crag gives a fierce, well protected technical test

GLEN NEVIS

GORGE CRAG

1. Plague of Blazes	E2 5b	***
2. In the Groove	E3	*
3. Travellin' Man	E2	***
4. Cosmopolitan	E5	***
5. Conscription	E1 5b	*
6. All Our Yesterdays	E1 5b	**
7. Mini Cooper	HVS	*

piece. It only succumbed after several attempts and held a reputation for many years. Start below and left of a hanging left-facing groove in the centre of the overhanging wall.

1. 15m 6a A bouldery start leads to a handrail leading out right to the groove. Follow this, exiting out rightwards to a spacious ledge.

2. 15m 6b Gain the thin diagonal crack from the right with a hard initial move, then go up to good holds just below the top.

5 Conscription   45m   E1 5b *
D.Cuthbertson, G.Latter   19 May 1982

limb the obvious wide crack on the left wall of the corner, then exit right on to a
dge and finish up an easy flake.

**ll Our Yesterdays 40m E1 5b ** **
.Cuthbertson, G.Latter 19 May 1982
 good, well protected climb which often stays dry even in the rain. Climb the cor-
er-crack, exiting right to finish up an easy flake (as for Conscription).

Mini Cooper 40m HVS *
/.Jeffrey, N.Williams, P.Hunter 11 Jun 1983
tart at foot of groove near the left side of the buttress below and right of the main
rag.
. 15m 5a Gain the groove by some steep moves, then go up to the terrace.
?. 25m 5b The corner leads to the top of the flake on the previous two routes.

WAVE BUTTRESS

NN 176 690) **Alt 320m South-West facing Map p142 Diagram p164**

Looking east from the car park towards Steall gorge (NN 175 689), this crag can
be seen on the open hillside of Meall Cumhann. The crag has a prominent quartz
patch in the centre and lies above and slightly right of Gorge Crag in the trees.
ts south-westerly aspect and relatively exposed position ensure fast drying, and
sometimes a midge free haven when the gorge is unbearable. The crag is generally
slabbier than most of the crags hereabouts, and is split into two buttresses by a
heather filled gully. The left-hand buttress has a very obvious right-slanting crack
of Crackattack. The right-hand buttress is smaller but is defined on the right by the
clean arete of Edgehog.

Approach: Follow the road to the car park at its end (NN 167 691), then the path
through Steall gorge and into the Steall meadows. Immediately turn left and head
up to the buttress, clearly seen above, using a steep zigzagging path up the hillside
left of a wide, open gully and an extensive area of rock buttresses The Meadow
Walls (below) are right of this gully.

Descent: By abseil, or by an indistinct path along the top, crossing the gully with
care (easiest low down) and down the right-hand side.

**First Wave 30m E1 5c ** **
E.Grindley, N.Williams 20 Apr 1982
The opening gambit on what was to become one of the finest crags in the area.
The left edge of the crag has a narrow left-slanting ramp with a series of ledges and
short walls above. Start at some quartz blotches. Boulder diagonally rightwards to
the foot of the ramp, then climb this and follow a direct line to finish up a steep
wall on good flakes.

On the Beach 30m E5 6a * **
M.Hamilton, R.Anderson Apr 1984
Bold open wall climbing with spaced protection in the upper half. Start from a
pedestal below a left-hand crack which ends at a horizontal break at mid-height.
Follow the crack moving slightly rightwards to the horizontal break. Step left and
follow the shallow runnel above to better holds at some quartz. Continue more
easily above.

**Ground Zero 30m E3 5c ** **
E.Grindley, N.Williams, C.Grindley, F.Gunn 9 May 1982
Varied open wall climbing, high in the grade with a bold lower section. Start just
left of the right-slanting crack. Climb directly up the wall past some thin flared
cracks, moving slightly right on good holds to the base of a diagonal crack come
ramp. Climb the crack in the groove past an awkward bulge, and finish up the
quartz staircase above.

GLEN NEVIS

WAVE BUTTRESS

164

1. First Wave	E1 5c **	4. Crackattack	E3 6a ***	7. Edgehog	E3 5c
2. On the Beach	E5 6a ***	5. Bewsey Crack	HVS 5a ***		
3. Ground Zero	E3 5c **	6. Walter Wall	E4 6a **		

Crackattack   30m   E3 6a ***
E.Grindley, B.Owen   14 Aug 1983
The right-slanting crack is well protected, with the crux at the top.

Bewsey Crack   30m   HVS 5a **
E.Grindley, N.Williams   23 May 1983
A shallow fading groove runs into a diagonal crack. Follow this into a sentry box near the top, and exit from this on good holds.

The following routes are on the right-hand section of the crag. An obvious left-slanting crack provides the line of **Think Vertical** (E3 6a), alas slow to dry, with the even more striking clean cut arete of Edgehog standing out on the right.

Walter Wall   30m   E4 6a **
K.Spence, J.McKenzie   28 Apr 1984
Serious though steady wall climbing up the shallow depression in the centre of the wall. Start at the toe of the buttress, as for Think Vertical. Go up this a short way, then move easily right across a scoop to reach good holds above. Climb boldly up the wall with no protection to a good horizontal break and protection. Hard moves past this lead to the 'Walter Wall bellyflop' on to a shelf. Exit rightwards.

Edgehog   30m   E3 5c ***
E.Grindley, N.Williams   26 Apr 1982
Grindley's finest and the most popular Extreme in the glen, partly because it used to be given E4. Gain the arete from the right, and follow it with a hard move past a flange on the left leading to a good resting spot. Continue steadily to a good horizontal break near the top. Easier climbing leads to a large ledge. It is better protected than first impressions would suggest.

(NN 176 688)   Alt 270m   South-West facing   Map p142

On entering the flat Steall meadows from the narrow confines of Steall gorge, a number of crags can be seen on the left. These are the Meadow Walls. The most striking feature is a large round pothole feature right of a slabby wall. Right of the pothole is a long wall overhanging towards its right end and bounded by a gully.

Approach: See Wave Buttress (above).

Descent: Go leftwards along a terrace and into the wide gully by the foot of Wave Buttress.

Reptile   40m   E2 5c **
D.Cuthbertson, K.Howett   21 May 1985
This route follows a left-slanting diagonal line up the wall left of the pothole and taking in the obvious cracks. Start to the right of the centre of the wall at a scoop containing a thin crack. Climb this to a ledge, trend left under a crack-line, and continue up a quartz wall to flakes at a junction with the final twin cracks. Follow these with some interest to the top.

Going for Gold   15m   E4 6a ***
E.Grindley   26 Aug 1983
A fine exercise in hand jamming, tackling the prominent crack through the centre of the roof left of the gully. The easiest approach is from the right along a terrace and across the gully. Climb the roof past some evil flared jams to a good horizontal flake near the lip, then continue up the wide flake-crack to the top. Very well protected; carry some large Friends for the upper crack.

BEN NEVIS
North-East
Buttress

Orion Face

Start of North-East Buttress obscured

Minus Face

First Platform

1. North-East Buttress	Very Difficult ***
2. Raeburn's Arete	Severe **
3. Bayonet Route	Hard Severe **
4. Minus Two Buttress, LH Route	VS **
5. Minus One Direct	E1 ****
6. The Long Climb	VS ***
7. Observatory Ridge	Very Difficult ***

BEN NEVIS

Although Ben Nevis is justly famous for its winter climbing, the summer season reveals huge crags of solid rock. The classic ridges provide extremely enjoyable expeditions in the lower grades, while the steep walls of Carn Dearg Buttress hold many of the most sought after high mountain rock climbs in Scotland.

The summer season is typically short. The snowfields of winter are slow to disappear, and they can form huge bergschrunds guarding the foot of the Minus and Orion Faces. The routes on Carn Dearg Buttress can be climbable from mid April, but the best time is any dry spell from mid June to mid September.

Maps: OS L41, E392. Harvey Superwalker Ben Nevis

SMC Climbers' Guide: *Ben Nevis* (2002)

Public Transport: Train and bus from Glasgow to Fort William; bus from Inverness to Fort William.

Amenities: Fort William is a tourist town with all the necessary facilities, a few of which are described below. There is an Information Office in Cameron Square (0845 225 5121).

Camping: Glen Nevis campsite (NN 125 722), (01397 702191). Wild camping in Glen Nevis is now discouraged.

Mountaineering Huts: CIC Hut – SMC (NN 167 722) is at 680m altitude under the cliffs of Ben Nevis; Steall hut – JMCS (NN 177 684) is a 3km walk from the head of Glen Nevis; Riasg – CC (NN 272 812) is at Roy Bridge and Waters Cottage – FRCC (NN 183 617) is in Kinlochleven.

SYHA Youth Hostels: Glen Nevis (NN 127 716), (0870 004 1120) open all year.

Independent Hostels: Farr Cottage Hostel, Corpach (01397 772315); Achintee Farm Hostel (01397 702240); Ben Nevis Inn (01397 701227); Calluna (01397 700451); Fort William Backpackers (01397 700711); Bank Street Lodge (01397 700070).

Climbing Shops: Ellis Brighams (01397 706 220), Nevisport (01397 704291) and West Coast Outdoor Leisure (01397 704291).

Climbing Wall: There is a 5m Bendcrete bouldering wall at the Lochaber Leisure Centre (01397 704 359).

BEN NEVIS

(NN 166 712)   Alt 1344m   Map p142

Approach: From Fort William follow the A82 north and turn off at Torlundy (sign-posted). Cross the railway bridge (traffic lights) then turn immediately right along a forestry road which leads to the North Face Car Park (NN 144 763) after 800m. Follow a track from the north end of the car park across a bridge and after 100m cross a stile on the right to reach a short path which leads up to the line of a disused narrow gauge railway. Follow this for 1km to reach another stile where a path leads up steep and muddy slopes on the left side of the Allt a' Mhuilinn to a small dam (NN 147 751) and follow the left bank of the Allt a' Mhuilinn to the CIC Hut. From Glen Nevis, park near the Youth Hostel (NN 127 716) and follow the easy tourist track to the broad col above Lochan Meall an t-Suidhe, the 'Halfway Lochan'. Skirt the lochan on the right and contour round below the North Face to the CIC Hut.

From the CIC Hut (NN 167 722), the most obvious feature on the left is the sky-line ridge of North-East Buttress. Below the ridge lie The First Platform and the Minus and Orion Faces, flanked on the right by Observatory Ridge. Largely hidden from the CIC, the massive Observatory Gully to their right separates North-East Buttress from the next major ridge line almost directly above the CIC – Tower Ridge. In turn, Tower Ridge is largely obscured in its lower half by the triangular bulk of the so-called Douglas Boulder. The big corrie facing the CIC is Coire na Ciste, its lower right flank dominated by the impressive slabs, corners and over-hangs of Carn Dearg Buttress. Higher up into the corrie, almost directly below the summit of Carn Dearg and partially obscured from the CIC, lie the Trident Buttresses.

NORTH-EAST BUTTRESS

(NN 171 716)   Alt 850m   North-East facing   Map p142

The First Platform is the clean slabby face at the lowest end of North-East Buttress. To its right lie the three slender buttresses of the Minus Face Right again, directly below the highest point on the buttress is the Orion Face, shaped like an inverted wedge.

1 North-East Buttress   500m   Very Difficult ★ ★ ★
J.Hopkinson, E.Hopkinson, B.Hopkinson, C.Hopkinson   6 Sep 1892
The most southerly of the great ridges on Ben Nevis offers a superb mountaineering expedition with the major difficulties near the top of the route. Start some distance to the left of the lowest rocks and the ridge crest.
    Scramble up to gain a broad ledge and follow it right to a level section on the

crest of the ridge, which is known as the First Platform. Follow the narrow ridge and turn a steepening by a shallow gully slanting up left. Trend right by short chimneys and walls to gain a sloping shelf on the crest of the ridge; the Second Platform. Above, the ridge is narrower and well defined and presents no real obstacle until a smooth overhanging wall is reached. This can be turned on the right by a corner with large steps, or climbed directly by working from left to right along a ledge until a bulge can be climbed on good holds.

The short step on the ridge above is the infamous Mantrap. The hardest pitch on the route can be turned on either side, but a direct ascent is recommended as both variations are inferior. Beyond the Mantrap climb the '40ft corner', or turn it on the left, to enter a small gully leading to easier ground above, and the summit.

First Platform

Alt 850m   North-West facing   Diagram p166

This clean slabby face has rough and friendly rock and dries fairly rapidly after rain. It is defined on the right by the gully of Slingsby's Chimney.

Descent: Reverse the broad east-slanting ledge back down into the corrie from the crest of North-East Buttress.

2 Raeburn's Arete   230m   Severe **

H.Raeburn, J.Inglis Clark, W.Inglis Clark   30 Jun 1902
The arete on the left side of the face provides one of the cleanest Severes on The Ben. A superb route that makes a good direct start to North-East Buttress.
1. 20m Start at the lowest rocks directly under the arete. Climb up to a black overhang, turn this on the right, and reach a grass ledge and belay.
2. 35m Follow the arete above to a stance.
3. 40m Traverse right for 6m, then climb up to regain the arete at the earliest opportunity.
4. to 6. 135m Follow the arete, with minor deviations, to the First Platform.

3 Bayonet Route   185m   Hard Severe **

G.G.Macphee, A.G.Murray   30 Sep 1935; Main Overhang Variation: B.P.Kellett   May 1943; Direct Start: J.R.Marshall, J.Stenhouse   Aug 1959
One of the most enjoyable climbs of its grade on the mountain. Start from a large grass platform which lies about mid-way between Raeburn's Arete and Slingsby's Chimney.
1. 35m Direct Start: Climb the prominent corner at the left end of the platform, and belay below an overhang.
2. 20m Move left onto the rib and climb to below the left edge of the main overhang.
3. 35m Main Overhang Variation: Climb a slab leading to a V-notch in the main overhang. Surmount this using cracks, exit right, then trend left above the overhang to reach a rib. Follow this until a right traverse leads into a grassy bay.
4. 35m Take the rib on the right of the bay to a belay.
5. 20m Continue up the rib in the same line.
6. 40m Climb a corner, exit on the left just above a prominent square-cut overhang, then continue by easier rock for 25m to the crest of the buttress.

Minus Face

(NN 169 716)   Alt 950m   North-West facing   Diagram p166

Right of the First Platform and Slingsby's Chimney lie three slender buttresses. Minus Three Buttress is the shortest buttress immediately right of Slingsby's Chimney. Minus Two Buttress is easily identified by a huge undercut nose at about

Ian Taylor on the Arete Variation to Minus One Direct, E1 5b
(photo Ian Taylor collection)

one-third height. To the right, the slim Minus One Buttress is separated from the Orion Face by the deep, narrow slit of Minus One Gully. The routes require around two to three days to dry after prolonged rain. Bergschrunds can cause problems after a winter of heavy snow.

4 Minus Two Buttress, Left-Hand Route   280m   VS **

B.P.Kellett, R.L.Plackett, C.M.Plackett   20 Jun 1944; Left Edge Variation: N.Richardson, R.T.Richardson, A.Walker   11 Jun 1988

A sustained climb following the left edge of the buttress in a magnificent situation. The original line followed the prominent cracks splitting the raised crest on the front face, then traversed to the left side of the buttress.

1. 30m 4a Move out on to the left rib and climb left via slabs and grooves to a flake belay in a niche on the edge of the buttress.
2. 40m 4c Descend to the right for a short distance, then move up and right and climb a bulging groove. Continue up a further groove on the very edge of the buttress, to reach a superb stance below an imposing wall.
3. 10m 4b Turn the wall on the left, then move up right to a belay.
4. 45m 4b Climb the slab above, keeping close to its left edge, until it is possible to reach a rib on the right and a belay. A memorable pitch.
5 to 8. 155m Climb easier and more broken ground to the crest of North-East Buttress (better to the left) and ascend or descend that route.

5 Minus One Direct   295m   E1 ****

R.O.Downes, M.J.O'Hara, M.Prestige   11 Jun 1956; Serendipity Variation: K.V.Crocket, I.Fulton   27 Aug 1972; Arete Variation: S.Abbot, D.N.Williams   28 Aug 1983 (FFA: W.Jeffrey, D.N.Williams   6 Jul 1984)

A magnificent climb with a distinct alpine feel, combining superb rock and situations with interesting route finding. A worthy contender for Scotland's best mountain route at the grade. Start in the centre of the lowest rocks of the buttress.

1. 25m Scramble easily to a belay under a left-facing corner.
2. 20m 4b Climb the corner, then exit right onto a smooth slab and belay.
3. 45m 4c Ascend a shallow groove in the wall above to a block at 6m. Pass this by a crack on its right (it is also possible to climb on its left), then climb by short walls, moving left to a niche. Step right and climb to the top of a vast plinth.
4. 25m 5b The first crux pitch. Traverse right on to a nose above the overhang and climb up to a ledge. At the right-hand end of the ledge is an undercut groove. Pull into this (crux) and climb it until it is possible to follow a ramp rightwards, to finish at a block belay on a platform overlooking the lower chimney of Minus One Gully.
5. 25m 5a Serendipity Variation: Traverse up and left, until a hard move leads to a recess. Make some devious moves up this, then break out right and climb up to a small grassy niche.
6. 20m 4c Arete Variation: Step left into a further recess and climb its slabby left wall. Climb the steeper rocks above until it is possible to break out on to right-trending slabs. Belay at a stack of detached blocks.
7. 15m 5b Arete Variation: On the left is a prominent slab capped by a long narrow overhang. Gain a foothold in the centre of the slab (second crux), move up to the overhang, then traverse left on underclings to the arete. Follow this to a small exposed stance.
8. 35m 4c Arete Variation: Climb a crack in the crest above, then continue more easily to a groove. Bridge strenuously up this to reach the great terrace.
9. 40m 4b Climb to the top of a 12m pinnacle, and move easily up to a leaning pedestal.
10. 45m Finish up the delightful knife edge arete to join North-East Buttress above the Second Platform, and follow it to the top.

Orion Face

(NN 169 715)   Alt 1000m   North-West facing   Diagram p166

Shaped like an inverted wedge, this face fans out from the narrow slit of Minus One

Gully to the deep Zero Gully on the right. The Basin, the depression in the centre of the face, holds snow well into summer. The name Orion derives from a fancied resemblance of the original routes on the face to the configuration of the stars in the constellation Orion, with the Basin corresponding to Orion's belt.

6 The Long Climb   420m   VS ***
J.H.B.Bell, J.D.B.Wilson   14 Jun 1940
An outstanding route of alpine proportions. The climb is neither totally clean or solid, and in anything but perfect dry conditions the route is likely to be significantly harder than the grade suggests. Choose a dry sunny day to savour one of the finest mountaineering expeditions in the country, but watch out for falling rocks from other parties! Start 30m left of Zero Gully below an easy angled ochre coloured rib.
1. and 2. 60m Climb the rib to a small platform.
3. 45m 4a From the left end of the platform, a rib leads steeply up to the base of the Great Slab Rib, an easily identifiable feature. Step round the rib on the left, then move up to the foot of the Great Slab Rib. Alternatively, climb the rib direct or the groove on its right side. Both variations are harder than the original line.
4. 30m Traverse right on to the crest of the Great Slab Rib and climb it by parallel cracks to reach a recess and belays. A superb pitch.
5. 45m Move out and up right, then climb more easily to the Basin.
6. 40m Cross the Basin and climb to the foot of the Second Slab Rib, a prominent feature which bounds the top right-hand side of the Basin.
7. 40m 4b Climb the rib by its slabby left edge. High up, turn a steepening on the left wall (4c if climbed direct), then regain the crest above. Climb an awkward wall on either the left or right side to a stance.
8. to 11. 160m The climb now continues on easier rocks, with much variation possible. The original route trends up left aiming, for the base of yet another great slab, some 60m high. This can be bypassed on the right to reach a niche, where a short difficult pitch leads to the top of the slab. Easier climbing then leads to the crest of North-East Buttress just below the plateau.

OBSERVATORY RIDGE

(NN 168 716)   Alt 900m   North facing   Map p142   Diagram p166

This is the long narrow buttress right of Zero Gully.

7 Observatory Ridge   500m   Very Difficult ***
H.Raeburn   22 Jun 1901
The most difficult of the classic ridges provides the finest climbing. From the lowest point of the ridge, climb easily to the right end of an obvious grass terrace (65m). Continue by slabs and walls, a little left of the crest, to steeper rocks that are turned on their right flank. Climb cracks and grooves to the easier angled crest of the ridge, and follow this with occasional difficulties to the plateau.

TOWER RIDGE

(NN 166 717)   Alt 800m   North-East facing   Map p142

Tower Ridge starts a short distance above the CIC Hut and rises steeply for 200m to the top of the Douglas Boulder, the gigantic rock pinnacle separated from the main ridge by the deep cleft of the Douglas Gap.

Tower Ridge   600m   Difficult ****
J.Hopkinson, E.Hopkinson, B.Hopkinson, C.Hopkinson   3 Sep 1892
A time honoured classic by virtue of its great length and the scale of its rock architecture, the ridge is usually climbed by skirting left round the Douglas Boulder to its east side, and climbing rocks above a grassy bay into a scree-filled gully leading to the Douglas Gap. This allows the route to be climbed in boots. From the Douglas Gap, climb a well polished 20m chimney to gain the crest of the Ridge. Pick the

BEN NEVIS

easiest line up the crest passing the inconspicuous Little Tower to the vertical rocks of the Great Tower. Go left along a level ledge about a metre wide (the Eastern Traverse) to enter the foot of a tunnel formed by a huge fallen block. From the top of the through route, steep but easy climbing leads to the top of the Great Tower. From the top of the Great Tower, make a slight descent and traverse the narrow crest to Tower Gap. The descent into the gap is quite tricky, but climbing out the other side is straightforward. Easy rocks beyond the gap lead to a final steepening, turned on the right.

Variation: **Douglas Boulder Direct Route   215m   Very Difficult **✱✱
W.Brown, L.Hinxman, H.Raeburn, W.Douglas   3 Apr 1896
An ascent of the great groove on the front face of the Douglas Boulder to the Douglas Gap gives a tremendous start to Tower Ridge. Start at the foot of the lowest rocks, well left of a smooth slabby wall, which is an obvious feature of the lower section of the face. Climb up easily by a large shallow groove to a point where the groove steepens to form an open chimney. Climb the chimney for 60m to well defined ledge. Traverse right along this and climb steep broken rocks to the top. From here, either down-climb to the right or abseil to reach the Douglas Gap.

SOUTH TRIDENT BUTTRESS

(NN 161 718)   Alt 1000m   East facing   Map p142

The most southerly and best defined of the three Trident Buttresses is bounded on the left by the scree filled Number Four Gully. The routes lie on the middle of three tiers, easily reached by slanting right from the foot of Number Four Gully.

Descent: Make a descending traverse left to reach Number Four Gully.

1 Sidewinder   75m   HVS ✱✱
J.R.Marshall, R.Marshall, A.Wightman   Jun 1964
The triple tiered corner that rises steeply leftwards across the face, gives strenuous but well protected climbing. Start left of centre about 15m right of a deep chimney groove easily identified by a small pinnacle at its top. Scramble up to the corner.
1. 25m 4b Climb the corner.
2. 20m 5a Continue in the line of the corner to an easy slab.
3. 30m 4c Finish directly by a crack and large flake to reach the crest of the buttress below the final tier.

2 Strident Edge   75m   VS ✱✱
N.Muir, D.Regan   Jul 1972
The formidable looking arete to the right of Sidewinder gives fine exposed climbing. It is easier than it looks and a little rattly in places, but it dries fast. Start by scrambling up to the base of the wall 5m left of Sidewinder.
1. 15m Climb up to a belay in the corner of Sidewinder.
2. 35m 4c Move out right and climb a steep crack immediately to the left of the crest of the arete.
3. 25m 4b Follow the left edge of the arete to the top of the middle tier.

3 Devastation   70m   E1 ✱
C.Moody, A.Nelson   12 Jul 1995
Fine varied climbing up the steep crack to the right of Strident Edge. Right of Strident Edge and 20m left of a huge corner is a big V-groove; **Spartacus** (VS 4b). Start at a smaller corner just to the right.
1. 40m 5b Climb the corner to reach a flake, then move left to a niche above an overhang which blocks the big groove. Continue up the steep crack which is a continuation of the big groove.
2. 30m 4a Follow a groove to the top.

4 The Slab Climb   90m   Severe ✱
B.P.Kellet   30 Jul 1944
Between Devastation and the huge corner is a big slab with a prominent crack

173

BEN NEVIS
Trident Buttressess

BEN NEVIS

South Trident

Central Trident

1. Sidewinder   HVS **
2. Strident Edge   VS **
3. Devastation   E1 *
4. The Slab Climb   Severe *

5. Steam   HVS *
6. Heidbanger   E1 *
7. Metamorphosis   E2 **

(actually two) which gives a superb pitch with surprisingly incut holds. Start below the slab.

1. 20m Climb leftwards up towards the corner of Devastation, then traverse right to a short wall below the main slab. Climb the wall to the base of the slab with its two thin cracks.

2. 40m 4a Climb the slab near the right crack towards an overlap. Traverse left into the left crack and climb it to a ledge (possible belay). Move left above an overhang to a flake-crack. Climb this and move left to an exposed position.

3. 30m 4a Gain and climb the groove above (as for Devastation).

Variation: **Original Finish**
Start from the possible belay on pitch 2 and climb the overhanging chimney-slot (strenuous) and grooves above, mossy in places.

CENTRAL TRIDENT BUTTRESS

(NN 161 719)   Alt 1000m   East facing   Diagram p173

This steep rounded wall of superb looking rock lies below and right of South Trident Buttress and is characterised by the large corner system of Metamorphosis near its right-hand end.

Descent: Reverse the ramp on the left side of the buttress, **Jubilee Climb** (Very Difficult) or make a single 50m abseil from a belay point near the top of Heidbanger.

5 Steam   90m   HVS *
S.Docherty, B.Gorman   1970
About 25m left of the prominent crack in the left arete of the buttress is a large right-facing corner with overlapping slabs on its right wall. Start below this.

1. 25m 4c Climb the corner to an overhang. Turn it on the left to reach a stance.

2. 30m 5a Climb the wall above for 6m, then traverse left into a small corner left of the main corner-line. Follow this to a left-sloping ramp and belay in a corner.

3. 35m 4c Traverse diagonally up right to a sloping ledge on the left. Continue left and climb the steep wall to the top.

6 Heidbanger   90m   E1 *
N.Muir, I.Nicolson   9 Jun 1970
A wandering line and low in the grade. The route climbs into the cave in the deep crack-line in the central arete, then continues up the wall above. Start mid-way between Steam and the base of the crack, just left of a steep groove.

1. 40m 4c Surmount a bulge and move right to the top of the groove after 6m. Climb the short corner above and move on to a slab. Traverse right across this to the arete, and turn this to reach the cave.

2. 20m 5b Take a crack leading out of the cave, then follow a left-trending line of weakness up the wall to the arete.

3. 30m 4c Ascend the big corner-line, then continue up a smaller corner to the top, passing a dubious flake.

7 Metamorphosis   105m   E2 **
S.Docherty, D.Gardner   Aug 1971
The hanging corner right of the cracked arete of Heidbanger gives a fine and sustained route. Start just left of the overhanging crack at the right-hand end of the face.

1. 35m 5b Move right up the wall to join the crack below a bulge. Surmount this and follow the crack-line to below a corner. Go right and up to the corner, and follow this to a ledge.

2. 30m 5a Continue up the corner past a recess to a ledge. Traverse right, then go up to a poor stance beneath a prominent flake.

3. 25m 5b Follow the flake and crack above, then trend right to easier ground.

4. 15m Finish by a corner and the wall above.

CARN DEARG BUTTRESS

(NN 163 722)   Alt 800m   North-East facing   Map p142   Diagram p176

Carn Dearg, with its overlapping slabs, huge corners, and sweeping overhangs has a rock architecture without equal in the United Kingdom and some of the most celebrated routes in Scotland on rough, solid and sunny rock.

The buttress is defined by the huge right-facing central corner-line of Centurion. To its right lies the shorter corner of The Bat and the deep chimney-line of Sassenach. Round the arete to the right and facing the Allt a' Mhuilinn, is the impressive but shady Titan's Wall. The lower left side of Carn Dearg Buttress has a curving subsidiary buttress with a prominent right-facing corner forming its right edge. Above and right of the subsidiary buttress rises the long, deep chimney-line of Route I. Away from the main drainage lines the rock dries dries fast but even at the height of summer some climbs seep for a while after heavy rain. The cliff receives the morning sun, so an early start will prove worthwhile.

Descent: Gain Ledge Route and follow it left to Number Five Gully. This often carries snow until late summer and care should be taken descending in rock boots. Much of the gully can be outflanked by climbing wet slabs on either side.

1 Ledge Route   450m   Easy * * *
J.S.Napier, R.G.Napier, E.W.Green   9 Jun 1895
An excellent scramble through magnificent scenery. Start up Number Five Gully, and break out right on the first ledge from the foot of the gully proper. Follow this until it becomes impracticable, then take a shallow gully that leads up and slightly left to a higher ledge. Follow the higher ledge to the right passing a large pinnacle block to reach the easy angled crest of the Great Buttress of Carn Dearg by a large cairn. Follow the crest of the buttress to the north-west summit of Carn Dearg.

2 Route I   215m   Severe * *
A.T.Hargreaves, G.G.Macphee, H.V.Hughes   17 Jun 1931
A fine chimney climb calling for determined use of an armoury of bridging and back and foot techniques, with the crux right at the top. Start a few metres up and left of the prominent right-facing corner on the right side of the subsidiary buttress.
1. 35m Climb to a ledge at 15m, then follow the right edge above to a larger ledge.
2. 10m Scramble up grassy cracks on the left to a large block belay.
3. 30m Traverse left and follow grooves to a recess. Continue up to the right, then move left to a platform.
4. 35m Scramble to the top of the subsidiary buttress and walk right to the foot of the upper chimney.
5. 20m Climb the chimney, finishing by a grassy groove to reach a recess.
6. 20m Ascend the right wall for 5m, regain the chimney and climb it to a stance and spike belay.
7. 20m Move left on to an exposed slab and climb it to the foot of the final chimney which leads to a broad ledge.
8. 45m Walk right and climb easy rock to the top.

3 Route II Direct   235m   Severe * * *
B.P.Kellett, W.A.Russell   9 Jun 1943; Direct Start: B.W.Robertson, G.Chisholm   19 May 1962
This superb outing traverses the central slabs from left to right, covering some fantastic ground for the grade. Start on a grass ledge below the slabby right wall of the prominent right-facing corner of the subsidiary buttress.
1. 30m Direct Start: Climb the centre of the smooth slab to a small ledge. Step right to a wall, then take a small slanting corner and traverse left to a stance. Finish up a small black crack to a flake belay.
2. 25m Direct Start: Continue straight up to a large block below a groove. Climb the groove, then traverse right round an arete to a shattered ledge.
3. 25m Direct Start: Move up to easier ground and a belay below the upper chimney of Route I.

BEN NEVIS

BEN NEVIS
Carn Dearg
Buttress

BEN NEVIS

4. 15m Climb the chimney for 10m, then traverse the slab on the right to reach a small stance and good belay.
5. 25m Move right to a large flake beneath the great overhangs.
6. 10m Traverse the flake (6m), then climb a rock rib to a thread belay on a plat-form. The same point can be reached by climbing directly above the flake and tra-versing right on vegetation, but this is not as good.
7. 40m Traverse right across the buttress, following the obvious line of weakness, to gain a platform on the edge of the buttress.
8. 30m Scramble up the edge.
9. 35m Enter a groove, and follow this mainly on the right wall to the buttress crest.

4 The Bullroar 285m HVS ****
J.R.Marshall, J.Stenhouse 1 Jun 1961
One of the finest mountain rock climbs in Scotland, this route makes a committing rising traverse across the central slabs giving superb climbing with tremendous exposure. It is not as popular as its better known neighbours which only adds to its attraction. The wet streak on the main slab dries early in the day, but returns by mid to late afternoon. Approximately 30m right of the prominent right-facing corner of the subsidiary buttress, is a large brownish right-facing corner with some large boulders at its foot. Start 3m right of this corner.
1. 25m 5a Pull over an awkward bulge into a widening groove, and continue to a flake belay.
2. 15m 4b Move left into a parallel groove and climb this until 5m below the over-lap at the top of the central slabs.
3. 15m 4a Traverse right along the slab under the overlap to a crack and climb this to a belay.
4. 45m 5a Descend slightly, then traverse right across the slab, passing a possible stance, to reach a descending traverse which leads to a belay above pitch 3 of Centurion.
5. 25m 4c Climb the crack above, then traverse right to a belay under the over-laps.
6. 30m 4b Traverse right under the overlaps on excellent small flake holds to eas-ier ground. Climb this to a large terrace above the chimneys of The Bat and Sassenach.
7. 10m From the left end of the terrace, traverse left to an area of shattered rock beneath an undercut groove.
8. to 10. 120m 4c Climb the groove and continue by a series of corners and slabby grooves to the top of the buttress.

5 Torro 215m E2 ****
J.McLean, W.Smith, W.Gordon 25 Jul 1962; FFA: I.Nicolson, I.Fulton Jun 1970
A brilliant route taking a complex but natural line up the sweep of slabs left of Centurion. Start just left of the foot of the rib forming the left wall of the Centurion corner.
1. 30m 5b Climb the overhanging groove to a flake. Continue up the groove to a larger flake, then climb it on its right-hand side. Move back left and continue up the groove to a good stance.
2. 25m 5b Continue up the widening fault above, then work up and left to the edge of a slab. Make a descending traverse left across the slab, move round an arete, then go up an overhanging groove through the overlap to a stance below and right of twin overlaps.
3. 25m 5a Move diagonally right round a bulge to a crack above. Climb this for 6m, then move slightly right and go up a slab to a good stance.
4. 20m 5c Climb a slight crack for 6m, step left on to a higher slab, cross this for 3m, and pull over the overhang above trending left (crux, slow to dry, but an in situ Friend can be used for aid). Take the groove above to a stance.
5. 35m 5a Follow the fault for 5m, traverse right across a slab to a crack, and climb this to an overhang. Climb through the overhang trending left, then finish by a groove to reach a grassy stance.

*The central slabs of Torro, E2 5c. Climber Charles French
(photo Tom Prentice)*

6. 15m 4b Continue up the fault to a grass ledge below the long overhangs. Junction with Route II Direct and Centurion.
7. 30m 5a Follow Centurion pitch 6 through the upper overhangs.
8. 35m 5b Traverse left to a steep black corner, then climb this to a grass terrace at the top. The sting in the tail!

6 Centurion   190m   HVS ★★★★
D.D.Whillans, R.O.Downes   30 Aug 1956
The classic of the crag gives an outstanding route following a superlative line up the great corner in the centre of the buttress. It takes its name from the smooth overlapping slabs which flank the route on the right, which bring to mind the armour on a Roman centurion. The route is very popular, and on a good day it is usual to find several parties on the climb. The second pitch is sometimes wet but the seeps are normally avoidable, and the penultimate pitch breaks through the first tier of the unlikely looking upper overhangs by some superb moves. Start at the foot of the great corner.
1. 15m 4c Climb the left wall of the corner by an awkward crack, to a fine stance on top of the rib.
2. 35m 5a Traverse into the corner and climb it to a belay on a slab in an over-hung bay. A brilliant pitch – the holds just keep coming!
3. 25m 4b Traverse left on to the edge. Climb easy grooves until level with the lip of a big overhang, then step back right on to the lip and move up to a stance.
4. 20m 4b Move back into the corner. Traverse left up across the wall below an overhanging crack and climb the arete on the left to a stance.
5. 40m 4a Climb slabby grooves in the same line past a block, then continue up easier ground to join the Route II traverse.
6. 30m 5a Climb up to the overhang. Move left on to a steep slab, and head up and left to another overhang. Step from a detached flake and traverse delicately

left on to a big slab. Climb easily up and right to a stance below the second tier of overhangs.

7. 25m 4c Traverse right for 6m and climb a spiky arete to a bulge. Surmount this, step left into an easy groove, and climb this to the terrace at the top.

King Kong   250m   E2 **

B.W.Robertson, F.Harper, J.Graham   2 Sep 1964; FFA: N.Muir, I.Nicolson   Jun 1970 using entry from The Bat

A fine climb taking an intricate line through the overlapping slabs to the right of Centurion. The route is long and sustained and route finding can be tricky, especially on pitch 3. The route originally started via a weaving line through the overlaps right of the start of Centurion, but these pitches are hardly ever repeated. Start as for Centurion.

1. 15m 4c Climb the left wall of the corner by an awkward crack, to a fine stance on top of the rib.
2. 15m 4c Follow the Centurion corner for 6m, then traverse right across a pink slab to belay on a perched block.
3. 30m 5c Move up and left on to a slab, climb an overlap and continue up to a crack. Traverse left on underclings and move up on to a higher slab. Climb this for 5m to a high runner, then hand-traverse down and right along a thin crack to a foothold below a smooth left-facing corner. Move up and right from here to a corner bulge. Swing round this and take a hanging stance on the left side of a small pinnacle shaped flake.
4. 35m 5b From the top of the flake, climb the slab on the left and pull up and right through a roof. Move up to the base of a shallow crack-line on the left side of the large red wall. Climb the crack and move right along the ledge at the top. Move up to belay at the top of The Bat corner.
5. 45m 5b The route now follows the crack and corner system 10m left of The Bat. Move up from the stance, then traverse 5m left to the crack system. Follow this over several bulges to a grassy bay. Go easily up the grassy bay to the foot of a steep crack cut by a roof.
7. 40m 5a Climb the crack through the roof and continue up the corner on the left, to belay below a corner-crack. Junction with Route II Direct.
8. 40m 4c Climb the corner, swing across to a spike, move left, then climb up to a stance and spike belay.
9. 30m Continue slightly right, then climb up to a grassy groove. Move left, then finish directly above.

The Bat   270m   E2 ***

D.Haston, R.Smith   Sep 1959

Another great classic based on the slim hanging corner to the right of the central slabs. The line is devious and complex, and the corner is reached by an intricate traverse from above the first pitch of Centurion. It was named after the great swooping falls taken by Haston on the first ascent, much of which was reputedly climbed at night. Start as for Centurion.

1. 15m 4c Climb the left wall of the corner by an awkward crack, to a fine stance on top of the rib.
2. 35m 5a Follow the Centurion corner for 6m, then traverse right across a pink slab to a perched block. Continue moving right along a shelf to a block belay.
3. 25m 5a Descend to the right for 3m to enter a bottomless groove, and climb a short wall to a triangular slab. Follow the V-groove above, then trend right along slabs to a belay beneath the left edge of the deep chimney of Sassenach.
4. 15m 5b The Hoodie Groove: Climb a steep shallow groove on the left of the chimney, then enter the main corner.
5. 30m 5b Climb the corner to the overhang, then launch into the wide corner-crack above. Continue boldly to a ledge and belay, trying not to emulate Haston.

Wilson Moir starting the crux corner of The Bat, E2 5b
(photo Niall Ritchie)

6. 35m 4b Climb the groove to the left end of a large terrace. For those not wishing to continue to the top of the buttress, it is possible to traverse right from here and make two abseils down Titan's Wall.

7. to 9. 120m Continue up the line of grooves above to the top of the buttress.

9 Sassenach   270m   E1 **

J.Brown, D.D.Whillans   18 Apr 1954; Patey Traverse: T.W.Patey, W.Brooker, W.Smith 1953

A magnificent old fashioned classic. It takes the prominent chimney-line towards the right-hand end of the front face and was the first of the big routes to be climbed on the buttress. It is somewhat neglected nowadays, which adds to its considerable atmosphere. The overhang guarding the base of the chimney-line is often wet and was originally climbed using aid (free at E3 6a). Because of this, a different start is described; the chimneys are best gained by taking the Patey Traverse from the first stance of Titan's Wall. Start as for Titan's Wall below the line of cracks 10m from the left edge of the wall.

1. 35m 5b Follow the central crack-line to an overhang at 15m. Pull over this and continue up the line of cracks, trending right, to a ledge. Traverse left along the ledge to a belay near the left arete. A superb pitch.

2. 10m 4c Patey Traverse: Traverse left round the arete and cross slabs to a ledge below The Banana Groove. Step down and left to a grass ledge below the great chimney.

3. 15m 5b Climb the chimney past a smooth tight constriction (crux) and belay where the angle eases. Good old fashioned climbing – beware of several large loose spikes.

4. 35m 5b Continue up the chimney to a large grassy terrace.

5. 20m Move right across the terrace and scramble up easy rock to the foot of a V-groove capped by an overhang.

6. 35m 4c Climb the groove for 10m, then move out left on to a ledge. Continue up the crack above to enter another groove with a wide crack.

7. 15m 4c Climb the groove, and step right at its top.

8. and 9. 90m 4b Continue up grooves to the top of the buttress.

10 The Banana Groove   105m   E4 ***

M.Hamilton, R.Anderson   21 Aug 1983

The striking curving groove in the towering buttress between Sassenach and the left arete of Titan's Wall. An excellent route with a sustained crux pitch. Start as for Titan's Wall below the line of cracks 10m from the left edge of the wall.

1. 35m 5b Follow the central crack-line to an overhang at 15m. Pull over this and continue up the line of cracks, trending right, to a ledge. Traverse left along the ledge to a belay near the left arete. A superb pitch.

2. 10m 4c Traverse left round the arete and cross slabs to a ledge below the groove.

3. 45m 6a Climb directly up the corner (possible detour on to the left wall at one point). Where the corner fades, climb the wall via cracks to a large precarious block. Pull up and left across a small overlap into a small right-facing groove. Pull out left on to a flat hold, then take a crack leading to a ledge. A stunning pitch.

4. 15m 5c Climb the overhanging crack above to the terrace. From here, either continue up Titan's Wall to join the final pitches of Sassenach, or make two abseils down Titan's Wall.

11 Agrippa   85m   E5 ***

P.Whillance, R.Anderson   29 Aug 1983

A bold and sustained route taking the overhanging arete left of Titan's Wall. Protection is well spaced and it is not a route for the faint hearted! Start below the slabby rib left of Titan's Wall.

1. 35m 5c Climb the rib for 15m to a small overhang. Gain the sloping ledge above, then follow a groove to a shelf below another overhang. Climb directly over this to the belay ledge at the top of pitch 1 of Titan's Wall.

*Keith Milne approaching the detatched flake on pitch 6 of Centurion, HVS 5a
(photo Tom Prentice)*

2. 25m 6b Follow the short slim groove on the left side of the arete, then climb a crack to gain better holds leading to a large dubious block. From a standing position on the block move precariously round on to the left wall of the arete and climb this with difficulty to a good ledge and belay.

3. 25m 5c Climb a slight groove on the right for a few metres then move up left across the wall to a flake-crack in the arete. Climb this to good holds, then move right to the ledge at the top of Titan's Wall (poorly protected). From here, either continue up Titan's Wall to join the final pitches of Sassenach, or make two abseils down Titan's Wall.

2 Titan's Wall   245m   E3 **

I.S.Clough, H.MacInnes   Apr 1959; FFA: M.Fowler, P.Thomas   Jun 1977
A brilliant route with two outstanding pitches following the line of cracks up the centre of the wall on the right side of the buttress. The second pitch is strenuous and very sustained, and overall the climb is high in the grade. It was first climbed as an aid route, and the first free ascent was a major milestone in Scottish rock climbing. It is normal to abseil down the line of the route after completing the first two pitches. Start below the line of cracks 10m from the left edge of the wall.

1. 35m 5b Follow the central crack-line to an overhang at 15m. Pull over this and continue up the line of cracks, trending right, to a ledge. Traverse left along the ledge to a belay.

2. 45m 5c Return right to the end of the ledge and arrange protection which will be good for a sideways pull. Climb the steep and sustained crack above, over a number of small bulges, until it eases. Continue directly to the top of the wall following the vertical crack with sustained interest.

3. 30m Climb up to the left, then move right to a groove. Follow this to the upper pitches of Sassenach.

4. to 6. 135m 4c Continue up Sassenach to the top.

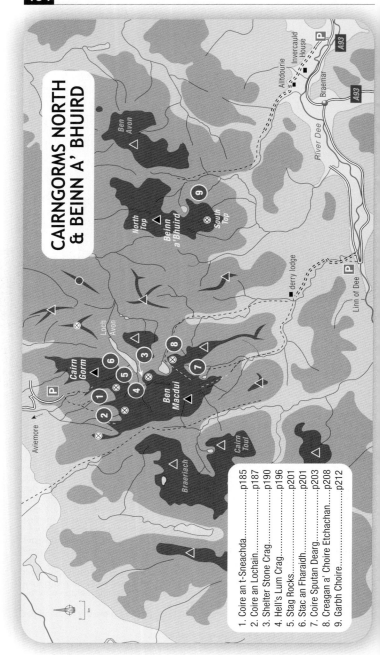

CAIRNGORMS NORTH & BEINN A' BHUIRD

CAIRNGORMS NORTH

The northern Cairngorms are a high massif of rolling plateau edged by steep corries with impressive granite cliffs. Typical of granite, the climbs combine slabby sections requiring good footwork and often with spaced protection, with steeper well-protected cracks requring a more forceful approach. The climate is drier than the western highlands, but the altitude, along with remnants of snow from the winter, means that mid June to mid September is the main season.

The crags in this chapter are usually approached from Aviemore to the north and include the Northern Corries of Cairn Gorm and the cliffs around the Loch Avon basin. Also included are the central cliffs of Coire Sputan Dearg and Creagan a' Choire Etchachan on Ben Macdui, which can be approached from the north or from Braemar to the south, and Garbh Choire of Beinn a' Bhuird which is normally approached from the south.

Maps: OS L36, E403, Harvey Superwalker Cairn Gorm

SMC Climbers' Guide: The Cairngorms Vol.1 (1995); The Cairngorms (projected 2006)

Public Transport: Bus and train from Edinburgh, Glasgow and Inverness to Aviemore. There is a regular bus service from Aviemore to the Coire Cas (Cairn Gorm) car park.

Amenities: The Aviemore and Strathspey area is well served for visitor facilities, some of which are described below. Information Offices in Aviemore (01479 810363), Kingussie (01540 661297) and Grantown-on-Spey (01479 872773).

Camping: The most convenient campsite is at Glenmore (NH 976 097). There is also a campsite at Coylumbridge (NH 815 106). Wild camping is allowed in the Cairngorms and is quite popular for the remote cliffs.

Bothies: For the remote cliffs, these are more popular than camping and are described under each cliff.

Mountaineering Huts: Raeburn – SMC (NN 639 909) is on the Dalwhinnie to Laggan road; Jock Spot's – JMCS (NN 667 947) on the Newtonmore to Laggan road; Milehouse – Ladies Scottish CC (NH 839 043) near Kincraig; Mill Cottage – Mill Cottage Trust (NH 846 047) near Feshiebridge and Karn House – FRCC (NH 894 133) Aviemore.

SYHA Youth Hostels: Aviemore (NH 893 118), (0870 004 1104), open all year and Cairngorm Lodge (at Glenmore NH 976 099), (0870 004 1137).

Independent Hostels: There are many in the area including: Glen Feshie Hostel – Glen Feshie (01540 651323); Slochd Mhor Lodge – Slochd (01479 841666); Carrbridge Bunkhouse (01479 841250); Fraoch Lodge – Boat of Garten (01479 831331); Lazy Duck Hostel – Nethybridge (01479 821642); Ardenbeg Bunkhouse – Grantown-on-Spey (01479 872824).

Climbing Shops: Aviemore has various, including Nevisport (01479 810239) and Cairngorm Mountain Sports (01479 810903).

Climbing Walls: Climb Caledonia, the Aquadome, Bught Park, Inverness (01463 667505) has a 9m leading wall and bouldering walls from slab to overhanging built in 2000. Glenmore Lodge, Glenmore (01479 861256) has a 6m leading wall and bouldering wall with a variety of angles (1993). There is an older wall (1990) at Dingwall Leisure Centre (01349 864226).

NORTHERN CORRIES

The main ski area is in Coire Cas, the eastern of the three northern corries of Cairn Gorm, and situated above the main car park. Coire an t-Sneachda is the central of the northern corries while Coire an Lochain is the westmost and highest.

COIRE AN T-SNEACHDA

(NH 994 033)   Alt 1000m   North facing

This corrie is separated from Coire Cas, the main ski area, by the Fiacaill a' Choire Chais and from Coire an Lochain to the west, by the Fiacaill Coire an t-Sneachda (unnamed on the 1:50K map). The corrie is best known for its winter climbing but also has some good rock climbing; not just the classic Magic Crack but also in the lower grades. Improving rock climbs are emerging as winter climbing erodes the turf from the ledges on the buttresses.

Approach: From Aviemore, follow the ski road to the Coire Cas car park. From the top of the car park, take a traversing path south-westwards and soon branch left and uphill on an equally good path, heading for the corrie. The path ends just before a boulder field which surrounds the corrie lochans. Move left and find the easiest route through the boulders (with difficulty) to reach a first aid box just beyond the lochans, 45mins.

There are three main rock masses in the corrie. High on the left is the Mess of Pottage and high on the right is Fiacaill Buttress. The described routes are on the two buttresses forming the central mass of rock. Aladdin's Buttress is situated above and left of the first aid box and Fluted Buttress is over to the right above the Goat Track, the path to the plateau and Coire Domhain.

Aladdin's Buttress

This is the obvious buttress in the centre of the corrie, characterised by some obvious corner-lines. The two main features to aid route location are the big left-facing corner of Doctor's Choice in the centre of the buttress and the wide chimney of Patey's Route near the right side. Between these two are three further corners, the central of which has a long finger crack on the slab to its right.

The Magic Crack   105m   HVS ***
G.S.Strange, M.Ross, J.Wyness, D.Dinwoodie   16 May 1981; Described start: A.Fyffe, M.Bagness   Jul 1984
An excellent route with its unique finger-crack. Climbed by an Aberdeen team, when surprisingly untouched by the locals. Start at a deep left-facing corner by a huge beak of rock.
1. 35m 4b Climb the corner and the broad blunt rib above to a platform and large spike.
2. 25m 5a Climb the rib a short way, then take the thin clean crack on the right. This leads into corners which run up to below the deep central corner.
3. 45m 5a Move right and climb the superb finger-crack. Cross an overlap and climb the cracked wall above to easier ground.

Above and to the right, the rock is more broken but shows three prominent ribs jutting up to the skyline; the right-hand and best defined is Pygmy Ridge. Approach near a wide right-slanting gully at the right end of the lower buttress. Scramble up the rock rib right of this and continue up grass to reach the right end of the upper buttress.

Pygmy Ridge   100m   Difficult **
H.Raeburn, W.A.Gordon, G.H.Almond, A.Roth   1 Apr 1904
The right-hand rib gives an excellent little climb. Start from its base and either climb the crest, better but slightly harder, or a little groove round on the right to join the crest. Continue up the well defined rib, cross a horizontal arete and finish up an upper tower on less good rock.

Fluted Buttress

The section of cliff between Aladdin's Buttress and the lowest point of the corrie rim is Fluted Buttress, cut by many gullies. Towards its right side is Fingers Ridge, with its distinctive two pinnacles high up near the plateau.

Fingers Ridge   140m   Difficult *
D.Bennet   Sep 1954
The slabby rib culminates in two obvious pinnacles (the Fingers). These are obvious from the first aid box but not from immediately below. Two diverging gullies,
the last gullies before the buttress ends, are the best locating feature. Crampon
points have cleaned the rock and the line is excellent, but the upper section is a
huge pile of wedged blocks and the start is a bit messy.
Start on the right side of the ridge, down from the foot of the diverging gullies. Go
up and left over slabs and ledges to a bay near the left edge of the buttress. Go left
and climb a rib overlooking the gully on the left, then take a short wall via a flake
to gain a large right-facing open groove left of some slabs. Climb this groove to a
narrow ridge, follow this past the fingers to a col, then a short wall leads to the top.

Fingers Ridge Direct   130m   VS *
A.Fyffe, M.Bagness   9 Jul 1984
Pleasant climbing on clean slabs, although escapable. Start just right of the normal
route on a section of clean low angled slab at the right side of the buttress base.
1. 35m 4b Climb directly up the pink slabs, cross an awkward bulge close to where
the normal route starts going left and reach an open groove in the centre of the face.
2. 20m 4b Climb the groove, then work up and right by cracks and small ledges
to a stance by the gully on the right.
3. 30m 4c Climb a diagonal crack in two sections to ledges. Climbing right of the
crack at times makes it 4b.
4. 45m 4b Climb thin cracks right of the right-facing corner of the normal route
(artificial) to join the normal route at the start of its narrow ridge.

COIRE AN LOCHAIN

(NH 985 025)   Alt 1100m   North facing   Map p184
This compact corrie lies below Cairn Lochan, the most westerly top of Cairn Gorm.
It consists of four main buttresses separated by obvious gullies. These form an arc
overlooking the corrie's most outstanding feature, the Great Slab; a huge easy
angled slab of pink granite which is visible from a considerable distance.

Approach: Leave the Coire Cas car park as for Coire an t-Sneachda but continue
traversing round Fiacaill a' Choire Chais and cross the burn which comes out of
Sneachda. Take either of two paths which ultimately lead to the lochans at the back
of the corrie. Head right and back left to the foot of the rightmost buttress. For the
first route (Daddy Longlegs), go to the lochans, then head up left to the leftmost
buttress, 1hr 30mins.

Descent: It is possible to climb with sacks and walk off. Abseil descents are possible from many routes (see each route).

The four buttresses are numbered from left to right. The Vent separates No.1 and
No.2 Buttress while the obvious diagonal fault of The Couloir in the centre of the
corrie lies between No.2 and No.3. Between No.3 and No.4 is a large recess
tucked in the corner of the corrie and housing the two branches of Y Gully.

No.1 Buttress

This is the buttress on the left side of the corrie. It has a steep right wall and the
rock has the blocky appearance that characterises this corrie.

Daddy Longlegs   70m   HVS **
G.Shields, B.Hall   25 Aug 1958 (5PA, 6NA); FFA: A.Nisbet, B.Davison   29 Aug 1983
Two good pitches but escape is possible at mid-height. The second ascent freed the
aid at a sensible grade, proving how hard it is to stop aiding once you've started.
Return to the start is down the slopes to the east and walking round under the base
of the buttress. Start up a steep groove on the left wall of The Vent about 15m

below its big chokestone.
1. 35m 5a Climb the groove, step right into a second groove and follow this past an overhang to ledges.
2. 10m Scramble up left.
3. 25m 4c Climb two consecutive vertical cracks in the wall right of a very obvious wide corner crack.

No.3 Buttress

The Vicar   70m   E1 *
G.Shields, S.Wilkinson   25 Jul 1968 (A2); FFA: A.Nisbet, B.Davison   29 Aug 1983
This route is on No.3 Buttress, approached as for No.4 but then traversing to the very steep wall facing it. S.Wilkinson was a vicar. Towards the left (lower end of the wall) is a large recess with a groove at either corner. The route takes a shallow corner and arete on the right wall of the recess, right of the right groove. A magnificent top pitch, but the start is usually slimy. There is usually an abseil point on the last crest before the plateau (50m abseil). Start as for the line of the right groove.
1. 35m 5a Climb a vile overhanging groove, then go up left towards the back of the recess. Under a second overhanging groove, traverse right and mantelshelf on to a ledge with large blocks. Leave the right groove and climb a steep crack to a second ledge directly above the first.
2. 35m 5a Climb the shallow corner directly above the belay, sometimes on the wall just to its left. Move out on to the arete after about 20m and follow this to the top.

No.4 Buttress

This is the largest and most important buttress, on the right side of the corrie. On its left side, it shows a fine steep wall cut by a series of compelling vertical lines of which the large central corner of Savage Slit is unmistakable. It is possible to do more than one of these routes by abseiling from the top of Savage Slit corner (abseil point often in place).

Bulgy   80m   VS 4b *
G.Shields, R.Doig   21 Aug 1968 (1NA); FFA unknown
Climb the left arete of Savage Slit, and finish up a wide crack through the obvious twin roofs.

Savage Slit   70m   Severe ***
R.B.Frere, J.D.Walker   17 Jul 1945
This very fine climb up an impeccable line, takes the wide crack in the big right-angled corner in the centre of the buttress. Better without a rucksack. Start below the corner.
1. 10m Climb the obvious line to below the corner.
2. 20m Climb the wide crack between the blocky walls.
3. 20m Continue in the same crack-line, or the wall on its right, to the top.
4. 20m Finish up a left-slanting gully and a short wall.

Prore   90m   VS *
G.Bradshaw, B.Taplin   5 Jul 1969
This route takes the obvious and spectacular curving arete right of Savage Slit at 4c, after climbing the first pitch of that route and finishing up its last pitch.

Fallout Corner   70m   VS **
T.W.Patey, R.Ford, M.Stewart   17 May 1964 (1PA); FFA unknown
An excellent climb up the impressive corner right of Savage Slit; low in the grade.

Prore, VS 4c. Climber Scott Muir
(photo Cubby Images)

Start below the corner.
1. 10m Go up to below the roof blocking the corner.
2. 30m 4b Cross the roof and climb the corner to its end.
3. 30m Continue in the same line to join Savage Slit, then continue to the plateau.

LOCH AVON BASIN

Loch Avon (pronounced A'an) lies in the heart of the northern Cairngorms, entrenched between Cairn Gorm, Ben Macdui and Beinn Mheadhoin. At its head is the spectacular square topped Shelter Stone Crag, although on the approach the slightly higher and pointed Carn Etchachan is more obvious. Set back to the right beside the approach is the slabby Hell's Lum Crag which runs round to Coire Domhain. East of Coire Domhain is Stag Rocks, closer above the loch. Further along the north-east side of the loch is a line of glaciated slabs just beneath the top of Stac an Fharaidh.

In the rocks below Shelter Stone Crag is the Clach Dhian or Shelter Stone itself, a huge boulder which can provide a good climbing base. It has a cairn on top and a path leading close to it from the Feith Buidhe, the burn running into the head of the loch. Some prefer to camp on good sites at the head of the loch, although day visits are more common.

General Approach: From Aviemore, follow the ski road to the Coire Cas car park. From the top of the car park, take a traversing path south-westwards and soon branch left and uphill on an equally good path, heading for Coire an t-Sneachda. The path ends just before a boulder field which surrounds the corrie lochans. Move left and find the easiest route through the boulders (with difficulty) to reach a first aid box just beyond the lochans. The Goat Track starts here and goes up right to the head of Coire Domhain. From there see individual cliffs.

SHELTER STONE CRAG

(NJ 001 013)   Alt 850m   North-East facing   Map p184   Diagram p192
This big cliff with its distinctive flat top, is one of the most impressive in the Cairngorms. Sometimes known as The Sticil, it thrusts out boldly between the scree filled Castlegates Gully on the left and Pinnacle Gully on the right.

Approach: Descend Coire Domhain and traverse across boulders to the foot of the crag, 2hrs.

Central Slabs

The magnificent and near flawless high angle slabs in the middle of the cliff offer sustained, clean, friction style climbing. They are just too steep to pad (although there are rumours!), so the routes follow obvious corner and crack-lines. The slab system is defined on the left by a big open vegetated corner, on the right by the lower chimney of The Citadel and above and below by the grassy ledge systems of the High Ledge and the Low Ledge. Route lengths are given between these two ledge systems. The Low Ledge is most easily approached from the bottom left (about Difficult).

Descent: From the High Ledge the best descent is by abseil. There are abseil points on the High Ledge above The Run of the Arrow (Cupid's Bow) and below its final flake. Both lead to an abseil point at The Run of the Arrow's hanging belay in the Thor diedre (better at present than the belay of Cupid's Bow 10m higher up). There are also abseil points down The Pin. It is also possible to climb Raeburn's Buttress, to the left, or Sticil Face, to the right, to the plateau. Neither are described here and both are equally exposed and unpleasant.

1 Thor   120m   E5 ***
M.Rennie, G.S.Strange   7 Sep 1968 (A2); FFA: R.Campbell, N.Craig   15 Jul 1989
A stunning route which climbs the eye catching diagonal diedre in the centre of the

slabs, thin and sustained but not too serious for a slabby Cairngorm E5. Start at a left-facing corner system which leads to the foot of the right-facing diedre.
1. 30m 5a Climb the left-trending corner system to an overlap. Cross this and go up to a step right past a loose flake, then reach the main overlap.
2. 20m 5b Traverse right into the main right-facing diedre and climb it to a hanging stance common to Missing Link and Cupid's Bow.
3. 25m 6b Continue up the diedre to gain a sidepull in an alcove (golo and peg); cross this (crux, thin) to belay on pegs on a flake.
4. 45m 6b Continue up the diedre via some hard moves to reach a good horizontal crack and a ring peg above the overlap. Hand-traverse the lip rightwards to good holds (also hard). Follow a weakness right past old rurps and a peg in a pocket into The Pin. Finish up The Pin.

2 The Missing Link   120m   E4 **
D.Cuthbertson, D.Jamieson   1981
This takes a diagonal line right across the slabs; sustained and serious for both climbers on pitch 3. Start at the left-facing corner system as for Thor.
1. 30m 5a Climb the corner system to the main overlap (as for Thor).
2. 20m 5b Traverse right into the main diedre and climb it to the hanging stance (as for Thor).
3. 35m 5c Traverse right and go up to follow a diagonal corner over a small overlap and up its continuation (poor peg runners) to reach a hollow flake. Traverse this to its end and pull into The Pin. Move down The Pin to a thread belay.
4. 35m 5b Finish up The Pin pitch 3.

3 The Run of the Arrow   90m   E6 ***
P.Whillance, T.Furnis   24 Jul 1982
Another excellent route with some bold climbing, taking the faint crack-line in the slab left of Cupid's Bow. An extraordinary on sight attempt by Dougie Dinwoodie had previously reached the crux traverse, retreating from a hammered nut (now gone). These desperate moves were soon solved by Pete Whillance after inspection. Start at the foot of the left-facing corner system leading to the right-facing Thor diedre.
1. 35m 5a Go up easily right for 10m, move left round a rib and follow a crack up to the base of the Thor diedre. Climb this a short way to a belay on pegs.
2. 30m 6b Swing left on to the rib and move up left to a thin crack-line. Follow this and the slab above to reach a small overlap on the right (crucial runners here; Friend 0, RP and a Wallnut 9 sideways). Make extremely delicate moves left from the runners, go up into a scoop, then follow a crack to sloping ledges on the left.
3. 25m 5b Follow the obvious right-slanting line to a junction with Cupid's Bow just below its final flake crack. Finish up this.

4 Cupid's Bow   85m   E5 ****
D.Dinwoodie, R.Renshaw   27 May 1978 (4 PA); FFA: M.Hamilton, R.Anderson   4 Jun 1982
A fine route, direct and central, low in the grade, which takes the bow shaped corner above the upper part of the Thor diedre. Originally climbed by Dougie Dinwoodie on sight without chalk, Friends or sticky boots and using peg runners (four for aid). Freed only four years later by Murray Hamilton and Rab Anderson in the modern style, illustrating a major change in Scottish climbing. Start immediately right of the left-facing corner system of Thor. Climb up rightwards about 5m to belay in a small niche.
1. 40m 5b Gain the grassy bay above and climb out of this via cracks on the left. Move right into a shallow corner and climb this to a pull out on to a rib. Go up and left to the hanging belay below a ledge in the Thor Diedre.
2. 45m 6b Climb the diedre to the ledge on the left at the foot of the 'bow'. Climb this corner with difficulty (peg runner at crux) until it is possible to gain the arete. Go up this to climb an awkward bulging section at the top of the corner, then follow the continuation of the bow to where it curves right. Step left and climb the

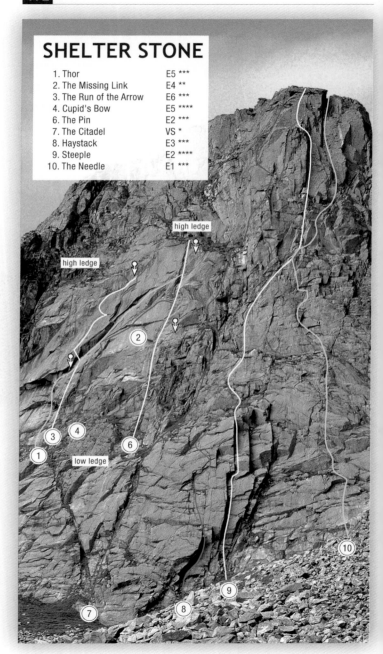

SHELTER STONE

1. Thor — E5 ***
2. The Missing Link — E4 **
3. The Run of the Arrow — E6 ***
4. Cupid's Bow — E5 ****
6. The Pin — E2 ***
7. The Citadel — VS *
8. Haystack — E3 ***
9. Steeple — E2 ****
10. The Needle — E1 ***

high ledge

high ledge

low ledge

steep slabby section to traverse right below the headwall. Finish back left by an obvious but small flake-crack.

Variation: **Direct Start: 5c**

Better but harder. Climb an obvious thin crack up a wall directly into the shallow corner.

Realm of the Senses 105m E7 ***

R.Campbell, G.Latter (pitch 2, original line) 29 Aug 1993; R.Campbell unseconded (L'Elisir d'Amore) 23 Jul 1994; Complete: J.Lines, P.Thorburn 1 Aug 1999

The hardest slab climb in the Cairngorms until Julian Lines climbed Icon of Lust (E8) in 2003. The two main pitches of this route were climbed as individual routes by Rick Campbell, with many attempts and falls, before Julian linked them up, leading both hard pitches to climb the whole route in a day.

1. 30m 5c Start as for Cupid's Bow direct start, but then follow a long right-curving line across the top of the wall on pitch 1 of The Pin to reach its belay.

2. 30m 6c Climb a left-facing corner running up and left with increasing difficulty (RP protection) to the overlap (good protection). Move left on non existent holds past two peg runners to join the Missing Link. Climb this past its two peg runners to gain a standing position on the hollow flakes and place crucial runners above the overlap. Step down before traversing left above the overlap to gain a flake leading to the Thor belay.

3. 45m 6b (L'Elisir d'Amore pitch). Follow Thor by continuing up the diedre to reach a good horizontal crack and a ring peg above the overlap. Hand-traverse the lip rightwards to good holds. Follow a weakness right past old rurps to a peg in a pocket. Leave Thor by making hard moves up left to a hold at the top of a pale streak (crucial Rock 4 in the back of the hold). Move left up a flake to its termination. Make a delicate move left to a good foothold in a red streak. Move precariously up the streak to a line of poor pocket holds that lead leftwards to a rest in a short groove and some poor RPs and a tiny cam. Climb the left wall of the groove to a ledge. Follow holds up and rightwards until they run out at a shield (RP 4). A flake groove is seen on the right; make an awkward move to gain this and continue up it to the top. Scramble up and right to a two peg belay in a short overhanging corner.

Icon of Lust (E8 6c) takes a more direct line through this route, and is probably the hardest slab climb in Britain, involving 25m of 6b with only a doubtful 00 Cam as protection.

The Pin 70m E2 ***

R.Carrington, J.Gardiner Aug1968 (1PA, 1NA); FFA: B.Cambell-Kelly, M.Kosterlitz 1970s

This route takes the striking crack-line near the right margin of the slabs and gives very fine sustained climbing. Climbed the same month as Steeple but a very different style of climbing. Start high on the Low Ledge below the crack.

1. 15m 5b Climb the crack directly up the wall to a stance.

2. 20m 5b Continue up the crack, crossing an awkward bulge, then go slightly right and continue to a good thread belay.

3. 35m 5b Go up and climb an overhanging wall to reach, then follow the continuously interesting crack to the High Ledge.

Main Bastion

The centrepiece of the cliff has some long routes which are generally sustained and strenuous, but well protected, including Steeple, one of the best multi-pitch routes in Britain.

Descent: Follow the cliff-top north-west past Pinnacle Gully and its distinctive Forefinger Pinnacle until close to the Garbh Uisge burn, then descend the last spur before the burn and make a traverse back to the cliff base. It may be worth carrying trainers for the long descent.

7 The Citadel   270m   VS *
R.H.Sellars, G.Annand   Aug 1958 (several aid points); FFA unknown

A traditional Cairngorms classic with some grass but an impressive line for the grade. The lower section starts up the shallow chimney bounding the right side of the Central Slabs; the upper is on the steep nose on the left of the great upper bastion.

Start below the chimney-line. Grassy cracks lead to Low Ledge. Continue up the chimney until overhangs force an exit to ledges on the left. The next pitch is the lower crux. Go up and left on slabs, then make a right traverse to a corner with a crack in the right wall. Move up this, then go right again to gain the slab above and a grassy fault leading to a belay (5a). Traverse right into an open corner, climb this and the corner into which it develops, to gain a ridge. Follow this, then go left to a stance by a huge flake. Next is the upper crux. Hand-traverse left, then climb the crack and chimney system above to a good stance (4c). Continue up the crack above, then traverse right with a step down to ledges. Climb the ensuing right-slanting fault until the left of two short chimneys leads to the plateau.

8 Haystack   280m   E3 ***
R.Carrington, I.Nicolson   1971 (1 PA); FFA unknown

A varied, steep, strenuous and superb route up the nose of the buttress. Start at the toe of the buttress. Low in the grade, with opinions equally divided between E2 and E3.

1. 30m 4c Climb the right-facing corner to below a short corner. (This is often wet and can be avoided by going 5m up the grassy gully as for Steeple).
2. 30m 4b Climb the short corner and exit left on to slabs. Continue up and left to a good grass ledge below a shallow corner.
3. 40m 4c Climb the corner, then move right and cross the overlap above via a prominent crack. Move left, then go up a right-sloping corner to terraces.
4. 40m 4b Follow short walls and grassy ledges left (approximately as for Steeple) to below a steep wall. The ramp pitch of Steeple goes rightwards from above here.
5. 40m 5c Climb the steep line of weakness (as for Steeple) but continue straight up through a slight break, then move right up a ramp (above the Steeple ramp) to a slight recess.
6. 45m 5a Make delicate moves left onto a ledge and climb pleasant cracks left to a break in the arete. Follow a crack, steep initially, to a ledge below an overhanging wall.
7. 30m 5b Climb a spectacular overhanging crack come groove, passing a prominent flake at the start of the difficulties.
8. 25m 5a Move right and climb a short vertical crack in the wall above (common with Steeple), then finish more easily.

9 Steeple   250m   E2 ****
Pitches 1-6 J.Porteous, K.Spence; Pitches 7-9 K.Spence, M.Watson   Aug 1968 (2 NA); FFA: J.Lamb, P.Whillance   May 1975

A truly magnificent route, in many ways the finest on the crag, taking a line connecting the obvious lower and upper corner systems. The rock is immaculate and the climbing very sustained and generally well protected. A contender for Scotland's best route! Start at a right-facing corner rising from the toe of the buttress and from about 5m up a grassy gully on the left of the corner.

1. 30m 5a Climb the corner, crossing a hard overlap (perhaps 5b) to belay above a second one.
2. 25m 5a Continue up the second corner and exit left.
3. 45m 4b Climb by short walls and grassy ledges to below a steep line of weakness which leads to a right-slanting ramp.
4. 35m 5c 'The Ramp' pitch. Climb up the steep line of weakness to reach a smooth slab leading right (Haystack continues up). Climb the slab rightwards

Emma Alsford on the big corner pitch of Steeple, E2 5b
(photo Alan Leary)

(sometimes seeps but still 'goes') to below an overhang, move right with difficulty (not obvious which way is easiest) to gain the ramp (it's still not all over!) and climb this to a belay. A superb pitch.

5. 45m 5a Climb a slabby ramp diagonally right to ledges. Go up the layback groove immediately above, then its continuation and move right to the foot of the impressive corner.

6. 40m 5b 'The Corner'. Climb the corner using a hidden crack to a niche, then continue to ledges on the left. Protection is good, but tiring to place.

7. 30m 5a Above, a thin and surprisingly difficult crack leads to easier cracks and ledges which in turn lead to the top.

10 The Needle 270m E1 ***
R.Smith, D.Agnew 8 Jun 1962

A classic climb, varied and quite strenuous, although not sustained. In 1958 The Citadel was climbed with aid at a mildish VS. Just four years later Robin Smith made a free ascent of The Needle – a big jump in standards. The main feature is the imposing top corner, where a long crack leading to a through route under the final chokestone, appears as a needle and eye when viewed from the lochside. Start directly below the corner about 30m up and right of Steeple.

1. 30m 4b Climb straight up the slab, then step left to a nose at 20m to reach a ledge and block belay.

2. 50m 5b Above are twin zigzag cracks. Gain these from the right and follow them to a steep wall at 40m. (Possible belay on the right side of the ledge below this wall). Climb the steep rib on the right to a stance below a grassy terrace.

3. 25m Cross the terrace and climb a slab until a flake leads left to a huge block.

4. 30m 5b Go up left for 5m, then move right into a flake-crack. Climb this until a narrow ledge leads left to a bulging crack. Follow this crack to a stance.

5. 20m 4c Go up from the left end of the ledge to gain a slabby ramp and climb this diagonally right to ledges (as for Steeple, whose layback cracks are above), then move right.

6. 35m 5a Gain and climb a shallow corner via 'the crack for thin fingers', break out right, then go up and left by blocks and ledges.

7. 20m 4c Go up grooves to the foot of the chimney-crack.

8. 35m 5a Climb this, the Needle Crack, to a ledge.

9. 25m Continue by the line of the chimney to thread a pile of chokestones and emerge on the plateau.

HELL'S LUM CRAG

(NH 995 017)   Alt 920m   South-East facing   Map p184   Diagram p199

The smooth water streaked crag overlooking the head of the Loch Avon basin offers a fine selection of middle grade routes on excellent rock. On the left-hand side, the huge Hell's Lum gully cuts deeply back into the cliff. The gully is most easily seen from the south and gives the crag its name; hell's lum or chimney.

The crag is prone to seepage, particularly from snow patches above the cliff in early summer. August and September are more likely to provide dry conditions, although the detached nature of Grey Buttress means it dries much faster. Once the hillsides have dried out the Main Face can dry quickly, but in wet summers it may never dry.

Approach: Descend Coire Domhain until the ground steepens sharply then cross the stream and find a way down through rocks to cut diagonally under the cliff. Rucksacks can be left above the steepening in Coire Domhain, allowing less of a descent for their collection. 1hrs 30mins.

Main Face

The approach leads to the right end of the face where the first obvious feature is a huge left-facing corner leading up into the watercourse fault near the right end of the cliff. Between this and a curving gully system is an area of fine pink slabs crossed by overlaps. The first two routes climb these slabs.

1 The Devil's Alternative   180m   E1 **
A.Fyffe, R.D.Barton   1 Aug 1981
This direct line on the right of the slabs gives bold and thin slab climbing on excellent rock. RPs useful. Start at shallow cracks on the right side of a lower band of greenish slabs.
1. 45m Climb the cracks to a huge terrace below a big overlap which crosses this whole section of cliff.
2. 45m 5a Twin cracks rise above the right side of the overlap (there is another set near its left end). Gain these from a scoop on their right and follow them to the next overlap (Auld Nick crosses rightwards here). Work left through the overlap on to a glacis.
3. 45m 5a Above is a stepped wall. Zigzag up this to a short left-facing corner, above which moves up and right lead to the next glacis.
4. 45m 5a Climb into a niche in the grey wall above, go left to a horizontal crack, then follow easier ground and a rib to the top.

2 Auld Nick   160m   Severe ***
G.Brown, I.Houston, I.Small   11 Oct 1965
A excellent, open and sustained route. All the pitches can be split. Start on the left side of the greenish lower slab, at an easier crack-line which is sometimes wet.
1. 45m Climb the crack to below the main overlap.
2. 45m Climb a right-facing corner and a crack to the next bulge, go right on a horizontal crack, then move diagonally right.
3. 20m Climb a left-facing corner by a series of steps to below a right tapering roof.
4. 30m Go past the roof on the right and continue leftwards to a big block. Move left past the block to gain the right side of a big ledge. Climb up to another big ledge. Climb the wall above the centre of the second ledge by a thin crack to below a huge grey block.
5. 20m Finish on either side of the big grey block. Scramble to finish.

Left of this section is another left-facing corner system extending high up the cliff and starting from the top of a bay. On the left side of the bay is a turfy diagonal fault leading left on to the main face.

3 Prince of Darkness   150m   E1 **
R.D.Barton, A.Fyffe   10 Aug 1984
This route climbs the first line left of the corner system, involving a prominent right-facing and roofed corner system halfway up the face. It has a particularly fine penultimate pitch. Start by the foot of the turfy diagonal fault.
1. and 2. 70m 4b Climb a thin crack in the green slab and follow cracks and corners to below a prominent red slab.
3. 30m 4c Climb cracks in the big red slab to a good ledge.
4. 20m 5b Work up into a right-facing corner with overlaps, then climb this to a ledge on the left.
5. 30m 4c Return right into the continuation corner and crack, which leads to the top.

4 The Clean Sweep   160m   VS ***
R.Smith, G.Tiso   Sep 1961
A great route up the pink leaning corner overlooking Hellfire Corner. This is not very obvious from the cliff base, but appears as an obvious corner above a big block when reached. Below the start of the diagonal fault is a green whaleback buttress.
1. 30m 4c Go up the corner on the left of the buttress for a short way to gain a groove. Go up the groove to cracks on the crest, which leads to the top of the buttress.

2. 45m 4a Step over the fault and climb slabs and corners to a huge block below the pink corner.

3. 45m 4c Climb the corner and the continuation fault; a superb pitch.

4. 40m 4b Continue by cracks, corners and bulges up the round grey edge above to near the top and a short easy pitch to finish.

5 Hellfire Corner 185m VS **
G.Annand, R.H.Sellers 14 Sep 1958 (1PA); FFA unknown

This excellent route follows the main left-facing corner system in the middle of the face. When fully dry the route may be Hard Severe, but the crux, an inverted V-slot high in the corner is often wet. Start at a prominent crack at the very lowest point of the cliff base, about 20m left of the start of the turfy diagonal fault and 10m left of Clean Sweep.

1. and 2. 60m 4b Climb the crack which runs into a left-facing corner, then go up this to the diagonal fault.

2. 45m 4a Climb the short deep left-facing corner into another corner system, then climb this to below a large overhang.

3. 20m 4b Go up the depression and the continuation corner until an awkward move leads to a platform where this merges with the main corner.

4. 20m 4b Climb the steepening corner, then go through the overlap by airy chimneying moves before moving right to easier ground.

5. 40m Climb the big fault to the top or, better, finish up the right-facing corner left of the big fault.

6 Salamander 155m HVS **
D.Dinwoodie, J.Tweddle 18 Sep 1971

This direct line gives fine climbing on clean water washed rock, but it is very slow to dry. Start below a short but obvious right-facing corner about 10m up the cliff and 30m left of the start of Clean Sweep.

1. 40m 4b Climb into the corner and follow it to a ledge. Continue in the same line to go through a steeper section by a bulging slab to reach a platform.

2. 20m Follow easy rocks to the diagonal fault.

3. 20m 5a Climb twin cracks up steep slabs left of an obvious corner to a platform.

4. 20m 4b Go through the overlap by the short black corner, then follow the crack to the obvious recess.

5. 30m 4b Continue to a shallow groove and follow this to break through the upper overhangs by a striking chimney slit.

6. 25m Continue up the open funnel to easy ground.

Grey Buttress

This clean, compact area of rock lies at least 100m up and left of the lowest point of the cliff between the huge Hell's Lum gully on the left and the left-hand of two narrow chimneys (Deep Cut Chimney) on the right. It is very quick drying because of its detached nature.

Since the middle pitches are the best, an abseil from their top allows the best part of a second route to be climbed. Exorcist and Evil Sprits are easily combined with the abseil point retrieved.

The routes start from a terrace above some broken ground at the base of the cliff. The buttress has at mid-height a near horizontal line of four roofs separated by five corner breaks, the rightmost two breaks being right-trending slabby ramps.

7 Hell's Lump 110m VS **
J.R.Marshall, J.Stenhouse Sep 1961

A good route taking the right-hand ramp. Start at a pink and green slab set between two corners and about 45m right of the Lum.

1. 15m 4a Climb a quartz band up the slab to a large flake.

2. 30m 4c Continue by the groove and crack above for 12m, then move up right

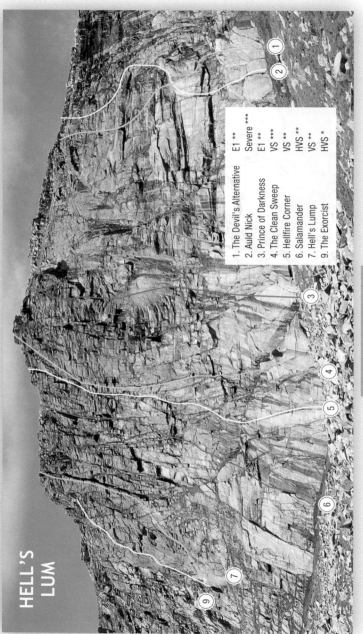

HELL'S
LUM

CAIRNGORMS NORTH

1. The Devil's Alternative   E1 **
2. Auld Nick   Severe ***
3. Prince of Darkness   E1 **
4. The Clean Sweep   VS ***
5. Hellfire Corner   VS **
6. Salamander   HVS **
7. Hell's Lump   VS **
9. The Exorcist   HVS *

and turn the square roof by the crack on the right. Gain a grassy bay, then climb up to the recess above.

3. 25m 4a Climb cracks and corners trending slightly right, then gain the rib adjoining Deep Cut Chimney.

5. 40m 4b Finish up the rib adjoining Deep Cut Chimney.

8 Evil Spirits   110m   E2 *

A.Fyffe, R.D.Barton   26 Jun 1986

This route gives some good climbing up the left-hand ramp, which passes the right end of the biggest roof of the system. Start just right of a right-facing corner which defines the left side of the pink and green slab.

1. 15m 5a Climb green rock just right of the corner to a horizontal crack, go right to a corner, then continue to the large flake.

2. 35m 5c Climb into a deep crack (as for Hell's Lump) and continue directly into the corner above. Climb this to the roof, traverse left, then go up to the next corner which leads to a ledge above the corner of The Exorcist.

3. 15m 5a Go diagonally left, then descend to an obvious overlap and pink rock. Climb diagonally up this to its end and go up to a stance above the crux groove of Good Intentions.

4. 45m Finish as for Good Intentions.

9 The Exorcist   100m   HVS *

A.Liddell, R.Smith   Jun 1975

This route trends right to take the leftmost left-facing corner high in the centre of the face and at the left end of the four roof system. Start at the right-facing corner which defines the left side of the pink and green slab.

1. 20m Climb the corner to grassy ledges.

2. 35m 5a Climb a wide crack in the recess above (close to Good Intentions), then go diagonally right to gain the corner via a shallow groove. Climb the corner, which has a prominent crack in its right wall, to a roof, then break right to a ledge on the rib.

3. 45m Climb the rib above to easy ground.

10 Good Intentions   120m   VS *

W.March, M.McArthur   12 Sep 1969 (1NA); FFA unknown

The main feature of this climb is a slabby ramp leading to an isolated corner on the rounded crest which curves round into the Lum. Very quick drying and with good positions. One very hard move has overhead protection. Start at green rock under the crest.

1. 25m 4a Climb the green rock and over a wedged block to gain the ledge below and right of the ramp.

2. 25m 4c Go diagonally left through a bulging recess to gain the ramp and climb this to the corner.

3. 10m 5b Climb the corner, hard to start, to a ledge.

4. 35m Go diagonally left to a ledge below a wall with a prominent V-groove overlooking the Lum (or climb the arete and traverse left to the groove, 4b).

5. 30m Climb the groove which is capped by blocks.

11 Chariots of Fire   45m   E4 **

J.Lyall, A.Nisbet, J.Preston   4 Aug 1991

A sensational route on the impressive left wall leaning over Hell's Lum gully, with some flaky rock to add to the excitement. The route overhangs all the way but the crux is short and well protected. Start immediately above the main pitch in Hell's Lum gully, best reached by abseil from a 'viewing block' overlooking the gully.

1. 15m 5b Climb out right into a shallow corner, actually a big flake. Follow this briefly, then go right again into another corner and climb this to below a roof.

2. 15m 6a Make a high traverse left on to the overhanging wall, then pull up to good holds (crux). Traverse left to a spike, then go up a line of flakes leading left to a small ledge.

3. 15m 5a Continue up the flakes, then go straight up over the bulge to the viewing block.

STAG ROCKS

(NJ 003 022)   Alt 870m   South facing   Map p184

Stag Rocks is the collective name for the cliffs lying on the south side of Cairn Gorm, between Coire Raibert and Coire Domhain. They look out over the head of Loch Avon and face south towards Loch Etchachan. The rock is rough and quick drying, and climbing may be possible here in the spring when other cliffs are still in winter conditions. Afterthought Arete is the most westerly climb (Coire Domhain end) on the cliff.

Approach: From Coire Domhain make a descending traverse eastwards to find the prominent Y shaped gully (NJ 000 022) at the west end of the crag and descend this to the foot of Afterthought Arete. Alternatively, descend Coire Domhain and traverse round under the cliffs. 1hr 30mins

Afterthought Arete   150m   Moderate * * *
R.H.Sellers, M.Smith   Sep 1956
The best route of its grade in the area, following the left-hand and most regularly shaped arete bounding the right side of the wide Y shaped gully. Start round to the right of the lowest rocks and scramble up left to the crest. Follow the crest fairly closely, with moves a couple of metres on either side at times to avoid unreasonable difficulties, to reach a steep wall towards the top. This can be passed either by a groove on the right or just on the left and keeping nearer to the crest above (perhaps Difficult).

Final Selection   60m   Difficult * *
R.H.Sellers, M.Smith   Nov 1956
An excellent little climb on the last defined arete near the top of Diagonal Gully, the scree filled gully in the middle of the crag. Usually approached from above, often after Afterthought Arete, it is an awkward scramble down on steep grass. The right side of the arete is steep but the route climbs the left side, which is a cracked slab angling into the big right-facing groove. The crux is the very start, especially if damp. Start up the large groove, then break right to the arete. Continue up the edge and cracks on the left of the edge to a platform on the right, just below the level of the obvious overhang. A corner on the right then leads to the top.

STAC AN FHARAIDH

(NJ 014 030)   Alt 890m   South-East facing   Map p184

These cliffs lie on the south flank of Cairn Gorm, overlooking Loch Avon near The Saddle at the head of Strath Nethy. It is an area of glaciated slabs which give largely friction climbs but with overlaps for variety. Typical of granite slabs, there are some bold sections. The slabs themselves are divided into east and west sections by a shallow grassy fault. The west section has much grittier rock and no climbs are described here. As with Hell's Lum, there may be wet streaks until the snow patches above have melted (normally July) but a sunny morning assists drying.

Approach: From Aviemore, follow the ski road to the Coire Cas car park. From the car park, go up Fiacaill a Choire Chais to Pt. 1141. Make a descending traverse round the south-west side of Cairn Gorm and across the spur leading to Pt. 1082 to pick up a stream leading down to Loch Avon. Leave rucksacks and descend by the west bank of the stream; this starts with easy scrambling but can be very wet and slippery, 1hr 30mins.

Whispers   120m   VS * *
J.Cunningham, G.Shields   1969
A pleasant, popular and quick drying route following cracks on the left edge of the

Whispers, VS 4c, Stac an Fharaidh. Climber unknown
(photo Allen Fyffe)

slab. A little vegetation doesn't spoil the route. Start near the left edge of the east section at the second crack from the left.

1. 40m 4a Climb the crack to an easing in the angle.

2. 45m 4b Continue up the same crack system, very close to the left edge at one point, to a huge flake below a steep grey wall.

3. 35m 4c From the top of the flake, traverse about 6m right, then move diagonally right through the bulge on to the slab above. Go diagonally left, then straight up to finish.

The next two routes start near a large boulder at the centre of the base of the crag.

Pushover   130m   HVS **
J.Cunningham and Glenmore Lodge party   1969
John Cunningham picked a bold central line for the first route on the crag. Start at the crack on the left of the large boulder.
1. 45m 4c Climb the sustained and poorly protected crack to below the crescent shaped overlap.
2. 15m 5a Pull onto the overlap and move left until the upper slab can be gained, then move up to a ledge.
3. 35m 4c Trend up and left to a steeper wall, and climb this by a series of cracks to below mossy blocks.
4. 35m 4b Climb over the blocks and go up slabs to a chimney. Finish up the wall above.
Variation: **Alternative Finish**
From the top of the second pitch, climb up and right to surmount a nose of rock by a seam and continue up the slab (45m). Continue up a corner, then move up and go left to the chimney and so to the top.

Pippet Slab   130m   Severe **
J.Cunningham, W.March   14 Jun 1970
A good route but sparsely protected in places. The first 5m are the technical crux. Pitch 3 is slower to dry but the variation dries quickly. Start at the crack on the right of the large boulder.
1. 45m 4b Climb the crack system to below the steep wall.
2. 30m 4a Go diagonally left until a move can be made onto the slab above the wall, cross this, then regain the line of the crack and bear slightly left to below an overlap.
3. 40m Go up the shallow stepped right-facing corner system to a niche in the steeper section.
4. 15m Continue in the same line to the top. It is necessary to continue some way back to find anchors.
Variation: **Direct Variation   VS 4b **
A.Nisbet and party   1987
Superb rock and quick to dry, but with minimal protection. Once above the overlap, climb the smooth slab forming a vague rib left of the normal route.

Linden   50m   Severe *
W.March, L.Rae, S.Matthewson   4 Jun 1970
A good little route, suitable for a second route of the day, which lies high on the right of the slab, taking a ramp-line left of a vegetated chimney. In a large grass bay up on the right is a big shield of rock lying against the slab. Above and right of the shield is a flake-corner with a blunt arete to its right.
1. 25m Follow thin flakes up the blunt arete. A short steep crack leads to a sloping stance.
2. 25m Climb the ramp by the layback crack, then the continuation corner.

BEN MACDUI

Coire Sputan Dearg and Creagan a' Choire Etchachan are on the south side of the Ben Macdui massif in the central Cairngorms. They are more remote, but can also be approached from either Aviemore to the north or Braemar to the south.

COIRE SPUTAN DEARG

(NO 000 988)   Alt 990m   South-East facing   Map p184   Diagram p205
Coire Sputan Dearg lies at the head of Glen Luibeg, high on the south-eastern flank of Ben Macdui. In spring and early summer, its dark buttresses stand out boldly against the old snow and are often clearly visible from as far away as the road

CAIRNGORMS NORTH

between Braemar and Linn of Dee.

'Sputan' is a unique corrie with an open and sunny situation and an unusually friendly atmosphere. The granite is rough, clean, sound and very quick to dry and there is no better place in the Cairngorms for routes at the lower grades. Although the climbs are short (30 to 150m) descents are quick and easy, making it possible to accomplish many routes in one visit. The Hutchison Memorial Hut (see Creagan a' Choire Etchachan below) is the closest reliable shelter for Coire Sputan Dearg. There are one or two draughty 'howffs' amongst the boulders in the corrie which are suitable for dry summer weather and camping is also possible.

Approach from Aviemore: Follow the ski road to the Coire Cas car park. From the top of the car park, take a traversing path south-westwards and soon branch left and uphill on an equally good path, heading for the first aid box in Coire an t-Sneachda. Follow the Goat Track to the head of Coire Domhain. Take a line across the plateau linking flat areas about 1km east of the path to Ben Macdui and cross-ing the Feith Buidhe and Garbh Uisge Beag and Mor burns (difficult navigation) to reach a small lochan at (NO 001 991). This is very close to the top of Glissade Gully, the likely descent. Main Spout, with access to Spider and Terminal Buttresses, is about 300m to the north-east and distinguished by rocks on its far side which are clearly seen from the plateau. 2hrs 30mins.

Approach from Braemar: Park at a new car park (NO 063 898) in the woods near the Linn of Dee. A signposted path leads from here to join a track from the Derry Gates (no vehicle access) to Derry Lodge. Follow the track throughout if using a bike; a worthwhile saving of energy. Then follow the Lairig Ghru track for 3km and fork right up a steeply rising path until some 150m short of the Luibeg burn. Follow the path up the burn. 3hs 30mins on foot, 3hrs by bike (on foot from Derry Lodge).

Grey Man's Crag

The largest and leftmost (looking up) of the main buttresses has some of Sputan's longest and best climbs. The frontal face is split by numerous grooves and narrow slabs which tend to lean left towards the very steep wall on its left side. The first route is left of Grey Man's Crag proper.

1 Crystal Ridge   120m   Difficult **

R.Still, Miss E.J.Lawrence   1 Sep 1948

A grand and popular little climb. As closely as possible, follow the crest of the great slab angling into and bolstering up the upper left flank of Grey Man's Crag. The ridge has a steep left wall.

2 Amethyst Pillar   100m   HVS **

R.J.Archbold, D.M.Nichols   10 Jun 1979; Crux crack: J.McArtney, J.Stenhouse   13 Jul 1964

This direct line gives an excellent steep climb. Start 50m up and left from the end of the cliff base, at the foot of a prominent left-slanting chimney-fault.

1. 40m 4c Move out right to steep slabs, starting about 5m below a curious round niche. Climb up the wall above (a big groove is now 3m to the right). Go left and pull over a bulge into an obvious hanging corner. Step left at a small roof, then go down left and traverse along a flake ledge to its end.

2. 25m 4b Above is a shallow cracked groove with a bulge. Climb the groove and exit right on to a ramp which ascends from a depression in the big groove to the right. Follow the ramp up left to its top.

3. 35m 5b Go up right to an obvious vertical crack above a rock pedestal. Overcome the initial bulge and continue directly up the crack to slabs which lead to the top.

3 Grey Slab   115m   Hard Severe ***

M.Higgins, J.C.Innes, B.T.Lawrie   14 Sep 1963

This excellent route follows a conspicuous corner trending left up the centre of the buttress. Near the top, it climbs the right side of a large slab which gives the route

205

BEN MACDUI - Coire Sputan Dearg

1. Crystal Ridge — Difficult **
2. Amethyst Pillar — HVS **
3. Grey Slab — Hard Severe ***
5. Hanging Dyke — Very Difficult **
6. Snake Ridge — Hard Severe *
7. The Fly — VS 4c *
8. Terminal Wall — Hard Severe *

A. Grey Man's Crag
B. Glissade Gully
C. Main Spout
D. Terminal Buttress

CAIRNGORMS NORTH

its name. Scramble up broken rocks to a good platform 10m below the corner.
1. 10m Climb a shallow depression and move awkwardly right to below the corner.
2. 20m Climb the corner to a grass platform.
3. 40m Continue up the corner to an overhang. Turn this on the left and go up to a ledge (possible belay). Climb by the corner at the right edge of the Grey Slab, until forced to move left at its top.
4. 45m Step down and enter the chimney on the left. It is better (but 4c) to climb a short slab and enter the chimney higher up. Finish up the chimney.

4 Ferlas Mor　125m　Hard Severe **
J.Mothersele, G.S.Strange, D.Stuart, B.T.Lawrie, D.Dinwoodie　22 May 1971
A direct line between Grey Slab and Hanging Dyke. The climbing is as good as Grey Slab and the standard similar, but the line is less prominent. Start as for Grey Slab.
1. 10m Climb Grey Slab, pitch 1. For an independent start, climb the layback corner right of the normal start (5a).
2. 30m Swing up right and climb grooves and ribs on the edge overlooking the Grey Slab to a basalt fault. Climb the fault to a ledge and belay below the crux of Hanging Dyke.
3. 40m Move left and continue up grooves, exiting onto the crest on the right, level with the top of the Grey Slab.
4. 45m Continue to the top on the skyline, via a short easy chimney and an arete.

5 Hanging Dyke　120m　Very Difficult **
A.Parker, J.Young　29 Mar 1949
A popular route following the backbone of the buttress by a geological dyke. Start to the right of the lowest rocks at the foot of a broad slab; the dyke goes up the centre of this slab. Follow the dyke to a small ledge, then climb a grass filled crack to a good stance. Climb a wide slab inclining left by a series of parallel cracks to a sloping corner. The dyke steepens and forms a rib to the left of the groove. Climb the rib for 20m on small holds (crux) until the dyke falls back into a chimney. Follow the continuation of the dyke up left on the crest for a further 30m.

Snake Ridge Area
Glissade Gully is the easy scree gully right (east) of Grey Man's Crag. Snake Ridge is on the section of cliff right of this.

6 Snake Ridge　130m　Hard Severe *
W.D.Brooker, D.A.Sutherland, C.Hutcheon　25 Jun 1949
Right of Glissade Gully are twin ridges. The left ridge is split by a prominent chimney into two sections low down and the right ridge is Snake Ridge. This is one of the original classics of the corrie, with a short crux. Snake Ridge is named for its fancied resemblance, when seen from the top, to a snake head down. For easier recognition, its lower rocks fan out into three ridges giving a fair impression of inverted Prince of Wales feathers. The left side of the ridge is low and angles easily into a grassy gully running alongside. Start on the left feather.
1. and 2. 60m Follow the crest directly to a platform below a step on the ridge.
3. 15m Climb this on the left to a stance on a spike on the right.
4. 25m Go up to a short wall and use good holds to pull into a groove (crux). Continue right up the groove to the crest or, easier, leave the groove and climb to a good hold on the left.
5. 30m Continue to the broken upper buttress.

Spider Buttress
This is the slabby buttress left of the Main Spout, a wide open gully near the right end of the cliff. Its main feature is a steep clean cracked wall above a terrace

Amethyst Pillar, HVS 5b, Coire Sputan Dearg. Climber Stuart Campbell
(photo Chris Cartwright)

and right of overhangs. It is best reached by traversing in from halfway down Main Spout.

7 The Fly   45m   VS 4c *
D.Dinwoodie, B.T.Lawrie   19 Jun 1971
A technical but well protected pitch on fine rock. The object is to reach a prominent S shaped crack high on the steep cracked wall. Start at the base of the wall. Climb a crack up left, then move up right to gain a horizontal crack. Traverse right across the wall and climb easily up left to the deep S-shaped crack. Climb this, then the slab above or the deep flake crack on its left.
Variation: **5a**
Instead of traversing across the wall, climb a finger crack which leads more directly to the S-shaped crack.

Terminal Buttress

The right flank of the Main Spout sports numerous short ribs and walls which diminish in size towards the plateau. Terminal Wall lies on the largest piece of rock at the foot of the Spout.

Descent: A grassy shelf slants down from the final crest of Terminal Wall into the Main Spout.

8 Terminal Wall   70m   Hard Severe *
B.T.Lawrie, J.McArtney   8 Sep 1963
This fine exposed route, high in the grade, ascends a series of cracks and grooves on the left edge of the big wall which forms the base of the buttress. At the left corner of the wall is a short gully. Start just right and round the corner from the gully. Either climb a crack and move right or climb straight up a smooth wall on the right (harder) to reach and go over an overhang on an unusual formation of huge jugs, then go up to a sloping ledge leading right. Go straight up from the end of this ledge and make an awkward move left around a corner. Finish by cracks and blocks just right of the crest, then the crest itself.

9 The Hin'most   80m   VS 4c *
R.J.Archbold, G.S.Strange   20 Jun 1976
On the wall right of Terminal Wall. Climb the first pitch of Terminal Wall to the belay ledge. Make a long rising right traverse following obvious parallel folds. Where the folds almost meet the flanking gully, go up left to the foot of a prominent crack in the centre of the wall. Climb this crack, starting on the wall to its right.

CREAGAN A' CHOIRE ETCHACHAN

(NO 016 997)   Alt 850m to 900m   East facing   Map p184   Diagram p210

This fine crag of mostly slabby granite is situated high on the east facing slopes of Creagan a' Choire Etchachan (1108m, a top of Derry Cairngorm), just a few hundred metres left of the southern path to Ben Macdui. The Hutchison Memorial Hut (NO 024 998) is a simple, open shelter built in 1954 and is ideally located amidst wonderful scenery.

Approach from Aviemore: Follow the ski road to the Coire Cas car park. From the top of the car park, take a traversing path south-westwards and soon branch left and uphill on an equally good path, heading for the first aid box in Coire an t-Sneachda. Follow the Goat Track to the head of Coire Domhain and descend to below the Shelter Stone.

Alternatively from the Coire Cas car park, ascend Fiacaill a' Coire Cas to the plateau. Descend Coire Raibert and follow the path round the head of Loch Avon towards the Shelter Stone. Follow a path over the col between Beinn Mheadhoin and Carn Etchachan to the outflow of Loch Etchachan and descend to the cliff, 3hrs.

Approach from Braemar: Park at a new car park (NO 063 898) in the woods near the Linn of Dee. A signposted path leads from here to join a track from the Derry Gates (no vehicle access) to Derry Lodge. Follow the track throughout if using a bike; a worthwhile saving of energy. About 200m beyond Derry Lodge, turn right at the public telephone, cross a bridge and follow the forest and subsequent road up into Glen Derry. A path branches left from Glen Derry to the Hutchison hut. 3hrs 30mins on foot, 3hs by bike.

The large buttress at the left-hand end of the crag (The Bastion) is bounded by the prominent slabby trench of The Corridor on its right. Talisman is on the right end of this buttress. The middle section of crag has less continuous rock but at the right end is the great sweep of the Crimson Slabs, with the soundest and cleanest rock.

1 The Talisman   100m   Hard Severe ***
W.D.Brooker, K.A.Grassick   24 Jun 1956
An excellent route following the defined right edge of The Bastion on the brink of The Corridor, approaching via a huge slab on The Corridor side. Steep and clean with continuous difficulties, it dries quickly after rain. Start from a platform beside a huge block set against the wall 10m up The Corridor.
1. 35m 4a Climb the crack behind the block to a ledge. Move right and climb straight up until it is possible to traverse left across the huge slab to the crest.
2. 20m 4b Detour left round an overhang and climb a corner to regain the crest. Move left to a groove and go up to a short overhanging corner. Climb the corner to a good stance (crux, maybe 4c).
3. 45m 4a Follow the crest directly, starting on the face overlooking The Corridor. Scramble to the plateau.
Variation: **Direct Start   40m   HVS 5b ***
A.Nisbet, S.Kennedy, N.Mollison   13 Jul 1981
Although not in keeping with the standard of the normal route, this sustained start has a well protected crux and is worthwhile in its own right. The line follows the obvious corner system just left of the arete below Talisman. Start at the lowest rocks. Climb the corner to an overlap (peg runner), then take the continuation corner on the left. Traverse back immediately across a steep wall on good holds to reach the arete which is followed to the stance after the traverse on Talisman.

2 Talking Drums   115m   E2 **
C.MacLean, A.Nisbet   4 Jul 1986
Good sustained climbing with a spectacular finish up the steep Corridor Wall right of The Talisman.
1. 40m 5b The direct start to The Talisman.
2. 25m 4c Take the obvious thin crack leading diagonally right past a triangular block and through the girdling bulge. Move slightly left and go up to a poor belay under the headwall.
3. 25m 5a Gain the base of a shallow groove, the first feature right of the Talisman arete, via two shallow scoops. Climb the groove to its top, then move right and up on hidden holds to a hand-traverse line leading right to a mantelshelf and an in-situ peg belay.
4. 25m 5b Make a delicate move up to gain a small ledge and peg runner, then swing down right and across the wall to the base of a corner-crack. Follow this to finish.

Crimson Slabs

This spectacular sweep of slabs is the finest single feature of the crag and provides some of the best climbing in the area. Continuity of the slabs is broken by two great corners, The Dagger on the right and Djibangi on the left. Away to the right, a steep raking terrace ascends to a platform near the top of The Dagger and provides a useful but loose means of descent for those wishing to avoid the inferior upper tier of slabs. The corners of Djibangi and The Dagger are slow to dry, however their right ribs dry quickly and provide equally good routes.

210

BEN MACDUI
Creagan a' Choire
Etchachan

terrace

3. Scalpel   E1 *
4. Djibangi   VS **
5. Sgian Dubh   HVS **
6. Stiletto   E2 **
7. The Dagger   VS *
8. Scabbard   VS ***

Scalpel 85m E1 *
D.Dinwoodie, G.S.Strange 11 Jul 1977; Direct Finish (as described): A.Nisbet, A.Ross 20 Oct 1985
The very shallow tilted corner in the middle of the slab left of Djibangi gives a fine sustained pitch which is quite bold at the top. Just right of the red chimney which bounds the Crimson Slabs on their left is a curved overlap. Start just right of twin corners leading up to this.
1. 40m 4c Climb the arete overlooking the corners to a ledge. Continue up the edge of the overlap, over a small bulge, then step right to a small ledge below the shallow corner.
2. 45m 5b Continue up the shallow corner to its end at an overlap. Step right to place good runners, then return and make a rising traverse left (crux) to the arete of a curving corner. Go up cracks just right of the arete to progressively easier ground. Go right to join Djibangi and descend via the terrace, or continue to the top.

Djibangi 140m VS **
J.Y.L.Hay, R.Wiseman, A.Cowie 22 Jul 1956 (2PA); FFA: unknown; Last 2 pitches: M.Main, M.George, E.Brown 1963
The left-hand of the two great corners gives the easiest route on the slabs, and the most intriguingly named. The first pitch of Sgian Dubh provides a direct start, better but harder than the normal route. Start at a grassy alcove (containing a recessed right-facing corner) beneath the main corner.
1. 20m Follow a diagonal line up left to a large platform overlooking the red chimney on the left.
2. 25m Trend right and climb a small corner set in the middle of the slabs. Easier climbing now leads to a good stance in the main corner. Pitches 1 and 2 are often combined.
3. 35m 4c Climb the corner directly past an overlap. Exit by pulling out right onto the rib. (It is now possible to follow grassy grooves right to join The Dagger, then to descend the terrace.)
4. and 5. 60m Step back left into the corner and climb it for a short way. Work up left to gain an obvious groove and follow this to a huge block. Climb round the block and continue up a rib to easy ground.

Sgian Dubh 110m HVS **
A.Nisbet, M.Bridges May 1978; First pitch: A.Fyffe, M.D.Y.Mowat, R.Burnett, W.Forbes Oct 1966
The arete right of the Djibangi corner dries quickly after rain. Start at the grassy alcove as for Djibangi.
1. 35m 4c From its left side, follow a series of shallow left-facing corners (the lower continuation of Djibangi corner) to below the main corner.
2. 35m 5a Climb the arete overlooking the corner. It is easier to move away from the arete briefly in the middle section.
3. 40m Follow grassy grooves right to the terrace.

Stiletto 110m E2 **
M.Forbes, M.Rennie 17 Aug 1966 (3PA); FFA: D.Dinwoodie, A.McIvor 1976
One of the hardest routes by the team of Mike Forbes and Mike Rennie, who climbed many of the remaining face lines in the Cairngorms in the late '60s, often using some aid but creating many of today's classics. It gives sustained and technical climbing, but has a well protected crux and is low in the grade. Mid-way between Djibangi and The Dagger, an impressive thin vertical crack splits the slabs.
1. 25m 4b Climb the lower continuation of the crack or the first pitch of The Dagger to below the crack.
2. 40m 5c Climb the crack past two hard sections.
3. 45m Traverse right into The Dagger and follow it easily to the terrace.

The Dagger 130m VS *
T.W.Patey, J.Y.L.Hay 4 Sep 1955 (4PA); FFA: unknown
The right-hand corner gives a classic pitch and is the line of the original route on the

Crimson Slabs; something of a breakthrough at the time. Start in the grassy alcove, as for Djibangi.

1. 25m 4b Traverse right and a little up for 5m. Move back left into a short corner, then go slightly left again to easier ground leading up and right to the base of the corner. An easier alternative is a vegetated line coming in from the right.

2. 35m 4c Climb the corner to a hanging stance on a huge spike below an overhang. A 50m abseil from here reaches the ground.

3. and 4. 70m Avoid the overhang by moving left below a bulge, then regain the grass groove above the bulge and scramble to a large platform below the last slab (the terrace descends from here). Climb the slab by a crack slanting right, then continue straight up to the top.

8 Scabbard 105m VS *
M.Forbes, M.Rennie Sep 1966

A fine exposed route following the rib to the right of The Dagger. It dries very quickly after rain. Start by a clean-cut, right-facing corner directly below the right bounding rib of The Dagger.

1. 20m 4c Climb the corner, then move left to a stance level with the foot of The Dagger corner.

2. 35m 4c Climb an obvious finger-crack, then further cracks to a small overlap. Continue up the edge to the huge spike at the top of The Dagger.

3. 50m 4b Move right, descend a little and pull out right to an edge. Climb a series of cracks and blocks to reach the terrace at its highest point.

BEINN A' BHUIRD

GARBH CHOIRE

(NJ 107 015) Alt 950m North-West to North facing Map p184

The huge massif of Beinn a' Bhuird includes the highest summit of the Eastern Cairngorms. For climbers who seek remote seclusion, there can be few finer places in this country than the lonely Garbh Choire of Beinn a' Bhuird. Hidden on the northern slopes of this complex mountain at the head of Slochd Mor, the corrie reveals its secrets only to the determined few. The inclusion of routes in 'Classic Rock' has guaranteed regular visitors. Although the use of a bicycle now makes a day visit an option, the best experience is to go light and spend two or three days.

Two superb buttresses of clean rough granite are situated at each end of the main face of the corrie: the friendly Squareface high at the east end and the impressive Mitre Ridge at the west end.

Approach: From the A93 Braemar to Aberdeen road, starting from Invercauld Bridge. Leave the main road 100m east of the gates to Invercauld House (signposted Keiloch) and park in a Pay and Display car park on the right (£2 in 2005). Cycling is now recommended and bikes can be taken as far as the top of Glen Slugain. Follow the road, initially tarmac, until just before a farm. Follow a track on the right (signs) and descend to rejoin the original road beyond the farm. Take the second track on the right (signposted Glen Slugain) and follow it through forest and a gate into the glen. A new track going through Glen Slugain becomes a good stalkers path at the ruined Slugain Lodge and arrives in Glen Quoich.

Keep to the path past a huge boulder called Clach a' Chleirich to the Sneck (col) between Ben Avon and Cnap a' Chleirich, then contour left avoiding rock ribs by descending. About 4hrs (including the cycle). There may be restrictions during the stalking season (see Environment notes).

Descent: It is common to climb with sacks and walk off. But if approaching over

The Dagger, VS 4c, Creagan a' Choire Etchachan
(photo Niall Ritchie)

the top and leaving sacks, descend at the back of the corrie, which is north of Mitre Ridge. For Squareface Buttress, which is often approached from the plateau, make a grassy scramble down in front of the route. The continuation of this line goes down to the corrie floor, so this is the approach from below.

Squareface Buttress

Going westwards from the Sneck, a series of ill-defined ribs and buttresses lead up to the steep north face where the rock is appalling, crumbling and vegetated. The name Squareface is derived from the 100m rectangular west face which overlooks a large grassy amphitheatre, the High Bay. The route Squareface lies on this slabby west face and is well seen from the plateau. Routes on this buttress can therefore make a convenient second route.

Squareface   90m   Very Difficult ***
T.W.Patey, J.M.Taylor   Jul 1953
This little gem of a route combines continuously exposed climbing with impressive situations and is remarkable for its low technical standard. The face dries quickly after rain. The left side of this face is a stepped arete bordering the north face. Start just round the crest of the arete.
1. 40m Climb cracks and grooves to a large platform, then follow the arete to below an overhang.
2. 25m Launch out on to the wall by a 10m traverse, past the first obvious vertical crack, then climb straight up and return left to a platform on the edge.
3. 25m Return to the face and follow cracks up right for 10m to a short horizontal crack. Just to the right a deep fissure cleaves the final section. Either climb the fissure (Severe), or layback a flake on the right for 4m, then leave it for a shelf on the right, thence gain the top by an awkward traverse.

Angel's Edgeway   70m   VS *
W.B.Gault, A.Kane   Aug 1959; As described: B.S.Findlay, G.S.Stange, 17 Jun 1989
Fine exposed situations but arguably just variations on Squareface.
1. 30m 4a A vertical crack leads directly to the stance below the overhang at the top of pitch 1 of Squareface. Climb slabs left of the corner formed by the crack. Where these steepen, move right and follow the crack through a bulge to belay on Squareface.
2. 15m 4b Climb close to the edge and belay on the platform (as for Squareface).
3. 25m 4a Follow Squareface to the short horizontal crack. Move left and layback a hollow flake to the top.

Mitre Ridge

This is one of the finest pieces of rock architecture in the Cairngorms. It thrusts out boldly between its gullies, 200m from the scree to the plateau in two walls meeting at an acute angle and topped by three towers.

Mitre Ridge   220m   Hard Severe *
E.A.M.Wedderburn, P.D.Baird, E.J.A.Leslie   4 Jul 1933
One of the great classic ridges of the Cairngorms. Although there is some vegetation and a little loose rock, it is a fine natural line with rewarding situations. After the first pitch (avoidable up on the right), the climbing is not more than Very Difficult.
The first pitch takes the big groove set mid-way between the lowest rocks and the right corner of the ridge. Start up slabs and follow the corner directly to a short bulging wall. Climb the wall in the corner to a small stance (35m). Follow the general line of a rising shelf to below a deep-cut chimney on the west face. Climb the chimney and enter a shallow gully which leads to a shoulder on the ridge. A short wall blocks progress. Make a delicate traverse right, then go straight up to the steep

wall below the First Tower (30m).
Above and to the left is a large grass platform which may be gained directly by a short inset right-angled corner or, slightly easier, by moving left across a slab and climbing a splintered chimney. Climb the wall above the platform and ascend right to the col between the two towers. The Second Tower can be passed on the left but much better is to follow a shelf to the right-hand corner and climb a very exposed crack on the west face. Step back left from the crack and finish straight up. Finish along a narrow horizontal arete over the final tower.

The west wall of Mitre Ridge is very steep and impressive, but with more holds than expected. Two obvious corner gully systems run up either side of a 100m subsidiary cuneiform shaped buttress which stands out from the wall of the ridge above the First Tower. Cumming-Crofton Route follows the left-hand corner to the arete between the First and Second Towers.

Cumming-Crofton Route   165m   Severe **
M.S.Cumming, J.W.Crofton   4 Jul 1933
This steep and sustained climb is the most outstanding pre-war route in the Cairngorms, climbed on the same day as the long sought after Mitre Ridge. Start directly below the corner.
1. 30m Go straight up to a small platform, then climb the prominent chimney, which has a hanging flake forming a constriction at mid-height, to a stance in a cleft at the top.
2. 15m Traverse right for 10m via a short smooth groove. When stopped by a vertical wall, return left by an airy traverse across a wall and over a bulge into the main corner.
3. 25m The general line is now up the corner. Climb the wall just to the right of the corner for 5m, then step left into the corner-crack and climb to a broad platform.
4. 30m Climb a crack in the left wall, then traverse right and follow a sloping ledge to a short wall. Pursuing the same line, follow a loose gully to the ridge between the First and Second Towers.
5. and 6. 65m As for Mitre Ridge, climbing the Second Tower on the right.

Right of the right-hand corner is a very steep wall with a prominent roof system at 30m.

Slochd Wall   110m   HVS **
M.Rennie, G.S.Strange   31 Aug 1969 (mostly aid); FFA: B.T.Lawrie, A.Nisbet   3 Jul 1979; Described finish: R.J.Archbold, H.Towler, D.J.Wallace   31 Jul 1982
This superb route follows the large vertical corner leading up from the left end of the roof system and offers technically interesting climbing on steep rock with surprising holds. Higher up, the corner diverges into two corners providing the left-hand and right-hand (original) finishes. Although both finishes are good, the left-hand finish makes a more sustained route. Start at the foot of the gully which bounds the face on the right.
1. 15m Climb the gully to the first depression and traverse on to the wall via a grass shelf to gain an obvious stance.
2. 30m 5a Follow a crack rightwards and climb a steep slab trending slightly left alongside a small corner (old bolt runner) to a big overhang. Swing right under the overhang into a shallow corner and climb this (crux) into the main corner.
3. 15m 4c The original route continues up the main corner (5a), but it is better to traverse left to enter and follow another corner until it is possible to step right to a large ledge.
4. 20m 5a Climb the rib at the left end of the ledge for a short way, then swing left to regain the corner. Go straight up, turn the overhang on the left, then move diagonally left to the arete; belay a little higher.
5. 30m Continue up the edge and finish by a final crack.

CAIRNGORMS SOUTH

The smaller group of hills south of Braemar, Ballater and the valley of the River Dee is dominated by Lochnagar, although the biggest and best cliff, Creag an Dubh Loch, is not on Lochnagar itself. All the cliffs in this chapter are granite and the climbing style is similar to that in Cairngorms North. Statistically, the climate is drier than the western highlands, but the altitude, along with remnants of snow from the winter, means that mid-June to mid-September is the main rock climbing season. Also included in this chapter are the roadside crags at the Pass of Ballater and the Glen Clova crags on the southern flanks of the group, due north of Dundee.

Maps: OS L44, E388, Harvey Superwalker Lochnagar and Glen Shee

SMC Climbers' Guide: *The Cairngorms Vol. 2* (1995); *The Cairngorms* (projected 2006)

Public Transport: There are many buses from Aberdeen to Ballater, but nothing up Glen Muick.

Amenities: For Glen Clova, see that section. The nearest town to Lochnagar and Creag an Dubh Loch is Ballater, which has hotels, shops, a campsite and petrol.
Camping: There is a campsite in Ballater (NO 370 953) but camping is not allowed in Glen Muick; wild camping near the cliffs is allowed.
SYHA Youth Hostels: None in Ballater. Braemar (NO 149 914), (0870 004 1105), Inverey (NO 077 896), (0870 004 1126)
Independent Hostels: None in Ballater. Braemar Lodge Bunkhouse (01339 741627), Rucksacks Braemar (01339 741517).
Climbing Shops: Braemar Mountain Sports (01339 741 242).

LOCHNAGAR

(NO 252 858)   Alt 880m   North to East facing

Lochnagar is one of Scotland's most famous mountains. A clear view of its north-east corrie and the semi circle of cliffs round the loch, as seen both from lower Deeside and from the north approach over the Lecht, has inspired both writers and climbers. Lochnagar's infamy attributed to its vegetation and loose rock is not altogether unfounded. But once on to the steeper ground and away from the ledges, the rock is sound and although mossy in places, there are fine features which give natural lines. The general north-east aspect and vegetated ledges means the climbs are quite slow to dry (apart from Eagle Ridge) despite the east coast climate, but in dry weather the atmosphere of the corrie makes it a special place to climb.

Approach: The car park at Spittal of Glen Muick (fee) is accessed from Ballater and gives unhindered access at all times, even during the stalking season. From the car park, walk through the wood past the visitor centre, turn immediately right (signpost) and follow a private unsurfaced road across the River Muick to a T-junction beside an outbuilding of Allt-na-giubhsaich Lodge. A path follows a fence westwards from this outbuilding. Take this path which leads through pine trees to join a landrover track. This is followed all too obviously out of the pines and up the open hillside to the Muick-Gelder col. Branch off left from the track on a well marked path to the col between Meikle Pap and Cuidhe Crom. Follow a rough path descending leftwards into the corrie. Follow this path to reach the First Aid Box, situated on a platform below the screes under the cliffs. About 2hrs 30mins.

Descent: Quickest is by the main (right) branch of The Black Spout.

The most obvious feature is the wide and boulder filled Black Spout gully on the right, heading towards the summit of the mountain. The Black Spout Pinnacle is left of it, the actual pinnacle being small and very high up. Left of here is the partly

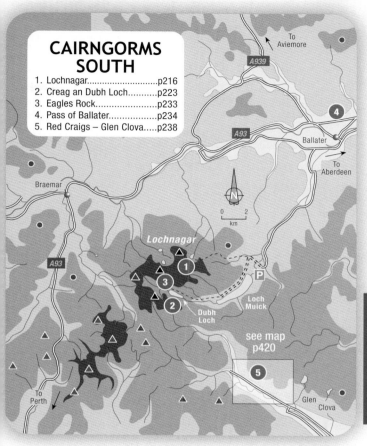

To Aviemore

A939

A93

Ballater

To Aberdeen

Braemar

A93

N

0 ... 2
km

Lochnagar

1

3

2

Dubh Loch

Loch Muick

P

see map p420

5

To Perth

Glen Clova

CAIRNGORMS SOUTH

hidden Raeburn's Gully, before reaching the smooth Tough-Brown Face, easily distinguished by a huge rockfall scar on its left side. Continuing left is the deep Douglas-Gibson Gully, the second largest gully in the corrie and sometimes snow filled into July. Overlooking Douglas-Gibson Gully on the right is Eagle Ridge.

Eagle Ridge   200m   Severe ★★★★
J.H.B.Bell, Miss N.Forsyth   Jul 1941 (1PA); FFA: (probably) S.Thompson, Mrs Thompson Jul 1944, (or) W.D.Brooker, D.Sutherland   1949
The narrow soaring crest gives one of the finest climbs in the country, and very popular. One of Bell's great routes, which proved there was some good rock on Lochnagar. There are several hard sections but they are well protected with good holds or cracks. The ridge dries quickly after rain. The longer pitches can be split. Start just inside the screes of Douglas-Gibson Gully.
1. 50m 4a Climb an obvious 20m groove, the lowest on the right wall of the gully. Easier climbing follows up a shallow gully and an awkward short chimney leading towards the grassy face on the right.

2. 50m 4a Head back left towards the crest by a groove, then by its right rib before moving right to a corner which leads to the crest.

3. 15m 4a Here the ridge steepens in a rugged tower. Climb the crest, then its steep right edge on huge holds before moving left to a splendid sentry box. A fantastic pitch.

4. 30m Climb the crest over the 'Whaleback', then just right of the crest to the base of a corner.

5. 10m 4a Climb the corner, the top of which ends in an airy knife edge forming the crest. The vertical wall against which the knife edge abuts is traditionally the crux. Climb it by a crack on the left to reach another level arete with a ledge on the right

6. 45m 4b Climb the crest to another wall and stay on the crest by going left on to a small concave slab. Climb this and steep blocks leading to a high step into a groove, crux. A Friend 4 protects this well, but it is possible to avoid this by easier ground to the right. Go left and up easy slabs to finish.

BLACK SPOUT PINNACLE

Diagram p221

The Pinnacle's lower slabs form an apron of continuous rock which stretches upwards for about 100m until the angle eases and the rock becomes broken and vegetated toward the summit of The Pinnacle. Moving up right into the Black Spout, the slabs become progressively steeper and merge with the very steep Black Spout Wall, roughly triangular shaped with Black Spout at its base and the two sides formed by the limits of the steep rock.

Climbs started on the lower slabs reach The Springboard, a large platform of vegetated ledges about 35m above Black Spout. The routes can finish here at an in-situ abseil point (sling and nuts, which may need replacing) leading back into the Black Spout; so several routes can be climbed in a day. Alternatively, finish up The Link (described below).

2 Pinnacle Face 95m VS *
J.Smith, J.Dennis 4 Sep 1955

A classic route with some fine climbing and a little vegetation, following a not too obvious line covering a fair area of the impressive lower slabs. Climbed the same day as The Dagger (Creagan a' Choire Etchachan) and a similar breakthrough onto one of the Cairngorm's intimidating smooth faces. Start low down on the left wall of the Black Spout, where steep walls turn into steep slabs at a rib with grooves either side, the right groove being a well defined sharp V starting 5m up.

1. 35m 4b Climb the shallow left groove, starting as an awkward wall, to reach a short chimney at 20m. Continue via the chimney, then by cracks trending left.

2. 25m 4b Climb a short distance to a corner and pull onto the right-hand slab. Work left up a slabby fault to a large grass stance.

3. 25m 4b Continue left a short distance, crossing an obvious fault, to twin cracks. Climb either crack, finishing at the top of the right-hand crack. Continue up the right-hand crack, then traverse right on flakes to a niche.

4. 10m 4b Climb the steep corner above to a ledge. From here, an easy traverse right on grass ledges leads to a descent to The Springboard.

3 Pinnacle Grooves 70m VS **
R.J.Archbold, G.S.Strange 29 Jun 1975

Good well protected climbing, following a prominent corner-groove which lies directly above the well defined V-groove.

1. 30m 5a Climb the prominent V shaped right-hand groove. At its top, move right up a ramp to its top. Layback up the left side of a flake to step into the main groove

Eagle Ridge, Severe 4b, Lochnagar. Climber Alison Rothwell
(photo Andy Tibbs)

on the left. Climb the groove to a step left.

2. 15m 5a Continue up the groove to a grass ledge on the right.

3. 25m Step left, then go up for about 10m until a series of grass ledges leads right to easy ground just above and left of The Springboard.

4 The Nihilist   45m   E1 *
B.T.Lawrie, D.Innes   Aug 1976

This good route packs a lot of climbing into its short length. Where The Black Spout narrows, a smooth vertical wall lies directly below The Springboard. The climb follows a diagonal line up rightwards close to the left edge of the smooth wall, then ascends the prominent twin grooves above to The Springboard. Start 12m right of the V-groove of Pinnacle Grooves, immediately left of the smooth wall.

1. 25m 5b Climb to obvious holds and make a difficult move left before swinging up to a large ledge. (Or go up a V-groove with a flat bottom just to the right – harder). From a higher ledge, gain a steep narrow slab with a bulging wall above then traverse right to a possible mantelshelf ledge. Ignore it and continue right eventually to gain the main groove and descend a little to a belay.

2. 20m 5a Make a long stretch to steep cracks above an obvious hooded overhang. Relatively easy climbing now leads up right to a hard exit by a wide crack to The Springboard.

5 The Link   120m   VS
K.A.Grassick, W.D.Brooker   16 Jun 1956: Direct finish (as described): G.Muhlemann, G.S.Strange   29 Jun 1974

This traditional continuation to Pinnacle Face is a little mucky in places. Initially it follows the furthest right of three faults above The Springboard, then takes a line of grooves and cracks to finish left of the summit crest. Start at the top of The Springboard in the rightmost fault.

1. 20m Enter a V-groove by a short awkward right traverse. Climb the groove to a stance on the rib on the right.

2. 30m 4c Make a few moves up the rib, then step back into the groove and climb it to below a prominent triangular overhang. Move up and right round a huge block to a small recess under an overhang. Climb the overhang, then follow a good crack slightly right to behind another huge block.

3. 35m 4c A big vegetated groove slants left and a prominent crack continues right. Follow the crack, and near its top move out left. Go awkwardly left to a steep groove and climb this to a large overhang. Pass this on the right using a sometimes rotating block.

4. 35m 5a Escape is possible by swinging up and traversing left between two overhangs, but it is better to climb the overhang above by good cracks.

Variation: **Independent Start to The Springboard**

Either up a corner bounding the right side of the smooth vertical wall (4c) or a ramp with overlaps but good cracks a little higher up Black Spout (4a).

6 Black Spout Wall   170m   E3 ***
D.Dinwoodie, R.A.Smith   8/10 Aug 1976 (2PA); FFA: B.T.Lawrie, N.Morrison   Sep 1983

A atmospheric route which climbs the formidable wall to the right of the previous routes (ie. further up the Black Spout) and finishes by cracks in the steep upper gable wall. There is a great overhung recess in the middle of the wall and the route follows the obvious crack-line in the pillar to the left.

1. 40m 5c Traverse along a small ledge to a deep crack and climb this to a block at 15m. Climb the bulge above and continue up a smooth dwindling groove to cracks (protection and a big in-situ peg, seen from the base). Descend to the lip of the overhang and swing left into the scoop at the base of a ramp. Climb the ramp and the overhang at its top to reach better holds. Go down diagonally right to a ledge and peg belay directly above the initial cracks; a great pitch.

2. 30m 5c Climb into and go up the corner above, climb a bulge into the groove above, then climb this to exit out left to ledges close to The Link. This pitch is a

LOCHNAGAR
Black Spout
Pinnacle

4. The Nihilist	E1 *	
5. The Link	VS	
6. Black Spout Wall	E3 ***	
2. Pinnacle Face	VS *	
3. Pinnacle Grooves	VS **	
A. The Springboard		

bit mossy.
3. 40m Climb out and up right by slabby shelves to gain the arete above the great overhangs. Climb this to the little ridge at the top of a chimney-crack which comes up from the right.
4. 25m 5c To the left is the 'inhospitable crack', which goes left, and directly above is a forking crack system. Climb the long right fork to the apex of the wall.
5. 35m Climb the crest to the top of The Pinnacle.

CREAG AN DUBH LOCH
Central Slabs

1. Dinosaur/Pink Elephant   HVS **
2. The Blue Max   E1 **
3. Cyclops   HVS ****
5. Black Mamba   VS ***

A. Crescent Groove
B. Quartz Corner

The Terrace

CREAG AN DUBH LOCH

(NO 235 825)   Alt 730m   North-East facing   Map p217

This huge precipice more than a kilometre wide and 300m high overlooks the Dubh Loch, an upper loch feeding Loch Muick, set in the high secluded valley between the extensive White Mounth plateau to the north and the cone topped plateau of Broad Cairn to the south.

The rock is a very sound grey or pink granite typified by a roof tile formation of colossal glaciated slabs. Progress is generally dependent on well defined crack-lines with tenuous slabby linkages where these fade out. The cliff will not dry while there is snow along the plateau rim, so spring is not the best time to visit, unless the winter has been mild or dry. Once dry, individual days of rain will have little effect but longer periods will require several days of dry weather, although some of the steeper routes dry faster. The cliff catches the sun until about mid-day, so an early start is worth the effort. There is little worthwhile climbing below VS, but the VS plus climber will find many routes of outstanding quality, on one of the finest cliffs in Britain.

In summer it is possible to camp at the Dubh Loch; the best site is by the beach at the far end of the loch, nearest the cliff. There is also a fine howff for two in the boulders under the Central Slabs.

Approach: The car park at Spittal of Glen Muick (£2 in 2004) is accessed from Ballater and gives unhindered access at all times, even during the stalking season. From the car park, follow the track straight ahead, heading towards the south shore of Loch Muick. Just before the loch gain a small path on the right, go over the river and cross to the track running along the north shore which is followed to Glas-Allt-Shiel. Continue up the pleasant birch strewn valley on a good path which ascends beside the Allt an Dubh Loch. The Dubh Loch has small paths on either side but the south side is definitely quicker for the Central Slabs; 2hs 30mins. A bicycle is highly recommended. Turn right past the visitor centre then left along the north shore of Loch Muick and leave it just beyond the end of the wood; about 2hrs.

Descent: Central Gully is the usual descent but requires care as it is quite loose and can contain snow early in the summer.

CENTRAL SLABS

This huge sweep of granite in the centre of the cliff presents over 300m of cracked and overlapping slabs. The angle is just too steep for friction climbing, so the routes must follow natural lines. Nevertheless, the style is delicate and enjoyable, with the overlaps providing variety. The continuity of the climbs is broken by a terrace system at mid-height, effectively dividing the routes into two distinct halves. Routes are interchangeable at this point and it is possible to traverse off right to the Moderate but very grassy buttress situated near Central Gully. This escape makes the slab climbs less serious than the more committing routes on Central Gully Wall.

Route finding above The Terrace is more difficult than on the lower slabs. The key features to find the continuation starts above The Terrace are the big corner of Pink Elephant which is in line with the lower section and the crescent-shaped groove of Cyclops which is well to its right. The upper pitches are slow to dry, particularly in early summer after a snowy winter.

◀ **Dinosaur – Pink Elephant   320m   HVS ＊＊**
J.W.Stenhouse, B.T.Lawrie   25 Jul 1964 (Dinosaur); J.Grieve, A.Fyffe   14th Jun 1969 (Pink Elephant)
The lower part of Dinosaur (the first route to tackle these intimidating slabs) and the upper section of Pink Elephant provides the best route on the left side of the main slabs; unfortunately the big upper groove (crux) is slow to dry. Start at the lowest rocks.

1. 25m Climb broken cracks to a grass rake. Alternatively, scramble up the rake from right to left.
2. 40m 4b Follow the main crack system above (5m left of a thinner crack) to a stance 5m below the long lower overlap.
3. 40m 4c Surmount the overlap above and go up the slab over an awkward bulge. Go up slightly higher and follow a toe traverse left (it is a mistake to go too high here). Step up left, then go slightly down left into the obvious shallow corner. Climb this using the left rib to the top of a big flake.
4. and 5. 80m 4c Dinosaur now goes left into Dinosaur Gully and finishes up the grassier edge left of the upper slabs. Instead, switch to Pink Elephant and go up to a grassy niche and climb the bulging corner above. Break right over the big left-slanting overlap to reach slabs, then follow the obvious line up into Dinosaur Gully and follow its right branch to The Terrace.
5. 20m 4b There is an obvious central corner; climb this to under bulges.
6. 45m 4b Continue up grooves above, go through the overhang by a short bulging slot and continue up slabs.
7. 25m 5a Climb a tapering slab leading up left to the right end of a big grass ledge below the upper overhangs. Traverse right to a slabby knife edge, then drop into the big upper groove.
8. 45m 5a Climb the groove, negotiating a steep step by the left wall, then regain the groove. Finish up the groove or the rocks on the left.

2 The Blue Max   305m   E1 **

B.W.Robertson, A.Fyffe, W.T.Wilkinson   16-17 Sep 1967 (various aid points); FFA: J.Fraser and party   May 1975

This route gives very fine and sustained climbing, but the crux section is not the natural line. It breaks through the main overlap, some 70m up, at an obvious gap with a rockfall scar. Scramble up the grass rake to a large block.
1. 40m 5a Climb the crack-line straight above the block over a difficult bulge. Continue up cracks and move right into a long corner.
2. 35m 5a Climb the corner to small ledges and go up to make a thin traverse right over a smooth slab to a stance under the main overlap (junction with Cyclops).
3. 25m 4c Ascend beside the rockfall scar (loose) and traverse right below the overlap, then go up cracks to belay below the next overlap.
4. 40m 5b Traverse left to a huge diamond shaped block in the overlap. Climb the block by its right side to the upper bulge, step right and go over the bulge by a crack which twists back into the groove. Continue up the groove to belay on the rib; a superb well protected pitch.
5. 40m Continue up the rib, then go straight up the succeeding crack and corner to a roof. Turn the roof on the right by cracks leading to a small ledge. Go up walls on the left for 10m to a good ledge. Now scramble up turfy ledges and short walls to smaller grassy ledges (The Terrace) below a short off-width groove leading to a larger crescent-shaped groove, (not obvious from below), on the right edge of the upper slabs – the line of Cyclops.
6. 40m 4c Turn the crescent shaped groove of Cyclops on the right by a smaller groove (or a wide V-groove round the right edge) to a union below short twin grooves. Climb the left-hand groove and continue slightly left by the short cleft of Cyclops to a ledge (possible belay). Climb cleaned cracks up and left to a grass ledge (junction with Black Mamba).
7. 40m 4c Gain the slab above and cross it left to the short Quartz Corner (actually pegmatite). When the corner becomes vegetated, exit onto its right rib and climb this to below grassy grooves.
8. 45m 4b Climb the grooves, moving onto their right wall towards the top to reach broken ground.

3 Cyclops   290m   HVS ****

G.S.Strange, M.Freeman   19 May 1973

This fine direct route takes a straight line of cracks up the lower slabs. On the upper slabs the route gains a crescent-shaped groove on the right edge of the slabs. The groove is obvious from afar, but not easily identified from directly below. It is strange that the cleanest and most direct of the lines was climbed last. Start at the top of a tongue of slab encircled by a ring of grass, which lies at the foot of the grass rake of Dinosaur.

1. 30m 5a Climb the left-hand of twin parallel cracks right of a brown corner to pull onto a hanging flake from the right side. Go up the edge to under a small overlap.

2. 40m 4c Climb the bulge above, then follow the obvious crack to a scoop with a constricted groove above. Climb the groove over a grass plug and continue to a stance under the main overlap.

3. 30m 4c Ascend beside the rockfall scar (loose) and traverse right below the overlap to gain a crack-line and follow it through the next overlap to a grassy ledge.

4. 40m 4c Continue up the wide crack-line to where it steepens in the pink waterwashed rock above. Climb the fine cracks direct to turfy ground.

5. 20m Go left up turfy ledges, then directly up short walls to smaller grassy ledges (The Terrace) below a short, steep off-width groove leading to a larger crescent-shaped groove on the right edge of the upper slabs.

6. 45m 5a Climb the awkward off-width groove (technical crux) and the crescent groove above to its top (junction with Blue Max). Go left by a short cleft to a ledge (possible belay). Climb cleaned cracks (junction with Black Mamba) up and left to a grass ledge.

7. 40m 4c Gain the slab above and cross it left to the short Quartz Corner. When the corner becomes vegetated, exit onto its right rib and climb this to below grassy grooves.

8. 45m 4b Climb the grooves, moving onto their right wall towards the top to reach broken ground.

4 Slithy Tove 65m E3 *
D.Dinwoodie, D.Hawthorn 1 Jul 1986

An eliminate between Cyclops and Black Mamba, without an independent finish; either abseil from a peg on Black Mamba or continue up, The Blue Max being the nearest in grade. Sometimes climbed as a second route of the day. The 6a traverse is fairly safe, whereas the start of pitch 2 is very poorly protected.

1. 25m 6a Climb the right-hand twin of the Cyclops crack for about 10m, then make a thin traverse right from the last runners and go up to a big hold. Continue up a crack-line to a ledge close to Black Mamba.

2. 40m 5a Climb the crack above and slightly left into a corner. Move out left and pull up a bulge to gain a deep curving crack. Climb this and the bulge at the top, then continue easily to Black Mamba.

5 Black Mamba 320m VS ***
A.Fyffe, J.Grieve 7 Jun 1969

The traditional route of the slabs, the first of five new routes by this team in a week. To the right of the grass ring of Cyclops is a grass ledge 15m up the slabs. Start from a grass base at a low point in the slabs.

1. 15m 4c Climb a delicate shallow crack-line to reach the left end of the grass ledge (technical crux).

2. 45m 4b Climb directly up the crack system above to gain a long corner. Climb this and pull out left to a stance under the main overlap.

3. and 4. 90m 4b Climb the overlap using the cracked groove on the right and follow cracks to ledges. Step round a big flake and go up cracked slabs to a shallow gully containing a large pointed block. Continue up easy slabs leftwards to turfy ground.

5. 20m Go left up turfy ledges, then directly up short walls to smaller grassy ledges (The Terrace) below a short off-width groove leading to a larger crescent-shaped groove, (not obvious from below), on the right edge of the upper slabs – the line of Cyclops.

6. 40m 4b Climb up and diagonally left under small bulges left of the crescent-shaped groove to gain a pink rib and slabs close to Pink Elephant.

7. 25m 4b Traverse back right to join the cleaned cracks of Cyclops and The Blue Max and follow them left to a grass ledge.

8. 40m 4c Gain the slab above and cross it left to the short Quartz Corner. When the corner becomes vegetated, exit onto its right rib and climb this to below grassy grooves.
9. 45m 4b Climb the grooves, moving onto their right wall towards the top to reach broken ground.

CENTRAL GULLY WALL

Diagram p228
This is the great convex face forming the right side of Central Gully. There are two major facets, the 250m frontal slab face with its big raking crack-lines and the shorter but steep wall impending over the gully. At the bend in the face between the two facets is a transitional zone, a maze of roofs and hanging slabs taken by routes like the classic Cougar. These extend over a tremendous overlapping wall guarding the mouth of the gully and contain some of the most impressive granite routes in the country.

At the top of most of the climbs there is a scrambly finish up a chaotic region of blocks and greenery below the rim. After prolonged rain, weeps continue to ooze down from this area for several days; if a line has wet streaks it is usually a waste of time embarking on it. The section from the Naked Ape to Vampire is the quickest to dry; Mousetrap also dries fairly quickly. The routes are described from the gully wall downwards and across the front face (left to right).

1 Goliath   150m   HVS ＊＊
B.S.Findlay, M.Rennie   7 Jun 1969 (4PA); FFA: I.Nicolson and party   1970
The great corner of **The Giant** is easily identified by the scar of a big rockfall which removed its top pitch. This varied route breaks through the guarding walls and slabs left of the corner of The Giant to finish up a big diagonal slabby corner in the upper cliff. The climbing is mainly slabby, but in an impressive position. Black Mamba's first ascent was on the same day. Further up the gully from The Giant is a vertical wall with a vast wedged block. Start up and left from the block, where a slab runs out across the wall.
1. 40m 4b Climb diagonally right, then traverse right across the slabs to below a small corner in the steep wall.
2. 40m 5a Climb the steep corner and move up to a shelf (crux); step left and continue up the fault-line to a belay on the right.
3. 40m 4b Go across the slab on the left, then climb to a ledge leading left to a huge slab. Climb the slab for 10m and continue to a stance about halfway up the great corner.
4. 30m Traverse right to finish up fine cracks splitting the slab. Scramble to the plateau.

2 The Naked Ape   100m   E5 ＊＊＊
P.Whillance, P.Botterill, M.Hamilton, R.Anderson   1 Aug 1982
This magnificent route offers bold climbing in an impressive situation up the big arete right of The Giant. Start below a groove leading directly up to the main corner system of The Giant. It is now common to miss pitch one and scramble into the belay for pitch 2 from the ramp below The Giant, then to abseil off from above the difficulties (see below).
1. 35m 5b Climb the groove and where it forks, keep right up a flake-crack to reach a ledge at the top of the initial ramp of The Giant.
2. 30m 6a Above is a smooth groove right of The Giant. Bridge the groove initially, then boldly climb its left-hand rib (crux) until it is possible to step back across right. Move up right onto the steep slab, traverse right to the arete and step up to a peg runner. Continue traversing right along an obvious foot ledge, then step up to a good ledge (junction with Ascent of Man and Voyage of the Beagle).

Goliath, HVS 5a, Central Gully Wall. Climbers unknown
(photo Stephen Reid)

CREAG AN DUBH LOCH

Central Gully Wall

2. The Naked Ape   E5 ***
3. The Ascent of Man   E5 ***
4. Cannibal   E6 ***
5. Voyage of the Beagle   E5 ****

A

○

2
3

7

4   5   6

8

10

6. Cougar   E3 ****
7. Vampire   E2 **
8. The Mousetrap   VS ***
9. Dubh Loch Monster   E1 **
10. King Rat   E1 ***

A. Rockfall on The Giant

9

3. 25m 6a Follow a left-slanting slabby corner to a niche below a roof and place a runner in the lip. Climb delicately down left to a good foothold near the arete. Step up and climb a break in the overhang to gain a sloping ledge. Climb a short steep wall to a ledge in a niche.

4. 10m 5b Climb the overhanging crack above to a large ledge and flake with slings for an abseil descent. A 50m abseil reaches the ramp underneath The Giant and scramble down.

If wishing to go to the plateau, then step up right and climb cracks to enter a groove system. Follow this to a grassy terrace at its top (5a). Scramble up right to the plateau.

The Ascent of Man   100m   E5 ***
M.Hamilton, R.Anderson   24 Jul 1982

An extremely fine natural line up the obvious groove and crack-line in the huge steep wall between The Giant and Cougar. Sustained and strenuous. Start below the line.

1. 30m 6b Climb a short crack, then traverse right along a ledge to gain the lower groove. Follow this up and traverse left across a slab to regain the crack. Climb this to a break in the roof, pull into the groove, then follow it to a hanging peg belay; it is best to belay a little lower down to incorporate good wires.

2. 30m 6a Step up and move across right to gain a subsidiary groove (if wet, climb the arete on its left, and return to the main groove as soon as possible – 6a, unprotected). Climb this and move left to climb a crack which leads to a leaning wall. Step up left to a ledge (this is where The Naked Ape belays at the top of its second pitch).

3. 15m 6a Climb the short crack above and hand-traverse right into a groove and go up this to its top. Climb a short corner to a traverse line.

4. 25m 5a Follow this traverse line up left along a slab and down into a recess with a large detached block (junction with The Naked Ape and its abseil point).

Cannibal   140m   E6 ***
M.Hamilton, R.Anderson   9 Jun 1984

A hard route with increasingly difficult pitches, all of high quality. The name may have been a reference to competition with Dougie Dinwoodie, who was planning to climb the route with Murray Hamilton. Below The Ascent of Man is a big overhanging alcove; start at a prominent arete which forms the right edge of the alcove, about 15m up from Voyage of the Beagle.

1. 30m 5c Climb the crack just left of the arete until moves can be made round the arete into another crack. Climb this until it fades, then step left to gain a crack on the crest. Climb this steeply to a stance on the slab above.

2. 10m 6a Move up left and gain holds which lead to a peg runner below the roof. Pull out right until a crack above the roof leads to a stance and peg belay on the higher slab.

3. 30m 6b Move up to a left-slanting corner and climb this to a roof. Traverse left and pull into the recess above, peg runner, then pull over its right wall onto the Cougar Slab; belay as for Cougar at the right end on the slab.

4. 40m 6b Above and slightly right is a stepped corner. Climb the first step, then swing right to the arete and move up until the corner can be regained. Continue up the corner and pull out right below a steep nose. Climb the wall right of the nose to gain a short crack, then pull onto a block on top of the nose. Follow a slab left below a roof to a stance.

5. 30m 5a Climb the crack above, then scramble to the top.

Voyage of the Beagle   130m   E5 ****
M.Hamilton, R.Anderson   12 Aug 1983

This superb, sustained and exposed route takes the very prominent line under Cougar to link with the top pitches of The Naked Ape. It offers slabbier climbing than other routes on this part of the wall. Low in the grade. It was previously known as the Boysen Line after an earlier failed attempt. Start 5m left of Cougar at a groove.

1. 25m 5c Climb a flake-crack on the right to gain the groove. Follow the groove, initially with difficulty, then more easily up the continuation to a small square-cut ledge.
2. 30m 6a Continue up the fault, then go out left before regaining the fault by a diagonal crack (crux). Follow the fault to the start of the slab. Climb across the slab to beside old pegs.
3. 40m 6a Climb leftwards on an upper slab to place high runners. Return to the belay and step down to gain a lower slab. Cross the slab to the arete, step sensationally left round this and climb straight up to enter a groove (on The Ascent of Man). Climb this to its top; to protect the second it is advisable to split the ropes and return right on the upper slab to place another runner. Move left to gain a groove leading to the stance on The Naked Ape at the end of its second pitch. Take care with rope drag.
4. 25m 6a Follow The Naked Ape (route 2) pitch 3.
5. 10m 5b Follow The Naked Ape pitch 4 to the abseil point (or continue to the plateau, initially 5a).

6 Cougar 135m E3 ****
M.Rennie, P.Williams 15-16 Jun 1968 (about 16PA); FFA: D.Cuthbertson, M.Hamilton Jun 1977
The Central Gully Wall below The Giant soars up for about 100m in a series of monolithic slabs and roofs. This magnificent climb takes a curving line of diedres near the right end of the wall, then cuts in over the main section by the huge hanging Cougar Slab to thread the maze of roofs above. The climbing is exposed, very sustained and intimidating despite good protection (although spaced on pitch 4). The 1977 ascent demonstrated the free climbing possibilities on this wall. Start at the foot of Central Gully on top of a mound with embedded blocks, common with Vampire.
1. 30m 4c Make a short right traverse into the initial corner and climb it (often wet) into a notch. Continue up left and work up to a ledge under an overhanging wall (common with Vampire).
2. 40m 5c Follow cracks leading up left over a bulge and go up the steep corner-line above to the Cougar Slab.
3. 35m 5c Traverse the slab left by a crack and step down into a recess below a short overhanging corner-crack. Climb this strenuously, then continue left by great flakes to under a short impending recessed wall.
4. 30m 5c Climb the wall to gain a girdling slab under the final bulging band. Move right and mantelshelf onto a block. Above is a crack with a protruding stone; climb it to reach an overlap. It is possible to climb straight up at 5c, but better to make a left traverse under the overlap bridging a slight gap. Continue traversing left to reach a good rounded spike and from this make a step up and traverse left under a bulge until it is possible to move up then left to a good ledge under a roof. Scrambling remains to the plateau.

In the case of retreat, a 45m abseil from the base of the overhanging crack (Cougar Slab) will just reach the gully bed (50m abseil from the top of the crack).

7 Vampire 225m E2 **
D.Dinwoodie, G.S.Strange 8 Oct 1972 (4PA, 1NA); FFA: B.T.Lawrie, A.Nisbet Jul 1977
A fine sustained route, although slightly dirty in places. Start as for Cougar.
1. 30m 4c Climb the first pitch of Cougar.
2. 40m 5a On the right, the bulge is split by an overhanging crack with a jammed flake at its base. From the jammed flake, pull right round the bulge and climb the corner above to a grass ledge with a good stance just above.
3. 40m 5b The big corner above is E3 5c and dirty, so step back down to the grass ledge, traverse right along the ledge, then go up to a slab on the right. Go diagonally right up slabs and a bulge to reach a blaeberry ledge after 20m. Make a toe traverse left across a tiny dwindling ledge, go up a corner to bulges, then break out left by a short wall and slab to a grass stance (poor protection).
4. 25m 5b Move left up a slab and climb a short recessed corner. Climb the slot

above and go up a slab to exit right. (Alternatively move right and climb a steep crack to the same point, 5c; or start up the crack and move left above the slot, 5b).
5. and 6. 90m 4c It is now easy to move left to broken ground, then right to the plateau but better climbing is had by continuing trending right and climbing slabby ground (5a).

8 The Mousetrap   180m   VS ***
J.R.Marshall, R.Marshall, R.Anderson   Nov 1959
This fine natural line is well protected, fairly quick to dry and offers the easiest way up the frontal face. It was considered the hardest route in the Cairngorms at the time. It uses the obvious grassy recess right of the grassy mound above the foot of Central Gully, which leads up to a big crack system. At the lowest point of the frontal face is the big King Rat recess; start up left from this at a deep easy groove leading to an array of cracks.
1. 35m 4a Climb the groove, traverse left above a slab, then go up to belay below and left of the main crack.
2. 45m 4c Move up right and climb the wide crack (crux), or use the rib on the right before moving back left, and so to the recess above. Continue up the recess to belay near the top.
3. 25m 4c Climb the steep flake corner on the left, move up to cracks and follow these to a stance.
4. and 5. 75m 4c,4b Continue up the crack-line to easier ground.

9 Dubh Loch Monster   200m   E1 **
I.Nicolson, D.Knowles   18 Jun 1970 (1PA); FFA: J.Lamb, P.Whillance   1975
The line of the thin solitary crack to the right of The Mousetrap cracks, some way left of the King Rat system, gives excellent sustained pitches of 5a with one move of 5c. Start just below and right of the easy groove of The Mousetrap.
1. 30m 4b Climb cracked slabs to under a chimney break.
2. 40m 5c Climb the chimney (crux), then continue up an awkward wall and follow the crack-line to under a big overhanging notch.
3. 10m 5a Move left and climb the arete, returning right to a big ledge.
4. 25m 5a Follow cracks to above a double bulge; climb the first bulge, move right 2m and climb the second with difficulty. Go up slabs to under a short wall.
5. 45m 5a Move left to a break and climb this to gain the slab above. Move left 2m and pull over a short wall into a corner. Follow the corner for 5m, then the rib on the right over two bulges, the second being turned on the left, then move right to a ledge.
6. 50m Climb slabs diagonally right to a crack at the right end of an overlap. Go up the crack, then climb a steepening corner. Follow the crack above to easier ground.

0 King Rat   220m   E1 ***
A.F.Fyffe, J.Bower   9 Jun 1968 (5PA); FFA: P.Thomas, M.Fowler   Jun 1977
This is the very fine crack system running straight up the frontal face. From below, the route is dominated by a big roof 50m up; the disproportionately hard moves through the roof are the route's only blemish. Climbed with 2 points of aid, the route is VS. Start close to the left wall of the big recess at the lowest point of the face, directly below the big roof.
1. 40m 4b Climb steep rocks at the back of the recess for some 15m, then traverse the left wall using flakes to a ledge on the open face (a more direct line continues straight up the recess to the slabs below the roof, 5a). Climb straight up the crack-line to a big grass ledge.
2. 20m 5c Move right from the ledge and go up cracked slabs to a shallow cave under the roof. Move awkwardly up left into a corner and climb this to a ledge.
3. and 4. 50m 4b Now follow the general line of the cracked ribs above, until under a short vertical wall. Go left up slabs to below a short leaning corner.
5. 10m 4b Climb the corner and move right to ledges.
6. 30m 4c The obvious right-trending line with a prominent peg is **Waterkelpie Wall** (E1). Climb a short wall to gain a slab under the roof, surmount the bulge

some 2m left of the roof, then traverse a narrow slab right above the roof and go up to ledges.

7. and 8. 70m 4b Move into the upper crack system and follow it to grass ledges. Scramble away left and up to the plateau.

EAGLES ROCK

(NO 235 835)   Alt 770m   South facing   Map p217

These slabby rocks form a long discontinuous cliff high on the White Mounth escarpment, opposite Creag an Dubh Loch. The rocks are rather dwarfed by the main cliff, but they are nevertheless a useful alternative when the condition of either rock or climber is not at its best, or for a second route. The climbs are short and quick drying on granite friction slabs, although not pure padding. In addition, the aspect ensures that the routes catch a good deal of sun, a point worth bearing in mind in cold weather or in the afternoon when the sun has left the Creag an Dubh Loch cliffs.

A LIKELY STORY SLAB

The main feature of the cliff is a big waterfall away to the left. Also prominent is the open and easy angled Diagonal Gully near the right end. A Likely Story Slab is the greenish disc of overlapping slab to the right of the lower part of Diagonal Gully. The approach is obvious.

Descent: The easiest descent is to traverse into Diagonal Gully. The 'modern' descent is to abseil from a thread (in-situ) situated in heather up and right of the finish of A Likely Story. 60m ropes are useful for the abseil, although a less direct abseil can be made with 50m ropes.

The Stretcher   70m   E2 *
D.Dinwoodie, A.McIvor   4 May 1975

In the centre of the lower slab is the obvious corner of A Likely Story; this route climbs the poorly protected slabs to its left. Start at a curious white trickle mark near the lowest left corner of the slab.

1. 20m 5a Climb to the first overlap, move left along the lip and go up a tiny corner just left of a scoop (Fraud Squad). Belay on the left.

2. 30m 5b Move about 5m right over slabs and go up to a short crack running back left to the main overlap. Climb the crack and the double overlap direct, then trend slightly right and back left to a ledge under a sharp nose in the upper overlap. An easier but indirect alternative is to traverse left after the double overlap, then to climb up to the ledge.

3. 20m Climb through the overlap just right of the nose and go up right to a grassy crack leading to heather.

Fraud Squad   70m   E2 *
A.Ross, G.Reilly, C.Harper   16 Jun 1984

In the centre of the lower slab is the obvious corner of A Likely Story; this direct line just left of it gives good climbing. Start just right of a curious white trickle mark near the lowest left corner of the slab.

1. 30m 5b Climb direct to the first overlap (as for A Likely Story). Traverse left for 3m through the overlap and climb a scoop with horizontal quartz bands. Exit left from the top of the scoop (bold), return right above it for 2m and climb directly to a crack which penetrates the main overlap just right of a V-notch.

2. 30m 5b Climb the crack through the double overlap and go slightly right to follow a pocketed blind crack (or the slab on its immediate right) to the base of a thin curving flake. Above this, traverse left to belay.

Cougar, E3 5c, Central Gully Wall. Climbers unknown
(photo Niall Ritchie)

3. 10m 4c Go through the upper overlap just left of a good thread and finish up mossy cracks.
Variation: **Direct Start   E3 5c**
J.Lines, C.Ord   12 Jul 2000
After climbing direct to the first overlap, pull straight over and go direct up the centre of the rippled scoop. Continue direct to the belay. Bold.

A Likely Story   80m   HVS ***
G.N.Hunter, D.F.Lang   25 Aug 1968 (2PA); FFA: A.Fyffe, J.Grieve   Oct 1970
This little gem, the best and most popular route on Eagles Rock, dries very quickly. Start in the middle of the lower slabs.
1. 30m 5a Go up slightly left to an overlap, move right 2m and cross the overlap to climb to an obvious corner leading to a ledge.
2. 20m 5a Go up by a flake to gain the corner above and follow this up to make a delicate right traverse under the overlap into a notch. Pull through the overlap and go up into a triangular depression.
3. 30m 4b Traverse left along a slab below a steep wall, then climb an obvious crack in the slab.

PASS OF BALLATER

(NO 367 971)   Alt 300m   South facing   Map p217

These cliffs have a delightfully sunny aspect and provide good routes of VS and above on clean solid granite. The cliff dries very quickly after light rain, particularly the western tiers, and it is usually possible to climb here from March through to December. It can be too hot on a warm summer day, with the rock feeling quite sweaty if it is also still and humid. The pass is a useful alternative for those heading for Lochnagar or Creag an Dubh Loch and finding mist or showers. The very keen have even climbed here after a failed visit to a wet mountain cliff. But this is actually one of Scotland's better outcrops for those climbing VS and above, and well worth a visit for its own sake. The climbing is often strenuous, with big holds or smooth walls, but there are many more deep cracks than in the mountains; excellent protection can be found on most routes. On a humid day it is noticeable that the starts of some of the popular routes are becoming slightly polished.

Approach: The cliff is easily located on the north side of the B972 (five minutes by car from Ballater). A car park lies below the central section. The cliffs are divided into three sections, the western and central areas are clearly visible from the car park, while the smaller eastern section is hidden by trees. The western section is approached by walking until directly underneath, then going straight up past the far end of the tiers. Each tier can be reached by traversing under it. The central section is approached direct, 5 to 10mins.

WESTERN SECTION

Diagram p236

The western section is divided into three tiers. It is common to leave sacks on the sunny terrace below the upper tier. The small lowest tier begins just above the scree and consists of only a small slab. The middle tier has a huge slab on the right-hand side, bounded on its left by an impressive broad pillar distinguished by the vertical quartz seam of Rattlesnake running up its right edge. The upper tier, below which runs a broad terrace, has the easily recognisable features of Smith's Arete and the right-angled corner of Little Cenotaph located centrally, with the diagonal crack of Black Custard to the right.

Middle Tier

At the west end of the tier are some shorter climbs, including the best selection of grades below VS. A right-facing blocky corner is **Jumbled Blocks Crack** (Very

Difficult). Moving right about 20m, a narrow chimney is reached before the cliff increases in height and steepens. Right of the chimney is the following route.

Lucky Strike   15m   HVS 5a *
M.Freeman, G.S.Strange, D.Stuart, R.Simpson   6 Jun 1971
Eight metres right of the chimney there is a very steep black streaked corner-line in two steps, forming the left side of the broad pillar. There is a tree on the ledge between the steps. Climb this to a spacious ledge and finish up the corner behind the tree. An excellent line, but unfortunately now polished.

Pretzel Logic   15m   E3 5c **
M.McDonald, B.Sprunt   1980
Climbs the overhanging corner high on the pillar. Start at a corner just past the right end of a huge flake on the wall (4m right of the flake traverse of the easier start). Bridge up the corner until a traverse across the wall gains a crack system. Follow this to the base of the final corner (possible belay), which provides an exhilarating finish.
Variation: **Easier Start**
About 3m right of Lucky Strike an obvious traverse on flakes leads up right across the wall to join the final corner. The traverse can be continued into Rattlesnake to give an exposed HVS.
Variation: **Direct Start**   8m   E3 6a *
B.Davison, N.Morrison   12 Jun 1983
The short overhanging groove in the true line of the route.

Rattlesnake   15m   E3 6a *
D.Dinwoodie, B.Lawrie   Jul 1981
Two metres right of Pretzel Logic direct start is a straight corner and crack-line near the right arete of the pillar. The initial crux corner gains the steep but easier quartzy cracks above.

Right of Rattlesnake is a long double overlap which guards the base of the slab. This ends in a recessed corner with a block (the much larger block which now lies below the crag used to be here). The following two routes start here, more deviously than before. They can be scary if the slab still has some early season muck.

Medium Cool   20m   VS 4c **
B.Lawrie, D.Dinwoodie   1971
A typical granite slab route, with some unusual moves but good rests to plan the next section. Pull out onto the right arete of the corner, then go up and traverse left above it to step down to a little tree on the slab between the two overlaps. Traverse left to a ledge (runners). Move back right and surmount the overlap. Climb to a big tree, then go up behind it on small holds.

Silent Spring   25m   E1 5a **
A.Ross, P.Garden   Sep 1982
A must for the keen slab climber. Follow Medium Cool to the runner ledge. From the highest point of the niche gain the upper slab via a scimitar shaped crack. Move up then right to the tree (high runner!). Often done by the start of Medium Cool, which is more natural. Follow the left-trending runnel to the top, no more runners. It can also be climbed directly up the slab from the niche, which is very fine but unprotected.

Upper Tier

Moving rightwards from the left-hand (western) side of the terrace are some hard smooth walls which end at two short crack-lines before reaching a break, 3m right of the right-hand crack.

Descent: Walk down to the west (easy) or scramble down east of Little Cenotaph.

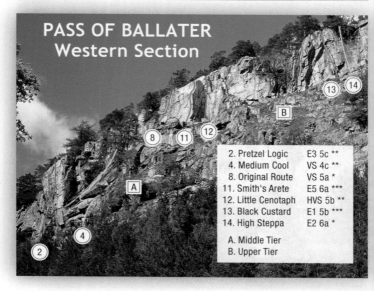

PASS OF BALLATER
Western Section

2. Pretzel Logic	E3 5c	**
4. Medium Cool	VS 4c	**
8. Original Route	VS 5a	*
11. Smith's Arete	E5 6a	***
12. Little Cenotaph	HVS 5b	**
13. Black Custard	E1 5b	***
14. High Steppa	E2 6a	*

A. Middle Tier
B. Upper Tier

6 Left-Hand Crack   8m   VS 5a *
S.Falconer and party   Jun 1975
The left of the two short crack-lines has some excellent holds.

7 Right-Hand Crack   8m   HVS 5a
S.Falconer and party   Jun 1975
Well protected. It leads into a corner which is easy enough but dirty.

8 Original Route   10m   VS 5a *
D.Duncan and party   Late 1960
Climbs the break, which starts with a bottomless corner. Make a difficult move to gain the corner and continue up right to a ledge. Finish by deep cracks above.

9 Fingerwrecker   10m   HVS 5c *
B.Lawrie, G.S.Strange   4 Aug 1979
Four metres right of Original Route is an obvious thin crack. Climb this (no cheating from boulders) and gain a scoop. Finish by Original Route. An aptly named route if you slip on the polished start.

10 Peel's Wall   10m   E4 6a ***
J.Peel, A.Barley   1977
The fine wall to the right of Fingerwrecker is a popular test piece. Gain an undercut flake and proceed to the horizontal break. Move straight up until an awkward long reach to a narrow ledge allows a committing move up and right to be made. A quick jibber up a short slabby wall leads to the top.

11 Smith's Arete   10m   E5 6a ***
R.A.Smith   1983
This is the striking arete right of Peel's Wall. Climb the edge to the horizontal break, which provides a welcome rest and runners. Finish directly up the slab above.

12 Little Cenotaph   10m   HVS 5b **
G.Muhlemann, G.S.Strange, R.J.Archbold   24 Aug 1975

A popular route which is distinctly easier for the taller. Climb the big right-angled corner by a wide variety of contortions to a ledge. Finish up the shallow corner on the left. If the upper corner is avoided, the grade is lowered to 5a.

Right of Little Cenotaph are some smaller walls either side of the descent ramp, then a tree filled groove and a slim corner. Right of this is a right-facing corner **Crumbling Dice** (E2 5c) bounding a steep wall with the following line.

Black Custard   12m   E1 5b ***
J.Mothersele, M.Freeman   Jun 1971
An obvious line where a quartzy crack slants up left to a black overhanging apex. Climb the crack up to the roof and pull over steeply into an easier groove. A well protected test piece which is still the scene of many a struggle.

High Steppa   8m   E2 6a *
B.Sprunt, M.McDonald   Aug 1980
The short but fine wall 3m right of Black Custard. Make a bold start up a thin crack just right of the arete to gain a friendly horizontal break. Attaining a standing position in the break can be frustrating. Finish straight up.

CENTRAL SECTION

Diagram p239
The central section, which is above and just right of the car park, is characterised by two obvious lines. In the centre of the cliff, on a south facing frontal wall, is the obvious corner of Bluter Groove, while on the left (gully) wall is the impressive capped corner of Anger and Lust. This gully wall faces west and gets sun in the afternoon and early evening. The routes are described from left to right i.e. descending the gully wall and across the front face.

Descent: Walk uphill, turn west and descend beside the gully wall. From the front face, it is quicker to descend to the east.

Cold Rage   20m   E4 6a **
D.Dinwoodie, C.MacLean   1983
Start by a big larch tree. Climb a thin crack just left of the corner of Anger and Lust to a niche (crux). Move left and climb straight up to a nose forming the right side of the final slot. Climb the slot and wall to the top. Low in the grade. The shallow groove just left of the normal start is E3 5c.

Hot Temper   15m   E5 6b **
W.Todd, G.Livingston   1986
A direct finish to Cold Rage. Where Cold Rage goes left from the niche, pull directly through the roof and climb the wall above with difficulty. Strenuous with reasonable protection, which is hard to place.

Anger and Lust   20m   E2 5c ****
FFA: R.A.Smith, A.Williams   Jun 1980
A classic route taking the obvious roofed corner near the bottom of the gully wall and just right of the larch. Climb the corner to finish sensationally by the deep crack splitting the left side of the roof. High in the grade.
Variation: **Right-Hand Finish   6m   E4 6b ****
FFA: D.Dinwoodie, W.Taylor   Oct 1985
From the bridging rest below the roof, traverse right along the lip of an overlap to a good jug. Step left and finish up the corner. Sensational and well protected.

Lech Gates   20m   E3 5c **
D.Dinwoodie, G.Livingston   1983
Start about 5m below Anger and Lust, below and slightly right of a smooth corner. Climb block flakes up right to a shallow corner. Use the crack on the right to move

up, then traverse left out of the corner to a poor resting place under a roof. Take a deep breath, pull round left, and sprint up the crack-line to a brutal finish.
Variation: **Direct start**
Climb the thin crack-line past a peg runner to join the original line at the resting place. Using this start makes the route slightly less challenging.

The cliff now changes aspect on to the frontal face.

19 Giant Flake Route   30m   VS 4c **
G.S.Strange, R.Simpson   17 Sep 1967
Just above the lowest toe of the crag is a small tree. Start about 10m right of the tree below a flake-corner. Climb a short but hard wall to the right end of a ledge system. Now the route is on giant flakes and technically easier. Go up the flake-corner to the line of big flakes which crosses the wall diagonally from left to right. Follow these to step down on to a sloping ledge. Climb onto big split blocks and continue steeply on big holds up the groove to the top.

20 Bluter Groove   15m   E3 6b *
M.Hamilton, P.Whillance, R.Anderson   Jun 1982
The most obvious groove in the centre of the tier. The hard lower section is initially climbed via the right arete, then step left to bridge up the groove. The steep upper crack is much easier. The desperate thin crack immediately left of the starting groove is **Bluter Crack** (E4 6c).

21 Blutered   15m   E1 5a **
D.Wright, A.Higham, G.Muhlemann   Jul 1976
This indirect ascent provides fine sustained climbing. Start approximately 5m up and right of Bluter Groove and follow an obvious traverse line across the wall to reach its upper part.

RED CRAIGS - GLEN CLOVA

Map p217, 240
The bulk of the rock climbing in Glen Clova can be found on the Red Craigs, a long drive but a short walk. With their sunny aspect and dry climate, they can be climbed on for most of the year, giving a variety of pitches of all grades. The climbing and the setting are almost Lakeland in character, the diorite varying from smooth and rounded to rough and angular, while the crags possess a sense of exposure which belies their roadside nature.

Amenities: There is little at the head of Glen Clova, save the Clova Hotel which serves food.

Accommodation: Carn Dearg MC hut – (NO 286 758). The Clova Hotel has a bunkhouse. A cheaper alternative is the spacious but draughty boulder cave below the South-East Crag.

Approach: Glen Clova lies in the southern Cairngorms; head first for Kirriemuir where there are signs for The Glens. Pass through the town and continue north, following signs for Glen Clova. On reaching the Clova Hotel, pass over the narrow bridge marked with a cul-de-sac sign and continue up the glen for 5km. On driving up the glen, a big mass of rock on the right is clearly seen, the main section of crag, also a rocky dome behind and to its left (The Doonie).

A clean and apparently full height section becomes, on closer inspection, a lower right section (South-East Crag) separated by a grassy gully from the higher and left Central Crag with a bright orange patch of rock (Empire of the Sun). Just to the left are two tiers of rock (Upper and Lower North-West Crag). The lower has a central depression and clean rib on its right (Proud Corner). The upper has some dark rock and impressive overhangs.Park on the roadside, either side of a grassy break in the boulders which leads to the right side of Lower North-West Crag. From here, access is obvious to the other crags, 10mins, 15mins to the Upper Crag.

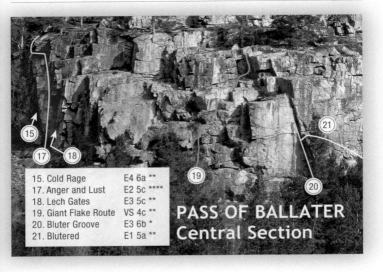

15. Cold Rage	E4 6a **
17. Anger and Lust	E2 5c ****
18. Lech Gates	E3 5c **
19. Giant Flake Route	VS 4c **
20. Bluter Groove	E3 6b *
21. Blutered	E1 5a **

**PASS OF BALLATER
Central Section**

LOWER NORTH-WEST CRAG

(NO 295 756)   Alt 380m   South-West facing

This crag contains some excellent pitches on good rock. The depression in the centre of the crag is bounded on the right by the prominent orange rib of Proud Corner. A steep nose on the right of the crag, right of an open corner, is Witches Tooth.

Descent: A small path traverses right across the top of a gully, then a short scramble to its continuation down the right side.

Wander   40m   HVS 5a *
W.K.Divers, K.A.Sturrock   Jun 1957
A good route following the thin crack and corner-line in the centre of the left face of the depression. Climb a thin vertical crack to a ledge, then move left to the foot of a shallow corner. Follow the corner to a tree (possible belay). Step out right above a lot of space and climb a crack in the steep exposed wall to ledges and the top.

Wandered   40m   HVS 5a **
N.Sheperd   1982
A good route giving some excellent moves in fine positions, although split by big ledges. Start as for Wander. Follow the thin vertical crack to the ledge below the corner. The steep flake-crack on the right leads strenuously to a large ledge in the back of the depression (possible belay). Step up into a recess on the left, step around the arete and climb the airy wall on good holds to the top.

Proud Corner   45m   VS 4b ***
G.Malloch   1950s
A tremendous route with exhilarating positions up the crest of the orange rib which forms the right edge of the depression. Quite bold, not a soft touch! Start below twin cracks in the right face of the depression. Climb the right-hand crack to a large ledge (possible belay). Move left onto the face and climb up the edge to a triangular slab (peg runner). Continue boldly to a small ledge (crux) and finish up the small corner above.

CAIRNGORMS SOUTH

RED CRAIGS - GLEN CLOVA

Witches Tooth   25m   E1 5b *
FFA: M.Hamilton, D.Brown   1976
A test piece up the prominent nose right of the big open corner. Climb the steep crack in the nose to enter a niche (crux). Step left to a corner-crack and follow this to the glacis and short wall above.

UPPER NORTH-WEST CRAG

(NO 294 757)   Alt 500m   West facing

This steep and intimidating crag contains some of the best climbing in the glen, partially due to its fine outlook high on the hillside. It is characterised by an over-hung recess in the middle, out of which cuts a deep diagonal cleft. Right of the recess and its right-bounding rib is the smooth Red Wall high up. Left of the recess is a big open corner high up, whilst below and left of the cleft, the large overhang belongs to Roman Candle. Generally the crag dries quickly after rain.

Descent: Go up and left to a small cairn and descend a gully left of the crag.

Just Another Sparkler   15m   E3 5c *
M.Hamilton, N.Sheperd   1985
The flake-line in the steep wall to the left of Roman Candle requires a determined approach. Strenuously gain and climb it to a difficult exit on to the slab above.

Roman Candle   25m   E4 6a **
D.Crabbe, J.Howe, D.Lang   1964 (aid); FFA: M.Hamilton, D.McCallum, R.Anderson   1983
The crack in the large overhang on the left of the crag is climbed by means of ape like manoeuvres. Wander up easy slabs to the corner in the roof. Climb this (technical crux) and hand-traverse to the lip (peg runner). Pull over (physical crux) on to the slab above.

Zigzag Direct   40m   HVS **
D.Lang   early 1960s (aid); FFA: S.Scott, I.Reilly   1974
A good independent start and direct finish to Zigzag, offering an excellent and exciting outing. Start at cracks in the slab below the large overhang of Roman Candle.
1. 20m 5a Move up and right across the slab to a large block (peg runner). Pull over this to follow the crack on the right to an airy pedestal at the top of the deep cleft.
2. 20m 5b Climb the large open corner above, exiting left at an obvious hand-traverse rail below the capping roof.

Zigzag Double Direct   45m   E2 **
S.Stewart, G.Farquhar, G.Ettle   1985 (first pitch climbed   1972)
A good route giving fine climbing and more impressive positions than the Kama Sutra! Start directly below the large open corner of Zigzag Direct.
1. 25m 5b Climb the steep crack-line through the roof to the large block of Zigzag Direct. Follow this to its belay.
2. 20m 5c Bridge up the corner above as for Zigzag Direct. Where this chickens out left, continue up to the capping roof and turn this obstacle on the right (crux) before stepping up left to the top.

Alder   40m   Hard Severe *
D.Brown   1951
An exposed route crossing some improbable ground for the grade. Start behind the Alder tree in the right side of the overhung recess.
1. 10m 4b An awkward start, maybe 4c, up wide cracks in the corner of the bay to a large ledge.
2. 30m 4a Climb first right towards a chimney, then back left up a flakey wall and straight up to the top.

The Red Wall   45m   E1 ***
FFA: M.Hamilton, D.Brown   1976
An excellent climb accepting the challenge of the central crack in the steep smooth red wall at the top right end of the crag. Start below a steep grey wall with a prominent flake which is at the right end and lowest point of the crag.
1. 25m 5b Either climb via the detached flake (5a) or tackle the steep flake-crack on its right (hard 5b and better) to reach the large sloping ledge. Continue up the quartz chimney above to the belay.
2. 20m 5b Step sensationally out right and climb the crack to the top.

CENTRAL CRAG

(NO 297 757)   Alt 500m   South-West facing

This fearsome crag is characterised by an impressively steep central wall with a steep nose on its left-hand side. The crag has some loose rock and a tedious descent.

Descent: This is via a scramble up the steep hillside to a fence. Follow a path rightwards until the scree filled descent gully is reached.

Empire of the Sun   30m   E4 6a ***
D.Dinwoodie, J.Hall   22 Sep 1986
An excellent route giving well protected aggressive climbing up the shattered

CAIRNGORMS SOUTH

orange patch of rock and the steep wall above. Start below the orange patch of rock. Go up slabs and climb directly up the loose orange rock by a crack to a slabby ledge. Grab the flake on the left, then move up and left to a good shake out at another flake. Move up right along a crack until it is possible to pull up to a small flat ledge (crux). Go straight up to a big ledge and belay. Finish up a short wall.

SOUTH-EAST CRAG

(NO 297 756)   Alt 400m   South-West facing

The crag contains the best low grade climbing in the glen, with three fine routes on perfect rock. It dries quickly and has an open aspect.

Descent: Go down the gully between this and Central Crag. Any hope of cutting back to the terrace without going back to the base of the crag are dashed.

The crag has a short steep left section and a bigger right section with the described routes. The routes lie above a terrace at 12m, on to which one can walk from the right. The lower wall can also be climbed, at 4c on the left through the right end of a steep wall or at 4b up a corner on the right.

**Flake Route   40m   Severe ** **
W.H.Ward, J.Ferguson   Aug 1939
Start up a steep chimney at the left side of the terrace. Above the chimney, follow a groove on the left to a perch. Surmount an overhanging block above and continue on top of a large flake (possible belay). From the flake, climb up and diagonally right to a small rounded ledge, then head for the top on good holds.

Central Crack   45m   Hard Severe * **
J.Malloch and party   1950s
Climb the thin corner-crack which runs directly up the face right of Flake Route. Superb.

**Parapet Route   45m   Hard Severe * **
G.S.Ritchie, J.Ferguson   Sep 1940
An awkward start leads to good open climbing. Start below a small corner just right of Central Crack. Climb the corner and overhanging chimney above to reach a steep crack. Pass this by going left and back right to the continuation crack. Or climb the crack direct, VS 4b. Continue straight up to a huge flake (possible belay) and finish up the arete above.

THE DOONIE

(NO 290 758)   Alt 300m   South-West facing

The Doonie is the dome shaped mass of rock above the quarry, consisting of upper and lower sections separated by a large diagonal terrace.

Approach: Park in the quarry and follow faint paths up the hillside, 5mins. The Upper Doonie lies above and right, 10mins.

Lower Doonie

(NO 289 758)   Alt 300m   West facing

The crag has a steep main face with a tree filled gully to its left.

Descent: To the right, down the diagonal terrace (or abseil).

**Guinness   50m   E1 ** **
F.Old, G.Malloch, F.Anderson, A.Ferguson   1958; FFA: G.Reilly, I.Reilly   1976
The classic route of the crag gives fine varied climbing on good rock. Start at the left-hand side of the main face, at the foot of a grey concave slab below a

prominent beak overhang.

1. 20m 5a Gain and boldly climb the concave slab directly to a good belay ledge.
2. 15m 5b Attack the black leaning corner above. If successful, continue up and left to a grassy ledge.
3. 15m 5a Finish up the wide crack on the right (peg runner).

Variation: **Alternative Finish   5b ***
M.Hendry (some aid)   1960s
From the top of the black leaning corner of the second pitch, move up and right below the beak overhang to finish up right-sloping cracks.

Special Brew   50m   HVS
G.Malloch   1950s (sling for aid); FFA: G.Reilly, I.Reilly   1975
A good though a little overgrown route taking an exposed line up the centre of the main face. The direct takes the central left-facing corner while the other left-facing corner to the right is taken by **Heinekin** (E1 5b). Start just right of Guinness, below a pink right-sloping ramp.

1. 15m 4a Follow the ramp to a ledge and peg belay.
2. 20m 5a Climb up and left to a small ledge (peg runner) below overhanging cracks. Thug up the cracks to gain a sloping ledge and small corner (peg runner). Traverse horizontally right to a large ledge.
3. 15m 4c Stand on the large detached block on the right-hand side of the ledge and continue sensationally to the top.

Special Brew Direct   60m   E3 **
N.Sharpe, G.Ettle   1985
A sustained and well protected direct line through Special Brew.

1. 15m 4a Special Brew, pitch 1.
2. 45m 5c Climb directly up the corner above the belay (first crux) to the large belay ledge at the top of Special Brew pitch 2. Step off the left-hand side of the ledge and continue directly up the wall (second crux) to the top.

Upper Doonie

(NO 291 759)   Alt 350m   South-West facing

This crag contains some fine Extreme climbing. The most obvious feature is the large central alcove bounded on the left by a blunt overhanging arete **DRI** (E6 6a) and with a slanting roof fault on its right wall. Routes in the central alcove area can take a while to dry out after wet weather.

Descent: Abseil descents can usually be made from convenient trees, or walk off to the left and descend the diagonal terrace below the crag.

Vindaloo   40m   E1 5b ***
J.Thompson, J.Cadger   6 Aug 1972 (aid); FFA: 1986
This route gives fine contrasting climbing up the clean slabs and steeper wall above, left of the central alcove. Start 5m left of the arete, at the foot of a grey slab. Climb the initial steep crack and the left side of the slab above (the central line with a peg is E4 6a) to gain a square black sentry box (possible belay). Move out right and over a bulge to a layback crack which leads strenuously to the top.

The Whoremistress   40m   E4 6a ***
G.Farquhar   1988
The central line in the alcove gives a very good and sustained outing, one of Clova's best. Start in the alcove below a recess with a small thin tree. Climb the recess and V-groove above to a diagonal shelf. Move onto the ramp above with difficulty (poor peg runner). Either climb directly up to the left-hand side of an overhang (hard) or traverse right across the overhanging wall to a small niche and crack leading to the right-hand side of the overhang (harder). Surmount the overhang directly using a prominent small flake on the wall above (crux). Step into the wide vertical crack on the left and follow it to a ledge and tree.

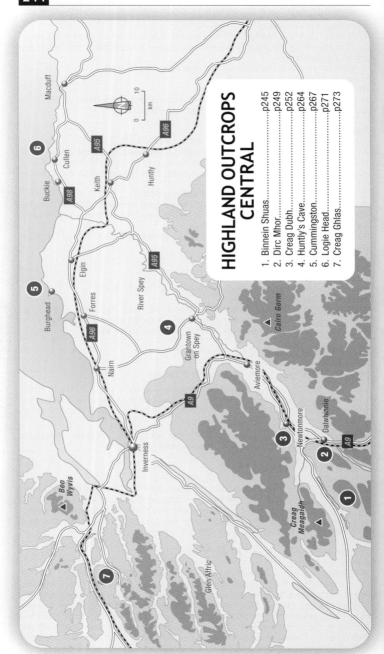

HIGHLAND OUTCROPS CENTRAL

HIGHLAND OUTCROPS CENTRAL

This chapter includes several outcrops and mountain cliffs away from the main ranges. They lie in an approximate line across the centre of the highlands, from Binnein Shuas in the west, through Strathspey (Dirc Mhor, Creag Dubh and Huntly's Cave) to the Moray Firth Coast (Cummingston and Logie Head) and Creag Ghlas in Strathconon, west of Inverness. They have much drier weather and good climbing, although higher options should be considered if the weather is good enough.

Maps: L42 (Binnein Shuas, Dirc Mhor), L35 (Creag Dubh), L36 (Huntly's Cave), L28 (Cummingston), L29 (Logie Head), L25 (Creag Ghlas)

SMC Climbers' Guides: *Highland Outcrops* (1998), *North-East Outcrops* (2003), *Northern Highlands Central* (projected 2006)

Public Transport: Possible, but complicated and time consuming.

Amenities: The crags are spread over a wide area with Aviemore and Strathspey being central. See Northern Cairngorms for a selection of these amenities. There are Information Offices in Elgin (01343 542666), Grantown-on-Spey (01479 872773), Aviemore (01479 810363), Kingussie (01540 661297) and Spean Bridge (01397 712576).

Laggan

Midway between Fort William and Aviemore is Loch Laggan, with Creag Meagaidh to its north and many hills, including Binnein Shuas, to its south.

BINNEIN SHUAS

(NN 468 827)   Alt 500m   South-East facing   Diagram p246

Best known for the classic Ardverikie Wall, this fine and accessible mountain cliff overlooks the beautiful Lochan-na-h-Earba, in a superb setting. The rock is micro granite and very different to the schists predominant in the area. The cliff has more of a west coast climate than the easterly crags in this chapter, so if the forecast is showers in the west, it may not be a good choice. But the sunny aspect and relatively low altitude mean that the rock dries quickly.

Approach: Park in a lay-by at the south-west end of Loch Laggan, just west of Moy Lodge, on the A86 from Newtonmore to Spean Bridge. Follow the track over the River Spean towards Luiblea, but branch off left before the house (high locked gate with a stile; you need to lift your bike over) to follow an older track to a small reservoir, then left to the sandy shores of Lochan-na-h-Earba. From here a faint path rises steadily up the hillside to the base of the cliff, 1hr 30mins. Using a bike saves 20 to 30mins and the return is a doddle.

Descent: Walk westwards along the top of the cliff (small path from Ardverikie Wall) until the path cuts back down a ramp and under The Fortress.

THE FORTRESS

This is the pale recessed wall capped by roofs, defined on its left by smooth clean slabs and on its right by Hidden Gully. A wide grassy terrace, The Garden lies directly below the central roofed area. The steep right-hand side wall is cut by a prominent crack-line and forms the start of the left wall of Hidden Gully.

1 Kubla Khan   110m   Hard Severe **
G.N.Hunter, D.F.Lang   25 Jun 1967
A fine climb up the first slab left of the central roofed area. The descent from Ardverikie Wall passes below, so it is often climbed as a second route, although many make a single 50m abseil after the first two pitches. Start just right of a vegetated dyke.

BINNEIN SHUAS
The Fortress
& Ardverikie Wall

1. Kubla Khan — Hard Severe **
2. The Keep — E1 *
3. Storming the Bastille — E3 *
4. Ardanfreaky — E4 *
5. The Fortress Direct — HVS **
6. Delayed Attack — E3 6a ***
7. Ardverikie Wall — Hard Severe ****

A. Hidden Gully

1. 20m 4b Climb a steep vertically grooved wall on rounded holds to a large grass ledge.
2. 40m 4b Climb the pale grooved slab above until forced to move left on to a small ledge in a recess.
3. 10m Go straight up to the terrace.
4. 40m 4a Climb the overhang and easy lichenous slabs to finish.

The next three routes lie above The Garden, accessed from the left by a scramble up a grassy ramp and corner containing a rowan tree.

2 The Keep   130m   E1 *
D.F.Lang, G.N.Hunter, M.D.Main   16 Jul 1967
This route follows the left edge of the central roofed area of The Fortress. Low in the grade.
1. 10m 4b Climb the crack in the left wall above the rowan tree to reach a block belay on the slab.
2. 45m 5b Continue by grooves on the edge of the buttress until confronted by twin cracks splitting the vertical wall above. Using both of these gain the flake above and continue up the fault-line, passing a loose block and an easy slab to a belay on a grass patch.
3. 30m 4a The slab above leads to the terrace.
4. 45m Follow the hog's back ridge to the top.

3 Storming the Bastille   80m   E3 *
M.A.Charlton, A.A.Moist (1PA, later freed)   17 May 1984
Unusual climbing up the spectacular off-width crack cutting through the roofs.
1. 40m 5c Make a hard entry into the bomb bay crack and follow it to the roof. Back and foot the chimney through the roof to a steep slab and climb this to good finishing holds.
2. 15m Climb the easy corner to a ledge and tree belay.
3. 25m 5a Follow the diagonal crack to reach a slab and the top.

4 Ardanfreaky   105m   E4 *
M.A.Charlton, A.A.Moist, J.Griffiths   27 May 1984
A wild trip through the roofs, capable of generating a surprising variety of emotions. Start below cracks in the slab below the corner extending down from the right-hand side of the main roofs.
1. 20m 5c Climb the steepening right-hand crack past vegetable oddments until it is possible to move right into the corner. Layback up this to a ledge.
2. 20m 6a Pull over the juggy roof above into a corner. Traverse left under the bigger roof to a strange down-pointing spike. Step up to the roof and traverse across the wall in a wild position into a short hanging corner, which succumbs after a struggle. Exit left onto a ledge.
3. 40m 5b Follow the diagonal crack above rightwards, then climb a slab to a tree belay.
4. 25m Climb the corner-crack above to the top.

The following routes start at the base of the crag, down and right of The Garden and left of Hidden Gully.

5 The Fortress Direct   125m   HVS **
T.Patey, R.Ford, M.Stewart   May 1964; Direct: R.Carrington, J.R.Marshall   Jul 1970
A fine route with sustained climbing up the right edge of The Fortress. Start round on the right wall above a jumble of huge boulders next to a large roof. Go beyond the boulders and cut back left to reach the start.
1. 20m 5a Climb a hanging groove to a higher roof and pass it on the left to get into another groove with a small sapling over the lip. Continue up the groove until it is possible to traverse left on to a large grass ledge.
2. 30m 4c To the left of a short right-facing corner are twin cracks. Climb these to

a diagonal crack leading right to The Garden. Belay at the right end.
3. 30m 5a Gain a triangular niche up and right and exit via a fine crack issuing from its lip. Step right at the top and go direct to a ledge.
4. 45m Climb the edge to the top.

6 Delayed Attack   40m   E3 6a ***
G.Goddard 30 Jul 1983
The impressive corner and deep diagonal crack in the side wall gives an outstanding climb, perhaps four stars if the weeds re-growing in the lower crack were cleaned out. Start at a vertical crack leading up to the hanging corner in the centre of the wall. Climb the crack and pull over the small roof (crux) into the corner. Exit from the corner via the diagonal crack with painful jamming to reach the right end of The Garden.

EASTERN SECTION

This is the large expanse of slabs and grass stretching rightwards from Hidden Gully.

7 Ardverikie Wall   180m   Hard Severe ****
G.N.Hunter, D.F.Lang   24 Jun 1967
This much sought after classic is one of the best routes of its grade in Scotland. It takes a fairly direct line up the smoothest and cleanest section of slab, the line of a coloured streak with some bold slab climbing on pitches 2 and 4. The easiest line is described but those feeling confident can just go straight up. The route is much harder in the wet and not recommended.

Start where the path first reaches the cliff base, immediately right of the base of Hidden Gully, where there is a very worn patch of ground below a steep knobbly rib (and 8m left of an obvious boulder lying against the slab).
1. 10m 4b Climb the rib, then go into a corner-line on the right which leads to a ledge with a large flake under the roof.
2. 35m 4a Traverse left to the rib and climb steeply up cracks, then climb rightwards above the top of the roof to reach the slab. Take the easiest line up the immaculate slab, going first right then diagonally back left to a ledge and flake belay.
3. 35m 4a Follow the flake-groove on the right to a bulge. Step right onto a ledge and pull over the bulge above. Continue for 3m to a small ledge and large flake at the base of a diagonal grass rake.
4. 35m 4b Make tricky moves out right across a blank looking slab below an obvious diagonal crack to gain good holds in the middle of nowhere. Go slightly left up an ill-defined rib into a shallow left-trending ramp-groove. This leads to a spike belay in a large scoop. A stunning pitch.
5. 25m 4a Climb the left side of the scoop, then follow the right-leading overlap above to pull over near its top. Go left up the slab to the terrace.
6. 40m Climb easy slabs to finish.

Strathspey

Most of the crags in this section are located close to the A9 as it passes through Dalwhinnie, Newtonmore and Aviemore.

DIRC MHOR

(NN 591 861)   Map p244

This impressive ravine, a giant meltwater channel, cuts a slice through the hills to the north-west of Dalwhinnie. Guarding the entrance to the north end of the defile

Ardveriekie Wall, Hard Severe 4b, Binnein Shuas. Climber Miranda Grant
(photo Cubby Images)

HIGHLAND CENTRAL

is the Sentinel Rock. The rock is similar to Binnein Shuas, a fine grained micro granite with pegmatite intrusions.

Approach: Follow the A889 north out of Dalwhinnie for about 2km, where the road ascends a steep hill. Parking is possible at the top of the hill opposite an estate track. Follow the track through the gate, pass below an estate house, and once past its grounds strike uphill to regain the track. Follow it until it drops down towards the Allt an-t-Sluie, then follow the banks of the burn up the glen until the deep gash of Dirc Mhor is seen on the left. From here it is best to climb the hillside through deep heather left of a birch wood around a small waterfall, then traverse right along the line of the highest trees to contour into the base of Sentinel Rock. Following the base of the defile has a section of boulders and heather but is only slightly slower and increases the chance of finding the last dinosaur, 1hr 30mins. There may be restrictions during the stalking season (see Environment notes).

SENTINEL ROCK

(NN 592 861)   Alt 550m   North-West facing

The pride of the Dirc. This barrel shaped 60m buttress presents a fine front face with a prominent arete, the line of The Man with the Child in his Eyes, and split into thirds by two ledges. The right side of the buttress is defined by a huge corner in the upper half, climbed by Positive Earth. The routes finish at a prominent area of large boulders which is easy to find from above.

Descent: Ascend broken ground, go over the top of the hillock, and walk back round the northern end of the Dirc to the base.

Working Class Hero   80m   E2 **
A.Fyffe, K.Geddes, A.Liddell   1 Aug 1980
This route takes the spectacular ramp and corner up the left wall, a great line but a bit mucky. Start at the toe of the buttress at the base of a big slanting slab.
1. 15m 4b Climb the big slab to its top.
2. 30m 5b Gain and climb a small right-facing corner in the overhanging wall above, which leads to the clean-cut ramp come corner-line. Follow this to a niche and exit to the right up a crack on to a large ledge cutting the front of the buttress.
3. 35m 4c Step up to the large ledge which leads diagonally right across the face to a corner. Climb this to the top of a pinnacle, then traverse diagonally right using a thin crack and from its end traverse back hard left. Easier rock leads to the top.

The Man with the Child in his Eyes   80m   E5 **
K.Howett, G.E.Little   24 Jun 1995
A sensational route climbing the left arete of the front face of Sentinel Rock. Start as for Working Class Hero at the big slab.
1. 15m 4b Climb the big slab to the belay.
2. 30m 6b Climb a small groove in the wall just right of the corner of Working Class Hero for 4m until it is possible to span out right around the arete to gain a big flat topped flake. Move up to join Fanfare for the Common Man at the left end of its first belay ledge. Climb the arete past a quartz fin where hard moves gain an obvious hold in the arete. Follow the thin crack on the left side of the arete with sustained difficulty until an exit left near the top gains a belay at the left end of the large ledge above.
3. 15m 6a Follow slabby rock up and left to gain the thin crack near the arete. Continue up this.
4. 20m 4c Trend leftwards to the base of a left-slanting ramp, then follow the crack directly above to broken ground. Scramble rightwards to reach a boulder strewn terrace.

Fanfare for the Common Man   80m   E5 ***
G.E.Little, K.Howett   16 Jul 1994
Another fine route on the left-hand side of the front face of Sentinel Rock. Start at

the lowest point of the crag, as for Working Class Hero.
1. 25m 5a Climb the easy angled slab (as for Working Class Hero) for 10m to the point where an obvious flake-crack breaks the right wall. Ascend this, then traverse right along a fault to step up onto the right-hand of two sloping rock ledges. Move left to take an awkward belay at the junction of the two ledges. Climbing direct from the fault to the ledges via a short steep diagonal crack is 6a.
2. 20m 6b Step up on to the higher ledge, then move to its left end below a slight groove. Climb this to a thin horizontal crack. Pull up bulging rock with increasing difficulty to a hairline horizontal crack, then make committing moves left and up to gain better holds. A sequence of good holds lead to the large ledge. A brilliant pitch.
3. 20m 5c Climb easy rock just right of the belay to gain a right-trending ramp shared with Working Class Hero. Follow this to the start of a less distinct left-trending ramp. Ascend this to a deep incut hold below bulging rock. Go straight over the bulge to a thin flake, then move left to gain a flange. Move left and go up to a ledge.
4. 15m 4a Climb a left-trending stepped groove, then scramble back right and go up to gain the wide block strewn terrace.

Positive Earth   80m   E2 *
M.Burrows Smith, A.Fyffe   23 Aug 1981
This climb traces a line up the right side of the front face, finishing up the big corner. Start at the lowest point of the crag below an overhanging corner.
1. 20m 4c Climb the corner until it steepens and escape up the right wall on to a large slab. Follow a line diagonally up the wall above to belay at the obvious large blocks.
2. 20m 5b Move slightly left into a niche. Climb the thin diagonal crack which leads leftwards with a hard move to reach a good small triangular ledge. Go up the wall above on good holds leading into the base of the big corner.
3. 15m 4a Climb the corner and exit left under the roof to belay on the large ledge on the front of the buttress.
4. 25m 5a Climb the fine vertical crack above to finish.

The line of cliffs continues beyond Sentinel Rock on a smaller scale, forming two large open bays. In the buttress right of the second bay is a very smooth and clean-cut open corner, sitting about 10m above a vegetated lower groove which is flanked by two small rowan trees. To the right of this corner the cliff continues in its upper half as a series of corners between smooth slabby walls. A lower tier of less attractive rock guards any entry.

After Many a Summer   50m   E2 5c *
G.E.Little, K.Howett   31 Jul 1994
Start below the corner between two small rowans. Climb the easy groove to the start of the corner. Excellent climbing up the corner leads to hollow flakes on the slabby right wall. Climb slightly above these to an incipient diagonal crack cutting the right wall. Move right with difficulty to a resting position at the base of a short rock ramp. Move up the ramp and make bold moves to surmount bulging rock (crux) and gain a short corner on the left. Go up to climb the wide finishing crack. About 12m of steep heather must be ascended to reach the belay (included in the overall length of the climb).

Scorched Earth   50m   E1 *
J.Horrocks, K.Howett   25 Jun 1995
The clean-cut slab sandwiched between two corners right of After Many a Summer. Start as for that route.
1. 20m 4c From the start of the big corner, scramble rightwards along the grass ledge with the right rowan, then climb the slabby wall leading up and right to an easy slab. Traverse right and go up to beneath the open chimney on the right of a sandwiched slab. Chokestone belay.

2. 30m 5b Climb the centre of the slabby wall via a vertical crack-line and large knobbles to the easier central slab. Go up this slightly left to near its left arete just below the top of the crag. Step right into a short ramp and pull out with trouble. Belay 15m back at a small outcrop of rock.

CREAG DUBH

(NN 672 959)   Alt 350m   South-South-East facing   Map p244

With more than 100 routes of up to 100m in length, Creag Dubh is the finest and largest roadside crag in Scotland. The horizontally stratified mica schist gives steep and exposed routes on generally flat or slightly incut holds with spaced protection, giving 'Creag Death' a reputation for exhilarating and occasionally scary climbing. This guide has upgraded some of the routes (again!) so no-one should be scared of it, although it is not a good choice for beginners; the protection requires too much calculation and there is little below Severe. However, the confident VS leader will find some memorable routes and the choice increases with the grades. A varied rack is useful, ranging from micro wires to extra camming devices, particularly small ones on the harder routes.

The crag dries quickly, although some areas are affected by seepage and the smooth rock is lethal in the wet. There is some loose rock in places and helmets are recommended. Following many of the routes to the top of the crag would involve an unpleasant grassy finish and a long descent, so it is common to abseil from trees. There are many old slings in-situ, but they and the trees they are attached to, should be treated with great caution.

Creag Dubh is also famous for its risqué route names. Dougal Haston and the Edinburgh Squirrels added 18 new routes in May 1965. The total was 36 by the end of 1965 and the refusal of the SMC to publish outcrop routes so infuriated the Squirrels that they published a guide themselves (*Creag Dubh and the Eastern Outcrops*, 1967 by Graham Tiso) and gave the routes obscene names to break another SMC rule.

General Approach: From Newtonmore follow the A86 to Spean Bridge for 5km to a lay-by on the north side of the road, directly below the crag and opposite a small gate leading to a large field at the west end of the western of two lochs. Arriving from Fort William or Spean Bridge in the west, the crag is even more obvious. The usual approach path starts from the lay-by and wanders up the hillside to below Great Wall.

To assist orientation on a first visit, go through the small gate on the opposite side of the road from the lay-by on to a grassy knoll. High on the right is Sprawl Wall slanting diagonally down the hillside with a black streaked wall at its lower right end. To the left and nearest the road is the long and continuous Central Wall. It is defined on its right by the Lower Central Wall with its distinctive growths of ivy, on its left by an impressive waterfall (obvious in all but a drought) and in the middle by the tall, smooth and light coloured Great Wall. Lower and some distance further left, only seen by evading the trees, is Bedtime Buttress with a big roof at its upper right and its Upper Tier just visible in profile behind.

BEDTIME BUTTRESS

The walls of the furthest left (west) and lowest buttress are not visible from the Central Wall Area, but the large roof at the top right of the buttress is often seen in profile.

Approach: Walk along the road to a gate opposite and just east of the gatehouse to the Creag Dubh Lodge (400m west of the lay-by). Cross the gate and follow a stalking track through the trees, then continue as it ascends beside a stream until the trees thin and Bedtime Buttress can be seen. Approaching from the Central Wall

Acapulco 45m E4 ***
D.Cuthbertson, R.Anderson Jun 1981
A brilliant bold outing through the roof. Start just right of Oui Oui at the foot of the wall.
1. 10m 5c Climb a left-slanting quartz seam to a ledge. A serious pitch and the scene of several bad accidents, but it can be avoided by climbing to the right or left to gain the ledge.
2. 35m 6a Move right to a groove. Climb this and step right onto the wall. Climb the wall veering left to reach for a 'schisty flange' on the lip of the roof about 5m right of the arete. Hand-traverse right to gain an obvious block, then pull over and get on to a ledge. Climb diagonally leftwards into the middle of the wall to finish direct up a tongue of quartz. It is also possible to gain the block from directly below at same grade.

The peg and tat above a break in the centre of the roof is **Independence** (E2 5c); a bold and quite serious trip up the big wall.

The following routes are on a lower section of Waterfall Wall which extends rightwards towards Central Wall. Descent is easiest by abseiling from the many trees that grow on the steep hillside above the crag.

Tip Off 40m VS 4c *
D.Bathgate, I.A McEacheran Mar 1965
This route takes an obvious groove forming the left side of an overhung recess. This is about 50m down and right of the previous route, beyond a buttress. Scramble up a corner to belay below the groove. Go up the groove until an obvious step left gains a shallower groove which leads to the top and the tree belay (abseil descent).

Right of the recess is a horizontal ledge 10m up and with many trees. The lower wall can be missed by scrambling up to the main pitch from the left. Descend by abseil from a tree above and left of the finish.

Smirnoff 50m HVS *
D.Bathgate, J.Brumfit (1PA) Nov 1965; FFA: Unknown
A good technical route which climbs an obvious tapering stepped corner above the ledge. The well protected corner has to be gained from a tree (falling off will provide a Tarzan impersonation). Older climbers who find it hard (it is!) swear the tree is growing further away from the wall! Start beneath some quartz on the lower wall (or climb an easier start further left).
1. 15m 4c Climb to the left end of a long overhang and cross it just left of the quartz. Trend right to a tree belay below the corner.
2. 35m 5a Climb the tree for a high runner, then step on to the wall and move right to pull over a roof into the base of the corner. Continue up the corner (peg runner) to finish.

Great Wall

Creag Dubh's centrepiece is defined on its left edge by a tree filled groove. To its right lies the prominent twisting rib of King Bee, which is interrupted by a roof at one-third height. However, it is the central wall further to the right, with its wildly folded beds of mica schist, shot through with seams of quartz, which grabs the attention. The most obvious feature is a triangular niche in the centre of the wall, which is visited by a number of routes, the most famous being Inbred. The wall left of the niche is covered in fine hard and serious routes.

Descent: By abseil (see descriptions), or go eastwards down the broad wooded shelf below Sprawl Wall. To gain the base of Lower Central Wall go lower and further left than appearance suggests (an indistinct cairn marks the line).

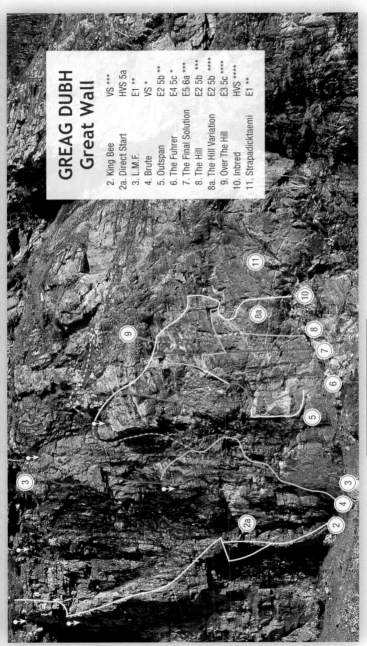

GREAG DUBH
Great Wall

2. King Bee	VS	***
2a. Direct Start	HVS 5a	
3. L.M.F.	E1	**
4. Brute	VS	*
5. Outspan	E2 5b	**
6. The Fuhrer	E4 5c	*
7. The Final Solution	E5 6a	***
8. The Hill	E2 5b	****
8a. The Hill Variation	E2 5b	
9. Over The Hill	E3 5c	****
10. Inbred	HVS	****
11. Strapadicktaemi	E1	**

259

HIGHLAND CENTRAL

1 Men Only   60m   E2 *
D.Cuthbertson, A.Taylor   9 Sep 1976
Highly spectacular climbing with adequate protection on the hardest section, although the roof is well protected.
1. 20m Start up the gully left of King Bee to a small ledge on the left of a green coloured wall. An easier start is 10m to the left.
2. 40m 5b Traverse right into a groove on the green wall. Climb this and the overhang above to a ledge with a small tree. Move right and climb a shallow groove to a roof. Pull over and traverse left to a ledge and flake. Ascend the flake and the wall to an overhang. Turn this on the right and continue to a junction with King Bee (in situ point for 50m abseil).

2 King Bee   110m   VS ***
D.Haston, J.Moriarty, A.Ewing   Apr 1965
A classic, and the best climb of its grade on the crag. Protection is adequate and good on the technical crux. Descend via one abseil after pitch 2 (in-situ) or two abseils after pitch 3, from trees left or right of the finish. Start at the foot of the chimney which runs right of the rib.
1. 25m 4c Climb the rib to a small tree, then move left and up to a roof. Move left again and climb to a tree under a bigger roof. Traverse right between the roofs and go up to a ledge.
2. 35m 5a Step left and climb the wall trending slightly left (passing an optional belay back in the chimney) to a small bulge out left. Pull through this (technical crux), then climb a vague arete trending leftwards to an exposed belay.
3. 20m 4c Pull up right to the roof above the belay. Pass it strenuously on the right to reach easier ground. From here, trend either left or right depending on the choice of abseil tree (as described above).
4. 30m 4b For those who choose to continue, pull up the wall above the right-hand tree, then slant left on good rock to reach the upper grass slopes.
Variation: **Direct Start   HVS 5a**
An exciting option on big holds. Where the normal route moves left at the first small tree, continue straight up the slight arete, pulling strenuously through the roof to join the parent route at the belay. A Friend 3 is useful.

3 L.M.F   70m   E1 **
F.Harper, B.March   10 Oct 1971
An exciting direct line up both tiers of wall and high in the grade. 'Lack of Moral Fibre', or something else! Start immediately left of the birch tree but right of Brute.
1. 35m 5b Ascend the steep wall direct to the belay ledge of Brute. Climb up around the left side of the roof above to a shattered crack (peg runner), then follow this to a ledge with five bolts.
2. 35m 5b Climb up into the left-hand of two quartz grooves before transferring to the larger right groove and climbing this (peg runner) to a right end of a roof. Traverse left a short way before heading direct to the abseil tree.

4 Brute   45m   VS *
T.Sullivan, N.Collingham   Oct 1959
A typical Creag Dubh route; steep, strenuous and rather intimidating. Start at an open groove 3m left of the birch tree.
1. 15m 4c Climb the groove, then step right and go up to a ledge.
2. 30m 5a Go diagonally right under the roof until it is possible to climb it using a crack at its smallest point (excellent runners, including a peg). Continue up until it is possible to move left and up a slab to the bolt abseil point of LMF.

The next routes all start from the raised grass ledge right of a large birch tree. Descent is a 45m abseil from the tree at the top left end of the wall.

Outspan 45m E2 5b **
R.Barley, B.Griffiths 13 Apr 1971
A 5b boulder problem start is followed by sustained and serious 5a climbing, snaking its way up the left side of the impressive main section of the wall. Start at a short thin crack 10m right of the birch tree and leading to a very white quartz blotch at 3m. Gain a loose block at 4m, pass it and gain a handrail. Follow it leftwards for 4m, then ascend directly up the steep black wall on good holds (serious) to gain a horizontal break. Follow this back rightwards to a bulge (peg runner). Step over this, go up right to a large flake, then ascend diagonally rightwards across the centre of the wall to a junction with Inbred on a long ledge. Follow the easy line diagonally leftwards to the tree abseil as for Inbred.

The Fuhrer 45m E4 5c *
D.Cuthbertson, I.F.Duckworth 17 Jun 1979
A serious outing even by Creag Dubh standards, although technically not too testing. Start as for Outspan at the thin crack. Climb past the loose block at 4m to reach another block and make thin moves leftwards up the quartz to gain a plaque-like block above. Stand on this and move right to the peg runner on Outspan. Follow Outspan over the bulge and go up right to a large flake. Climb the quartz wall diagonally left to a grotty ledge. The steep shallow groove in the headwall leads to the tree. Abseil off.

The Final Solution 45m E5 6a ***
S.Monks, W.Todd May 1987
A superbly serious outing up the middle of the wall. Steve Monks nabbed this central line from Grant Farquhar, who made the second ascent unknowingly a few days later. Start left of the boulder at the foot of The Hill. Climb the wall just right of the vertical quartz streak by bouldery moves to gain a small ledge immediately left of The Hill. Step up left and climb directly up the bulging wall on improving holds to gain a handrail running out right into a small niche and protection (phew!) Continue directly above, passing through the second niche of The Hill, to the long ledge on Inbred, then follow this to the tree.

The Hill 50m E2 ***
K.Spence, J.Porteous Sep 1967
A magnificent and intimidating climb, serious on the first pitch and very exposed on the second. Kenny Spence's debut on the crag, very bold for the time. Start at a boulder below some rust coloured rock, left of the crack of Inbred.
1. 20m 5b Ascend to a small ledge (tape runner), then continue direct up the bulging wall past a poor peg runner to enter a small groove. Climb this until it is possible to traverse right into the triangular niche of Inbred.
2. 30m 5a Traverse leftwards to a smaller niche. Continue by a slightly descending weakness into a second niche. Climb straight up on big holds to below small roofs (The Final Solution continues above), then make a descending traverse left to another slight niche. Now on easier but still very steep ground, climb fairly directly up the wall (joining Outspan and later Inbred) until moves left gain the abseil tree.
Variation: **45m E2 5b** ****
A single pitch version is possible by missing out the traverse into the triangular niche to belay. Instead climb direct from above the peg runner into the smaller niche of the second pitch, then follow the normal route, starting with the descending traverse left into the second niche.

Over The Hill 45m E3 5c ****
D.Cuthbertson, R.Kerr Nov 1980
A direct version of The Hill giving a superb sustained pitch. Follow The Hill Variation past the peg runner and into the small niche. Move up and right to a small spike. Traverse left and ascend the wall up a difficult thin crack to join and finish left up Inbred to the tree.

HIGHLAND CENTRAL

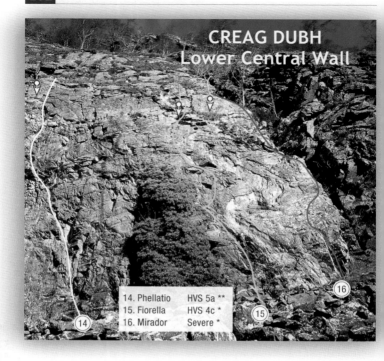

CREAG DUBH
Lower Central Wall

14. Phellatio	HVS 5a **
15. Fiorella	HVS 4c *
16. Mirador	Severe *

10 Inbred 105m HVS ★★★★
D.Haston, T.Gooding Oct 1964

A tremendous route, steep and intimidating but on big holds, if a little reachy at the start. High in the grade but the protection is adequate (i.e. you won't hit anything!), especially with a Friend 2.5 placement in the wall below the niche. Dougal Haston's ascent was one of the first routes at Creag Dubh, up the steepest part of the most impressive wall on the crag; it soon gained a reputation. Start at a thin crack leading to an obvious triangular niche on the right side of Great Wall.

1. 25m 5a Climb the crack to a peg runner, then move left and go up to pull into the triangular niche from the left. Step down and move out right, then go up to a ledge.

2. 35m 4b Climb over the bulge at the left end of the ledge to gain a long ledge, then continue diagonally left to a tree belay. It is common to abseil from this tree, or:

3. 45m 4a Climb the slabby wall on the left to finish.

11 Strapadicktaemi 50m E1 ★★
D.Cuthbertson, R.Anderson 10 Sep 1976

Juggy and exciting climbing, pitch 1 being less technical but distinctly more serious than Inbred. Start as for Inbred.

1. 25m 5a Ascend the initial bulge on Inbred, then follow an obvious right-slanting crack to a rest. Go up a short crack to a long narrow ledge, then continue over the bulge above to belay as for Inbred.

2. 25m 5a Move right to gain a left-slanting crack. Follow this to a small overhang, then traverse left to another crack which leads to the top.

To descend, traverse grass ledges up and left, then descend to the abseil tree.

Lower Central Wall

The lower wall comprises three sections divided by a wet chimney with holly and a deep narrow gully. The left section consists of an excellent steep black wall on which lies Ticket to Ride. Between the wet chimney and the gully is another fine steep wall climbed by Phellatio. This is bounded on the right by a thick growth of ivy, the most distinctive feature. The wall right of the gully is more broken and has a prominent straight pine with a dead top at its base.

Descent: Abseil is recommended since there are convenient trees near all the routes on the left-hand section, although it is possible to scramble to the broad wooded shelf.

12 Rib Direct   110m   Very Difficult
B.Halpin, T.Abbey, S.Tondeur
A reasonable route, the only one at its grade, with a good final pitch. Also the first route recorded at Creag Dubh. Start at a left-slanting crack.
1. 10m 4a Climb the crack with a tricky start to a tree belay.
2. 25m The obvious groove leads to a ledge and tree belay under an overhang.
3. 45m Turn the overhang by a crack on the left and continue to a ledge and tree belay.
4. 30m Traverse right onto the rib which leads to the top.

13 Ticket to Ride   35m   E3 5b **
D.Cuthbertson, A.Taylor   9 Sep 1976
An excellent sustained pitch with barely adequate protection up the black streaked wall right of the quartz. Start below the quartz streak and ascend up and right across it to a good spike. Go direct to a small niche, move left through a horizontal quartz streak and climb the steep wall slightly rightwards to a grass ledge.

14 Phellatio   40m   HVS 5a **
A.Ewing, I.A.McEacheran   May 1965; Direct finish (as described): K.Crocket, C Stead   1972
A fine direct line up the wall right of the wet chimney provides a sustained and fairly serious pitch; runners are good but spaced. Start at a left-slanting groove 10m right of the chimney and 4m left of the ivy (not the groove immediately left of the ivy). Ascend the groove and continue up a bulging wall to a ledge (possible belay). Continue fairly directly up the wall above to finish right of a tree (abseil descent). Going direct to the tree is harder. Going left from the ledge is less intimidating but not as good.

15 Fiorella   35m   HVS 4c *
F.Harper, A.McKeith, J.Knight   Nov 1965
A very serious but good quality pitch. Start immediately right of the ivy crop below a left-slanting groove. Climb the groove to a bulge. Traverse right, then pull through the bulge and traverse back left beyond the initial groove. Climb the wall above (possible ground fall), then work rightwards to a tree belay.

16 Mirador   30m   Severe *
I.A.McEacheran, J.Knight, R.S.Burnett   May 1965
Start at the foot of a short groove on the left-bounding arete of Fred. Climb the groove, then move right on to the arete and follow it to the ledge and a tree belay. Abseil off.

Right of the deep gully is a wall with a big pine tree sitting on an elevated ledge below its centre.

17 Goutes d' Eau   25m   E2 5b *
D.Cuthbertson, R.Anderson   Jun 1981
A fine exposed pitch requiring some faith to gain the arete right of the gully.

Scramble up to the ledge with the big pine. Start 3m left of the pine. Climb the wall and pull over a bulge to a spike on the right. Traverse left across the slab to a small groove in the arete. Climb the arete, then go up the easy wall to a grass ledge. Finish diagonally up right on grass to reach an abseil tree.

SPRAWL WALL

This is the distinctive black streaked wall at the far right-hand end of Creag Dubh. Fewer routes are described than in the Central Wall Area and they are slightly less accessible, however the quality is just as good.

Approach: From the lay-by, walk rightwards up grass to a small flat area (2mins), from where there is a good view of Sprawl Wall. Continue rightwards beyond the worst of the boulders and fight a way up to its right-hand end (near Tree Hee), 10mins. To reach Sprawl Wall from Central Wall, traverse rightwards along the base of the cliff with a slight descent before one can go up through trees to the wall.

Descent: A 50m abseil reaches the ground from the top of Jump So High Direct. A long traverse right from the top of Tree Hee gains a faint path leading back to the foot of the crag.

Jump So High Direct   40m   E2 ***
F.Harper, A.McKeith, A.Ewing   May 1965 (5PA); FFA: G.Shields and party   early 1970s;
Direct start: K.Spence, J.Porteous   Sept 1967
This crack-line near the right end of the black streaked wall, gives superb strenuous climbing, with generally good protection. Scramble in from the left above a lower wall to reach a 4m left-facing corner at the bottom right end of the black streaked wall.
1. 25m 5c Climb a crack in the corner (avoiding the temptation to step off left) and make a long reach for a crack. Continue up black rock to reach the foot of an overhanging crack and climb it to the belay ledge. An easier alternative for shorties to the long reach move is to step delicately right on to a hanging slab, move further right to join the normal route, then return left to the overhanging crack.
2. 15m 5b Climb a thin overhanging crack above and trend right to finish.

Tree Hee   70m   Severe **
H.Small, J.Graham   Apr 1965
A delightful climb on excellent rock, climbing the slabs right of the black-streaked wall. There is some vegetation, but it is easily avoided. The lowest point of the buttress is an overhanging wall. Start at the right end of this.
1. 30m Make a left-rising traverse above the overhanging wall, then follow a shallow groove to a ledge and belay on the left edge.
2. 40m Move up and right past a holly tree. Ascend a slab to an overlap, then move up left to belay on the terrace.
Direct Variation: **50m   VS 4b**
I.A.McEacheran, J.Knight, R.S.Burnet   Apr 1965
From halfway along the initial rising traverse, climb directly up near some quartz. Join the normal route just right of the holly, then climb directly up the slab and through the upper overlap by a steep V-groove.

HUNTLY'S CAVE

(NJ 024 327)   Alt 300m   North facing   Map p244
This impressively steep crag of blocky schist, is as popular for its ability to stay dry in showery weather, as it is for its middle grade routes. Despite all the overhangs, most routes are easier than they appear as the rock strata dips slightly downwards giving large and numerous holds, and protection is generally very good. The crag lies in a sheltered wooded gorge and midges can be a problem at the cliff base. Huntly's Cave itself lies in a jumble of boulders at the downstream end of the main crag.

Approach: Where the A939 Grantown-on-Spey to Nairn road runs through a cutting, there is limited parking at its south (Grantown) end (NJ 024 325). From here, a stile leads to a path down across a disused railway line to the top of the cliff. A muddy path on the left (facing out) leads to the foot of the climbs, 3mins.

Routes are described from the right side of the crag downwards.

Pete's Wall   12m   E2 5c **
The climbing is sustained, strenuous and a little reachy, but very well protected, with small Friends useful. Whether Pete Boardman found it any easier with flowers growing out of the cracks, than most folk do nowadays is hard to say. Climb the wall right of Right-Hand Groove to the smallest point of the long roof. Cross this with difficulty and continue up the wall above.

Right-Hand Groove   10m   Very Difficult *
Climb the obvious groove over a jutting block to finish by a horizontal tree.

Slot Direct   10m   Severe *
A steep and enjoyable route which goes directly up the deep V-groove to the left.

Lime Street   20m   E4 5c *
Lower down is an overhung bay below a chimney-corner with huge overhangs. The overhanging right wall of this bay gives a fine, strenuous and well protected route which loses a star for escapability. Pete Livesey did this route while doing his MIC assessment at Glenmore Lodge, probably to impress the assessors. Start off blocks at the foot of the chimney-corner (Double Overhang). Move right and pull through a roof at a flake. Return left (subtract a grade for continuing to Double Overhang for a rest) and climb the central crack-line which curves left to join Double Overhang above its second roof. Just before Double Overhang, make a long reach up right and climb walls to the top. Going into Double Overhang here is allowed. Total exhaustion or your money back.

Double Overhang   20m   HVS 5a ***
The classic of the crag. An awesome line which is not quite as hard as it looks. Climb the obvious corner which is blocked by two large roofs.

Diagonal   25m   VS 4c **
A good climb up the bottomless corners left of Double Overhang. Climb Double Overhang to the first roof, traverse left and gain the left-facing corner either by a low line (strenuous) or a high line (technical). Go up the corner and move up to the next corner (it is common to belay here). Traverse right under the final roof to finish.

Diagonal Direct   25m   E1 5c *
Start right of Cave Route on the frontal face. Climb a scooped green wall to gain the first corner of Diagonal. Go up this and exit right to an optional belay under a roof. Climb a thin crack over the roof (crux) and go up the wall above.

Slabby Groove   25m   HVS 5a *
A fine route, daringly named but less strenuous than many here. Start as for Diagonal Direct but trend leftwards to the arete. Step left round the arete and pull awkwardly into a shallow groove. Continue up the stepped rock behind to finish up the bottomless crack of Cave Route.

Cave Route   25m   Hard Severe 4b ***
The other classic of the crag, often split into 3 pitches. The final section is unusual and very exposed, sometimes with a noisy audience of young jackdaws. Start at a recess near the left end of the cliff. Climb the slabby corner on the right to gain a ledge. Go up the corner at the back of the ledge for 2m, then traverse the banded

wall leftwards to the prow. Move up and right to the cave below the huge final roof, then go right and finish up the bottomless crack. From the cave, thin people can escape through the squeeze chimney running leftwards or the one at the foot of the bottomless crack. But those who get stuck must remember jackdaws eat meat!
Variation: **Cave Direct: VS 4b** ***
Climb the corner direct from the right end of the first ledge to the cave.

Moray Firth Coast

These sea-cliffs offer pleasant and easily accessible climbing in one of the driest and sunniest parts of the country. As such they are excellent poor weather alternatives.

CUMMINGSTON

(NJ 130 692) Partially Tidal Mostly North facing Maps p244, 268

While its softish sandstone does not offer the highest quality routes, Cummingston has some of the driest and sunniest weather in Scotland, and is often dry when other areas are not. The routes are short and sometimes overhanging, frequently with difficult undercut starts, but big fluted holds and other wind eroded features also produce many routes in the lower grades. A spare length of rope or long slings can be utilised for top-roping on the belay stakes, although erosion is causing unpleasant sandy finishes to some of the more popular climbs. In recent years the cliffs have become popular for bouldering and a guide by Iain Macdonald can be downloaded from <www.scottishclimbs.com>. The cliffs lie above a tidal beach of sand, gravel or rock, the quality of the landing often being variable from year to year.

The Moray Mountaineering Club recorded the first routes in the 1950s, followed by Moray Sea School and RAF personnel. John Mackenzie and friends started intensive development in the late 1970s followed by Aberdonians, particularly Dougie Dinwoodie, in the early 1980s.

Approach: From Cummingston village turn north towards the sea at the first turning 100m east of the white war memorial with a cross on top. Turn left and then right to reach an unsurfaced car park overlooking the sea. A childrens' play park and mobile toilets are conveniently at hand for a day out with the family. Descend to the old railway line (kiddies' slide optional) and follow it left (west) along a cutting for about 200m until its right wall disappears. Follow short tracks down to a pebble beach seen below, 5mins. Continue further left for The Stacks Area (the big stack is clearly visible) or turn back right to the Prophet Walls.

PROPHET WALLS

The rock in this section is usually sound and many of the better leads are here. The area can be reached at almost all tide levels from the beach. The three corners taken by Left, Central and Right are set in the right side of a projecting buttress and are obvious on the approach. Beyond them (east) is an overhung bay containing the best hard routes. At the left side of the overhung bay is a corner leading to a roof **The Gripper** (HVS 5b). The smooth little hanging corner right of The Gripper and left of the roofs is **Aesthetic Ape** (E4 6a).

1 Orange Ape 20m E2 5c
D.Dinwoodie, A.Ross 1984
The obvious undercut corner at the back left of the bay.

2 Bat's Wall 15m E4 6a **
D.Dinwoodie 1984
The classic of the Prophet Walls takes the crack-line up the back wall right of the

Double Overhang, HVS 5a, Huntley's Cave. Climber Alastair Buchanan (photo David Buchanan)

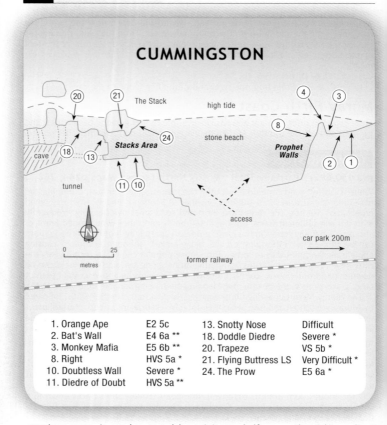

CUMMINGSTON

The Stack

high tide

stone beach

Stacks Area

Prophet Walls

cave

tunnel

access

car park 200m

former railway

metres

N

0   25

1. Orange Ape	E2 5c	13. Snotty Nose	Difficult
2. Bat's Wall	E4 6a **	18. Doddle Diedre	Severe *
3. Monkey Mafia	E5 6b **	20. Trapeze	VS 5b *
8. Right	HVS 5a *	21. Flying Buttress LS	Very Difficult *
10. Doubtless Wall	Severe *	24. The Prow	E5 6a *
11. Diedre of Doubt	HVS 5a **		

previous route. It can be started by gaining a shelf up on the right or direct (harder). A well protected route, mercilessly strenuous with a wicked finish, sometimes sandy. Rarely flashed on sight.

3 Monkey Mafia 15m E5 6b **
L.Johnston 1998
A strenuous and technical outing but mostly well protected, taking the hanging crack leading leftwards out of the deep cave on the right of Bat's Wall. Gain a sloping ramp from either left or right (or harder direct), then move up to the roof. Undercut leftwards with some technical moves. Gain the freedom of a groove and finish with difficulty.

4 The Prophet 15m E2 5c **
J.R.Mackenzie, I.Dalley 16 Feb 1980
Start at a small inset corner at the left side of the projecting buttress. Climbs its right arete, then pull into a left-facing corner which leads up to the roof. Surmount the roof and finish more easily. Low in the grade.

5 I-Ching 20m E3 5c *
D.Dinwoodie, D.Hawthorn, A.Ross Dec 1984
Climb the fine arete left of Left. Protection is just adequate, so perhaps E2.

6 Left   20m   VS 5a *
J.R.Mackenzie, R.Brown, M.Birch   29 Jul 1978
On the right face of the projecting buttress are three corners. This is the left one, (surprise, surprise).

7 Centre   20m   Hard Severe 4b **
M.Birch, J.R.Mackenzie   29 Jul 1978
As for Left to an overhung flake, then step right and climb the corner directly. Intimidating rather than difficult.

8 Right   15m   HVS 5a *
J.R.Mackenzie, R.Brown   29 Jul 1978
The right-hand corner.

9 Bay Watch   80m   6b **
N.Clement   1980s
A complete left to right boulder traverse of the Prophet Walls providing a fine and technically demanding stamina exercise. Start at the far left side of the bay by some boulders and follow the chalk!

STACKS AREA

At the west end of the pebble beach is the large sea-stack with good routes on the walls opposite it and further along. This area of cliff is the most popular with a large selection of easier routes and good bouldering. Unfortunately its popularity has eroded the cliff-top, so the routes are prone to being sandy. The first routes are on the long steep wall opposite the largest stack, ending at a tunnel. A roofed corner left of this wall and not far above the beach is **The Nest** (E2 6a), often done as a boulder problem up to the 'nest'.

0 Doubtless Wall   10m   Severe *
M.Birch, J.R.Mackenzie   Mar 1979
Climb the left end of the wall to gain a ledge at two-thirds height, then continue on smaller holds to the top.

1 Diedre of Doubt   12m   HVS 5a **
Climb a fine corner in the centre of the wall directly from the undercut base and finish up the poorly protected smooth corner above. There is a less strenuous start on the right (the start of Diedre of Double Doubt). The undercut base (low cave) offers a number of fine bum scraping boulder problems. The left side of the corner's left arete is **The Artful Dodger** (HVS 5a).

2 Diedre of Double Doubt   12m   E2 5b *
Gain and climb the short diedre up and right of Diedre of Doubt and just below the cliff-top. Climb strenuously up the centre of the wall, arrange gear awkwardly (only E1 if you trust it) and make the crux move up the small wall to the diedre.

Beyond the tunnel and the stack, the cliff takes a step out towards the sea forming a big arete and preventing access during high tide. Right of the arete, a series of heavily sculptured walls and grooves lead rightwards to a rounded undercut wall left of the next cave entrance.

3 Snotty Nose   12m   Difficult
The big arete (close to the stack) is loose but still popular.

4 Cornflake Wall   12m   Moderate *
The wall just right of twin grooves **Old Peg Groove** (VS 4c) and left of a left-facing corner has excellent holds but an awkward start for the grade.

HIGHLAND CENTRAL

15 Rice Crispie Wall   12m   Difficult
The steep sculptured wall next right provides an example of verticality without difficulty. Start from a bare rock platform at the base of the cliff and climb directly up a bulging rib.

The next three routes are in a recessed section left of the obvious rounded undercut wall. The recess is bounded on either side by corners, **The Groove** (Difficult) on the left and Doddle Diedre on the right. The back wall of the recess contains a more recessed section with an obvious narrow chimney capped by a roof Blockbuster.

16 Bombproof   12m   Severe *
Start at the base of The Groove and climb the overhanging wall on the right on big holds (avoid bridging into The Groove) to a direct finish on cleaned plates.

17 Blockbuster   12m   Very Difficult
Climb the chimney-crack to the roof (excellent thread runner). Exit right to stand on a spike on the right arete. Finish obviously as for Doddle Diedre. A harder alternative is to pull direct through the roof on big holds to the left.

18 Doddle Diedre   12m   Severe *
Climb the fine corner and exit left below the top. Perhaps only Very Difficult. Well protected; Friends are useful (though not essential).

19 Stegosaurus   12m   VS 4c **
D.McCallum, J.R.Mackenzie 25 Feb 1979
The aptly named spiky arete between Doddle Diedre and the undercut wall is both exciting and strenuous.

20 Trapeze   12m   VS 5b *
The wall about 2m right of Stegosaurus, surmounting a roof at half-height, is **Gibbon** (HVS 5c), usually climbed as a boulder problem. This route is a shallow corner above the centre of the wall. A powerful start leads into the corner and an easier finish. Again usually a boulder problem. The hanging arete at the right end of the undercut wall is **Gorilla** (5c).

THE STACK

The largest of the stacks is cut off by the highest tides, but normally the top is accessible.

Descent: By abseil or descend a chimney-corner on the east side (Moderate).

Captain Birdseye (E2 5b) climbs the left edge of the landward face to a niche, finishing directly up a bulge and groove above. The centre of the face is **Fingers Wall** (E3 6a, or E3 5b starting on the left).

21 Flying Buttress, Left Side   10m   Very Difficult *
Start at the top right of a low sloping shelf on the landward face. Climb a corner to a ledge, then go up a short wall to the top.

22 Flying Buttress, Right Side   12m   Difficult
The opposite side of the same corner-crack.

23 Flying Groove   12m   VS 4c *
M.Birch, J.R.Mackenzie, D.Gilbert 12 May 1979
Right again is another groove, difficult to climb elegantly. The rock is a little suspect.

24 The Prow   12m   E5 6a *

D.Dinwoodie 1987
The big overhanging prow on the east side is unprotected but perhaps only 5c. Climb out on massive holds, then go up the left edge to gain and pass the lip. The landing is unthinkable.

LOGIE HEAD

(NJ 528 682) Map p244

This attractive cliff consists of upturned beds of metamorphosed rock, forming steep walls and prows jutting into the sea. Holds are generally positive and protection plentiful, although care should be taken with the thinnest flakes and there is the occasional loose block. The best routes are in the middle grades and powerful arms are not needed, though finger strength is an advantage.

The rock dries quickly and stays dry during blustery showers from the west, making Logie Head a popular retreat in poor weather. Most of the routes are accessible at high tide (although the Star Face might need an abseil approach) and nesting seabirds are rarely a problem.

Approach: From Cullen Caravan Park (NJ 516 674), to the east of the town and signposted from near the town square. From the tarmac car park beside the Park entrance walk east round the site beside a football pitch to gain a track leading northwards to a wide, open grassy bay. Logie Head is the obvious rocky headland forming the east side of the bay. A good path leads round eastwards and crosses the neck of the final rocky crest of the headland to gain a smaller rocky bay on the far side. The main east face of the ridge faces across the bay, 20mins.

EMBANKMENT ONE

Non-tidal   East facing
This is the furthest inland of the walls on the east side, above a grassy area and the first reached on the approach. The attractive appearance and position away from the sea makes it the most popular section of cliff. Embankment Two (no described routes) lies seaward and is separated from Embankment One by a grassy ramp.

Descent: Scramble down a ramp and short wall just to the left of the climbs.

The cliff is characterised by a left to right diagonal break, the line of **The Central Belt** (E1 5b); an enjoyable rising traverse and the longest route here. Another diagonal break crosses it right to left. The next four routes finish by the three crack-lines above the top left part of this diagonal break.

Bladder Wrack   10m   Severe 4b
A.Robertson 1982
Climb a tricky crack straight up to and finish by the wide leftmost upper crack.

Sea Urchin   10m   Hard Severe 4b
A.Robertson 1982
Climb the more obvious break in the wall just right of Bladder Wrack and follow the second upper crack from the left.

Sea Link   10m   Very Difficult *
A composite of the previous two routes makes a worthwhile easier climb. Climb the initial break of Sea Urchin to the diagonal break. Step left below the bulge and finish up the top wide crack of Bladder Wrack.

Poacher   10m   VS 4b **
A.Robertson 1982
A fine pitch, sustained and well protected, low in the grade.. Start just left of where the diagonal break meets the ground. Climb the wall to the break. Pull through the bulge by a short diagonal crack, then go up the main crack leftwards to the top. It

HIGHLAND CENTRAL

is the same standard to go right above the diagonal crack to join the finish of Cullenary Delight.

Cullenary Delight   10m   VS 5a ***
A.Robertson   1982
Another fine pitch up the vague crack-line on the right. Start where the diagonal break meets the ground and the grassy ramp dividing Embankment One and Two slants up right. Climb past a small flaky recess at head height into the left-slanting crack-line and follow it with some technical moves up and left at mid-height, where the crack is less defined.

Sunnyside Up   10m   HVS 5a *
D.Lawrence, R.McHardy, N.Morrison, A.Nisbet, A.Robertson   1982
Climb the short crack starting just right of Cullenary Delight, then move right into a well defined crack and finish up this. A direct start up the lower crack is 5c.

Fisherman's Tail   10m   Hard Severe
S.Steer   1982
Climb the more broken wall right of Sunnyside Up, starting right of a defined crack.

GULLY WALL

Non-tidal   East facing
Logie Head ends in a long ridge jutting out to sea. The seaward end is split into two by a gully hidden from view except from the crest. Despite being a little gloomy and sometimes slow to dry, there are some good routes on the gully's left wall (viewed as approached).

Sea Pink   12m   VS 4c *
A.Robertson   1982
The obvious crack starting well left of the wedged block at the foot of the gully.

Sea Anemone   12m   E1 5b **
A.Nisbet, D.Lawrence, R.McHardy, N.Morrison, A.Robertson   1982
Start on top of the huge wedged block at the foot of the gully and take the faint crack-line veering slightly left up the right end of the slab. A superb sustained pitch with good protection, although there is some lichen.

Star Zone

Tidal (most routes possible)   East facing
This open sunny wall is continuous with the left gully wall and has the best rock at Logie. Below the wall is a rock platform which is partly submerged at high tide, but routes are still accessible. At mid-tide the wall is best approached down the gully itself (an awkward scramble). At low tide it is most easily approached along the base of the Embankment walls. At high tide, or for entertainment, an approach can be made along the West Face, then through the Black Hole (Moderate). An abseil rope from the top of the wall is the best option when several routes are planned.

Black Hole   15m   Difficult *
A.Robertson   1982
An odd excursion. Climb a short corner and flakes for about 5m to gain the hole. Go through the hole to easy ground on the west side of the ridge and climb a slanting groove above to the ridge crest.

Moray Eel   10m   VS 4b **
A.Robertson   1982

Start in the centre of the wall and climb a line of flakes up and left to gain the obvious steep curving crack finishing at the top of a ramp which comes up from the Black Hole.

Rising Star   10m   HVS 5b ***
D.Lawrence, N.Morrison, R.McHardy, A.Nisbet, A.Robertson   1982
Start as for Moray Eel and gain the thin crack in the centre of the upper part of the wall. A delightful route.

Fallen Star   10m   VS 4c ***
A.Robertson, D.Lawrence, R.McHardy, N.Morrison, A.Nisbet   1982
A wee classic. Start just left of the edge of the wall. Climb up left to a flake and then follow a right-slanting crack to finish in a fine position at the top of the arete.

Fading Star   10m   HVS 5a *
N.Morrison, D.Lawrence, R.McHardy, A.Nisbet, A.Robertson   1982
An eliminate up the right edge of the wall, artificial but very enjoyable. Climb the edge near the arete forming the end of the wall to a pocket at 3m. Step up left towards the crack of Fallen Star, then move back right to gain a small ledge on the arete. Continue up the edge to finish. Climbing the arete direct, keeping the right hand on or round the arete the whole way, is E2 6a.

Dark Star   10m   E1 5b **
R.McHardy, D.Lawrence, N.Morrison, A.Nisbet, A.Robertson   1982
A fine line in a good situation. The left branch of the ridge ends in a steep, narrow, black wall facing north and dropping straight into the sea. This is split by two parallel cracks. Make a hard move up the left-hand crack to a jug. Swing right and finish up the right-hand crack.

The Cull   8m   E1 5b *
A.Nisbet, D.Lawrence, R.McHardy, N.Morrison, A.Robertson   1982
This ferocious leaning crack lies at the seaward end of the West Face, reached by scrambling down from near the start of the descent gully. Start by stepping off a rock pedestal.

Strathconon

This long valley north-west of Inverness has several crags in its lower reaches. But it saves its best for the clean slabs of Creag Ghlas, some 20km up.

CREAG GHLAS - WEST BUTTRESS

(NH 246 545)   Alt 500m   South-West facing   Map p244   Diagram p274

Clean rock, sustained climbing and a sunny aspect characterise this unusual mountain crag on the south-west face of Sgurr a' Mhuillin above Glen Meinich. The smooth schist slabs, sometimes cut by deep parallel cracks, and steep sidewalls offer a unique style of climbing. Cams of all sizes are useful, particularly the smallest ones in some of the recent routes.

Approach: Park near Glenmeanie (NH 282 526) and walk or cycle along the forested Gleann Meinich until below the crag and ascend 250m of steep ground fairly direct to it. East Buttress appears about 500m before West Buttress and is bigger, but somewhat rambling. About 1hr with a bike. There may be restrictions during the stalking season (see Environment Notes).

Descent: Either down the steep heather gully at the south-east end of the cliff, which can be tricky in the wet, or by a shallow scree filled gully at the north-west end. Abseils can be used for the short routes and after the main pitches of some of the longer routes.

HIGHLAND CENTRAL

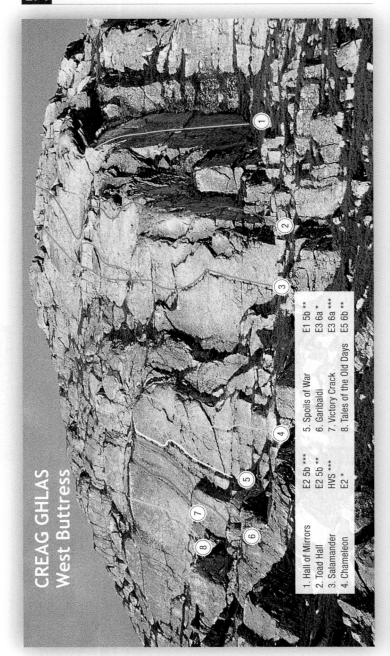

CREAG GHLAS
West Buttress

1. Hall of Mirrors   E2 5b ***
2. Toad Hall   E2 5b **
3. Salamander   HVS ***
4. Chameleon   E2 *
5. Spoils of War   E1 5b **
6. Garibaldi   E3 6a *
7. Victory Crack   E3 6a ***
8. Tales of the Old Days   E5 6b **

The climbs are described from right to left. There are several additional routes on slabs on the upper right side of the crag. These are separated on the left from the main sector of slab by a big sidewall with the following route. The nine hours spent cleaning it was worthwhile, as you're bound to agree.

1 Hall of Mirrors   80m   E2 ***
R.Brown, G.Cullen, J.R.Mackenzie   30 Oct 1993
The excellent and sustained first pitch offers the best climbing on the crag. The pitch is low in the grade and well protected but requires a double rack of Friends from 0.5 to 3. Take an old sling if you intend abseiling from the top of the first pitch. Start centrally below an obvious crack system in the striated sidewall.
1. 50m 5b Climb cracks and flakes to a small overlap. Pull over and follow the main crack to a hanging belay by a small spike about 6m below the large overhung ledge.
2. 30m 4a Continue to the large sloping ledge and move left on to the arete. Climb this by delightful flake-cracks to an awkward step right. Continue up and left to the right end of the heather terrace above. Scramble down, then up to reach the descent gully.

2 Toad Hall   145m   E2 **
D.McGimpsey, A.Nisbet, G.Nisbet   3 Sep 2000
An excellent first pitch on the sidewall and right edge of the main slab. Start at a ledge beneath the central rib of the West Buttress where a broken groove forms the right edge of the main slab.
1. 45m 5b Step up right on to a higher ledge, then climb to heather below the right sidewall of the rib. Step left immediately on to the sidewall and climb this, initially close to heather but soon diverging into a crack-line about a metre from the arete. Follow this, sometimes using the crack to the right, to gain the arete at a ledge. Follow the arete (crux, runners in the crack to the right) to a ledge on the left and belay.
2. 20m 4c Climb the right edge of the main slab, then continue on the main slab trending left before returning back right to the top of the slab.
3. 20m Scramble up left to a big flake at the foot of the next slab.
4. 20m 5b Go 5m further left to gain and climb a right-slanting crack to a terrace (an initial runner high on the left is recommended).
5. 40m 4b Climb a line of flakes up the next wall. Go left to a big flake at the base of the final blocky wall. Stand on it and climb the wall above.

3 Salamander   150m   HVS ***
J.R.Mackenzie, R.Brown, C.Powell   12 Aug 1994
An enjoyable route taking a central line and giving sustained climbing which is quick to dry. To the left of Toad Hall is a sweep of smooth slabs split by a prominent dog-leg crack.
1. 40m 4c Climb the crack which is noticeably harder after the dog-leg to a narrow ledge; a superb well protected pitch.
2. 25m 4c Trend up right on hidden edges to a narrow heather ledge and creep left along this to some holds. Climb the bold slabby wall above, exiting left along a diagonal crack.
There are two methods of climbing the next pitch.
3a. 40m 5a Climb up to hollow flakes and go straight up to a curved overlap. Traverse left under this and pull over on the left to shelves. Climb up a delicate wall to a narrow rake and a hollow flake right of a hidden corner.
3b. 45m 5b Step right and climb a thin crack which is difficult for the first 6m,but eases with the lessening of angle. Take a line directly to the overlap above and turn this delicately by the right edge. Easy climbing up left leads to the hollow flake.
4. 25m 4c On the left is a hidden corner; climb up the edge and step left (often wet but possible) on to the slab and undercut into the corner. Climb this excellent corner with interest to the rock glacis below the top wall.
5. 20m 4b Left of a big block is a superb narrow chimney which narrows to a crack. Layback the edge, which is easier than it looks, to finish up a short steep crack.

4 Chameleon   60m   E2 *
J.R.Mackenzie, R.Brown   31 Aug 1998
Left of the heathery corner that lies left of the Salamander slab is a another steep
slab with a shallow right-trending curved overlap. The route takes shallow cracks
running straight through this feature. The first pitch is optional but avoids heather.
Start below the overlapped slab to the right.
1. 15m 4b Climb two short slabs to move left to a short crack below the overlap.
2. 45m 5c Climb up to and through the overlap (small Friends) to the base of a
thin crack. Climb this well protected crux to a wobbly flake and small ledge. Move
up rightwards through an overlap and make a delicate step up right to the edge
which is followed more easily to the heather ledge. An excellent sustained pitch.
Either scramble off leftwards along the exposed ledge or continue to the top as for
Victory Crack or Salamander.

5 Spoils of War   45m   E1 5b **
R.Brown, J.R.Mackenzie   4 Nov 1995
This is a fine pitch up the very pronounced right-hand crack near the right edge of
the long smooth slab left of Chameleon. The terrace below it can be reached by
climbing a chimney-corner or more easily the next corner left, then scrambling up
a break in the wall. Start to the right of the crack to avoid heather. Traverse left by
a flake hold to the main crack. Climb the crack past a wide section to a little tree
and step left to the crux section which is parallel and holdless but very well protected. Scramble off left along a narrow ledge.

Left of Spoils of War and below the narrow ledge is another section of smooth slab
with some fine hard routes, including the popular Victory Crack. Descend by abseiling pitch 1 of Victory Crack or scrambling off left.

6 Garibaldi   40m   E3 6a *
D.McGimpsey, A.Nisbet   29 Aug 2000
A fine thin crack immediately left of Spoils of War provides some thin moves. Climb
a detached narrow slab immediately below and right of Victory Crack. The boulder
problem start is climbed from the base at 6a or avoided on the left at 4b (15m,
optional). Climb the crack, which is well protected by very small cams, to the ledge
(25m). Rather close to Victory Crack but feeling quite independent at the crux.

7 Victory Crack   70m   E3 ***
J.R.Mackenzie, R.Brown   20 Aug 1995
Next left is a straight crack with the crux where it should be – right at the top! The
easier pitches 2 and 3 are rarely climbed. Originally found very hard when freshly
cleaned but has now become popular, even with some who normally keep to 5c.
1. 25m 6a The crack is sustained but well protected by wires and small cams.
2. 20m Step right from the belay and gain a crack that runs right of a roof forming a hidden corner. Climb the corner.
3. 25m 4b Climb up the broken slab behind the stance, reaching an unprotected
quartz studded slab above which is followed to below a curving crack left of the
corner pitch of Salamander. Scramble off leftwards to reach the glacis above or finish up the final two pitches of Salamander.

8 Tales of the Old Days   30m   E5 6b **
R.McAllister, D.McGimpsey, M.Harrison   Sep 1998
A bold thin line to the left of the Victory Crack area. Start in a slabby recess below
a 'crescent moon' crack above. Climb the thin slab to gain the right edge of the
crack and go up this to a good pocket at half-height (first good gear). Move up and
right to an awkward mantelshelf where a long stretch or dyno gains the top break
and poor cams. Follow this leftwards to a short finishing crack. Scramble off left.

*Chameleon, E2 5c, Creag Ghlas. Climber Andy Jones
(photo John Mackenzie)*

SKYE

A trip to Skye feels special. Not only is the atmosphere different to the mainland, but the volcanic rocks are different too. The traditional venue is the Cuillin, unique in Britain for the volume of exposed rock forming its jagged peaks. Formed from extremely rough gabbro, the mountains offers some superb long routes in the easy and middle grades, which are often more friendly than their steep angle indicates. In recent years there has also been extensive development of Skye's mainly dolerite sea-cliffs. The routes often follow steep natural lines and are mainly above VS, although an effort has been made to include some easier routes as wet weather options.

As an exposed west coast island, Skye has the extremes of weather, both good and bad. With a wind off the sea, the Cuillin are often in cloud, with the potential for heavy rain. But with a wind off the mainland, Skye is usually sunny, or at least dry when the rest of Britain is wet. The phrase "all or nothing" comes to mind for the mountains. The sea-cliffs are well away from the mountains and the rain can pass quickly. This choice makes climbing in Skye more attractive, although going at short notice on a good forecast is still the best. May traditionally has the best weather and the statistics prove it, but some recent Mays have been poor and the summer months good.

Skye may be notorious for midges, but they are no worse than anywhere else in the west, and a breeze keeps them away.

Maps: OS L23 (South Skye), L32 (North Skye), E411 (Cuillin and Elgol), E407 (Neist), E408 (Kilt to Rubha Hunish). Harvey Superwalker Skye The Cuillin, Harvey Superwalker Storr and Trotternish (Kilt to Rubha Hunish)

SMC Climbers' Guide: *Skye and the Hebrides Vol.1* (1996)

SMC Scramblers' Guide: *Skye Scrambles* (2000) has many easy rock climbs

Access: By car this is usually via the now toll free bridge at Kyle of Lochalsh. A year round car ferry runs between Mallaig and Armadale, (7 sailings per day in summer).

Public Transport: Train to Kyle of Lochalsh from Inverness; also Mallaig from Glasgow-Fort William. Bus from Glasgow and Inverness to Portree and on to Sligachan. Two post buses per day to Glen Brittle (not Sunday). There is also a post bus from Broadford to Elgol and a Portree circular route via the north of Skye (not Sunday).

Amenities: Skye caters well for visitors, with a wide variety of accommodation. The main tourist office is in Portree (01478 612137), with seasonal offices at Broadford (01471 822361) and Dunvegan (01470 521581).

Camping: Both Sligachan (NG 485 301) and Glen Brittle (NG 412 206) have a shop. Two sites at Dunvegan (NG 261 478, NG 252 471) are handy for Neist, and Staffin (NG 496 668) is useful for Kilt, Staffin, Flodigarry and Rubha Hunish.

Mountaineering Huts: Glen Brittle War Memorial Hut – BMC & MCofS (NG 412 216).

SYHA Youth Hostels: Glenbrittle (NG 409 225), (0870 004 1121), also at Armadale, Broadford and Uig.

Independent Hostels: Sligachan Bunkhouse (01478 650204), Croft Bunkhouse and Bothies in Portnalong (01478 640254), The Waterfront Bunkhouse in Carbost (01478 640205), Portree Independent Hostel (01478 613737), Dun Flodigarry Hostel (01470 552212), Dunvegan Hotel bunkhouse (01470 521497).

Hotels: The Sligachan Hotel, The Old Inn at Carbost and the Flodigarry Country House Hotel are popular for bar meals.

Shops and Petrol: Not a problem except that there is no petrol in Glen Brittle. There is 24hr petrol in Broadford. Island Outdoors, in Portree sells climbing equipment as does Cioch Direct in Straun.

Cuillin Area

Glen Brittle and Coire Lagan contain the best climbs in this area and naturally

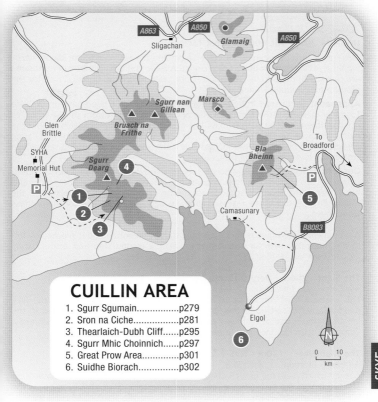

0   10
km

SKYE

dominate this section. Other excellent routes exist in this area, but they are not found in such a concentration as in these two corries and only a few are described.

COIRE LAGAN

When thinking of rock climbing on Skye, the routes on Sron na Ciche immediately spring to mind. Easily accessible from the Glen Brittle camp site, these are the most popular destinations in the whole of the Cuillin, offering some of the best lower and middle grade climbs in Scotland on rough slabby gabbro. A climb up the three tiers of the Cioch Buttress, with lunch on the Cioch itself, makes one of the best outings in Scotland.

SGURR SGUMAIN

(NG 448 206)   Alt 947m
This mountain lies south-west of Sgurr Alasdair and throws out a long well defined north ridge giving enjoyable scrambling from near the lochan in upper Coire Lagan, straight to the summit.

High on the mountain the impressive north face looks west into upper Coire Lagan and has many routes. Separating Sgurr Sgumain from Sron na Ciche is a wide boulder filled gully, the Sgumain Stone Shoot. On Sgurr Sgumain but overlooking the lower part of the Sgumain Stone Shoot, is the West Buttress.

West Buttress

(NG 444 207)   Alt 600m   West facing

This crag stands between upper Coire Lagan and the Sgumain Stone Shoot, catching the eye on the walk up to Coire Lagan. A route could be climbed here (if sacks are carried) en route to the Thearlaich-Dubh crags of Coir' a' Ghrunnda, saving the plod up the Sgumain Stone Shoot.

Approach: Either start from the camp site and follow the good path up to Coire Lagan or start from the Memorial Hut and break off right from the Sgurr Dearg (Inaccessible Pinnacle) path to pass just above Loch an Fhir-bhallaich to join the path. Continue to the lip of the corrie and walk rightwards over undulating glaciated rock in front of the loch to reach the start of a right-rising rake which crosses the lower part of the buttress.

Descent: There is no easy descent back to the base so carrying sacks is recommended. The quickest descent is to break off right (south) on to boulder slopes and head over to the Sgumain Stone Shoot on the right. To return to the start of the routes, find the top of the rake and follow it back across the base of the buttress (Moderate).

A prominent blaze of white rock marks the start of the routes and is reached by following the rake, with an awkward start, over a second step and across slabby ground back left (Difficult).

The Slant   200m   Very Difficult *
A.H.Greenbank, J.Wilkinson, D.Murray   1 Sep 1958
This pleasant climb on sound rock follows a natural line which crosses the face diagonally left. Start under the white blaze, a pitch to here is included in the length. Climb a shallow chimney and continuing cracks and ramps to a chimney. Climb the open chimney and finish up a wall of very rough rock.

The Klondyker   130m   HVS **
A.Tibbs, D.Bearhop   3 May 1988
A route which picks the best climbing around the more natural line of Sunset Slab. The top half of the face gets the sun around lunchtime. Start about 8m below the white blaze, directly below the shallow chimney on The Slant.
1. 30m 4b Climb diagonally left up a slab to a corner left of the chimney on The Slant. Layback up the corner until it is possible to move right to a cracked slab which leads to a belay at the foot of a steep impressive wall.
2. 30m 5a Climb a small corner and cracks to gain the left side of a large sloping ledge about halfway up the steep wall. Gain the weak crack-line above from a perched block on the left, then follow this and the wider crack above through an overhang to a large ledge and an old peg at a junction with Sunset Slab. An improbable pitch for the grade.
3. 15m 4a Climb the groove above the peg (as for Sunset Slab) until an easy left traverse leads to a ledge at the foot of an obvious groove with a yellow left wall.
4. 30m 5a Move left around an edge into an exposed position and climb up left past an overhang to a basalt recess. Climb to a small well positioned ledge, then go up a short wall to a belay.
5. 25m Move right and finish up the painfully rough arete.
Variation: **Variation Finish**
4a. 30m 5a The obvious groove with a yellow left wall, avoided by pitch 4.
5a. 30m 4c A second yellow groove.

Sunset Slab and Yellow Groove   170m   VS 4c *
J.D.Foster, D.C.Blake   13 Jul 1951 (Sunset Slab); I.S.Clough, D.J.Temple, M.Battle, B.Fein 30 Jun 1964 (Yellow Groove)
A popular climb, although the crux crack is slow to dry. Start below the white blaze.

1. 45m Start up The Slant, or the slab on its right, to reach a steep break on the right wall.
2. 20m Climb the break for 10m, then traverse easily right to a groove with an old peg at its base. The original Sunset Slab now traversed right from here to join the line of a continuous dyke (Very Difficult). If the crux crack is too wet, take this line with the possibility of returning left to the grassy ledge above (reversing the upper escape).
3. 10m Climb the groove to a corner below an overhanging crack.
4. 20m 4c Climb the wall left of the crack to a ledge, then continue by the crux upper crack to a grassy ledge. If wet, it is easy to switch on to The Klondyker, although this is slightly harder. There is an escape right from the grass ledge, either easy low down or by a tricky groove.
5. 15m 4b Climb an easy slab, move round a corner and climb a steep groove. Traverse under an overhang to a broad ledge with a vertical yellow wall on the left.
6. 10m 4a Move right to a stance and belay on the arete.
7. 30m 4a Climb the arete, avoiding the steep upper section on the right.
8. 20m Climb a steep corner to easier rocks and the top.

SRON NA CICHE

Map p279   Diagram p284
Deservedly the most famous cliff on Skye, Sron na Ciche offers an unrivalled col-lection of routes of all grades and lengths with the additional attraction of a rela-tively short approach from Glen Brittle. Like many of the Cuillin cliffs, it has a massive appearance that leads to confusion in mist. There is no substitute for a reconnaissance on a clear day, both from the path leading to upper Coire Lagan and by identifying the starts of climbs from the base of the crag. The cliff gets the sun from mid-afternoon onwards (Cioch Buttress), an excuse for a late start!

General Approach: From the camp site follow the good path up towards Coire Lagan. There is a right fork for Sron na Ciche, initially not obvious, at 350m alti-tude and where there is a short section of particularly white gravel. Alternatively, start from the Memorial Hut and break off right from the Sgurr Dearg (Inaccessible Pinnacle) path to pass just above Loch an Fhir-bhallaich. A short distance beyond the loch, take the lower of two options to join the good path from the camp site. The Sron na Ciche branch cuts rightwards off the main path about 10m below where it joins. Take a slightly rising traverse to the burn, then head up increasingly steeply to below Western Buttress.

Western Buttress

(NG 442 202)   Alt 500m   North-North-West facing
Some of the longest mountaineering routes on Skye can be found on this huge and rather featureless rockface. Route finding is part of the challange and will be appre-ciated more or less, depending on how close you are to your top grade.
The buttress is identified by its two left-slanting diverging faults, Cioch Gully and Central Gully and a third parallel fault, West Central Gully, which lies to their right. Central Gully begins as an easy angled shallow chimney which leads up to a large depression of slabs at half-height, The Amphitheatre, then continues to the plateau.

Descent: The routes are best climbed with sacks to allow descent by walking off.

Routes are described from right to left.

1 Median   300m   Very Difficult ✱✱
E.W.Steeple, H.E.Bowron 1909
One of the best routes of its grade in Skye, this excellent climb has some poorly protected pitches and needs basic route finding ability. Some of the climbing is on

SKYE

basalt, so much harder in the wet. Start 40m right of Central Gully; the route name is scratched on the rock at the foot of a long crack-line. The start of Central Gully is not obvious from the cliff base, especially in mist, so this crack is at a break between overhangs low down on the crag.

Climb the crack and continue to West Central Gully (90m). Go briefly up the gully to the foot of a deep chimney cutting rightwards through slabs. Climb the chimney to its end (40m). Above is a big overhanging wall. Follow the chimney-line leftwards beneath it for 45m, and belay on the more open crag above. Climb a wall some 5m to the right, then traverse right and go up to a belay at the foot of an easy angled slab. This leads left to the base of the big fan shaped corners which form such a noticeable feature from the corrie floor. Belay at the foot of the corners and go rightwards up a depression, often greasy and poorly protected, until the line turns left again up a chimney (45m). A further two pitches follow either the chimney, or the buttress on its left, to the terminal arete.

2 Trap Face Route Direct 300m VS 4c **
J.B.Burrell, C.N.Cross 1914; Direct: J.Holmes, W.Trafford 12 Sep 1976
A harder mountaineering route with the same plus points as Mallory's Slab and Groove. The lower section of the route climbs through the Diamond Slab, the diamond shaped area defined at its top by West Central Gully, at its bottom by Central Gully and on its left by Mallory's Slab and Groove. Start left of Central Gully and about 15m right of Cioch Gully at a small overhang.

Climb the overhang, then follow easier slabs to Central Gully. Go 5m up the gully, then climb straight up to cracks in the middle of the slab, belaying 10m below them. Climb the cracks through an overlap and belay in the basalt dyke 3m above and right. Climb the slab above to a large overhang, then pull onto a glacis under the overhang via the left-hand corner of a brown wall; belay. Turn the overhang by the right-hand of two grooves and 5m up, layback the finger crack right of the groove to exit from the overhang; belay. The next two pitches take the large overhang above, followed by a chimney, then go up left and belay on top. Continue straight up and follow the dyke to join Mallory's Slab and Groove. Finish up this, or keep to its right.

3 Mallory's Slab and Groove 300m Very Difficult **
G.H.L.Mallory, D.R.Pye, L.G.Shadbolt 1918
This is classic Skye, a long mountaineering route up acres of rock, with route finding part of the fun. Start just right of Cioch Gully and a large overhang at an improbable cracked corner. Climb this fine corner on good holds and its continuation crack out on to slabs. Climb the slabs leftwards until forced into Central Gully, followed for about 20 to 30m to a prominent crack going up to the right. Climb this (or on its left if wet) to a steep section. Bend left and return right by a big flake to reach a continuation crack-line. Follow this, passing left of a huge overhang (where West Central Gully peters out) into a gully which starts above. Finish up the arete on the right. Going left gains Amphitheatre Arete.

4 Amphitheatre Arete 270m Moderate **
J.N.Collie 1907
A sporting mountaineering ramble; stars are subjective. Start up and left from Cioch Gully, almost level with the base of Cioch Buttress. Climb a right-slanting watercourse into Cioch Gully, go up it a short way, then leave it and ascend slabs towards The Amphitheatre. Pass Central Gully (don't go up it!) which crosses the base of The Amphitheatre, and instead of going up the corner above (wet and smooth), walk right for about 50m to below the nose of the arete. A tricky slab gains the easier arete, which is followed to near the top. Here some careful route finding is necessary where the route bends left.

Direct Route, Very Difficult, Eastern Buttress. Climber Bob Black
(photo Andrew Fraser)

SKYE

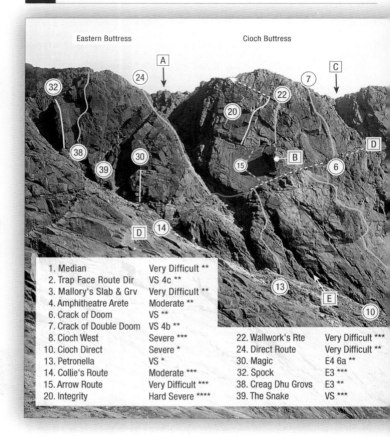

Eastern Buttress   Cioch Buttress

1. Median	Very Difficult **	
2. Trap Face Route Dir	VS 4c **	
3. Mallory's Slab & Grv	Very Difficult **	
4. Amphitheatre Arete	Moderate **	
6. Crack of Doom	VS **	
7. Crack of Double Doom	VS 4b **	
8. Cioch West	Severe ***	
10. Cioch Direct	Severe *	22. Wallwork's Rte	Very Difficult ***
13. Petronella	VS *	24. Direct Route	Very Difficult **
14. Collie's Route	Moderate ***	30. Magic	E4 6a **
15. Arrow Route	Very Difficult ***	32. Spock	E3 ***
20. Integrity	Hard Severe ****	38. Creag Dhu Grovs	E3 **
		39. The Snake	VS ***

Cioch Buttress

(NG 445 204)   Alt 570m   North-West facing

The superlative central buttress is a massive area of steep slabs and grooves in three tiers, the Lower Buttress, Cioch Slab and The Cioch, and Cioch Upper Buttress, separated by terraces. It dries quickly, although there may be wet streaks after rain until the sun appears during the afternoon.

Any combination of routes on the different tiers may be made. The combination of Cioch West, Cioch Nose or Arrow Route, followed by Integrity or the less good but easier Wallwork's Route, makes a four star outing. The Lower Buttress may be missed by approaching along The Terrace (Collie's Route), which also provides a descent from the top of the Lower Buttress. The shorter routes on the Cioch Slab must be climbed to reach Cioch Upper Buttress. First described are three routes high on the right of the three tiered section.

Approach: From Western Buttress go left and uphill along the cliff base to a level and well worn area below the Lower Buttress. It is distinguished by a small rock shelter below the gully of Cioch Direct. The Cioch itself is impossible to spot in the morning without the contrast of sunlight.

SRON NA CICHE

Western Buttress

A. Eastern Gully
B. The Cioch
C. Central Gully   F. Cioch Gully
D. The Terrace   G. The Amphitheatre
E. Little Gully   H. West Central Gully

SKYE

Crack of Doom Area

The aptly named crack and a route either side have a different approach. Alternatively, a route on the Lower Buttress can be climbed first.

Approach: Start up Amphitheatre Arete (route 4) to reach Cioch Gully and climb it to a point 10m above a grass ledge which leads rightwards from below a large chockstone in the gully. Here is the Direct Start to Crack of Doom, which can be bypassed by continuing up Cioch Gully and climbing a Severe slab to The Terrace below the routes. A good climbing approach is up most of Cioch West (route 8) to the top of pitch 6, then descend a rib right of a small gully, finishing in the gully to arrive in Cioch Gully near Crack of Doom's Direct Start. After other routes on the Lower Buttress, descend from The Terrace under Arrow Route to a lower and smaller terrace, then follow this left (facing out) to the top of pitch 6 of Cioch West (Moderate).

Descent: Head left over a slight summit of Sron na Ciche, then continue up. The first big gully reached is Eastern Gully. Unless you want a hard time, go on up to descend the next one, the Sgumain Stone Shoot, which seems a long way, but is unmistakable because the way to its top is blocked by a smooth slab which must be descended over to the right. A long descent – trainers recommended.

5 Rib of Doom   75m   VS 4c ** *
C.M.G.Smith, A.Cleland   Jun 1949
This is the fine rib to the left of Crack of Doom; the description is from The Terrace.
Follow Crack of Doom to a point below the crack. Traverse towards the rib, gaining it via a subsidiary groove. Follow the rib in a tremendous position to the top.

6 Crack of Doom   165m   VS **
D.R.Pye, L.G.Shadbolt   Aug 1918; Direct Start: B.Ritchie, C.D.Milner   Jun 1936
This is a historic and famous climb. Or is it infamous, since the actual crack is an
insecure thrutch, memorable for its polish and dampness, but the rest makes up
for it. The actual crack can be seen from the corrie as a prominent curving crack. It
is the lower continuation of the upper glacis (top of Integrity) which drops off right
beyond the top of Archer Thomson's Route. The Direct Start is described (see
Approach above).
1. 20m Climb a square corner to a short slab and hence to a line of holds leading
diagonally right to an open 'V'. Climb this by its left side to a small stance and
belay by a detached block.
2. 20m Descend again to the foot of the 'V', climb right around another slab, then
go up a steep corner to a narrow ledge.
3. Traverse briefly right from the ledge, then ascend a steep shallow groove which
joins the lower continuation of Crack of Doom. Follow this for about 15m to the
Terrace.
4. 12m Climb the crack to a chockstone.
5. 4b Above, the crack steepens and narrows, forming the crux. This is strenuous
and can be hard if grease is present on an already polished surface. It is possible
to avoid the crux by Severe climbing on the left wall.
6. The climb finishes at the foot of the sloping glacis; exit up left, or there is a Hard
Severe direct finish up the wall above.

7 Crack of Double Doom   90m   VS 4b ** *
D.H.Haworth, I.E.Hughes   21 May 1947
An excellent classic climb despite some dubious rock, described from the Terrace.
A clean-cut fault with a prominent inverted V lies right of Crack of Doom. Start
immediately right of Crack of Doom and follow the fault to the apex of the slab.
The climbing gets progressively harder with the crux in the last 10m below the
apex. Above the slab, a crack runs leftward up a steep right-angled corner. Climb
the corner to the top.

Lower Buttress
Routes are described from right to left.

8 Cioch West   210m   Severe ** **
C.F.Holland, H.R.C.Carr, Miss D.E.Pilley   1919
A fine climb, if polished in places, giving constantly interesting climbing with a
splendidly exposed crux. Start at the right side of the level area below a notch like
chimney (CW scratched on the rock).
1. 35m Climb polished grooves into a strenuous chimney. Above, easier grooves
lead to a stance on the left.
2. 30m Climb a slab back into the easier grooves which lead to an overhung ledge
below an off-width crack.
3. 20m 4a Climb up right across a steep slab on polished incut holds to reach a
fine ledge which encircles the upper bastion of the climb. Scramble right, then walk
to a flake on the wall.
4. 20m Climb up (or walk further right and climb back left – easier) to reach a
right-trending break, followed with interest to ledges.
5. 15m 4a A shallow chimney on the left leads to the crux, an exposed left traverse that leads onto a narrow ledge; a fine pitch.
6. 45m Continue left along the ledge to its end, then climb easier rock slightly

right, then straight up and over a small crest to a short nose overlooking Cioch Gully (possible to escape left here along the obvious line).
7. 40m 4a Climb this unlikely bulging wall to easy slabs, which are climbed straight up to the ledge system running below The Cioch itself. It is recommended to continue by Cioch Nose (route 19), which climbs straight up from here onto The Cioch. Alternatively, scramble left and slightly down to reach Arrow Route.

9 Crembo Cracks   155m   HVS **
D.Gregory, R.Hutchinson   27 Jul 1958 (1PA); FFA: unknown
This superb but serious climb is easily identified by a pair of cracks rising above the level area left of Cioch West and right of the chimney-gully of Cioch Direct.
1. 40m Either climb the right-hand crack (which has an inverted V 10m from the base) and follow the dyke up left to a ledge (4b) or, far better, climb the left-hand jamming crack to step up left on a nose and follow a slabby corner past flakes to the same ledge (4c).
2. 35m Continue up a very pleasant chimney and cracks to the base of a steeper slab. Traverse right to a ledge and climb the steep corner-crack to the grassy ledge of Cioch West.
3. 40m 5a The route now attacks the unlikely wall above, sometimes easily identified by signs of retreat! Climb the steepening corner above to a square corner at the base of the wall, old peg runner. Traverse 5m delicately right across the slab to a hidden corner. Climb the steep creaky flakes above and go up a series of awkward poorly protected steps, passing an old peg, crux. Now climb the impressively situated bulge above by the undercut wobbly flakes, taking care with the cuddly jug above. Step up right to a fine ledge. A serious but excellent pitch which requires steady climbing.
4. 40m Continue much more easily over slabs to the foot of the steep little wall of Cioch West.

10 Cioch Direct   150m   Severe 4a *
H.Harland, A.P.Abraham   1907
An open chimney-gully which starts 10m up and left of the level area. Heavy traffic in the past has caused the inevitable polishing and this can be detrimental in the wet. There are two main methods of attack for the lower section: Poise and Elegance, or Elephantine Struggles. Either way, climb the open chimney-gully, following a polished corner and a long easy groove, before climbing a series of entertaining chimneys. The top chimney is the tight crux, the scene of an historic rockfall on the first ascent. Above, a sloping shelf leads up and left to a jumble of boulders which include a yardarm. Traverse left across a broken slab, then climb parallel cracks on impeccable rock to easier slabs and the terrace.

11 Cioch Grooves   150m   HVS **
I.G.McNaught-Davis, G.H.Francis   21 Sep 1957
A superb climb, varied and exciting, the only drawback being the possible escapes into Cioch Direct. Start up and left of Cioch Direct at a grass ledge running right onto the buttress. A prominent crack near a corner lies parallel to Cioch Direct.
1. 30m 4c Climb the crack to where it steepens, then step left to a parallel crack which is followed to easier slabs. Traverse right to near the crux chimney of Cioch Direct.
2. 25m 5a Traverse back left below a steep wall and go up this on the left to a block. A thin traverse right, crux, enables a delicate step on to the slab above. Belay below a fine crack which lies immediately left of Cioch Direct.
3. 25m 4b Climb the crack to easier slabs.
4. and 5. 70m Continue up the left-hand crack, then follow easier slabs to the terrace.

12 Bastinado   90m   E2 *
J.Cunningham, J.Allan, W.Smith   16 Jul 1956 (1PA); FFA: unknown
A good and well protected climb needing a positive approach. Start 8m right of the

gully which forms the left end of the buttress (Little Gully).
1. 35m 4c Ascend to an obvious crack, which slopes slightly left, then climb it to a broad grassy ledge.
2. 10m 5b Climb the corner direct, then trend left to a sloping ledge.
3. 10m 5b Step left to below a groove which overhangs at its lower end. Climb this strenuously until good holds allow a move right to a triangular corner and belay.
4. 35m 4b Climb a crack immediately behind the corner to a small rock ledge. Continue up a crack to the terrace.

Petronella   70m   VS 4c *
G.H.Francis, E.A.Wrangham   29 Jun 1952
This fine little climb lies on the small buttress between Little Gully and the big gully which separates Cioch Buttress from Eastern Buttress (Eastern Gully). From the screes, climb an awkward prominent crack which curves leftwards up the centre of the buttress. The overhangs above are turned by a shelf followed by an airy pull up.

Cioch Slab & The Cioch

This is the middle tier of Cioch Buttress. Right of Eastern Gully lies the massive Cioch Slab; pockmarked with weathered augite crystals, and composed of the finest gabbro. At its right end lies a noble tower, one of the Cuillin's most famous landmarks, The Cioch. It rests, somewhat implausibly, on the slab, cracked around the base but presumably very stable. Cioch Gully curves in behind The Cioch and terminates, although the fault-line continues as a shelf running diagonally left across the top of Cioch Slab to terminate in Eastern Gully.

The Cioch is a superb viewpoint and should be visited at least once by every climber. After Sean Connery's sword fight on the summit in the film Highlander, a plastic sword remained on the summit for many years.

Approach: Via a route on Lower Buttress or via The Terrace (Collie's Route).

Descent: Reverse the upper section of Collie's Route, or make a 40m abseil from the neck of The Cioch (25m plus easy down-climbing also works) to reach The Terrace.

Collie's Route   Moderate **
J.N.Collie   1906
A devious route through amazing scenery for the grade. From the base of Eastern Gully, go up left until just above the debris of a recent rockfall (about 60m altitude) where the Sgumain Stone Shoot starts to become defined. An awkward initial step gains The Terrace. Follow The Terrace across Eastern Buttress into Eastern Gully. Here a curving polished shelf leads right to the base of the Cioch Slab, rising above a grassy ledge. Climb deep cracks on very polished rock, following the left edge of the slab for 50m to the edge. Easy blocks now lead back into Eastern Gully which is followed to the narrow shelf which runs across the top of the slab. Traverse right easily and downwards along the exposed 'Collie's Ledge' and gain The Cioch itself by a highly polished arete (The Neck). Climb to the top by the chimney a few metres west of The Neck. Descend by the same way. The best option is now to return to Eastern Gully and go up it to the top. This involves a wriggle behind a chockstone and other entertainment to finish by the right fork.
Variation: **Very Difficult**
A recommended variation climbs the steep slab up right of the cracks to Collie's Ledge, instead of entering Eastern Gully.

Arrow Route   60m   Very Difficult **
I.Allan   1944
From 5m left of the base of Slab Corner, follow a diagonal crack out left across the

Cioch Grooves, HVS 5a, Cioch Buttress. Climber Stuart Buchanan
(photo David Buchanan)

slab easily for 15m to belay at a triangular flake. Now climb up and left towards a hidden shallow ramp utilising the magnificent dimples. Either finish up the ramp or, slightly harder, climb another break to the right. No longer the unprotected pitch it used to be, it is possible to place well spaced protection. If feeling brave, follow the first pitch and then batter straight up before you notice the lack of protection.

16 Cioch Slab Direct   45m   VS 4b **
A fine direct line up the slab some 5 to 10m left of Slab Corner, virtually unprotected. If confident, find a quick line up the lovely rough slab, with a crux bulge at the top.

17 Slab Corner   45m   Difficult *
The big polished corner to the left of The Cioch is less exposed and consequently very popular, but distinctly harder in the wet.

18 The Highlander   30m   E6 6b **
G.Farquhar, G.Latter   1992
A stunning pitch up the frontal arete of The Cioch. Climb easily up slabs to the arete. Climb boldly up the right side of the arete to an obvious hole (runners in the flake to the right). Continue via a thin diagonal crack to a resting ledge (crucial Friends). Move up to a large flat hold on the arete (poor micro nuts) and attempt to stand on it. A tricky mantelshelf gains the upper slabs and easy ground; belay on top of The Cioch.

19 Cioch Nose   45m   Very Difficult **
An airy climb up the western edge of The Cioch and a satisfying continuation to Cioch West. Start from The Terrace and climb a groove to slabs above. Move left to a delicate slab and go up this to mantelshelf the edge above. Gain and climb the knife edge to the top.

Upper Buttress
This steep slabby wall above and left of The Cioch, is cut by impressive overlaps and pierced by several prominent and challenging crack-lines taken by some of Skye's finest routes.

Approach: The easiest is via The Terrace and Collie's Route.

Descent: Follow a ramp rising up left to reach the plateau. Turn left and join the descent from the Crack of Doom area. Pass Eastern Gully and descend the Sgumain Stone Shoot (see p285).

20 Integrity   75m   Hard Severe ****
D.H.Haworth, I.E.Hughes   11 Jul 1949
A magnificent classic breaings through intimidating slabs gives the best climb of its grade in Skye. Start about 6m up the shelf left of the grass patch behind the Cioch.
1. 40m 4b   Surmount a strenuous overhang on good rough holds to arrive on the slab above. Continue up the thin crack in a superb position, excellently protected. A little block overhang inset by a corner is awkward, belay on the flat ledge above.
2. 35m 4b   Continue up the crack more easily. Purists will take the top, steeper, crack direct (VS 4b). The normal line bypasses this with a step to the right.

21 Trophy Crack   80m   HVS **
P.Walsh, H.MacKay   16 Jul 1956
This well protected climb takes the excellent crack to the right of Integrity, above the grass patch. Start by a pinnacle at the base of the crack.
1. 40m 5b   Go over the initial steepness, then follow a groove and a short overhang. A layback above is followed by the crux and a step left to a good ledge.
2. 40m 4b   Climb the much easier crack above. Either climb the big overlap direct

(5a), or step left through a narrow sentry box and climb the slab above. Step back right to the main crack, which widens before finishing on the glacis.

22 Wallwork's Route   75m   Very Difficult ***
W.Wallwork, H.M.Kelly, J.Wilding   1915
A splendid route of character which used to be graded Difficult when real men and women wore nailed boots. Start at the grass patch behind The Cioch. Traverse right along a broken rake, then swing left along a tottering pile of blocks; belay under a roof. Pull over on excellent holds to a platform. Above is a fearsome crack. Avoid this by stepping right into a right-angled corner capped by a small roof. The corner is surprisingly tricky but well protected and leads over the roof to a stance. Follow a wide crack through a slab and outflank a roof by a traverse right, above which lie perched blocks and the upper glacis.

23 Archer Thomson's Route   75m   Very Difficult **
J.M.A.Thomson and party   1911
Another of Skye's traditional Diff's but easier than Wallwork's. Start on the grass patch behind The Cioch. Follow Wallwork's Route for 25m, then break out on to the steep shelf on the right which finishes at the base of the upper glacis.

Eastern Buttress

(NG 446 204)   Alt 650 - 750m   Diagram p284
The leftmost and highest section of Sron na Ciche rises from the Sgumain Stone Shoot at its base, to form a broad ridge defined on the right by the deep slit of Eastern Gully, which separates it from Cioch Buttress. Eastern Buttress is at quite a high altitude and it can be rather colder here than one might expect, particularly on Vulcan Wall.

West Face

South-West facing   Diagram p284
Despite its south-west aspect the wall overlooking Eastern Gully is shaded by Cioch Buttress until the afternoon. The routes are accessed from The Terrace (Collie's Route).

Approach: From Western Buttress follow the cliff base below Cioch Buttress to the Sgurmain Stone Shoot. Some 60m above the base of Eastern Gully, just above the debris of a recent rockfall, an awkward initial step gains The Terrace.

Descent: The safest descent is to head to the summit crest and turn left to reach the Sgumain Stone Shoot, which is a straightforward descent over large scree and boulders, painful in rock boots. The slabby left to right ramp cutting across the top of Vulcan Wall can also be descended into the Sgumain Stone Shoot. It is also possible to descend Eastern Gully with an abseil and a narrow through route.

24 Direct Route   180m   Very Difficult **
E.W.Steeple, G.Barlow, A.H.Doughty   1912
This very popular classic gives an exhilarating climb following the edge of the buttress overlooking Eastern Gully as closely as possible. A variety of starts are possible from the broad ledge at the start of the Eastern Terrace, but none are entirely obvious. The crux is a steep wall near the top, which should be avoided in the wet by climbing loose flakes to the right and traversing back left above.

Right of Direct Route, two striking open corners rise above The Terrace and are accessed by climbing broken rocks to their base.

25 Trojan Groove   25m   HVS 5a *
I.Heys, K.Roberts   Jul 1965
Climb the left-hand of the two corners to join Direct Route.

26 Helen   35m   E3 6a **

S.Hill, C.Moody   31 Jul 1994

This excellent route, so called because it lies between the Trojans and the Spartans, climbs the formidable looking arete between Trojan and Spartan Grooves. Climb the initial bulge of Spartan Groove, then move up left to a slanting crack which starts from a horizontal crack. Climb the slanting crack, crux, then the wall just right of the arete to finish up the arete to join Direct Route.

27 Spartan Groove   40m   E1 5b **

I.Heys, K.Roberts   Jul 1965

Climb the right-hand of two corners, following it to a left-trending overhang. Traverse with difficulty under this and continue to join Direct Route.

Variation: **E1 5b**

P.Hunter, S.Drummond   8 Aug 1980

A direct alternative is to pull through the overhang by an undercut to a small ledge left of the overhang; gain the slab above and finish more easily.

28 Jack o' Diamonds   100m   Hard Severe **

D.Leaver, C.E.N.Wilson   Jul 1953

A very good climb, well seen from The Cioch and named after the diamond shaped block left of a deep 20m chimney.

1. 35m Start in Eastern Gully, 12m above The Terrace, and climb open rocks direct to the foot of the 20m chimney.

2. 20m Climb a steep wall left of the chimney and, after a mantelshelf at 5m, follow a steepening groove to the conspicuous diamond shaped block. Trend right across the top of the block, then follow a short crack to the top.

3. 35m Follow a line of blocks and grooves directly above to the foot of the final V-chimney.

4. 10m Climb the chimney to join Direct Route below its crux pitch.

29 Shangri-La   130m   VS ***

I.S.Clough, A.Nicholls   20 Jun 1964

A superb classic climb following a fine series of corners. Start from Eastern Gully, 30m above the terrace, where there are two lines of grooves parallel and right of the deep 20m chimney which is obvious on the approach up the Eastern Gully. The left-hand line of grooves is **Searcher** (Very Difficult or VS direct). This route takes a series of corners on the right. Easy grooves lead to a stance below a steep wide crack. Ascend this, or the wall on the left, to gain the grooves above via awkward cracks (4b); flake belays. Climb the excellent corner above and take the final overhang direct in a fine position (35m 4b). Climb the deceptive groove to a wide platform (20m 4b). Above are two corners; climb the strenuous left one (20m 4c). Finish up easy rocks.

Magic Wall

North facing   Diagram p284

About 50m up the Sgumain Stone Shoot from the start of The Terrace (Collie's Route) and about halfway to Vulcan Wall is an area of recessed rock. Routes are described left to right.

30 Magic   45m   E4 6a **

D.Cuthbertson, G.Latter   1982

Superb well protected climbing up the prominent left-hand crack. Climb the flake and slab leading to a small overhang in a corner, move right and go up the crack to a corner which leads to the top.

31 The Conjuror   45m   E3 5c *

R.Anderson, M.Hamilton   24 May 1983

The right-hand companion crack, 6m right of Magic. Follow the thin crack up the wall to gain a corner. Climb the corner to a roof and follow the crack to the top.

The right-slanting crack to the right is **Presdigiteur** (HVS 5a).

Vulcan Wall

North-West facing   Diagram p284, 294

The impressive slabby wall at the top left section of Eastern Buttress contains the best collection of harder routes in the Cuillin.

Approach: From Western Buttress follow the cliff base below Cioch Buttress to the Sgumain Stone Shoot. The wall lies some 160m up the stone chute.

Descent: The safest descent is to head to the summit crest and turn left to reach the Sgumain Stone Shoot. The slabby left to right ramp cutting across the top of Vulcan Wall can also be descended into the Sgumain Stone Shoot.

Routes are described from left to right.

32 Spock   70m   E3 ***
P.Hunter, C.Lees   18 May 1980
A dramatic route with excellent bold climbing at the bottom of its grade. Start 5m left of Vulcan Wall.
1. 40m 5c Climb overhanging cracks on the arete, then continue up the arete on small holds through a shallow groove to belays above an obvious roof.
2. 30m 5a Go diagonally right to finish up the steep crack left of Vulcan Wall.

33 Vulcan Wall   70m   HVS ****
H.MacInnes, D.J.Temple, I.S.Clough   1957 (aid); FFA: unknown.
A magnificent route. Start at 'VW' scratched on the rock.
1. 20m 5a Climb to a ledge and block belay.
2. 40m 5a Move up to a ledge to the left of the block, then continue by a line of cracks to a small ledge on the right (possible belay – The Chambre Finish rises above this ledge). Make a rising traverse left to bigger holds; a sustained pitch.
3. 10m Traverse left to the edge of the wall and climb to a glacis. Belay well back.
Variation: **The Chambre Finish   25m   E2 5c ***
G.Latter, D.Cuthbertson   1982
A purist's finish giving a logical conclusion. Where the normal route goes left onto easier ground, ascend the thinner and left-hand of two parallel cracks above; the right-hand crack is taken by Uhuru.

34 Uhuru   70m   E3 ***
K.Howett, T.Prentice   22 Jul 1990
Excellent climbing up the fine crack-line in the silver streaked wall right of Vulcan Wall. Start at cracks just left of the prominent vertical crack in the slab (Dilemma).
1. 25m 5c Climb to a small overlap and follow the crack above to a hard move right to the Vulcan Wall ledge. Traverse left to a flake block.
2. 45m 5c Step right off the block, climb cracks and go right over a curving overlap. Move up and right to pull into the main crack, then follow it with difficulty to better holds. Continue up the excellent crack to finish right of a large precarious block.

35 Clinging On   65m   E4 **
K.Howett, S.Muir   12 May 2001
Another superb direct line with a long and sustained pitch, if rather squeezed in. Start at the prominent vertical crack in the slab (Dilemma).
1. 55m 6a Climb the crack to its end (as for Dilemma). Make a move up, then gain the obvious vertical crack just on the left. Follow this to where it fades into tiny cracks and gain an obvious small protruding block above. Step on to the block and step left to a foot ledge on Uhuru. Step back right and gain a thin crack and follow

SKYE

SRON NA CICHE - Vulcan Wall

32. Spock	E3 ***	36. Dilemma	E3 ***
33. Vulcan Wall	HVS ****	37. Pocks	E3 **
33a. Chambre Finish	E2 5c *	38. Creag Dhu Grooves	E3 **
34. Uhuru	E3 ***		
35. Clinging On	E4 **		

it with difficulty to gain better holds. Follow these up right into a final crack to under the roofs. Traverse 2m left past the roofs to a vertical crack.

2. 10m 5a Climb up and left to under a projecting block. Take the hand-traverse out left to the top.

36 Dilemma 80m E3 ***
M.Fowler, P.Thomas 21 Jun 1977

A delicate slab with spaced protection, followed by a strenuous overhanging jam crack. The dilemma is which holds lead to protection and which do not. Start at the prominent vertical crack in the slab.

1. 45m 5c Climb the crack until level with the stance of Vulcan Wall. Continue up

the crack to its finish, then climb up right to an overlap. Move under the overlap into a faint groove, then climb over the overlap to gain a descending traverse line which leads to a small niche just left of the large stance on Creag Dhu Grooves.
2. 35m 5c Follow the crack diagonally left up the slab, then struggle up its continuation through the impressive overlaps.

**7 Pocks 85m E3 ** **
C.Moody, N.Smith 7 Jun 1992; Pitch 1: G.Szuca, C.Moody 13 Jun 1988
Fine varied climbing but an indirect line.
1. 35m 5b Start up Creag Dhu Grooves, then climb the crack on the left to where Dilemma crosses the overlap. Move right under the overlap to a ledge, step right, then climb the overlap and move up right to the belay on Creag Dhu Grooves. A superb pitch.
2. 50m 5c Climb a steep crack, just right of Creag Dubh Grooves, to a slab and follow this rightwards to an arete **Zephyr** (E5 6a). Cross the arete to continue up right to finish up a crack in the steep upper wall.

**8 Creag Dhu Grooves 95m E3 ** **
H.MacInnes, I.S.Clough 1957 (aid); FFA: G.Reagan, R.McHardy 1977
Another superb climb up the chimney between Vulcan Wall and the huge flake on the right, although the difficulties are short and the chimney prone to dampness. Start on the ledge below Vulcan Wall at the corner of the wall and great flake.
1. 40m 4b Climb the chimney behind the flake to a chockstone, then continue to a large ledge above the flake.
2. 10m 5c Climb the superb technical corner.
3. 20m 5c Continue up the equally good corner to a good ledge.
4. 25m Continue to the top.

9 The Snake 105m VS * **
W.Sproul, J.Renny, J.Hall 9 Aug 1965
The classic medium grade route of the crag has a stunning middle pitch, but there are some hard moves above protection. The route follows a very obvious fault line formed by a dyke, starting 3m right of the prominent flake to the right of Creag Dhu Grooves.
1. 35m 4b Follow the fault to a belay.
2. 35m 4c Continue up the fault to a belay in a groove.
3. 35m 4a Finish up the dyke to the crest of the buttress.

COIR' A' GHRUNNDA

THEARLAICH-DUBH CLIFF

(NG 451 206) Alt 850m South-West facing Map p279

This is the next large corrie south of Coire Lagan. It is a wildly impressive place with huge areas of glaciated slabs and an excellent example of a terminal moraine. In its bowl is a lochan surrounded by huge rough boulders. At its back left side is a cliff below the ridge down from Sgurr Thearlaich. This is the ridge with the notorious Thearlaich-Dubh gap (T-D Gap), so the Thearlaich-Dubh Cliff seems a good name, although the left section is really on Sgurr Alasdair.

Approach: The traditional route is to walk round into the base of the corrie and up to its lochan, then gain the cliff through boulders. However an approach via the Sgumain Stone Shoot is marginally shorter and allows a route on Sron na Ciche (say Direct Route on Eastern Buttress) to break the long approach. Follow the route up to the base of Sron na Ciche, then continue rising under the cliff base to follow the Sgumain Stone Shoot to the col at its top. Traverse northwards into the top of Coir' a' Ghrunnda on a hint of path, at times being forced down by crags, to reach a spring below the cliff. This is a gorgeous spot for eating and drinking, especially as this crag is much sunnier than Sron na Ciche (and therefore dries quicker).

SKYE

Descent: Returning to the cliff base from routes left of the T-D Gap is not easy, so finishing by Commando Crack with sacks leaves you close to the top of The Great Stone Shoot (the col between Sgurr Thearlaich and Sgurr Alasdair) and descending it into Coire Lagan is definitely quickest. To return to the cliff base in rock boots, the shortest is to abseil into the T-D gap (but this can be crowded) and descend its gully. From routes right of the Gap, descend the ridge until it levels off and scramble back under the cliff (much easier). Returning to Glen Brittle from the cliff base, it is perhaps easier (certainly different) to descend the walkers' route out of Coir' a' Ghrunnda. The route starts to the right of the burn draining the corrie, leaving the burn quite soon and following cairns across rough ground to reach a small moraine valley which descends above the main burn and leads (eventually) to a good footpath.

The crags present a very steep frontage of well defined grooves and walls. Despite its imposing appearance, there are incut holds. Heading left from the T-D Gap Gully is a big groove, starting from the same point but trending left. Next is a steep buttress with a very prominent left-facing corner and an obvious overhanging gully, some 50m left of the T-D Gap, forming its left side.

Con's Cleft   60m   HVS ***
J.McLean and party   1965
The prominent corner, starting 7m up from the base of the buttress, gives a very good climb with good protection. Con Higgins told John McLean about the line and was not pleased when it was climbed, or with the route name.
1. 15m 5a Climb with increasing difficulty to an overhang, then gain the crack above (crux, beware of a loose block) leading to a ledge.
2. 10m 4c Climb the crack to another ledge.
3. 35m 4c Continue up the crack directly. At one point make a couple of moves on the right wall to avoid loose rock, then regain the crack immediately.

The Asp   75m   E1 5b ***
J.McLean and party   1965
An excellent well protected climb which takes a steep crack-line in the wall to the left and 7m right of Commando Crack. The crack is not obvious from a distance. Climb the crack, largely by chimneying, to an overhang, then pull out on to an inclined ledge beneath the overhang. Move up to the overhang where a difficult move left (crux) gains the upper crack (large Friend protection); belay on a ledge above. Climb the crack above, then scrambling leads to the top.

Commando Crack   105m   Severe ***
A.C.Cain, B.L.Dobson   Jul 1950
A very good and quite exciting climb which takes a twin cracked chimney, to the right of a cave. It is 20m left of the big overhanging gully. Start below a crack between two overhangs.
1. 10m Climb the rib right of the crack for 3m, traverse left into a chimney, then climb to a pinnacle high on the left.
2. 20m Ascend the right wall for a few metres, then traverse into the chimney. Ascend the awkward overhang to a belay on the left.
3. 10m Continue up the crack on the right to a sentry box below an overhanging chockstone.
4. 10m Thread the chockstone, climb the nose on the left and climb to a stance.
5. 25m Layback the right-hand crack, then cross to the left-hand crack, which is followed by a short scramble.
6. 30m Easier climbing leads rightwards to the top of the Stone Shoot.

The next two climbs are on the buttress right of the T-D Gap.

Quiver   90m   Very Difficult **
J.Hammond, R.Morden   16 May 1951

A climb with some fine positions. Start under a small overhang near the left edge of the buttress and make a short traverse right, then follow a shallow groove until a corner leads on to a terrace. At the left end of the terrace is a steep slab topped by two overhangs. Climb a crack in the slab and take the first overhang direct. From under the second overhang, step left on to the edge of the buttress, and follow it to a stance and belay. Continue up easier rocks until progress is barred by another series of overhangs. Traverse across the left wall of the buttress to a projecting nose, then finish by a steep shattered groove.

Grand Diedre   70m   VS ***
H.MacInnes, I.S.Clough, D.Pipes   1 Jun 1958
This excellent, popular and well protected climb takes the prominent diedre running up the buttress. One of the best short routes in the Cuillin. Start below the diedre.
1. 20m 4c Climb an initial right-facing diedre. If wet, climb a cracked slab on the right, then go left to the main diedre (4b).
2. 30m 4b Continue up the diedre across an overhang to a small ledge.
3. 20m Follow the diedre directly to the top.

SGURR MHIC CHOINNICH

Map p279

COIREACHAN RUADHA FACE - FLUTED BUTTRESS

(NG 448 214)   Alt 700m   North-East facing

The northern cliffs of Sgurr Mhic Choinnich offer climbing that is remote and dramatic rather than top quality. Were it not for the long approach from Glen Brittle and the necessity of three days drying time after wet weather, they would be much more popular. But they make a good contrast to the popular Sron na Ciche.

Approach: From Glen Brittle and Coire Lagan, scramble up easy rocks to the right of the An Stac screes to reach the main ridge at the start of the rise up to Sgurr Mhic Choinnich. Descend the evil Rotten Gully, which is on the left side of the cliff (facing out). It can be also abseiled on 50m ropes from the ridge crest to easy ground. Traverse right (facing out) onto a terrace below Fluted Buttress and above a lower cliff.

Go left (facing in) along the terrace from Rotten Gully, passing a smaller buttress and a gully to reach the larger Fluted Buttress with its characteristic 'flutes' and a huge right-angled corner **Cocoa Cracks** (E2 5c) on its front face. Routes are described right to left.

Fluted Buttress   210m   VS 4b **
W.D.Brooker, C.M.Dixon   1 Aug 1950
This splendid route offers exciting climbing which is not high in the grade. About 60m up on the right-hand section are three flutes which give the climb its name. Start on the terrace to the right of the corner of Cocoa Cracks.

Climb a little rib for 7m, then traverse up under overhangs for 15m to where the overhang can be climbed to a ledge above (30m). Follow the ledge to the right, then go up an easy angled chimney. Climb this to where it steepens under the flutes, then traverse out right to a slab (The Gangway) below a huge overhang. Follow the slab rightwards, with the overhanging flute on the left and the wall of the buttress dropping into the gully on the right, until the slab steepens. Traverse out to the wall on the right where delicate and exposed climbing, crux, leads right and up to an easement above the overhangs. Follow a broken groove, trending back left to the centre of the buttress, then climb a short groove to a terrace with a cairn at its left end.

Either continue up The Escape Route, Difficult slabs on the right edge of the buttress or, better, climb the little rib left of the cairn. Climb a crack in the crest to an overhanging nose. Climb its right wall by a hard crack in a groove (4c), step left to a ledge, then go back right to an easy groove. From a recess at the top of the groove, traverse right to a ledge and go along it, moving up and right over two little corners.

Dawn Grooves   170m   HVS **
R.W.P.Barclay, W.D.Brooker   22 Aug 1958
An excellent line of grooves forming the boundary where the front wall meets the south-east face of the buttress. Some folk are happy with the original grade of VS 4c. Start at a prominent crack which forms a chimney after 40m.
1. 25m 5a Climb the crack to a niche and belay.
2. 15m 4b Climb up on the right edge of the niche and up steeply into the crack above, then traverse onto the exposed wall on the right to reach the platform which crosses the face.
3. 45m 4a The easier but steep chimney directly above is **Crack of Dawn** (VS 4c). The platform steepens to the left to form grooves. Climb the groove to below a point where the main groove becomes a clean-cut V (Mongoose Direct) and throws a lesser groove up to the right.
4. 20m 4b Traverse 5m right to a crack in the right wall of the lesser groove. Climb the crack up the slabby edge of the buttress to a good ledge.
5. 20m 4a A steep 15m wall leads to a ledge girdling the upper part of Fluted Buttress. (This route can be joined here by either climbing up for 15m or by escaping right along the ledge). Traverse 12m left to a chimney marking the line of the grooves.
6. 15m 4c Climb the chimney to an overhang, step left and climb a steep crack up and right to ledges below the final corner.
7. 15m 4b Climb the hanging corner and a V-corner above to ledges, 20m of scrambling gains the crest of the summit ridge.

Mongoose Direct   195m   E1 5b **
J.Lamb, P.Whillance   1974; Direct: M.Fowler, P.Thomas   20 June 1977
This fine climb climbs the great cleft in the south-east wall of Fluted Buttress. It is a drainage line and is often wet. Start at a corner-crack 5m left of Dawn Grooves.
1. 25m 5a Climb the crack to a sloping ledge.
2. 20m 5a Continue up a similar crack, then move up a slab to a belay beneath the deep groove of the main cleft.
3. 35m 5b Climb a crack in the right wall, then the groove itself. Where it splits in two at a junction with Dawn Grooves, climb into the prominent clean-cut V-groove of the left-hand branch, crux, to a stance in a niche on the left.
4. 35m 5a Continue up the chimney-groove to a spacious ledge.
5. and 6. 80m Step up left across the overhang in the chimney-line, then continue up the fault to easy ground.

King Cobra   165m   E1 **
C.J.S.Bonington, T.W.Patey   14 Aug 1960
This is one of Skye's most famous routes, remote and with good situations. Unfortunately it is not sustained and the rock quality is not up to the standard of Sron na Ciche, making it feel quite serious. Left of the cleft of Mongoose Direct the south-east wall ends in a big bay, from the back of which springs a meagre gully. Scramble up the gully for 45m and just below where it steepens, traverse easily right to a large flake at the foot of a 25m diedre.
1. 25m 4c Climb the right wall of the diedre to a big ledge.
2. 25m 5b Traverse right into another diedre and climb this, crux. It soon eases, then easier climbing leads to belays.
3. 15m 4b Climb up a rib on the right (loose) to a comfortable shelf below a big overhang overlooking Dawn Grooves.
4. 35m 5a Climb the wall 5m right of the continuation groove to a slab below the roof. Traverse right to avoid the overhang, then climb a ramp to a V shaped groove

which leads to large overhangs. Climb out on the left wall of the groove, swing across to jammed spikes on the left, then climb a short chimney on good holds.
5. 40m 4c Traverse left across a slab into a chimney which leads to a good ledge on the right. Continue up the chimney to a large platform.
6. 25m Climb a further chimney set in a narrow buttress to the top.
Variation: **Direct Finish   E3** *
B.Davison, H.Day   28 Jun 1992
For those needing an extra challenge.
3. 45m 5c Climb pitch 3 but go to the shelf at the left end of the big overhang. Go through the left end of the overhang into a groove, crux, and follow this to a ledge with a chockstone in a wide corner-crack.
4. 50m 4c Climb the corner and a chimney to a large ledge, then climb a corner behind the ledge to easy ground a short way from the top.

BLA BHEINN

(NG 529 217)   928m   Map p279

Bla Bheinn or Blaven is a magnificent mountain with twin summits less than 300m apart, the south-west top being just lower than the main summit. To it north-east is the rocky Clach Glas, the traverse of which across to Bla Bheinn is a classic mountaineering outing.

General Approach: From a car park at NG 561 216, follow a path along the north bank of the Allt na Dunaiche to where it crosses the main stream. Different routes diverge from here and are described below.

Clach Glas – Bla Bheinn Traverse   Difficult ***
This is a superb expedition, like a miniature version of the Cuillin Ridge Traverse. For either traverse, route finding is perhaps more of the challenge than the climbing. The words of an early guide should be heeded: "Many strangers who tackle the two peaks in thick mist fail to carry out their programme". The hard sections are short but there is plenty of exposed scrambling. Graded for walking boots, which are appropriate.

After the initial path, head up into Choire a' Caise and gain the bealach north of Clach Glas. Don't go to a right-hand bealach which marks the western end of Sgurr nan Each. Turn the first wall of rock easily on the left. Now keeping to the ridge, climb the exposed arete to a crest, then steeply descend leftwards by grooves to a full stop just short of a little col. Find a way down! Ahead the ridge broadens, so go up right and traverse slabs to reach a stone chute which ends at an exposed and narrow col. Ahead, a wall of about Severe standard is the most sporting line, but an easier alternative is to take the slanting gully inset into the wall a little further down to the right. This leads over Moderate humps and bumps and arrives at a narrow neck. Slant up a scree-covered ledge and either go round an exposed edge on the right or climb two awkward parallel cracks in a steep wall, both leading to easier ground. Continue up slabs and broken rocks to the summit of Clach Glas.

Traverse the airy summit and descend the south-east ridge, firstly down a crack in a slab, then by a narrow arete, The Imposter. At the bottom, a little overlap gives an exposed move to reach easy ground on a shattered horizontal crest. Continue on to the next section, which needs the most careful route finding. The key is to cross over to the Loch Slapin side and descend a shallow gully in an exposed position. Reach a rake which leads right to a notch. Following the crest here leads to an awkward final drop (which can be abseiled) to the notch. An awkward short tower out of the notch has good holds and leads to a traverse past the final pinnacle, and so to the small grassy bealach known as the Putting Green.

From the Putting Green (695m), the complex north-east spur rises up to Bla Bheinn. This also requires good route finding. Follow an easy path on the left side of the ridge for 60m, which avoids the initial step, then continue easily up to a small col. Climb the short wall above on good holds. Traverse scree rightwards for

SKYE

Stairway to Heaven, E5 6a. Climber Kevin Howett
(photo Tom Prentice)

about 60m, past a steep chimney to a narrow stone chute. Climb this back left to an enclosed cul-de-sac on the right. Continuing on up reaches the prominent Half-Crown Pinnacle, sometimes called The Horn, but the best route climbs the narrow boulder filled gully above the cul-de-sac for 20m by its right wall, moving right on superb holds at the top. Now cross some big stones rightwards and descend slightly to enter the upper section of a large stone chute. Ascend this leftwards to a cairn at a saddle on the east ridge (795m), where the major difficulties cease. Turn right and follow the upper section of the east ridge to the summit of Bla Bheinn.

GREAT PROW AREA
(NG 534 217) Alt 650m South-East facing Map p279

A complex series of buttresses and gullies lie to the immediate right (north-east) of the east ridge of Bla Bheinn. It contains the mountain's most famous feature, the distinctive and well named Great Prow. The Great Prow route itself dries quickly apart from the first pitch.

Approach: Follow the path up the Allt na Dunaiche, then struggle up the unpleasant scree slopes towards the Putting Green at the bealach. It can be quicker to ascend by Bla Bheinn's "Normal Route" and take the recommended descent route from a large cairn once the Great Prow is reached.

Descent: The gully on the right of The Great Prow (looking up).

Sidewinder 110m Severe *
I.S.Clough, A.Sivers, J.Greenwood, D.J.Waller 16 Sep 1968
This good climb follows the left extremity of the big left wall of The Great Prow, left of the big corner of Jib. Start at a short slabby groove in the wall left of Jib which leads to a crack in its right wall.
1. 30m Climb the crack and its right fork to a stance.
2. 15m Continue up grooves to a ledge.
3. 35m Continue in the same line for 20m, then follow a fault diagonally right to a pedestal.
4. 30m Climb the wall to the top.

Jib 130m E1 **
M.Boysen, D.Alcock May 1969
This excellent route follows the big corner to the right of Sidewinder. After an intimidating start the climbing eases; protection should be placed at the earliest opportunity! Start 5m right of the true chimney-crack below an overhung gangway.
1. 40m 5b Climb the left-trending gangway, then go up a steep wall to a ledge. Traverse left past the ledge into the main line.
2. 40m 4c Climb the crack with continuous interest in a fine position.
3. 15m 4c Climb the chimney above to a stance.
4. 35m 4b Climb the fine groove on the right to the top.

Stairway to Heaven 120m E5 **
M.Fowler, P.Thomas 19 Jun 1977
A great Skye classic, with some impressive and quite serious climbing and some dubious rock. Start below the main chimney-crack, left of the normal start of Jib.
1. 30m 5b Climb the groove and chimney through the Jib traverse, then traverse left to a niche.
2. 20m 4c Follow the crack above to a further niche.
3. 30m 6a Move up to a fault-line and follow this leftwards until it is possible to climb the overhang by a short crack. Traverse right with difficulty to a narrow ledge, then climb diagonally up right to a short crack which leads to a stance and peg belay on a slanting gangway. A serious pitch.
4. 40m 5b Follow the crack, climb an overlap, then move up in a tremendous position to a flake covered wall which leads to a ledge. Finish up the wall and move right to the top.

The Great Prow 105m VS *
T.W.Band, P.W.F.Gribbon, N.S.Ross, W.Tauber 15 Jun 1968
Despite its classic status and great position, the climbing could be better. Beware of loose rock in places. Start below an overhanging chimney-corner.
1. 35m 4c Climb the awkward crack to exit onto a slab, then climb the slab to a belay at its top.
2. 40m 4b Continue up the crack above to a pedestal ledge.
3. 10m Move back down from the pedestal, level with an orange coloured slab, then follow a thin diagonal fault up the wall leftwards to the crest.

SKYE

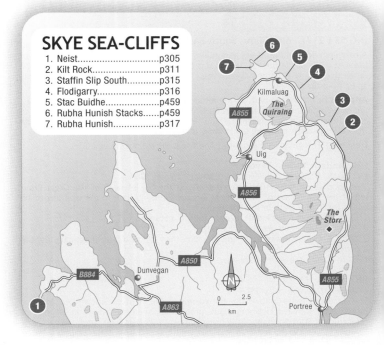

4. 20m Continue up a ramp until a crack on the right leads back to the crest and the summit.
Variation: **Twilight Slab   VS 4c** **
A.J.Kennedy, G.Rooney   6 Jun 1975
From the cracks on pitch two, below the orange slab, traverse left across the prominent slab on the front of the Prow; belay on the edge. Continue up and right to a large block, then go straight up to join the original line for the final pitch.

Skye Sea-Cliffs

The development of Skye's coastline cliffs has given it a new rock climbing dimension. Most are well away from the mountains and often dry when the Cuillin are cloud bound. Most of the climbing, save for the first two areas described below, is on non-tidal dolerite escarpments.

SUIDHE BIORACH

(NG 515 123)   Non-tidal   South facing   Map p279   Diagram p304

The Elgol peninsula south-east of the Cuillin is one of the driest parts of the island. The rock is jurassic sandstone, with climbing more reminiscent of Northumberland than Torridon. Some routes dry quickly, others are affected by seepage. The crag was spotted from a fishing boat and then explored by several locally based climbers including Rob MacDonald, Dominic Partridge and Neil Smith, without realising that Noel Williams and Willie Jeffrey had been before them.

Approach: Turn west at Broadford, and continue for 24km to one of the car parks at the road end at Elgol. Walk south (best to head 100 to 200m from the coast) to reach the cliff in 20mins. A massive cracked block, shaped like India, juts out from the cliff-top. Immediately west of this is the obvious corner of Jamie Jampot, which gives the most convenient abseil approach to the routes; it is best to take a spare rope. Paradise Ledge is near the top of this corner. It is also possible to scramble in from either end at low tide. It is usually possible to get to all of the climbs from the abseil, although in very high tides access to the last three routes could be awkward.

1 Veritas Splendour   25m   E3 *
S.Hill   1993
The obvious arete left of Jamie Jampot.
1. 12m 5c Climb the leftward curving crack and pull strenuously on to the left wall of the arete. Move up and back right more easily to a belay.
2. 13m 5c Climb directly up the arete and belay on Paradise Ledge.

2 Crack of Zawn   25m   HVS/E1 5b *
R.MacDonald   1992
The crack left of the Jamie Jampot corner, with a thin step left.

3 Jamie Jampot   25m   VS 4c **
R.MacDonald, D.Partridge   1992
Rob and Dominic's first route was approached by boat giving a ground (sea) up ascent. The prominent corner-crack is a sustained and interesting, continue to the top or step left onto Paradise Ledge.

4 Digitalis   25m   E3 5c **
D.Partridge   1993
The wall right of the Jamie Jampot corner has a bold start and a finger pocket move up high which is slow to dry.

5 India   30m   E3 **
N.Smith, D.Partridge   1993
This great route starts up the prominent corner to the right. It is strenuous, but well protected. The lower pitch can be damp.
1. 5c Climb the corner through the stepped roofs, and gain an airy stance and belay across on the right.
2. 5c Move back left along the lip of a roof to gain a short crack. Climb the overhang above and finish up the prominent jamming crack in a superb position.

6 Altar-Ego   30m   E1 *
D.Partridge, R.MacDonald   1992
This route starts immediately right of the corner of India, and finishes up the right-hand side of a big roof.
1. 5b Climb the left side of a pillar on large holds. Continue up the blanker wall above (crux), moving right at the top to gain the stance on India.
2. 4b Move up right into a corner, and climb to the roof. Undercut rightwards in an exposed position, and finish more easily up a deep cleft.

7 Rapid Learning Curve   30m   E6 6b ***
N.Hancock, M.Smith   Sep 1999
This sensational, well protected climb forces its way through the triple tiered roof and up the smooth headwall. The 'locals' had top roped this but understandably wimped out of the lead. Ascend on good holds to a cramped rest below the final roof, move out to a fingery crux turning the lip, then climb the headwall on gradually improving holds. Take a good selection of cams, wires and long slings to reduce drag on the lower runners.

8 Tree Route   30m   E2 5b *
D.Partridge, S.Bally   1994
This fine route follows a steep crack-line to the right. Climb the very steep crack to an overhang. Surmount this (crux), and continue past the tree to the top.

SKYE

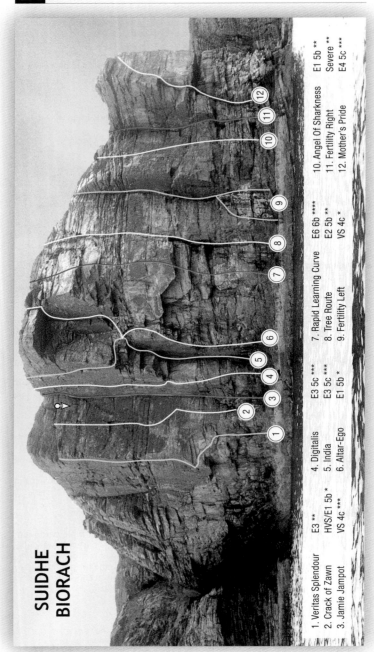

SUIDHE BIORACH

1. Veritas Splendour — E3 **
2. Crack of Zawn — HVS/E1 5b *
3. Jamie Jampot — VS 4c ***
4. Digitalis — E3 5c ***
5. India — E3 5c ***
6. Altar-Ego — E1 5b *
7. Rapid Learning Curve — E6 6b ****
8. Tree Route — E2 5b **
9. Fertility Left — VS 4c *
10. Angel Of Sharkness — E1 5b **
11. Fertility Right — Severe **
12. Mother's Pride — E4 5c ***

9 Fertility Left   30m   VS 4c *
D.N.Williams, W.Jeffrey   11 Jul 1987
The prominent left-facing corner. The direct start is wet but straightforward, or start on the left.

10 Angel of Sharkness   25m   E1 5b **
M.Philp, N.Smith 1994
The obvious crack in the wall left of Fertility Right.

11 Fertility Right   25m   Severe **
D.N.Williams, W.Jeffrey   11 Jul 1987
This pleasant climb takes the next prominent left-facing corner.

12 Mother's Pride   25m   E4 ***
D.Partridge, R.MacDonald   1994
Dominic and Neil were working on the same North Sea Platform but Neil went back to work before bagging this route. At the same time Dominic finished his stretch and was tipped off about the climb. The climbing is outrageous, up the seriously overhanging prow at the right-hand end of the face.
1. 5c Climb the crack leading to a roof. Swing up through this to land on a ledge.
2. 5c Climb the groove above the ledge. Swing right (crux) on to the face. Continue directly up the crack-line on wilting arms.

SCHOOLHOUSE BUTTRESS - ELGOL

(NG 516 137)   Non-tidal   South or East facing

These quick drying routes are two minutes from the road but rather public.

Approach: From one of the car parks at the road end at Elgol, walk past the school (on the shore side) and continue past a cottage. A prominent arete is just past the cottage.

Bee Keepers Bother   16m   E1 5b *
S.Park, L.Whitmarch, L.Varney   29 Jul 1994
Climb the arete and swing left on to a ledge. Continue up the corner left of the arete.

Schoolhouse Buttress   20m   VS 4c *
W.F.Alexander, J.Ashbridge   12 May 1987
This climbs the slabby right side of the larger overhanging buttress further on. Good climbing but a couple of loose holds. Climb past grass to reach an undercut flake, step left and follow the flake, then an obvious crack. Just left is **Apiary Arete**, climbed at a similar grade.

NEIST

Map p302, 308
Skye's most westerly point is an impressive dolerite sea-cliff sporting hundreds of mostly single pitch routes. Most of the climbs described dry quickly and are bird free, although there can be fulmars on the second pitch of Supercharger. Midges can be troublesome, but Neist often catches a breeze and the grass (midge cover) is shorter than Skye's east coast cliffs.

Access: From Dunvegan drive west through Glendale and Waterstein to the road end at Neist, 18km from Dunvegan.

BAYWATCH AREA

(NG 132 477)   Alt 50m   South-West facing   Map p308

These pleasant routes are fairly popular as the cliff-top is 2mins from the car park!

SKYE

Approach: Go halfway down the concrete ramp from the car park, then duck under the railing and follow the path hard left. Cross a stone wall, **Juniper Rib** (Severe) starts 12m before the wall, and continue along the crag to a faint rib marked by a triangular roof at one-third height just left of the crest.

1 Baywatch   25m   Hard Severe 4b
D.N.Williams, P.Duggan   12 Oct 1994
Climb a groove in the crest of the rib, then the crack just left of the crest.

2 Sonamara   25m   VS 4c *
D.N.Williams, S.Abbott, L.Taylor   15 Apr 1995
A little further right there is a more prominent rib with a recess on its right-hand side. Climb an obvious groove on the left side of the rib.

3 Transitive Nightfall of Diamonds   25m   Hard Severe 4b
A.Holden, R.Holden   17 Jul 1997
Start at the first rib right of Sonamara, just to the left of the crest. Climb a series of slabs pleasantly to the top, keeping to the left of the crest. Protection is spaced.

THE FIN

Non-tidal   North-East and South-West facing
East-south-east of the car park, a narrow rock ridge known as The Fin forms the south-west wall of an impressive chasm (NG 136 476). It is approached by slanting downhill from the car park in about 5mins.

4 Heavenley's Pleasure   45m   E5 6b ***
M.Garthwaite, D.Gregg   21 May 1992
This superb route climbs a crack on the south-west face of The Fin; 6c for short climbers.

The next two routes are on the north-east wall of the chasm opposite The Fin. Stakes are in place at the top.

5 California Dreaming   35m   E1 5b ***
W.McCrae, D.Armstrong   30 Dec 1981
Fantastic climbing up the prominent crack-line towards the back of the chasm, opposite the fin, unfortunately there is often wetness low down.

6 Breakfast in America   40m   E3 6a **
D.Armstrong, P.Whillance   29 Dec 1981
A steep open groove lies 9m to the right of the previous route. Climb easily up to below the groove, then follow a very thin crack in the right wall of the groove to reach ledges. Ascend a short easy corner to the top.

AN T-AIGEACH

Non-tidal   West facing
The hump of An t-Aigeach (the stallion) lies between the car park and the light-house. 10mins from the car park.

7 Supercharger   110m   E3 *
E.Grindley, C.Grindley, W.Jeffrey, D.N.Williams   22 Aug 1981
This fine line gets a lot of traffic, but loose rock can still be encountered on pitch three. The large platform at the foot of the route is above high tide level. It can be

SKYE

Nick Hancock on the first ascent of Rapid Learning Curve, E6 6b, Suidhe Biorach
(photo Nick Hancock collection)

reached from either direction at very low tide, although it is best to abseil down the line of the route. Start at the top left-hand end of the platform below a crack.

1. 25m 5b Climb the crack and groove over a bulge. Climb a short corner to belay on the left.

2. 25m 5a Move up left onto a ledge, then move right to gain a steep corner. Ascend this and pull out at the top into an easy groove on the right. Follow the groove and traverse right to a large stance.

3. 35m 6a Ascend a steep crack to gain a flake-line leading up left to a corner below a big stepped roof. From the top of the flake make a fingery move out right on to the face. Climb right and up, with little protection, to the right-hand end of the big roof. Follow cracks up overhanging wall. Swing past the roof and pull strenuously into a leaning groove on the left. Continue to an airy stance on the left.

4. 25m 5a From the left side of the ledge, climb an awkward crack. Easier climbing up a broken arete and grass leads to the summit.

FINANCIAL SECTOR

(NG 129 484) Alt 80m West facing

There is some superb varied climbing in this bay. George Szuca enthused about the area for years. Noel Williams then saw the potential and climbed a number of routes with Stevie Abbott, and Willie Jeffrey. Other investors were Emma Alsford (Hurricane Hideaway), Colin Moody and Neil Smith (Bad Dream) and Tom Bridgeland (Piggy Bank).

Approach: From the car park head north-west across the moor passing the coastguard lookout. The cliff-top is 100m beyond this, just before the moor levels out into bog, 10mins. A more scenic approach is to follow the cliff-top west-north-west from the car park. A slightly longer approach is to descend the ramp towards the lighthouse. Turn right and cut through a gap in the drystone dyke, then follow sheep tracks below the Upper Cliff. The sector is just beyond another drystone dyke. Abseil in with a spare rope. It is possible (but not pleasant) to descend Tower Gully, a gully with a small stream, just north of the sector.

Various stakes are seen at the top. Looking down and left (south) is a drystone dyke below a pillar which forms the south end of the bay. Routes are described from Tower Gully southwards.

8 Bad Dream 60m E3 5c ***
C.Moody, L.Gordon Canning 17 Jun 1997 (first pitch); N.Smith, R.Lupton, C.Moody 19 Jul 1997 (complete)
Walk north from the sector, under the cliff to reach the north facing corner which overlooks Tower Gully. A compelling line.

1. 35m 5b Climb the corner to the overhang, traverse right to climb a short corner-crack and move on to the ledge on the right. An excellent pitch.

2. 25m 5c Step back left and follow the obvious fault, finishing by jamming the left side of the summit block.

Towards the north end of the bay is a hanging curtain of basalt. This is well right of the terminal pillar, which has a large basalt pedestal at its base. The buttress to the right of the curtain has two grooves.

9 Earthbound 30m HVS 5a *
C.Moody, M.Tweedley 13 Jun 1996
Start up an easy slab, then climb two successive steep cracks to gain the left-hand groove which leads to the top.

10 Terminal Bonus 30m HVS 5a *
S.Abbott, D.N.Williams 6 May 1996
Move up left to gain the right-hand groove. Follow the lovely groove, steep to start.

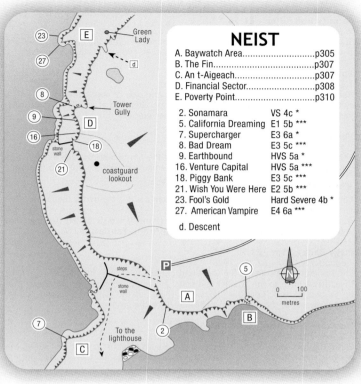

NEIST

2. Sonamara	VS 4c	*
5. California Dreaming	E1 5b	***
7. Supercharger	E3 6a	*
8. Bad Dream	E3 5c	***
9. Earthbound	HVS 5a	*
16. Venture Capital	HVS 5a	***
18. Piggy Bank	E3 5c	***
21. Wish You Were Here	E2 5b	***
23. Fool's Gold	Hard Severe 4b	*
27. American Vampire	E4 6a	***

d. Descent

Green Lady

Tower Gully

stone wall

coastguard lookout

steps

stone wall

To the lighthouse

P

N

0   100
metres

SKYE

1 Insider Dealing   30m   HVS 5a **

D.N.Williams, S.Abbott   16 Jul 1995

The buttress to the right has two overhangs high up separated by a pillar. This quality route finishes up a prominent groove right of the right-hand overhang. Start below the overhangs and ascend the left side of a small alcove. Continue up and rightwards to gain a slight recess. Pull over a bulge and then step up leftwards on to a slabby ramp. A short distance above move hard right to gain the main groove come crack-line. Climb this passing the overhang.

Midas Touch (HVS 5a) is a worthwhile, slightly easier alternative. Start up Insider Dealing then climb the left-slanting slabby corner.

2 Shocks and Stares   25m   VS 4b **

D.N.Williams, S.Abbott   1 Jul 1995

Scramble up below the right side of the buttress. Follow the prominent hand crack that slants slightly left, then goes up the rib.

About 50m to the right are two fine buttresses. There is a 6m pinnacle below the right-hand buttress.

3 Bridging Interest   30m   HVS 5a ***

W.Jeffrey, D.N.Williams   4 Aug 1996

This classic gives sustained climbing. Climb the black corner left of the left-hand buttress.

14 Security Risk   30m   E1 5b **
W.Jeffrey, D.N.Williams, A.Holden   16 Jun 1996
Start up Powerbroker, then follow the flake-crack out left to the edge. Work out the easiest line up the buttress to finish up big ledges. Protection could be better.

15 Powerbroker   30m   E1 5b **
S.Abbott, D.N.Williams   6 Apr 1996
Good climbing up the groove on the right-hand side of the left-hand buttress; a side runner can be placed to protect the start. Step left at a bulge around half-height; there are useful holds left of the upper groove.

16 Venture Capital   30m   HVS 5a ***
S.Abbott, D.N.Williams   16 Jul 1995
This great route starts at twin cracks right of the 6m pinnacle. Make a few moves up the left crack then step right and continue up, and over the bulge to the top.

17 A Fist Full of Dollarite   30m   E1 5b *
Climbs the right-facing corner just right. A Camalot 4 is handy for the last section.

To the right is a north face. The short bulging chimney and steep, left-slanting ramp is **B.C.C.I.** (E2 5c *). The strenuous crack just right is **Fat Cats** (E2 5c *).

18 Piggy Bank   25m   E3 5c ***
T.Bridgeland, E.Ash   23 May 1998
This brilliant route starts at the south end of the bay. A huge boulder leans against the cliff; clamber up the boulder and belay at the top. Step down right, then move up to two pockets. Continue rightwards (bold) to the base of a curving ramp. Follow the ramp, then move up right and climb the groove.

19 Hurricane Hideaway   25m   E1 5b ***
E.Alsford, P.Donnithorne   8 Jun 1997
Climb the corner left of Wall Street, then take an obvious traverse left. Climb the hanging corner to the roof and undercut rightwards to gain a short meaty finishing corner.

20 Wall Street   30m   E2 5c ***
S.Abbott, D.N.Williams   1 Jul 1995
Another brilliant route! It climbs the wall right of the Piggy Bank buttress. Climb the cracked wall left of centre until forced to trend rightwards. Climb straight up till just below the roof, and step left to a right-facing corner. Swing out left to pass the roof, and continue to the top.

21 Wish You Were Here   32m   E2 5b ***
G.Szuca, G.Armstrong   Sep 1990
A short distance south of the stone wall there is a shallow recess set into the steep face high up. This route climbs a striking crack forming the right-hand side of the recess, turning a roof at the top on the right.

POVERTY POINT

(NG 129 488)   Non-tidal   South & West facing

There is a wide range of grades here, useful for climbers who want an easier time than the Financial Sector. The rough crystalline rock is similar to the other sea-cliffs at Neist, although quite different to the Financial Sector with its oddly shaped holds.

Approach: Looking north from the Financial Sector two coastal peninsulas can be seen, Poverty Point then the shorter more distant Destitution Point. Walk past the top of the Financial Sector and the loch, then go down an easy grassy gully past a squat pinnacle (The Green Lady). Continue down and left slightly to reach the cliff-top, less than 30mins from the car park. The cliff forms a bowl to the west of the main prow; a shorter cliff runs north from the west end of the bowl. Abseil to the base via an extra rope.

22 Any Spare Change?   20m   Severe *
C.Moody   20 Apr 2003
The central crack in the short cliff.

There are recessed corners either side of the crack; the right-hand one is **Thrift is a Virtue** (Severe *). The stepped wall to the right of Thrift is a Virtue has one move of Severe. **Broken Wing** (Very Difficult *) climbs the crack in the yellow recess at the right end of the cliff.

23 Fool's Gold   16m   Hard Severe 4b *
C.Moody, C.Grindley   31 May 2003
At the right end of the face is a short pinnacle. Start at the right side of the pinnacle and move up left behind it. Continue up to the yellow bulge and move up right through it.

The twin cracks to the right are the line of **Homer** (HVS 5a *).

24 Giro Day   25m   E2 5b **
C.Moody, M.MacLeod   20 Jul 1997
Climb the crack left of a shallow chimney; the bulge is awkward.

The shallow chimney is **Superlager for Breakfast** (VS 4b *).

25 Recovery Day   25m   E1 5b **
C.Moody, L.Gordon Canning   1 Jun 1997
The corner-crack 4m right of the chimney curves to the left. High in the grade.

26 Fight Club   25m   E3 6a ***
P.Benson, F.Bennet   15 Apr 2001
A fine jamming tussle up the left-hand crack of the prow, facing Fool's Gold.

27 American Vampire   25m   E4 6a ***
P.Benson, F.Bennet   15 Apr 2001
The right-hand crack. Sustained climbing leads to the overhanging hand crack with the crux at the top.

SKYE

KILT ROCK

(NG 507 662)   Alt 50m   South-East to East facing   Map p302   Diagram p313

The southern and most spectacular of the three cliffs described on Skye's Trotternish peninsula, Kilt Rock gives atmospheric, often strenuous climbing on quick drying dolerite. Protection is usually great, although it is easy to run out of gear before the top and it can be windy, although this keeps the midges away. Ed Grindley kicked off development with Dick Swindon and Noel Williams, joined later by Pete Hunter and Willie Jeffrey.

Approach: From Portree drive north and turn right into the Kilt Rock viewpoint car park. Cross the burn and follow the cliff-top north. Alternatively park north of the viewpoint at a phone box. Walk along the road for 150m to a gate on the right. Go through the gate, and with a fence on the left at first, head north-east for 400m, crossing a fence after about 200m. Reach a cliff-top fence at its high point with bushes behind. The descent gully is just to the north (left). Just over 10mins walk either way.

There are a number of iron stakes in the thin cliff-top soil, so do not rely on single stakes. In most cases it is best to arrange a belay with a separate rope before climbing. Scramble down the gully which is about 4m wide. Where the gully gets wider there is a short left-facing corner-crack on the left.

1 The Electric Bagpipe 33m HVS 5a ***
D.N.Williams, P.Hunter 16 Jul 1983
This delightfully varied climb starts at the short left-facing corner-crack. Climb the corner and continue up the front or left-hand side of the giant flake above. From the top of the flake layback up the crack on the right. Step left on to the wall and climb to a ledge. Move up and right to finish.

2 Clandestine 38m VS 4c *
D.N.Williams, C.A.Hill 28 May 1983
A pleasant route which slants rightwards across the lower gully wall. Exposure increases as height is gained. Start up The Electric Bagpipe (crux), then move right and up to a triangular recess. Step right again to another recess and climb the left-hand of two parallel cracks. Climb the left side of a pedestal to the top.

3 Secret Service 42m HVS 5a **
D.N.Williams, P.Hunter 13 Jul 1983
Near the bottom of the gully a ledge runs horizontally right across the wall. Traverse out along the ledge and round the rib. Follow the crack up slightly left then climb the right-hand of two parallel cracks. Finish up the right side of the pedestal.

The next four routes all finish on a prominent slab near the top of the wall.

4 Tartan Terror 40m E2 5b **
P.Hunter, D.N.Williams 13 Jul 1983
Start up Secret Service but step right about 6m up to gain the crack.

5 Skyeman 40m E2 5b ***
P.Hunter, D.N.Williams 16 Jul 1983
The crack immediately to the right offers sustained climbing.

6 Godzilla 40m E3 6a ***
E.Alsford, P.Donnithorne 1 Jun 1999
The groove next right, with fine sustained climbing but some tricky moves low down.

7 Wide Eyed 40m E2 5b **
E.Grindley, C.Grindley 22 May 1983
The corner come chimney-crack to the right.

The following routes are best approached by abseil and have hanging belays or poor stances at the start. It is worth belaying on the abseil rope and prudent to tie a big knot in the end.

8 Edge of Beyond 45m E2 5c ***
P.Hunter, W.Jeffrey 10 Jul 1983
Climb the next groove right of Wide Eyed, with a wildly exposed excursion on to the left bounding arete at half-height. The top is 3m west of Grey Panther.

9 Grey Panther 45m E1 5b ****
E.Grindley, D.N.Williams, P.Hunter, W.Jeffrey 9 Jul 1983
A popular classic, strong climbers say HVS others are convinced that it is E2! It climbs a fairly prominent recess with angled walls immediately right of the previous route. Ascend twin cracks in the back of the recess, the top is 5m north east of the twin boulders.

KILT ROCK

3. Secret Service	HVS 5a **	7. Wide Eyed	E2 5b **
4. Tartan Terror	E2 5b **	8. Edge of Beyond	E2 5c ***
5. Skyeman	E2 5b ***	9. Grey Panther	E1 5b ****
6. Godzilla	E3 6a ***	10. Internationale	E3 5c ****

10 Internationale   45m   E3 5c ****
R.Swindon, E.Grindley   1 May 1983
A very sustained and photogenic route up the centre of Kilt Rock. Climb the conspicuous jamming crack right of Grey Panther to a horizontal break. Continue directly and move right to finish. It is difficult to carry enough large protection devices. Finish 3m east of Grey Panther.

11 Road to Ruin   E2 5b **
E.Grindley, R.Swindon, D.N.Williams   31 Apr 1983
Round the corner right of Internationale is a wide chossy gully. This route climbs the prominent jamming crack to its left. Move right near the top and finish beside the gully.

STAFFIN SLIP SOUTH

(NG 499 675)   Alt 30m   North-East facing   Map p302

This cliff lies just north of Kilt and offers similar climbing, although the northerly aspect means the rock is not as clean. However, it can be sheltered in a souwesterly with light showers passing overhead. Two buttresses can be seen by looking south from the road end at Staffin Slipway, this is the extensive left-hand crag. Dougie Dinwoodie climbed the first route in 1987. Over the next two years Ed Grindley and an army of Lake District climbers produced twenty more routes. Sadly the long routes don't get enough traffic and some are overgrown; the routes described here are still clean.

Approach: From Portree drive north past Kilt to Staffin; after the shop look for a right turn to Staffin Slipway and park there. It is best to take the pathway that slants up left from the car park to reach the top of the right-hand crag. Go along the top of that crag, then descend an easy grassy gully at the western end of Staffin Slip South.

The right-hand end of the crag is quite short, but further left its height increases impressively to nearly a full rope length. The routes are described from right to left. The first three cracks are the off-width **Babe** (E2 5b), **Lateral Thinking** (E1 5b **) and **Hand Jive** (E2 5c **).

Jugs of Deception   18m   E4 6a *
M.Tweedley, C.Moody   10 Jun 1996
The pillar left of the three cracks is climbed using thin cracks, a change from the usual hand jamming. The final bulge is climbed by a layaway off the edge to reach a hidden hold on the right.

Lat up a Drainpipe   17m   HVS 5a **
G.Libeks, E.Grindley, S.Suthorn   30 May 1988
Just round to the left of the previous routes is a corner recess with twin cracks.

Swillington Common   19m   E2 5c **
I.Blakeley, G.Libeks, C.Downer   28 May 1989
This is the second crack to the left of Lat up a Drainpipe. The awkward black crack between is **The Avon Man** (E2 5b *).

About 30m left is a grassy corner with an overhang high up on the right; this is **Easy Day for a Lady** (HVS 5a). Left of this an impressive pillar is half the height of the crag. Between the two is the following great route.

Grey Panther, E1 5b, Kilt Rock. Climber Paul Moores
(photo Cubby Images)

Gorbachev   45m   E2 5b *****
E.Grindley, G.Libeks, S.Suthorn   29 May 1988
Climb the obvious twin cracks. **Woman of the Eighties** (E3 5c ***) is the finger crack just right.

East Chimney Crack   40m   HVS 5a ****
J.Hargreaves, W.Birkett   May 1988
Climb the shallow chimney formed in the corner at the left end of the cliff. Good climbing and worth checking out in showery weather. The crack just right is **Green Vote** (E3 5c **), passing a rowan tree at two-thirds height.

FLODIGARRY

(NG 465 729)   Tidal   South and East facing   Map p302

This cliff offers a variety of routes on dolerite in nice rocky surroundings; Spantastic is a must. The usual team, Noel Williams and Willie Jeffrey did the first routes in 1989, Ed Grindley also climbed here the same year.

Approach: Some 6km north of Staffin lies the tiny settlement of Flodigarry. Drive north past the turning to Flodigarry Hotel for 1km, and park 200m before a white roadside house (NG 459 727). Traverse a hillside north-eastwards until just short of a rock topped knoll. The crest is gained up on the right (second small col before the knoll), where a stye crosses a fence. A path descends an unlikely ramp through an upper cliff to reach a forward pointing right-angle in a lower fence. Directly below is a bay with a stumpy stack. The top of a south facing slabby wall is easily seen; Spantastic climbs this wall.

The right arm of the fence runs round the rim of the bay to a visible easy grassy descent into the bay. The left arm of the fence runs along a crest over the top of South Tunnel Buttress, above the top of a shrub filled depression with abseil stakes at the top of Rock Island Line, then continues towards North Tunnel Buttress but turns downhill away from it.

1 Newspaper Taxis   40m   Severe *****
D.N.Williams, P.Duggan   6 Jul 1990
Climb a fairly prominent broad rib of clean rock in the back wall of the bay opposite the stumpy sea-stack, pleasant and straight forward. Approach down the grass slope at the south side of the bay, at high tide abseil in, there are belay stakes on the grass slope above.

Facing the stumpy sea-stack is a south face containing the following two routes. A large tunnel runs right through the back of the buttress, and several narrower crevices lead off this at right angles on the seaward side. Canoeists have paddled through the tunnel at high tide. Numerous stakes have been placed at the top.

2 Spantastic   40m   HVS ****
D.N.Williams, W.Jeffrey   26 May 1990
This memorable route climbs the astonishing pillar spanning the southern entrance to the tunnel. The pillar has a narrow base which may not support it for much longer. Abseil down to a leaning niche just below the pillar.
1. 20m 4c Fix a high runner before setting off up the pillar. The technical grade assumes a complete lack of imagination. Continue up the recess above, then break right to a good stance.
2. 20m 4b Continue up ledges trending right. Where the ledges lead horizontally right, make a steep move up the wall and climb slightly leftwards past the left end of a horizontal roof. Finish more easily.

3 Lucy in the Sky   40m   HVS 5a ****
D.N.Williams, W.Jeffrey   26 May 1990

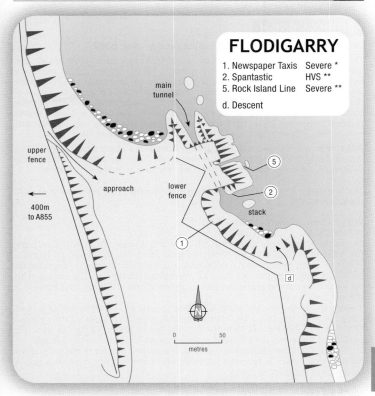

FLODIGARRY

1. Newspaper Taxis   Severe *
2. Spantastic   HVS **
5. Rock Island Line   Severe **

d. Descent

main tunnel

upper fence

approach

lower fence

← 400m to A855

stack

0   50

metres

SKYE

This good route climbs the obvious crack in the wall to the right of Spantastic. Start in the leaning niche as for Spantastic. Traverse very delicately right until it is possible to pull up onto a small ledge. Continue more easily slightly leftwards to gain the main crack. Climb this and at the top go up the left side of a leaning pedestal. Join Spantastic on top of the pedestal, then move up the wall and slant left past the roof as for that route.

4 Election Chimney   40m   Hard Severe *
D.N.Williams, P.Duggan, C.Clark   3 May 1990
This route ascends a prominent chimney opposite the rock island on the right-hand half of the crag. Start from a ledge by the left wall of the chimney above the high water mark. Ascend the chimney (crux), step out right at the top and continue by the easiest line to finish rightwards.

5 Rock Island Line   40m   Severe **
D.N.Williams, W.Jeffrey   7 May 1990
Pleasant balance climbing to the right of Election Chimney). Abseil from the shrub filled depression, just north of the top of the other routes, to a ledge opposite the rock island. (At low tide it is possible to step onto the island.) At high tide start from a tiny triangular foot niche a few metres higher. Climb up very slightly rightwards at first and continue directly to a grassy finish.

RUBHA HUNISH

(NG 410 761)   Alt 20m   North-West facing   Map p302

The northerly tip of Skye is one of the most picturesque parts of the island, and well worth a visit even if you don't intend to climb. Some smallish stacks are described in the sea-stacks chapter, although they are somewhat dwarfed by the main cliff, but they pair up with Master of Morgana at a lower grade than most of the routes. The lower part of the cliff is rather friable in places, but most of these routes have had a number of ascents. Willie Jeffrey and Noel Williams (again!) climbed Whispering Crack. Bill Birkett climbed some fine routes with various partners including Dave Birkett, who produced the hardest route on Skye at the time.

Approach: Leave the road at Duntulm on a bend by a phone box (NG 422 743). A path starts from the right side of the sheep fank, head north-west to a trench like depression. Go down through the cliffs; the best path is on the left, 35mins.

The first routes lie on an impressive crag immediately to the right (north-east) of the descent path.

Willey's Last Stramash   75m   E4/5 **
W.Birkett, G.Sharp   21 Sep 2003
Climbs the great corner system just left of centre. A route of two halves with the first offering a classic pitch on denatured rock, not unlike Mousetrap on Gogarth. Whilst technical difficulties are reasonable and the climbing good, concentration on the limitations of the rock must be maintained throughout. The second pitch has excellent rock and protection and some sensational climbing. Start beneath a shallow cave like recess.
1. 40m 5b Steep grass and easier rocks lead to a corner. Climb to the black cave. Large Friends in the gas pockets offer reasonable protection. Move up and right out of the cave to pull into the right-hand corner-groove above. Climb this until it is possible to move into the left-hand corner-crack which is followed to a ledge.
2. 35m 6a Climb the impending corner with sustained interest to the roof. Gain a hand-traverse which is followed leftwards across the lip until moves up gain a crack. Climb the crack to the top.

Northern Lights   72m   E2 ***
W.Birkett, A.Sheehan   9 Sep 1991
This route starts up an obvious groove system just right of centre. On the face to its left at one-third height is a long narrow roof. Start at a diamond shaped block. The very impressive line of **Drifting Too Far From Shore** (E8) starts 10m to the left.
1. 15m Move up, then climb diagonally left across a grassy bay. Step left and move up to gain a groove and stance on the left side of a pinnacle. A rather loose and grassy approach pitch to the groove line proper.
2. 35m 5a Move up on to a pinnacle and climb the crack come groove system above to the top of a large pinnacle. Continue up and step left awkwardly to exit the groove about 4m below a roof. Move up, then step right before climbing to the roof. Gain a handhold on a flat topped block just below and right of the roof. Pull right into a corner groove and ascend this for 3m until an exit left can be made. Continue up the groove directly above the overhang and pull over blocks on to a heathery ledge. Step up and left to a perfect eagle's nest stance, and peg belay.
3. 20m 5c Follow the leaning and tapering ramp, which leads steeply leftwards to the top. A superb pitch.

Friends in the North   80m   E2 **
N.Robinson, W.Birkett   31st May 1996
This fine climb also starts at the diamond block and finishes up the central of three leftward-leaning crack systems.
1. 20m 4a Climb up to a right-trending grassy ramp. Follow this to beside a small

pinnacle at the base of the corner-crack proper.

2. 35m 5b Climb the corner-crack on excellent rough rock. Step right at the over-lap, continue up the corner-crack in the dark reddish rock, which terminates in a pinnacle column abutting the headwall. Step up and left to gain a ledge. Move left to a short corner-groove.

3. 10m 5a Climb the corner-groove to an easy leftward traverse which leads to a deep crack.

4. 15m 5c Step left to gain thin parallel cracks. Follow these up the wall past a heathery niche to finish up a short groove formed by a large block.

The remaining routes lie south-west of the descent path. The first route is reached by leaving the descent path early on. Head downhill and then go round left a short distance to the base of a distinctive rock bastion.

Master of Morgana   70m   HVS **
A.Holden, M.Hudson   31 Aug 1996

A superb well protected line following the right-hand side of the face and finishing up the obvious cleft on the skyline. Start below the right-hand of two deep chimneys at the right side of the rock bastion.

1. 30m 4c Gain the chimney and climb it on improving rock to a ledge on the left. Climb a series of grooves trending left to reach a blocky ledge and nut belays.

2. 40m 5b Climb the crack above the stance to reach a higher ledge. Traverse left to gain a leftward rising ramp leading to a horizontal break. Hand-traverse back right to gain the bottom of the final crack. Climb this (crux) to a spectacular grovelling finish.

Northern Exposure   90m   E2 **
W.Birkett, C.Thorpe   31 May 1993

This excellent climb ascends the longest and most continuous section of rock at Rubha Hunish. It lies over 100m to the south-west of the previous route, and is reached by scrambling over boulders and grass at the base of the cliff. There is a rib of rock a short distance to the right of the start, after which the wall becomes noticeably reduced in height. Start at the bottom of a great crack come groove line soaring up through a sizeable double roof.

1. 30m 5a Climb the discontinuous crack within a groove to a small overhang and foot ledge.

2. 50m 5b A big pitch in every sense. Above the small overlap the crack becomes continuous and rises to an overlap guarding the deep hanging corner. This in turn rises to a double stepped roof. From the belay move into the crack and climb it with lots of determination. Some hard moves allow a little roof to be gained beneath the corner. Surmount this and follow the corner to the first stepped roof. Over this to the top roof which extends 3m out from the face. Move out left across this and pull out strenuously and on up to a great chockstone. Belay on top of this.

3. 10m 4c Climb the wide crack directly above to a stake.

Whispering Crack   55m   E3 ***
W.Jeffrey, D.N.Williams   6 May 1989

This route starts some distance right of Northern Exposure and climbs a prominent leftward-curving crack on a clean section of wall set at a higher level than the rest of the cliff. It is a brilliant line through a blank wall, and gives a remarkably sustained climb. Willie Jeffrey fell off the crux in 1987; the route was climbed twenty anxious whispering months later. It is best to arrange a belay at the very the top of the route before climbing, using stakes well back from the cliff edge.

2. 10m 4b Start on the left and climb up trending right to join the crack where it becomes better defined. Go up to a small ledge and take a semi-hanging belay on in-situ pegs backed up with nuts.

3. 45m 5c Climb the crack and gain a pod with difficulty (crux). The crack gives continuous interest above. Eventually reach a flake ledge on the right wall, which proves surprisingly difficult to make good use of. Move left and continue with very little respite until the top is gained.

SKYE

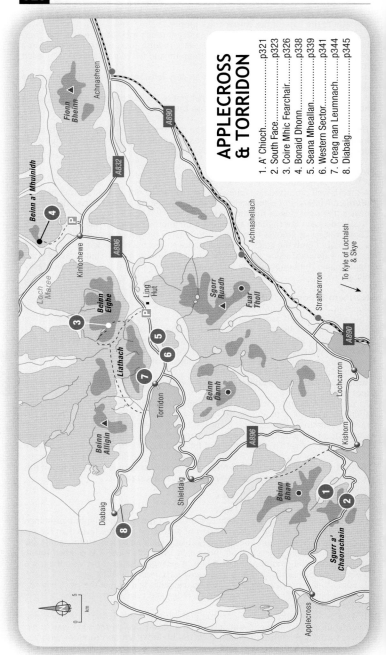

APPLECROSS & TORRIDON

APPLECROSS & TORRIDON

The spectacular glen of Torridon has the three great mountains of Beinn Eighe, Liathach and Beinn Alligin on its north side. Beinn Eighe has the classic Triple Buttresses as well as harder routes on the steep flanking quartzite walls. But Torridon also has some great outcrop climbing on Diabaig, Seana Mheallan and Creag nan Leumnach. After a long day in Torridon, try some accessible mountain routes on Sgurr a' Chaorachain in Applecross, the famous Cioch Nose being arguably the best route in Scotland at its grade. The recently acknowledged quartzite cliff of Bonaid Dhonn sits nearby at Kinlochewe.

Maps: OS L24 (Applecross, Diabaig), L25 (Torridon, but Explorer or Harvey better), L19 (Bonaid Dhonn), E428 (Applecross), E433 (Torridon, Bonaid Dhonn), Harvey Superwalker Torridon covers north side of Glen Torridon

SMC Climbers' Guide: *Northern Highlands Vol.1* (1993), *Northern Highlands South* (projected 2007)

Public Transport: Awkward – there is one post-bus per day from the railway stations at Achnasheen and Strathcarron.

Amenities: Kinlochewe has a shop, cafe, petrol, hotel (bar meals) and a small climbing shop, Moru, at the village hall just on the Torridon road. Torridon village has a shop and post office. The Beinn Damph bar at Annat has bar meals and petrol. Applecross has a hotel with excellent bar meals, petrol and a shop.
Camping: Torridon village (NG 905 558) and Applecross (NG 711 443).
SYHA Youth Hostels: Torridon (NG 904 559, (0870 004 1154).
Independent Hostels: A bunkhouse is attached to the Kinlochewe Hotel (01445 760253).
Climbing Hut: Ling Hut – SMC (NG 958 562) is in Torridon, near the start of the Coire Mhic Fhearchair path.

Applecross

SGURR A' CHAORACHAIN

(NG 797 417) 792m

The high road leading to the Bealach na Ba gives easy access to the central of the three Applecross peaks.

A' CHIOCH

(NG 795 426) Alt 300m (Lower), 400m (Upper) South-East facing

This sandstone bastion which forms the end of the north-east ridge of Sgurr a' Chaorachain is a classic photo from the road and is bound to attract the rock climber, especially when its impressive profile can be climbed at Severe to give the classic Cioch Nose route. It is composed of excellent rough sandstone, beautifully clean on its upper frontal face, though more vegetated in the lower reaches and on the flanks. There are several other good climbs in the Severe to HVS grades. Cioch Nose in particular is easier than it appears, with a generous supply of holds, and the superb views make it arguably the best climb of its grade in the Northern Highlands. The cliff catches sun and wind and consequently dries quickly, particularly true of Cioch Nose. Those with energy after Cioch Nose can climb the very accessible Sword of Gideon on the way home for a magnificent sandstone day.

Approach: The recommended approach is from the top in order to include the fine traverse of the A' Chioch ridge on the return to the car. Park at the big car park on the summit of the Bealach na Ba. Walk back south-east for about 300m, then go up the locked landrover track almost to the radio mast on the lower summit of

APPLECROSS

Sgurr a' Chaorachain (776m). From the last bend about 100m short of the summit, cut left and after about 100m reach the north-west corner of the corrie which forms the south side of the A' Chioch ridge. A short steep descent on bits of path gains the top of the corrie floor. Descend the corrie, passing under the steep but vegetated south flanks of the A' Chioch ridge, until nearly at the lip of the corrie. Go up over boulders to below the gully which comes down from A' Chioch and reach a small path along Middle Ledge to the start of the routes.

The easiest line is hard to find but take the lower of two ledges which form Middle Ledge – the terrace between the Upper and Lower Tiers of the buttress. Middle Ledge gradually narrows as it comes on to the front of the buttress. A short step up on to the upper of the two ledges gains the start of Cioch Nose, only a few metres along the ledge. For the Lower Tier, angle down left from the lip of the corrie to its base (or perhaps approach from the road below).

Descent: The immediate descent from A' Chioch is down the gully on the south side of the col behind A' Chioch (South Gully), but this requires two short abseils. A longer scrambling route can also be found by traversing terraces rightwards from near the top of the gully. But it is expected that parties will continue up the A' Chioch ridge.

Upper Tier

Snothard 90m VS **
C.W.Dracup, R.Hobbs May 1969
This route with fine clean rock starts from Upper Ledge, best gained by climbing the first pitch of Cioch Nose which arrives on Upper Ledge at its start. Alternatively, climb easier but vegetated ground well to the left. Low in the grade. Start at the foot of a groove 5m left of the chimney of Cioch Nose.
1. 35m 4b Climb the groove until it is possible to move left onto a slab on the lip of a conspicuous overhang. Climb the slab to a ledge and continue up a steep corner to belay.
2. 25m 4b Move left and climb a crack past three overhangs.
3. 30m Easier climbing leads to the top.

Cioch Nose 125m Severe ****
T.W.Patey, C.J.S.Bonington 12 Aug 1960
This is the classic of the area, a most enjoyable climb. Climbed by Tom Patey, who imported Chris Bonington as a partner for a hard route, and was delighted when "it was only Difficult". Best climbed as a circuit from the Bealach na Ba (car park), therefore including the long upper ridge (see below). Some technical moves on each of the first 3 pitches, but very well protected, therefore low in the grade. The route is enjoyable in the rain, as the friction remains good, but the grade rises to about VS. Start from Middle Ledge about 20m right of the low roof where the rocks become cleaner. Here the path returns from a lower ledge to the foot of the wall (CN scratched on the rock).
1. 30m 4a Gain and climb a wide crack (Hex 10 or 11 useful) to a ledge. Move left up over a block and climb consecutive tricky corners to the Upper Ledge. Belay here, then transfer 6m right to below a short V-chimney with an undercut base.
2. 15m 4a Climb the chimney and exit on the right, continuing up right over clean easy rock to a splendid ledge.
3. 35m 4a Step out right on to exposed ground, then diagonally right for 5m on excellent holds to a peg runner. Step up, then traverse left until one can go straight up to a ledge below a small overhang (or a more direct left-trending line, only slightly harder). Pass the overhang on the left and return right immediately above it to a big ledge.
4. 45m A straight up line is now possible but the normal route is to walk 10m right and belay (CN again scratched on the rock). Climb onto a big block. Move up, then step round the arete to the right and take the natural left-trending line of grooves and flakes to the top of A' Chioch.

Variation: **Direct Start 50m Hard Severe ★★**
T.W.Patey, H.MacInnes 9 Jun 1968
From the ordinary start continue walking along Middle Ledge, where it becomes narrower, underneath steep rock with overhangs, until a large dark diedre is reached.
1. 40m 4b Climb up 5m, then traverse left on steep rock to gain a short vertical crack. Climb this to reach the rib on the left edge of the diedre. Follow the rib and wall above on good holds to a ledge.
2. 10m Go left and up to the second stance of the normal route.

A' Chioch Ridge Continuation 500m+ Very Difficult & scrambling
The most enjoyable route is to continue to the top of the mountain instead of descending South Gully. If so, cross the neck connecting A' Cioch to the ridge behind and scramble up vegetation and short rock steps to reach a steep wall girdling the nose of the ridge. Climb this on its left edge using alternating sides of the arete (Very Difficult) or up the centre (Severe). The ridge soon levels out and then climbs gradually, with several summits and sharp gaps, avoidable if wished by clever route finding, to the summit. A direct line on the crest of all the towers gives moves up to Severe.

Cioch Corner 125m HVS ★★
C.W.Dracup, R.Hobbs 25 May 1969
This climb is perhaps best combined with Cioch Corner Superdirect, on the lower tier (described below). The crux is short. Start at the large dark diedre as for Cioch Nose Direct.
1. 35m 5a Climb directly up the diedre to the roof, step right to a ledge and go straight up to a grassy recess.
2. 40m 4c Follow the line of grooves over a bulge. Climb a pleasant slab on the right of the corner, then return to the corner-line. Climb a chimney-groove to a grassy bay.
3. 40m 4a Climb more easily, with a final steep corner.
4. 10m Scramble to the top.

Lower Tier

Cioch Corner Superdirect 160m HVS ★
J.E.Howard, C.Rowland May 1970
The climb takes the obvious line of grooves which runs the full length of the lower tier below Cioch Corner. It is best combined with the latter to give an excellent, sustained climb of seven long pitches. The climb has a lot of interest and can be recommended in dry conditions. There is some vegetation in the grooves but it doesn't spoil the climbing (say those who have enjoyed the route). Start at the foot of the grooves by a huge pinnacle. Climb directly up the groove line all the way in 4 pitches (5a, 5a, 4c, 4b) to reach Middle Ledge.

APPLECROSS

SOUTH FACE

(NG 788 413) Alt 400m South facing Diagram p324

This is the crag that rises steeply on the right of the road to Bealach na Ba at a point opposite the waterfalls in the floor of the corrie. Best known for some of the most accessible multi pitch climbs in Scotland, on clean sandstone which is often warm and dry. Although Tom Patey first climbed on the crag when he soloed Sword of Gideon in 1961, it was only developed by instructors, including Ben Beattie and Terry Doe, from the outdoor centre at Applecross in the early '70s, followed soon after by others.

Approach: There is a small incut parking place below the top end of the crag with room for about three cars. The buttresses are visible from here, 5 to 10mins.

SGURR A' CHAORACHAIN
South Face

1. Gideon's Wrath	E1 *	3a. Direct	E1 5b **
2. Lost Supper	E1 5b **	4. Bumblytwo	VS **
3. Sword of Gideon	VS ***	5. Bumblyone	Severe **

The crag consists of six buttresses numbered from left to right. No.1 is the best, having a broad 40m wall of excellent clean rock in its middle section (Patey's Wall). This is the most obvious area of clean rock halfway up the nearest buttress to the car park. No.2 is more broken, hidden behind No.1 from the car park, and is separated from No.3 by a square-cut, mossy gully. Nos.3 and 4 are narrow pillars separated by a narrow gully with caves. These are close together and left of the skyline buttress, which is No.5, a much larger buttress coming down almost to the road.

Descent: From No.1 Buttress, go left (north, towards the Bealach na Ba) down a big grassy ramp (small path) until directly above the car park. From Nos.3 and 4, which finish higher, descend another grassy ramp north until the No.1 Buttress ramp and small path can be seen below. Descend to it and follow as before.

No.1 Buttress - Patey's Wall

The lower 45m of No.1 Buttress gives delightful climbing of about Very Difficult up to a ledge at the base of the steep middle section which forms a clean reddish wall (Patey's Wall). Or walk on to this ledge from the left. The climbs are described from here (except Sword of Gideon). Several routes are possible by making a 35m abseil from the top of their difficulties back to the ledge. Finish by an easy pitch to the descent terrace (as described for Sword of Gideon).

1 Gideon's Wrath   40m   E1 *
K.V.Crocket, C.Stead   21 Aug 1971
Start towards the left end of the main ledge, where the reddish wall takes a gentle curve and forms a slight crest (3m right of a white patch under a small roof). Here is a shallow left-slanting groove 5m up the wall. Good climbing, low in the grade. The first pitch is not well protected but perhaps only 5a.
1. 15m 5b Gain a higher ledge, then climb up into the groove. Go up the short groove, then traverse 4m left and move up to below an overhang.
2. 25m 5b Climb the overhang above and follow a line trending right to reach a short wide crack. Continue up and right to finish just right of the biggest bulge.
Variation: **Direct Finish   5a or 5b** **
T.Doe, A.Brooks   19 Jun 1973
Harder than the original way. Instead of the 4m traverse on pitch 1, go up a thin crack to a triangular niche, then trend right to join Lost Supper at the small roof and peg. Finish up this direct (5b) or on the right (5a) – see Lost Supper.

2 Lost Supper   35m   E1 5b **
T.Doe, J.Duncan   25 May 1973
A fine direct line on good rock, if a little lacking in protection. Immediately right of Gideon's Wrath is a patchwork of short cracks in a grey piece of rock 5m up. Climb up through these and continue up to a small roof with an old peg and tat. Either pull through the roof to easing ground (5b), or from immediately under the roof, traverse right for 3m to a break up a tiny ramp. Climb this to the easing ground. The traverse version reduces the overall grade to E1 5a, technically easier but still with an exposed feel.

3 Sword of Gideon   100m   VS ***
T.W.Patey   11 Oct 1961
This is the original route of the crag, immaculate rock, good protection and very enjoyable. Start at the lowest point of the buttress.
1. 45m Easy climbing on perfect rock leads to the terrace above the lower tier.
2. 15m 4c Starting from near the right end of the terrace (the original start is at the very right end), climb a shallow corner bending slightly left, then traverse left for 4m to beneath prominent cracks.
3. 20m 4b Climb the two short cracks to easier ground and pick a line to a ledge.
4. 20m Pick a line to the descent terrace.
Variation: **Direct Start   12m   E1 5b**
Gain the thin groove with difficulty (although the tall may think HVS 5a) and climb it directly to the prominent cracks in the upper part of Sword of Gideon.
Variation: **Original Start   4b**
An easier but less direct start reduces the route to 4b. This is the line that Patey soloed on the first ascent and certainly is the best choice if damp. Start just right of the normal route at the wall's right arete. Climb a parallel line to the normal route, then traverse left to join its traverse, which then becomes the crux.

No.3 Buttress

4 Bumblytwo   140m   VS **
B.Beattie, K.Hiles, E.Gautier   Jun 1970
Some fine climbing but poorly protected in places. Start at the foot of the buttress.

APPLECROSS

1. 25m Climb two walls to a spike on the left. Abseil tat indicates that it has been undergraded at Severe in the past.
2. 20m 4b Make a delicate step up on to a sloping ledge, then traverse right to climb delicate and unprotected ground to a ledge.
3. 25m Continue straight up and avoid a steep wall by going left up a ramp to a ledge.
4. 25m 4a Step up and traverse right to slabby ground. Go up this to a crack, climb this, then go back left to the centre of the face and up left to a large block.
5. 45m 4a or 4b The next pitch is up a steep wall which is avoidable on the left. Either step across a gap and climb a groove (4a) or for a better but harder finish, go further up and left, trend right across smooth pink rock to finish straight up (4b, unprotected, possibly HVS). Finish more easily.

No.4 Buttress

5 Bumblyone   130m   Severe **
T.Cardwell, B.Beattie, C.Brooker   27 Jun 1970
Start at the left corner of the buttress.
1. 45m 4a Go right up a ramp to an obvious flake-crack. Better but 4b is to start off a block on the right and climb a steep wall to the flake-crack. Climb the crack to a terrace, then up the easier crest to a tree.
2. 30m 4a Climb a corner to a ledge, then a clean wall (or as two pitches, both 4a).
3. 55m Easier up the crest.

Torridon

BEINN EIGHE

COIRE MHIC FHEARCHAIR

Map p320
Coire Mhic Fhearchair, on the north side of Beinn Eighe, is one of the finest corries in Scotland and is justly famous for its magnificent Triple Buttresses. Secluded from the road by a relatively long approach, they dominate the lonely corrie and offer routes of great length and character. Some of the climbs are among the best in Britain.

Approach: Start from the Coire Dubh car park in Glen Torridon (NG 959 569). The best approach for first time visitors, for whom the panorama of the cliff from Loch Coire Mhic Fhearchair is not to be missed is to follow the well made Coire Dubh path between Liathach and Beinn Eighe. Fork right at a cairn about 2km beyond some stepping stones and follow a path contouring below Sail Mhor and rising gradually to the lip of the corrie. This takes about 2hrs and a further 40mins to the foot of the Triple Buttresses.

For the more technical routes on the Far East Wall and Eastern Ramparts, a direct approach over the top from the south is quicker and rucksacks can be left at the top. Follow the Coire Dubh Mor path for about 2km until it flattens out and the hillside on the right becomes scree covered. It is best to follow a stream which bounds the scree on the left; initially on the stream's right as far as the first rock band, then cross to its left and finally trend further left to reach grassy fields below Coinneach Mhor. Go to the east cairn of Coinneach Mhor, then descend to the col leading to Ruadh-stac Mor (or cut the corner on the east and go more direct to the col). From here, descend the scree gully into the corrie.

Gideon's Wrath, E1 5b, Sgurr a' Chaorachain. Climbers unknown
(photo Andy Nisbet)

Far East Wall

(NG 950 602) Alt 800m North-East facing

This is the wall in the top left of the corrie when viewed from Loch Coire Mhic Fhearchair. It has some excellent routes on sensationally steep quartzite, which is usually easier than it looks. The main wall catches the afternoon and evening sun and requires a spell of dry weather to stop some seeps.

Descent: The left-hand scree gully from the col below Ruadh-stac Mor is the most convenient. It is possible to descend in two abseils if a second climb is contemplated and the top is known.

1 Moonshine 95m E4 ***
C.Forrest, A.Nisbet 10 Jun 1988
The main pitch takes a shallow overhanging groove left of the bulging nose of an impressively steep and apparently smooth pale wall towards the left end of the crag. Sustained technical climbing but arguably only E3. Start on the long grassy ledge under the buttress, about 10m from the left end, by a small rock scar.
1. 25m 5b Go straight up the wall, then move right into a flake-line and follow this to belay by the horizontal break.
2. 35m 6a Go diagonally left to gain the base of the groove. Climb the groove with increasing difficulty to a foothold on the left arete. Climb straight up until level with a huge overhang on the left, then move right and up to a ledge.
3. 35m 5b Climb the short awkward corner above, then move left and up a long easy wall to finish.

2 Angel Face 95m E2 ****
C.Forrest, A.Nisbet 1 Jun 1988
A highly recommended route taking a sensational and improbable line above the bulging nose of the wall. Protection is good apart from bold moves to gain the tiny ramp on pitch 2. Take plenty of small nuts. The line was always admired by Andy Nisbet but thought impossibly smooth until a quick abseil revealed holds and cracks. Start at the left end of a long flake which is embedded against the right side of the lower wall on the long grass terrace.
1. 15m 5a Climb a narrow ramp leftwards, move right into a shallow groove, and climb it to a grass ledge at the base of a bigger groove on the right.
2. 35m 5c Take the left-leaning groove to the horizontal ledge. Traverse left about 5m along the fault to a small pedestal. Climb the wall above, then move left to gain a tiny ramp. Up this to a crack, then make a long step left into the base of a thinner crack. Climb the crack to a small roof. Traverse delicately left under the roof to the edge of nowhere, then return unexpectedly right to a belay above the right end of the ledge.
3. 45m 5b Climb the crack, and when it becomes unfriendly move slightly right and up to a large flake-ledge. Go on up the wall above to a smaller flake-ledge. Traverse left to a large block. Now trend rightwards across slabbier ground to a steep blocky finish.

3 Seeds of Destruction 95m E3 ***
A.Nisbet, W.Todd 9 Jun 1988
A superb route with very sustained climbing up the wall left of The Reaper. A double set of medium sized RPs is useful for pitch 2. Start as for The Reaper and Angel Face, at a large detached flake.
1. 15m 5a As for Angel Face.
2. 20m 5c Climb the left-leaning groove to the horizontal fault and traverse left to the pedestal of Angel Face. Move right past a poor peg runner and pull over a bulge into a shallow corner. Belay on the right under a smooth groove.
3. 30m 5c Climb the groove to a big ledge on the right. Step down and traverse left until a left-facing corner can be gained. Climb the corner to the right end of the large flake-ledge of Angel Face. Climb the wall above to the next ledge.
4. 30m 5c Go up to a small rock scar, then steeply up and left to a rest at a

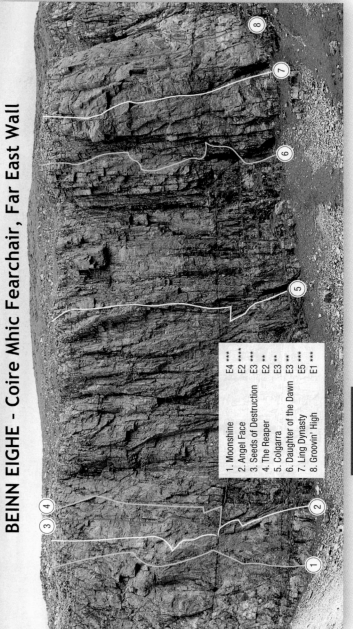

BEINN EIGHE - Coire Mhic Fearchair, Far East Wall

1. Moonshine   E4 ***
2. Angel Face   E2 ****
3. Seeds of Destruction E3 ***
4. The Reaper   E2 **
5. Colgarra   E3 **
6. Daughter of the Dawn E3 **
7. Ling Dynasty   E5 ***
8. Groovin' High   E1 ***

TORRIDON

horizontal break. Traverse right, then go up into a curving groove on the right. Above this go straight up steep blocky ground to finish.

4 The Reaper   95m   E2 **
B.Sprunt, G.Strange   17 May 1980

The original route on this wall takes a bold line up the vertical crack towards the right side. On the first ascent, Brian Sprunt launched up the crux without protection and only salvaged the strength to make the final moves by hooking his chin on a ledge (he may have gone more direct!). The first section up to the horizontal fault was subsequently used by Angel Face and Seeds of Destruction.
1. 15m 5a As for Angel Face.
2. 25m 5c Climb the left-leaning groove to reach the prominent horizontal fault (as for Angel Face). Traverse right until below the left side of the large recess above. Climb steeply to reach a crack (which is not visible from the fault) in the left side of the recess. Climb the crack and belay in a niche.
3. 25m 5b Continue up the crack to a ledge on the left.
4. 30m 5a Go up right into a shallow corner, move further right then zigzag to finish up an obvious chimney.

5 Colgarra   100m   E3 **
R.Archbold, G.Cohen   21 Aug 1976; FFA: S.Blagbrough A.Nisbet 14 Jun 1988

This very steep route goes up the centre of the cliff, starting at a deep slit cave. In its upper reaches it takes a hanging chimney visible from below immediately right of a big left-curving corner. Another route of great character.
1. 20m 4c Climb the left side of the cave and up diagonally left to a grass ledge.
2. 20m 5b Traverse right beyond the line of the big left-facing corner **Rudolf** (E2 5c), then go up past the horizontal fault and pull into the main corner. Follow this to a step right and belay at a large jammed flake.
3. 10m 5a From just above the belay swing right onto the steep wall and go up a flake-crack to a smaller flake.
4. 20m 6a Climb the thin groove above to reach good holds leading up and left into the hanging chimney, which is climbed to a grass ledge.
5. 30m 5b Climb up and slightly left to a small overhang, over this and follow a crack (not the ramp on the left) to easy ground.

6 Daughter of the Dawn   100m   E3 **
A.Nisbet, G.Nisbet   28 May, 1993

A sensational line up the vertical wall between a mossy fault-line leading into a gully and a big chimney-line, **Kami-kaze** (VS 4c), defining the left side of a steep grey pillar forming the right end of the cliff. A direct finish awaits. Start at a damp overhung recess about 30m left of a deep slit cave.
1. 25m Climb up the recess until it is possible to traverse right to a shallow groove. Go up this then right to belay below the big chimney-line.
2. 20m 5c Traverse 5m left and go up left to a smaller ledge. Step right into a crack in a pale wall and climb it leading into a corner and tiny ledge at its top.
3. 10m 5c Pull out left into another corner and up this to a roof. Pull out left again and go up to a ledge on the left.
4. 45m 5b From the right end of the ledge, climb up flakes, pull out right, place high runners and traverse right into a big left-facing corner, followed slightly left to a wide notch at the top.

7 Ling Dynasty   110m   E5 ***
G.Livingston, A.Nisbet   Jul 1987

To the right of the big chimney-line, the steep grey pillar is cleft by an obvious chimney-line in the lower part. **Birth of the Cool** (E1 5b) follows this line then breaks right through a belt of overhangs and finishes up a prominent corner. This

Groovin' High, E1 5b, Coire Mhic Fhearchair. Climber Jo George
(photo Cubby Images)

route starts up the obvious chimney-line and continues straight up a magnificent crack and through the big roof above. Very sustained, perhaps only 6a, and well protected but requiring stamina to place all the protection. Start at the wet slit cave at the base of the chimney.

1. 25m 4c Climb loose rock on the left side of the cave.
2. 15m 5a Continue up the steep chimney-crack to a ledge.
3. 15m 5b Climb a steep crack and the wall on the right to a good ledge.
4. 25m 6b Step left into the crack and climb it to a roof. Pull out rightwards into the continuation of the crack and climb it to the big roof (very sustained). Traverse right to a belay (which is more comfortable than it looks) at the right end of the roof.
5. 15m 6a Return left and climb the wide crack in the roof. Go leftwards up the thin ramp above to belay.
6. 15m 4c Move right and up a corner to the top.

8 Groovin' High 90m E1 ***
R.Archbold, J.Ingram, G.S.Strange 7 Jul 1973

A superb route following a big corner on the right side of the steep grey pillar. The first ascentionists thought this might be the best route in Scotland! Start 6m right of the slit cave of Ling Dynasty.

1. 30m 4c Climb short walls and corners to a large ledge below the big corner.
2. 20m 5a Climb the steep corner.
3. 40m 5b Continue by the fine corner system above to reach a small ledge at 20m (possible belay). Continue in the same line to the top.

9 Sumo 85m E3 ***
A.Cunningham, A.Nisbet 20 Jun 1987

This takes the vertical crack-line and wall just right of Groovin' High, with an excellent crux pitch, clean, technical, well protected and very sustained. Start 2m right of Groovin' High.

1. 30m 4c Climb corners and short walls to the large ledge 3m right of Groovin' High. Crawl right to belay.
2. 30m 6a Climb a steep corner, then the crack-line to enter a groove below a roof. Move left to good holds and re-enter the groove beside the roof. A strenuous bulge leads to a belay.
3. 25m 5b Take the shallow groove above to horizontal cracks. Traverse right into a corner, climb it and return diagonally left until above the belay at a small roof. Finish rightwards up a slight ramp and back left on big holds to the top.

Eastern Ramparts

(NG 947 602) Alt 800m North-West facing

When viewed from Loch Coire Mhic Fhearchair this wall forms the left flank of East Buttress, the left-hand of the Triple Buttresses. The face gets the morning sun and is slow to dry, but the VS and HVS routes make an alternative for climbers finding seeps on the harder routes. The wall is long and complex and the climbs are not easy to find on first acquaintance. The face is cut by a prominent ledge, the line of the Upper Girdle, which starts near the left end.

Descent: The quickest descent is the steep broken ground at the east end of the cliff (about Difficult), or by two abseils down any route. The easiest descent is down the scree gully from the col below Ruadh-stac Mor, beyond the Far East Wall.

10 Olympus 70m HVS **
A.Nisbet, N.Spinks 18 May 1980

At the left end of the cliff, just before it falls back towards Far East Gully, there is a slim V-groove with an overhang at 30m **Cornice Groove** (VS 5a). Its right arete and roof is **Corniced Arete** (VS 4c). This route, sustained but easier than it looks, takes a line up the middle of the imposing wall right of Corniced Arete making for

a vague depression about three-quarters of the way up the cliff. Start near the beginning of the prominent ledge just left of a large right-facing corner **Claustrophobic Corner** (E1 5b).

1. 35m 4c Move right and back left above the initial roofs to reach ledges. Go left on to pale rock, then climb up and right to reach a small flakey ledge below a steepening in the wall.
2. 35m 4b Climb the wall and a shallow corner on the right before swinging up left on to a ledge beneath an obvious 6m flake-crack. Climb the crack, move 3m right and finish up the wall.

11 Pale Rider 110m E1 **

A.Nisbet, B.Lawrie 10 Aug 1986

This takes the most prominent crack-line on the wall left of The Pale Diedre; a grade of E4 was expected but the rock was helpful as usual. Climbed by the same team on the day after Elastic Collision (Seal Song Bay, Reiff) and considered a more important route. Yet it has had only one repeat while Elastic Collision has had hundreds. How times change! The crack-line is characterised by two projecting blocks just at the point where its angle eases. About 35m right of the start of the prominent ledge is a clean pale, right-facing corner in the lower tier **Eastern Promise** (VS 4c). Start some 50m to the right of this below a left-facing corner, which is below and a little to the left of the pale diedre which features prominently in the middle of the upper cliff.

1. 45m 4c Climb directly up to the base of the corner. Immediate entry is barred by a detached block, so go up left and enter above the block by delicate moves across pale rock. Follow the corner to the Upper Girdle and belay 10m further left just below and left of the crack-line, about 20m left of The Pale Diedre.
2. 35m 5b Climb the crack to a small ledge beside the projecting blocks. Go easily up right to belay on a large ledge.
3. 20m 4c Return left to the original line, which has a blank section below a bulge. Instead go left round an edge and straight up the wall above to belay below a short chimney on the left.
4. 10m 5a Climb the wall on the right to finish.

12 Paleface Wall   100m   E3 **
S.Blagbrough, A.Nisbet   14 Jun 1988
A direct line up the pale wall left of Pale Diedre. A series of fine technical pitches on the best rock. Start at a 6m pinnacle below a rib, in whose left side is set the initial corner of Pale Rider.
1. 45m 5b Climb the front face of the pinnacle. Go up the wall above, then right and back left into a shallow corner on the crest of the rib. Go up this to The Upper Girdle.
2. 20m 5b Some 10m left of The Pale Diedre is a clean right-facing corner. Gain this from the left and climb it to a ledge.
3. 10m 5c Climb the shallow corner above the right end of the ledges to jugs. Move left and go up to a ledge.
4. 15m 5c Climb the crack above the right end of the ledge. Move left round a roof and make a thin move left before going straight up to a big ledge.
5. 10m 5b Climb the horizontally faulted wall directly above (strenuous). A rattling flake is a crucial hold. Sometimes wet but avoidable.

13 The Pale Diedre   105m   E2 ***
B.Sprunt, G.S.Strange   18 May 1981
This is the obvious line in the middle of the upper part of the cliff. Climbed the day after The Reaper, this was a fine weekend. Olympus was climbed the same day by Andy Nisbet, who was inspired to return for many routes. Start below and slightly left of this at the foot of a right-facing diedre. A most enjoyable climb.
1. 40m 5b Climb the diedre directly to overhangs at 24m. Move left then go up right to below the pale diedre.
2. 40m 5c Climb the diedre; excellent!
3. 25m Finish up the easy groove on the right.

Triple Buttresses

(NG 945 603)   Alt 700m   North facing (mostly)   Diagram p336

These buttresses dominate the view from Loch Coire Mhic Fhearchair and offer some of Scotland's best mountaineering lines. They are composed of a lower plinth of sandstone topped by two tiers of quartzite divided by a fault taken by the **Upper Girdle (Severe)**, a sensational 700m route across all three buttresses, which starts at the left end of the Eastern Ramparts. The steep quartzite walls may sometimes be climbed with surprising ease using big flat holds. The routes can be climbed in the wet (given a grade in hand), as the horizontal holds on the quartzite are rough (although the cracks are slippery).

Descent: Reverse one of the high level approach routes back to the car park. The easiest descent to the cliff base and the Loch Coire Mhic Fhearchair path is down the scree gully from the col below Ruadh-stac Mor, beyond the Far East Wall.

14 East Buttress (quartzite)   210m   Difficult ***
G.B.Gibbs, E.Backhouse, W.A.Mounsey   Jun 1907
An enjoyable, classic climb up the crest of the buttress, often climbed in boots. It has an imposing appearance but the holds are very positive and it is only slightly harder in the wet. The lower sandstone tier is harder and often wet, so is best to

avoid all its difficulties on the left and traverse in along the terrace forming its top (Broad Terrace). This is easy but with one wet and exposed section; using a rope is advised. Start about 10m from the terrace's right end. Climb the steep face on good holds to a large ledge (30m). Continue up an interesting and varied series of pitches, often slightly right of the crest, to the top. A short vertical corner right of the crest is the crux and also the last difficulty before scrambling. Keeping further left is Very Difficult and also good.

Central Buttress

As always, there are three tiers, sandstone, lower quartzite and upper quartzite. Any combination of routes on each tier can be made but some old and new combinations of consistent grade are described.

**15 Central Buttress (Piggott's Route) 270m Severe 4b ** **
A.S.Piggott, M.Wood 1922
This is the line nearest the crest and most commonly followed, often referred to as 'Central Buttress'. A classic route in all senses, taking a magnificent line up the crest of the buttress but quite vegetated in the sandstone and many ledges with loose blocks on the quartzite. When damp (or wet, when it is still possible), it is recommended to use the start of Hamilton's Route as described below or to miss out the sandstone by starting up West Central Gully. This is about Moderate but not exposed and soloing is assumed for the recommendation.
The route starts up the sandstone via the obvious diagonal line running up from right to left (not so obvious from directly underneath). Start on the grass terrace just above the lowest rocks, about one-third of the way from the right-hand end, where a pinnacle block leans against the face. Climb from the block to a terrace, move right and reach a black cave clearly visible from below (30m). From the top of the cave follow the grassy rake up left to Broad Terrace and the quartzite.
Continue quite close to the arrival point, from the highest point of the grass on Broad Terrace, in a bay just right of the crest. Climb up trending left to a stance in a corner (20m). Traverse left to the crest, round it, and up an exposed chimney on good holds. Go up easy ground to the foot of the final tier.
    The route up the final tower takes a big groove which starts just left of the crest and bends up right to follow the crest. Climb a big open groove over several short steps to a platform. On the right is a short overhanging chimney-crack with a crack to its right. Climb the chimney with great difficulty (sack hauling and combined tactics may help; or avoid it by a diversion on the right on to the frontal face, particularly useful in the wet), and move up to an obvious crack. Go up right on big blocks towards the frontal face, then pull up left to a flake on the wall and overlooking the crack. Step left under a bulge to the top of the crack and then a bay. Climb a short overhanging wall on the right or, easier, go left to a big pinnacle and right to the top.

**16 Central Buttress (VS Route) 280m VS ** * **
A.Nisbet, N.Spinks (Central Corner) Sep 1976; J.Colverd, E.Gillespie, A.Nisbet (first quartzite tier) 23 Mar 1998; Top tier unknown.
Constructed as a VS line on all tiers and offering arguably the best climbing (particularly for a VS leader!). The big corner (Central Corner) in the sandstone is high in the grade (especially with rucksacks) but the quartzite tiers are much easier. Start via the very prominent diedre on the left flank of the sandstone tier.
1. 50m 4a Climb to the terrace below the corner, then a right-slanting line to the base of the corner itself.
2. 50m 4c The corner provides a superb long pitch; the pitch can also be split. Walk right along Broad Terrace until about 40m right of the crest (and Piggott's) where the highest sandstone forms a platform 10m above Broad Terrace. This is below the right-hand of two right-facing corners which each start about 20m up.
3. 20m 4a Climb on to the platform and straight up to the left end of a ledge (same as Hamilton's Route).

TORRIDON

BEINN EIGHE
Coire Mhic Fearchair
Triple Buttresses (quartzite tier)

Eastern Buttress

Central Buttress

Western Buttress

sandstone tier

sandstone tier

14. East Buttress — Difficult ***
15. Central Buttress (Piggott's Route) — Severe 4b **
16. Central Buttress, "VS Route" — VS ***
17. Central Buttress (Hamilton's Route) — Severe 4a ***
18. West Buttress — Severe *
18a. Easier Route — Difficult

4. 20m 4b A fairly direct line up the wall above, slightly right, then left to finish up a corner.

5. 40m 4a Climb steep blocky ground.

6. 40m Scramble to the Upper Tier.

7. 30m 4b Start just right of the crest and a block resting against the face at a small right-facing corner with jammed flakes (ie. between Piggott's and Hamilton's). Climb this and a wider corner-crack above. An easy way leads left to Piggott's. Instead, move out right on to the crest.

8. 30m 4a Follow the crest steeply on good holds to the top.

7 Central Buttress (Hamilton's Route)   270m   Severe 4a ***
J.F.Hamilton, W.Kerr 4 Jun 1936

The other traditional line, up the right side of the buttress, more sustained but no harder. Not as good a line but better climbing, particularly on the Upper Tier. An easy but pleasant route up the right-hand side of the sandstone has been chosen as a start **Slab Route** (Difficult), although Hamilton did not start this way.

Start at the right end of the grass terrace below the face, about 10m left of West-Central Gully. Climb slabby rock parallel to the gully, choosing the easiest line on good rock, for 70m to meet a barrier slab beneath Broad Terrace. Trend left up this, spaced protection, to the Terrace close to where the route continues.

Start about 40m right of the crest (and Piggott's) where the top of the sandstone rises above Broad Terrace and forms a platform 10m up. This is right of an obvious right-facing corner in the centre of the wall which starts about 20m up. Climb to reach the quartzite and straight up to the left end of a ledge (20m, 4a). Or reach the same point by going right and back left, easier but some loose rock. Traverse right along the ledge (about 15m), then trend up right to the edge of the buttress, overlooking West-Central Gully (20m). Go up a big groove slanting back left and continue to below a short bulging corner. Traverse back right round an edge to climb a short corner (or climb the bulging corner – 4b). Continue on easier ground to the base of the final tower.

Start this about 10m right of the crest below a huge flange of rock curving up right. Go diagonally right on flakes to gain the right end of a ledge on top of a large detached flake below the flange. Climb slabs diagonally rightwards (4a) to reach and follow big open chimneys to the top, keeping always on the right side of the buttress.

8 West Buttress, Ordinary Route (quartzite)   300m   Difficult or Severe *
G.S.Bower, J.B.Meldrum Jul 1919

The sandstone tier of West Buttress is quite formidable so the described route misses it out and still provides some good situations, although not as good a climb as the other buttresses. Start up the block filled gully on its right (Fuselage Gully) and scramble up this to Broad Terrace (top of the sandstone). Go left along this until just short of the crest. Climb on the right of the buttress crest, with short walls and occasional interest, to the base of the final tower.

This is characterised by a steep wall on the frontal face, sometimes referred to as a 'domino shaped block'. The direct route climbs this but it can be avoided by walking right and climbing back left up a huge corner at Difficult (overall). For the direct, climb a clean 9m wall strenuously on good holds. This leads to a recess on the left of the tower, whence an easy move left gives access to a flake-crack slanting up right. Climb this, with a fine exposed finish behind an enormous projecting block. Climb the wall above to the top.

BEINN A' MHUINIDH

(NH 032 661)   Alt 692m   Map p320

This hill, which lies just north of Torridon and south-east of Slioch, divided from it by the picturesque Gleann Bianasdail, has a fine quartzite cliff. The views up Loch Maree, across to Slioch and back to Beinn Eighe are superb.

TORRIDON

BONAID DHONN

(NH 022 657)   Alt 450m   West-North-West facing   Map p320

An impressive plaque of steep clean rock forms the centrepiece of the cliff. There are positive holds and good cracks typical of quartzite, but the compact nature of the rock here means that there are also bold fingery sections. The cliff gets the sun from mid afternoon onwards. The rock is clean and dries quickly, save for the centre of the wall (Dream Ticket) which is a drainage line. The described routes are best approached by a long abseil; the abseil point is fairly easy to find, even for first time visitors.

Approach: Park at Incheril, 1km east of Kinlochewe (NH 038 624). Follow a path leading north-west along the north side of the Kinlochewe River towards Loch Maree. After about 3km and just before reaching Loch Maree, a quartzite cliff with a distinctive waterfall (marked on the maps) is seen at NH 024 648. Head up the south side of the burn below the waterfall to reach the top of the cliff.

Follow the cliff-top northwards until almost at its high point. Here is a slight bay under the last rise (NH 022 657, alt 550m, marked by a cairn in 2005). At the bottom right of the bay, tucked under a small outcrop, is a platform from where a big south-facing sidewall of a corner can be seen on the right. This platform is the abseil point, requiring medium to large wires and 8m of slings to reach the cliff edge. The abseil is close to 53m, so 60m ropes are ideal but 50m ropes and a short scramble down can be used with care. The abseil is down Dream Ticket and leads to a large boulder which is at the start of the routes.

The Creep   70m   HVS **

J.Cunningham, W.March   13 May 1971

A good climb up the right edge of the wall; not well protected on the first pitch.
1. 40m 5a Move up and right on grass ledges, then traverse right across the wall until near the right arete. Go up to a ledge (peg runner) then straight up the wall to a roof and belay on the right.
2. 30m 4c Climb the overhanging corner directly above the belay and finish up a splendid steep crack.

Dream Ticket   65m   E3 ***

T.Prentice, C.French   17 Jul 1996

Fine sustained wall climbing on very clean rock, in a superb position. Following rain the line dries slower than the rest of the cliff, but this can be checked on abseil and the route left for the afternoon sun. Protection is good, but spaced and a double Friends 0.5 to 2 are useful.
1. 45m 5c Climb ledges to a prominent pair of thin cracks, then move up and right to the left end of a long overlap. Return back left into the centre of the wall and continue to a small overlap level with the top of the Vertigo flake. Pull over this, climb the crack above and follow the scoop right, to the right edge of the wall.
2. 20m 5b Move back left and follow the right edge of the wall and easier ground to the top.

Vertigo   70m   E1 5b ***

J.Cunningham, W.March   13 May 1971

A flake-crack and upper wall give an excellent and quite bold route. Low in the grade.
1. 30m 4c Climb the flake-crack to a small ledge at its top.
2. 20m 5b Traverse left and step on to a steep grey wall. Climb up and slightly left until it is possible to pull on to the steeper wall above. Climb this until an awkward move left is made into the obvious short corner 5m above; climb the corner to a belay.
3. 20m 4b Climb over an overlap above, then move up and right towards an obvious easy corner. Avoid this by climbing a slab on the left to the top.

Crack of Ages, E2 5b, Seana Mheallan. Climbers unknown
(photo Blair Fyffe)

leading to a crack in a steepening is **Fleeced** (Hard Severe 4c). Immediately right of Fleeced is a steep wall with a rightward-slanting crack-line (HVS 5a), then a crack rising from a triangular slot (E1 5b) and a left-facing corner just right again. Beyond the corner is a left-slanting stepped corner forming a hanging slab.

TORRIDON

Unmasked   20m   Hard Severe 4b **
S.Kennedy, C.Grindley   16 Jul 1994
Climb the left-slanting slabby corner, starting on the right and going left round an arete (or more direct).

To the right is a corner with flakes on its left wall, a possible descent. To the right is a fine steep wall with **Outswinger** (E2 5c), a corner with two stepped roofs on the left side of the wall and **Nasal Abuse** (E1 5b) up the right side of the wall.

The Age of Confusion   20m   E3 5c **
C.Moody, L.Gordon Canning   17 Jun 1998
The rib between Nasal Abuse and a big corner (Mechanical Sheep). Start left of the rib. Move up right to a horizontal break (Camalot 4 useful). Reach up then right to a crack. Follow the crack, step left before the final overhang and climb the arete.

Mechanical Sheep   20m   E2 6a **
C.Moody, R.Watson   3 Jul 1994
The obvious corner with an overhang at one-third height and another near the top.

Sustained but very well protected passing the first roof (crux). Unfortunately the rock is a little dirty. The named animal was from a car insurance advert made at the much photographed Bealach na Ba.

Clockwork Rat   20m   E2 5b *
A.Nisbet, C.Watkins   13 Jul 1999
Strenuous but well protected. Start up the corner of Mechanical Sheep but move right to gain a crack in its right wall. Follow the crack round the right arete to a roof and rockfall scar. Go through the left side of the roof and finish up the continuation crack.

Clingfilm   15m   Very Difficult *
C.Moody   3 Jul 1994
About 30m right is a narrow clean buttress containing a blocky crack.

There are several other sandstone crags in Torridon, each recently developed and with some very good routes, and Creag nan Leumnach has been chosen as sunny rather than particularly better. Others are Kinlochdamph Crag (NG 869 477), Creag na Speireag (NG 863 531), Creag an Fhithich (NG 892 538), Creag na Botaigeann (NG 928 533) and Hairpin Crag (NG 880 573).

CREAG NAN LEUMNACH

(NG 899 569, L24)   Alt 270m   South-South-West facing   Map p320
The crags can be seen directly above Torridon village shop at the top of an open gully filled with boulders. There are two long crags; the lower is very steep; the crag directly above gives some easier climbs. Like all the sandstone crags, many lines seep and may take at least a couple of days to dry after heavy rain (but Warmer Cleaner Drier is quicker).

Approach: Climb straight up the gully. The boulders are generally solid and better than the heather and bracken, 30mins.

LOWER CRAG

The crag is divided into two sectors by a big right-slanting break (possible descent, or a chimney at the right end of the crag).

Left Sector

The arete at the left end is **Global Warming** (Severe). The slanting corner-crack just right is **Blind as a Frog** (E2 5b). The wall to the right is **Squeezin' Yir Hied** (E4 6a).

The Vanishing Frog   30m   E5 6b **
I.Taylor   8 Aug 1996
Climbs the streaked rounded nose in the centre of the wall right of Squeezin' yer Heid. Bold and unobvious. Start up the second groove right of a wide flake-crack to gain a break. Climb the shattered wall to the next break and using hidden holds above, make a hard move rightwards round the nose. Climb the right-hand side of the nose until a move left at the top gains a ledge.

A thin crack between Vanishing Frog and the big right-slanting break (descent) is **Kermit's Crack** (E3 6a).

Right Sector

Torridown Man   25m   E2 5c ***
C.Moody, I.Taylor   25 May 1994
An excellent route, well protected. In the centre of the wall right of the slanting

break is a steep crack. Climb the crack to a ledge (strenuous), step left and climb another crack (technical), move left and climb a third crack.

Warmer Cleaner Drier   20m   E2 5b **
C.Moody, I.Taylor   23 May 1994
A fine line, quick drying. Climb the steep jagged crack at the right end of the wall, trending right then back left.

UPPER CRAG

Descent is at the right (east) end. The left half of the crag features a prominent leaning block on the terrace below. **Block and Beak** (HVS 5b *) passes a small overhang above the block on the left and follows the groove and crack-line above to finish at the beak (a small feature on the skyline). **Completely out to Lunge** (E5 6b *) climbs the shallow scoop right of Block and Beak, starting up it to a ledge, then going right to a small ramp and the wall above. The **Great Brush Robbery** (E4 6a *) climbs a chimney up the left side of a huge block against the cliff before moving left to flat holds, straight up to a ledge and finishing up a cracked wall. **A Million Years B.C.** (E1 5b *) moves right from the top of the block to climb the obvious crack in a left-facing corner.

DIABAIG

Map p320

Diabaig has some of the best outcrop climbing in Scotland, although there are few routes below VS. The setting is exquisite, above a picturesque inlet and village at the end of the road north of Loch Torridon. The rock is excellent gneiss, usually rough, clean and slabby but occasionally overhanging and juggy. Protection is often excellent. The only disadvantages are the long approach drive and possible midges in the summer, although the crag is open and sunny. The rock is quick to dry after showers but there is a little drainage and many routes seep for a day after heavy rain. The first routes, imaginatively named One, Two and Three, were climbed by Allan Austin (of Almscliff fame) and Ed Grindley only in 1975, but Diabaig was pretty remote in those days. The routes were later published in the SMC Journal, which encouraged visitors like Colin Moody (Boab's Corner), Murray Hamilton (The Pillar) and Andy Nisbet (Dire Wall and Northumberland Wall). Later Kev Howett adopted the place, liking the thin slabby style of climbing.

Approach: Follow the road through Torridon village and past Beinn Alligin, to park just before the pier at Lower Diabaig. From here the craggy hillside is obvious, but the Main Cliff and the Domes face away from the village. Walk to the end of the road and follow the right of way path towards Inveralligin (signposted through a garden). Walk up the wooded hillside and follow the path through a gate – access to Diabaig Pillar is by descent to the right. Further up, the path reaches an open gully. Follow it a short way, then turn south, gradually descending until the steep slabs of the Main Cliff are visible up on the left. To reach the Condome and Charlie's Tower, continue a little further along the path and cut up left.

DIABAIG PILLAR

(NG 800 596)   Alt 40m   West facing

Diabaig Pillar, the most prominent section of cliff visible from the village, is an impressive steep wall fairly low on the hillside which faces out to sea. The approach path to the Main Cliff initially runs up near its left side. Access to its base is by scrambling down and right through bracken. From below, a large inset slab is obvious at its top left. Between this and the pillar is a sharp arete, the line of Dire Wall.

Dire Wall   35m   E2 ***
A.Nisbet, R.F.Allen   May 1984
A fine route, but not as pure a line nor as well protected as The Pillar. Unaware of

the ascent of The Pillar, this line was chosen as cleaner, but was still mossy and Andy Nisbet took a fall when a hold broke off. Start about 3m left of The Pillar on clean rock, at a small step in the cliff base.

1. 20m 5a Go up and left to the edge of a groove which comes up from ground level (or climb the groove). Continue up to join The Pillar but soon move left to the base of the arete.

2. 15m 5b Climb the arete.

Variation: **Slab Finish**

After pitch one, continue out left across the slab – much easier and a bit of a cop out.

The Pillar   35m   E2 5b ****
M.Hamilton   1983

A superb quick drying route up the continuous wall of the pillar. It is hard to believe there was a lot of moss on the first ascent as the route is now held up as an example of a perfect outcrop route. Despite its intimidatingly smooth appearance, there are good holds and runners, and it provides a sustained pitch at the lowest limit of the grade. Start from a bay below the wall. Climb to and up a crack in the centre of the wall (same as Dire Straights) until it is possible to make a short traverse left towards the top of a groove which comes up from ground level (or start as for Dire Wall). Gain an intermittent crack-line which trends right into the centre of the wall and climb straight up.

Dire Straights   35m   E2 5b **
S.Jenkins, M.Moran   31 May 1991

A parallel line up the wall about 5m right of the Pillar. Not as sustained as The Pillar, but with a poorly protected section. The start of this route, perhaps finishing up a corner on the right **Upper Corner** (HVS 5a) was climbed by Joe Brown and Ginger Cain around 1980. Start as for the Pillar, but instead of moving left continue up a bulging crack, then an easy ramp, and then thin cracks in the upper wall to finish at an obvious V-notch.

MAIN CLIFF

(NG 801 595)   Alt 80m   South facing (mostly)   Diagram p348

The superb main cliff is a 70m wall of steep rough slab bounded on the right by a wet gully and split just below half-height by a less steep section with patches of vegetation. The routes generally have two pitches with belays at this halfway point. The routes are well protected and on near perfect rock. Being less than vertical, good footwork is the key to success.

Descent: The easiest descent is to make two abseils down the line of The Black Streak (in-situ threads, please leave any krabs). The alternative is an intricate and often muddy scramble. Traverse right from the cliff-top and cross the gully to gain a vague ridge. Descend a shallow gully just beyond the ridge until the ridge can be crossed rightwards (back towards the routes) and finished steeply.

The left-hand side of the crag has a heather ledge at about 20m which angles across the crag to about 5m from the ground at its finish in the centre.

1 Route Three   80m   E1 **
J.A.Austin, E.Grindley   4 Aug 1975

This route ascends to the heather ledge then traverses right to gain an obvious crack-line (more distinct than Route Two) which springs from a triangular roof near the lower right end of the heather ledge. The lower part of the crack is Brimstone. Start just left of a tree which has collapsed to horizontal, 8m left of Route Two.

1. 15m 4b Climb a right-facing blocky corner formed by a rib to the heather ledge below a prominent holly.

Northumberland Wall, E2 5c, Diabaig. Climber Mark Glaister
(photo Cubby Images)

DIABAIG - Main Cliff

1. Route Three   E1 **
2. Brimstone   E2 **
3. Route Two   HVS ****
4. Northumberland Wall   E2 ***
6. The Black Streak   E1 ***
7. Route One   HVS **

2. 30m 5b Step right and climb up the wall for 3m until it is possible to traverse right into a scoop below a turfy ramp. Follow this rightwards to join the crack. Climb the crack-line to belay below where it steepens.
3. 35m 5a Follow the crack to the top.

2 Brimstone   75m   E2 **
J.Lyall, A.Nisbet   1 Sep 1991
An enjoyable route, starting up the crack initially avoided by Route Three. Protection on the first pitch is good but fiddly and the route is high in the grade. Start below the right end of the heather ledge.
1. 35m 5c Gain the heather ledge and traverse left. From the apex of the triangular roof, pull out left into the left of two thin cracks. Move up, then return to the right crack and follow it to a junction with Route Three. Follow it over a quartz bulge, then move right to the Route Two belay.
2. 40m 5b Follow Route Two until it is possible to go left under an overlap. Where it ends follow a thin crack to the top.

3 Route Two   75m   HVS ****
J.A.Austin, E.Grindley   4 Aug 1975
Highly recommended – sustained, well protected and the best introduction to the wall. Start below the right end of the heather ledge.
1. 35m 5a Climb to the right end of the ledge, then pull awkwardly up right into the start of the crack. Follow it, then go slightly right to a large grass clump below a thin crack.
2. 40m 5a Climb the crack.

4 Northumberland Wall   70m   E2 ***
A.Nisbet, R.McHardy   May 1984
This follows intermittent cracks between the more continuous cracks of Route Two and The Black Streak (nearer the former). Thin and sustained, with small but good wires to be found. High in the grade – it feel harder than The Pillar. Named because Richard McHardy and Andy Nisbet were told by someone observing the ascent that Northumberland climbers had done it the month before; no one else has ever claimed it!
1. 30m 5c Start up a short left-facing corner, pull left over its capping roof to a shallow groove topped by a thin horizontal crack. Traverse back right and follow the intermittent cracks to belay beside a small tree (common with other routes, also on the abseil descent).
2. 40m 5c Climb the faint crack just left of the tree to the first overlap and traverse left underneath it to its end. Climb a faint crack and subsequent cracks above.

5 Wall of Flame   70m   E4 **
K.Howett, C.Thomson   10 June 1987
Climbs a rather blank and intimidating section of wall. Possibly E5, but depends if you find a high runner for the crux. Start just right of the initial corner of Northumberland Wall.
1. 30m 6a Go up the wall just right of the arete to a faint diagonal line running right. Follow it to its end, then pull over a bulge and a small overlap, stepping right to reach a large flat hold (just left of the crux of Black Streak). Go direct up a blank slab to an impasse below an isolated overlap. Go diagonally left (crux) to gain the base of a thin crack and up to belay as for Northumberland Wall, Route One and Black Streak.
2. 40m 6a Climb the slab left of Northumberland Wall to join that route at the left end of an overlap. Climb a faint crack and subsequent cracks above (as for Northumberland Wall).

6 The Black Streak   65m   E1 ***
J.A.Austin, R.Valentine   9 Aug 1976
An excellent route following a thin crack-line just left of the big right-facing corner.

Start just left of the big corner. Don't miss the second pitch, which is even better than the first.
1. 25m 5c Go up to and follow the thin crack (crux, overhead protection) to reach the common belay.
2. 40m 5b Climb the faint crack just left of the tree. It leads directly into a prominent crack which forms the right boundary of a black streak.

**7 Route One   70m   HVS ** **
J.A.Austin, E.Grindley   3 Aug 1975
Start 5m right of the big right-facing corner.
1. 30m 5a Climb the wall until it is possible to traverse left to the holly. Step left on to the face and climb it diagonally left, then a long step left to a fault leading to the common belay.
2. 40m 5a Climb a thin crack which starts just right of the tree. Move right and back left at a hard section after about 10m. Climbing the hard section direct is 5b. There is an easier (4c) alternative start to the pitch up a groove to the right.

THE DOMES

Continuing along the path beyond the Main Cliff, an apparent dome of smooth rock becomes visible beside the top right end of the slope under the Main Cliff. This is the Condome. To the right of this is a recess beyond which the cliff turns again to form a long face parallel to the Main Cliff but of less continuous rock; Boab's Corner is on this.

**Condome   30m   E4 6a ** **
K.Howett, D.Cuthbertson   29 May 1987
Climbs the discontinuous crack on the left of the dome. Start just left of the large boulder at the base of the cliff. Gain and climb the obvious hanging crack, move left to ledges on the edge, then return right to climb the upper crack. It is possible to climb direct to the ledges, missing out the hanging crack, at E3 5c.

**The Con-Con   30m   HVS 5b ** **
Climb the crack right of Condome, soon becoming right-curving twin cracks, to a ledge. Move right into a left-facing flake-corner and follow it leftwards to the top, the technical crux being the thin crack at the top (avoidable on the right). Sustained, some say E1.
Variation: **Direct   E2 5c ** **
D.Etherington, A.Nisbet   29 Jul 1990
From the ledge, continue direct past small right-facing overlaps.

The direct line from the Condome to Boab's Corner is blocked by a steep wall (5b up!), so a downward loop must be made. The quickest descent from Boab's Corner is to follow an overlooking ramp down to a terrace and finish down the short gully between this face and the Condome.

**Boab's Corner   60m   VS ** **
C.Moody, R.Sharples   24 Apr 1982
The best of the easier climbs, taking the slabby wall near the bottom end of the long face via an obvious right-slanting, stepped and capped corner for its second pitch. Start at a short corner and climb to an oak.
1. 30m 4b Step right and climb straight up cracks in the wall on the right to the base of the groove.
2. 20m 4c Go up the groove. This is hard for the short, but can be avoided on the right by a short corner, returning immediately. Finish up slabs.

The Con Con, HVS 5b, Diabaig. Climber Andy Tibbs
(photo Al Matthewson)

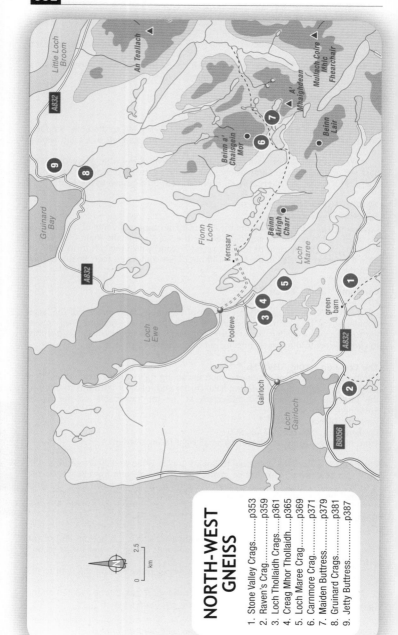

NORTH-WEST GNEISS

NORTH-WEST GNEISS

The west coast area between Torridon and Ullapool is the heart of gneiss country. The major crag at Carnmore with its magnificent upper wall has been established for many years, but many of the one pitch crags based around Gairloch and Gruinard were only developed in the '90s. Slightly older were the two pitch Creag Mhor Thollaidh and Raven's Crag, along with the shorter but very roadside Gruinard Jetty Buttress.

Many of the gneiss crags are on smooth domes with rough slabby rock, providing middle grade routes. Raven's Crag, however, and parts of Jetty Buttress have more holds and lower grade routes. But there are some 'half-domes' too with very steep sides, like Loch Maree Crag and Lochan Dubh Crag (Dome Crag) with their sustained face climbs. Routes are generally quick drying, useful in the west coast climate, although the area has much less rainfall than the Fort William and Glen Coe areas further south. The midges can be very bad on still cloudy days but many of the crags are open and sunny, so a breeze and fine weather solves the problem.

Maps: OS L19, E434 (Stone Valley on E433, Carnmore on E435)

SMC Climbers' Guide: *Northern Highlands Central* (projected 2006)

Public Transport: Access by public transport is possible but not recommended for this area.

Amenities: There is an all year Tourist Office at Gairloch (01445 712130). Gairloch is a fair sized place with shop, chip shop and petrol. Old Inn is the best pub. Poolewe is more favoured by climbers, with an outdoor shop (no hardware) at the Slioch clothing factory. Also the Bridge Cottage Coffee Shop and a swimming pool.

Climbing Wall: Gairloch Leisure Centre, open from 5pm, but quite old (DR, 8m high, 1994), (01445 712345).

Accomodation: The area can also be visited in a day from Ullapool or Torridon (see those chapters).

Camping: Gairloch (NG 797 773), Poolewe (NG 862 812) and Laide (NG 903 918).

SYHA Youth Hostels: Carn Dearg is 4km west of Gairloch (NG 763 776), (0870 004 1110).

Independent Hostels: Sail Mhor Croft, Camusnagaul (NH 064 893), (01854 633224) open all year.

Loch Maree & Gairloch Area

These crags lie in an area defined by the A832, where it leaves Loch Maree for Gairloch at Slatterdale and then returns close to the loch near Tollie Farm. Many smaller crags have been developed, but these are the best.

STONE VALLEY CRAGS - MEALL LOCHAN A' CHLEIRICH

This hillside of fairly accessible gneiss crags lies above the road between Loch Maree and Gairloch and has a splendid outlook both to Baosbheinn and the sea. The crags are a suntrap and due to their hummocky formation, many routes dry rapidly after rain. The proximity to the mountains means, however, that the crags often catch showers when crags nearer the coast are dry. The planting of a million trees in the area as part of the Millenium Forest project will eventually alter the open-ness of the site, but all in all this is a very pleasant place to climb.

The crags are clearly visible from the road but the best walls are in profile. So although local climber Steve Chadwick climbed here in 1984, the main development waited until Bob Brown saw the clean arete of Open Secret glinting from the path and returned with John Mackenzie. The pair climbed the most obvious lines, soon to be followed by others on the smaller walls and some of the harder lines, among them Blyth Wright, Graeme Ettle and Ian Taylor.

Approach: The crags lie to the south of the A832 west of Loch Maree. Park at a car park around a green barn (its colour in 2005) at NG 856 721. Follow the Poca Buidhe track, which has a signpost indicating the Bad na Sgalag Native Pinewood, for about 1km and the crags will be seen facing south-west on the craggy hillside of Meall Lochan a' Chleirich. There is a hint of a path leading across the upper of two bridges and towards Stone Valley Crag, about 40mins.

Clearly seen from the car park are the Domes high up at the back and a prominent arete (on Rum Doodle Crag, not described). The pale clean arete of Stone Valley Crag is a key locating feature. It is barely seen from the parking place but becomes increasingly obvious the further up the track one goes, as does the clean wall on its right with the best climbs. There are many other routes here on good rock, but not of the same length or line.

RED WALL CRAG

(NG 868 717)   Alt 230m   South facing

This is the steep wall left of Stone Valley Crag. The rock is more fissile but essentially sound.

1 Bold as Brass   20m   E3 5c ** **
J.R.Mackenzie, R.Brown   9 May 1996
Climbs the obvious red coloured pillar bounding the left side of the wall. Gain a ledge just left of Flaming June. Climb direct from the ledge, near the right arete of the wall (bold with RP protection), to reach a thin curved crack. Make thin moves up the crack and easier to the top.

2 Flaming June   25m   VS 5a *
R.Brown, J.R.Mackenzie   11 Jun 1995
A steep line with devious but good climbing left of a groove with trees. Start on a short rib just right of Bold as Brass. Climb up to a small ledge at its right end. Continue to an obvious flange above, then traverse right to a ledge with small trees. Climb up the flake-crack and step left into a niche below a small roof, then step back right towards heather. Climb up and left into a well positioned open corner to a ledge. A short arete provides a pleasant finish.

3 Lucky Strike   20m   VS 5a ** **
R.Brown, J.R.Mackenzie   3 May 1996
Start just at the bottom of a heather ramp which slopes up right. Follow the obvious groove, bearing left to a nest of hollow spikes at its top. Climb the seemingly blank wall up and right on hidden holds to the ledge.

STONE VALLEY CRAG

(NG 868 717)   Alt 250m   South facing

This is the biggest and best crag, barely seen from the car park but easily identified from the approach track by the pale clean arete of Open Secret which lies down and left of the apparent summit crags. The base of the crag is a short steep wall with a short crack on the left, a central chockstoned gully and some cracks on the right near a little tree. Above this wall the angle falls back into undulating steep slabs with a prominent water washed groove right of centre.

Descent: Easiest by the open grassy gully on the left.

4 Touch and Go   20m   HVS 5a *
J.R.Mackenzie, R.Brown   11 Jun 1995
The obvious inset slab formed left of the crest. Start in the slab's centre and climb straight up (keeping away from the right edge), then slightly left to finish up its left-bounding corner. Reach the crest and the main slab at a niche. Step right and finish up the crux of Open Secret.

STONE VALLEY CRAGS

The Domes

Stone Valley Crag

Red Wall Crag

1. Bold as Brass   E3 5c **
3. Lucky Strike   VS 5a **
4. Touch and Go   HVS 5a *
5. Open Secret   Hard Severe 4b ***
9. Inside Information HVS 5a *
10. The Flashing Blade E3 6a *
11. Cat Burglar   E4 6a ***
12. The Thug   E2 5b **

N-W GNEISS

5 Open Secret   40m   Hard Severe 4b ***

S.Chadwick and partner   1984 (line uncertain), A.Brooks, T.Doe, D.Jones   18 Jun 1989

This fine route climbs cracks in the crest which forms the left edge of the main slab. The 1989 ascent started up the corner of Bald Eagle; finished by Open Secret and named it Singing Stone Slab, but the musical block has been trundled by someone unaware of its history.

1. 15m 4a Climb a short crack on the left of the lower wall and trend left to below the crest.

2. 25m 4b Climb the crack to where it bends right. Now follow a thin snaking crack which trends left up the steep slabby headwall.

6 Bald Eagle   40m   HVS 5a **

R.Brown, J.R.Mackenzie   11 Jun 1995

The seemingly bald slab right of Open Secret gives a very good route, despite feeling close to that route. Climb the initial pitch of Open Secret to the base of a corner on the right (or start from here, either reached by scrambling up left from the foot of Open Secret or traversing easily to it from the descent). Climb the corner and at its top step left and climb a thin crack to its end. Climb straight up over two small bulges above to a thin crack. Climb the thin crack to its termination, then straight up the red slab.

7 Blood Feud   40m   E1 *

J.R.Mackenzie, D.S.B.Wright   30 May 1997

Another fine route but rather squeezed in. Start at the foot of the lowest wall, to the right of Open Secret's initial crack, below a ledge with a cleaned lip and a small tree. Quite hard for those who have trouble finding the key hold.

1. 20m 5b Climb to the tree. Climb the bald wall behind the tree via a crack but make a blind reach straight up where the crack veers right. Step left and continue up the fine slab to the left end of a heather ledge.

2. 20m 5a Climb the left side of a scoop and the thin crack above. Continue up to finish up a crack in the headwall slab (the corner-crack on the right being Inside Information).

8 Stone Diary   40m   HVS *

J.R.Mackenzie, R.Brown   14 May 1995

Start just left of the central chockstoned gully in the lower wall.

1. 20m 5a Gain a plinth and climb the steep rib between the gully and a smooth pod. Step left above and friction up a fine slab to a heather ledge (belay as for Blood Feud).

2. 20m 5b From the middle of the ledge move up rightwards on friction. Reach left to a good hold over the bulge above. (Pitch 2 of Blood Feud is close on the left and the more obvious line.) Continue up and finish up the crack as for Blood Feud.

9 Inside Information   45m   HVS *

R.Brown, J.R.Mackenzie   14 May 1995

1. 20m 5a Climb the steep jamming crack on the right of the lower wall to exit by some blocks. Step left and climb an easy rib to avoid the heather, stepping right at the top to belay below the water worn groove.

2. 25m 5a Climb the excellent groove. Step left and climb a flake-crack to an awkward exit by a little corner.

THE DOMES

(NG 869 717)   Alt 300m   South facing   Diagram p355

Higher up above Stone Valley Crag are two dome like crags which form the summit buttress and are separated by a gully. Near the base of the left dome and immediately left of a big corner is an overhanging wall with left and right-slanting cracks forming a V above a lower wall.

Open Secret, Hard Severe 4b, Stone Valley Crags. Climber John Mackenzie (photo John Mackenzie collection)

10 The Flashing Blade   20m   E3 6a *
G.Ettle, I.Taylor   14 Jun 1997
The thin crack forming the left-slanting section of the V. Start up a right-slanting mucky groove and turn left to the base of the crack. The crack involves a very hard move but is well protected by small Friends.

11 Cat Burgler   20m   E4 6a ***
I.Taylor, G.Ettle, R.Brown   24 Jun 1997
The formidable looking wall between the two more definite cracks of the V. Superb sustained climbing, but better protected than it looks; high in the grade. Start up The Flashing Blade and then step onto the wall, following a thin overhanging crack all the way.

12 The Thug   20m   E2 5b **
R.Brown, J.R.Mackenzie   9 May 1996

358

RAVEN'S CRAG

1. Hydro Hek — Hard Severe *
2. Lonmore — Severe *
3. Stage Fright — HVS *
4. Charlestone — Severe **
5. Lucy — Very Difficult **
6. Entasis — Very Difficult *
6a. Direct Finish — VS 4c *

Climbs the striking right-slanting crack of the V. Start left of the crack at a right-slanting groove (as for the previous two routes). Climb the groove to a small ledge below the crack. The crack yields to a no frills approach with the crux at the top. Finish up a straightforward arete or scramble off left.

RAVEN'S CRAG

(NG 797 712)   Alt 120m   South-West to West facing   Map p352

A typical gneiss dome, but less steep and with more holds than many in the area and therefore, like Gruinard Jetty Buttress, a good place for lower grade routes. The rock is good and rough, despite a smooth appearance and it dries quickly, although one can climb in the wet.

The crag was discovered by Gairloch resident Steve Chadwick and extensively climbed by him and his partners in the '80s. Originally published without stars, visits by others have been limited but its quality is slowly being recognised.

Approach: Just south of Gairloch take the B8056 to Badachro. After 2km, just before the Shieldaig Lodge Hotel (there is a big parking area just after it, but some folk park on the verge), walk up a track on the left (signposted) across a small ford. Ignore a track on the right after 100m, then ignore a small path on the left after another 50m, but continue up the main path till it opens out, then levels off and there are slabby crags close on the left. From here, the slabby right end of the crag is seen in profile about 300m away on the right; head direct to it, 30mins.

Climbs are described from right to left.

1 Hydro Hek   50m   Hard Severe *
G.Powell, S.Chadwick   Jul 1982
Start at the right end of the crag, just left of a large flake and beneath a clean plaque of slab on the upper wall.
1. 20m Climb clean brown slabs to the base of the plaque.
2. 30m 4a From the right side traverse up left across the plaque and continue up leftwards towards the top.

2 Lonmore   55m   Severe *
A.Smailes, S.Chadwick   Jun 1983
The middle of the wall is divided at about 15m by a heather terrace with a prominent tree. From here two diagonal faults rise up left, the left one leading to another tree high up, with a triangular niche up on its left. Quite vegetated but the climbing is good.
1. 15m Climb directly to the tree on the heather terrace.
2. 30m 4a Move up left to the diagonal fault. Climb this to the high tree and niche. Climb left out of the top of the niche to a ledge.
3. 10m Finish easily rightwards.

3 Stage Fright   55m   HVS *
I.Davidson, S.Chadwick   1985
The clean, blank looking wall left of Lonmore's upper section. Start at the base of a heather break which leads up left under the blocks of Lucy.
1. 25m Climb a vague crest on the right side of a clean area of slab to reach the right end of a higher left section of heather terrace.
2. 30m 5a Climb steeply up the wall to join the final moves of Lonmore. A good variation is to move left from the middle of the wall. Continue easily to the top.

4 Charlestone   50m   Severe **
S.Chadwick, H.Emerson   Aug 1981
Takes a direct line up the centre of the crag, featuring a water worn scoop left of the clean wall of Stage Fright. Start 5m left of the base of the heather break.
1. 25m 4a Climb a convex slab to the break. Continue up a line of weakness

composed of a shallow groove, a crack-line and a steeper wall to the higher left section of the terrace and below the scoop. Or climb the first pitch of Stage Fright, as good and slightly easier.

2. 25m 4a Climb straight up on good holds left of the scoop to an easier finish. Or swing right from a big hold into the water worn scoop and follow it up left to the same finish.

5 Lucy   60m   Very Difficult **
S.Chadwick, I.Davidson Sep 1984

Huge blocks at 15m mark the line up to a high and prominent rowan tree. Take the cleanest line to the blocks and pass them immediately on the right to gain a left-slanting depression. Follow this up to a heather ledge on the left (the belay of Entasis). Go right to the tree. Abseil from the tree (45m) or finish rightwards.

Variations: This is the best line on this central area of slab but the slab is climbable in many places at Very Difficult. The original line started as for Charlestone, then took a left-slanting line of weakness to the heather ledge.

At the left end of the crag there is a large grass ledge with a tree about 15m up, forming part of a left-slanting rake. Below and right of the tree on the grass ledge is a broken scoop in the lower rocks. Above and right of the tree are two right-slanting ramps, the lower being much wider.

6 Entasis   60m   Very Difficult *
M.McKay, R.A.Napier 3 Apr 1986

Start just right of the broken scoop at a small red ramp.

1. 35m Start up the ramp, then climb directly up slabs to reach a heather ledge at the top of the wider rocky ramp running up right from the tree (belay as for Lucy).

2. 25m Finish rightwards to the tree, as for Lucy.

Variation: **VS 4c ***
D.Conway, R.A.Napier 6 Apr 1986

2a. 25m Climb a left-slanting line to the smaller ramp and continue above, about 5m left of the tree and on good clean rock.

Dark Slab

Round the left end of the crag is a dark slab of clean rough rock, which provides some good short routes. An abseil rope allows all the routes to be done quickly; otherwise scramble off left to descend.

7 Jutting Blocks   20m   Very Difficult *
D.Lang 1991

At the right side of the slab are prominent jutting blocks. Climb to and pass the blocks on the right (or slightly harder on the left), then continue to the top.

8 Leac McCac   20m   VS 4c **
D.Neville, S.Chadwick 1982

Start left of the jutting blocks and climb the smoothest and cleanest section of slab direct. Hardest at the start but limited protection in the middle.

9 Ricicles   20m   Severe 4a *
D.Neville, S.Chadwick 1982

Climb the slab direct keeping just left of its smoothest section and trending right towards the top.

10 Special K   20m   Severe *
D.Neville, S.Chadwick 1982

Climb the slab by a right-slanting line, crossing Leac McCac and Ricicles.

RAVEN'S CRAG
Dark Slab

7. Jutting Blocks	Very Difficult *
8. Leac McCac	VS 4c **
9. Ricicles	Severe 4a *
10. Special K	Severe *

LOCH TOLLAIDH CRAGS

(NG 850 780)   Alt 150-200m   North-West facing   Map p352   Diagram p363

This collection of gneiss crags overlooks Loch Tollaidh and is well seen on the south side of the road between Gairloch and Poolewe. The different crags offer a variety of the climbing styles typical of gneiss from smooth rough slabs to overhanging walls on positive holds. The crags get the afternoon sun and there is little drainage, so they dry relatively quickly and the rough rock means the easier routes are still possible when damp. Their open nature allows the breeze to blow, speeding drying and reducing the midge problem. This and their convenient grouping has made the crags the most popular in the area. Several visits by Rab and Chris Anderson in 1995 and 1996, assisted by Dave Cuthbertson on some very hard routes on the Gairloch Wall, brought the first publicity. In fact the first routes were climbed during the war by the Highland Field Craft Training Centre, based in Poolewe. The locals soon claimed some routes, particularly Jim Buchanan from Poolewe soon to be joined by very keen and able climber Paul Tattersall, who moved to the area to work at the local lighthouse and started a very active exploration.

Approach: Park near the east end of Loch Tollaidh and cross the Tollie burn near the outflow of the loch. Head across boggy ground to the crags. Wellies may be useful after wet weather, 15mins.

RAVEN'S NEST

(NG 849 783)

This is the first crag reached after crossing the outflow from the loch and walking across the boggy ground. A large eyrie in the middle of the crag is an obvious feature. The right edge of the crag is formed by a fine 40m slab – a metal stake at the top of the slab indicates an old abseiling site.

**Raven's Edge   40m   Very Difficult **

Start at the right edge of the steep wall, where it turns round into a big clean slab. Follow the left edge of the slab throughout. The top is less clean.

Assault Slab   40m   Very Difficult *
Clean rough rock and good protection; the start is the crux. Follow the same first 5m as Raven's Edge, then trend right up the centre of the slab, passing the right side of a curving corner. Other variations are possible.

GAIRLOCH WALL

(NG 849 781)

Lying just to the right, this wall is located above a slight rise in the slope, just above some large boulders. Undercut at its base, the cliff has a vertical wall at its left side and a ramp slanting up rightwards from beneath the undercut section. The base of the crag is sheltered from the elements.

El Passe   35m   E6 6a *
D.Cuthbertson, R.Anderson   12 May 1996
The obvious crack-line up the right side of the vertical wall, where a slime streak springs from a niche at the start. Swing right into the niche from good holds and continue up the unobvious wall to reach a break and protection. Step right and climb the fine overhanging crack to easier ground and a belay just short of the top.

Old El Pastits   35m   E6 6b *
R.Anderson, D.Cuthbertson   11 May 1996
The obvious undercut crack-line up the middle of the leaning wall. Pull into the crack and awkwardly place a crucial Rock 6 above the obvious slot, then continue to a point at mid-height where a span across left gains a jug. Pull up right, then climb the crack to the top.

DINOSAUR BUTTRESS

(NG 849 781)

At the right end of several crags is an area of fine reddish rock, beyond which the crag merges into the hillside before rising up towards Fraggle Rock. The base of the crag is very boggy.

**In the Pink   30m   HVS 5b **
S.Chadwick, G.Powell   1981
The obvious crack in the middle of the crag, strenuous at the start above wet ground.

Red Faced   30m   E1 5b
K.Clark, I.Davidson   1992
The next crack just around the edge to the right leads to a finish up an easy corner.

**Flushed-out   30m   HVS 5a **
J.Buchanan, D.Neville   1992
The crack and shallow groove at the right end of the crag.

FRAGGLE ROCK

(NG 848 778)

This crag, visible in profile on the skyline from the road, lies higher up at the far right end. A huge shattered block lies just out from the base of the crag. The left and lower end of the crag is split into two smaller tiers but the best climbs are where the crag reaches full height. Here is a big corner, rather vegetated, right of a horizontal cave and nearly opposite the huge shattered block. The base of the right wall of the corner holds a slab leading to two roofs near the right arete.

LOCH TOLLAIDH CRAGS

A. Raven's Nest
B. Gairloch Wall

C. Dinosaur Buttress
D. Fraggle Rock

E. Inlet Wall
F. Hidden Crag

Kermit   25m   E1 5b *
J.Buchanan, J.Henderson   Jun 1992
Climbs the right wall of the big corner. Gear is spaced but perhaps only 5a. Start near the corner at the left edge of the slab. Climb straight up towards the top of the corner, then trend right up the middle of the wall.

Sprocket   25m   E2 5b **
J.Buchanan, J.Robinson   Jun 1992
Climb the centre of the slab (poorly protected) to the first roof, move right, then pull left through the right end of the roof and go up to the next roof. Move out right and climb cracks to the top. The original ascent was less direct.

Fraggle Roll   25m   HVS 5a *
T.Doe, J.Buchanan   Jun 1995
Round to the right are some cracks and corners based around a big holly bush. Climb a short leaning crack whose right side forms a pedestal to the left end of the holly bush, then a corner left to the pedestal and an overhanging corner above.
Variation: **Direct Finish (Roll Up)   E3 5c ***
L.Hughes, A.Cunningham   27 Apr 2001
Climb through the holly and up the groove and crack above.

INLET WALL
(NG 844 789)

The leftmost crag of a group close behind an inlet of the loch and seen from the car park to be facing the road and just right of Fraggle Rock. Most easily reached by heading right from Dinosaur Buttress.

Lifeline   30m   E3 5c **
P.Tattersall, C.Meek   23 Aug 2000
The route follows the obvious crack-line, with a cleaned ledge part way up.

HIDDEN CRAG
(NG 850 780)

This crag overlooks a flat boggy area and is quite hidden. It lies just behind

N-W GNEISS

Dinosaur Buttress and is best reached from its right side. A tall, reddish coloured wall is cut by a number of prominent crack-lines.

Wild Iris   35m   E4 5c *
P.Thorburn, J.Preston   3 May 2000
Climbs the steep wall to the left of Water Lily. Start up a hollow pillar and boldly tackle the wall above to finish up the left edge of the upper slabs.

Water Lily   40m   E2 5c **
A.Winton, A.Gorman   Aug 1994
A well protected crack-line that runs up and slightly left from a series of soggy sods of turf. The start is usually wet but on jugs. The finish is thin but try not to escape right to Buena Vista.

Buena Vista   40m   E2 5b ***
A.Winton, S.Chadwick   Apr 1994
The vertical crack-line which lies immediately right of the wet sods. Sustained and well protected.

CREAG MHOR THOLLAIDH

(NG 864 776)   Map p352

Overlooking the shore at the north-western end of Loch Maree, this rugged gneiss hillside has numerous crags dotted about it. Set amidst picturesque surroundings, the crags have an atmosphere akin to the Lake District and offer a variety of fine, easily accessible routes on excellent rock. Although the biggest crag in the area with some marvellous multi pitch routes, it has never gained the popularity of crags such as Diabaig. In part this is due to some jungle starts, stubbon heather and a sheltered position which can generate a serious midge problem, particularly in the trees at the base of the Lower Crag.

However, the jungle starts often lead to fine open climbing and the midges can be avoided by visiting in spring. The Upper Crag is more open and can be midge free on a breezy day. The crags catch the morning sun and are fairly quick to dry. Although Philip Tranter was an early visitor, the latent possibilities were first realised by Tom Patey and Brian Robertson, of the Edinburgh Squirrels. Chris Jackson from Sheffield soon climbed here and these two teams explored for many years. In the late '80s, Rab Anderson and Murray Hamilton from Edinburgh and Dougie Dinwoodie and Alasdair Ross from Aberdeen climbed some of the harder routes.

Approach: About 2km south of Poolewe, on the Gairloch road, a single track road (signposted Tollie Bay) branches off to run past Tollie Farm and end at a small car park close to the water's edge. For access from the car park and descent, see each crag individually.

LOWER TOLLIE CRAG

(NG 869 779)   Alt 30-60m   East facing   Diagram p367

The crag is easily seen from the car park. Follow the track towards the loch shore, then head direct for its right end through trees, 5mins.

Descent: Descent from the main central wall is by traversing right through deep heather to reach a shallow gully filled with jungle which runs down the north-west side of the crag. Descent from the left end of the crag is best by abseil from a tree just right of the top corner of Stoney Broke (when looking up, the largest and nearest tree on the cliff-top left of Stoney Broke).

Buena Vista, E2 5b, Loch Tollaidh Crags. Climber Iain Small
(photo Chris Cartwright)

N-W GNEISS

On arrival a two grooved arete, overhanging at its base, marks the right end of the lower section of the crag. A wall with the first route leads left to an obvious, steep and often slimy corner. Moving left, the crag reaches its maximum height.

1 Cloud Cuckoo Land   25m   HVS 5b *
G.Nicoll, R.Anderson   9 May 1987
The obvious crack-line through the first break in the steep lower wall about 10m left of the arete. Climb a short corner, pull through the roof at a block jammed in the crack and follow the continuation crack to step up left and finish by a corner-crack.

2 Gudgeon   70m   E2 ***
C.Jackson, T.Proctor   18 Aug 1971; FFA: R.Anderson, C.Greaves   22 May 1988
A good route with an excellent second pitch taking the thin crack up the right edge of the high section of crag. Moving left from Cloud Cuckoo Land, the crag base descends to its lowest point at a damp black wall. Beyond this it rises up quite steeply and 10m up is a black recess with a big tree at its base. Start at a tree right of the obvious fault of The Trip, at a recess.
1. 20m 5b Climb the tree and step up left to climb a short corner. Move right, climb a groove then go right below the roofs to a stance on the edge where a grassy ramp comes in from the right.
2. 30m 5c Step left to climb the corner-crack to a horizontal break, then step across right and climb a thin crack-line in the wall to a belay on the left of a large flake.
3. 20m 5a Climb the flake, step right then climb cracks to the top.

3 Decadent Days   70m   E2 ***
R.Anderson, M.Hamilton   May 1983
A superb route following a thin crack-line directly up the crag. Start as for the previous route at the tree.
1. 40m 5c Climb the tree and step up left to climb the short corner until it is possible to step left onto the lip of the roof to reach the thin crack-line. Follow the crack to the obvious diagonal crack slanting left across the face.
2. 30m 5c Step up left to the diagonal crack then move right to gain thin cracks which are climbed to the top.

4 The Trip   85m   E1 *
C.Jackson, B.Andrews   7 Sep 1967 (1PA); FFA unknown
This route takes the obvious shallow groove and crack in the left section of the highest part of the crag. A superb line which would be a three star HVS with a good clean, but there is heather in many of the cracks. Start at the base of the broken groove, 5m left of the recess of Gudgeon.
1. 35m 5a Climb the groove to an oak tree. Continue up the groove (crux) and up a small chimney.
2. 25m 5a Continue in the same line, initially over perched blocks to the base of a large flake. Go up for 4m, then traverse right to a niche.
3. 25m 4c Climb the right-slanting crack behind the stance for 4m, step left to avoid an unpleasant heathery rake and continue up in almost a straight line, following the zigzag cracks leading to a heathery shoulder.

5 The Hand Rail   80m   Hard Severe 4a **
T.W.Patey, M.Galbraith   15 May 1966
The left margin of the highest part of the crag is marked by the obvious right-angled corner of Stoney Broke. Below this is a heathery depression from which a well defined vegetated fault-line slants up right onto the main face. Go about 30m up left from The Trip and walk on to a ledge, then descend easily rightwards into the depression (or climb direct using a tree 15m left of The Trip). Go up to belay. The route gives two fine pitches going out right below roofs and with good exposure.

CREAG MHOR THOLLAIDH

1. Cloud Cuckoo Land   HVS 5b *
2. Gudgeon   E2 ***
3. Decadent Days   E2 ***
4. The Trip   E1 *
5. The Hand Rail   Hard Severe 4a **

6. Rain in the Face   E3 **
7. Stoney Broke   HVS *
8. Each Uisge/Across The Lines   E4 **
9. Teddy Bears' Picnic   E1 **
10. The Bug   E2 5b ***
11. The Heretic   E3 5b **

N-W GNEISS

**6 Rain-in-the-Face   75m   E3 ** **

D.Dinwoodie, A.Ross   27 Aug 1987

A superb pitch up the obvious blunt arete right of Stoney Broke, gained from The Handrail.

1. 40m 5a Climb the vegetated fault of The Handrail to beneath the roofs. Hand-traverse a big jagged block to a hanging belay at the foot of the arete.

2. 35m 6a Make awkward moves out to the arete to a slim groove (hidden peg runner). Climb the groove to the roof and move right to gain a thin crack-line, which springs from the end of the roof and is climbed in a fine position, close to the arete, to easier ground.

7 Stoney Broke   70m   HVS *

J.Cunningham, W.March   9 May 1970

The large right-angled corner marking the left edge of the highest section of the face. Start 12m left of The Handrail on the grassy approach terrace.

1. 40m 5b Climb a short wall to a heather patch, then go up diagonally right to climb a sloping ramp leading towards the corner. A small ledge is gained after a struggle with some bushes and the corner is then climbed to an overhang where a move onto the right wall and up gains a ledge and tree belays.

2. 30m 5a Continue in the corner with occasional detours onto the left wall and wide bridging to avoid some heather.

**8 Each Uisge – Across The Lines   50m   E4 ** **

D.Dinwoodie, A.Ross   27 Aug 1987 (Each Uisge); R.Anderson, C.Greaves   8 Jul 1988 (Across the Lines)

This combination provides an excellent sustained route up the steep slab left of Stoney Broke. Start from a terrace 5m above the approach terrace, right of some huge blocks and below a direct line leading to an obvious wide crack in the slab.

1. 25m 6a Immediately right of this direct line, move up to small wedged blocks and a short thin crack, then step right and gain the horizontal break above. Continue to the next break, then climb directly to another break beneath a roof; step up left then up to holds at the next break and easier ground. Continue to a horizontal break, step up left, then go up right to another break and peg belay.

2. 25m 6a Climb slabs up right then straight up to another horizontal break, peg runner. Step right and climb a thin crack with difficulty to the abseil tree.

UPPER TOLLIE CRAG

(NG 870 777)   Alt 120m   East facing   Diagram p367

This lies a few minutes walk beyond and uphill from Lower Tollie Crag. Continue uphill along the line of its base. First reached is a huge tree filled corner; the main wall is beyond this. Continue up until out of the trees; it has a much more open aspect. The most obvious features are a prominent left-slanting tree filled chimney-fault and an obvious crack on its right. On its left is an intermittent crack-line in a smooth slabby wall (The Bug).

Descent: By the easy slopes on the left.

**9 Teddy Bears' Picnic   75m   E1 ** **

C.Jackson, R.Conway   30 Jun 1985

A good route which cuts through the chimney-fault and the obvious crack, but by a natural line. Start immediately right of the intermittent crack-line.

1. 25m 5b Climb the obvious right-slanting corner-ramp over a roof towards the chimney-fault, step up left to gain a horizontal break, then pull up to holds and climb a short crack to reach a tree belay in the chimney. The original route followed the ramp all the way into and up the chimney.

2. 20m 5b Step down to gain and follow a right-rising crack-line across the wall to belay in the obvious crack beside a perched block.

3. 30m 5a Traverse right to climb a crack leading up to the right edge, step right and continue up easier rock to the top.

10 The Bug 50m E2 5b *
P.Botterill, J.Lamb 11 Jun 1974
A tremendous route taking the intermittent thin crack-line in the wall left of Teddy Bears' Picnic. Similar atmosphere and standard to Diabaig Pillar. Climb the crack over a small bulge to a ramp. Follow this briefly rightwards then step back left and go up to another bulge. Climb this on good holds (or easier via the ramp on the right) to reach delightful, delicate and occasionally run out thin cracks in the slabby wall. Unfortunately, all good things come to an end. Belay where the angle eases. Scramble up slightly right to the top. The best descent is down heather to the left.

11 The Heretic 55m E3 *
C.Jackson, R.Conway 30 Jun 1985 (line uncertain but less direct); R.Anderson, G.Nicoll 10 May 1987 (as described)
Good though sparsely protected climbing up the wall left of The Bug. It takes the main feature of the face, a huge right-leaning shallow scoop.
1. 45m 5b Start 3m right of the obvious chimney at the left of the crag. Climb easily to two blocks in a heathery break. Stand on the two blocks and step right to a shallow slabby groove. Climb this (poor protection) to gain a ramp (runner placement in the Bug up right). From a good hold at the base of the ramp, move up then left to the start of a diagonal crack which is climbed past a shallow scoop. Stand in the crack where it becomes horizontal and continue above, first right then left, to a diagonal break. Move up to another diagonal break and pull over on to a slabby ledge.
2. 10m Go easily up right, then up and off left.
A direct start over the initial bulge and up to join the normal route is unprotected 5c, or 6a truly direct.

WHITE WALL CRAG

(NG 875 772) Alt 100m North-East facing

This is a white wall overlooking the loch two-thirds of the way towards the more obvious Loch Maree Crag.

Approach: From the parking place, go down and follow the shore until forced up after a short distance. Return down and follow the shore, mostly on the pebbles if the loch is low. But in the spring, before the bracken has grown, an old path above the shore is better. Leave the shore when the slope above becomes less steep. The crag is immediately seen; go up through the trees to it, 30mins.

The central fault is full of trees, and the right side is crossed by several diagonal cracks. The clean left side is split at mid-height by a diagonal crack.

The Shimmer 30m E4 6a *
K.Howett, J.Horrocks 7 Jun 1992
This gives superb face climbing up the clean left side of the wall, sustained and thin but without any desperate moves. There is good protection for the hard sections. Start 5m from the left edge at a thin wiggly crack leading to a patch of black rock below a small ledge at 6m. Climb the crack to the ledge. Step left, then follow the line up and right to a small flake. Traverse right and gain the diagonal crack, then follow this left with surprising difficulty to near its end. Step back right, then go diagonally up and right (again with difficulty) to gain a thin crack to finish. Tree belay and abseil descent.

LOCH MAREE CRAG

(NG 879 789) Alt 60m North-East facing Map p352

This is one of Scotland's most impressive crags; an awesome wall with good holds and ideal for those with stamina. Development of the crag was due to the enthusiasm of Kev Howett, although the tough grades, particularly E4 for Spirit Air, have

N-W GNEISS

spared it becoming popular. The routes have been upgraded. None have been given four stars although Spirit Air and Ariel may be worth it; future ascents with the new grades may generate sufficient enthusiasm.

Approach: From the parking place, go down and follow the shore, mostly on the pebbles if the loch is low. There are a couple of places where you are best to leave the shore briefly, one quite soon and one near the access to White Wall Crag. But in the spring, before the bracken has grown, an old path above the shore is better. The going in general is rough and it may take an hour to reach the crag, 45mins in the spring or if the loch is low.

Descent: By abseil, using in-situ gear. There are slings and krab in the holly forest (and on the tree in the diagonal break).

Left of the crag's prominent overhanging arete is a gently impending wall with a right-rising diagonal fault, a big holly near its top and a holly forest at its very top.

Spirit Air   50m   E5 6a ***
K.Howett   1987
A stunning route, unremittingly sustained and strenuous, which takes the crack up the left side of the overhanging arete. Start at the base of the arete. Go up an easy groove and where this ends pull directly up the wall to gain the crack, which is followed in a mind blowing situation with continual interest until it fades out. Move up to reach and follow a line of good holds leading diagonally leftwards to a white shield of rock (not particularly obvious from the base). Here a diagonal crack continues across its base to join Ariel (an option for those running out of steam). Instead, climb the right side of the shield to reach up right for good holds and follow them diagonally left to below the holly forest at the cliff-top.
Variation: **E4 6a**
To make the route E4, split the route into two 25m pitches by sneaking round the arete to the right after about 25m. There is a fine airy nook which gives a good belay stance, not hanging.

Destitution Man   50m   E4 5c **
K.Howett   1987
The first crack-line left of Spirit Air is steep and strenuous in its lower half. Start below the crack with a bushy sapling at 5m. Climb the crack through the bulges, trending right past blocks to follow the right-hand cracks diagonally up right, with brief excursions onto the right wall. Join Spirit Air at the white shield and finish up this (or take the diagonal crack going left to join Arial).

Arial   50m   E3 5c ***
K.Howett, G.Ridge, J.Horrocks   30 May 1992
An excellent route which gives sustained and strenuous climbing up the fine crack-line up the centre of the impending wall immediately below the abseil point. Start as for Destitution Man. Climb the crack past the sapling and through a bulge, then continue directly. The crack-line becomes more defined, then bends right into a jagged flake-crack. Continue in the same direct line, up a shallow groove in the centre of the face, passing just right of the big holly in the diagonal fault to the holly forest at the top.

Carnmore Area

The Letterewe Forest, commonly known by climbers as Carnmore after its most famous crag, has some of the best climbing and wild walking in the Northern Highlands. The distances can be quite large; indeed, the mountain frequently cited as being the most remote Munro summit is within this area. A good idea is to plan a long weekend (or more); the approach effectively takes half a day.

The Carnmore area is actively used for stalking between 15th September to 15th November and visitors may find access restricted during this period. There is no stalking on weekends. The owners have recently re-roofed the barn at Carnmore and a sign states, "Walkers and climbers are welcome to use the barn".

Approach: The usual approach to the barn is from Poolewe via Kernsary, a walk of about 4hrs. The approach is shorter if one starts by cycling from Poolewe to Kernsary and along the vehicle tracks beyond it. Go past Kernsary and along the track leading east to a fork by a plantation. Go right through the plantation for just over 1km to where a path leaves on the right (cairns). Follow this path to the edge of the plantation and on across moorland above the Allt na Creige. This is a new path, at a higher level than that shown on the current map and provides easy walking on a good hard surface all the way to Carnmore. Continue along the path south-east to the foot of Srathan Buidhe and cross the stream in this narrow glen to follow the path as it drops below the North-East face of Meall Mheinnidh towards Fionn Loch. Cross the causeway to Carnmore.

CARNMORE CRAG

(NG 980 775)   Alt 350m   South-West facing   Map p352   Diagram p376

The outlying shoulders of the flat topped Beinn a' Chaisgean Mor (857m) drop away steeply to form Carnmore Crag. Unimpressive from a distance, its scale and ferocity only grow apparent to the climber drawing near to Carnmore Lodge. It is one of the few major Scottish crags to catch the sun for most of the day, and generally dries quickly after rain. The cliff is mostly solid pale gneiss – rough and gnarled, and, at its most accommodating, eroded into pockets, buckets, and letter box slots. The most popular routes are Fionn Buttress, Dragon, and Gob, and it is worth bearing in mind that all three contain very exposed traverses – not recommended for inexperienced seconds.

Descent: Either to east or west. The west descent is probably the least knee jarring. There will usually be short damp sections except during a dry spell. Traverse well over from the top of the crag and descend an easy gully system to grass slopes. It is important not to start descending too soon. The east descent lies down the grassy slopes of the ravine. A big gully compels a slight ascent from the top of the crag, over a couple of rocky crests, before descent of vague paths overlooking the ravine. Lower down either cut back west to the base of the crag, or continue down into the lower reaches of the ravine.

The crag is roughly C- shaped, the Lower Wall and Upper Wall being divided by the grassy Central Bay, with Fionn Buttress forming the left-hand upright.

FIONN BUTTRESS

This is the massive nose forming the most continuous piece of rock on the crag. It is climbed by the following superb long route.

1 Fionn Buttress   240m   VS *
M.J.O'Hara, W.D.Blackwood   7 Apr 1957
Although initially vegetated, this route unfolds to give an exposed and varied climb on perfect rock. Harder climbers may be disappointed because the pitches don't match Dragon or Gob but a great mountaineering experience for the VS leader. Start from the highest point of the heather in a bay under the Great Chimney, at the base of a steep, clean slabby wall capped by a prominent roof.
1. 30m 4b Start up the right of the slabby wall for a short way. Traverse right into a corner, climb its right wall and go round onto a ledge. Climb the crack in the wall on the right for 3m then step right onto a slab. Cross this and belay at a chockstone in the chimney beyond.
2. 25m 4a Go up the right wall and then grass trending right. Climb a flake leaning against grey slabs to its top.
3. 15m 4c Climb the slab, then left to a ledge and back right as high as possible for 2m. Then go up to an overhung ledge.
4. 25m 4c Go left to a recess (usually wet) with large bollards. Go up the wet red corner above to a grass recess.

N-W GNEISS

5. 25m 5a Go up corners or walls above to reach the prominent overhang which is surmounted by sensational moves 3m from its right end (crux). Move right above to a stance.

6. 25m 4b Traverse right across the face to a stance on the true nose of the buttress.

7. 20m 4b Gain a flake up on the left by a steep groove above the belay. Above it move a little left, then go up right.

8. 20m 4a Follow the slabs above on the crest to reach a niche.

9. 20m 4a Go up the crest to a heather ledge and perched blocks below an overhanging slab.

10. 20m 4b Climb over the blocks and go up the slab on to a shelf. Move right to its top corner.

11. 20m 4a Finish up the wall above and then left to the top.

LOWER WALL

This is the extensive band of rock below the level of the Central Bay, and includes all the rock to the right of Fionn Buttress. The main landmarks are two broad ribs, the First and Second Ribs. Both are prominent in the morning light and both merge into slabs higher up. The First (left-hand) Rib is bounded on the left by a prominent curving red fault, The Red Scar. The Second Rib has a prominent yellow scar right of its base, bounded on the right by the very steep and obvious recess of Balaton. This has a prominent vertical black streak on its right wall. Right of this is a more vegetated area and right again the distinct shield of overlapping slab and wall is taken by Penny Lane and Strawberry Fields. The Lower Wall routes generally boast some good steep climbing, followed by pleasant slabs which peter out in the Central Bay.

2 Black Mischief   130m   VS *
B.E.H.Maden, R.D.Sykes   19 Jun 1966

An enjoyable climb and a useful preamble to Gob. Between the First and Second Ribs is a recessed area of cliff with a heathery bay. Start at the foot of an obvious black groove at the top right corner of the heather bay. This groove is capped on the right by a conspicuous square-cut overhang.

1. 25m 4c Ascend easily to the first bulge in the groove proper and surmount this on the right. Continue up the groove past another bulge and exit left to a stance.

2. 25m 4b Climb up right where the groove steepens at 6m; good spike. Move delicately right under a bulge onto a slab. Traverse diagonally across this to a conspicuous ledge on the skyline. Climb the crack above and exit right with difficulty onto a grass ledge level with and to the right of the square-cut overhang.

3. 20m 4c Climb the cracked wall above, (hard above a good ledge at half-height on the right). Continue more easily to large ledges.

4, etc. 60m Easier climbing leads to the Central Bay.

3 Balaton   105m   HVS **
W.Gorman, C.Higgins   May 1966

Takes the very steep crack at the right side of the recess right of the Second Rib (and yellow scar), then traverses left under a roof to climb the obvious big corner-line at the back of the recess. This is the best line on the Lower Wall, making a fine combination with Dragon.

1. 25m 5a Climb the crack to a belay on the right.

2. 10m 5b Descend a little, step across a crack, and traverse a steep band of slab to belay at the foot of the large corner.

3. 35m 4c Climb the corner to a slab, traverse right, turn an overhang, then move up left to below a big roof. Break out right, then go up to a stance and belay.

4. 45m Move up and left of a rib on the skyline, then continue by slabs to the Central Bay.

Balaton, HVS 5b, Carnmore Crag. Climber Graeme Ettle
(photo John Lyall)

Variation: **E1 5b**
3a. More sustained but still good quality. Where the route goes right, continue direct up the groove, then join the original route below the big roof.

The remaining two routes on the Lower Wall lie on a distinctive pale shield of overlapping wall and slab. This is separated from the scrappy vegetated area by a grassy rake which curves up left as a steep fault.

4 Penny Lane   70m   HVS **
R.J.Isherwood, E.Birch   Jun 1967
Gain the grass rake by grassy slabs or an easy traverse from the right. Belay up at the left end of the rake. The route traverses right along the steep wall under a roof.
1. 30m 5a Traverse right along a big flake and continue traversing above a lower roof to go round the corner into the central groove.
2. 25m 4b Go diagonally left under the top overlap and climb over it into a groove.
3. 15m Finish right up slabs to the grassy Gangway.

5 Strawberry Fields   45m   HVS *
G.Macnair, R.Jones   Jun 1967
Start near the right end of the grass rake below a black corner going up to a large roof.
1. 25m 5b Climb the wall on the left of the corner for a few metres, traverse into the corner and climb up to the roof. Move left and go up on quartz to a second smaller roof. Step right onto the arete and go up to a stance.
2. 25m 4b Climb the slabs above trending left to a bulge. Climb this into a grassy crack and go up slabs to easy ground.

Central Bay

The Central Bay is an area of heathery slopes and scraps of slab. Great care is needed in wet conditions. Apart from approaches via the Lower Wall routes, access or exit can be most easily made either by the Gangway (a series of exposed ledges and steps running from the right, passing above the pale shield of rock containing Penny Lane), or by broken ground to the right (facing up) of a slabby ramp which runs from near the base of Carnmore Corner up rightwards under The Orange Bow to the cliff-top. This is also exposed and rather loose (Moderate), but the best way back into the bay from the cliff-top. Access for a second route on the Upper Wall is possible by making a largely free 50m abseil down the line of Red Crack (the top of Carnmore Corner is easily found from above on account of the springs) landing on slabs just right of the easy traverse left on pitch 1 of Gob. From here it is 20m of easy down climbing to the true start of Gob and access to other routes.

Upper Wall

The very steep upper band of the crag provides fine climbing with considerable exposure. Its left wall is bounded by the out thrust nose of Fionn Buttress. To the right its height gradually dwindles. The most obvious features are: A big corner set into Fionn Buttress and running up to the great roof above the Dragon Slab **Green Corner** (VS 4c); A pale easy angled slab at the bottom left. Dragon climbs the slab to the top right corner then takes cracks up the wall above, to the right of a towering corner system; A great roof roughly halfway up the central wall and descending slightly from left to right. Gob climbs up to traverse under this roof from right to left and the unmistakable Carnmore Corner, to the right. There are twin cracks in the back and it is usually wet. Its scale is diminished by a tongue of scrappy terrain extending up from the bay. The jutting right arete is taken by The Orange Bow.

6 Fian Grooves   110m   E3 *
T.Rankin, G.Robertson   4 Jun 2000
An excellent route based on the bulging arete immediately left of the big corner

set into Fionn Buttress (Green Corner). Start at the base of the corner.
1. 45m 5c Go left into an obvious clean groove and follow this to an overhang. Swing out left along a handrail and pull round the left end of the overhang into another groove. Move up the wall on the left, then back right to a crack which is followed to an awkward mantelshelf. Continue straight up the crest to the base of a corner. A fantastic pitch.
2. 20m 4b Climb the corner with surprising ease to a terrace and junction with Green Corner.
3. 20m 5c Above is a shallow leaning groove. Gain this from the left, then follow it to step left to belay.
4. 25m 5a Go directly across a ramp behind to enter and climb a constricted groove to easier ground.

7 Death-Wolf   110m   E6 **
G.Livingston, D.Dinwoodie   9 Aug 1986
There are two flake gangways cutting through the great roof above Dragon Slab. This route takes the right-hand one, then climbs the steep wall above, trending right then left. A very strenuous undertaking, climbed over two days, a nut being left in place overnight at the lip.
1. 40m Climb the Dragon slab to its top, then traverse 10m left from the left end of the narrow ledge to a peg belay under the gangway. (This could be reached by a direct ascent of the slab).
2. 30m 6b There is no rest on this pitch until 10m above the roof. (The gangway is often wet lower down but this can be avoided on the outside). Climb the gangway out over the lip of the roof, into a little scoop with a hidden sidepull in a crack. Go straight up the wall to a flaky jug then move right and up onto a resting ledge. Climb the little arete and groove above to a belay ledge close to the right arete.
3. 25m 6a From the right end of the ledge move up and across left, then up left to gain isolated knobbles. Traverse right by a thin horizontal crack to gain better holds and pull out right to easy ground. Move up left to the left end of a big heather ledge.
4. 15m 5c Climb the wall above the belay (unprotected for some distance), veering left under an obvious scooped groove and up the wall to the top.

8 Abomination   100m   HVS **
J.McLean, A.Currey, J.Cunningham   22 Jul 1966
There is a towering corner system formed where the bulging wall of Death-Wolf thrusts out from the main wall. Abomination takes the obvious plummeting groove in the undercut sidewall. Although intimidating, it is not as hard as it looks. A fine climb.
1. 35m Climb the Dragon slab rightwards to its top.
2. 35m 5b From the ledge climb the right-hand groove for a few metres, then step left and climb the hanging crack for 20m to a ledge. Climb the crack on the right with increasing difficulty to a sloping ledge.
3. 30m 4c Continue up the groove to a ledge; climb a chimney to below a square-cut roof; move right and up a slab on loose flakes to the top.

9 Dragon   95m   HVS ****
G.J.Fraser, M.J.O'Hara   22 Apr 1957
The classic original route on the Upper Wall, high in its grade and much harder then Gob. Superbly exposed, it takes an improbable line and is not for nervous seconds. Mike O'Hara thinks E1, but a majority say not. Above and right of the big corner system is a huge jutting triangular roof. Dragon takes obvious cracks right of the main corners to turn the roof on the left. Start at the base of the pale grey slab.
1. 35m 4b Climb to a grass patch then trend right up the slab to belay on a narrow ledge under the main wall. (Alternatively, the slab can be missed out by climbing a short chossy groove at the top of the right retaining wall).
2. 35m 4c Climb a groove for 5m, passing the small roof which fills it, on the right. Traverse left out of the cracks a short distance above the roof to gain easier grooves. Pedestal belay 9m up on the right.

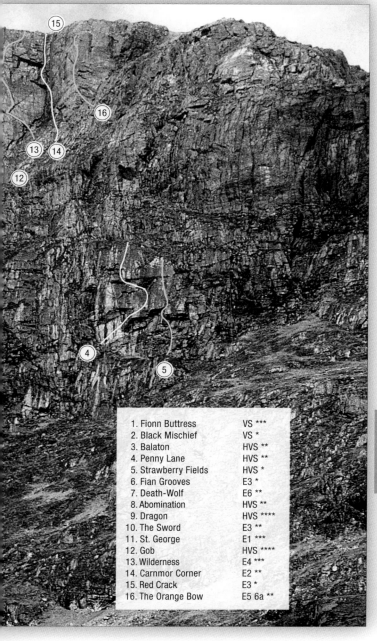

1. Fionn Buttress   VS ***
2. Black Mischief   VS *
3. Balaton   HVS **
4. Penny Lane   HVS **
5. Strawberry Fields   HVS *
6. Fian Grooves   E3 *
7. Death-Wolf   E6 **
8. Abomination   HVS **
9. Dragon   HVS ****
10. The Sword   E3 **
11. St. George   E1 ***
12. Gob   HVS ****
13. Wilderness   E4 ***
14. Carnmor Corner   E2 **
15. Red Crack   E3 *
16. The Orange Bow   E5 6a **

3. 15m 5a Climb a steep short wall to reach a yellow chimney up on the left. Climb this and exit left at the top to a tiny perch under the great roof. Traverse the steep wall on the left to belay in a little bay. (Seconds falling from the traverse might have to prussik!).

4. 10m Traverse round left and up to the top.

10 The Sword 80m E3 **

R.J.Isherwood, E.Birch   Jun 1967 (3PA); FFA: G.Duckworth and party   1980

An atmospheric and very direct route taking the big groove above the cave right of the Dragon Wall. One of the best natural lines at Carnmore, but with some poor rock. Start at the right end of the ledge above Dragon Slab.

1. 35m 5c Traverse right for about 3m on the lip of the overhang, then climb up and right to gain the main groove. Climb the groove to a small stance at the Swallow's Nest of Gob. Alternatively, use the original start (5c): Climb the wall for about 5m, then traverse right to the arete. Continue delicately down and right across a steep slab, then right and up to reach the main groove.

2. 20m 6a Climb up and right through the steep break in the roof to gain the rib and go up to a stance.

3. 25m Climb the shallow groove above to the top, the original finish of Gob.

11 St. George 90m E1 ***

A.G.Cram, R.Schipper   28 May 1967

This route takes the fine steep crack-line in the wall right of the cave of Sword.

1. 20m 5b Climb a short wall to the foot of the crack, which has an overhang at 8m. Climb the groove to the overhang. Pull round this into a sentry box and climb the wall on the left to a superb stance on top of a big doubtful flake.

2. 40m 5a Climb the groove for 6m, then traverse left to another obvious groove. Go up this for 8m, traverse left round the arete to join The Sword, and climb up to the Swallow's Nest under the roof. Now joining Gob, move left to a pulpit belay.

3. 35m 4c Take the obvious break right through the roof. Finish direct up the left-slanting fault.

12 Gob 110m HVS ****

D.Haston, R.Smith   Apr 1960

The line of least resistance on the Upper Wall, snaking left under the main roof to find a break. A classic, with all the best that Carnmore has to offer, huge holds and tremendous exposure. VS climbing in an impressive position and comparable in difficulty to Dream of White Horses at Gogarth. Start at the right end of the main face, where the Central Bay begins to rise up into the base of Carnmore Corner.

1. 30m 4c Traverse left along an overhung ledge to a break in the overhang; go up right and climb a shallow corner to a belay.

2. 45m 4c Traverse away left by the easiest line under the great roof to negotiate an out thrust shield of rock (the Swallow's Nest) where The Sword and St. George come up from below. Continue the traverse to a good pulpit belay not far right from Dragon's pedestal.

3. 35m 4c Take the obvious break up and right through the roof. Finish direct up the left-slanting fault, or:

3a. 45m 4c The original finish. After going right through the roof traverse away right to finish up a steep corner.

13 Wilderness 80m E4 ***

M.Lawrence, D.Mullin   May 1980

A diagonal crack-line (unclimbed) cuts across both walls of Carnmore Corner. **Jivaro Crack** (E4) is the thinner crack running vertically above the diagonal one on the left wall; this route climbs the wall to its left on immaculate rock. It was climbed on-sight and has had few repeat ascents. Start by scrambling up to an obvious diagonal break running up left.

1. 20m 5c Climb the break, which has an awkward bulging start.

2. 35m 6a Go up the diagonal crack a short way, then traverse horizontally left on

jugs to the base of a thin crack. Climb this, then go straight up into a groove sys-tem which is followed out left to a scoop. Step across the scoop on to the arete and follow this past twin cracks to a ledge and belay at the base of a corner.
3. 25m 5a Climb the corner, right of the original finish of Gob.

14 Carnmore Corner   65m   E2 *
R.Carrington, J.R.Jackson   19 Jun 1968 (1PA); FFA: R.Perriment, A.Hodges   1975
There is a spring in the hollow at the top of this climb so a lengthy spell of good weather is needed for it to dry up. Although relatively short, the Corner is a route of some character; steep and intimidating. The obvious direct start is nearly always wet and slimy so the route starts to the right before moving left into the corner. A curving fault with two recesses undercuts the right wall. Start below and left of the lower one.
1. 40m 5b Climb slabby rocks up and left, then go up steeply into a niche just up left from the second recess (old pegs). Go straight up for a short way, then quit the crack-line to follow a diagonal line, starting as a small ramp leading up left into the corner. Belay below the big overhang.
2. 25m 5a Move left, up and delicately back right and finish up an easier crack.
Variation: **Direct Start   50m   E3 5c ***
G.Latter, L.Arnott   22 Jul 1997
A brilliant varied pitch, though one of the last routes to dry on the cliff. Start at some horizontal pockets high on the slab, about 8m above the start of Wilderness. Climb the corner and hand-traverse right on a large block at its top to gain the nor-mal route. Continue up this, then direct up an awkward hand crack (wet) to finish up the easier final corner.

15 Red Crack   65m   E3 *
D.Dinwoodie, A.Nisbet   21 May 1988
Climbs the right-hand crack-line all the way. It is quicker drying than the corner.
1. 20m 5a Climb Carnmore Corner to a belay in the niche.
2. 45m 6a Continue straight up the crack-line to a resting place at a niche under a big bulge. Climb the bulge (crux) and follow the easier fault to the top.

16 The Orange Bow   35m   E5 6a *
D.Dinwoodie, D.Hawthorn   16 Jun 1985
The impressive arete right of Carnmore Corner. Start at ledges up on the right. Traverse out left along a slabby shelf and negotiate a tricky bulge to move up left to big footholds under the bulging edge. Swing out left on flakes and climb a vague intermittent crack-line up the overhanging wall for 10m to good runners before the crack peters out. Traverse right and up slightly for 5m to gain the edge and a rest. Climb up the edge, as the angle eases, and finish up the left-slanting crack.
Variation: **Left-Hand Start   25m   E5 6b ***
D.Dinwoodie, A.Nisbet   22 May 1988
This good pitch gives the route some length, but is probably harder than the edge itself. Start below and left of the first recess of the curving fault undercutting the right wall of the Corner. Move up to the recess and swing up right on to a plat-form. Go up onto a bulging wall, swing left and up to a resting place. Peg runner on the right. Pull up to a good pocket, move up left to a flake, then make a hard move across right to jugs. Poor peg runner. Climb straight up the wall to gain a hor-izontal fault and a resting place. Traverse right and slightly down to a flake-crack and hanging belay (peg above) under the 'vague crack' of the edge pitch.

N-W GNEISS

MAIDEN BUTTRESS

(NH 001 762)   Alt 500m   South-West facing   Map p352   Diagram p380

This is a small but well formed mass of rock on the south-east side of Carnan Ban. Climbing on the buttress is pleasant due to immaculate rock and a sunny aspect. Most of the climbs have one or two difficult pitches at the start, then become eas-ier. The rock is good clean gneiss. It is visible from the Dubh Loch causeway, but is

MAIDEN BUTTRESS

1. Ecstasy	Severe ***
2. Sleeping Beauty	VS *
3. Dishonour	Very Difficult **
4. Tweedledum	Severe

more or less concealed in the small basin that holds Fuar Loch Beag. It is well seen from the lower part of the north-west ridge of A' Mhaighdean, the path up which passes above the opposite shore of the lochan.

Approach: Access is easy from Carnmore by the Shenavall path to just beyond the zigzag, then across the ravine and up to the col, passing beneath the Barndance Slabs. The buttress is visible across the lochan from this col.

1 Ecstasy   95m   Severe ***
M.J.O'Hara, R.E.Kendell   20 Aug 1955
A climb of particular quality. Start at the foot of the first rib to the left of the bottom left corner of the buttress. The rib widens rapidly upwards into a V of slab bounded by vertical walls.
1. 30m Go up the left edge of the slab for 14m, well past an obvious diagonal finger crack, then swing out right on to an ascending hand-traverse. Follow it past an obvious niche above, go round a rib, then climb a small slab and corner to gain a large ledge and block.
2. 15m Go up the slab above, first right then back left above an overhang to reach and climb a groove.
3. 30m Continue easily up the buttress edge to below a steeper slab.

4. 20m Climb the slab, first delicately right, then left and up the edge.

2 Sleeping Beauty   110m   VS *
A.Nisbet 8 Aug 2001
Right of the prominent V-slab of Ecstasy is a recessed inverted V. This route climbs the right corner of the V, then the crack-line above. Start from the first platform left of the bottom left corner of the buttress.
1. 25m 4b Climb the corner to a ledge below a vertical section with a small overhang.
2. 20m 4c Climb this vertical section leading to the top of the V, then the crack-line above to a big ledge.
3. 20m 4b Climb the crack above, initially overhanging.
4. 45m 4a Continue up the crack over two steep sections.

3 Dishonour   115m   Very Difficult **
M.J.O'Hara, Miss M.M.Langmuir 10 Apr 1955
A close second to Ecstasy in terms of quality. Start at the foot of the left edge of the front face of the buttress.
1. 20m Climb the slab up the left edge to a steeper wall. Belay to the right.
2. 20m Move around the edge onto a large flake, then step back right onto the front face and climb to a small ledge in a niche. (A harder alternative is to climb the wall direct.) Continue straight up the slab to a ledge with a large perched block.
3. 25m Move up right into an easy chimney, climb this then go diagonally left to a ledge under an overhang.
4. 25m Go up right then back left above the overhang, then straight up a narrowing groove to a ledge. Take a groove on the right to reach a large terrace.
5. 25m Climb just right of twin cracks in the wall above and up a second wall by a crack to easy ground.

4 Tweedledum   115m   Severe
R.E.Kendell, M.J.O'Hara 19 Aug 1955
Start 5m right of Dishonour.
1. 20m Climb the slab between two vegetated cracks and belay on the left below a steeper wall.
2. 10m Move right to the overhang and climb it on the right. Belay in a niche on the left.
3. 20m Climb the rib on the right then a chimney on its right.
4. 20m Continue up the chimney.
5. 20m Traverse left on ledges above overhangs, then go up the broad scoop. Climb a short V-groove to a large terrace.
5. 25m Climb easily on the left of the central turfy gully, finishing up a steep 'boulder problem' wall on good holds.

Gruinard Crags

Map p352
The numerous crags within the areas bounded by Gruinard Bay offer some excellent and easily accessible climbing. Unless already local, the north approach through Dundonnell is quicker because of faster roads. The rock is typical gneiss, generally rough and with good protection cracks. Since many of the crags are on isolated summits, there is limited drainage and most routes dry very quickly after rain; occasional wet holds tend not to affect the grade. Though most of the outcrops, apart from the impressive Lochan Dubh Crag, are short, the view over the bay makes it a lovely place to climb. Three kilometres to the north is the roadside Jetty Buttress. Like many crags in the area, locals such as Dave Neville and Jon Robinson climbed here before John Mackenzie and Bob Brown rediscovered them, soon to be followed by Rab and Chris Anderson who climbed many of the harder lines. Most notable are the outstanding Major Domo and Dead Calm (both E6) on Lochan Dubh Crag.

N-W GNEISS

GRUINARD CRAG

(NG 957 900)   Alt 110m   North-West facing

This crag, which is both bigger and better than it looks, is well seen from the road 300m north of the car park but not from the car park itself. Not to be confused with Inveranvie Crag which is more easily seen and well to the right, nearer Inveranvie River.

Approach: It is best reached by skirting leftwards across the knoll directly behind the Gruinard Bay car park (NG 952 900). Cross the fence at the left end of the car park and follow the fence up, then left. Where the fence runs horizontal, make a slightly rising traverse leftwards and the crag soon comes into view, 15mins. Lochan Dubh Crag can be easily reached from Gruinard Crag by curving up right from its base (the profile of Lochan Dubh Crag appears very soon) and following a flat area (marked on the map) south-eastwards.

LOWER CRAG

A smaller smooth wall with a big flake on its left side.

**1 Halcyon Days   20m   VS 4c ** *
R.Brown, J.R.Mackenzie   14 May 1994
The recessed break on the left has a prominent flake forming its right edge. Layback the flake to a large jug. Step right on to the blank looking wall which is covered in holds and either exit easily right up a heathery groove or, better but harder, finish up the steep slab on its left.

**2 Utopia   15m   HVS 5b *
R.Mackenzie, R.Brown   14 May 1994
This is the thin vertical crack near the right edge. Climb the wall right of the lower crack, trending left to join the crack at half-height and finish up it.

UPPER CRAG

Steep and exhilarating climbing, often easier than it looks and generally well protected. Some lines have a a bit of heather higher up but this is a minor blemish.

Descent: Unpleasant – abseiling might be preferred. Descend diagonally rightwards (south) down a steep vegetated ramp until near the base, then cut back left.

**3 Paradise Regained   50m   E1 ** *
J.R.Mackenzie, R.Brown   23 May 1994
The open chimney on the left side of the crag with a holly tree at its base. Sustained but varied climbing with a bold section; high in the grade.
1. 30m 5b Climb the rib just left of the holly and step right into the groove above. Climb the groove and short chimney to a hard mantelshelf onto the ledge on the right. Step right and back left climb a scoop to an easing. Move 2m left to a blunt rib and climb a short crack, then continue slightly leftwards up the slab to a pair of jammed blocks.
2. 20m 5a Climb the wall above the topmost block and follow rough rock to the nose which is passed on the right.

**4 Pistolero   25m   E3 5c ** *
R.Anderson, C.Anderson   25 May 1997
The shallow corner come groove line immediately right of Paradise Regained is **Quick on the Draw** (E5 6a). This route takes the intermittent cracks in the wall immediately right of Quick on the Draw. Better holds and protection than it looks. Climb direct by a bold slab to the left end of the roof system. Alternatively, start up The Big C for 3m and move left or the short corner of Quick on the Draw and

GRUINARD CRAG

1. Halcyon Days	VS 4c **	6. Gunslinger	E2 5b *
2. Utopia	HVS 5b *	7. Red John of the Battles	E2 5b ***
3. Paradise Regained	E1 **	8. Overlord	E1 5a **
4. Pistolero	E3 5c **	9. How the West Was Won	E4 6a **
5. The Big C	HVS 5a *	10. Stand and Deliver	E5 6a ***

383

N-W GNEISS

swing out right. Pull through the roof with difficulty; continue up the cracks above to a heather ledge. Traverse right to descend.

5 The Big C   30m   HVS 5a *
R.Brown, J.R.Mackenzie   3 May 1994
This is the central line taken through the niche. An atmospheric route with a big feel, but with a little heather. Start directly below the niche and climb a shallow corner to step left into the niche. Swing right on to the airy wall and follow the right-trending line to below a stunted holly (above and left of the more obvious holly at the top of the crack of Red John of the Battles). Climb up to the tree and step right. Climb a crack above and finish by a sporting mantel to its right.

6 Gunslinger   25m   E2 5b *
G.Ettle, J.Preston, D.McGimpsey, P.Thorburn   30 April 2000
Climbs up to and over a protruding tongue of rock below the right end of the roof formed rightwards from Big C's niche. Climb the wall above to finish up the mantel of Big C.

7 Red John of the Battles   25m   E2 5b ***
J.R.Mackenzie, R.Brown, A.Nisbet   28 May 1994
Right of The Big C is a straight crack running up an overhanging wall. Climb this strenuously with excellent holds and runners to gain a ledge and holly. Continue slightly left to finish by the 'sporting mantel' of The Big C.

8 Overlord   25m   E1 5a **
R.Brown, J.R.Mackenzie, A.Nisbet   28 May 1994
To the right of Red John is an overhanging corner. Climb into the corner and up it to some blocks. The daunting wall above is climbed leftwards into a hidden crack and the climb finishes up a right-slanting ramp. Strenuous but very well protected.

9 How the West Was Won   25m   E4 6a **
R.Anderson, C.Anderson   27 Jul 1997
To the right of Overlord is a thin crack-line ending at hanging flake-blocks. Gain the start of the crack from a groove in the centre of the wall, pull out left on to a ledge then step right and climb the crack to where it stops. Move left, gain a ledge, then step right to climb the wall and a short slab.
Variation: E5 6b **
P.Thorburn, J.Lowther   16 Aug 1998
Go on to the flake-blocks and directly up the wall above on spaced holds and protection.

10 Stand and Deliver   25m   E5 6a ***
R.Anderson   24 May 1997
The thin crack-line up the right side of the wall right of Overlord, just left of the fissure at the right end of the crag. Sustained and generally well protected but with a sting in the tail.

LOCHAN DUBH CRAG

(NG 960 894)   Alt 140m   South facing

This high quality crag is situated in a secluded spot overlooking Lochan Dubh. It is also known as Dome Crag, although Half Dome might be more accurate, since it is dominated by an awesome overhanging wall, with more amenable ground either side.

Approach: The crag is reached from the Gruinard Bay car park (NG 952 900) by the path up the Inverianvie River, then following the stream up to Lochan Dubh. It can also be reached from the base of Gruinard Crag by a traverse curving up right and across a flat area south-eastwards to the crag which is soon seen in profile.

LOCHAN DUBH CRAG (DOME CRAG)

1. The Silk Road — E2 *
2. Call of the Wild — E3 5c **
3. Dead Calm — E6 ***
4. Major Domo — E6 ****
5. Nick the Niche — E1 5b **

N-W GNEISS

1 The Silk Road   50m   E2 *
J.R.Mackenzie, R.Brown   14 Apr 1994
Left of the main overhanging wall is a short but prominent corner, which provides a fine technical problem as the second pitch. The first pitch is up the lower over-hanging wall, starting on the right rib of a slight recess in the centre of the wall (5a up the recess, an alternative).
1. 20m 5b Climb up steep orange rock to a bulge. Move right round the bulge and back left on to its top. Continue up easier rough rock to a smooth corner.
2. 10m 5c Climb the smooth corner to mantel onto the airy slab on the right.
3. 20m Pull over the bulge on the right and climb rough rock to the top.

2 Call of the Wild   50m   E3 5c **
M.E.Moran, M.Welch   28 Apr 1995
Climbs the left-hand weakness of the central wall. A committing start but the tech-nical crux through the roof is well protected. From an ivy filled recess (well below the main ivy) pull over the roof to the right on a large loose looking flake, and climb the impending wall to a resting ledge. Layback through the flaked roof above, and swing left to easier ground and belays (35m). Easy scrambling to the top (15m).
Variation Start: **E4 6a**
G.Latter, P.Thorburn   12 May 1996
Provides a very sustained route. Start up Dead Calm, then trend left above the low roof and up the wall to the resting ledge.

3 Dead Calm   50m   E6 ***
R.Anderson, C.Anderson   6 Aug 1995
The obvious discontinuous crack-line in the centre of the wall provides a stunning route.
1. 30m 6b Follow the line past a blankish section to an easing and continue up bulging rock above to easier ground where moves up, then left gain a large niche.
2. 20m 4c Climb up rightwards and follow the best line to the top.

4 Major Domo   50m   E6 ****
R.Anderson, C.Anderson   3 Aug 1995
The striking niched crack-line up the right side of the overhanging wall provides a tremendous climb. Well protected with as many small wires as you can muster. Originally redpointed, it has seen very few flashed ascents.
1. 25m 6b Climb the niched crack-line to a ledge (knee lock rest at half-height).
2. 25m 5b An easy groove slants up left. Climb the buttress on the right via a cen-tral line which trends left and up to a ledge. Climb a juggy crack in the final short wall to reach a platform.

5 Nick the Niche   45m   E1 5b **
J.Robinson, D.Neville   1989; As described A.Andrew, M.E.Moran   26 May 1995
This excellent route follows the first line of weakness right of the overhanging wall. To the right of the overhanging wall is an easy angled corner topped by a large block. Start up the corner, step right and climb to a small ledge. The overhanging wall above is split by a thin twin cracks. Climb the wall immediately on their right and gain a large niche (possible belay). Climb the crack out of the top left corner of the niche (crux) to easier ground.

JETTY BUTTRESS

(NG 961 926)   Alt 30m   Varying aspects   Map p352   Diagram p388
This gneiss crag is generally rough but smooth on some of the steep walls and

N-W GNEISS

The Silk Road, E2 5c, Lochan Dubh Crag. Climber Jason Walker
(photo Chris Cartwright)

388

JETTY BUTTRESS

1. Route Major   Hard Severe 4b *
2. Route 6   Hard Severe 4a **
3. Munroron   Very Difficult *
4. Lilly the Pink   Hard Severe 4a *
5. North-West Arete   HVS 5a *
6. Crab Crack   HVS 5a *
7. Anthrax Flake   VS 4c **
8. Charlie's Corner   VS 4b **

definitely roadside. The rock dries quickly and the wide range of grades and easy access makes it a popular crag. It has a much longer history than others in the area. The first recorded visit was by J.H.B.Bell in 1946 when he climbed Lilly the Pink, though it's doubtful whether he would have approved of the subsequent name. Kinloss MRT members climbed here in the '60s, also Tom Patey, but the buttress was only written up in the '70s by Joint Services Mountain Training Centre parties based at Dundonnell. Dundonnell MRT members have also climbed here for many years (Right Charlie) and more recently the remaining harder lines have been climbed by John Mackenzie and Paul Tattersall.

Approach: It is very easily seen only 50m inland from the road. Park on the verge, 30 seconds!

Descent: The easiest descent is over the top of and down beside the North Wall.

NORTH WALL

The wall at the top left of the crag.

1 Route Major   20m   Hard Severe 4b *
Good but a little scary. Start approximately 8m below (towards the road) the bottom post at the start of the fallen fence where there is pale rock leading to a grey concave slab. Climb a small corner (another corner 2m right is harder), then move right and pull over a small pale wall using an embedded flake. Gain and climb the grey slab (poorly protected) passing its headwall on the left. Finish up the slabby final wall. Climbing the headwall direct is unprotected 4c.

2 Route 6   20m   Hard Severe 4a **
An intimidating wall, but the holds are good. Start two-thirds of the way down the North Wall by a small black cave, an obvious feature. Climb the wall just right of the cave (perhaps 4b), then step down and left across its top on to the impressive wall. Trend left to a small groove in the centre of the wall. Climb the groove, then a diagonal crack rightwards. Return left to finish.

3 Munroron   30m   Very Difficult *
Climb the centre of a thin bottle shaped rib, an easier angled line above the pink rock of Lilly The Pink. Finish up the clean continuation slab on the left. Nice climbing on the rib, although it is easy to step off.

4 Lilly the Pink   30m   Hard Severe 4a *
J.H.B. and Mrs. Bell   Aug 1946
A fine open climb. Start to the left of the north-west arete in a depression. Follow the red quartzy rock up the centre of the depression and continue on clean slabs to the top.

5 North-West Arete   35m   HVS 5a *
A little disappointing for such an obvious line. Climb the well defined crest, tenuous at first, between the North and Front West Wall, then directly up the slabby ground above.

FRONT WEST WALL

The frontal face.

6 Crab Crack   35m   HVS 5a *
A good start but quickly over. Start 5m right of the arete. Climb to a heather ledge at 3m (would be better if cleaned, or start to the right). Step right and climb a thin crack with a bulge at mid-height to reach slabby ground. Climb a scoop on the right to join North-West Arete. Another crack just to the right is VS 4c but a little overgrown.

N-W GNEISS

7 Anthrax Flake 25m VS 4c **

The classic of the crag, with some strenuous moves up the flake. Start in the centre of the wall, 5m right of a shallow right-slanting ramp, at the right side of a black depression. Climb pale coloured rock up to prominent flake-cracks and a large detached flake. Climb the left edge of the flake to its top, then finish direct.

8 Charlie's Corner 25m VS 4b **

Another fine route, strenuous but good holds and protection. Start at the obvious corner to the right of Anthrax Flake by a wall and tree. Climb the corner to a ledge on the left. Continue up to the left of the main crack, then step back right into the crack above an overhang (which can be climbed direct at HVS 5a, but overgrown with ivy).

9 Right Charlie 20m E2 5c **

F.Fotheringham, J.Robinson 1980s

The best of the harder routes; well protected. Start 8m to the right of Charlie's Corner. Pull though the initial bulge with difficulty and climb a short corner. Move left on a hollow flake and up to the big ledge above. Step right to a shallow corner directly above the start. Climb this, step left and finish directly up the obvious crack above (ignoring an escape left).

10 Gaffers Wall 25m E3 *

J.R.Mackenzie, R.Biggar 16 May 1999

Between Right Charlie and a crack and corner to the right is an overhanging wall providing an excellent steep route. Start 3m right of Right Charlie.
1. 10m 5b Surmount the initial overhang and step left on to a shelf. Climb up to and over a slanting flake-crack to gain the ledge just right of Right Charlie.
2. 15m 5c Climb up the shallow fault above, parallel with Right Charlie.

Short West Wall

Right of the arete is a south facing wall with some easier routes, then a smaller west facing wall with chimneys, trees and the following route at its right side.

11 Starwood 20m HVS 5a **

A crack immediately left of the arete and with a small tree growing 2m up. Fight the tree and climb the crack with an innocuous move at the top to a ledge (possible belay). Climb the back wall to a triangular block, trending right on to a large flake on the arete and then up the edge of the south wall and back onto the arete to finish in an excellent position.

BACK WEST WALL

After a second south facing wall is this steep smooth wall.

12 Gogmagog 20m E5 6a **

P.Tattersall, A.Katzenmeier May 1998

An impressive route up the clean left side of the wall, very bold until past the lower roof, with good but spaced protection above. Climb up to the big grassy tree filled ledge. Climb the centre of the wall above, going directly up to a small slanting roof, which is climbed at its lower right-hand end. Move up and right towards a big detached flake but avoid this by staying to the wall to its left to reach a good ledge. Boldly climb the vague cracked seam on the right on improving holds.

Major Domo, E6 6b, Lochan Dubh Crag. Climber Niall McNair
(photo Cubby Images)

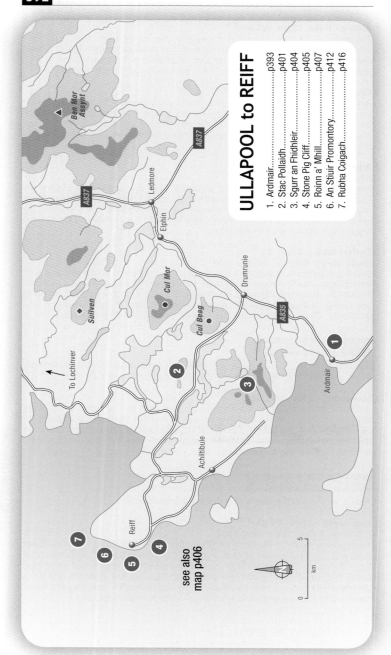

ULLAPOOL to REIFF

Ben Mor Assynt

A837

A837

Ledmore

Elphin

Cul Mor

Suilven

Cul Beag

Drumrunie

A835

To Lochinver

Achiltibuie

Reiff

Ardmair

see also map p406

N

0 ——— 5
km

ULLAPOOL TO REIFF

These crags and mountain cliffs of Torridonian sandstone lie in Coigach, an area best known for its distinctive and dramatically isolated hills emerging from a low gneiss moorland. North of Ullapool the first crag is the rough, almost gritstone like Ardmair Crags. Deeper into Coigach is the famous miniature mountain of Stac Pollaidh and the classic Nose of Sgurr an Fhidleir, followed by the Reiff sea-cliffs whose friendly crags and excellent rock are increasingly popular. The climate is not nearly as wet as Fort William, especially the Reiff peninsula, but prone to cloud and drizzle when high pressure is located over England.

Maps: OS L15 (Ardmair on L19), E439

SMC Climbers' Guide: *Northern Highlands North* (2004)

Public Transport: Bus from Inverness to Ullapool is straightforward. Then 2 per day (one Sat) to Achiltibuie and Reiff, passing Ardmair and Coigach.

Amenities: There are Information Offices at Lochinver (seasonal, 01571 844 373) and Ullapool (01854 612 135). There is also a convenient Tourist Information Centre at Kessock in the first lay-by on the A9 just north of the Kessock Bridge, near Inverness (01463 731505).
Camping: Ardmair Point (NH 108 984), (01854 612 054); Achnahaird, near Reiff, Coigach (NC 015 137), (01854 612 135); Achmelvich, Assynt (NC 058 248), (01571 844393).
Mountaineering Huts: Naismith Hut – SMC (NC 216 118) is at Elphin; Taigh nam Famb – Grampian Speleological Group is also at Elphin.
SYHA Youth Hostels: Achininver (NC 042 056), (0870 004 1101); Achmelvich (NC 058 247), (0870 004 1102); Ullapool (NH 129 940), (0870 004 1156).
Independent Hostel: Ullapool Tourist Hostel, West Argyle Street, Ullapool (01854 613 126)
Hotels: The Fuaran Bar (Altandhu, near Reiff) is a favourite with climbers and has a live folk music programme. The Ceilidh Place, West Argyll Street, Ullapool is a popular coffee shop, also with bookshop, restaurant and live folk music.
Shops and Petrol: Ullapool has all facilities. There is a climbing shop in Ullapool, North West Outdoors, West Argyle Street (01854 613 383). Petrol at Ullapool is more expensive than Inverness, but there is none at Reiff.
Climbing Wall: A 7m wall (quite old, DR, 1990) at the Lochbroom Leisure Centre, Quay Street, Ullapool (01854 612 884).

ARDMAIR - CREAG AN UILLT GHAIRBH

(NH 117 987)   Alt 60 to 100m   South-West facing   Diagram p395, 397

These 25m high buttresses of generally good quality Torridonian sandstone are situated close to the A835 about 5km north of Ullapool, overlooking the stream draining north-west from Lochan Sgeireach into Loch Kinaird at the fish farm just beyond Ardmair. The aspect provides sun from late morning onwards and the crags dry relatively quickly after rain, apart from a few drainage lines.
    Most of the climbs follow cracks with good jamming and protection, the rock between the main cracks tending to be more inhospitable. Unless proficient on gritstone, taping the hands may prove useful on the harder routes and starting at a lower grade may allow greater appreciation of the quality of the routes.
The crags are described in the order they are approached from the road, the first routes being on the buttress seen in profile from the car park.

Approach: From a new car park below the crag (NH 115 987) follow a small path, somewhat overgrown in summer, which starts at the left end of the old road bridge and follows the left bank of the burn. The first buttress seen is scrappy with an overhanging base (no routes). Next is a long buttress (Fish Farm Walls) with several tiers separated by heather ledges and finishing with a roof high on the right before an easy gully separates it from the next buttress. Here the path takes a zigzag, leaving the burn and going to the base of the buttress below the roof. The path then traverses the hillside immediately under all the buttresses, Big Roof Buttress being the last, 15 to 25mins.

MONSTER BUTTRESS

This is the first main buttress reached after the path reaches the cliff base, beyond the long buttress with its roof. It has a small bulging buttress with short routes below its left side. The substantial main buttress is characterised by a big left-slanting fault on the left, starting out of a big recess. The rock is poorer quality here than on the other buttresses but this makes it sensationally steep. Forming the right side of the main bay is a greenish thin pillar.

Descent: Traverse right under a small upper tier until easy scrambling leads into the fault below Dancing Buttress.

1 Le Petamine   30m   HVS 5a *
A.Cunningham, K.Geddes   15 Jun 1996
Takes a ramp-line leading right out of the big left-slanting fault, with a tree near its start. Start up the left-slanting fault to its second bay, then gain the tree and climb out rightwards onto the line. Move awkwardly round a big block and finish up the top corner in a gripping position.

2 Gravity's Rainbow   25m   E1 5b **
A.Fyffe, A.Cunningham   Jul 1989
A very good route, steep and exposed, up the right side of the narrow green pillar. Climb a right-facing corner. Go up then move left under a roof, up twin cracks then go right up a ramp. Return left on to the crest of the pillar and finish up a crack.

DANCING BUTTRESS

The next buttress to the right offers pleasant generally well protected climbing and a good introduction to Ardmair, but the routes are still more strenuous and difficult than they first appear. The buttress has a very obvious flat ledge, the Dance Floor, at about three-quarters height.

Descent: From the Dance Floor, walk or crawl off rightwards. There is one quite exposed section under a roof where all fours may be the safest means of progress!

3 Moondance   20m   VS 4c *
R.Mansfield, A.Fyffe   26 May 1989
This is the deep dog-leg crack in the centre of the cracked wall. Start at a fault about 2m left of the prow. Climb the fault and the crack which springs directly from its top. When it finishes continue up a thin crack (right of a tree in a corner) to the Dance Floor.

4 Sculptress   20m   HVS 5a **
L.Healey, R.Mansfield   20 May 1989
The thin parallel cracks in the wall just left of the nose. Start just right of Moondance. Climb the right side of the wall to reach and follow twin cracks, staying just left of the nose all the way to the Dance Floor.

5 Primitive Dance   20m   E2 5b *
A.Fyffe, J.Hepburn   19 May 1989
The right-hand crack in the prow gives interesting and quite varied climbing including a wide crack. Start in the open corner in the prow. Climb the crack and follow the line up and right until able to move back left onto the beak. Climb the right-hand crack on to the Dance Floor. The slot in the overhang above and subsequent crack is a possible second pitch (10m 5a).

ARDMAIR
Monster & Dancing
Buttresses

Dancing Buttress

A

6
5
4
3

1. Le Petamine   HVS 5a *
2. Gravity's Rainbow   E1 5b **
3. Moondance   VS 4c *
4. Sculptress   HVS 5a **
5. Primitive Dance   E2 5b *
6. Just Add Lib   HVS 5a **

A. Dance Floor

Monster Buttress

2
1

ULLAPOOL

**6 Just Add Lib   20m   HVS 5a ** ✱✱
L.Healey, R.Mansfield   19 May 1989
The obvious flakes and ramp on the wall right of the nose. Start below the shallow scoop at 2m. Climb gradually steepening cracks to an obvious perched block, pull onto this and continue trending right along sloping ramps to the final shallow V-scoop. Climb this to the Dance Floor.

To the right lies the orange impending and generally inhospitable Arapiles Wall, divided from the following buttress by a steep fault full of trees.

BEAST BUTTRESS

This buttress has a steep front face with a distinctive left-slanting diagonal crack starting by a small pillar, the line of Unleash the Beast, and a slabbier left wall.

Descent: Walk right to an obvious easy way down.

7 Market Day   25m   E1 5b ✱
I.Taylor, S.Ryan   12 Apr 1988
A good route taking the pronounced scooped corner on the slabbier left wall of the buttress. Climb on to a ledge then up the large scooped corner to a small roof. Pull over this and continue more easily up the two short walls above.

8 On the Western Skyline   20m   E4 6a ✱✱
A.Cunningham, A.Fyffe   Sep 1989
Good, sustained climbing up the blunt left arete. Start on the left of the wall and climb a short awkward corner on to the edge leading to a ledge. Move right on this to a flake leading to a thread (difficult to use unless in-situ). Move up and left then back right to finish direct up the top crack of Neart nan Gaidheal.

9 Neart nan Gaidheal   20m   E5 6a ✱✱
A.Cunningham   Aug 1989
An obvious and difficult line up the left-trending thin crack left of Unleash the Beast; low in the grade. Start at a short overhanging niche and climb direct through the final bulges onto the ledge. Walk off left or finish by one of the other routes.

10 Unleash the Beast   25m   E4 6a ✱✱✱
R.Mansfield, L.Healey   19 May 1989
The obvious diagonal crack-line on the front face is strenuous, technical but very well protected. Bridge up between the pillar and the crack until a hold on the right wall allows entry into the crack. Follow the crack on jams to the large ledge. Either finish up the continuation crack or walk off to the right.

BIG ROOF BUTTRESS

The most extensive and best buttress with the unmistakable jutting nose of Burning Desire, which gives one of the finest lines in the area. The rock is generally excellent and protection is also good. However, the climbs tend to be more strenuous than they first appear, with a preponderance of flat and sloping holds. The first climbs are on the Sidewall, the left side of the buttress running uphill at right angles to the main crag.

Descent: Walk down the nearest side, the big roof being the division. From the terrace, go off right by scrambling on the uphill side of a big squat, blocky tower. There may be an in-situ thread for abseil at start of the descent on the left.

11 Acrimonious Acrobat   20m   E1 5a ✱✱✱
R.Anderson, C.Greaves   27 May 1989
A steep crack and groove where the wall reaches full height, an excellent, well

ARDMAIR
Big Roof Buttress

19. Skeletons   E3 5c, ***
20. Burning Desire   E5 6b ****
21. Space Monkey   E2 5c ***
22. Tunnel Vision   E1 5b **

23. Town Without Pity   E2 5c ***
24. Buried Treasure   E1 5b *
25. Dangerous Dancer   E3 6a **
26. Exasperated Escapologist E5 6a **

16. The Friendly Groove HVS 5b **
17. Terrace Crack   VS 4c **
18. Relax and Swing   E2 5c *

protected and sustained climb. Climb the obvious corner to the left end of a long roof, then move left into the main crack and follow it steeply to the top.

12 Twitching Twister   20m   E3 6a *
R.Anderson, T.Prentice   17 Jun 1989
Right of Acrimonious Acrobat. Climb a thin crack to the right of a large block beneath the roof. Step left and up to the break, cross the roof and continue up the groove above.

13 Convoluted Contortionist   20m   E4 6b *
R.Anderson, C.Greaves   28 May 1989
The obvious wide crack through the roof near the right of the wall, finishing up the excellent crack above, gives a thought provoking roof and jamming problem. Taping up may be considered essential! Having tried and failed miserably on the roof crack, a good 'spooky' alternative is; swing right on to flakes on the right wall and move up to hand-traverse right on a block. Pull up and left into the top crack – E3 5c.

14 Bolshie Ballerina   20m   E2 5b *
R.Anderson, C.Greaves   27 May 1989
The right-hand crack in the wall above the roof of the previous route. Start just right of Convoluted Contortionist and climb easier rock and a short fierce corner-crack above the tree to a traverse left to gain and climb the fine crack to the top.

15 Grumpy Groper   45m   E1 5b *
R.Anderson, C.Greaves   4 Jun 1989
Good climbing up the wall and slab just left of the right edge of the Sidewall. Climb a vague groove, pull over the bulge and continue to a heathery ledge via the obvious crack. Ascend the wide crack above then its continuation to reach easier ground.

The main front wall of the buttress starts with the distinctive brown Terrace Wall. This lies below a heathery platform with lots of small trees which extends right to a detached tower.

16 The Friendly Groove   40m   HVS 5b **
A.Fyffe, A.Liddell   20 May 1989
The obvious groove in the crest between the side and front walls. Generally very well protected. Climb the groove and cracks to a horizontal break, cross the roof at a crack and continue up leftwards to the top. Alternatively finish the route on the terrace by moving right above the roof.

17 Terrace Crack   15m   VS 4c **
A.Fyffe, R.Mansfield   27 May 1989
Near the right end of the wall is a fine flake-crack running up and rightwards. Climb this then move right to finish on the terrace.

18 Relax and Swing   10m   E2 5c *
A.Cunningham, R.Mansfield   3 Jun 1989
At the right end of the terrace above the tower and above some large blocks is a prominent short slanting corner with a leaning left wall. This provides some good climbing.

Beyond the tower is the roof section with its collection of fine crack, corner and groove lines which form the finest features of the cliff, pride of place going to the stunning roof crack.

Burning Desire, E5 6b, Ardmair. Climber Lawrence Hughes
(photo Cubby Images)

2 Walking on Air   60m   E5 ★★★★
R.Anderson, T.Prentice   26 Aug 1989
A tremendous route giving technical climbing up the crack-line and stepped corner splitting the main overhang. A large Friend is necessary for the belay. Start just right of a block on the ledge, below twin cracks on a very red section of the wall.
1. 30m 6a Climb the cracks with difficulty to better holds and continue until it is possible to traverse left into a crack and corner. Below the break, a scoop and rib on the right lead to a belay in the horizontal break.
2. 30m 6c Step on to the large block and climb to a triangular niche. Climb the crack with difficulty and move up awkwardly into a niche. Follow the stepped corner until it is possible to step left to finish up the wide crack.

3 Mid Flight Crisis   65m   E4 ★★★
R.Anderson, C.Anderson   2 Sep 1989
Another excellent route crossing Walking on Air from right to left. The second pitch takes the superbly situated crack on the prow, right of a hanging corner **Felo de Se** (E2 5c). Again, large Friends are required. Start at the crack-line right of Walking on Air.
1. 30m 6a Climb the right-hand of two cracks for 4m, then move left to the other crack. Continue up and right, then back left to follow the crack to the horizontal break, left of the large block.
2. 35m 6b Move up and left to an awkward right-facing corner, make hard moves left to swing into a left-facing niche. Climb the diagonal fault to a niche, old peg, pull directly up to a wedged block and climb the crack to the top. The crux can be bypassed at about 5c by traversing left at the awkward right-facing corner for 3m or so and climbing a crack to the niche.

4 Expecting to Fly   40m   E4 6a ★★★
T.Prentice   30 May 1988
A fine route with a strenuous and delicate crux in an exposed central position. It follows the grey groove and diagonal crack breaking through the band of over-hangs right of the mossy recess. Start at the upper terrace above the short rock step. Climb easy rock and flakes on the right before moving back left into the main crack-line which leads to the hanging groove below the roof; micro wires useful. Use a flake-crack to gain a bridge in the groove. Steep moves bring good layaways, which lead with difficulty to a niche. Continue up the crack.

UPPER NO.2 BUTTRESS

This is the small overhanging buttress on the right at the top of the wide gully dividing West (No.1) Buttress from the rest of the mountain on the south side.

Cold Shoulder   25m   E2 5c ★★
C.Lesenger, A.Cunningham   Jul 1996
At the right end of the buttress is a large recess. Climb the very steep crack-line out of the right side of the recess. Move left at the final bulge and back right to finish.

NO.2 BUTTRESS

Alt 500m   South-West facing
Down and right of West (No.1) Buttress, this crag presents a series of steep groove and crack-lines finishing on the right, beyond a sharp arete which forms the toe of the buttress, with the prominent corner and cracked slab of Vlad The Impaler.

Vlad the Impaler   75m   HVS ★
A.Fraser, J.Dickson   29 Sep 1985
Enjoyable crack climbing up the cracked slab and corner right of the toe of No.2 Buttress.

ULLAPOOL

1. 40m 5a Climb wide cracks up the centre, then the right side of the slab to a surprising exit to a detached summit.
2. 35m 4b At the back of the large ledge above is a twisting crack. Climb this and finish up an easy arete.

Cat on a Hot Tin Roof   60m   E3 *
A.Crofton, G.Robertson   Aug 1998
1. 40m 5c Climb the thin cracks left of Vlad the Impaler's first pitch until they join that route after 15m, then continue up Vlad to the platform.
2. 20m 5c Left of Vlad's second pitch is a prominent hanging finger crack. Climb this to a step left at the obvious foothold. Move up using the left arete before stepping back right and pulling through the bulge to the easier crack above. Sustained and well protected.

Wingless Warlock   55m   E1 *
R.Everett, D.Gaffney   9 Sep 1989; Pitch 2: T.Prentice, S.Richardson   14 May 1988
Left of the toe is an overhanging alcove (dry in the rain). Left and up is a recessed area with a big rockfall scar. Left and up again is a long wall with a raised terrace below its right end. A pinnacle can be seen above the wall. This route takes the cracked groove just left of the left end of the terrace.
1. 25m 5b An awkward steep groove and bulge leads to ledges in the main groove line. Move up to a very steep crack, then step right to a crack in the arete. Climb this and its flake-crack continuation to exit right on to a ledge.
2. 30m 5b Climb the corner above and continue by delightful cracks and corners to the very summit of the pinnacle.

SGURR AN FHIDHLEIR

(NC 094 055)   Alt 703m   Map p392
This superb pointed peak lies just north-west of Ben More Coigach and is clearly seen from the minor road from Drumrunie to Achiltibuie. The Nose of Sgurr an Fhidhleir provides a great mountain route up a dominant feature, with some easy sections and some vegetation. Dry conditions are recommended.

Approach: Park by the roadside at NC 139 068. Near the east end of Loch Lurgainn there are stepping stones just left of where a fence crosses the burn. There is also a bridge on the other side of the fence (NC 138 067). A small path leads across boggy ground to the Allt Claonaidh to follow its south bank to Lochan Tuath below Sgurr an Fhidhleir. There may be restrictions during the stalking season (see Environment Notes).

Descent: From the summit descend to the col to the south and then north-east down slopes towards Lochan Tuath.

The Nose of the Fhidhleir   245m   HVS **
N.Drasdo, C.M.Dixon   May 1962
This fine route, one of the classics of the area, has a long history. It was the scene of a remarkable early attempt by Ling and Sang, and it later repulsed such redoubtable names as Baird, Parker and Young, who were forced into long detours. The line follows an obvious grassy groove twisting up the centre of the buttress to the Pale Slabs and then finishes directly up the spur in a magnificent position. It is best seen from the subsidiary lochan beyond Lochan Tuath. Start at the base of the buttress, a little right of the crest, aiming for grooves in the slabs above.
1. 50m 4b A fine pitch up a slab, left of the grassy groove, leads to broken ground.
2. 50m 4b Follow the grassy groove to a fine cave below a roof.
3. 30m 4a Step right and follow the groove to easy ground below the First Pale Slab.
4. 20m Follow steep grass rightwards to the grassy groove on the right. Go up this to a little bay.
5. 15m Traverse the grass ledge left to the Hansom Cab stance.

6. 15m Climb the Second Pale Slab via the grassy groove on the left (or the finer crack to the right) to a good ledge.
7. 15m 5a From just right of the edge, step on to the slab with difficulty, then go up left to a groove and good ledge above.
8. 25m 4c Step right and surmount the overlap by an old peg runner. Climb the slabs above just right of the arete to a ledge.
9. 25m 5a Take the steep corner above to the final thin crack up a little wall (old peg runner, crux). Easier climbing leads to the top.

Reiff Sea-Cliffs

Map p406

These cliffs lie on the Rubha Mor Peninsula, accessed from the village of Reiff (NB 965 144). Although the sandstone north of Ullapool tends to be softer than in Torridon, Reiff's sea washed cliffs match the rock in Torridon for quality. The routes are often short, but the rock is clean and wave cut platforms make for easy access to most of the cliffs. With many routes possible in a day and much fine bouldering on offer, the area has become very popular. There are several hundred routes in the SMC's comprehensive guide. Being away from the mountains, the weather tends to be better than inland.

STONE PIG CLIFF

(NB 972 131)   Tidal   South facing   Map p406
This lies below (west of) the road from Altandhu to Reiff and is hidden from view.

Approach: Driving towards Reiff where the road rises high above the coast, a large boulder silhouetted on the horizon can be seen up on the right looking like a pig gazing out to sea (use your imagination!). There is limited parking near the lay-by just south of it. Walk to the first lay-by just past it, then another 30m before heading straight down to the coast. The most obvious feature from the cliff-top is a big overhanging wall.
   Descend a slabby corner about 20m right (facing out, north) of the overhanging wall, just before a small inlet, not the much bigger inlet further away. Walk back south at lowish tide. At mid-tide, all the routes can be reached by abseil.

The big overhanging wall with a long roof system at 8m is bounded on the right by a deep dank chimney separating it from a squat tower. The first route is a crack-line on the right wall of the tower.

Strongbow   20m   E2 5c *
K.Geddes   Jun 1989
Follow the crack throughout, which forms a shallow corner in the lower half. A fine overhanging well protected pitch.

Left of Strongbow is an undercut arete. **Headstrong** (E4 5c) starts up Strongbow, then heads out to the prow. **Die Another Day** (E5 6a) climbs the bulging wall, starting up its left arete, then hand traversing right.

Sonique   15m   E4 5c *
L.Hughes, A.Cunningham 5 May 1998
Near the right side of the big overhanging wall is a vague crack-line with twin cracks at one-third height. Start below the right end of the roof system and climb to the left of the cracks via horizontal breaks to a small overlap. Move right into the line at a small niche and finish by long reaches on flat holds.

Manumission   15m   E4 6a *
L.Hughes, A.Cunningham   18 Jun 1998
Start at an upside down V-slot at the cliff base. Climb a right diagonal crack above

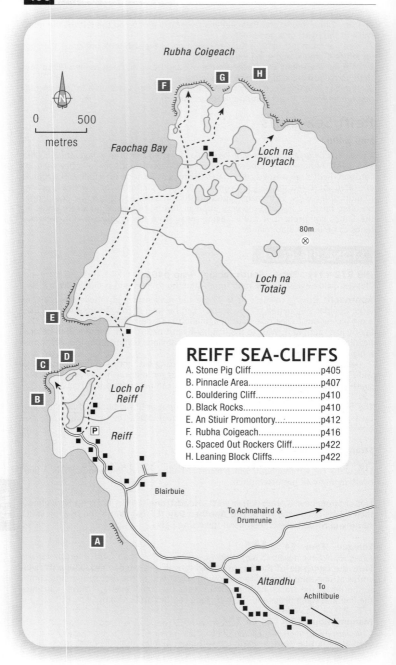

Rubha Coigeach

F G H

Faochag Bay

Loch na Ploytach

80m ⊗

Loch na Totaig

E

C D

B

Loch of Reiff

Reiff

P

0   500
metres
N

REIFF SEA-CLIFFS

Blairbuie

To Achnahaird & Drumrunie

A

Altandhu

To Achiltibuie

a small pool to a large ledge. Climb the roof above at the widest point and up slightly rightwards into a crack-line and shallow right-facing corner to finish.

If You See Kay   20m   E3 5c **
A.Cunningham, L.Hughes   14 Jun 1998
Climbs a right-slanting deep crack above the roof. Start centrally and climb the initial wall to the large ledge. Pull through the middle of the roof via twin right diagonal cracks and move right into a right-curving line. Go steeply up this to finish.

Miss Moneypenny   15m   E5 6a ***
L.Hughes, A.Cunningham   14Jun 1998
A central line up the wall. Climb the initial wall to the right of a deep off-width to a break. Pull over a roof moving left and back right into the line. Climb a very steep crack-line to the top.

Tinsel Town   15m   E2 5c *
A.Cunningham, J.Pickering   May 1989
Climbs the very left end of the wall. From under the left end of a huge recess, move up left to enter an obvious short groove with difficulty. Step right on to a ramp and from the top of this under the bulges, swing left on to the left arete of the wall (Icarus) to finish.

Icarus   15m   VS 4c **
A.Cunningham, J.Pickering   May 1989
Climbs the left arete of the overhanging wall, by thin cracks and pockets near the right edge of the slab round the corner.

The slab is bounded on the left by a stepped corner **Naloxone** (VS 4b *). Left of Naloxone is another corner, overlap and hanging groove **Automaton** (HVS 5a *)

Daunts Arete   15m   Very Difficult **
A.Cunningham   Aug 1989
The slab arete left of the left corner, gained by a curving crack in the right side. Good climbing.

ROINN A' MHILL
The headland nearest the village has four climbing areas; the Pinnacle Area, The Point, the Bouldering Cliff and Black Rocks.

PINNACLE AREA

(NB 962 149)   Non-tidal (mostly)   South or West facing   Maps p406, 409

A popular area, sunny and quick drying, and visible from the end of the road. The routes are short and it has a friendly feel, although lacking the excitement of the bigger crags. This is a good place for beginners, with fine slab routes and the pinnacle itself.

Approach: Walk round the left (south) side of Loch of Reiff and head for the visible crag. 7mins.

First reached is the First Geo, a narrow boulder filled inlet with a number of corners and steep walls on its east side and an easy slab on the west. Immediately after is the Second Geo.

Second Geo

This is a larger inlet with an impressive undercut headwall and a long wall on the east side, which terminates at a sea washed promontory. The west side of the inlet comprises a fine exposed slab and the pinnacle itself.

REIFF

1 Tangle of the Isles   10m   Hard Severe * *
B.Lawrie   1970s
Good sustained climbing up the prominent clean-cut black corner in the middle of the east wall. Reach it by descending a broken fault just to its left (as seen from the top of the slab opposite).

The next routes are on the impressive headwall, reached by descending a ramp on the east side. **A Walk Across the Rooftops** (E3 5c **) follows the hand-traverse leftwards across the overhanging headwall to finish up vague cracks at the end (big Friends useful). **Immaculate Deception** (E1 5b *) starts at the bottom of the slab on the west side under the headwall by a protruding block. Steep positive climbing over the small roof leads into a left-trending crack.

The Slab

Approach as for the headwall above, or traverse round from the pinnacle. Unfortunately the approach is nearly as hard as the routes. An easy abseil might be quicker.

2 Slab and Corner   20m   Difficult *
B.Lawrie   1970s
Follow the corner throughout.

3 Jellyfish Slab   20m   Difficult * *
B.Lawrie   1970s
Pleasant climbing up the middle of the slab.

4 Edge of the Sea   20m   Very Difficult
A.Fyffe, B.Fyffe   Oct 1988
Exposed climbing up the left edge of the slab. Take a diagonal line out to the edge from near the middle of the slab.

The Pinnacle

The best approach is to follow the easy descent to the north and walk round under the Pinnacle Walls. The pinnacle platforms are above the high tide level, but a rough sea combined with high tide may cut off the platform; in this case use Descent Corner (Difficult) on the Pinnacle Walls (see below).

5 Moonjelly   10m   Very Difficult * * *
B.Lawrie   1970s
Excellent bold padding up the vague central scoop on the pinnacle slab. Descend by down-climbing or abseil.

Pinnacle Walls

These are the walls opposite the pinnacle and extending round to the north. The wall round to the north from the pinnacle is bounded on its left-hand side by **Descent Corner** (10m Difficult).

6 Channering Worm   10m   E3 5c * *
N.Morrison, B.Lawrie, M.Forsyth   1980s
The wall opposite the base of the pinnacle slab (Moonjelly) gives superb varied climbing. Pull over the roof and snatch for the 'crazy spike'. Leave this reluctantly and make hard moves up and right to finish via the easier left-slanting diagonal crack.

7 Yellow Dogs   10m   E3 5c *
A.Cunningham, K.Geddes   Nov 1988
The grossly leaning groove tucked into the left side of the Worm Buttress. An

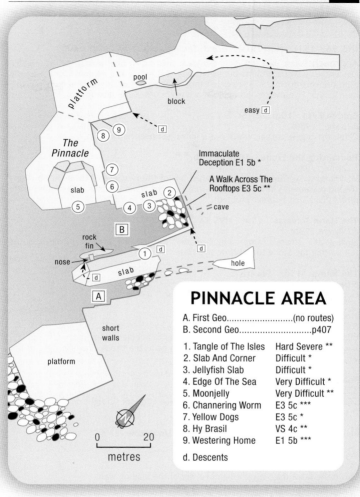

PINNACLE AREA

A. First Geo.........................(no routes)
B. Second Geo...........................p407

1. Tangle of The Isles   Hard Severe **
2. Slab And Corner   Difficult *
3. Jellyfish Slab   Difficult *
4. Edge Of The Sea   Very Difficult *
5. Moonjelly   Very Difficult **
6. Channering Worm   E3 5c ***
7. Yellow Dogs   E3 5c *
8. Hy Brasil   VS 4c **
9. Westering Home   E1 5b ***

d. Descents

0   20
metres

excellent workout! Climb the groove direct and hand-traverse the break out to the right edge. Fight to stand on the ledge and reach for the top.

**8 Hy Brasil   10m   VS 4c ** **
B.Lawrie   1970s
This climbs the arete to the left, where the wall turns from south to west facing. Start left of the fine arete and follow the first obvious line out right on to it. Finish direct. An alternative start is up a corner just right of the arete, exiting on to it (5a).

**9 Westering Home   10m   E1 5b ** **
B.Lawrie, N.Morrison, M.Forsyth   1980s
Climb the crack just left of the arete. Good stuff, delicate at the top.

BOULDERING CLIFF

(NB 963 151)   Non-tidal   North facing generally   Map p406

Approach: Walk past the Pinnacle Area, then north near a ruin to find a gully. Descend this, wet and slimy but not as bad as it looks, and the main area is on the right (looking down). Six metres left (now looking up) of the descent gully is a corner (VS 4c). Five metres left again is a bigger corner, the next route.

10 Golden Eyes   10m   E1 5c *
B.Lawrie   1980s
Climb the bigger corner, which has a ledge just over halfway up.

11 Romancing the Stone   10m   E3 6b **
B.Lawrie   1984
Very hard moves up the thin crack just left of the next arete. Either finish direct (Friend placements in the break), or finish up The Hand Traverse. The bottom arete direct gives a 6c boulder problem.

12 The Hand Traverse   15m   HVS 5a **
B.Lawrie   1980s
Start at the obvious ramp-fault. Gain and traverse the break rightwards across Romancing the Stone to finish up the arete.

13 The Ramp   15m   Severe *
B.Lawrie   1970s
Good climbing up the right-slanting fault-line.

14 Hole in the Wall   10m   E2 6a *
B.Lawrie   1980s
Climb the middle of the wall left of The Ramp to a 'hole' at 4m, move left and layback a shallow flake to its top. A long reach gains the break. Traverse right to finish.

15 Toad in the Hole   20m   E5 6a **
A.Cunningham   Jul 1990
Climb Hole in the Wall to the first break, then continue straight up the middle of the narrow wall.

Next left is an amazing grossly leaning wall **Undertow** (E7 6c)!

16 Wyatt Earp   20m   E4 6a ***
M.Hamilton, R.Anderson   Jul 1985
This route takes the big right-hand corner of the leaning wall.

17 The Crack of Desire   20m   E3 6a **
D.Dinwoodie   Jul 1985
The right-slanting diagonal crack-line, near the left end of the next north facing wall. Climb to the large break via the lower corner-crack. After the bulge above, break out on to the left wall to finish direct.

18 Desire Direct   20m   E4 6a ***
M.Hamilton   Jul 1985
Follow the diagonal crack of The Crack of Desire all the way.

BLACK ROCKS

(NB 964 151)   Partially tidal   North facing   Map p406

Basically an extension of the Bouldering Cliff past the landslip inlet. Black Rocks

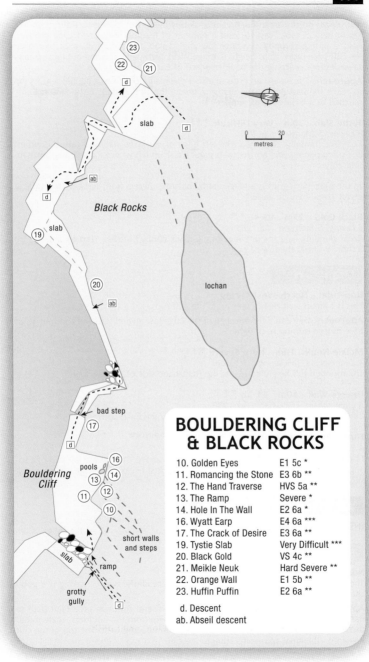

Black Rocks

slab

slab

lochan

Bouldering Cliff

bad step

pools

short walls and steps

slab

ramp

grotty gully

BOULDERING CLIFF & BLACK ROCKS

10. Golden Eyes   E1 5c *
11. Romancing the Stone E3 6b **
12. The Hand Traverse   HVS 5a **
13. The Ramp   Severe *
14. Hole In The Wall   E2 6a *
16. Wyatt Earp   E4 6a ***
17. The Crack of Desire E3 6a **
19. Tystie Slab   Very Difficult ***
20. Black Gold   VS 4c **
21. Meikle Neuk   Hard Severe **
22. Orange Wall   E1 5b **
23. Huffin Puffin   E2 6a **

d. Descent
ab. Abseil descent

REIFF

first trends north-east through various slabby buttresses and steep walls, then, rising in height, turns east to form a number of leaning aretes and wide grooves, before ending abruptly at a huge low angled slab. For a short distance thereafter the cliff once more gains height (Orange Wall) eventually petering out into scrappy zawns before reaching the boulder beach of Camas Eilean Ghlais.

Approach: The easiest access is to abseil down a groove from a big block at its top to reach the east end of the platform below the cliffs (tidal). Tystie Slab is easily reached as a large area of slab.

19 Tystie Slab   30m   Very Difficult ***
B.Lawrie, N.Morrison Jul 1985
Excellent climbing. Start near the left edge of the large slab and take the easiest line using pockets and horizontal breaks. Finish up left where the slab narrows considerably.

To the right (facing in) is a black slabby buttress. Access from Tystie Slab is tidal; a direct abseil may be easiest.

20 Black Gold   25m   VS 4c **
B.Lawrie, N.Morrison Jul 1985
Great climbing near the left edge of the black slabby buttress. Start by pulling into a short V-slot at the lowest point.

Orange Wall

Non-tidal   North-West facing
This is a steep wall clearly seen from the cliff-top.

Approach: Descend a flake-trough in the huge low angled slab and continue to its base before turning back right.

21 Meikle Neuk   10m   Hard Severe **
A.Cunningham, J.Pickering Oct 1988
The rounded full height corner at the right-hand side of the big wall.

22 Orange Wall   10m   E1 5b **
A.Cunningham, J.Pickering Oct 1988
Climb up to a ledge at half-height and finish by the flake above.

23 Huffin Puffin   10m   E2 6a **
A.Cunningham, J.Pickering Oct 1988
Good climbing; hard to start and well protected above. Start at the left end of a triangular niche at the foot of the wall. Up to the first break by a large pocket, move slightly right and finish direct.

AN STIUIR PROMONTORY

(NB 964 157)   Maps p406, 414

SEAL SONG AREA

Non-tidal   South facing   Map p414
The crag is sheltered, easily accessible and has a sunny aspect, making it a good choice on a doubtful day.

Approach: Follow the east side of Loch of Reiff and continue on a faint path to the beach of Camas Eilean Ghlais. Keeping well up from the boulders, circle round the head of the inlet and rise up onto moorland heading west. The top of the cliff is seen on this final approach, 30mins.

A line of fine cliffs run west from the head of a dry boulder inlet, to an impressive leaning wall above a large sloping tidal platform. The wall visible on the approach has two parallel cracks near its left arete, Seal Song and Elastic Collision. The arete itself has a diamond shaped slab cut out of it.

24 Razor's Edge 15m E1 5b *
B.Lawrie, N.Morrison, K.Murphy Jul 1985
Right of the right crack is a chimney-slot high up. Start right of this below a small sharp-edged undercut flake. Climb up to and pull left round the flake to gain a crack leading into the chimney. High in the grade.

25 Elastic Collision 15m E3 5c ***
B.Lawrie, A.Nisbet 9 Aug 1986
Equally fine climbing following the right-hand crack. Technically easier but more sustained than Seal Song. Named after a yo-yo on the first ascent, but the second ascent excavated a big jug.

26 Seal Song 15m E3 6a ***
N.Morrison, B.Lawrie, K.Murphy Jul 1985
Good strenuous and sustained climbing up the left-hand crack.

27 Diamond Back 20m E1 5a *
B.Lawrie 1980s
The diamond-shaped slab cut out of the arete. Start immediately left of Seal Song and climb a short wall to a ledge. Follow a ramp-line for a short distance until it is possible to step right on to the hanging diamond shaped slab.

Further towards the sea and over a small rock ridge is an even more impressive wall with horizontal breaks and a left-slanting crack forming its right side.

28 The Executioner 12m E2 5b **
B.Lawrie, N.Morrison, K.Murphy Jul 1985
Good sustained strenuous climbing following the left-slanting crack. Named since Kevin Murphy fell on a finger jam and had to be rushed to the nearest health centre to seek repairs.

29 Modern Thinking 15m E4 6b **
G.Livingston, K.Geddes, A.Cunningham Aug 1987
Tremendous climbing up the obvious stepped corner-line at the left end of the impressive wall. Gaining the corner-line direct is the crux. The original line (6a) started 4m right of the arete and climbed up to the first horizontal break. Move left and up to a hand-traverse, which leads back right into the base of the corners.

MINCH WALL

Non-tidal West facing Map p414
Approximately 80m north of the Seal Song Area is an area of short walls above an extensive platform.

Approach: Descend an obvious break at the south end of the walls.

The routes are described from the descent, north to the corners of Where the Green Ants Dream, right to left when facing the cliff. Walk north under an overhanging capped wall, then a bottomless corner in a slight crest and just left of this is a deep crack starting through a roof at 3m.

30 Judicial Hanging 10m HVS 5b **
A.Cunningham, K.Geddes Aug 1987
The obvious deep undercut crack is harder than it looks.

REIFF

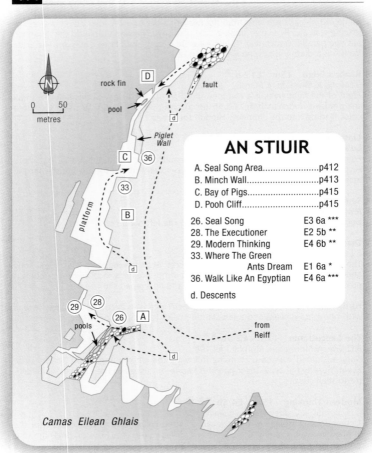

31 Dunskiing   10m   VS 4c *
K.Geddes, A.Cunningham Aug 1987
Start just left of the previous route and climb into and up a shallow corner. Move left round the final short prow.

Left again is a full height overhanging wall and at its left margin is the following route.

32 Jim Nastic   12m   VS 4c ***
K.Geddes, A.Cunningham Aug 1987
A spectacular route. Start at the left end of the overhanging wall. Climb over ledges trending right to a platform at mid-height. From its right end, finish via a thin crack in the slab. A direct finish can be made at the same grade up a crack at the left end of the platform.

The platform ends at a step, also the wall ends here at an arete.

33 Where the Green Ants Dream 20m E1 6a *
B.Lawrie 1970s
Set into the left arete of the Minch Wall is a line of corners. After a hard boulder problem start, follow the easier corners to the top.

BAY OF PIGS

This area is really a continuation of the Minch Wall, set back on the platform forming a bay of fine steep walls. Access is to continue along from Minch Wall, scramble down leftwards (facing out) at the north end of the steep walls, or abseil.

34 Reiff Encounter 20m E3 6b ***
P.Whillance, C.Fanshaw 1990
About 8m left of Green Ants is a thin crack splitting the huge undercut base. Hard moves through the undercut lead to a peg runner. Combined tactics will reach the peg! Move up on good holds to a ledge and finish rightwards.

Free Base (E5 6b **) is a fierce right-slanting crack-line near the right corner of the bay.

35 The Thistle 12m E5 6b ***
G.Livingston, A.Cunningham, K.Geddes Aug 1987
The impressive and deceptively steep crack in the left wall of the bay, right of the obvious corners of Egyptian. Well protected, but very powerful moves at the top thin crack.

36 Walk Like an Egyptian 18m E4 6a ***
A.Cunningham, K.Geddes Aug 1987
Guess the climbing style! The obvious line of corners at the back of the bay. Climb the corners until it is possible to graunch up the bomb bay groove to finish easily leftwards.

37 Cleopatra's Asp 14m E5 6a **
W.Moir, B.Lawrie Jun 1991
Start from the upper platform left of Egyptian. Hand-traverse the break rightwards to a resting ledge on the edge. Move back left to climb the right side of the wall to horizontal breaks (good Friends). Make a hard move up to gain a jug below the next horizontal break. Move up and right to a fighting finish!

POOH CLIFF

The climbs here lie approximately 100m north of the Bay of Pigs, where the rock heightens and steepens above a series of narrow platforms, to eventually run out onto a storm boulder beach at the north end. The routes are quite short, around 8m in height, but include some fine routes around the VS to HVS range.

Approach: Walk north along the cliff-top from the Bay of Pigs, and descend a fault-line on to a boulder beach at the north end of the cliff. It is also an easy scramble down to the south end of the cliff.

The routes are described from the boulder beach end southwards, left to right when facing the cliff. A narrow platform runs under the cliff, broken by a triangular step roughly in the middle.

38 Short Sighted Severe **
A.Cunningham, J.Pickering Aug 1987
Climb the shelfy groove near the left end of the cliff, with an awkward mantelshelf start.

REIFF

39 Tigger   VS 4b *
A.Cunningham, J.Pickering   Aug 1987
The cliff now heightens above a raised platform. From the left end of the platform take a steep thin crack in the left wall.

40 Pooh Corner   VS 4c ***
A.Cunningham, J.Pickering   Aug 1987
The excellent black corner above the middle of the raised platform.

41 The Ramp   Severe *
A.Cunningham, J.Pickering   Aug 1987
An obvious left-slanting ramp-line at the right end of the raised platform.

42 Sticky Fingers   VS 4c **
A.Cunningham, J.Pickering   Aug 1987
On the wall right of a wide crack in a corner, climb a shallow scoop direct over a bulge and finish leftwards.

On the right, the platform narrows above the pool into an awkward raised triangular step. Two routes start from the step, HVS 5b on the left and VS 5a on the right.

43 Eeyore   HVS 5a ***
A.Cunningham, J.Pickering   Aug 1987
Past the triangular step the platform widens once more, with a fine concave wall on the right. Steep unobvious climbing up the middle of the concave wall. There is an easier line further right, really a separate route.

44 Jelly Wobbler   E1 5b **
A.Cunningham, J.Pickering   Aug 1987
Follow the awkward finger crack in the left-curving black corner 10m right of a groove at the right end of the concave wall.

RUBHA COIGEACH

Maps p406
Rubha Coigeach is the most northerly point of the Rubha Mor peninsula with some of the best climbing on the coastline. It offers a varied selection of routes of up to 25m at all grades and is well worth visiting.

Approach: Approach as for An Stiuir until above the beach at Camas Eilean Ghlais, then continue straight on to a croft. Go straight on (gently uphill) from the croft, aiming for cairns on the slab left of a boggy slot to reach cairned summits. As soon as the point is visible in the distance, the profile of the Golden Walls is obvious. Head directly towards them, rough in places, to join the coast path at Faochag Bay. Rounding Faochag Bay, cross the burn draining from Loch na Faochaig and contour round over a shoulder to descend steeply into a boulder strewn fault on the left. Follow this north to the Golden Walls, 1hr.
   On a first visit, the best approach to Spaced Out Rockers Cliff and Leaning Block Cliffs is via the Golden Walls area, following the cliff round to the east as described below. For a subsequent visit, it is quicker to cut inland from Faochag Bay and head north past the ruined crofts of Faochag, passing the east side of Loch Learain to the cliffs. Loch Learain drains into the large bay mentioned below.

There are numerous good camping spots in the area, particularly around Loch na Foachaig, with usually plenty of driftwood for fires along the rocky shoreline of the bay.

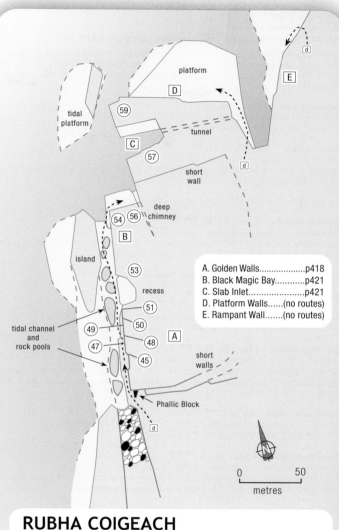

platform

tidal
platform

D

C 59

57

tunnel

short
wall

54 56 deep
chimney

B

island

53

recess

51

49 50

47 48

45

tidal channel
and
rock pools

A. Golden Walls...................p418
B. Black Magic Bay............p421
C. Slab Inlet.......................p421
D. Platform Walls......(no routes)
E. Rampant Wall.......(no routes)

A

short
walls

Phallic Block

d

E

d

d

N

0   50
metres

REIFF

RUBHA COIGEACH

45. Murphy's Law	HVS 5a **	54. Necronomican	E1 5b ***
47. Carnival of Folly	E2 5b **	56. Black Magic	VS 4c ***
48. Moronic Inferno	E3 5c **	57. The Ali Shuffle	VS 5a **
49. Split Personality	E4 5c ***	59. Atlantic Crack	E3 5c ***
50. Crann Tara	E3 5c ***		
51. The Rite of Spring	E3 5c ***	d. Descents	
53. The Road to Nowhere	E4 6a ***		

GOLDEN WALLS

(NB 977 180)   Non-tidal   West facing   Diagram p419

Where the cliff begins, a curious small 'phallic block' protrudes above a flat platform. Walk along the platform under the cliff, crouch to pass under a low nose and
where the platform opens out again is a big corner with a rounded back and
cracked left wall.

45 Murphy's Law   15m   HVS 5a **
K.Murphy, D.Dinwoodie, B.Lawrie   1985
The prominent corner, strenuous at the top.

46 Halcyon Daze   15m   HVS 5b *
K.Murphy, D.Dinwoodie, B.Lawrie   1985
The wall to the left of Murphy's Law, finishing by an obvious hole like feature at
the top. Technical to start.

The rounded pillar left of Halcyon Daze is **Verushka** (E3 5c).

47 Carnival of Folly   15m   E2 5b **
D.Dinwoodie, B.Lawrie, K.Murphy   1985
The bulging wall left of Verushka. Start just left of the pillar and trend right up an
obvious line of holds to finish near the top of the pillar.

Next is the fine Golden Wall, with four obvious crack-lines.

48 Moronic Inferno   15m   E3 5c **
B.Lawrie, D.Dinwoodie, K.Murphy   1985
The rightmost crack, low in the grade. The lower section is straightforward. Hurry
past the upper bulge on good holds.

49 Split Personality   15m   E4 5c ***
A.Nisbet, N.Ritchie, S.Blagbrough   Aug 1987
The thin crack just left is technical to start, hard in the middle and steep at the top.
Well protected but sustained. Various attempts were required, hence the name.
Flashed on the second ascent, by Roger Everett.

50 Crann Tara   15m   E3 5c ***
B.Lawrie, D.Dinwoodie, K.Murphy   1985
The next crack, with the right-hand finish.

51 The Rite of Spring   15m   E3 5c ***
B.Lawrie, D.Dinwoodie, K.Murphy   1985
Gain a round hole 3m up, traverse left into the line and finish via a wee corner.
Quite bold at the start, but the diligent will find a few runners.

The next section of cliff forms a large recess with a huge detached flake at the left
side of a higher ledge at its base.

52 The Road to Somewhere 15m   E5 6b **
W.Moir, P.Allen   12 Jun 1993
Climbs the vague arete which forms the left side of the recess. Step off the big flake
and climb a crack-line, then the arete to the top. Sustained and superb.

53 The Road to Nowhere   15m   E4 6a ***
B.Lawrie, D.Dinwoodie, K.Murphy   1985
A fine climb following a shallow groove in the wall just left of the vague arete and
right of an obvious right-facing corner. Climb a strenuous crack on the right to a
horizontal break and make a difficult move over the overlap into the groove above.

REIFF – Golden Walls

45. Murphy's Law   HVS 5a **
46. Halcyon Daze   HVS 5b *
47. Carnival of Folly   E2 5b **
48. Moronic Inferno   E3 5c **
49. Split Personality   E4 5c ***
50. Crann Tara   E3 5c ***
51. The Rite of Spring   E3 5c ***
52. The Road to Somewhere E5 6b **
53. The Road to Nowhere   E4 6a ***

Leave the groove with difficulty and climb boldly via a flange to a horizontal break (Friend runner). More awkward moves lead to the top.

BLACK MAGIC BAY

Tidal   North-West to North facing   Map p417

Beyond The Road to Nowhere, the crag base becomes tidal and progress requires scrambling, so access is easier by abseil. The following two routes are actually at the very end of the Golden Walls crag, just before the cliff cuts back inland to a high platform.

54 Necronomican   25m   E1 5b *
B.Lawrie, D.Dinwoodie, K.Murphy   1985
At the cliff-top, find a very deep chimney which leads down to the rock platform. Between it and the end of the offshore island is a large flat area of rock. The route is the west side of a slightly detached projection (the east side is obviously easier, with ledges – Difficult). Abseil down the line. The route is the large corner below. Very enjoyable and well protected, but watch out for turbulent tidal water near this end of the cliff.

55 The Presence   25m   VS 4c **
B.Lawrie, D.Dinwoodie, K.Murphy   1985
Start as for Necronomican but follow an obvious right-slanting ramp to finish via an exciting sustained 3m wall.

56 Black Magic   15m   VS 4c *
B.Lawrie, N.Morrison   1984
The route is up the black north facing wall between the chimney and the easier line at the east side of the projection. It offers smart climbing up the centre of the wall.

The right side of the slabby wall left of the chimney is **The Comeback** (VS 4c *), climbable at low tide only.

SLAB INLET

Tidal   North facing   Map p417

North of Black Magic Bay, the next main feature is a narrow inlet with a distinctive low angled slab forming its seaward (north) side. The landward side is a 12m black wall with three shallow corners.

57 The Ali Shuffle   12m   VS 5a **
B.Lawrie, A.Nisbet   Aug 1986
The right-hand and most prominent corner on the landward side. Very well protected. Approach by abseiling down the line.

58 Break Dance   12m   E2 5b *
B.Lawrie, A.Nisbet   Aug 1986
Climb the wall to the left of The Ali Shuffle and just right of the arete. Friend runners in every break!

On a north facing seaward wall on the opposite side of the small promontory to the slab, just round the corner where the promontory turns from west (facing the island) to north (facing the Atlantic) is a corner with a deep fissure and a crack in the right wall. Approach by abseil down the fissure to a big ledge only visible at low tide.

REIFF

The Rite of Spring, E3 5c, Golden Walls, Reiff. Climbers Alan Scott & Alan Shand (photo Grahame Nicoll)

59 Atlantic Crack   12m   E3 5c * * *
A.Nisbet, B.Lawrie   11 Aug 1986
A magnificent overhanging crack right of the fissure, mostly finger width, with the most technical move at the top.

SPACED OUT ROCKERS CLIFF

(NB 980 180)   Tidal   North facing   Maps p406, 417

This wall is on the far side of the large bay into which Loch Learain drains. It is not the wall facing the approach, but that facing away from it, opposite a west facing wall with a huge block poised to slide at its top (not the Leaning Block!). Continue round the top of the first cliff to have a close look at the wall. The line of Spaced out Rockers is stunningly obvious; a crack-line traversing 60m left across the vertical wall.

Approach: For the direct approach from Reiff see Rubha Coigeach approach, above. From the top of the Golden Walls or Slab Inlet go some 300m to the east to a large bay biting back inland. Descend the steep grassy slopes at its back and head out over boulders, low tide required, from where a bit of exposed soloing leads to the start of the route at a big niche just round the corner, left of the edge. Alternatively, scramble down into a gully north-east of the cliff and return under the poised block to the route (mid-tide).

Spaced out Rockers on the Road to Oblivion   65m   E4 * * * *
D.Hawthorne, K.Murphy   1985
A stunning right to left diagonal line across the big undercut wall, giving the longest and best route on the peninsula. Originally graded E2 but repeats failed. An ascent by G.Latter, D.Hollinger on 21 Aug, 2000 raised the grade to E4. Start at a big roofed recess just left of the right edge of the wall, gained from the west face by soloing leftwards round ledges.
1. 20m 5c Traverse horizontally left until below the left end of a ledge system. Make hard moves up to gain the ledge, and belay at the right end.
2. 45m 5c Go to the left end of the ledge and up to a prominent handrail, and follow this until it is possible to gain a higher handrail, which cuts through an obvious niche to finish in the corner. The pitch was originally split but the 2000 ascent claims this was unethical. A large rack of Cams (mainly size 1.5 to 3) will be found more than useful.

LEANING BLOCK CLIFFS

(NB 981 181)   Partially tidal   North facing   Map p406

This area offers excellent climbing, with solid crystalline sandstone running to steep walls split by fine cracks, corners and breaks and fine views across to Suilven, Canisp and Quinag. Despite the aspect, the majority of walls dry very quickly after rain, and during the summer months, most routes catch some sun.

Approach: For the direct approach from Reiff see Rubha Coigeach approach, above. From the top of the Golden Walls or Slab Inlet go some 400m east past the large bay biting back inland, which contains the Spaced Out Rockers Cliff. The Leaning Block is a square tower leaning against the cliff face and consequently is not obvious until directly above it on the cliff-top. Then a narrow gap is seen between it and the mainland. West of it is a tidal bay above a tidal platform with north and west facing walls while east of it, there is a north facing wall before the cliff decreases.

East of the Leaning Block walk easily down slabs (slippery if damp) to boulders below the east wall of the block. At low tide, it is possible to walk under all the routes. High tide will affect access to routes beyond Cyclops on the leaning block itself, although it is possible to squeeze through the block chimney to climb the routes around Wall of Silence and The Africaan Problem.

The north facing wall east of the block is characterised by an angled corner at its right end.

Empty on Endorphins 15m E1 5b **
A.Cunningham, J.Pickering   Jul 1990
Start under the left arete of the wall on top of a large boulder. Strenuous but well protected initial moves over the undercut base leads to the huge break. Take a left-slanting diagonal line to the top, quite bold, keeping a couple of metres right of the arete.

Brave Heart 15m E2 5b **
R.Mansfield, N.Ritchie   Jul 1990
Climb the middle of the wall to a short roof at half-height. Pull over and finish straight up the hard wall on improving holds.

Olympus 15m E2 5c *
A.Cunningham, J.Pickering   Jul 1990
The deep widening crack straight up from the start of the corner.

Coigach Corner HVS 5a **
R.Mansfield   Jul 1990
The angled corner, initially a ramp, then much steeper.

Next is the Leaning Block, a fine lump of rock partially detached at one side (and standing on a bunch of small boulders) presenting a remarkable chimney which may be traversed and used as access from the sloping platform at mid to high tides. The routes here are some of the best in the area.

Blind Bandit 12m HVS 5a *
N.Ritchie, A.Cunningham   Jul 1990
Start on a block under the east facing wall and climb straight up by a flake and hor-izontal breaks to a roof. Pull through the left end of the roof and trend rightwards up the bulging wall to finish.

Cross-Eyed 15m E2 5b **
R.Mansfield, N.Ritchie   Jul 1990
Starting off the same block, follow an obvious line curling right to a huge thread on the arete and finish via a diagonal crack on the seaward face. Very strenuous, but well protected.

Cyclops 15m E2 5c **
A.Cunningham, J.Pickering   Jul 1990
The east arete of the block. Start at the lowest point of the arete and climb via a series of breaks to the huge thread. Finish up a short groove on the left.

Losgaidh 15m E3 5c **
D.Dinwoodie, B.Lawrie, M.Ross   Jun 1989
Another good sustained and very strenuous climb. Start under the centre of the north facing seaward wall and climb up heading for a groove in the middle. Climb this to the top.

The next routes lie on the overhanging west facing wall of the Leaning Block and are all extremely photogenic.

The Gift 12m E5 6a ***
R.Mansfield, A.Cunningham, N.Ritchie   Jul 1990
Excellent powerful climbing up the left arete of the west wall. Start at the edge of

the raised platform, step left onto the seaward face and up into a cave. Move back right and make hard committing moves up the arete to a jutting block and a hands-off rest, if you can find it! Another hard move leads to jugs and the top.

The Screamer   12m   E4 6a ***
A.Cunningham, R.Mansfield   Jul 1990
The wall between Wall of Silence and The Gift. Start mid-way between the two and climb bulges to the big break. Move diagonally left past a semi-rest at a hand ledge to a short wide break. Trend right and up to the final wide break to finish up left. Steep, strenuous exciting climbing protected with small and large Friends.

Wall of Silence   12m   E3 5c ***
N.Ritchie, W.Moir   Jul 1989
Fine sustained climbing following an obvious crack-line right of centre. Named after a disagreement over the grade (Wilson Moir said E1 5b).

Block Chimney   12m   Very Difficult **
J.Lyall   Jul 1990
Interesting and fun climbing up the west end of the chimney.

Immediately right of the Leaning Block chimney is a superb steep black slab running to surprising holds and giving the next three routes. Small camming devices are useful.

The Africaan Problem   15m   E1 5b **
A.Cunningham, J.Pickering   Jul 1990
Start at the extreme left end of the slab by the entrance to the chimney. Trend right to a big ledge and climb up via a shallow gnarly flake to finish left under a stepped roof.

The Good, the Bad and the Ugly   15m   E2 5c *
R.Mansfield, N.Ritchie, A.Cunningham   Jul 1990
Climb the middle of the steep slab, starting up a short corner-crack and finishing easily by a short left-facing corner.

Van Hoover's awa'   15m   E1 5b **
N.Ritchie, R.Mansfield   Jul 1990
Start 3m left of an obvious crack near the right edge. Trend left on good holds up to half-height and finish direct.

Round the corner is a west facing wall.

Sunshine on Reiff   15m   E1 5b *
N.Ritchie, W.Moir   Jul 1989
Follow a scooped line up the left edge of the wall.

Golden Fleece   20m   E1 5b **
C.McLean, B.Lawrie   Jul 1989
An obvious crack-line on the wall to the right.

Waigwa   20m   HVS 5a *
W.Moir, N.Ritchie   Jul 1989
The black pocketed cracked wall a few metres to the right.

REIFF

The Screamer, E4 6a, Leaning Block Cliffs. Climbers Nathan Martin & Jo George (photo Cubby Images)

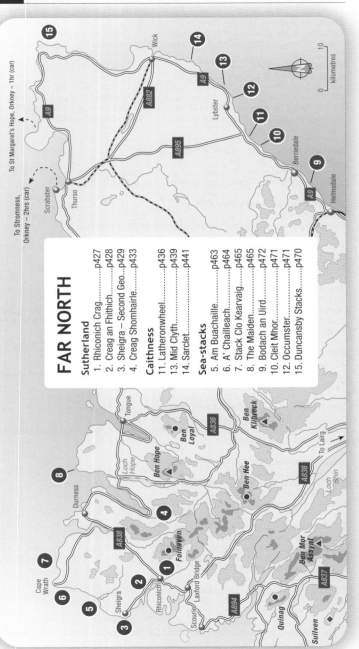

FAR NORTH

FAR NORTH

The far north of Scotland feels very remote but the west side (Sutherland) can be reached from Inverness in around two hours via Lairg and the east side (Caithness) slightly faster up the A9.

Maps: OS L9 (Sheigra, Rhiconich & Creag Shomhairle), OS L11 (Mid Clyth, Latheronwheel), L12 (Sarclet).

SMC Climbers' Guide: *Northern Highlands North* (2004)

Public Transport: For Sutherland a once daily bus goes from Inverness via Ullapool to Rhiconich, Kinlochbervie and Durness. An alternative is by train from Inverness to Lairg, followed by once daily bus to the same places. For Caithness there are regular buses from Inverness to Wick up the A9. The train is not helpful.

Amenities: Wick has all amenities, Dunbeath and Lybster have shops and cafes. Also see Ullapool to Reiff chapter for amenities further south.

Tourist Offices: Durness (seasonal, 01971 511259); Ullapool (01854 612135). There is also a convenient Tourist Information Centre at Kessock in the first lay-by on the A9 just north of the Kessock Bridge, near Inverness (01463 731505).

Camping: Scourie (NC 154 447), (01971 502060) is quite expensive, but has a restaurant/bar. Sheigra (NC 182 601) has no facilities but is by the crags. Oldshoremore is closed (2003); Durness – Sango Sands (NC 406 679), (01971 511761); Wick (ND 354 512), (01955 605420) Riverside Caravan Club, Janetstown; Dunbeath (ND 165 299), (01593 731441), Inver Caravan Park.

Mountaineering Huts: The Naismith Hut – SMC (NC 216 118) is in Elphin; Taigh nam Famb – Grampian Speleological Group is also in Elphin.

SYHA Youth Hostels: Durness (NC 417 672), (0870 004 1113), Helmsdale (ND 028 155), (0871 330 8525).

Independent Hostels: Lazy Crofter Bunkhouse, Durness (all year), (01971 511202).

Hotels: There are many; the Rhiconich Hotel is central for Sutherland and three at Lybster are central for Caithness.

Petrol: Petrol is more expensive north of Inverness, so best fill up there, where there is the last 24 hour station. Petrol is available during the day at Scourie, Kinlochbervie, Durness and Wick.

Sutherland

Described here are two of many recently developed roadside crags near Rhiconich, the established superb sea-cliffs at Sheigra and the mountain cliff of Creag Shomhairle, although hardly a high or distant mountain. The crags are composed of rough Lewisian gneiss, often steep and positively juggy. An approach via Ullapool is longer but allows the climbing in Coigach and Reiff to be visited on the way.

RHICONICH CRAG

(NC 259 519)   Alt 70m   West facing   Map p426

An accessible crag of crystalline gneiss, obvious from the road just south of Rhiconich. The crag has a distinctive deep left-slanting chimney on its lower left side.

Approach: Park in a wide truck area in front of a building on a bend just north of the Rhiconich to Kinlochbervie junction on the A838. Ascend the hillside opposite to its crest and find the crag after a second crest (or park on the old road on the north-east side of the river and follow a path up the river bank until the crag is seen above), 10mins.

Short But Beautiful   35m   HVS *
B.Birkett, H.Lancashire   22 Aug 2000
Start just right of the deep chimney.
1. 20m 5a Climb a slabby gangway right of the chimney to a shelf on the edge. Move up into a steep crack and follow it past the left end of a small overlap to a large ledge.

FAR NORTH

2. 20m 5a Step left and climb the wall direct left of a chimney with a holly. Pass a large detached block and continue easily.

Moral Turpentine   35m   E1 *
J.Walker, N.Wilson   1996
Start at the base of an obvious left-slanting crack.
1. 20m 5b Follow the crack left to reach the large ledge (or move out right just below the ledge).
2. 15m 5b Climb the chimney, painful passing the holly. Originally climbed finishing left of the holly up Short but Beautiful (this is recommended).

Black Gold   35m   E3 5c **
H.Lancashire, B.Birkett   22 Aug 2000
Well protected climbing directly up the central black streak, then straight through a bulge above. Start at the same place as Moral Turpentine. Pull over the first bulge, then follow the streak directly past two obvious pockets to a second ledge. Move up thin cracks, rock right and step up (crux), then continue in same line to enter awkwardly the diagonal chimney. Stand up and attack a steep crack to an exciting finish on great holds.

The Road North   35m   E2 5c **
B.Birkett, D.Allan   21 Aug 2000
Sustained and quite bold climbing, low in the grade. Start immediately right of the left-slanting crack. Pull up on a flake and move right to the first overlap. Climb through this and up to a triangular niche in the next little overlap. Stand above this, then pull over the next overlap onto the slab above to gain a vague crack. Climb directly up the slab and steep cracks above (avoiding easier ground) to heather.

Gneiss Too   18m   HVS 5b *
B.Birkett, D.Allan   21 Aug 2000
Start on a heather covered block at the base of the smaller right-hand end of the crag. Climb straight up past a small left-facing corner to finish right of a small nose. Starting further right is easier, perhaps reducing it to VS.

CREAG AN FHITHICH

(NC 258 538)   Alt 80m   North-West facing   Map p426

The crag on the dome shaped hill looking down Loch Inchard has three good and separate sections of rock. It is better and bigger than it appears from the road.

Approach: Leave the A838 at Rhiconich and follow the B801 north for about 2km to park on the right just before a bridge below the crag at the south end of Achriesgill. Start beside the stream and head up the hill to the crags, 5mins.

Gaff   25m   HVS 5a *
N.Wilson, N.Stevenson   27 Jun 1996
The prominent diagonal crack in the grey wall which forms the left section of the crag, is more sustained than it looks. Start at a steep groove right of the crack. Climb the groove, then the crack to finish left of the vegetated niche at the top.

About 100m further right and slightly up is a fine steep ruby coloured wall with a very distinctive wavy band of black striated gneiss low down in the centre.

The Swirl   35m   E3 5c ****
M.Charlton, A.Cater   May 1997 ; Route as described: G.Latter   4 Jul 2000
A spectacular climb with some bold and strenuous climbing. Climb large pockets just left of the black wavy band to a ledge. Continue up the superb pocketed wall passing left of an overhung slab and a niche to finish up the cracked wall. A steep heathery finish leads to a small tree (sling and maillon in-situ). Descend by abseil. It is possible to move right on to Sapphires below the hard looking top wall.

Sapphires   35m   E3 5c ***
G.Latter   30 Sep 2002
Excellent well protected climbing. Start a few metres right of The Swirl. Climb easily up leftwards on pockets, then by a crack to the base of the prominent fault cutting through the central overhanging section. Ascend leftwards on jugs to pull
rightwards up on to an overhung slab. Break through the roof at its highest point
and move up into an overhung niche, then traverse spectacularly left along a good
break. Move up and left on steep heathery ground to the abseil point.

A Diamond is Forever   35m   E5 6a **
H.Lancashire, T.Rogers, B.Birkett   20 Aug 2002
A tremendous pitch on excellent rock, taking a direct central line on the crag.
There are three hard contrasting sections, with good rests between. Start below a
light coloured left-facing groove low down. A full set of cams from size 00 to 3.5
are useful, if not essential. Steep moves leftwards and then back right lead to the
base of the groove. Move up into the groove and use holds on the wall to its right
to reach a good small obvious pocket. Swing up left to a good blunt spike and easier ground. Move up the slab to the right to a short corner. Climb up and then out
left to two good pockety holds on the wall. Steep moves up on undercuts lead to
small sharp holds. Hard moves left lead to an easing in the angle. Move up and
right to beneath a steep crack. Using a combination of the crack and the wall to its
right, enter a steep groove above to a thank god hold. Continue up the groove and
surmount an overhang to exit leftwards on to a slab and easier heathery ground.

Russet Wall

Continuing further right for about 100m is an excellent smooth wall, well endowed
with letter box slots and pockets and with blocky overhangs either side. Direct
access to this wall is quickest by parking in a lay-by 300m before (south-west) the
bridge and going up the hillside to the right end of the crag, 5mins. To reach the
cliff base traverse right across heather and down the right edge of the crags.

Dragonfly   25m   HVS 5a **
G.Latter, A.Warner   4 Jul 2000
An exciting climb on excellent holds. Climb the left side of the smooth wall, trending leftwards, then up a short flake-corner and through more bulges to break
through the final bulge past a couple of protruding flakes. A direct start climbs a
fingery wall to the corner (E3 5c).

Apple Pie   25m   E1 5b *
H.Lancashire, B.Birkett   13 Aug 2002
Start as for Dragonfly but continue direct up the wall right of the corner and
through steep ground right of the protruding flakes.

Horseshit Direct   25m   HVS 5a **
G.Latter, A.Warner   4 Jul 2000; Direct: J. and D.Preston   15 Jun 2002
Start towards the right side of the wall. Climb up and move left along a diagonal
break. Go straight up the wall on good pockets to finish up a layback flake through
the final bulge, pulling on to an easy slab above.

SHEIGRA

(NC 186 605)   Map p426

Near the village of Sheigra, just north of Kinlochbervie, a headland of gneiss inter-
rupts the more usual sandstone. There are several geos and walls here and one in
particular, The Second Geo, provides one of the most impressive walls in Scotland,
vertical to overhanging and covered in jugs (hence the large number of stars). The
walls are quick drying but like any sea-cliff, can hold condensation. The holds are

so good that the routes can still be climbed in the damp if a grade is added.

Approach: From Rhiconich on the A838, take the B801 to Kinlochbervie and just upon reaching it, turn right for Oldshoremore and Sheigra, which is at the end of this road (8km). At Sheigra turn left to the campsite and sandy beach. Park as near the end of the road as allowed (near a small cemetery). The headland is on the right (north). Go into the campsite and to the last gate before the road reaches the beach. A fence traverses the right slope and then turns uphill; this leads to the First Geo. The fence then cuts back below the horizon and goes over the crest to the Second Geo. For direct access, cut the corner and head straight for the upper part of the fence. Follow the fence over the crest and down to a 3m sandstone erratic boulder, from where the routes are clearly seen.

SECOND GEO

(NC 179 602)   Non-tidal   North-West facing   Map p426

This consists of an impressive orange west face at its northern end running down a huge slab to sea-level and a large cave. At the top of the easy slab is the sand-stone boulder. The orange wall runs into a series of black corners at the south end of the cave with the corner route of Dark Angel bounding the orange wall.

For routes left of the cave (Juggernaut to May Tripper), start from the slab; for routes from Geriatrics, above the cave, abseil the cave. On the rib of Lucifer's Link left of the main black corner of Shark Crack, abseil on to the Black Pedestal, a good incut ledge at the base of **Black Knight** (HVS), 3m above the sea. The only belay is a rusty peg, so use a separate abseil rope and tie on to it!; for Shark Crack and Fingers, abseil down Shark Crack to the slabby lower section.

1 Juggernaut   25m   E2 5b *
R.Anderson, C.Greaves   22 May 1989
Three easier routes (VS) lie at the top end of the wall. The right-hand, **Sideline**, climbs up into a big left-facing corner which bounds the very steep section of the wall. This steep, quite bold, but low in the grade route starts a few metres down from Sideline and climbs the steep wall. Continue in the same line past the left side of a large hole to finish up steep cracks just right of the arete of the big corner.

2 Juglust   25m   HVS 5a **
The easiest line up this steep wall still gives plenty of excitement. Start up Bloodlust Direct to the large hole. Join Juggernaught and follow it straight up to the right corner of the big ledge of Sideline. Try not to step onto it for a rest but stay on the overhanging wall, trending right away from Juggernaught.

3 Bloodlust Direct   25m   E2 5b ****
P.Nunn, P.Fearnehough   May 1978; Direct: D.Cronshaw, J.Ryden   1988
Start at the point where the slab meets the top of the cave and gain a small ledge. Go up a shallow corner and left up a gangway to the large hole. From the hole, go diagonally right (the original continues right, E1 5b) and back left up the bulging wall above on good pockets to finish direct.

4 May Tripper   25m   E1 5b **
R.Anderson, C.Greaves   22 May 1989
Start as for Bloodlust Direct to gain the first ledge. Climb diagonally right follow-ing a zigzag quartz vein to gain and follow a small ramp to a large hidden pocket right of a black streak (the left-hand of two wide ones). Move up to finish direct (easier but not as good to go out right).

5 Geriatrics   40m   E2 5c **
R.Carrington, M.Boysen   May 1987
From the Black Pedestal, traverse left into the next corner (Dark Angel) and con-tinue left across the lip of the cave on a quartz band. From its end move up and

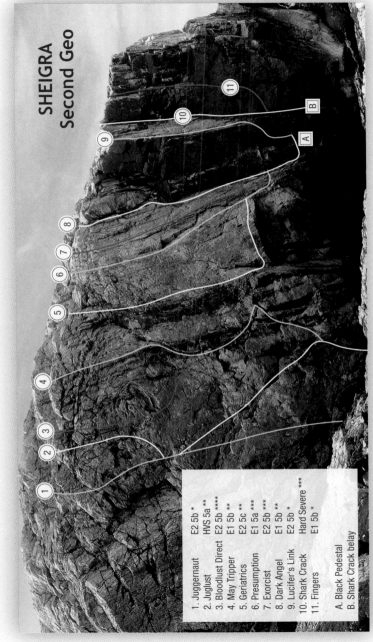

SHEIGRA
Second Geo

1. Juggernaut   E2 5b *
2. Juglust   HVS 5a **
3. Bloodlust Direct   E2 5b ****
4. May Tripper   E1 5b **
5. Geriatrics   E2 5c **
6. Presumption   E1 5a ***
7. Exorcist   E2 5b ***
8. Dark Angel   E1 5b **
9. Lucifer's Link   E2 5b *
10. Shark Crack   Hard Severe ***
11. Fingers   E1 5b *

A. Black Pedestal
B. Shark Crack belay

continue left in a spectacular position to a ramp at the left end of the cave roof. Climb direct up the wall above, right of the right-hand black streak (or move left and climb the black streak).

6 Presumption   40m   E1 5a *******
P.Nunn, R.Toogood   May 1983
Follow Geriatrics to the end of the quartz band and climb via black streaks above to a small ledge below the obvious shallow left-curving arch forming a higher groove. Climb the groove to the arch and finish direct just left of the top groove.

7 Exorcist   40m   E2 5b *******
R.Carrington, M.Boysen   May 1987
Climb Dark Angel to just past the first bulge. Traverse horizontally left to reach black streaks. Continue up the black streaks to gain a higher faint groove which is followed to the top.

8 Dark Angel   30m   E1 5b ******
P.Nunn, R.Toogood   May 1983
Step left from the Black Pedestal to climb the fine groove to the large upper shelf (possible belay). Make steep moves up the hanging corner above to finish (crux).

9 Lucifer's Link   35m   E2 5b *****
P.Nunn, P.Kershaw   Jul 1983
Climb the rib on the right of the Black Pedestal all the way in impressive surroundings. Sustained.

10 Shark Crack   30m   Hard Severe *******
R.Dearman, K.Bridges, P.Nunn   Jun 1971
The crack in the main corner right of the Black Pedestal. Start from a ledge on the right of the lower slab reached by abseil. An improbable appearance but excellent holds.

11 Fingers   30m   E1 5b *****
R.Dearman and party   Mid 1970s
The black wall right of Shark Crack is split by a thin crack. Climb the crack with a final steep section.

CREAG SHOMHAIRLE

(NC 382 507)   Alt 100m   West facing   Map p426   Diagram p435

This interesting cliff lies some 5km from the head of Loch Eriboll. The crags run for about 2km above a pleasant wood, the best climbing being at the south end, where the described routes lie. The rock is excellent gneiss.

Approach: Follow a track up Strath Beag to Strabeg Cottage. To get a good view of the crags it may be better to cross to the west side of the river.

Descent: Make a pleasant traverse right across slabs to the top of **Windy Corner**. This is the broken gully to the right of the main face, which provides a convenient descent (60m, Difficult); it is usually abseiled after scrambling down about 5m to an in-situ abseil point.

1 Black Gold   85m   E1 *****
R.Anderson, C.Greaves   21 May 1989
This good route takes the obvious black streak in the wall left of the big left-slanting ramp. Start below a crack at the left end of the wall. There is a diagonal crack to the right.

Geriatrics, E2 5c, Sheigra. Climbers Iain Small & Jason Walker
(photo Chris Cartwright)

FAR NORTH

1. 20m 5a Gain the crack and climb it to a small ramp, step up right and continue to just below a heathery ledge. Move right to the ledge and a holly bush.

2. 35m 5a Follow a ramp up left and across above a roof to the black streak and move up right into the base of a slim corner. Climb this and continue directly up the black streak to a ledge and tree belay.

3. 30m 5a Move right to gain and climb a corner system leading back above the belay to reach a small holly bush. Traverse up right to the arete and climb this in a fine position to the top. Descend by abseil or traverse off right.

2 The Ramp   105m   VS *
R.How, J.R.Sutcliffe   28 May 1969

This takes the obvious diagonal fault rising up left from a point about 50m left of the right end of the face. The 4c crux on pitch 2 is hard for both leader and second, but the rest is much easier.

3 Bardo Thodol   95m   E2 ***
G.Cohen, G.Macnair   1 Aug 1984

Above the start of The Ramp is a great slab which is taken by this route. Some say it is even better than Land of the Dancing Dead; certainly the style is different, this route being exposed both in terms of position and protection. Start 8m left of Dancing Dead.

1. 40m 5b Climb blocks passing the overhang to gain a slab. Traverse left and go up and left to a small ledge. Go right, then directly up to a stance on the great slab at the bottom of its right-bounding corner.

2. 25m 5a Climb the slabby corner, traverse left under the roof until near the left edge, then go up a short wall to a stance.

3. 30m 5a Climb up to a steep crack and follow this leftwards to the edge. Go up a short wall in a fine, exposed position to ledges.

4 Land of the Dancing Dead   90m   E1 ***
C.Jackson, T.Proctor   21 Aug 1979

There have been suggestions of E2 5b and E1 5c but top end E1 5b has been selected for this excellent route. At the right end of the face there is a clean rib with a very steep wall to its left. This route takes the corner-crack on the left of the rib. There is a Damoclean flake about 20m up. Start below the crack.

1. 35m 5a Climb up the crack to a hanging flake, move left and follow its continuation to a sloping ledge. Traverse back right into the corner and follow this to a small stance on the left.

2. 25m 5b Climb the corner-crack direct (very strenuous but well protected). Move left to a spike belay.

3. 30m 5a Continue up to a roof and layback round it to easier ground.

5 Tank Top   45m   E6 6b ***
M.Hamilton, R.Anderson   28 Jun 1986

This climbs the awesome thin crack-line just right of Land of the Dancing Dead. If it is wet, note how far out behind your head the drips land! Climb Land of the Dancing Dead for 10m, then move right to a small stance. Move up and slightly right until moves left can be made underneath the roof; pull over this and follow the crack to the top.

To the right of Tank Top the cliff turns a corner. The obvious gully used for descent, Windy Corner. Right again there is another steep section of cliff, the South Face.

6 The Roost   60m   VS **
Caithness MC   1962

This is the very obvious crack in the middle of the South Face. Start towards the right end of the heather ledge below the face.

1. 30m 4c Trend left up a strenuous curved crack, on magnificent rock, to a second heather ledge with a holly tree.

CREAG SHOMHAIRLE

Windy Corner descent

1. Black Gold   E1 *
2. The Ramp   VS *
3. Bardo Thodol   E2 ***
4. Land of the Dancing Dead   E1 ***
5. Tank Top   E6 6b ***
6. The Roost   VS **
7. Hot Pants   E4 6a *

FAR NORTH

2. 30m 4a Continue to beneath the main overhangs and make an exposed traverse left round the buttress into an open corner, which is followed to the slabs above. Either traverse left and descend Windy Corner, or scramble 100m to the top.

7 Hot Pants   55m   E4 *
M.Hamilton, R.Anderson   28 Jun 1986
The obvious roof crack right of The Roost.
1. 30m The Roost, pitch 1.
2. 25m 6a Move right and climb the crack to the top.

Caithness

These sea-cliffs lie between Dunbeath in the south and Wick in the north. The setting is pleasant, the cliffs have a generally sunny aspect and the weather is dry, although prone to haar in the spring. The rock is sandstone, generally strongly layered and horizontally banded, with camming devices often crucial for protection. A visit to this little known area is sure to delight.

LATHERONWHEEL - BIG FLAT WALL AREA
(ND 188 388)   Tidal & Non Tidal   South through to East facing
A sheltered and picturesque spot with excellent climbing on fine sandstone.

Approach: Some 4km north of Dunbeath, turn off the A9 into Latheronwheel village. Follow the road to the harbour and park. The cliffs are reached after a walk south of 500m. Cross the old bridge and follow the path up the hillside, through a wall, then alongside a fence. Go through a gate and 200m or so further along the fence the top of the Big Flat Wall becomes visible. Routes are described north to south, right to left.

PENINSULA WALL

A narrow peninsula extends north-eastwards from the Big Flat Wall to form a south facing wall. On the other side of this peninsula is a dry bay containing a group of four stacks. The peninsula is penetrated by a tidal through-cave, to the right of which is a shelf with two arches, or caves above it.

Access: Walk down the gully at the back of the dry bay and around the end of the peninsula to the shelf. Only the left end of the cliff is affected by the sea.

**Positive Mental Attitude   15m   VS 5a ** **
J.Sanders, G.Stein   7 May 1998
The wall left of the first arch and just right of the second arch. Gain a ledge then climb the overhanging wall on jugs.

**Don't Think Twice   15m   HVS 5a ** **
J.Sanders, A.Robertson   29Aug 1998
At the end of the shelf left of a crack and just right of the arete, climb horizontal breaks to beneath a small roof. Pull through this and steeply gain a ledge and easier ground.

The next routes lie on the wall left of the through cave and just right of the Big Flat Wall. Access is best by abseil from the obvious large block, down the crack of **Pippet at the Post** (Severe 4b) to a good ledge.

Imperial Lather   15m   E1 5a * **
R.Anderson, C.Anderson   26 Jun 2005
Just right of Pippet at the Post, climb a thin crack, then step right and steeply climb

Don't Think Twice, HVS 5a, Latheronwheel. Climber Rab Anderson
(photo Chris Anderson)

Crypt Robber   35m   E2 5c ***
R.Wallace   3 Jul 2003
The deep chimney. Climb from a ledge in the chimney onto the right face. Trend left until directly under a roof. Make strenuous moves over the double roof to a great position bridging onto a massive spike. Follow the chimney above with decreasing difficulty.

A Paddler's Tale   35m   E4 5c ***
G.Robertson, T.Woods, D.Porter   28 Jun 2003
The slim right-hand pillar, a superb outing. From the base of the deep chimney climb up and right on to the pillar and follow it, at times boldly, to better holds and an easing of the angle. Continue up cracks then move onto the right arete and finish up this.

East Face

This face is crowned by overhangs, is split by a prominent groove and has small ledges at its base. It can be viewed from the top of the adjacent Djapana Buttress.

Time Bandit   35m   E4 6a ***
T.Woods, G.Robertson   5 Jul 2003
A brilliant sustained pitch snaking past the big overhangs on the left. Start on ledges just up and left of the base of the prominent groove, below a smooth wall. Climb boldly up the middle of the wall on improving holds and pass a strange protruding blob on its left-hand side. Move up, then traverse left under the overhangs to gain blind cracks which lead to a prominent flake. Follow the flake to a rest by a wobbly hold below overlaps. Undercut up and slightly left, pull over, then step back right to better holds and the top.

Groove Armada   35m   HVS 5a ***
T.Woods, G.Robertson, D.Porter   28 Jun 2003
The prominent groove is climbed direct on good holds, turning the overhangs on the right. Sustained, well-protected climbing in an impressive situation.

The Sarclet Pimpernel   35m   HVS 5a ***
D.Porter, T.Woods   28 Jun 2003
Another impressive climb taking the cracks left of the right-hand arete. Start up Groove Armada and make a rising traverse along a crack to the arete. Move up the arete, then back left into the cracks and climb these to the top, avoiding loose rock by moving left to finish as for Groove Armada up the right side of the overhang.

DJAPANA BUTTRESS

Non-tidal   North facing

This square buttress lies at the end of a huge natural arch and can be seen from the top of Big Buttress, to which it is joined by a precarious rock bridge.

Access: Walk out across the narrow top of the arch and abseil to ledges.

Northern Alliance   20m   E3 5c **
G.Robertson, T.Woods   28 Jun 2003
The striking arete left of Djapana. Climb the edge using cracks just to its right all the way to a strenuous finish; not as hard as it looks.

Djapana   20m   E3 5c **
O.Slarke   1994
The demanding crack-line up the centre of the buttress.

The Sarclet Pimpernel, HVS 5a. Climber Jo George
(photo Cubby Images)

FAR NORTH

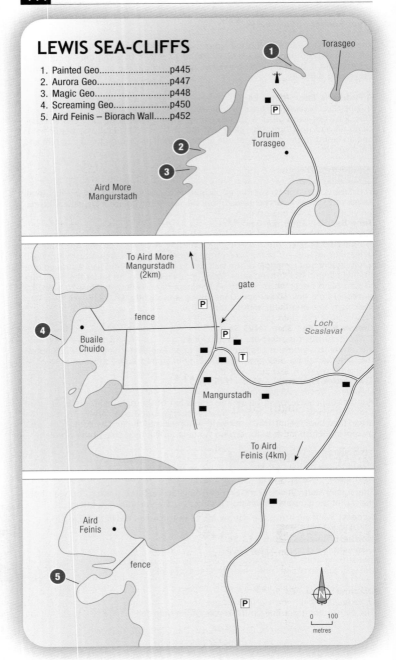

LEWIS SEA-CLIFFS

Torasgeo

Druim Torasgeo

Aird More Mangurstadh

To Aird More Mangurstadh (2km)

gate

fence

Loch Scaslavat

Buaile Chuido

Mangurstadh

To Aird Feinis (4km)

Aird Feinis

fence

0   100
metres

LEWIS & HARRIS

For those with a spirit of adventure the lengthy and expensive journey to the Outer Hebrides should be well rewarded. As well as the great climbing, this is somewhere to relax and soak up the atmosphere.

Maps: OS L13, E458

SMC Climbers' Guide: *Skye and the Hebrides Vol 2* 1996

Access: By Caledonian MacBrayne ferry from Ullapool to Stornoway, or Uig (Skye) to Tarbert (Harris) <www.calmac.co.uk>. The 5 day return offers good value for money, whether travelling as a foot passenger or with a vehicle.

Public Transport: A car is pretty much essential but a bicycle could be used and a bus/post bus serves the area <www.cne-siar.gov.uk/travel>.

Amenities: There is one shop and petrol station in the Uig area at NB 058 339 and everything plus two major supermarkets in Stornoway. There is a community centre and cafe in Uig. For all other local information go to <www.visit hebrides.com> or <www.cne-siar.gov.uk>. The latter site also has details on the only climbing wall, in Stornoway.

Camping: There are two campsites in Uig with facilities, both are beside lovely beaches. The best is at Traigh na Beirigh NB 100 360 and the other is at Traigh Uuige NB 048 328.

Lewis Sea-Cliffs

The sea-cliffs along the west coast of Lewis offer excellent climbing on fine gneiss, amidst impressive Atlantic surroundings. The cliffs are extensive, so to give a flavour of the area the climbs described are on the principal and most accessible headland in the main Uig area, about one hour's drive from Stornoway via the A858 and B8011. The climbs are mainly single pitch and generally involve abseil approaches, so it is advisable to bring a separate rope for that purpose. Geodha, shortened to Geo, is the term for rocky inlet or zawn. Be prepared for the weather and the Atlantic to decide whether you will climb. The walking in the hills and along the coast is excellent and there is also surfing, fishing, flora, fauna and archaeology to provide alternative distractions.

Aird Mor Mangurstadh

This is the large headland to the west of the beautiful expanse of sand at Traigh Uuige. The headland extends around to the sands at Traigh Mangurstadh.

Approach: Follow the B8011 past the shop at Timsgearraidh and Uig sands. Continue past the turning for Carnais and take the road off right to the hamlet of Mangurstadh. Follow the road up right, go through a gate and continue to where the road ends at an aerial, park by a small shed. On rounding the final bend just before the aerial there is a small 'window' where the only mobile telephone signal for miles can sometimes be picked up.

PAINTED GEO

(NB 006 334)   Non-tidal (mostly)   South-West & North facing

The stretch of coast to the north of the aerial contains Painted Geo, a large, picturesque geo, which offers a number of good quality climbs. It has the shortest approach in the area and is generally sheltered and unaffected by the tides.

Approach: Walk north across flat ground and in a minute the ground literally opens up with the striking Painted Wall obvious on the far side. A large tidal pool sits at the bottom of the geo.

PAINTED WALL

A beautiful wall of colourful banded gneiss. In the shade the wall can look as if it is seeping, however, this is normally just dark streaks of colour. The wall consists of a steeper upper half on which the routes are located and an easier-angled lower half, which can be climbed easily to reach the base of the routes. The most obvious features are, on the left, the right-facing **Director's Corner** (VS 5a) and in the centre, the crack of Motion Control with the right-slanting pink vein of Painted Wall to its right.

Access: Abseil directly to ledges beneath the routes, or scramble down the descent gully on the south side, cross the geo and climb to beneath the routes.

Mick's Corner   25m   VS 4c *
M.Tighe, J.Paterson   May 1979
From a good ledge beneath the line of Directors Corner, trend leftwards on slabby rock and climb the shallow corner at the left side of the wall.

Dauntless   21m   E5 6a **
G.Latter, D.Cuthbertson   7 May 1985
Some 6m right of Director's Corner, climb a quartz wall to a break. Continue to a second break, then go left into a scoop to the right of a flake at about one-third height. Now go back right, aiming for twin diagonal breaks near the top. Follow these strenuously to finish. Difficult and sustained but reasonably well protected.

Motion Control   20m   E2 5c **
M.Tighe, B.Newton   1980s
The central crack is climbed from a good ledge at its base.

The Painted Wall   20m   E4 5c ***
D.Cuthbertson, G.Latter   5 May 1985
From the ledge at the foot of Motion Control go up and right across some horizontal breaks, then cross the pink quartz band and follow it to the top, crossing it again.

The Dreaded Dram   25m   E3 5c **
D.Cuthbertson, G.Latter   7 May 1985
Climb an obvious short black groove and its continuation to the steep upper section. A series of short vague cracks leads to the final easy moves of Painted Wall. Protected by small wires.

BLACK WALL

This atmospheric wall drops into the sea at the mouth of the geo. The rock is excellent, although the aspect means it can be greasy early in the day. Seen from the opposite side, a right-slanting crack is obvious, with a wide crack and left-slanting, pink quartz streak to its right.

Access: Abseil to a small ledge for Black Foot and down the groove of Feint Chance to a common ledge for the other routes.

Black Foot   30m   E2 6a **
N.Dazell, J.Ashdown   May 1993
Climb the right-slanting crack through a bulge, trending right, then move up to a ledge with difficulty. Follow the obvious line left to the top.

Vein Hope   40m   E2 5c *
R.Anderson, C.Anderson   6 Jul 2000
Gain, then climb the wide crack (Friend 6 useful though not essential) and continue up the left slanting line.

Feint Chance   40m   E2 5b *
R.Anderson, C.Anderson   6 Jul 2000
From the recess beneath the wide crack pull out right and move up to ledges. Step
left and climb the groove to the top. **Long Shot** (E1 5b) climbs the wall and
grooves on the right.

Aurora Geo & Magic Geo

The stretch of coast that runs south-westwards from the road end, contains two of
the area's major geos, Aurora Geo and Magic Geo, which are located in a rocky
headland, some 10mins from the road.

Approach: Contour the hillside southwards, cross a small burn and head down to
a depression. Scramble up slabs to the flat highpoint to locate Aurora Geo and then
just to the south, Magic Geo.

AURORA GEO

(NB 002 329   Map p444

A deep and narrow geo into which the sea surges to smash into a sea cave.

EAST FACE & NORTH WALL

Non-tidal but swell affected   South-East & South-West facing

In the north-west corner of the geo are two obvious corner-lines, to the right of
which is an arch over the sea cave.

Access: Abseil down the corners to ledges.

Newton's Law   30m   E1 5b *
B.Newton, M.Tighe   Jun 1974
The prominent, open, two-stepped corner is climbed, either from a ledge at its
base, or by a traverse in from the foot of the right-hand corner.

Star of the Sea   30m   E1 5b **
M.Tighe, B.Newton   Jun 1974
The impressive zigzag corner formed in the angle between the faces is climbed
directly. Sometimes wet, but a fine pitch nonetheless.

Romancing the Moose   30m   E5 6a **
G.Huxter, K.Pyke   7 Sep 1996
A route of contrast in a committing situation directly above the sea-cave. From the
corner, teeter gingerly along the lip of the hanging slab to a good rest beneath the
roof (RPs). Jam wildly rightwards through the roof to gain an awkward crack, from
the top of which moves right gain the headwall, which is climbed steeply through
quartz bands to good finishing jugs in the centre.

WEST FACE - CIOCH WALL

Non-tidal (mostly)   North-West facing

On the landward side there is a recessed section of tar black rock, generally less
than vertical and characterised by a Cioch-shaped block towards its seaward end,
best viewed from the other side of the geo. A fine ledge runs beneath the wall, from
the block to the base of an obvious chimney. Since the routes start well above the
sea, this can be a good and rather impressive place to climb when the swell is up.

Access: Locate the top of the Cioch-shaped block, then abseil to the fine ledge.

President's Chimney   20m   Very Difficult *
M.Tighe, J.Paterson   1970s
The obvious, deep chimney at the left end of the recessed section.

LWIS & HARRIS

Immaculate Crack   20m   Hard Severe **

I.Sykes, I.Sutherland   1970s
The crack to the right of President's Chimney.

Things Are Looking Up   25m   E2 5c *

G.Latter, R.Campbell   Jun 1993
The vertical crack-line and fault to the right of Immaculate Crack.

The Roaring Foam   25m   E3 5c **

Some 4m right of the chimney, follow the thin crack which veers rightwards in its upper half, sustained and well-protected.

The Chicken Run   20m   VS 4c *

M.Tighe, J.Paterson   May 1979
Climb the wall to the right of the slimy wide crack, finishing by a thin crack.

Funky Chicken   20m   E1 5b **

M.Tighe, J.Paterson   May 1979
The fine straight crack, which starts 2m left of the Cioch block.

MAGIC GEO

(NB 001 329)   Map p444

Immediately south of Aurora Geo is another deep geo, featuring an overhanging, west-facing wall of grey rock and an east-facing slabby wall, on the seaward side of which is a narrow red wall at the entrance to the geo. The tide empties the sea from the floor of this geo.

RED WALL

Non-tidal   South-West facing

This is the butt end of the promontory separating Aurora Geo from Magic Geo. It is characterised by three diagonal crack-lines, best viewed from the opposite side.

Access: Abseil directly, or take the West Face abseil, gain the floor of the geo, cross the gap and scramble to the large ledge below the wall.

Flannan Crack   25m   VS 4c **

M.Tighe, J.Paterson   May 1979
The obvious right-slanting crack up the left side of the wall.

Campa Crack   30m   HVS 5a *

D.Cuthbertson, P.Moores   7 Jun 1985
Climb the crack on the right directly with the main difficulties at the start.

Limka   35m   E1 5b *

P.Moores, D.Cuthbertson   7 Jun 1985
From the right end of the ledge trend up and right following the obvious line to finish up the arete.

EAST FACE

Partially tidal   South-East facing

This is the slabby wall that runs to the back of the geo. It can be approached from the base of Red Wall, or via the West Face approach.

Flannan Slab Direct   45m   E1 5b **

Start near the left end of the wall, beneath the mid-point of a large slanting over-hang 15m up. Climb a shallow groove with difficulty (crux) to better holds in

Flannan Slab, VS 4c, Magic Geo. Climbers Chris & Rab Anderson
(photo Cubby Images)

another groove that leads to a large ledge on the left arete, below the left end of the slanting overhang. Step back down and traverse right to easier ground, then move up to a series of left-facing flakes and corners. Follow these up and left, then climb the slab just right of the final arete to the top.

Flannan Slab   50m   VS ***
M.Tighe, J.Paterson   May 1978
Start to the right of the centre of the face, beneath the line of a thin crack.
1. 25m 4c Climb the crack up the wall on the right to a ledge, poorly protected. Go up and left to another ledge and belay on the ledge above.
2. 25m 4c Gain and climb a short left-facing corner, then traverse left and go up to good holds at an obvious traverse line, which leads leftwards under the overhangs.

WEST FACE

Non-tidal (mostly)   North-West facing

The left side of this face is an impressive steep wall of grey rock, patchworked with long, thin crack-lines. In the centre the rock steps back to form a right-angled corner, then some chimneys and another corner running up the left side of a black wall.

Access: To the south of the face, abseil down the black wall from a flat platform to good ledges and an easy ramp that leads to the floor at the back of the geo.

LEWIS & HARRIS

The Magician   40m   E5 6a ***
J.Moran, D.Pearce   5 May 1985
This impressive route, high in its grade, climbs the crack to the left of a long thin crack that almost touches the ground and is to the left of a short corner-ramp in the centre of the face. Start some 7m right of the corner at the back of the geo. Climb boldly up and left to gain a red band and the start of the crack. Climb the sustained and strenuous crack, well-protected, veering right towards the top.

The Sorcerer   40m   E5 6a **
J.Moran, D.Pearce   5 May 1979
Another bold route. Start up The Magician, then climb a ramp on the right and go back left to a flakey corner. Pull over this, then traverse right to finish up a groove.

Island Life   25m   VS 4c *
R.Anderson, C.Anderson   Jul 2000
The right-angled corner in the centre of face. From the base of the black wall scramble up leftwards and along a large, tapering shelf to belay at the foot of the corner. **Island Fling** (VS 5a) is a spectacular finish taking the obvious incut ledge and slanting crack on the left to finish by pulling round the arete in a fine position.

SOUTH WALL
Non-tidal   North facing
A prominent mitre-shaped wall, whose edge comes out of the sea. A crack runs up the centre of the wall and is easily gained by traversing in to its base.

The Black Crack   40m   E1 5a *
Lochaber MC   1970s
Start from small ledges just above the waterline, at the base of a wide groove at the foot of the wall. Climb the groove to the base of the main central crack, then climb this to the top passing a water filled hold.

BUAILE CHUIDO - SCREAMING GEO
(NB 002 317)   Map p444
The highest point on this stretch of coast and the biggest cliff hereabouts. It is an awesome place with climbs ranking amongst the best in the country. The Mangersta Slabs enjoy a sunny aspect, as does the West Face, or Screaming Wall. The Lower Tier of the North-West Face, however, only catches the sun late on. Salt spray affects these cliffs since they face full-on into the westerly seas, consequently it may be better to climb here late in the day.

Approach: Park considerately at Mangurstadh where the road forks and doubles back on its way to the aerial, or on the other side of the gate across the road. Head across the fields aiming for the highpoint of Buaile Chuido. Cut around leftwards below this to locate a curious but impressive bothy on the cliff edge, in the angle of the slope below the highpoint, where the slope descends towards the Middle Platform, some 15mins from the car. Permission to stay in the bothy should be sought in the house close to the parking spot.

Access: Descend a rock ramp slightly to the left and scramble down to the left end of Middle Platform, which in turn provides abseil anchors for access to the climbs at sea-level.

MANGERSTA SLABS
Tidal   South-West facing
The slabs lie below and to the right of the southern end of the Middle Platform.
Access: A right-slanting diagonal abseil from the corner at the right end of the

Middle Platform gains a fine sea level ledge. Some routes in the Very Difficult to HVS grades lie on the short walls above the spacious Middle Platform, something to keep one occupied when the seas are rough.

Claymore   30m   HVS 5a **
I.Sykes, I.Sutherland   1970s
The line of slim corners and cracks just right of the abseil. Climb a right-facing corner to a ledge at 6m. Step right into a thin crack and climb an awkward bulge to a ledge on the left. Move back right and go up a shallow groove to a small footledge. Traverse left to better holds, then climb a small left-facing corner and trend left over a bulge.

Moscow Mule   30m   E2 5b *
D.Cuthbertson, L.Clegg, C.Henderson   Jun 1988
From the ledge at 6m on Claymore, follow a hand-traverse line to the left edge. Climb a crack for 1m or so, then make a trying move left across an overhang to a jug. Finish up the groove above.

NORTH-WEST FACE - UPPER TIER

Non-tidal   North-West facing

This face extends around the arete at the left end of the Middle Platform, towards the sea cave at the back of the geo.

Access: Directly by abseil.

Hughys' Cocktail Mixture   25m   E3 5c **
L.Clegg, D.Cuthbertson, C.Henderson   Jun 1988
The pink crack in the left wall of the corner at the end of the girdling break. Pull round the overhang in a fine position and layback the crack above. Sustained but slightly easier climbing follows, with some deviation to finish.

NORTH-WEST FACE - LOWER TIER

Tidal   North-West facing

The steep face beneath the Middle Platform, which runs towards the sea cave.

Access: Abseil from good boulders and cracks on the Middle Platform. A Very Difficult escape route takes the right side of the wall.

Suffering Bastard   25m   E4 6a ***
D.Cuthbertson, L.Clegg, C.Henderson   Jun 1988
The prominent crack system leading to the centre of the Middle Platform gives a brilliant, well-protected pitch. An undercut start leads to overhanging cracks, which are climbed with an awkward transfer into the left-hand crack. Finish up a superb bomb-bay groove; Friend 4 useful.

Killer Fingers   30m   E4 6a ***
D.Cuthbertson, L.Clegg, C.Henderson   Jun 1988
Immediately right of the central overhanging face is an obvious slab with a layback crack above. An undercut start and two-stepped corner lead to a crack on the right side of the slab. Climb the crack and arrange protection. Now step down and hand traverse left. Make a difficult move to reach the layback crack, which leads to the top. The boldness of the climb depends on how far up the crack protection is placed before the traverse left.

WEST FACE - SCREAMING WALL

Tidal   West facing

The impressive wall that extends leftwards from the angle in the face, out over and beyond the massive sea cave. The first routes are at the left end of the Lower Tier.

Approach: As for North-West Face – Lower Tier.

The Screaming Ab Dabs   75m   E6 ****
D.Cuthbertson, L.Clegg, C.Henderson   Jun 1988
A magnificent and committing climb which follows an impressive line up the right side of the big cave before attacking the overhangs above. The crux is short but hard and in an intimidating position. Start at the left end of the Lower Tier on the left wall of a corner.
1. 20m 5c The Yosemite Crack. Climb an undercut groove, then move left to the obvious white crack. This leads to a perfect ledge and belay.
2. 25m 5b Traverse of the Gods. Traverse left along the horizontal break with lots of exposure, then move up to a ledge on the right. Make a rising left traverse across an orangy-brown-coloured wall to a small ledge at the girdling break. Large Friends are useful for the belay.
3. 30m 6b/c The Moonlight Cooler Pitch. Move right over a bulge and follow a line of black pockets going left to a large but secure block under the roof, possible belay. Traverse right and use undercuts to gain the obvious ramp hold above the lip (Friend under the roof and a Friend 00 in a small diagonal quartz crack above the roof). Pull over the roof with difficulty and continue slightly left to better holds beneath the next overhang, which is climbed by means of a horizontal crack to finish up the quartz corner above. Beware of rope drag.

The Prozac Link   50m   E4 ****
H.Jones, G.Huxter   29 May 1996
One of the best E4s in Scotland, this is a serious undertaking that would be difficult to retreat from.
1. & 2 As for The Screaming Ab Dabs.
3. 50m 5c Follow pitch 3 of The Screaming Ab Dabs as far as the large block under the roof. Move left round the front of the block onto large holds. Continue traversing left beneath a curious down-pointing flake, advisable to belay here to avoid rope drag, then onto a pink quartzy wall with difficulty. Climb directly up the quartzy wall and finish up the ramp rightwards. A direct finish climbs the crack left of the ramp to maintain the diagonal line and add a fine bit of extra climbing.

The next route lies on the wall on the other side of the massive arch, above good ledges reached by a 45m abseil from large blocks above the centre of the wall.

Grant's Bad Hair Day   50m   E2 **
H.Jones, G.Huxter   29 May 1996
1. 20m 5a Traverse right until below a shattered corner, then move up this and onto the front face of a precarious block. Move up to a ledge and belay.
2. 30m 5b Follow fault lines easily up and left, aiming for the left-hand end of a big overhang. Move left around the arete beneath the overhang in an exhilarating position and continue easily up and left to finish up a cracked corner.

Lighthouse Arete   45m   Hard Severe **
The obvious ridge at the left end of the cliff, where the rocks turn to face north. Gain the foot of the ridge by abseil and climb it in two pitches.

AIRD FEINIS - BIORACH WALL - THE 'V' ZONE
(NB 992 290)   **Non-tidal but swell affected**   **North-West facing**
Map p444

This is located on the southernmost promontory of the Aird Feinis headland to the

The Screaming Ab Dabs, E6 6c/c, Screaming Geo. Climbers Dave MacLeod & Scott Muir (photo Cubby Images)

south of Aird Mor Mangurstadh. It is a long black wall running the length of the promontory, best viewed from directly opposite. The climbs are located towards the far end around a deep, dark V-slot. Fine rock and good ledges above the high tide mark make this a useful venue. A small stack sits out in front of the wall and tends to break-up some of the Atlantic rollers. All routes were climbed by R.Anderson, C.Anderson, 18 & 19 Jul 2001.

Approach: The headland and its cairn come into view just after the narrow walled-in section of the road. Park on the verge a few hundred metres further on, directly opposite the cairn. Walk towards the fence and before reaching it go left and walk along the promontory, 10mins.

Access: Abseil down the left wall of the V-slot. It is possible to scramble down the right end of the cliff.

Biorach Corner   20m   HVS 5a *
The leaning corner left of the V-slot.

Outer Limits   20m   HVS 4c **
The crack in the right side of the left arete of the V-slot.

Anti Matter   20m   E1 5a **
The crack-line running up the left wall at the entrance to the V-slot.

Black Hole   20m   E1 5a **
Move up into the V-slot and climb the black seams up the left wall.

The Singularity   20m   VS 5a *
The V-slot via the left-hand exit.

Atlantic Highway   20m   E1 5a **
Climb the outer arete some 5m right of the V-slot; first on the left, then on the right.

Fulmar Loops   20m   HVS 4c **
The wide, recessed groove-line with seamed rock just to the right. Climb the right side and finish more directly.

Gannet Chops   20m   VS 5a **
The corner-groove right of Fulmar Loops to finish directly up cracks.

U-Tern   20m   Severe 4b *
The corner-groove just right of Gannet Chops.

BEINN NA BERIE - LITTLE BIG WALL

(NB 109 367)   Non-tidal   West facing
The hillside at the eastern end of the magnificent Traigh na Beirigh sands is dotted with small crags and minor bits of rock. One of these is a small, insignificant look-ing wall, which on closer acquaintance is found to be composed of smooth, near perfect gneiss. There is no sea to worry about so it is a useful little venue. Especially since there is also some bouldering and the campsite is at the other end of the beach. It is possible to drive across the machair by one of the tracks near the house to get right up to the beach.

Tunes of Glory   20m   E5 6b ***
R.Anderson   9 Jul 1999
A superb route up the staggered crack-line running up the left edge of the wall. Climb the first crack, move right to the upper crack, Friend 0, and up to the top.

Barrier Reef   20m   E5 6a **
R.Anderson   16 Jul 1999

Brilliant climbing up the pocketed central wall. Gain the first pocket, then the large pocket. Move left to another large pocket, good protection, then go up right to a thin crack and continue to the break and then the top. Some large Friends are useful for the pockets.

Lewis & Harris Hills

Two of the country's finest crags are located here and are often combined with a trip to the sea-cliffs

LEWIS: CREAG DUBH DIBADALE

(NB 046 239)   Alt 180m   North-East facing

Creag Dubh Dibadale is located in the Uig Hills of Lewis. It is never overhanging in the same sense that Sron Ulladale is, but for quality it is unsurpassable and arguably one of the finest mountain crags in Scotland. Although extensive, almost a kilometre in length, few lines of weakness break the cliffs' defences. The climbing is sustained and requires a bold approach, particularly as protection is often scarce due to the compact nature of the rock. The cliff faces north-east, so an early start is worth the effort. After prolonged periods of rain the cliff can take four days of good weather to dry. Midges can be a problem. There is good camping beside the lochan below the cliff.

Approach: On foot, or mountainbike from the B8011 by following a track that starts close to the western end of Uig sands at NB 031 313. The track is barred by a locked gate a short distance along it. Follow the track for 7.8km up Glen Raonasgail to its bealach (col), then strike steeply up left and head almost due east to a grassy col. Drop down south-eastwards into the corrie until the crag impressively looms into sight overlooking the end of Loch Diobadail 2hrs 30mins.

In the centre of the highest part of the cliff, above an obvious tongue of red slabs, the wall is marked by black streaks and features a flying saucer-shaped depression high on the face. This area is bounded on the left by a prominent crack-line.

Via Valtos   150m   E1 **
A.Ewing, W.Sproul   1970; FFA: R.Archibold, G.Cohen   1974
The prominent crack-line on the left side of the steep central wall, often wet.
1. 40m 5a Climb straight up the crack to a grass patch.
2. 35m 5b Move out onto the left wall, then go up to an overhung corner with a sloping slab above.
3. 30m 5a Step up and right, go left into a crack, then straight up to a ledge.
4. 45m Go right then left to gain and climb an overhung corner, then move left into a crack. Continue by a chimney and finish more easily.

The Big Lick   175m   E3 ***
M.Fowler, A.Meyers   1Jul 1981
This impressive and very sustained climb takes an almost direct line above the left side of the flying saucer-shaped depression. Start at the upper left-hand side of the tongue of slabs.
1. 25m 5c Step right onto the front of the tongue and climb past the overlap. Trend left across groove-lines to reach a good jug beneath a black bulge at the top of the most prominent groove. Thin moves lead left, then go up to a thin flake, which leads to a ledge.
2. 20m 5b Climb the groove above the left end of the ledge to its capping overhang. Move round the right-hand side of this to a ledge, then move up to belay on the next one.
3. 45m 5b Surmount the overhang directly above the stance to gain the area of slabby rock. Climb this directly to a stance at the upper right-hand extremity of the black flying saucer-shaped depression.
4. 20m 5b Gain a pinnacle flake on the right and step left from its top to climb boldly up the wall of quartz. Continue more or less straight up to a good ledge

about 10m below overhangs.

5. 25m 5c Step down left from the stance and traverse horizontally left on an exposed sloping ledge. Climb a corner for 4m, then move left again to belay on a ledge beneath a light-coloured area of rock.

6. 40m 5c Above are three groove-lines. Gain a sloping ledge in the middle groove by an awkward move. Continue with difficulty until it is possible to move into the left-hand groove, which gives easier climbing to the top. It is also possible to climb the left-hand line, which is cleaner and in a superb position.

LEWIS: GRIOMABHAL - TEALASDAIL SLABS

(NB 012 220)   Alt 250m   North facing

These prominent slabs, visible from most of the Uig coastline, are set in a magnificent position overlooking the dark waters of the Dubh Loch at the head of Glen Tealasdail. The rock is clean and sound and gives excellent slab climbing leading directly to the summit cairn of Griomabhal (497m). It is possible to climb virtually anywhere and the route described is a pointer in the right direction. As usual with this style of climbing, protection and belays can be scarce. The cliff dries quickly although it is usually possible to weave around any weeps, connecting the available dry rock. The Main Slab is steeper in its lower part while the upper section changes rock type to a tapering unbroken sweep of quartz. The Main Slab is separated from the shorter East Buttress on the left by a steeply inclined grassy terrace

Approach: Follow the B8011 through Breanais to its end at the slipway at Camus Mol Linnis (NB 9935 2343). Walk up south-eastwards to reach the third streamway in the upper reaches of Glen Tealasdail and follow this to the Dubh Loch, 2.5km, 1hr to 1hr 30mins. Steep grass leads to the foot of the slab.

Descent: Griomabal's flanks afford easy descents, although the left-hand west flank, over the back of East Buttress, allows one to collect gear left at the bottom.

Islivig Direct   240m   Severe ***
R.Sharp, W.Sproul 8 Jun 1969
An adventurous day out amidst lovely surroundings, this route takes a direct line on the Main Slab, from the foot of the lowest slabs to the summit, following a crack and corner system. Various combinations are also possible, utilising all of or bits of, the routes to the left; **Lochlann** (VS ***) and **Comes the Breanish** (HVS ***). All finish on the upper quartz slab where they find independent lines on go-anywhere rock.

HARRIS: SRON ULLADALE

(NB 080 133)   Alt 160m   North-West Facing

The Sron is located in the hills of North Harris and sits sphinx-like at the head of Glen Uladal where a long north running ridge terminates abruptly in an imposing mass of overhanging rock, which towers 270m above Loch Uladal. The Sron is without doubt one of the most impressive pieces of rock in the British Isles.

Approach: From Tarbert, follow the A859 towards Stornoway and after 4km turn left along the single track B887 to Hushinish and follow this to NB 053 078, just before Amhuinnsuidhe. A tarmac road on the right is signposted to Chliostair Power Station. Park here, or 400m up the tarmac road where there is a locked gate and a right fork to a fish farm, both have limited parking. Walk, or cycle along the track past the power station to a dam at the southern end of Loch Chliostair (3.1km, 45min). Now on foot only, follow a good track along the east side of the loch and then by the west bank of Loch Aiseabhat before dropping down to the Sron (4.3km, 1hr 15mins). There is good camping and 'bivi' boulders at the foot of the Sron, be prepared for midges!

Descent: Traverse right beyond the end of the cliff following intermittent deer tracks to descend a grassy gully containing a rocky rognon. There is another more

prominent gully to the right.
The North-West Face is massively overhung and in its centre is a deep-set line of
roofed grooves, the line of The Scoop.

The Scoop   205m   E6 ****
J.Dawes, P.Pritchard   1987
A serious and committing climb of awe-inspiring steepness. Retreat could be complicated after Pitch 4, but it is still possible to abseil off after pitch 3. Start to the
left of Stone by scrambling up some delicate slabs to an in-situ peg belay below
the line.
1. 20m 6b A rude awakening! Step down from the belay and move up to an overhang. Climb this and a short wall, passing an old bolt, with a delicate pinch move
onto a sloping ramp. Ascend the awkward overhanging wall above, then move
right to a hanging belay.
2. 25m 6a Move right and climb a short steep crack in the back of the groove to
a ledge with numerous pegs, possible belay. Step right and go up a cracked rib to
enter the fine open corner above and climb this to a comfortable ledge on the left.
3. 25m 6a If you thought the rock on the pitch below was suspect, you had better hand the lead over to your partner! Climb the groove to a roof, make thin
moves left and continue to a hanging belay below the main corner.
4. 25m 6b Climb the flying groove out left by a series of wild layback and undercut moves. The groove above leads to an overhang, turned on the left by means of
an extremely exposed 'barn door' move round the arete – and you thought the
pitch was finished! Now continue strenuously up the thin crack and huge flake to
the sanctuary of a lie-down ledge.
5. 15m 6a A well balanced pitch. Step down onto a huge flake and traverse left
in a sensational position. Continue the traverse line with increasing difficulty to a
hanging belay in a corner below the left end of the roof.
6. 25m 6a The welcome respite. An awkward move leads into the groove above.
Take the left arete to a slab, then follow a slim undercut groove right to a good
ledge under the capping roof.
7. 20m 6a A serious pitch. Move right and up to peg runners. Climb back down
and traverse right to a bulge. Make a series of committing moves through the bulge
to the sanctuary of a line of jugs leading to a belay on the lip of the overhang.
8. 50m 5a Traverse left under the block overhang and go up to a ledge, turning
any difficulties on the left. Now climb rightwards to the edge, which leads to sal-
vation.

To the right of The Scoop an obvious nose divides the North-West Face from the
longer West Face. The following route climbs the prominent corner-crack in the
upper third of the face, right of the obvious recessed V-groove.

Stone   200m   E5 ***
K.Spence, J.Porteous   May 1969; FFA: M.Fowler, A.Meyers   1981
Start at an obvious open corner in the lowest rocks at the left end of the face, below
and right of the recessed V-groove. The fifth pitch is one of the finest on the island.
1. 25m 5a Climb the corner to a large flake on the right wall.
2. 35m 4b Descend a little, traverse right on the slab beneath the overlap, then
go up an obvious break to a slab under a further roof.
3. 25m 5c Traverse left on a slab under the roof to a ledge. Go left again and climb
an overhanging quartz groove. Exit left below its top to a ledge and belay.
4. 25m 4a An easy quartz ramp leads to a ledge below a big corner with twin cracks.
5. 45m 6a Climb the corner crack to a bulge which bars access to the upper crack.
Either climb a wide crack on left, followed by a traverse right to gain the upper
crack, or move right over the bulge and by means of a thin overhanging crack gain
the upper section (harder). The upper section is sustained and strenuous but very
well protected. Belay on the upper of two grass ledges below a corner.
6. 45m 5b Climb the corner until a small ledge on the right arete can be reached.
This permits a right traverse into easier grooves leading to the top.

SEA-STACKS

The 1967 television ascent of the Old Man of Hoy highlighted the added challenge and excitement offered by a sea-stack, over a rock climb with a simple walk-off. Here was a mountaineering style environment where a knowledge of tides, complex rope work and difficult abseils all came into play, on terrain where the rock was often less than perfect. Since then many dramatic sea-stacks have been climbed, mostly in the north and among the islands, giving Scottish climbing another unique facet that has become surprisingly popular.

Most require calm weather and a lot of preparation due to the sea, so a single minded tour of the north is a big gamble. But if the sea state suits grab the chance! Although swimming, often utilising wet suits, is the romantic approach, the use of boats is becoming more popular, from inflatables to hiring a boatman. The possibility of an epic is part of the excitement, provided it doesn't actually happen!

Skye

Skye has many stacks but those on the west coast like Macleod's Maidens, are of poor rock. The following are on the north-east tip of the island, are of mostly good rock and could be combined with trips to the nearby sea-cliffs – see Skye chapter.

STAC BUIDHE

(NG 448 745)   Map: OS L23   Map p302

This distinctive stack, marked and named on the 1:50k map, lies on a large platform which is well clear of the sea at low to mid-tide. Approach from a small turning area at NG 448 738 (about 150m beyond an old building at the roadside where a track twists up to a viewpoint).

Approach: By a 50m abseil from the cliff-top opposite. Reliable fence post anchors 30m back will require an extra rope. Cross a narrow channel easily to reach the platform. Be sure to shake hands with the resident on the summit.

Descent: By abseil.

North Ridge   25m   VS 4b *
G.Muhlemann, S.Richardson   8 Jun 1991
Traverse round the left side of the stack just above the high tide mark to a ledge below a groove just east of the north arete. Climb columnar ribs and the well protected groove to a pull through with some loose rock and finish up the ridge to the summit block.

Original Route   25m   VS 4c
E.Grindley, G.Libeks, N.Williams   2 Jun 1990
Traverse round the left side of the stack and gain a higher ledge below a groove. Climb this north-western face by this obvious groove with horizontal columns. Make a delicate traverse out left (crux) to gain the ridge which soon leads to the summit block.

South-West Face   30m   HVS 5a *
A.Holden, M.Hudson   25 Jun 1995
Start on the same big ledge as the previous route and traverse 5m right to a prominent groove. Climb this, taking care with the dubious block at its finish, then move right up the ramp before finishing up easier ground.

Rubha Hunish Stacks

Map: OS L23   Map p302

There are several 30m stacks on the north-east side of this headland, the northerly

Climbers on Original Route, VS 5a, Old Man of Stoer
(photo Cubby Images)

tip of Skye. The stacks are quite small, especially when one has walked past the impressive mainland cliffs, but their exquisite situation feels completely isolated and untouched.

Approach: Leave the road at Duntulm on a bend by a phone box (NG 422 743). Follow the path which starts from the right side of the sheep fank and head out to the headland. The top of the South Stack can be seen on the approach but the North and Split stacks are near the tip of the headland.

SOUTH STACK

(NG 413 766)

The first stack encountered on the north-east side of the headland is approached by swimming across a narrow channel. Either take stakes and abseil direct; a Tyrolean can then be set up, or scramble from the south and make a longer swim. Descend from the stack by abseil; the south ridge can also be down-climbed. Both routes are good but loose at the top. **Willie Hunish** (25m VS) climbs the mainland face. **Maol Groove** (30m VS 4c *) climbs a left-facing groove on the seaward face.

MIDDLE STACK

This is 50m north of South Stack. It was originally reached by means of a grappling hook from the headland. Alternatively abseil down the cliffs north of a prominent corner to a small platform, then swim 10m. **Original Route** (30m VS 4b) climbs the mainland face via the central groove until near the top, then traverses left, up and back right to finish. **Eilean Groove** (35m E1 5b) is a sustained climb up the well defined north-facing corner. The top 5m is very loose; 15m of rope wrapped round the summit is the belay, also used for the abseil descent.

For the return to the cliff-top, the prominent corner is **The Planning Department** (VS 4c), while a crack above the left end of a black ledge to the south (an alternative start for the swim) is **The Exit** (Severe); the wall on its right is **Stage Right** (VS 4c). All are good routes.

SPLIT STACK

(NG 409 769)   Tidal

This is close to the land and not immediately obvious as a stack, although close inspection shows it to being two stacks split by a narrow gap. North Stack, close to the north, is more obvious. Split Stack is reached by a gully to its south at low tide.

Approach: Either scramble down the gully to reach a bay which can be very greasy, or abseil.

Descent: By abseil, or Tyrolean back to the mainland.

Trodday Wall   30m   Hard Severe 4b *
G.Muhlemann, S.Richardson   25 Sep 1993
At the base of the descent gully, at mid to low tide, climb up 5m to gain the rift that separates the two summits of the stack. Climb through the rift seaward and turn right to traverse round on to the seaward face. Follow a line of holds just left of centre to reach the south summit.

Forty   30m   E3 5c
C.Dale, L.Sell   29 May 2002
Go through the rift but turn left to traverse the north-east face of the northern summit on easy ledges. Continue to gain the slender north-west face, overlooking the north stack. The route starts here. A well protected sustained climb on perfect rock, easy for the grade. Climb the central crack come groove until moves can be made rightwards to gain a ledge on the arete. Climb the steep wall just right of the arete on huge holds to the top of the north summit. The excursion can be continued by traversing to the south summit (Severe) and abseiling from here.

For the return to the cliff-top, a narrow chimney opposite the south end of Split Stack and a huge flat boulder is **Workout** (VS 4c), a depression just right of the centre of the bay is **Delicase** (VS 4b), a narrow chimney towards the right end of the bay is **The Narrows** (HVS 5a), while the right-hand corner-crack is **Back Bay Crack** (VS 4c). The latter is directly opposite the narrow rift of Split Stack. Again, good routes on good rock.

NORTH STACK

An involved and committing outing. On the south-west face is a chimney-rift which closes near the top and effectively divides the stack into two disproportionate legs. At low tide with calm seas this can be reached by boulder hopping with a tricky channel to finish, but this does not allow very long for an ascent and return. **Original Route** (E2 5b *) climbs the rift, pulling out left at two-thirds height. **Shiant Corner** (HVS 5a) climbs the prominent left-facing corner on the north-east face. Approach by swimming from the north-west corner of Split Stack to gain a small platform on the south-east corner.

West Coast & North Coast

OLD MAN OF STOER

(NC 016 353)   Map: OS L15   Tidal

From its slender base this impressive sea-stack bulges at mid-height before tapering to a pointed summit. The stack lies on the Stoer peninsula north of Ullapool and Lochinver and offers a superb VS on large rough grained sandstone holds, which make the climbing easier than it appears.

Approach: Drive to the lighthouse at the end of the road on the west side of the Stoer peninsula, from where a walk of about 3km leads to the Old Man. Scramble steeply down the 90m face opposite the Old Man to a broad shelf. There is a channel of about 8m wide at its narrowest point, which usually has to be swum. It is advisable to establish the times of the tides and to take an extra rope since a Tyrolean is necessary (but sometimes a rope is in place; it may need tensioning). It will only be at the lowest of tides that a dry crossing is possible on boulders about 50m to the right. A Tyrolean may be used to bring across the rest of the party and protect the retreat. With such a low tide, it is possible to walk round the back to the south side and set up a Tyrolean to here; this misses the hardest pitch. A longer swim also reaches here.

Descent: Fifty metre ropes only allow a single abseil from the top if an anchor just below the top is used (but 60m is always enough). Otherwise, abseil directly to the first belay ledge (45m). Traverse a thin ledge on the landward face to another abseil point and abseil again to the base.

Original Route   65m   VS **
T.W.Patey, B.Robertson, B.Henderson, P.Nunn   Jun 1966
1. 20m 5a From 4m up the landward face follow twin horizontal cracks left on to the south-west face, then climb straight up on good holds to a big ledge on the arete.
2. 20m 4b Climb a steep slab above the ledge to a fringe of overhangs, pass these by a crack and step left to reach ledges; continue for 10m to a cave above a large chockstone.
3. 10m 4b Traverse round the edge on the right to the landward face and trend up right, avoiding the first upward break, to reach a small ledge.
4. 15m Climb the V-chimney above to easy ground and finish up a corner-crack.

Diamond Face Route   60m   E1 *
R.Edwards, B.Gordon   1st Jun 1987
Start from the belay at the end of the Original Route's initial traverse, on the left edge.

Even the most accessible sea-stacks offer excitement and challenge above and beyond the norm. Approaching the Old Man of Stoer in rough and calm seas (photos: above, Cubby Images; below, Tom Prentice)

1. 30m 5a Climb a chimney and crack directly above to a ledge just to the left of the second belay of Original Route. In the same line, enter a pod and then a wide continuation crack. Avoid the roof on the left and climb up rightwards to the cave of Original Route pitch 2.

2. 30m 5b Surmount the roof above to gain a groove leading up and right to a large ledge, possible belay. Stand on top of a block on the left and stretch up to the next break. Trend up and left to an obvious corner above the right side of a roof. At its top a short traverse right gains the summit belay.

North-West Corner   60m   E2 **
M.Fowler, C.Newcombe   29th Aug 1987
This takes the right arete of the landward face, as seen from the cliff-top. Cams are essential, preferably take a double rack.

1. 15m 5c Climb the poorly protected arete on its left side, with difficulty at 6m, to a ledge and large cam belay.

2. 20m 5b A flake just left of the arete allows holds to be gained leading up right to a resting place on the arete. Move up right round to the right-hand side and follow a left-slanting crack to regain the crest. Move left to a fine belay ledge.

3. 25m 6a Climb the obvious left-trending ramp past two old peg runners (very hard) to a ledge at its top (junction with Original Route). Move out right to a large ledge just left of the arete and follow the arete to the top.

AM BUACHAILLE

(NC 201 652)   Map: OS L9   Tidal   Map p426

This impressive stack is more of a challenge than the Old Man of Stoer. It lies about 1km west of the south end of beautiful Sandwood Bay, located about 8km north of Kinlochbervie. At low tide there is an 8m channel between the shore and the stack. In the absence of a Tyrolean rope or ladders, swimming is required. It is important to establish the time of low tide, and to make the ascent fairly quickly, otherwise retreat could be very problematic.

Descent: By abseil down the landward face.

Direct Route   50m   HVS **
T.W.Patey, J.Cleare, I.Clough   23 Jul 1967; Variation: P.Nunn, D.Peck, C.Rowland and about 10 others   Jul 1967
Start just left of centre.

1. 15m 4a Climb overhanging rocks up and on to the prow on the right. Continue straight up until steep rock forces a traverse along a horizontal ledge on the left. Climb up to gain a large ledge by a left-facing corner.

2. 25m 5b Make an awkward move up across the right wall of the corner to gain a ledge above on the right. Move back left to the inset crack above the corner, which is climbed on dubious rock to a ledge below a deep overhanging crack. Climb the crack.

3. 10m 4c Continue more easily to the summit.

Variation: **VS   30m   5a **
2a. This better protected pitch makes the route low in the grade and was the line taken on the second ascent. Leave the corner by traversing rightwards along a break to reach a steep crack. Ascend this and continue by a central line before moving slightly left to the ledge below the deep overhanging crack. Climb the crack as above.

Atlantic Wall   50m   E1 **
S.Richardson, R.Clothier   15 Sep 1990
An intimidating and exposed route on the seaward face, with good rock and protection. The first ascensionists were forced to bivouac at the top, cut off by the tide and high seas. Start below the south face at the left end of the rock plinth.

1. 15m 5a Climb a small left-facing corner to a roof. Traverse left to the arete and climb this to an exposed stance.

2. 15m 4c Climb the strenuous overhanging flake on the west face above and continue more easily to a large ledge beneath the steep final wall. Belay up right beside a huge detached block.

3. 20m 5a/b Climb the thin crack above the block to a horizontal break. Traverse left to the continuous crack running up the left side of the wall, which leads to easy ground. A fine pitch.

Cape Wrath Stacks

Cape Wrath is mainland Scotland's wildest section of coastline and has some impressive stacks requiring calm weather.

Approach: The most convenient access to Cape Wrath during the summer season (May to September and weather/tide dependent) is by passenger ferry (signposted) across the Kyle of Durness, followed by a minibus taxi to Cape Wrath lighthouse. The minibus will drop-off and pick-up where required. Durness Tourist Office (01971 511 259).

A' CHAILLEACH

(NC 249 737)   Map: OS L9   Map p426
This spectacular slender 25m stack lies just off the coast about 2km south of Cape Wrath. It is much easier than appearances suggest. Swim the short gap to reach the south face of the stack but beware of surprising swells and tidal currents. A simple Tyrolean is possible.

Descent: By abseil.

South Face   25m   Hard Severe ✳✳
S.Richardson, G.Muhlemann, M.Fowler, N.Dugan   17 Jun 1989
A fine atmospheric route spiraling across the landward face. Start on the left edge facing the mainland. Climb up right into a line which reaches the arete facing the nearest point of the mainland. Follow this to the final overhanging wall, which is avoided on the right.

Seaward Face   25m   E1 5b ✳✳
M.Moran, M.Furniss   Jun 2001 (Original Route); R.I.Jones, A.J.Porter   2 Jun 2002 (Direct Finish)
Climb the black groove on the right-hand side to its top. Make a large airy step out left and pull around the corner on to the wall on good flakes. Pull through the roof above (crux) to easier vertical ground and a good jug. Climb direct to the top.
Variation: **Original Finish   HVS 5a**
Traverse left under the roof using a flake on to the east face to finish up the final moves of the South Face route.

AM BODACH

Am Bodach is more of a huge block hugging the coast just to the south of A' Chailleach. The climbing is nothing special but it is conveniently close.

South Face   40m   Difficult
G.Muhlemann, S.Macintyre, S.Richardson   27 May 1989
The stack can be reached at low tide, in a calm sea, by stepping over a narrow channel. The south side of the stack gives an obvious line of steep cracks and good holds. Descend by the same route.

There is also good quality climbing on the gneiss mainland cliffs near A' Chailleach. Almost directly opposite A' Chailleach is a rock tower, under which is the access for the swim to the stack. The south-west arete is **Photographers** (VS 4b ✳). About 30m north is another tower and in between is a geo with a big ledge at the bottom and a fine pool. The next two routes climb out of this geo. **Slightly**

Impeccable (VS 4c **) climbs the fine black corner on the south side. Equinox (HVS 5a **) climbs the northerly corner-line leading to the top of a tower. The fine back (north) wall of this second geo has a prominent groove about halfway along with a small sea inlet below, and a big ramp Red Ramp (Hard Severe) running across the easterly section at two-thirds height. Sea Fury (E2 5b ***) takes a lower diagonal line below this.

STACK CLO KEARVAIG

(NC 295 737)   Map: OS L9   Tidal   Map p426

This superb 40m stack stands at the western end of the Clo Mor cliffs overlooking Kearvaig Bay and is easily visible from the road to the Cape Wrath lighthouse. It has three tops, the so called Landward Stack and Seaward Stack are connected at the base by huge wedged boulders, the highest block being visible from the light-house road. The third top is in front of the Seaward Stack as seen from the road and again is connected at the base to the other two. Calm seas are unusual and currents can be strong. During the breeding season, the stack has a large number of guillemots and razorbills and climbing between April and August is not recommended. Stars have not been given, largely due to ignorance.

Approach: A boat can be hired in Durness from James Mather (01971 511 284), or contact Durness Tourist Office (01971 511 259). Excellent sea conditions are required before the boatman will agree to this big commitment.

Descent: By abseil.

The Seaward Stack   55m   HVS
M.Fowler, C.Watts   18 Jun 1989
Start from a large platform at the north-east end of the stack.
1. 35m Move round the corner on to the seaward face and trend right, then back left, to gain a short right-angled corner with a crack in the back. Climb this to a ledge next to the left arete (as seen from the seaward side). This ledge is level with the highest of the wedged boulders between the two summits.
2. 20m 5a Move up right to a ledge and follow a short but awkward open right-slanting groove. Easier ground leads to the top.

The Landward Stack   60m   HVS
G.Muhlemann, S.Richardson   18 Jun 1989
1. 35m As for The Seaward Stack.
2. 15m 5a Traverse horizontally across the wall to reach the highest of the wedged boulders. Cross this to the landward stack and climb a right-angled corner to a ledge.
3. 5m 4c Climb the corner to the top.

Whiten Head
(NC 503 687)   Map: OS L9   Map p426

At Whiten Head are two quartzite stacks, known collectively as The Maiden (NC 497 686).

Approach: A boat can be hired in Durness from James Mather (01971 511284), or contact Durness Tourist Office (01971 511 259). The Eastern Stack has a cave through its base. The landing is tricky and is best done on the landward side. Landing on the Western Stack is easier and can be made almost anywhere on its east side.

THE MAIDEN - WESTERN STACK

Descent: Abseil from the north-west pinnacle to ledges on the west side.

Waterfront Wall   55m   Severe ***
M.Fowler, C.Newcombe   28 May 1988
A superb route on solid rock up impressive terrain normally reserved for much

harder climbs. Start on the north-east (seaward) corner of the stack.

1. 25m Climb up (line variable) on good holds to a depression beneath a steep band, stance on the right.

2. 20m Surmount the small overhang above the stance and move left to a short discontinuous crack-line. Climb this for 6m to overhangs and traverse left to a sensational stance on the arete.

3. 10m Easier ground to the top.

THE MAIDEN - EASTERN STACK

This was the scene of the tragic accident to Tom Patey, abseiling after the ascent of the Original Route. March's Route was taken on a trip to recover the abseil rope left by the original party.

Descent: By a single free abseil from the lower edge of the slanting top.

Original Route   55m   HVS *
P.Nunn, T.W.Patey, B.Fuller, C.Goodwin, C.Rowland   Jun 1970
From the large platform on the landward side, traverse left along the west side of the stack just above sea-level to a stance at the bottom of a groove on the north side.

1. 35m 4c Climb a steep groove but avoid an overhanging crack by a traverse up right and up a steep wall for 8m. Traverse left into the crack-line and continue to a good square ledge (possible belay). Climb the wall above on easier ground to a second ledge and belay.

2. 20m 4a Climb the ramp above and loose flakes to the summit.

March's Route   55m   HVS **
W.March, J.Cunningham   1970
A fine steep route taking the prominent line up the west face. Start from the large tide washed platform about 5m left of the cave running through the stack where initial overhangs guard access to a scoop and a right-trending ramp.

1. 30m 5a Surmount the overhangs trending left and move back right into the scoop. Follow the prominent right-trending ramp-line to capping roofs and move right and up to ledges. Follow these left to beneath the prominent central fault cleaving the upper part of the face.

2. 25m 5a Ascend the steep corner-line to a dangerous big loose block and make an exit left to easier ground leading to the summit.

Orkney

Orkney is home to some of Britain's most dramatic stacks, by far the biggest being the Old Man of Hoy. But a few days stack bagging can be enjoyed by including the Castle of Yesnaby and North Gaulton Castle. Some photos, topos and extra information, particularly on other stacks in Orkney, can be found on <www.orkney-seastacks.co.uk> and in the SMC Climbers' Guide: *Northern Highlands North*.

Access: Most climbers don't take a car but use taxis or buses where necessary. Northlink <www.northlinkferries.co.uk>, (01856 851 144) or (0845 6000 449, reservations) operate three ferries per day during the week (two per day at weekends) between Scrabster and Stromness (Orkney Mainland).

Amenities: Orkney Tourist Information Office (01856 872 856), or <www.visit orkney.com>.

Hoy

The western shores of Hoy boast some of the most spectacular coastal scenery in the British Isles and on a clear day, the view from the Scrabster ferry alone makes

Climbers on the crux pitch of the East Face (Original Route), E1 5b, Old Man of Hoy
(photo John Lyall)

the long drive feel worth the effort. There is much rock climbing on the mainland cliffs at Rora Head (ND 173 992), as well as highly adventurous routes on St John's Head (HY 187 034) – see also SMC Climbers' Guide: Northern Highlands North.

Access: A passenger ferry (01856 850 624) runs between Stromness and Moaness (in north Hoy). It leaves Stromness from a pier about 200m from the Scrabster ferry berth (small sign) and operates four per weekday in summer, two at weekends. A taxi is then taken to Rackwick Bay. A taxi sometimes comes to meet the ferry but bookings are best made in advance (01856 871 315) or (01856 791 262). Including the travel from Scrabster, it is not generally possible to climb the Old Man over a normal weekend.

Amenities: Rackwick Bay is the starting point for the walk to the Old Man of Hoy. There is a beautifully situated bothy on the edge of the beach in the centre of the bay and it is also possible to camp next to the bothy. Alternatively, Rackwick Youth Hostel has eight beds (01856 873 535).

OLD MAN OF HOY

(HY 177 005)   Map: OS L7   Non-tidal

Approach: From the northern end of Rackwick Bay the coastal path zigzags up the hillside then makes a rising traverse before descending past Rora Head on the left to reach the cliff-top overlooking the Old Man of Hoy. Descend with care via a narrow 'sheep track' slightly to the north of the lookout point (1hr 30min).

Descent: By abseil down the East Face route. To avoid a bottomless abseil during the descent either leave a doubled rope on pitch 2 to pull yourself across to the stance (perhaps with prusiks), or use 60m ropes and reach the ground direct. Often there is a rope in place; if not and doing the South Face first, one would still have to be placed!

East Face (Original Route)   135m   E1 ***
R.Baillie, C.Bonington, T.W.Patey   18 Jul 1966
The landward face of the stack provides a memorable outing with some excellent climbing on mostly good rock (nowadays). Aid was used on the first ascent and large Friends are useful today (two 3.5 and two 4 ideal). A pull on the wedge at the lip of roof two reduces the grade to 5a. Start at the end of the boulder ridge linking the stack to the mainland.
1. 25m 4b Climb a shattered pillar to a large ledge, The Gallery.
2. 30m 5b Descend rightwards, then traverse right to gain the foot of the great crack. Climb the crack passing roofs at 10m and 20m. Step right at the top to a triangular alcove.
3. 20m Step right and move back left over easy ledges to regain the crack-line which is followed for 8m to a large ledge.
4. 40m 4b Near the right-hand end of the ledge climb up a short way and traverse delicately left to another ledge. Climb the chimney in the corner, then wriggle right along a horizontal ledge until easy ledges lead to grass below the final crack. Other lines on this pitch can be taken.
5. 20m 4c Climb the sensational corner-crack splitting the upper section of the stack (the best pitch).

South Face   160m   E2 **
J.Brown, I.McNaught Davis   8-9 Jul 1967
A fine sunny route on acceptable rock.
1. 20m 4b As for the Original Route to the Gallery.
2. 30m 5b Climb the corner on the left, go up the steep wall above (bold) to a flake on the left. Climb this to a ledge, then walk 12m left to blocks below a shallow chimney-crack.
3. 25m 5b Climb the shallow chimney to a ledge and cave (bivvy on first ascent).
4. 40m 5b Surmount the roof of the cave (strenuous) and continue up a chimney-

crack to a ledge. Pull through an overhang, move right and climb a corner and face above to reach steep grass leading to a crack at the top of the grassy Haven.
5. 30m 4c Climb up and left to a ledge, then a big flake on the left, to further vegetation. A series of ramps and ledges lead up to an easy chimney and the south summit. An alternative on better rock is to traverse right to join the Original Route at the base of its corner. Finish up the corner.

Orkney Mainland - Yesnaby Area

The Castle of Yesnaby and North Gaulton Castle are both near Yesnaby, which lies about 8km north of Stromness. Brass's Taxis (01856 850 750), is a Stromness based firm, much nearer to Yesnaby than the Kirkwall firms. O2 and Vodaphone mobile phones work at the old military buildings for summoning the return taxi ride. Alternatively, there is a long but wonderfully scenic approach along the cliff-tops from Stromness. The Castle of Yesnaby is 10-15mins walk south from the car park at the end of the road.

CASTLE OF YESNABY

(HY 219 153)   Map: OS L6

Approach: This most impressive 25m stack is approached by abseil and a swim; calm seas are required. Starting at about half ebb tide gives the best sea conditions. There are two choices for an abseil point. The direct abseil is to ledges at the base of the cliffs on the north side of the bay (same as for the surrounding cliffs). A separate rope is required and the anchor points are awkward but it is possible to set up a Tyrolean. An easier abseil and an easy climb out, but a longer swim and no Tyrolean, is to abseil down the north side of a loose headland just to the south on to much bigger sea-level platforms. Walk as close to the castle as possible and swim; at very low tides the base of the direct abseil can be reached.

South Face Route   25m   E2 5b **
J.Brown and party   Jul 1967 (1PA); FFA; unknown
An excellent route, but quite bold now the pegs are rusty. Take the right side of the south face to about half-height to the second ancient piton, then continue directly up cracks to the top. The original route moved left from the second piton.

Meditation   25m   E2 5c *
G.Latter, T.Pringle   10 Jul 2002
Good climbing up the left side of the south face, with a short well protected crux. Start in the arch and move easily up right on to a large ledge. Move out left on good holds, then climb a difficult wall on sloping holds to better holds leading up to an easy flake-groove. Finish up this.

Yes Please   25m   E3 6a **
M.Fowler, J.Freeman-Attwood, C.Jones   19 Jul 1996
The route takes the flying finger crack in the seaward edge of the stack. Start on the right-hand side of a sloping ledge at the seaward end. A very fine pitch. Move up and swing round to the left-hand side on a good hold (poor peg runner). Climb boldly up right to a resting place on the arete. Follow the strenuous finger crack on excellent rock through an overhang and up a final overhanging hand jamming crack.

Landward (East) Arete   25m   E2 5b **
Climb directly up the landward arete, passing a hard move at two-thirds height. Low in the grade.

There is a large amount of climbing on the mainland cliffs, some of high quality – see SMC Climbers' Guide: Northern Highlands North.

NORTH GAULTON CASTLE

(HY 217 134) Map: OS L6

This dramatic stack is situated roughly halfway between Outertown (Stromness) and the car park at Yesnaby, about 2km south of the Castle of Yesnaby.

Approach: The most convenient approach is from Mousland farm (HY 229 128), perhaps reached by taxi. Follow the signs for Birsay as you leave Stromness, then take the Cauldhame road. From here it is 1.5km walk to the cliff opposite the stack. An elaborate rope technique similar to Patey's method for reaching the top of The Great Stack of Handa (a huge Tyrolean traverse) was used to reach the base of the stack on the first ascent. A direct abseil approach can be made from stakes (not in-situ), using an extra rope as back-up. A 60m abseil rope is more convenient. This is followed by a 40m swim.

Descent: Use blocks on the north side of the stack as an anchor to descend the south face. Fifteen metres of abseil tat may be required. There is a route back up the mainland cliff which climbs the wall to the right of the ledge on poor rock to join and finish up a left-slanting groove at two-thirds height (Hard Severe).

**The Original Route 50m HVS 5a ** **
P.Minks, C.Phillips Easter 1970
The precise line taken by the first ascentionists is unknown but the following route was climbed in 2002 (access by boat) and 2003 (swim and conventional Tyrolean). Start on the tidal platform at the base of the landward arete.
1. 20m 5a Climb a left-facing corner 5m to the left of the arete and pull on to a good non-tidal ledge at 5m (crux). Alternatively climb the arete direct to the ledge (unprotected, 5b). There is a bolt on the ledge to raise the Tyrolean rope in case of rising tide. Climb up easy ground to a large platform about a third of the way up the landward arete.
2. 30m 4c Traverse left to an open book corner and climb this to another big ledge. Traverse left for 5m and climb a big fault in the centre of the broad landward face of the stack to the summit (loose near the top).

Far North and Caithness East Coast

DUNCANSBY STACKS

(ND 400 719) Map: OS L12 Map p426

Duncansby Head is the north-east tip of Scotland, 3km from John o' Groats. There are several spectacular stacks. The largest, **The Great Stack of Duncansby**, locally known as The Muckle Stack, is the most southerly, but the climbing is poor (Very Difficult). Just north of this is Peedie Stack (Orkney dialect for peery, meaning small), an 85m wafer of rock. These can be approached by swimming, but a boat is easier.

Approach: By boat; asking in Scrabster about boats for hire has been successful in the past!

Peedie Stack 65m VS *
T.Cumpstey, W.Lacey, N.Smith, D.Young 17 Sep 1967; M.Fowler, P.Allison, N.Dugan, J.Lincoln 27 May 1989
A thin (but rather tall) sliver of rock. Later called Witches' Hat Stack (1989). The **West Ridge**, starting on the south face, has also been climbed (VS 4c). Start at the seaward end.
1. 25m 4b Climb up on the south side to gain the seaward arete at a ledge. A short steep wall leads to a further ledge from where 15m of shallow cracks lead to a belay just below and right of the start of a prominent shallow groove.
2. 40m 4c Move up and left into the groove and follow this past several dubious flakes to gain the arete again just below the top. Follow the arete to the top. Abseil descent down the line of the route.

Variation: **40m HVS 4c**
2a. Climb the arete left of the groove throughout.

East Coast Stacks
There are many stacks on the East Caithness coast, often of poor rock or bird infested, but the following are of reasonably good quality and have the big advantage of better weather and sea conditions when the wind is in the west. A boat can be hired at Lybster (ask at the harbour), which is between Occumster and Cleit Mhor, so both venues might be possible in a day for an efficient party, although the stacks can be reached by swimming.

OCCUMSTER STACK

Map: OS L11 Map p426

About 2km north of Lybster harbour (ND 245 350) is a group of stacks. Occumster Stack is the most northerly and most impressive, a slender finger of rock.

Approach: Abseil from a large boulder behind the fence to a rectangular platform, washed only at high tide (50m rope required). Access to the stack is by a 10m swim or Tyrolean.

Descent: From in-situ wires on the south wall.

Occumster Stack   25m   HVS 4c *
M.Fowler, N.Dugan, P.Allison, J.Lincoln   26 May 1989
Starting from a ledge on the south-east corner, the route follows a crack on the left side of the seaward face. Although the protection is reasonable, the rock has very sharp edged horizontal striations; falling is not recommended.

CLEIT MHOR

(ND 174 300) Map: OS L11 Map p426

About 2km north of Dunbeath (on the Helmsdale to Wick road) there are three stacks marked on the OS Map as Cleit Mhor. The central stack, Cleit Bheag, is the most appealing.

Approach: Either using a small boat from Dunbeath at low tide or via an abseil (bring your own stake) down the grassy cliff just south of the stacks and a swim. A boat can be hired at Dunbeath (see Bodach an Uird) or at Lybster for a combination with Occumster Stack.

Descent: By abseil (bring your own stake?).

Cleit Bheag   35m   E1 *
M.Fowler, C.Watts, N.Dugan   2 Oct 1989
The obvious crack on the seaward face is harder than it looks.
1. 25m 5b Climb easily to overhangs at 15m. A difficult section then leads to a chimney and a stance on the right.
2. 10m 4c Move left and climb the wall to the top.

Cleit Ruadh   15m   HVS 5a *
C.Watts, S.Sheridan, N.Dugan, M.Fowler   2 Oct 1989
The northern stack is short but pleasant, climbed up its seaward face. It would be a long swim; a boat might be better. A short technical wall at 6m provides the crux, well protected, then easier but a bit run out to the right arete and the top.

RAMSCRAIG STACK

(ND 145 264) Map: OS L17 Map p426

The stack is about 4km south of Dunbeath.

SEA-STACKS

Approach: Park at Ramscraig's road junction (ND 143 268). Descend an ancient 'cut' track in the steep grassy cliffs 100m north of the stack to gain a boulder beach. The stack is easily accessible at mid to low tide.

Descent: A 50m abseil.

Ramscraig Stack   50m   VS
C.Dale, L.Sell   14 May 2001
The route is based on the south-eastern arete, on generally sound rock and with mostly Friend protection.
1. 15m Climb the south-east arete to an obvious ledge.
2. 20m 4b Follow the ledge line rightwards, pass a bad step and climb a steep wall above to gain a grassy ledge. Follow this leftwards to the arete.
3. 25m Follow the crest of the arete.

BODACH AN UIRD

(ND 114 213)   Map: OS L17   Map p426

This fine but guano covered 30m stack, known locally as the Needle, lies 2km south of the village of Berriedale, which is about 18km north-east of Helmsdale. It is known as The Needle because the gap between stack and land (the eye) appears to fishermen at a known distance from port. It is also home to several thousand birds during the nesting season and should only be attempted from August onwards.

Approach: By boat from Berriedale. A boat can be hired at Dunbeath from Terry Merrill, (01593 731279). Land on the seaward side (more difficult at low tide).

Descent: By abseil to ledges on the east side of the stack.

South Route   35m   HVS *
M.Fowler, C.Watts   1 Oct 1989
The cleanest route taking a series of grooves on the south side of the stack. Start at the left of two obvious grooves.
1. 10m 5a Climb easily up into the chimney in the back of the groove. Traverse the left wall to a stance on the arete.
2. 15m 5a Climb straight above the belay for 3m and move right to climb a groove to overhangs. Traverse left to the left arete of the groove above the stance, and climb the wall above the overhang, trending right to a good stance.
3. 10m 4c Trend left on dubious rock to a shallow groove leading to the top.

Berwickshire Coast

A range of routes can be found on the greywacke cliffs surrounding Fast Castle Head on the coast south-east of Edinburgh – see SMC Climbers' Guide: *Lowland Outcrops*.

THE SOUTER

(NT 869 709)   Map: OS L67   Non-tidal

This easily accessed stack lies about 1.5km east of Fast Castle. The cliffs are heavily birded from April to August, although The Souter's seaward face is usually bird free.

Approach: Leave the A1107 at NT 828 688 for a minor road signposted Dowlaw. Follow this for 2km and park on the left before the entrance to Dowlaw Farm. From the parking place walk right around the farm, then follow a track towards the sea, passing through two gates. When it fades, trend left and go through a drystone wall. Now head seawards down fields to the coast opposite The Souter.

Descent: By abseil down the landward face from in-situ slings. These should be treated with caution and replaced if necessary.

*Chris Watts getting to grips with the bird poo, Bodach an Uird
(photo Simon Richardson)*

Ordinary Route   25m   HVS 5a *
I.Clough, J.Cleare   1970
This takes the seaward face starting from a raised platform. At high tide gain the platform by making an awkward traverse across the base of the south-east face. Climb the groove above the platform with difficulty to a ledge. Move up and right (peg runner) to a V-groove. Go left up this, then climb a diagonal crack and the wall above to the top.

Seal of Approval   25m   HVS 5a
R.Campbell   1 Apr 1990
This is on the south-east face of The Souter. Start above the bad step at the south arete.
1. 15m 5a Step up to a sloping ledge and climb an obvious crack over a bulge and small ledge to a continuation crack leading to the left side of a large ledge.
2. 10m 5a Pull over a bulge and continue up the crack on sharp holds to join the landward side near the top.